From the day Mussolini's Italy declared war on Britain in June 1940, the island of Malta was under siege. Its strategic importance was obvious to both sides, standing as it did in the central Mediterranean, athwart the supply route between Italy and Axis armies in North Africa. It had therefore to be bombed out of existence by the Axis powers, and preserved at all costs by the British.

That Malta survived was due in part to the courage and fortitude of the Maltese population and the airmen and soldiers who endured the Axis' bombing, contested the air-space above the island and maintained its defences. But without food, aircraft, ammunition and all the impedimenta necessary to warfare in a modern era, courage and fortitude would have counted for little. For despite the apparently overwhelming might of the combined airforces of Italy and Germany, British ships constantly reinforced the beleaguered island, turning Malta from a vulnerable outpost of the British Empire to a ravelin from which the enemy's communications with North Africa could in turn be interdicted.

The cost in men and ships was enormous; the logistical difficulties at times seemed insuperable, the strategic task a military and naval impossibility. The expenditure of vast resources to keep Malta alive and capable of acting offensively has attracted much criticism from historians armed with wisdom of hindsight. But the fact remains that it was done by the exertion of sea-power, of men-of-war and merchant ships acting as a single arm of British policy. It is this stark and determined effort that is detailed here.

Mistakes and miscalculations beset the planning and execution of operational plans on both sides. At times the importance of Malta was sidelined by events elsewhere, but Admirals Cunningham and Somerville, often with limited resources and frequently at both a strategic and a tactical disadvantage, doggedly maintained a remarkable campaign which, whatever the cost, ultimately proved successful, reaching its climax in the PEDESTAL convoy of August 1942.

This review of the contest of air-power against sea-power by a professional seafarer, emphasizing the part played by the Merchant Navy, has new resonance in the light of recent events in Europe.

Richard Woodman is well known for his Nathaniel Drinkwater series, ten other sea stories, a *History of the Ship* and a work on sea-power in the Napoleonic Wars. In *Malta Convoys*, he continues his study of British maritime services in the Second World War that he began in *Arctic Convoys*, published to wide critical acclaim in 1994.

Born in London in 1944, Richard Woodman first went to sea in 1960. His maiden deep-water voyage, aboard the cargo liner *Glenartney* (a veteran of a convoy to Malta), sparked an interest in the subject of this book. He spent over thirty years at sea and has extensive experience of command and operational planning. He now writes full-time and is a regular contributor to *Lloyd's List*.

Malta Convoys

1940–1943

RICHARD WOODMAN

John Murray
Albemarle Street, London

To the men of the British Sea Services
who served in Malta Convoys,
1940–1943, these pages are dedicated

———————

A useful chapter in naval history and tactics could be
written on the defence of convoys, by which it might
perhaps be made manifest, that a determined bearing,
accompanied by a certain degree of force, and a vigorous resolution to exert that force to the utmost, would,
in most cases, save the greater part of the convoy, even
against powerful odds.

Captain Basil Hall, RN (1788–1844)

Contents

Illustrations

(between pages 228 and 229)

The author and publishers would like to thank the following for permission to reproduce illustrations: Plates 1, 2, 3, 9, 11, 12, 14, 15, 17, 18, 19, 20, 21, 22, 23, 24, 25, 27, 28, 30, 31, 32 and 33, Imperial War Museum, London; 4, 10, 13, 16 and 29, National War Museum Association, Malta; 5, Private Collection; 6, Captain C.K.S. Aylwin, RN; 7 and 8, Commander Neville-Towle, RN; 26, Freddie Treves.

Preface

THE UPHEAVAL OF the Second World War produced a multiplicity of histories which range from intensely personal ordeals of private survival to the great crusade of the Grand Coalition. Between these extremes lie the histories of the war's constituent parts, of military, air and naval campaigns in which intelligence and logistics were vital factors in the outcome of pitched battle.

This book is primarily concerned with that part of the naval war in the Mediterranean centred upon the island of Malta. Specifically it is the history of the supply of the beleaguered island and of the naval operations and actions which this entailed. Such battles were mainly running fights, often lacking the grand names of capes or seas, and are easy to overlook; yet the amount of material resources committed to them was enormous, and much rested upon their outcome.

The supply and defence of Malta have attracted a degree of adverse criticism, a strong suggestion that the game was not worth the candle. It seems to me that such a viewpoint is skewed, for while the wisdom of hindsight, armed with the latest revelations of the archives, may suggest an alternative and ultimately superior course of action, such a chillingly objective analysis omits the very core of the matter. This is surely an admission of prejudice, an imposition of arguments or facts unperceived or impossible to divine at the time. It makes of criticism an arrogant overview, detaching the historian from the nuts and bolts of the events he is commenting upon. If the study of history is to have any value beyond a recondite attraction, it must be to inform the present in order to safeguard the future. And to do so must necessarily entail a realistic appreciation of the nature of decision-making at the time, and the admission to the story of that great and unquantifiable unknown, risk.

Great Britain engaged upon war in the Mediterranean at an extreme moment; the Western Front had collapsed, Anglo-French intervention in Norway had ended in defeat, and the defeat of her French ally threatened Britain. Having detached her army, devoid of its military equipment, from the beaches of Dunkirk, Britain confronted a combination of naval forces in Europe and the spectre of invasion. But the folly of the Fascist dictator of Italy gave Britain, led by the pugilistic Churchill, an opportunity to stay in the ring, and to hit back. When, as at Dunkirk and in Norway, she was savagely bloodied in the further disasters of Greece and Crete, something was again salvaged by her principal asset, her over-worked navy.

Notwithstanding its considerable weaknesses, and they were significant, the Royal Navy of the United Kingdom of Great Britain held the breach at this moment of national nadir. It accepted terrible losses until, by May of 1943, it had endured the worst of the maritime war and was fast being re-equipped. Only then did the Royal Air Force, alongside the United States Air Force, begin to assume its own offensive, with the augmented, reorganised and retrained British Army preparing for the Allied invasion of Europe.

Suffering alongside the Royal Navy throughout this bleak period, that heterogeneous flock of commercial ships which constituted Britain's 'Merchant Navy' was transmuted into a fighting force upon whose courage and integrity much depended. In the supply of Malta, these complementary yet hugely disparate sea-services were to achieve their most impressive synergy.

Between the fall of France in May 1940 and the full entry of the United States of America into the war in December 1941, the British Prime Minister Winston Churchill and President Franklin D. Roosevelt of the United States played a delicate and sometimes disingenuous game.[1] This involved drawing the teeth of the isolationists in Congress, and persuading American public opinion to move from detached disinterest to active support of Britain against Germany. In addition, the purchase of arms and war *matériel* from the United States by Great Britain helped American industry crank itself out of depression and into full productive gear. So, in her final days as an imperial power, Britain invested the last of her wealth in the American economy, enabling the United States to enter the war after the unprovoked Japanese attack on Pearl Harbor with revitalised industrial capacity, stimulation which enabled her to acquire a significant technological lead for the post-war world.[2]

President Roosevelt played a waiting game, helping Britain to fight her own war, which was also America's proxy war, and building British muscle until the United States could remain aloof no longer. When that time came, American might swiftly surpassed that of the small island kingdom, which indeed was left exhausted and economically ruined in her wake.

At that time, it is doubtful whether Churchill, a man full of flaws but of dauntless courage and unwavering resolution, saw himself and the people whom he led as the junior partners in the emerging alliance with the United States. It was he and the British people who stood between the horrors of German domination and the world at large, and they could still claim the support of the other members of the British Commonwealth of Nations. But after the evacuation of Dunkirk and the defeat in Norway, Churchill had no opportunities to carry the war into the enemy's camp, to convince the world that Britain might be bowed but was not broken. Ironically, during this grim time he was diverting to a Soviet Russia so recently party to the division of Poland with Germany, but now betrayed and invaded, supplies which would otherwise have re-equipped the denuded British army. Yet although this support for the Russians was conceived of as no less moral than material, it could easily be perceived as fighting a war by substitute, despite the heavy cost in ships and men of forcing the convoys through the Arctic Ocean. Churchill yearned to engage the enemy directly, as much for Britain's own sake as to convince the Americans and Russians that she was still capable of taking the offensive. He was guilty of insisting, against the advice of his Chiefs of Staff, on costly and ineffective stratagems, and ran great risks politically in so doing by drawing adverse criticism upon himself. He was also guilty of sacrificing British and Commonwealth men and arms, the very opposite of his intentions, when those stratagems miscarried. Such obduracy worried Roosevelt, and the relationship between the two leaders became strained over the subject of Mediterranean strategy in particular; but the German threat to the Middle East was real, and upon British presence there, even in adversity, depended reactions in Ankara, Madrid and Tokyo.

As Churchill wrote to Roosevelt in the summer of 1941, before the entry of Russia or Japan into the war, at a time when Axis arms had driven British and Commonwealth forces out of Greece: 'We must not be too sure that the consequences of the loss of Egypt and the Middle East would not be grave ... If all Europe, the greater part of Asia and Africa became, either by conquest or agreement under duress, a part of the Axis system, a war maintained by the British Isles, the United States, Canada and Australia against this mighty agglomeration would be a hard, long and bleak proposition. Therefore ... the vast balances may be tilted heavily to our disadvantage.'

In the event, Italy's precipitate entry into the war in June 1940 afforded Churchill the opportunity he sought: Lieutenant-General O'Connor's destruction of Marshal Graziani's 10th Army with his Anglo-Indian 13th Corps and the naval strike on Taranto in November were the first victories to lift the spirits of the British. Just as he had committed German forces to support the faltering Italians in Greece, Hitler sent Erwin Rommel's Afrika Korps to Cyrenaica. Thereafter Malta provided the base from which the supply lines for Rommel's troops were intermittently raided. The long, arduous campaign in the Western Desert culminated in late 1942 with Montgomery's victory at El Alamein. It was what Churchill called 'the end of the beginning'. In due course thereafter, Malta became the base from which the invasion of Sicily and Italy was launched.

The preservation and alteration of Malta from a strategic position considered indefensible to that of Allied bridgehead was a remarkable feat of arms, carried out in the teeth of Axis opposition. It was composed of three elements, the first of which, the defence of the island itself, rested upon the astonishing endurance of the Maltese and the courage of the airmen and ground crews struggling for mastery of the blue Mediterranean skies overhead. The second was the use of the island as an offensive base by the Royal Air Force, and by warships and submarines of the Royal Navy: the actions of these forces fatally compromised the Axis supply line from Italy to North Africa. But neither the maintenance of Malta nor the attacks on enemy logistics could have been achieved without the means to do so. Food, fuel, aeroplanes, guns, ammunition, medical supplies, spare parts, and those innumerable essential sundries without which modern warfare fails – all had to be conveyed to the island. It is this last element with which this book is concerned, for the attrition rate on the ships and men of the combined sea-services attempting to supply the island was huge.

American Anglophobes like Fleet Admiral King might dismiss this effort as of little ultimate value. Later historical analysts argue that the sacrifices made by the Maltese and the losses in ships, aircraft, men and *matériel* were too great a price to pay, or that the threat to the Middle East and the Persian oilfields was exaggerated. In point of fact, the disproportion of commitment was attributable not to the strategic value of Malta, but to the profligacy of war. The *threat* to Malta and the Middle East, as we now know, was very real. General Warlimont, deputy chief of operations for the Oberkommando der Wehrmacht, OKW, relates how the combined services staff at Hitler's own head-quarters were required to produce an appreciation of the options for future strategy in the Mediterranean following the German intervention in Greece. Put bluntly, the question was Crete, or Malta? The staff unanimously concluded that Malta should be seized, 'since this seemed to be the only way to secure perman-ently the sea-route to North Africa'. This forceful recommenda-tion was rejected by Hitler in favour of the ejection of the British from Crete, 'because of the danger of air attacks on the Rumanian oil fields'. Moreover, Hitler, with his eye ever on an opportunity, howsoever fantastic, considered that from Crete the Luftwaffe might mount air attacks which could open up 'far reaching pos-sibilities for offensive action in the Eastern Mediterranean', by which he meant a bombing offensive against the vulnerable British naval base at Alexandria, and Egypt beyond.[3]

A warning note as to the risks inherent in ignoring Malta was sounded by General Thoma, who was sent to North Africa in October 1940 to assess whether German forces should support the Italians. Thoma reported that any campaign would rely upon regular supplies, and that this matter would be decisive; British possession of Malta rendered the matter uncertain, and there-fore compromised the intended campaign. The objection was brushed aside by OKW with an alternative solution: instead of being invaded, Malta would be bombed into submission.

It was the failure of Hitler to appreciate the strategic import-ance of Malta that fuelled post-war doubts as to the wisdom of the British effort to sustain the island. Strategic assessments in London were congruous to those in Berlin: with an enemy base lying athwart a vital logistic route, the dispatch of reinforcements and supplies would always be a matter of doubt, and such a risk was foolhardy. But as late as February 1942, Hitler was still listening enthusiastically to Grand-Admiral Raeder's optimistic assessment of opportunities in the Mediterranean, where the success of German arms sent initially to rescue the Italians might now be turned to an offensive advantage which would ensure the collapse of the British Empire as German forces from the west linked hands with Japanese armies advancing from the east.[4]

In the event the so-called 'Grand Plan' was stillborn. By a great irony the outcome of Hitler's decision to invade Crete ultimately modified German thinking at a time when the neglect of Malta was having its fatal effect upon supplies of food, ammunition and fuel for Rommel's armour in North Africa. So great had been German losses in the airborne assault on Crete that the OKW baulked at a second such operation aimed at Malta. British resistance in Crete, though it ended in defeat, therefore contributed to the saving of Malta, which was to prove 'a more critical matter'.[5]

Malta's fate was decided in the summer of 1942. By April of that year, despite relentless bombing of the island, the Axis supply situation in North Africa had become desperate. That proponent of airborne warfare, General Student, approached Hitler with a plan for a joint German–Italian invasion of Malta. German paratroops would seize a beach-head which would then be quickly reinforced by an overwhelming Italian seaborne force of up to eight divisions. 'I hoped', recalled Student, 'to carry out the plan not later than August ... in June I was summoned to Hitler's HQ for the final conference on the operation. Unfortunately ... Hitler had just seen General Crüwell, who was just back from North Africa, and had given a very unfavourable account of the state of the Italian forces and their morale. Hitler at once took alarm. He felt that if the British Fleet appeared on the scene, all the Italian ships would bolt for their home ports – and leave the German airborne forces stranded. He decided to abandon the plan of attacking Malta.'[6]

The Italian navy threw away advantage after advantage, largely due, it seems, to the failure of Fascism to permeate its ranks. An uneasy truce between its officers and its ratings seems to have preserved its existence, but to have eliminated any real sense of being a fighting service. There were examples of high courage, but none of that tenacity of purpose which character-ised its enemy.

Had Hitler known, not so much the condition of the Italian forces, but the reduced state of the garrison and people of Malta that summer, he might have reached a different conclusion. A combined Italo-German invasion in August 1942 might well have succeeded for, as we shall see, Malta was within days of col-lapse. Thus, although it never actually materialised, the *threat* to Malta remained potent until the beleaguered island was finally relieved in the autumn of that year.

It is evident, then, quite apart from the clear obligation of the British crown to the people of Malta, that the retention of the island was of major importance to the Allied cause. Hitler's com-mitment of the Afrika Korps to North Africa made Malta the key-stone of the Mediterranean war. In the judgements of those burdened with the grave and unenviable responsibility of British leadership, there was no alternative to running the convoys by which the island was supplied. Malta came within a whisker of surrender, so close-run was the campaign in the late summer of 1942, and the grievous loss of men and ships which averted this disaster merits its own detailed history. While it is the great and sometimes good who make war, it is ordinary people who endure its vicissitudes and pay its price, whether in victory or defeat. Their vital contribution should not be forgotten, nor can it be diminished by criticism of the strategy to which they were committed.

I hope this book adequately recounts the sea battles waged the length of the Mediterranean to maintain Malta, both directly and indirectly. I have given only a general account of events else-where in the Mediterranean theatre, insofar as they affected naval operations and, in particular, the strength of the naval forces available to support Malta. I am deeply grateful to all those who have helped me, and trust they are content with the outcome. I have sought to do justice to them in the list of acknowledgements at the end of the book, where will also be found chapter notes containing sources and references, together with a select bibliography.

In an ever-changing world, I have thought it best for clarity to

retain the forms of names used during the Second World War.
Where British naval officers are concerned I have omitted decorations, adding only where necessary the initials indicating
service in a Commonwealth navy or any of the reserves. Where
during the course of my researches I have encountered inconsist-
encies, I have attempted to reconcile these according to what, in
my judgement, seemed the best information. If I have perpetu-
ated errors, as for those mistakes or omissions which I fear must
unintentionally enter these pages, I ask forgiveness.

Richard Woodman
Harwich, 1999

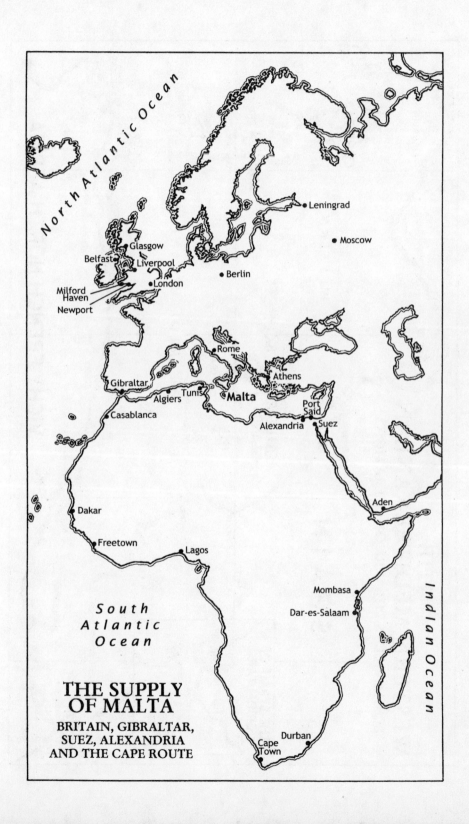

North Atlantic Ocean

Leningrad

Moscow

Glasgow
Belfast
Liverpool
Milford
Haven
Newport
London
Berlin

Rome

Athens

Gibraltar
Algiers Tunis **Malta**
Port
Said
Casablanca
Alexandria Suez

Aden

Dakar

Freetown
Lagos

Mombasa
Dar-es-Salaam

*South
Atlantic
Ocean*

Indian Ocean

Durban
Cape
Town

THE SUPPLY
OF MALTA
BRITAIN, GIBRALTAR,
SUEZ, ALEXANDRIA
AND THE CAPE ROUTE

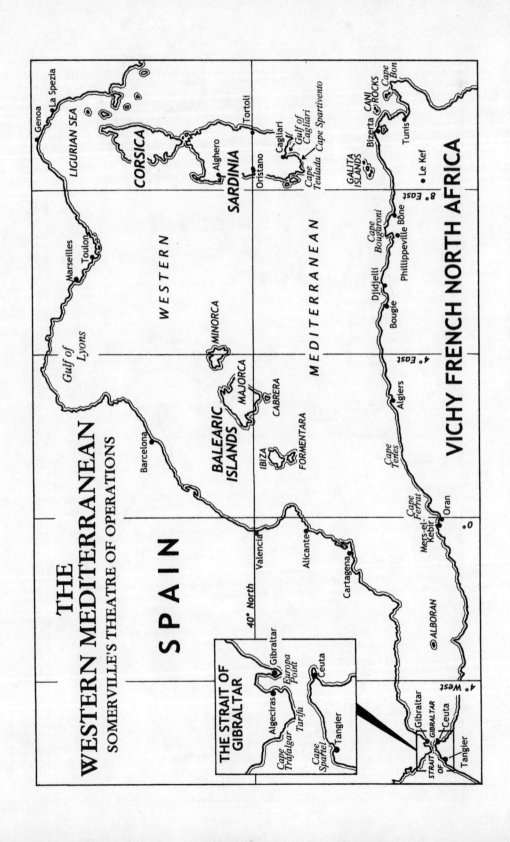

THE
WESTERN MEDITERRANEAN
SOMERVILLE'S THEATRE OF OPERATIONS

SPAIN

THE STRAIT OF
GIBRALTAR

VICHY FRENCH NORTH AFRICA

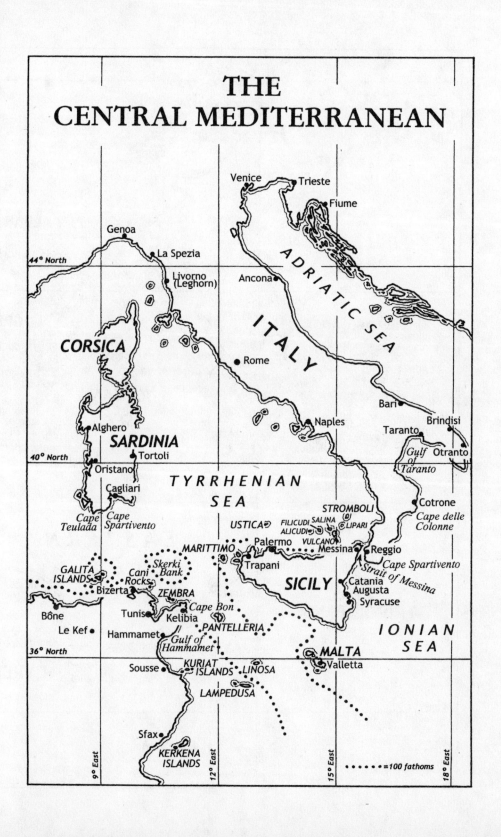

THE
CENTRAL MEDITERRANEAN

Venice • Trieste
• Fiume

Genoa
44° North • La Spezia
Livorno
(Leghorn) Ancona •

ADRIATIC SEA

CORSICA *ITALY*

Rome •

Bari •

Alghero Naples • Brindisi •
SARDINIA Taranto •
40° North • Tortoli *Gulf* Otranto •
Oristano • *of Taranto*
Cagliari • *TYRRHENIAN*
SEA Cotrone •
STROMBOLI *Cape delle*
Cape *Cape* *USTICA* FILICUDI SALINA *Colonne*
Teulada Spartivento ALICUDI LIPARI
MARITTIMO Palermo • VULCANO Messina Reggio •
Skerki Trapani • *Cape Spartivento*
GALITA *Bank* **SICILY** Catania • *Strait of Messina*
ISLANDS *Cani* Augusta •
Rocks Bizerta • *ZEMBRA* Syracuse •
Bône • *Cape Bon*
Le Kef • Tunis • Kelibia **PANTELLERIA** *IONIAN*
Hammamet • *Gulf of* *SEA*
36° North *Hammamet*
Sousse • *KURIAT* **MALTA**
ISLANDS LINOSA • Valletta
LAMPEDUSA

Sfax •
KERKENA
ISLANDS

9° East 12° East 15° East 18° East

• • • • • = 100 fathoms

THE EASTERN MEDITERRANEAN

THEATRE OF OPERATIONS OF THE
MEDITERRANEAN FLEET
(ADMIRALS CUNNINGHAM & HARWOOD)

40° North

A

tza
niki

AEGEAN SEA

ECE

TURKEY

ONIA

Athens
Piraeus

DODECANESE

CYCLADES

Cape
Malea

MILOS

RHODES

Kastellorizo

CYPRUS

LEBANON

IERA
KITHERA

Cape
Spada

Suda
Bay

SEA
OF CRETE

Lakania

KASOS

Canea
Heraklion

Scarpanto
Strait

Maleme

Kasos
Strait

Limassol

GAYDO

CRETE

34° North

MEDITERRANEAN

Beirut

SYRIA

Haifa

erna

Bomba

Gazala

Tobruk

Sidi
Barani

NILE DELTA

Port
Said

Port
Fouad

PALES-
TINE

Bardia

Sollum

Mersa
Matruh

Alexandria

Ismailia

Great Bitter Lake

El
Alamein

Cairo

Suez

NAICA

Suez Bay

28° North

25° East

35° East

EGYPT

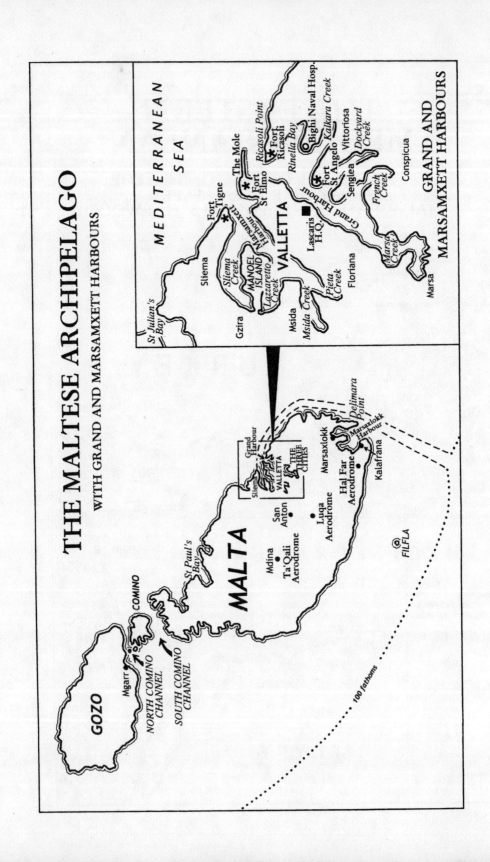

THE MALTESE ARCHIPELAGO

WITH GRAND AND MARSAMXETT HARBOURS

MEDITERRANEAN SEA

St Julian's Bay
Sliema
Gzira
Sliema Creek
Fort Tigne
The Mole
Ricasoli Point
Fort Ricasoli
Bighi Naval Hosp.
Rinella Bay
Kalkara Creek
MANOEL ISLAND
Lazzaretto Creek
Marsamxett Harbour
Fort St Elmo
Fort St Angelo
Vittoriosa
Dockyard Creek
Senglea
VALLETTA
Grand Harbour
Lascaris H.Q.
French Creek
Conspicua
Pieta Creek
Msida
Floriana
Marsa Creek
Msida Creek
Marsa

GRAND AND MARSAMXETT HARBOURS

MEDITERRANEAN SEA

GOZO
Mgarr
COMINO
NORTH COMINO CHANNEL
SOUTH COMINO CHANNEL
St Paul's Bay
MALTA
Mdina
Ta'Qali Aerodrome
San Anton
Luqa Aerodrome
Grand Harbour
Sliema
VALLETTA
THE THREE CITIES
Marsaxlokk
Delimara Point
Marsaxlokk Harbour
Hal Far Aerodrome
Kalafrana
FILFLA
100 fathoms

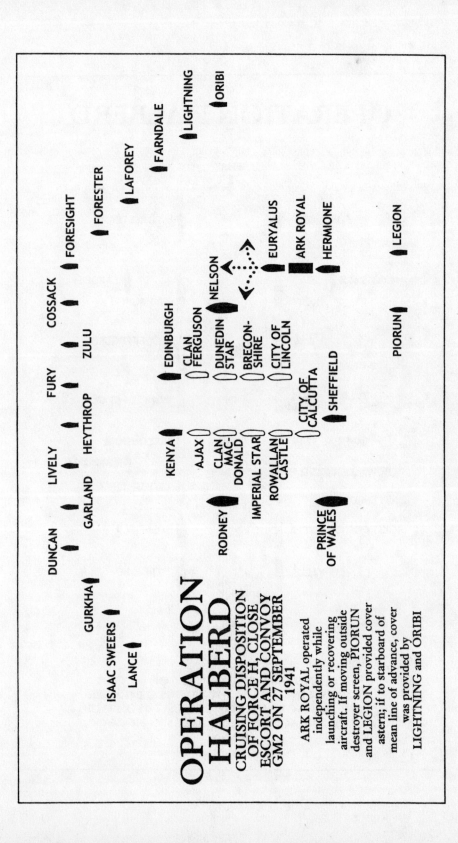

OPERATION HALBERD

CRUISING DISPOSITION OF FORCE H, CLOSE ESCORT AND CONVOY GM2 ON 27 SEPTEMBER 1941

ARK ROYAL operated independently while launching or recovering aircraft. If moving outside destroyer screen, PIORUN and LEGION provided cover astern; if to starboard of mean line of advance, cover was provided by LIGHTNING and ORIBI

LANCE

ISAAC SWEERS

GURKHA

DUNCAN

GARLAND

LIVELY

HEYTHROP

FURY

ZULU

COSSACK

FORESIGHT

FORESTER

LAFOREY

FARNDALE

LIGHTNING

ORIBI

RODNEY

KENYA

AJAX

CLAN MAC-DONALD

IMPERIAL STAR

ROWALLAN CASTLE

EDINBURGH

CLAN FERGUSON

DUNEDIN STAR

BRECON-SHIRE

CITY OF LINCOLN

NELSON

EURYALUS

ARK ROYAL

HERMIONE

CITY OF CALCUTTA

SHEFFIELD

PRINCE OF WALES

PIORUN

LEGION

OPERATION HALBERD

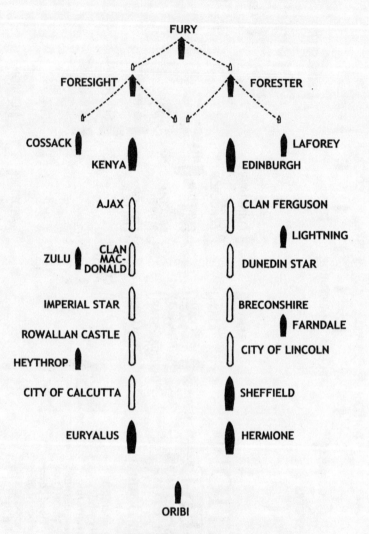

FURY

FORESIGHT

FORESTER

COSSACK

KENYA

LAFOREY

EDINBURGH

AJAX

CLAN FERGUSON

LIGHTNING

ZULU

CLAN MAC-DONALD

DUNEDIN STAR

IMPERIAL STAR

BRECONSHIRE

FARNDALE

ROWALLAN CASTLE

CITY OF LINCOLN

HEYTHROP

CITY OF CALCUTTA

SHEFFIELD

EURYALUS

HERMIONE

ORIBI

CRUISING DISPOSITION (No.17) OF CONVOY
GM2 DURING THE NIGHT OF 27/28 SEPTEMBER
1941. CONVOY AND CLOSE ESCORT CLOSED UP
FOR PASSAGE OF MINED AREAS IN SICILIAN
CHANNEL

1

'The adventure begins'

THE MEDITERRANEAN IS, as its name implies, an inland sea. The winds which disturb its surface are generated by the surrounding land masses and bring with them the characteristics of the terrain which creates them. The cold and 'masterly' mistral, which periodically roars south from the Rhône valley, churns the waters of the Gulf of Lyons with gale force. The hot and humid levanter drives westward between July and October off the Algerian coast and through the Strait of Gibraltar; the gregale, the 'Greek wind', blows strongly out of the Balkans over the Ionian Sea, Sicily and Malta whenever a depression forces its way through the central Mediterranean. The scirocco, a hot and evil spring wind, and the khamsin blow off the African coast, the former across the Gulf of Sirte from the arid highlands of Libyan Cyrenaica, the latter out of the Nile basin.

These winds can be dangerously strong and throw up heavy seas. It was the gregale which cast St Paul's ship upon the shores of Malta, the khamsin that afflicted Egypt as the Ninth Plague of the Old Testament, and the mistral that dismasted Nelson's *Vanguard* in 1798. In general, however, the Mediterranean is a pleasant place, considered benign by seafarers when compared to other seas. It is bisected by the boot-shaped peninsula of Italy which, with its barbican of Sicily, narrows the gap between Europe and Africa almost exactly half-way between Alexandria and Gibraltar, conveniently dividing it into two basins. Behind the heel of Italy, at the entrance to the Adriatic, lies the port of Brindisi; situated under the heel is the naval base of Taranto; and Reggio at the toe is opposite Messina on the Sicilian shore, the latter place giving its name to the narrow strait separating the two.

One hundred and eighty miles to the north-west of Sicily is the large Italian island of Sardinia, the southernmost point of which is Cape Spartivento. To the south-west, less than a hundred nautical miles distant, lies Cape Bon, hornwork of Tunisia and westward headland of the great bight in the coast of North Africa upon whose shores lie Tunis, Sfax, Tripoli (now known as Tarabulus), El Agheila at the head of the Gulf of Sirte (Sidra) and, as the coast swings north again, Benghazi. The Cyrenaican coast then turns east and here in succession Derna, Bomba, Gazala, Tobruk and Bardia are situated. Still further eastward, the Egyptian towns of Sidi Barani, Mersa Matruh and the great port of El Iskandarîya, Alexandria, interpose before the mouths of the Nile debouch into the Mediterranean. Here the flat, alluvial banks spread a great delta, beyond which Port Said and Port Fouad sit astride the entrance to the Suez Canal, the shipway to India and the Far East.

As equidistant to the westward of Sicily as Alexandria is to the east lies that contentious British possession, Gibraltar. Across its bay is Algeciras in Spain, in 1939 a dictatorship nominally neutral but with strong Fascist sympathies, making Algeciras a lookout post for spies keeping watch on the movements of the British fleet. To the south, across the six-mile-wide Strait of Gibraltar, is Morocco, its Atlantic port of Tangier once the dowry of a British queen, with its lighthouse at Cape Spartel.[1] Directly opposite Gibraltar stands the port of Ceuta, the gateway of North Africa. Between Ceuta and Cape Bon extended the then French colonies of Algeria and Tunisia upon whose coasts lay Oran, Algiers, Bône, and Bizerta. By the summer of 1940 these were in the hands of the Fascist Vichy French government, technically neutral but allied to the Axis Powers.

Sixty miles south of Sicily and about a hundred and eighty miles east of Cape Bon lies the small archipelago centred upon Malta. The island possessed strategic importance from earliest times, not merely because of its location but for the shelter of its harbours, the result of its geological constitution. Alternating stratae of soft globigerina limestone, with greensand and blue clay substrates between the hard layers of honey-coloured coral-line limestone, gave the island its ancient name of Melita, 'the honeyed one'. The oval-shaped island 'is a plateau, sloping gently towards the south east, tilted eastward from the west-coast cliffs, the highest point being no more than 800 feet above sea level'. Erosion over the millennia has produced deep re-entrants into which the blue Mediterranean flows, forming sleep sided inlets the greatest of which is known by the superlative name of Grand Harbour. In fact Grand Harbour, on the north-east coast, is the southern part of a greater inlet which is divided by the peninsula upon which stands Valletta, the Maltese capital, and which terminates in Fort St Elmo; the farther inlet is Marsamxett Harbour. This complex area has always been the island's most coveted asset.

Along the southern shore of Grand Harbour further deep inlets alternate with limestone prominences, each with its ram-parted city. French Creek and Dockyard Creek are separated by Senglea, Dockyard Creek and Kalkara Creek by Fort St Angelo. Bighi with its naval hospital separates Kalkara Creek from Rinella Creek, which culminates in Ricasoli Point, the southern jaw of the entrance to Grand Harbour, upon which was the radio station. Senglea, with its neighbours Vittoriosa and Conspicua, forms the conurbation known as the Three Cities. To the north and west of Valletta and Fort St Elmo lies the wider, less impressive Marsamxett Harbour, in the middle of which is Manoel Island, along whose southern shore passes Lazaretto Creek, the British navy's submarine base. Lazaretto Creek runs into Msida Creek which, on the outbreak of war, housed the torpedo store. To the north of Manoel Island is Sliema Creek, on the northern shore of which lies Sliema itself, its peninsula closing Grand Harbour from the north at Dragutt Point upon which stands Fort Tigne. In 1940 the whole area was densely populated, crowding round the harbour which since 1800, when the French were driven out, had been a favourite support base of the British Royal Navy's Mediterranean Fleet.

On the south-east corner of the island lies Marsaxlokk Bay, also known as Marsa Scirocco, a more exposed area with the town of Marsaxlokk on its northern shore. Upon its southern littoral stand Kalafrana, at the head of Pretty Bay, and Birzebugga, in whose limestone caves aviation spirit was stored during the war. In a line running roughly north-west from Marsaxlokk Bay along the plateau, at intervals of about two miles, lay the aerodromes of Hal Far, Luqa and Ta' Qali. From the exposed runways of this trio of neighbouring air stations operated the aircraft of the Royal

Air Force and the Fleet Air Arm which would defend the island, strike at the enemies' supply routes, and provide cover for the incoming convoys as they fought to succour Malta.

It was in Marsaxlokk Bay that the Ottoman Turks had landed to take Malta from its overlords, the Knights Hospitallers. Ejected from the Holy Land by the Turks, the Knights had finally retreated to Malta, gifted to them in 1530 by the Spanish Emperor Charles V in his capacity as King of Sicily and held against the Ottomans. The Knights built the forts of St Angelo and St Elmo, constructed the first curtain walls, and threw a chain boom across the harbour entrance in anticipation of attack. On 18 May 1565 the Turkish fleet arrived from the Bosphorus, to confront the six hundred Knights and their 7,000 auxiliaries with a force estimated at 35,000 armed men. The Knights were led by their Grand Master, Jean de la Vallette Parisot, who proved an outstanding commander. In Edward Gibbon's words, although the Knights 'neglected to live, they were prepared to die, in the service of Christ.'

Once ashore the Turks deployed their array, firing cannon shot against St Elmo, whose garrison of five hundred were ordered to resist to the last. Reinforced across the harbour they held out for a month against huge odds, but on 24 June the Turks seized St Elmo, crucified four Knights and floated the gruesome trophies across to St Angelo. Not to be outdone, the defiant defenders there are said to have fired back the heads of slaughtered prisoners. Malta was suddenly the cynosure of all eyes in the confrontation between the Cross and the Crescent. In distant England, Queen Elizabeth I ordered prayers for Malta to be read in all churches three times a week, for six weeks.

Meanwhile Vallette had obtained help from the Viceroy of Sicily and a relieving force landed along the coast on 7 September, raising the siege the following day. It was this feat of arms which caused the defence of the island between 1940 and 1943 to be called the 'Second Great Siege of Malta'.

In the succeeding years a fortified city was built behind St Elmo and named after Vallette. A great cathedral and magnificent *auberges*, each dedicated to the different nationalities of the Knights, provided the spiritual and communal accommodation the Order required. Further ramparts were raised about Fort St Angelo and the new city of Vittoriosa nestled behind massive walls, for the Turks remained masters of the eastern Mediterranean until, in October 1571, a combined Christian fleet under

Don Juan of Austria, an illegitimate son of the Emperor, defeated the fleet of Selim II, under the command of Ali Pasha, off Lepanto in the Gulf of Patras on the coast of the Morea.

The defeat of the Ottoman Turks and the expansion of western maritime powers across the Atlantic towards the Indies reduced the strategic importance of Malta until, two centuries later, the military energy of Revolutionary France confronted the restraining opposition of British sea-power. Once again the Mediterranean became a cockpit of war.

Although the Knights had continued to terrorise Turkish and Barbaresque shipping, by this time the Order had degenerated, their membership corrupted by an infusion of absent aristocrats who were mostly French and vanished in the Terror. By the end of the eighteenth century Tsar Paul I of Russia was manoeuvring for a position of titular ascendancy, to which the Grand Master was inclined to submit. But in May 1798 a French expeditionary force sailed from Toulon for Egypt; it was commanded by an ambitious young general named Napoleon Bonaparte. *En route* the French took Malta, to destroy nascent Russian hegemony and dissuade both the British and the Austrians from seizing the island.

French Knights with republican sympathies undermined Malta's defence, and the Order's French treasurer Bosredon de Ranjisat announced he could not in conscience oppose his own countrymen. There were three hundred Knights who, 'had their hearts been as anachronistic as were their institutions ... would have fought'.[2] The victorious French roistered among the 'ravishing beautiful and charming' women in the city of Valletta, which boasted a higher number of whores than any other contemporary European city. In less than a week Malta was the recipient of all the benefits of French republican civilisation, her youthful conqueror having dictated her new constitution before departing. He left behind a small garrison of 3,000 under Général Vaubois.

Meanwhile, casting about for the French fleet was a British squadron under Rear-Admiral Nelson, who finally caught up with his quarry and annihilated them in Aboukir Bay. A remnant trio of French men-of-war struggled into Valletta, their forlorn state fuelling the islanders' smouldering resentment of the Republic's arbitrary rule. When in September the French attempted to sell the treasures and relics of the Church of Our

Lady of Mount Carmel at Mdina, there was a popular uprising which drove the garrison into Valletta. The islanders were without arms but, seeing British warships offshore, put off in boats to beg assistance. Captain Saumarez of *Orion* sent back 1,200 muskets and ammunition taken out of the French prizes he was escorting. Soon afterwards a British squadron led by Captain Ball in *Alexander* arrived to blockade the French in Valletta itself. Lacking the resources for a full assault, Ball's seamen and marines landed guns and assisted the islanders, gradually stepping up this co-operation until, on 4 September 1800, having eaten everything edible, burnt ships for firewood and sent the population outside the walls to burden the besiegers, there was nothing left for Vaubois to do but surrender. He relinquished the island to Ball, who became Malta's first British governor. At the conclusion of the war in 1814 Malta formally became a British possession, under the terms of the Treaty of Paris. Nor were the Maltese unwilling, such had been the popularity of Ball's administration. *To Great and Unconquered Britain*, read an inscription raised in Valletta in 1814, *the love of the Maltese and the voice of Europe confirms these Islands.*

So began Malta's long relationship with the Royal Navy. And while the admirals agreed about the influence a British fleet operating from Malta could wield in the Mediterranean, the denizens of the lower deck loved Malta for the winning welcoming smiles of its people, for its sunshine, its wine, and the comeliness of its women. Valletta was to witness the high noon of imperial splendour when naval investment consequent upon the opening of the Suez Canal in 1869, which encouraged the regular transit of steamships bound for India and the Far East, radically improved Malta's economy, damaged by the long post-Napoleonic peace. Imperial policy added to the fortifications of Valletta and the island became of strategic importance when, at the end of the nineteenth century, Britain adopted the 'two-power standard' to determine the size of her navy – the Royal Navy having to be capable thereafter of matching the allied power of any two European navies. At the time this was prompted by fears of Franco-Russian alliance, but there was another rising power in the Mediterranean, that of a newly united Italy, whose genius for ship design, the leading exponent of which was Vittorio Cuniberti, put her in the forefront of technological development. Cuniberti's published works profoundly influenced naval thinking and partly inspired the design of the British battleship HMS *Dreadnought*. The commissioning of the world's first all big-gun battleship in 1906 rendered every capital ship in the world obsolescent.

Coincident with *Dreadnought*'s commissioning was the completion of the breakwater protecting Grand Harbour. Malta had become 'a main link in the chain of command with India by the Suez Canal, and a base for any service the government may require in the central or eastern Mediterranean ...' In fact, as tension in Europe increased in the period preceding the First World War, a debate took place on the defence of Malta and the size of the naval force to be allocated to it in time of war. The Royal Navy was beginning to feel the effects of overstrain in its obligation to protect world-wide commitments, particularly when confronted with the increasing power of the German High Seas Fleet.

When war broke out in 1914, Malta's part in hostilities was relatively subdued, though the uneasy naval alliance between France and Great Britain was centred upon Grand Harbour. Of greater significance was the fact that the German submarine menace in the Mediterranean was opposed from the island, an opposition accomplished partly by aircraft supported by three seaplane carriers, *Ark Royal*, *Manxman* and *Engadine*, and partly by the new Malta Naval Air Station. From these no fewer than 106 seaplanes were operating air patrols by 1918. Moreover, a shortage of convoy escorts was made up for by a flotilla of warships from Japan, then a useful ally, consisting of the cruiser *Idzumo* and fourteen destroyers, while additional anti-submarine forces were provided by American submarine-chasers. There were several major losses of warships to mines and torpedoes in Maltese waters, but the importance of the island fortress lay in its dockyard, which maintained men-of-war from the allied fleets of Britain, France, America, Japan and, occasionally, Russia, Greece and Italy. Troop transports, hospital ships, munitions ships and ordinary merchantmen visited the island on passage to the various theatres of war, the Dardanelles, Palestine and Mesopotamia, as well as in the course of maintaining the day-to-day traffic of regular commerce. Ship movements ran at about two dozen a day, with tankers bringing in oil for the newer vessels' bunkers, and fleets of colliers discharging coal for older ships. Maltese labour kept all this activity in motion by providing the infrastructure to support it, while the local minesweeping force was manned entirely by native ratings, who acquired a reputation for efficiency and courage.

In the unhappy period between the wars, Malta's strategic place in the world was confirmed. In 1925 the Turkish government objected to a frontier decision made by the League of Nations and threatened an attack on Iraq. As the responsible power designated by the League, Britain's task would have been to enforce Turkish obedience, and preparations were put in hand for a full naval expedition from Malta. In the event the matter cooled, but political upheaval in Italy was moving to a more heated climax, which was to impact disastrously upon Malta itself.

In 1921 the Kingdom of Italy was in a state of deep civil unrest. Terrified of the success of Communism in Russia and post-war Germany, King Victor Emmanuel II finally sought stability by caving in to pressure from the Italian Fascist Party, the chief opponents of the Communists. He requested their leader to become prime minister; Benito Mussolini assumed dictatorial powers the following month, to become the Duce, or leader, of Italy. The Duce permitted a limited but faltering democracy to totter on until 1924, but had imposed full Fascist rule by 1929, when the population was allowed to vote for 400 candidates all nominated by the Fascist Grand Council. Mussolini's programme of public works and reforms obscured the sinister implications of his rule, earning him the respect of men like Bernard Shaw and Rabindranath Tagore, plus the specious reputation of having compelled Italian trains to run on time. But the veil was rudely torn from the eyes of his admirers when in 1935 he ordered the invasion of Abyssinia (Ethiopia). The only remaining independent nation on the African continent after the scramble for colonies by the European powers, Abyssinia had maintained her integrity against previous incursions, including an earlier foray by the Italians. Ruled by the Emperor Haile Selassie, who traced his descent from the union of Solomon and the Queen of Sheba, the country was undergoing modernisation. Border clashes with Abyssinians on the frontiers of the Italian colonies of Eritrea and Somalia combined with Mussolini's desire to avenge the earlier Italian defeat and to gain a military reputation for himself. Despite the condemnation of the League of Nations, the Duce ordered General Graziani to invade, without a declaration of war. Graziani prosecuted a campaign using mechanised vehicles, aircraft and mustard gas, occupying the capital, Addis Ababa, on 5 May 1936. Haile Selassie went into exile as Mussolini appointed Graziani a Marshal, Duke of Neghelli and Viceroy of Ethiopia. This act of inexcusable aggression caused Italy to be ostracised by the Western democracies, while the increasing congruence of Italian Fascism and German Nazism made bedfellows of the Duce and the Führer, despite Mussolini's suspicion of Hitler. The Berlin–Rome 'Axis' was eventually strengthened in May 1939 by the agreement known as the Pact of Steel.

The tension induced by Mussolini's action in Abyssinia raised the political and naval temperature in Malta. Operations against Italy were mooted, including an attack on the naval base of Taranto, and caused fear of gas attacks among the civilian population. But it was the outbreak of the Spanish Civil War in 1936 which claimed the attention of the British Mediterranean Fleet, the chief duty of which was to evacuate British subjects; destroyers picked up isolated British nationals at odd locations.[3] Destroyers also played a leading part in this quasi-hostile situation. Long patrols were frequent, and HMS *Codrington* steamed for 104 days that year, covering 15,780 miles. These were arduous duties for peace-time commissions, but the peace was nominal. On 22 February 1937, HM Destroyers *Havock* and *Gipsy* were bombed, a more determined attack was made by Junkers bombers on *Gallant*, and *Havock* was later attacked by a submarine. No serious damage was done until 15 May, when HMS *Hunter* struck a mine off Almeria. The destroyer's bow was holed and her forward boiler burst. It was a nasty foretaste of what was to come, for Italian submarines were operating in support of the rebel Spanish Fascists, as were Italian troops ashore.

By the summer of 1938, British relations with Italy were precarious. Admiral Riccardi paid a courtesy visit to Valletta in a squadron consisting of two battleships and four destroyers, but the atmosphere of amity was contrived, for the two countries were mutually suspicious. Ever since the Abyssinian crisis, the British Code and Cypher School had been trying to crack Italian signals, and by 1939 the 'most secret' and 'book' cyphers of the Italian navy and one of the two codes used by Italian naval attachés had been broken, as had the 'book' code used in the Mediterranean by the Regia Aeronautica, Mussolini's air force.

These successes later yielded a short warning of Italy's entry into
the war, as soon as Mussolini decided upon it, along with intelligence of the strength and organisation of the Italian order of
battle.[4]

Suspicion of Italian motives further increased after her invasion of Albania over Easter 1939. On Good Friday, 7 April, Italy
occupied and annexed the country, deposing King Zog and
passing the crown to Victor Emmanuel III. Italian 'improvements' were put in hand, and though the invasion created 'a bit
of a storm in intellectual circles in Albania' and resulted in
'twenty or so persons [being] immediately sent to concentration
camps ... Public works are starting well,' Count Ciano gloated,
'the roads are all planned in such a way as to lead to the Greek
border ... the Duce ... is thinking more and more of attacking
Greece.'[5]

The acquisition of Albania was not just the 'lebensraum for
Italy' Ciano claimed.[6] But Italian military weakness, a lack of military hardware of all types, a crucial want of raw materials and
the incompetence, servility and mendacity of her commanders
began to expose the fundamental weakness at the heart of the
Pact of Steel. Furthermore, the situation was worsened by the
blockade imposed by Britain which embargoed, among other
commodities, seaborne imports of coal on their way to Italy.

But the easy success in Albania had its soothingly delusive
effect and provided a combination of circumstances which seems
to have acted as the necessary catalyst upon the Duce's volatile
mind and which was the precipitate for all his major decisions,
further enhanced by German victories in the north. The Duce's
fateful meeting with Hitler at the Brenner Pass on 18 March 1940
had exposed Mussolini 'more and more [to] the fascination of the
Führer'. This fascination, according to Ciano, was based upon
military success, 'the only success that Mussolini really values
and desires'. Moreover, it was a Fascist axiom that 'the prestige
of a leader victorious in war is never questioned'.

Apprehension of hostilities with Italy had been increasingly
felt in a Britain which saw in the German invasions of Denmark
and Norway, of France and the Low Countries, during April and
May of 1940, a terrifying efficiency. The defeat of the Anglo-
French forces in both theatres produced a sudden fear of Italy
taking a more active part alongside her victorious ally. And
whereas Italy had been widely thought to be opposed to war, at

the end of April the Italian ambassador in London informed Rome that 'responsible British circles thought that the outcome in Norway would influence the Italian decision to enter the war'.[7]

They were right: Mussolini became increasingly indignant at the deprivations caused by the British blockade and simultaneously excited by the idea of dominating the Mediterranean. On 28 May, as Belgium capitulated, he announced to his intimate circle that 10 June was the intended date of Italian entry into the war; this the British soon learned from their analysis of radio signals and decrypts of cypher traffic.

Even as the Duce spoke, the British Expeditionary Force was being evacuated from the beaches of Dunkirk, abandoning its equipment, while the fuming Guderian obediently halted on orders from a Hitler who still considered Britain would come to her senses and sue for peace. But by 6 June Operation DYNAMO had rescued the shambles of the British army from the beaches, Paris had been bombed, and Allied troops had begun to be withdrawn from Narvik. Two days later, as Norway fell, the heavy guns of the *Scharnhorst* and *Gneisenau* sank the British aircraft-carrier *Glorious* and her two escorting destroyers *Acasta* and *Ardent*.[8]

To the waiting Mussolini, it seemed the tide had at last turned against the British. He had long vowed vengeance upon Britain for so adversely affecting the Italian economy by blockade, especially of German supplies of coal: 'I shall make the British repent. My intervention in the war will bring about their defeat.' Such a grandiloquent claim was to be expected of Mussolini, but was also a manifestation of the widespread hatred Great Britain had aroused by her imperial might.[9] Ciano recorded these words with his customary apprehension, commenting: 'The Duce, alas, is still under illusions as to our chances of quick rearmament. The situation is still very difficult and lack of coal will only make it worse. Perhaps we shall enter the war, but we shall be unprepared and unarmed.' It was now too late for such regrets. Three months of vacillation, and of momentous success accruing to Hitler, provoked Mussolini to throw in his lot with Germany. His judgement, impaired most probably by the mental impact of tertiary syphilis and unencumbered by political opposition, succumbed to the fatal fascination of the German Führer and the lure of aggrandisement.[10]

Mussolini proved ready to rush 'to the assistance of the victor', as one diplomat observed. At the very moment when Hitler had halted Guderian in the hope of reaching an accommodation with Great Britain, Mussolini was intent upon a course of action which gave Churchill the opportunity to retaliate. The malleable Duce, dreaming of a new 'Roman Mediterranean Empire', seduced by Hitler's military successes, declaimed that 'to make a people great, it is necessary to send them to battle even if you have to kick them in the pants', further ruminating that 'if we do not take advantage of this occasion to pit our navy against the French and British forces, what is the use of building 600,000 tons of warships?' When Mussolini announced Italy's declaration of war from the balcony of the Palazzo Venezia, it did 'not arouse much enthusiasm'. 'I am sad,' Ciano went on, concluding his diary entry for 10 June 1940, 'very sad. The adventure begins. May God help Italy!'

The following day aircraft of the Regia Aeronautica took off to bomb Malta. Italian intelligence reports indicated that the island lay supine, for the Royal Navy's Mediterranean Fleet had withdrawn from the area three weeks earlier: Malta was considered too vulnerable.

In the years prior to 1939, Malta had been largely written off by the British army and air force as indefensible, and was evidently a low priority in the strained British defence budget. By early 1940 the island's garrison comprised only five battalions; there were three airfields but no fighters, though a flying-boat base was operational. In spite of the Admiralty's view that Malta's location and its dockyard facilities were vital to any Mediterranean conflict, the island was, at the outbreak of war, virtually defenceless.

Mussolini's opportunistic declaration of war radically altered the strategic importance of Malta, for its conquest would be essential to his ambitions in the Mediterranean. Conversely, the holding of Malta would frustrate him, and was essential to Britain's maintenance of both a defensive and an offensive capability in that theatre. The only way this could be achieved was through continuous replenishment of the island, not with military stores only, but with the necessities of life itself. With a native population of over a quarter of a million, to be increased by a large garrison, the support of Malta posed a major logistical problem to the over-stretched British. Supply was not a matter of a single achievement, nor a question of gradual augmentation: whatever was shipped to the island was rapidly consumed, one way or another. Food, fuel, ammunition, guns, medical stores, reinforcements, vehicles, aircraft and spares – all had to be forced through on a regular basis and each consignment required a prodigious effort, a concentration of merchant shipping with massive naval escort, to ensure its arrival. With this went its concomitant in modern war, as much air support as could be mustered: both fighter cover and aerial reconnaissance were crucial, either from the aircraft of the fleet itself, or from Gibraltar, Malta or Egypt.

These Malta-bound convoys were not ordinary convoys in the conventional sense. They were 'military convoys', often coded 'WS' – 'Winston's Specials' – and quite unlike the large, slow convoys of the 'Atlantic Bridge'. They were usually relatively small, with what were intended to be – and, let it be emphasised, needed to be – powerful escorts. If the escorts amounted to battle-squadrons, then the core of the convoys, the merchant ships themselves, were the cream of the British commercial fleet, fast cargo-liners whose owners were peacetime rivals and counted themselves among the household names of the shipping industry.

The requisite assembly of naval might was not always possible; British resources were very far from being limitless, nor were they as fit for their purpose as they might have been. There were competing demands at coincident times. In the critical period between the summers of 1941 and 1942, Britain was sending abroad five aircraft and fifteen tanks for every one she received from the United States of America, and these exported consignments were going to Soviet Russia, escorted by warships of the Royal Navy. Men-of-war, and in particular destroyers, dashed from the freezing wastes of the Barents Sea to the milder Mediterranean and back again, an exhausting shuttle punitive to men and ships. In both theatres the enemy's air, surface and sub-sea forces, operating on interior lines, were always potentially able to attack the thinly-spread British convoy defences. To sustain Malta between the major convoys, each of which amounted to a complex naval operation, single ships, both merchant and naval, were slipped through with small, vital consignments of essential supplies; significantly, only one such run involving a merchantman was successful. Even submarines were pressed into this service. Equally essential to Malta's preservation was a constant reinforcement of fighter aircraft, flown off from British and American carriers which steamed eastwards until within flying range of the island, whereupon their 'cargo' took off, often to arrive at their destination in the midst of an air battle.

Without this costly effort Malta would have been starved and might well have been bombed into impotence, as indeed the Axis came to consider it had been. In such a case nothing could have stopped exploitation of the short-sea supply route between Italy and Libya, and the campaign in the Western Desert might well have resulted in Britain's eviction from the Suez Canal. In this event, the concept of Axis hands linking across the Indian sub-continent, as postulated by OKW's 'Grand Plan', does not seem quite so impossible an outcome.

2

'The moral is to the material as three is to one'

COUNT CIANO WAS right to express misgivings about Italy's long-term prospects in a protracted war. Roughly a quarter of her coal and anthracite was imported; over three-quarters of her crude oil, two-thirds of her scrap steel, almost all her nickel and other rarer metals were brought in by sea. Much of Italy's imports came from sources within the British Empire or from countries allied to or associated with Britain, while the rest had to be conveyed through the bottlenecks of the Dardanelles, the Suez Canal, or the Strait of Gibraltar. It was comparatively easy for the British navy to close all of these.

Coal, which came from Poland in German ships, the British embargo of which so annoyed the Duce, could be transported overland, but the Germans, through whose territory it had to travel, had a prior claim on it. On the other hand, iron ore could be obtained from defeated France or from North Africa. Because of her geography and the difficulty of trans-Apennine communications, Italy depended upon her own coastal merchant shipping for mainland communications as much as for communications between her offshore islands. Deployment of the Italian army in North Africa only increased this dependence, requiring the services of her deep-water shipping. Although the Italian merchant fleet was considerable and quite capable of providing such service, Mussolini's precipitate declaration of war resulted in the internment of Italian merchant ships dispersed about the globe.

Nevertheless, even before the increase of Italian forces in Cyrenaica, command of the central Mediterranean was essential to Italy's participation in the Axis war effort. Such command centred on her naval and air forces. The Italian Fascists had begun a programme to produce a balanced fleet almost as soon as they came to power, an advantage they had over Hitler's Germany, and in 1939 contemporary opinion held the Italian navy, or Regia Marina, in some esteem. Their lack of aircraft-carriers was nullified by the disposition of Italy's air bases in the central Mediterranean. With some 1,200 aircraft in metropolitan Italy, a further 284 in North Africa and a handful in the Dodecanese, command of the air seemed assured, well able to support the Regia Marina in domination of the area. The Italian navy consisted, by way of capital ships in commission, of two old but modernised battleships of the *Cavour* class, with two more undergoing updating and two under construction. These, *Littorio* and *Vittorio Veneto*, with a main armament of 15-inch guns, were on the brink of completion. A substantial number of cruisers had been built in the 1930s to join some of older vintage. Seven were 'heavy' cruisers, mounting 8-inch-calibre guns and built to the 10,000-ton limit set by the 1922 Washington Treaty in an attempt to curb a naval arms race. These were lightly armoured, following a traditional Italian theory that speed was a more important element than the ability to absorb punishment. Four knots faster than their British counterparts, these ships were supplemented in 1928 by the laying down of the first of eleven 6-inch-armed 'light' cruisers. Of some 5,000 tons displacement, the *Condottieri* class were also thinly armoured, allowing them to exceed the contract-specified 37 knots on trials;[1] variants of slightly heavier tonnage followed. These light cruisers were intended to operate with flotillas of destroyers, and possessed a minelaying capability.

There were sixty-one destroyers armed largely either with four 4.7-inch guns and six torpedo tubes, or six 4.7-inch guns and four torpedo tubes. They varied between 1,000 and 1,600 tons and were capable of very high speeds. Lighter-armed and smaller 'torpedo-boats', which like their German namesakes were actually small destroyers, amounted to a further sixty-six ships. Moreover the Italians, who had earned a considerable reputation for underwater engineering skills, had a superior fleet of sub-marines, numbering 115 in June 1940. In technical terms their ocean-going submarines were capable of surfaced speeds of up to 17.5 knots (one was capable of 19), with submerged speeds of

9.5 knots. An Italian submarine had dived to an unprecedented record depth of 400 feet (120 metres) off the Gambia River, remaining submerged for 36 hours, thereafter circumnavigating Africa in a voyage of 15,000 miles. The four *Cagni*-class submarines, carrying fourteen torpedoes, were designed for the war against trade, and had sunk merchantmen during the Spanish Civil War. In comparative terms, the Italian submarine service could be considered a world leader.[2]

In addition to these warships the Italians possessed some corvettes, a quantity of auxiliaries, minesweepers and minelayers, patrol vessels, and fast attack craft. Chief among the last were the *Motoscafi Anti-Sommergibili* or *MAS* boats, swift dashing craft, similar to the German *Schnellboote*, whose characteristics suited the individually courageous panache of the Italians themselves.

The Italian fleet was disposed throughout a number of bases in metropolitan Italy, at Taranto, Naples, La Spezia, Brindisi and, at the head of the Adriatic, at Trieste. Insuline Italy boasted the Sicilian ports of Messina, Augusta and Palermo, and the Sardinian port of Cagliari. But there were warships based on Tripoli and Tobruk in North Africa, a squadron was deployed in the Red Sea, and another was stationed at Leros, an Italian island in the Dodecanese. Italy also held the Dalmatian ports of Zara, Lagosta and Saseno, the ports of Albania, chief of which was Durazzo, and the island of Rhodes. Moreover, Mussolini had made of the island of Pantelleria, which lay between Cape Bon and Sicily, 'a counter-Malta'.[3] Further fine harbours existed at Genoa and Pola. Thus, within the Mediterranean, particularly after the fall of France and despite the pre-emptive destruction of the French fleet by the British, the Italian Regia Marina appeared to enjoy local superiority, supporting the Duce's assertion that the Mediterranean was *Mare Nostrum*.[4]

However, since Italy had only been a unified state since 1866, the Italian navy had no long tradition from which to draw strength in adversity and, unfortunately, adversity was what it had principally experienced. In its first fleet action, at Lissa in July 1866, it had made a poor showing. This was doubly unfortunate, for the Italian fleet consisted of new ironclads and was pitted against an Austrian squadron among which were some obsolescent ships mounting muzzle-loading guns. Despite his superiority Ammiraglio Carlo di Persano lingered at Ancona, and in the end the younger Von Tegetthoff forced the issue. In a confused action in which ramming tactics were employed, the Italian fleet was savaged.

But while their navy was a youthful service, the general maritime tradition of the Italians was not. The great hero of their liberation, Garibaldi, was an accomplished seaman, and among other great Italian seafarers could be numbered Christopher Columbus, John Cabot, Andrea Doria and Alessandro Malaspina.[5] After Lissa, Italy produced a number of significant innovative talents. Italian flair for design and fitness for purpose has been a byword since the Renaissance. Benedetto Brin and Vittorio Cuniberti were directly involved in warship design, influencing naval theory outside Italy, while that genius of his age, Guglielmo Marconi, had a profound effect upon the history of mankind. Italian engineering skills ought to have made of the Italian fleet in being in 1940 a formidable weapon, for individual Italian courage was not in question. During the struggle for liberation there had been ample demonstrations of this, and the coming war was to provide more. Italian raids by manned torpedoes were to greatly embarrass the British Mediterranean Fleet at a critical moment, prompting Churchill to enquire of his staff why the British had nothing comparable.

The Regia Marina, however, was not what it seemed from outward appearances. There were constant rumours of corruption and misappropriation of funds during the building of some of the fleet, in which Ammiraglio Ciano, among others, seems to have been implicated. A lack of seaworthiness lurked in the design of one class of destroyers, but a more baleful influence on the conduct of the Italian navy was the Fascist state itself, with its excessive centralisation, the infighting which such a structure engenders and, most inhibiting of all, a blame-culture. It was widely said of the naval hierarchy that it was composed of better Fascists than admirals.

For the more junior officers and the lower ranks, on which the moral fibre of a fighting service most depends, Fascism had less appeal. Fewer benefits accrued at these levels to adherents to the creed, and many ratings were, if not Communists, then politically inclined to the left of centre and broadly opposed to the war. Fascism never gripped a generation of Italians, as Nazism did a generation of Germans; nor was the character of the Italians so easily regimented, nor they themselves so easily persuaded to leave the hearth and beat the ploughshare into a sword.

The Italian battle-fleet was largely composed of very fast and effective if often lightly armoured ships, well provided with fire-power and of sufficient numbers to inflict damage if it employed the hit-and-run tactics for which it was designed. Such tactics were entirely consonant with the dash and spirit of the Italian character and should have tied down enormous British resources. But it suffered from two major limitations, a lack of fuel reserves and a lack of leadership.[6] In hands deficient in drive and experience the Italian fleet was likely to perform less well than expected, despite the advantage of not having the French navy as an additional opponent. But, as a contemporary com-mentator sagely pointed out, 'naval efficiency springs first from tradition, and, second, from persistent support of a single ideal throughout the whole service'.[7] This was almost the only advan-tage the British navy had over the Italian in that first summer of 1940.

At the outbreak of war the Royal Navy was far less able than its obviously potent manifestations suggested. During the First World War it had been cheated of its anticipated second Trafalgar, and post-mortems on the major fleet action at Jutland persist to this day.[8] The impressive British Grand Fleet which, with an American squadron in its divisions, escorted the German High Seas Fleet into safe-keeping under the terms of the Armistice, did so with a triumphalism that gave the event the specious appearance of a great victory. In fact, such had been the influence of the German fleet-in-being that the British navy, for all its preponderance of super-dreadnoughts and battlecruisers in addition to the lesser panoply of naval might, had been so tied to home waters that it had relied largely upon the allied fleet of Japan, most of whose ships were British-built, to cover Britain's defensive commitments east of Suez. Under the terms of the Anglo-Japanese Treaty, as noted in the previous chapter, *Idzumo* and her destroyers were based at Malta, a measure of assistance welcomed within the Mediterranean itself. Nevertheless, the British Royal Navy appeared to have accepted many of the lessons of the First World War, in particular the importance of discovering a successful mode of defeating the submarine's ability to interdict the seaborne trade upon which Britain depended, and the growing importance of air-power.

Where the Royal Navy was concerned, air-power meant

seaborne aircraft. These had advanced beyond the seaplanes carried in *Engadine*, *Manxman* and *Ark Royal* at Malta in 1917, or the experimental biplanes launched off the forward turrets of battlecruisers. Although spotting and reconnaissance aeroplanes were to be carried in cruisers and battleships, the introduction of aircraft capable of delivering a torpedo attack in squadron strength prompted the development of the dedicated aircraft-carrier. A liner under construction in Britain for an Italian shipping company during the First World War, the *Conte Rosso*, was requisitioned, given a full-length flight deck and completed as HMS *Argus*, the first British carrier. She was commissioned at the end of the war and was followed by *Furious*, *Glorious* and *Courageous*. The Washington Treaty of 1922, which sought to curb the building of big-gun battle fleets, thereby delivered to the world's navies a number of redundant battlecruiser hulls, which were swiftly converted to carriers, and the origins of these three ships as aborted battlecruisers produced fast effective ships (the last two named were lost early in the war). They were joined by HMS *Eagle*, which had been laid down as a battleship for the Chileans, and finally the British added a purpose-built carrier, the smaller *Hermes*. With these six carriers Britain looked set fair to take the lead in naval aviation, but despite the Royal Navy's early adoption of aircraft it had subsequently fallen behind its rivals in the matter. It had also seriously compromised itself in respect of that other great lesson of 1914–1918, anti-submarine warfare.[9]

Ironically, the naval arms limitations of the Washington Treaty had had a baleful effect on British sea-power because, generally speaking, the British conformed more closely than any other signatory power with the terms of the treaty. In the wake of the carnage on the Western Front, the pacifist spirit of the western democracies influenced the political thinking of successive British governments, wrestling in any case with the enormous economic problems of a post-war slump. Disarmament was perceived as one solution, and the post-war First Lord of the Admiralty, Sir Eric Geddes, had instituted a drastic cost-reduction programme even before signatures were put to the disarmament treaty. Britain scrapped many of her greatest ships, including Beatty's flagship *Lion*, along with some two hundred destroyers and convoy escorts. With this reduction in ships went a corresponding loss of trained personnel across the whole spectrum of the naval hierarchy. At the same time, Britain had both to maintain a modern fleet in order to protect her empire, and to be seen not to have lost her ancient ability to keep a vast fleet in being.

Britain was also increasingly uneasy about her reliance upon the Anglo-Japanese Treaty, renewable in 1922, while across the Atlantic there was widespread Anglophobia in American naval circles – factors which were to warp the thinking of the British naval staff, lending too great a weight to the retention of capital ships at the expense of escorts and the protection of trade. At the same time, significant progress in the development of sonar (then known as asdic) having been made, to the point where the submarine menace was considered to have been overcome, anti-submarine warfare was relegated to a backwater of naval training and development, a fact which had a critical impact in the Mediterranean, as elsewhere.[10] Destruction of manpower and morale was in proportion to that of hulls.[11]

While Britain's means to support a large navy shrank, her detachment from Japan as a naval ally increased her obligations, with the added menace that Japan, already a formidable naval power no longer reliant on British hardware, was herself likely to prove a future enemy. Among the prescient, appreciations of imperial defence, hinging upon the neglected naval fortress of Singapore, were gloomy.[12] Indeed, the abandonment of the Far East was actively considered. It might have been thought that the great dominions of the British Empire should have contributed more, but the naval forces at the disposal of the dominion governments were insignificant at the outbreak of war, and defence of the empire actually depended upon the Mother Country, for whom such a liability was beyond her economic resources.[13]

Not only was Britain burdened by economic and strategic problems; she had lost her lead in technology.[14] Assumptions made by the Admiralty took no account of this. When naval rearmament was finally kick-started there was a rude awakening, and this deficiency became immediately apparent. The poor quality of British armoured steel, combined with a shortfall in its production, necessitated the purchase of 15,000 tons from Czechoslovakia. The new Vickers anti-aircraft gun turned out to be ineffective and Swedish 40-mm Bofors guns were hurriedly bought, together with 20-mm weapons from Oerlikon of

Switzerland. So limited and inexperienced had Britain become in the manufacture of guns and their mountings that in the late 1930s these could not even be manufactured under licence. Problems in the production of medium calibre high-angle guns for both destroyers and the secondary armament of cruisers were augmented by the Admiralty's obsessive preoccupation with coming fleet actions and its belief that attacks by aircraft could be dealt with by anti-aircraft fire – a convoluted paradox which produced some otherwise fine destroyers wholly unable to give themselves adequate air-defence, let alone provide it for anyone else!

The air threat had become as underrated as that of the submarine, as naval orthodoxy jigged its thinking back to the familiar and comforting track of opposing battle fleets engaged in a big-gun duel while destroyers dashed about delivering torpedo attacks. The submarine would be dealt with by patrolling cruisers while hunting groups, each based upon a carrier, would roam the oceans with spotting planes aloft. This theory was not without merit when properly applied but lasted scarcely a fortnight in its original form, for the carrier *Courageous* was torpedoed and sunk by *U29* on 17 September 1939. No such comforting theory sustained those charged with the rapid rearmament of the Royal Navy in the brief respite after Munich: a sub-committee examining bombing and anti-aircraft defence in January 1939 reported that, because of a shortage of gun-barrels, destroyers must be fitted with vintage 4-inch high-angle guns behind shields, instead of the more up-to-date, turret-mounted 4.7-inch weapons for which they were designed. Fortunately these proved adequate if not outstanding assets.[15]

Not only were the intended guns late, but so was the fire-control system. Just as the Royal Navy had gone into action at Jutland with a cheap fire-control system designed by a naval officer, in preference to the civilian inventor Arthur Pollen's 'Argo clock', a primitive analogue computer for calculating the off-set necessary to long-range gunnery, so the anti-aircraft system a generation later foundered on a poor high-angle control.[16] The fault lay in part with the Naval Ordnance Department, whose thinking relied upon the fact that no warship had been sunk by aircraft in the First World War, and the belief that the battleship could withstand bombs and torpedoes. Gunnery representation on the naval staff was minimal, while senior admirals seem to have been as contemptuous of scientific advice as their fathers. In 1925 anti-aircraft gunnery control research was vested in a lieutenant and two scientists, and an anti-aircraft department was not set up (at HMS *Excellent* on Whale Island, the Royal Navy's gunnery school) until 1935. Little was achieved, and the historian Commander Stephen Roskill, on joining the naval staff in early 1939, was 'appalled at the backwardness of our A[nti]A[ircraft] preparations for war'.

This backwardness was exacerbated by the inability of British engineering companies to design and produce such highly sophisticated precision equipment as the tachymetric control device required for accurate gunnery. There was no time to put the matter right; unlike the German and United States navies, which adopted tachymetric control, the Royal Navy went to war with the mixed ability of a grouse-shooting party. This appalling neglect and complacence was to seriously affect the fleet in the Mediterranean, and to contribute to the complete annihilation of Force Z off Singapore.[17]

It took some time for British industry to crank itself into the wholly mobilised war-economy it subsequently became. The rapid rearmament programme was at best a damage-limitation exercise, and quite incomplete when war broke out. Blood continued to be, in Kipling's unsurpassable phrase, 'the price of Admiralty'. Apart from the dramatic losses of the unmodified battlecruiser *Hood* and Force Z, there were lesser disasters. Late delivery of the much-vaunted sonar sets caused a severe shortage, while British torpedo performance left a lot to be desired, and there were frequent failures of these expensive weapons. Fortunately German torpedoes proved equally flawed, and while German shell quality had deteriorated since Jutland, British shell manufacture had improved, as had anti-flash devices. So too had interior hull subdivision and armouring, but programmes of renovation ran late, which proved fatal in the case of *Hood*.

In the matter of naval aviation, the Royal Navy was worst served. From its commanding position in 1918 the Admiralty had surrendered – not lost – its advantage. During the so-called rationalisation period of the 1920s, both the Royal Flying Corps and the Royal Naval Air Service had been disbanded. As far as the Admiralty was concerned, the RNAS had become too powerful and was full of headstrong, opinionated young men.

Moreover, in the view of the Admiralty Board, many of these young officers came from social backgrounds which Their Lordships considered humbler than was desirable in British naval officers. British military aviation was henceforth to be vested in the Royal Air Force, who would supply aircraft and an air command structure to carriers when required. Most ambitious flyers transferred eagerly from the deadening shadow of a purblind Admiralty to the new, vigorous RAF, depriving the navy of its own experts. To compound this folly, inter-war aircraft development in Britain was generally appalling,[18] and nowhere was this technological lapse more apparent than in the matter of aircraft for the Royal Navy.

Three years after accepting the specification for a fighter dive-bomber, the Blackburn Company could not better the production of sixteen Skuas per month before the end of 1938. When it did finally enter service, the Skua was already out of date. Messrs Fairey, who had produced the standard torpedo-bomber in the Swordfish, a wood-and-fabric biplane known affectionately as the 'Stringbag', attempted to fill the gap with a slow fighter known as the Fulmar and a biplane replacement for the Swordfish called the Albacore which did not enter service until 1941, and was by then thoroughly outclassed. Various other types of aircraft intended for carrier work were also obsolescent, and the Stringbag continued to form the backbone of the Royal Navy's carrier-borne strike-force for the first half of the war. Swordfish were flown off carriers in theatres as diverse as the Mediterranean and the Arctic, serving with distinction as bombers, torpedo-bombers and, when later fitted with radar, as U-boat killers. Part of their offensive capability as carrier-borne aircraft lay in their ability to absorb punishment, part in their slow speed and high manoeuvrability; but with their open cockpits they were hard on their young aircrews, particularly in the Arctic, and entirely at the mercy of faster fighters. While the Royal Navy therefore continued to rely upon them for aerial strikes, air-cover had to be provided by something better than the Sea Gladiators and other hopelessly inadequate fighters.

The most expedient solution was to produce a variant of the successful Hurricane and Spitfire, modified for carrier work. At best these models proved a stop-gap measure, for both the Sea Hurricane and Seafire were slower than their RAF counterparts and also too light for flight-deck operation, suffering from inadequate integral airframe strength and weak undercarriages. They were, however, the best that could be achieved at short notice. Later Grumann Wildcats, known to the British as Martlets, specifically designed for carrier work, were among the fine American aircraft which entered service with the Royal Navy; but it was some time before the eager young pilots of the Fleet Air Arm were able to fight their opponents in machines equal to their own mettle. Even the decision to modify Hawker and Supermarine fighters was a consequence of a greater event. After a campaign in the national press and a bitter battle fought behind the closed doors of Whitehall, the Admiralty regained control of its shipboard aircraft in July 1937. The post of Fifth Sea Lord was reconstituted, and although the Royal Navy never regained control of long-range maritime aircraft, which remained under Coastal Command, the Fleet Air Arm was established.[19]

The rapid expansion now extending the obsolete and neglected industrial plant of Great Britain in the production of warships, from basic corvettes to sophisticated carriers, was only one aspect of rearmament. It was necessary to man the new ships. In the late 1930s a scheme was introduced to enable merchant naval officers serving in the Royal Naval Reserve to transfer to the regular service on a permanent basis while other reservists, both officers and ratings, were called up. More officers were obtained from the volunteer reserve, amateur enthusiasts who were pro-cessed through the training establishment HMS *King Alfred* on the south coast, while volunteer reservist ratings also received specialist training at similar 'stone frigates' such as HMS *King Arthur*, a former holiday camp on the Lincolnshire coast. The general products of naval conscription, the 'H.O.' ratings who were to serve for the duration of 'Hostilities Only', provided the greater part of the rapidly expanding manpower requirement. Not all were imbued with the spirit of conformity upon which the Royal Navy had built up its fighting tradition. Though eager to overcome the enemy, they were equally eager to get the unpleasant job over with and return home to jobs, families and normality. Many capable men, though they resented the class system that consigned them to the ignominy of life on the lower deck, refused commissions, and most endured the rigours of their fate and indeed completed the task with the efficiency the Royal Navy demanded.[20]

The rejuvenation of the naval service took some time; building ships and working them up with competent crews was not something to be achieved overnight.[21] But the seaman's war started the day before war broke out, when the first convoy left Gibraltar for Cape Town. Within hours the first of many, many merchant ships was sunk: the Donaldson liner *Athenia* (13,581 grt), bound from Liverpool to Montreal, was torpedoed west of Ireland by *U30* (Leutnant Lemp). Merchant shipping losses were thereafter daily occurrences and, as the attrition rate mounted, the Royal Navy was also subject to a number of humiliating defeats which merely underscored the weaknesses and misconceptions that had guided Britain's naval thinking and investment between the wars.

It was fortunate for Great Britain that she was able to gain the overnight reinforcement of fifty Lease-Lend destroyers from the United States, in exchange for naval bases which America would need if Britain fell. It was fortunate, too, that she was able to produce sufficient corvettes from civilian building yards to beef up the wholly inadequate convoy escort force initially available for duty in the North Atlantic, without which the toll of merchant ships and merchant seamen would have been even higher than it was. But she was fortunate most of all in having a tradition with which even inexperienced officers and men identified, and which swiftly aided the process of assimilation. Blooded in this testing time, sick, resentful and exhausted they may have been, but they clung on and performed their tedious duties, gradually gaining both their physical and their moral sea-legs. The confidence that the experience of sea-time confers, the quality which adversity has of forming a ship's company, if ably led, into something greater than its constituent parts, gave to the Royal Navy the indispensable advantage it ultimately possessed. It was just as well, for the Royal Navy was about to enter a period of the most terrible losses, losses which, without a tradition of four hundred years, might well have destroyed its morale.[22] This morale was a crucial factor, a tradition old when Nelson hoisted his signal at Trafalgar of England's expectation that every man in the fleet should do his duty, and that every commander should engage the enemy closely. This fighting tradition imbued the officers and men of the Royal Navy, particularly the former, with selflessness in time of battle. It was an uncompromising and very effective *esprit de corps*, a means to an end which afterwards might be seen as amoral but which whipped in the lax, spurred on the over-cautious, and made of that self-confessed 'air of conscious superiority', so great a drawback in peacetime, a source of raw courage in action. It enabled the Royal Navy to survive the many disasters and vicissitudes which it was to endure, not least in the Mediterranean, for this tradition was a living continuum, a force for great moral effect.

But this ramrod stiffening was exclusive to the Royal Navy; it did not extend to the sister sea-service. While it might be induced in naval recruits, it could not be found among the merchant seamen whose ships were so desperately needed to carry the vast quantities of foodstuffs, raw materials, oil fuel, arms and ammunition required to keep British forces in the field and to keep Britain herself in the war. Most germane to the matter in hand, they were necessary to keep the island of Malta alive and fighting.

'The Merchant Navy' was a collective name given to that vast muster of merchant ships falling under the wartime control of the Ministry of War Transport (MoWT). It was a 'navy' only by courtesy, almost an invention of propagandists during the First World War, for in truth it was a collection of privately owned vessels which only the stern pressures of war melded into anything remotely resembling a navy. Its constituent parts were often very disparate; the lordly liners of the Cunard–White Star Line and the Peninsular and Oriental Steam Navigation Company, in which every deck officer was a master mariner, were at one end of a wide spectrum. At the other extremity were the 'pound-and-pint' tramp ships owned by hard-nosed, tight-fisted owners who paid the minimum wages to their crews and allowed no more than the subsistence victuals laid down as minima by the Board of Trade. This body, which regulated merchant shipping, surveyed its ships and certificated its masters, mates and engineers, exercised some statutory control over British shipping, provided such shipping was actually registered under the red ensign. Ship-owners functioned exploitatively, to profit from their ships, so were therefore generally unconcerned with matters of crew morale or conditions of service. The tradition of the merchant seaman was far older than that of his cousin in Crown service, for the Royal Navy had grown from merchant ships co-opted in time of war, but most were insensible of this ancient link. Seafaring in merchant ships was always hard, and enjoyed none of the popular esteem accorded to the Royal Navy's blue jackets. The Royal Navy *trained* for war; war caught the merchant marine going about its everyday business. The *Athenia*'s loss on the first day of hostilities, 3 September 1939, was followed by that of the *Bosnia* and *Royal Sceptre* on the 5th, *Rio Claro* and *Manaar* on the 6th, the *Pukkastan*, *Olivegrove* and *Gartavon* on the 7th, the *Winkleigh*, *Regent Tiger* and *Kennebec* on the 8th. And so it went on, until 7 May 1945, when the cargo ship *Avondale* was torpedoed by *U2336* in the Firth of Forth.

Many masters of fast merchant ships squeezed into the strait-jacket of a convoy felt the protection thus afforded to be inadequate, and they were often right. At the beginning of the war few escorts were available, and then only for a limited part of a convoy's passage. Convoy speed was usually no more than 8 knots in fair to moderate weather, a slow plod largely due to the decrepit state of much of Britain's merchant fleet, particularly the tramp ships best suited to bulk cargoes. Like so much of British infrastructure the so-called Merchant Navy, although the world's largest, had been in decline since the First World War.[23] A difficult economic situation had discouraged investment in new tonnage, while an increasing proportion of the world's goods were being carried in American and Scandinavian ships. By 1939, Norway owned the world's fourth-largest merchant fleet. The Japanese, moving into high industrial gear in the 1930s, introduced a 'scrap-and-build' policy which had doubled their merchant tonnage by the outbreak of war. The British government rarely granted subsidies to merchant ship-owners and, in the bust which followed the brief post-war boom, a series of mergers affected British shipping. The small one- or two-ship firms dwindled; there were a hundred and twenty in Cardiff alone in 1914, but by 1939 only twenty remained. Shipping became increasingly concentrated in the hands of a small oligarchy of Bibbys, Inchcapes, Brocklebanks, Holts, Ellermans, Runcimans, Denholms and Vesteys. These dynasties maintained their ships under a sufficient variety of house-flags to create the illusion that little had changed, but many of these mergers were at inflated prices, and as soon as the markets slumped, the owners were in trouble. Lord Kylsant's Royal Mail Group, which owned 15 per cent of the British flag fleet, collapsed in 1930 when government loans were called in. Kylsant himself spent a year in prison.

At the same time, Britain abandoned the gold standard and devalued the pound sterling. Little advantage was gained thereby, even when trade picked up with the first stirrings of rearmament, because of the excessive number of ships available, many of which had been laid up. The problem was compounded by foreign governments subsidising their own merchant shipping in order to earn invisibles; moreover, a large proportion of the British merchant fleet was acquired by foreign owners. In 1932 Fascist Italy underwrote its own ships, followed in 1933 by Nazi Germany, the Netherlands and France. In 1935 the British woke up, too late. A scrap-and-build policy was introduced for tramp ships that year. Ninety-seven old ships were broken up and replaced by fifty new vessels amounting to less than half the scrapped tonnage, but many of the old hulks had been deliberately purchased from foreign owners to profit from the scheme.

Part of Kylsant's problem had been his genuine concern for jobs. He had over-extended himself in the belief that he should protect his employees and in the hope that trade would pick up. In the event, the slump worsened, and a rescue operation was mounted by Richard Holt of the Ocean Steamship Group[24] and Sir Frederick Lewis of Furness Withy. Such well-motivated men were in the minority among ship-owners, the majority of whom had made huge profits in the First World War, largely from those of their ships which had been sunk and thus attracted government compensation. As for the unfortunate seafarers who took to the boats, their pay stopped the day their ship went down. This scandalous state of affairs prevailed well into the Second World War, until the poor morale of merchant seamen arising from the terrible successes of German U-boats compelled the authorities to end the appalling abuse.[25]

During the Great Depression between the wars, the world's merchant seamen, working in a truly global market-place, suffered badly. Destitution proved the lot of many, particularly those expecting employment in the large but idle commercial fleets of Britain and the United States. As a consequence of their plight, they acquired the reputation of being generally undesirable and in turn felt this ostracism acutely.

When in 1939 war immediately embroiled Britain's mercantile marine in the crucial matter of military and civilian supplies, the merchant seafarer found himself in great demand, elevated to strategic importance. Some men accepted this philosophically, others with rather less enthusiasm. In comparison with all other Allied services, it was the merchant seamen who died in proportionately greater numbers.

Thus it was that the British sea-services began the war. At its outbreak the British, the greatest exponents of sea-power in history, found their navy inadequate to the task ahead of it. Nevertheless, they understood the fundamentals well enough, for while the means by which sea-power is attained are constantly evolving, sea-power remains essentially 'the sum-total of ... weapons, installations, and geographical circumstances which enable a nation *to control transportation over the seas during wartime.'*[26]

This was achieved by the immediate introduction of convoys, without the long delay which had brought Britain to the brink of surrender in 1917. The convoy system, tried to extremity though it was, won the great battle of logistics. This was most critical across the North Atlantic, but other seas could also only be commanded by that control of transportation which was the key to sea-power, and it was the achievement of this that allowed Malta to be supplied, sustained and reinforced during the dark days of the war.

Despite the fact that the distance between Italy and the principal Axis ports of Tripoli and Benghazi was a matter of only a few hundred miles, whereas that between Great Britain and Alexandria by way of the Cape of Good Hope and the Suez Canal was many thousands, it was the British who maintained their communications. And it was, moreover, the British who, by interdiction from Malta, largely denied to their enemy those few vital hundreds of miles across the central Mediterranean.

The convoys which ran the gauntlet of enemy submarines, bombers and surface warships to sustain Malta from Gibraltar and Alexandria had to be fast, composed of merchant ships which could combine capacity with speed, and with the ability to discharge themselves when they arrived in the bombed-out recesses of Grand Harbour. Mercifully, British shipping houses possessed a large number of suitable vessels of a type known generically as cargo-liners. These smart, speedy ships usually ran scheduled services world-wide, often specialising in frozen meat or chilled fruit, heavy lifts such as plant and locomotives, quantities of liquids and oils. Their prevailing lading was 'general', break-bulk cargoes: they carried and handled almost any*thing* almost any*where*.

On the whole the crews of cargo-liners had not suffered the extremes of demoralisation which the years of depression had engendered among those manning the bulk-carrying tramps making up much of the Atlantic and Arctic 'lifelines'. They were usually on contracts, and thus escaped the uncertainty of the Reserve Pool, the Board of Trade's manning agency designed to find crews for all ships, including the worst. Many liner companies drew their crews from the Empire, so Chinese and Lascar deckhands and stewards, Sudanese firemen and greasers, along with whole crews from the Hebrides or the Shetlands, filled the ranks of the ratings up to petty officer. For the most part these men, whether they were *serangs*, *tindals*, *bandaddies*, *casabs*, tigers, lamptrimmers or plain sailormen, whether they were known by name, rank or number, gave exemplary service. The officers, as company employees, felt for their shipping companies a degree of loyalty comparable with the best ethics of the senior service, and a service is precisely what they were and how they thought of themselves. There were exceptions, of course, but there is no doubt that this attitude played a considerable part in the ready co-operation which largely characterised the relationship between the Royal Navy and its merchant counterparts in the Mediterranean theatre, a happier circumstance than, on occasion, prevailed elsewhere.

It was a combination which was to prove formidable. Technological decline, economic imperatives, government neglect and a lack of real investment by both industry and state had effectively compromised Britain's real standing as a sea-power as far as her ships themselves were concerned. But the quality of the men who manned all these ships, merchant and naval, like that of those in the submarines and aircraft operating from Malta, proved the Napoleonic maxim that 'the moral is to the material as three is to one'.

To this Malta owed her survival.

3

'Sustained by the volume of prayer'

JUST BEFORE SEVEN o'clock on the sunny morning of 11 June 1940 the air-raid warning sirens wailed out over Valletta, echoing mournfully between the ancient yellow ramparts. Grand Harbour was empty. The Royal Navy's Mediterranean Fleet had withdrawn to Alexandria and the Commander-in-Chief, Admiral Sir Andrew Cunningham, had left behind only the monitor *Terror* and the river gunboat *Aphis*, which had slipped round to Marsamxett Harbour. High above the crowds who now filled the streets with noisy excitement as they made for the doubtful shelter of shops, clubs and churches under the direction of a handful of special constables, seven Savoia Marchetti bombers escorted by nine Macchi 200 fighters caught the sun, like 'stars in the morning' according to a young Maltese observer, Joseph Attard. The air defences opened up: a rapid-firing pom-pom at Senglea, a Bofors gun manned by dockyard workmen, and then the deeper rattle of the AA guns of the monitor and gunboats filled the air with noise, and with the innocent-seeming puffballs of bursting shells high above. Simultaneously the first bombs began to fall, shaking buildings and sending shock waves through the limestone bedrock. There were to be eight such raids that day, mounted from airfields on Sicily, only sixty miles away. In addition to the barrage, a few obsolescent Gloster Gladiator biplanes roared aloft. They had been assembled from ten crated machines, spares for the Fleet Air Arm held in the dockyard for the aircraft carrier on the Mediterranean station. From Cunningham at Alexandria, Air Commodore Maynard urgently requested permission to use them. This was granted with 'the most cordial approval'. One Gladiator was soon shot down, but, as there were never more than three airborne they have become known as 'Faith', 'Hope' and 'Charity', 'and were flown by flying-boat and other pilots inexperienced in flying fighters'. They 'inflicted loss on the Italian bombers' and were 'sustained by the volume of prayer that went up for their safety from the Maltese'. Such were the island's airborne defences in the wake of the pre-war assessment that it was indefensible.[1]

What this conclusion failed to take account of was that Malta possessed the incalculable advantage of an indomitable population, and was composed of unyielding limestone. The Regia Aeronautica, adopting high-level bombing from 20,000 feet, aimed for the dockyard area, indiscriminately hitting the small houses around it and inflicting the first casualties upon the civilian population in an area which was one of the most densely populated in Europe. But the limestone was almost tolerant of enemy bombs. Easily quarried and mined when first exposed to air, it quickly hardened afterwards, and while Valletta and its environs were in the coming months subjected to the most violent and concentrated bombing assault, the islanders made of their native land a warren of subterranean shelters. The next day an Italian reconnaissance flight over the island was shot down. The battle for Malta had begun.

What Air Commodore Maynard's airmen, the ships' companies of *Terror* and *Aphis*, the slender defensive force of the Royal Malta Artillery, the King's Own Malta Regiment and the Malta Volunteer Defence Force achieved in the first crucial weeks of war with Italy confounded the pundits. While air force and army opinion were agreed that the proximate might of the Italians ought to overwhelm Malta, it seemed the island might not after all be completely indefensible. Though the aerodromes at Luqa and Hal Far were currently inadequate, there was little doubt that Malta had the potential to become an unsinkable aircraft carrier.

The Royal Navy took this view. Not only was it, collectively, fond of Malta, but it had for long relied upon the dry-dock in Grand Harbour. This, until the completion of a panic building programme just before war broke out, was superior to the dockyard repair facilities at Gibraltar and remained better than the floating docks at the Mediterranean Fleet's primary base at Alexandria.[2]

Under the terms of the Franco-British Alliance, Cunningham's ships were responsible for the eastern Mediterranean, hence their presence at Alexandria. The French navy, based on Toulon and the Algerian port of Mers-el-Kebir at Oran, was to hold the western basin. However, further British naval forces were also at Gibraltar, while French ships were with Cunningham at Alexandria. As it became increasingly clear that an Italian declaration of war could be expected, from 1 May British merchant ships were forbidden to pass through the Mediterranean, a measure seen by Ciano as 'a prelude to war'.[3] Meanwhile Cunningham's fleet had been reinforced, and by 10 June consisted of the battleships *Warspite*,[4] just returned to the Mediterranean after seeing action off Narvik, *Valiant*, *Royal Sovereign* and *Malaya*, the last two sent as reinforcements from the Atlantic. He also had at his disposal a squadron of elderly cruisers, the 3rd, *Caledon*, *Capetown*, *Calypso* and *Delhi*. This was augmented by the 6-inch-gun *Orion* and *Neptune*, sent from the West Indies and the South Atlantic respectively, *Gloucester* from the East Indies, *Liverpool* from China, and HMAS *Sydney* from the Dominion navy of Australia; these were formed into the 7th Cruiser Squadron. Also from the Far East were the carrier *Eagle* and the battleship *Ramillies*. The Home Fleet provided the anti-aircraft cruiser *Carlisle*, the netlayer *Protector*, sixteen destroyers and three sloops, while ten submarines came from eastern stations. HMAS *Stuart* was flotilla leader of an Australian group of old V- and W-class destroyers, bringing Cunningham's total strength in destroyers up to twenty-five, though a few of these were deployed east of Suez. Finally, Cunningham had under his flag units of the French fleet, namely the battleship *Lorraine*, four cruisers and three destroyers, commanded by Vice-Amiral Godfroy.

The Italian Regia Marina had been active since 6 June, laying extensive mine barrages, but it was not until the declaration of war on 11 June that six Malta-based British submarines, *Odin*, *Oswald*, *Osiris*, *Olympus*, *Orpheus* and *Grampus*, sailed to attack shipping off Italian ports. On the 13th, however, *Odin* was located in the Gulf of Taranto and sunk by the Italian destroyer *Strale*; three days later *Grampus* was destroyed off Syracuse by the torpedo-boats *Circe*, *Clio* and *Polluce*, and *Orpheus* was caught and sunk by the destroyer *Turbine* off Tobruk. British submarines from Alexandria patrolled the eastern Mediterranean and French submarines were also active, the *Saphir* laying mines which shortly afterwards sank two small Italian freighters. Elsewhere, east of Suez, British and Indian warships engaged Italian units with mixed fortunes.

On 10 June Cunningham sent the 2nd Destroyer Flotilla and two flying-boats to sea to prevent a close approach being made to Alexandria by Italian mine-laying submarines, but it was 19.00 hrs that evening before the official declaration of war arrived. Cunningham put his fleet under two hours' notice for steam, ordered the R-class battleship *Ramillies* to leave the floating dock, and next day, as the Regia Aeronautica made its first bombing raid on Malta, himself left Alexandria, flying his flag in the battleship *Warspite*. His squadron consisted of the flagship's sister *Malaya*, the carrier *Eagle*, the 7th Cruiser Squadron under his deputy, Vice-Admiral Tovey in *Orion*, with *Neptune*, *Sydney*, *Liverpool* and *Gloucester*, and the elderly cruisers of the 3rd, *Calypso* and *Caledon*, screened by nine destroyers. Cunningham made a sweep north towards Crete and then, with Tovey ahead, south towards Tobruk and Benghazi, in the hope of sinking Italian merchant shipping. He also hoped to try the mettle of the enemy air force, but although they were engaged by some minesweepers and batteries off Tobruk, only one distant plane was seen. Italian submarines proved more potent: the *Bagnolini*, Capitano di Fregata Tosoni-Pittoni, torpedoed *Calypso*, even though she was astern of a destroyer screen. Cunningham had entertained a slight expectation of encountering units of the Italian fleet and in this he was disappointed, but in fact two cruiser divisions sortied as a result of aerial reconnaissance. The 3rd left Messina accompanied by two destroyer flotillas, the 11th and 12th, and the 1st and 8th sailed from Taranto with the 9th and 16th Flotillas.[5] No contact resulted, though the French cruiser squadron under Vice-Amiral Godfroy, escorted by destroyers, swept north from Alexandria to the Dodecanese.[6] These operations concluded on 14 June, just as the Italian destroyers *Turbine*, *Nembo* and *Aquilone*, of the 1st Flotilla under Ruggieri, shelled Sollum on the Egyptian border near Bardia. A few days later the last joint operation between the French and British took place with a bombardment of Bardia itself. Tovey in the cruiser *Orion*, with *Neptune* and *Sydney*, was accompanied by the French battleship *Lorraine* and screened by the destroyers *Stuart*, *Decoy*, *Dainty* and *Hasty*. The same day two of Godfroy's cruisers, *Duguay Trouin* and *Suffren*, screened by British destroyers, swept along the coast to the westward but were disappointed, failing to locate any enemy vessels. The Italians presented a greater menace under water, for they were busy reinforcing their submarines. Ten of these were dispatched to patrol areas dispersed about the eastern Mediterranean and a further twenty-one into the western basin, where *Capponi* accounted for the Swedish freighter *Elgö*.

Cunningham, concerned about the loss of *Calypso* and the mines being laid in the approaches to Alexandria, had been keeping his remaining destroyers on anti-submarine operations, and on 27 June a group under Commander M. Thomas of *Dainty*, with *Defender*, *Ilex* and *Voyager*, sank the submarine *Luizzi* south of Crete where, two days later, they also accounted for *Uebi Scebeli* and damaged *Salpa*. Thomas returned quietly to Alexandria, for on board *Uebi Scebeli* he had captured the Italian naval code-book with tables for the following month; however, coup though this was, as a consequence of these British successes against their submarines, the Italians overhauled their cypher system shortly afterwards. The *Argonauta* had also gone missing, while *Anfitrite* and *Sirena* were damaged by Sunderlands of No. 230 Squadron on 28 and 29 June. The same day they hit *Sirena* the flying-boats sank the *Rubino* on her way back from Alexandria. The thorough reform of codes and procedures which the Italians subsequently undertook came 'as a great shock to intelligence authorities [in Britain] long accustomed to receiving a steady supply of Italian Sig[nals] int[elligence]'. And this blow fell 'at a time when Italy was expected to take the offensive with greatly superior forces ...'[7]

But these vicissitudes were overshadowed by events in France. While the bulk of the British Expeditionary Force had been evacuated from Dunkirk between 26 May and 4 June, some British forces had remained in France. The 51st Highland Division were hard-pressed by Rommel's 7th Panzer Division and, being refused permission to withdraw across the Seine by the French high command, were bottled up in the Havre peninsula by 11 June, to be captured alongside their French allies. Lieutenant-General Sir Alan Brooke was sent back to France with British and Canadian divisions as reinforcements to the weak 1st Armoured Division in an attempt by Churchill to stiffen French resistance and encourage the Allies to fight on.

It was too late: the cause was lost. The French capital was too close to the border with Germany, and as Paris was threatened, with gallant but sadly insignificant exceptions France collapsed. The government of Paul Reynaud sued for terms and finally capitulated, a cease-fire being ordered from 01.35 on 25 June.

The situation in the Mediterranean was transformed by the French surrender. Although several French warships reached Britain and Marshal Pétain and Admiral Darlan (of the new French government) insisted that French naval ships would remain in French hands, the terms of the armistice stipulated that the French navy would be disarmed under French or Italian control. It was imperative for the British that the French Fleet should not fall into the hands of the Germans, for in combination with either the Kriegsmarine or, more immediately, the Regia Marina, it would have constituted a formidable threat to a Britain now standing alone. In the Mediterranean, such a combination would have abruptly terminated any advantage the British might hold at sea, a point which, in the light of subsequent events, cannot be emphasised too strongly.

The immediate concern of the Admiralty was to increase the force at Gibraltar and close the Strait to French warships; thereafter it was necessary to consider neutralising the French fleet in its Mediterranean and overseas bases. The result was the formation of a powerful battle-squadron known as Force H – the only truly beneficial consequence of the Admiralty's obsessive preoccupation between the wars with capital ships, for it was organised, with breathtaking speed, by the end of June. Initially Force H was composed of the battlecruiser *Hood*, flying the flag of Vice-Admiral Sir James Somerville, the carrier *Ark Royal*, the battleships *Resolution* and *Valiant*, the light-cruisers *Arethusa* and *Enterprise*, with four destroyers. Force H was a 'detached squadron', and Somerville was responsible directly to London, not to the Flag Officer, North Atlantic, Admiral Sir Dudley North at Gibraltar. Since Somerville too was based at The Rock and put demands upon the dockyard there, this ambiguity caused some problems, not least because he alleviated his paucity of destroyers by raiding North's own meagre numbers. Although Somerville went on to play a major part in the supply of Malta, he initially arrived in Gibraltar after meetings in London during which he received instructions 'to secure the transfer, surrender or destruction of the French warships at Oran and Mers-el-Kebir, so as to ensure [they] ... did not fall into German or Italian hands'.[8]

As Somerville's ships proceeded east early on 3 July, Captain C. S. Holland was sent ahead in a destroyer to explain the imperatives to the French Commander-in-Chief. Amiral Gensoul refused to see Holland, and written notes were exchanged. In his reports to the French Admiralty Gensoul glossed over the temporising proposals of transfer or surrender, emphasising instead the British demand that he scuttle his ships within six hours or expose them to destruction by bombardment. Darlan ordered Gensoul to resist, and the British mined the harbour entrance to prevent him escaping. Somerville, who had arrived in force during the forenoon, postponed his ultimatum from 13.30 to 15.00. At 14.40 Gensoul agreed to meet Holland personally, but it was 16.15 before Holland arrived aboard *Dunkerque*. Meanwhile Somerville was ordered by the Admiralty, which had intercepted a signal instructing all French forces to concentrate on Oran, to 'settle matters quickly', and gave Gensoul until 17.30. Holland had obtained a half-hearted proposal from Gensoul that he should withdraw to Martinique or the United States, but this seemed a mere prevarication and Holland left, clearing the harbour as the French went to action stations. Twenty-nine minutes later, at 17.54, Somerville opened fire, and in a brief but violent bombardment destroyed the *Bretagne* and seriously damaged *Dunkerque*, *Provence* and some smaller ships. The battlecruiser *Strasbourg* and five destroyers escaped to Toulon, though attacked by *Ark Royal*'s Swordfish aircraft. The episode aroused intense antagonism in the French navy and horror in the Royal Navy itself. Somerville, a tough, blunt-spoken seaman, told his wife that he had '*begged* [the Admiralty] ... not to go to the lengths of opening fire ...' Moreover, he expected to be relieved forthwith for his failure in letting *Strasbourg* escape. It had been a 'filthy business' and he felt 'thoroughly depressed and unclean'.[9]

Further pre-emptive strikes were made at French men-of-war elsewhere, at Dakar and in the West Indies, with neutralising effect, but in the Mediterranean 'uncertainty regarding the disposal of the French warships continued for many months to cause serious anxiety to the British Cabinet and Admiralty ...'[10] This anxiety was not to end until after the invasion of North Africa in November 1942, and its seriousness caused the First Sea

Lord, Sir Dudley Pound, to consider the evacuation of the eastern Mediterranean; for Cunningham, confronted by potentially overwhelming odds, was now at the extremity of a tenuous supply line that extended round the Cape of Good Hope. Pound suggested the removal of the Mediterranean Fleet to Gibraltar, part by the direct route, part via the Cape, but Cunningham responded that, though such a move was 'practicable ... the consequences would be the loss of Egypt and Malta.'[11]

Churchill would have none of it, vetoing Pound's 'tentative proposal' with a minute to the Admiralty that 'it is of the utmost importance that the fleet at Alexandria should remain to cover Egypt from an Italian invasion which would destroy prematurely all our position in the East'. The Prime Minister went on to underline his view: 'Even if Spain declares war it does not follow that we should quit the eastern Mediterranean.'[12] Cunningham was of similar mind, independently concluding that 'his earnest hope [was] that such a decision would never have to be taken', for it would result in a 'landslide in territory and prestige'. The Chiefs of Staff concluded that the 'political, economic and military reasons for retaining the fleet in the Eastern Mediterranean outweigh the purely naval reasons for its withdrawal'. The matter was dropped. Admiral Cunningham had already embarked upon the task of reinforcing Malta.

4

'A moral effect quite out of proportion to the damage'

(Operation MA3, the Battle of Calabria, Operation MA5 and Convoys MF1 and MS1)

ON 10 JUNE 1940, the day of Italy's declaration of war, Malta's new governor, Lieutenant-General Sir William Dobbie, a man of stern religious faith, made a broadcast to the people of Malta, calling upon God's help and expressing his faith in the fortitude of the Maltese. Thereafter he turned his sapper's mind to husbanding the limited resources available, to organising civil defence and troop training, and to encouraging morale. In this he was successful. Though he was a Seventh Day Adventist, at the other extreme of Christian orthodoxy from the indigenous Roman Catholic population, the sincerity of his religious convictions was widely respected. He was supported by Air Commodore Maynard (whose commissioning of the crated Gladiators had, incredibly, earned Cunningham a reproof for the loan of Admiralty equipment to the Royal Air Force) and by Vice-Admiral Wilbraham Ford who, as Vice-Admiral, Malta, had charge of the dockyard and the port facilities. Ford was also to prove a man of resource, operating from his headquarters in the 'stone frigate' HMS *St Angelo*, the fortress at the seaward extremity of Vittoriosa.

These men faced a daunting task. As an island so close to Sicily, Malta was in an immediate state of siege, short of everything except water which, though not a single lake or river exists on the island, could be drawn up from subterranean sources. It was decided not to attempt to defend the island of Gozo, but 'the market garden and larder of Malta was kept under cultivation'.[1]

Up to the very day of Mussolini's declaration of war, French and Italian passenger aircraft were using Malta's undefended aerodrome of Hal Far, which was in running order. Ta' Qali was complete but neglected, and Luqa unfinished. Lewis guns were all that was available to defend them, and in a short time the handful of aircraft using them was reduced to almost nothing, for on 16 July Flying Officer Keeble and his Hurricane were shot down.

Nevertheless, the best had to be made of what was to hand. Fortunately some attempt to reduce the number of dependants had already been undertaken, a number of the wives and families of men on active service outside the island having been repatriated aboard the Orient liner *Oronsay*, homeward bound from Australia, prior to the outbreak of hostilities with Italy. However, many families remained in Malta, including Cunningham's own wife and nieces. To protect the population the ancient catacombs and the deep stores later cut by the Capuchins were greatly enlarged, extensive shelters were cut everywhere by tunnelling, and in all a total of thirteen miles, including a disused railway tunnel between Floriana and Mdina, were eventually brought into use. The island's limestone, from which most of the buildings were constructed, revealed another virtue in addition to its ease of working: it proved impervious to incendiary bombs.

Dobbie instituted conscription for able-bodied males, thus at a stroke bringing the potential realities of war home to a people generally contemptuous of the Italians, especially of Mussolini's grandiose claims over the archipelago, placing a highly familial people on a war-footing, and augmenting his garrison of one Maltese and four under-strength regular battalions. The Royal Malta Artillery had been blooded on the first day of air-raids, when a Savoia Marchetti roared in low and deliberately bombed an AA emplacement, killing all six men serving the gun.[2]

In the first weeks of war the Italians taught the Maltese to endure their bombs, and at the same time threw away the only real opportunity to storm the island they were to have. In this, its most extreme period of defensive destitution, Malta was almost helpless, lacking anything significant in the way of guns, soldiers or aircraft. But while Dobbie broadcast encouragingly to the people, courageously revealing the daily toll in casualties and

damage, almost a thousand miles away to the east Admiral
Cunningham, well aware of the desperation of her plight, prepared to bring Malta some aid.

It was first necessary to retrieve a number of merchantmen
stranded there by the war, and at the end of June it was the intention that two small convoys, a fast one of 13 knots and a slower
of 9 knots, should be run under the cover of an operation code-
named MA3.[3] The 7th Cruiser Squadron under Vice-Admiral
Tovey in *Orion* sailed from Alexandria on 27 June, with flying-
boats reconnoitring ahead. To provide heavy cover *Royal
Sovereign*, *Ramillies* and *Eagle* were also at sea, screened by eight
destroyers. At the same time the Italian destroyers *Espero*, *Ostro*
and *Zaffiro* were proceeding to Tobruk, laden with military supplies from Taranto. The Italian ships were spotted by aircraft and
Tovey's force increased speed to intercept. At 18.30 on 28 June,
some seventy-five miles west-south-west of Cape Matapan,
Tovey's cruisers came in sight of the Italian squadron steaming
due west at high speed. Tovey engaged at extreme range and
Capitano di Fregata Baroni swung his ship, the *Espero*, to cover
his consorts' escape. The barrage thrown at the retreating Italians
and their gallant defender was terrific. With *Orion*, *Liverpool*,
Gloucester, *Neptune* and *Sydney* 'pumping out' salvos, 'the ammunition just melted away'. Shells from *Sydney* sank *Espero*, but
such expenditure was, Cunningham wrote afterwards, 'tremendous … to sink this one 1,000 ton destroyer'.

When Tovey's ships returned to Alexandria there were only
800 rounds of 6-inch ammunition left in the Suez Canal Zone.
The nearest accessible reserves were 6,000 miles away at Durban,
South Africa. The 800 reserve rounds, doled out, only half replenished the shell rooms and magazines of Tovey's wanton cruisers.
The return of his ships also meant that the withdrawal of the
empty merchantmen from Malta was postponed. This was an
unhappy state of affairs, over which the Commander-in-Chief
agonised for three weeks, during which period the last act of his
tragic alliance with Godfroy was also played out. Relations
between the two navies had been cordial, and Cunningham
baulked at the idea of doing to Godfroy what Somerville was
preparing to do at Oran. Such action he considered 'almost inept
in its unwisdom', but the dangers of having Godfroy's ships
either in his rear or slipping over to the enemy were obvious.
Fortunately, the close contacts the two admirals had hitherto

enjoyed enabled a more amicable negotiation to take place. Matters came to a head on 3 July; Godfroy was undecided, and news arrived of Somerville's use of force against Gensoul. The Admiralty wanted a resolution at Alexandria immediately: 'Do not, repeat NOT, fail', London signalled. Cunningham seemed fatally compromised but, filled with indignation, he defied the Admiralty and played for time. By now Godfroy had learned the fate of the ships at Mers-el-Kebir. He repudiated all agreements, and ordered his partially defuelled ships to raise steam and prepare to fight their way to sea. For his part, Cunningham sent orders to all units for Draconian action if the French moved, and in the meantime engaged in the distasteful task of suborning the French officers and ratings. Messages were flashed and carried round on blackboards, captains of British ships chatted to their French opposite numbers. The pragmatic imperative of the British position began to coincide with the helplessness of the French. Staff officers gathered together, ratings held meetings. It was clear to the anxious Cunningham that the tide of opinion was turning against Godfroy's hard line. All the French captains visited their vice-admiral, and that afternoon, 4 July, he agreed to the demobilisation and internment of his ships.[4]

Having resolved this matter, Cunningham was now able to turn his wholehearted attention to the Maltese problem. In consultation with Dobbie he agreed to remove a further number of civilians, chiefly wives and families, including his own wife and two nieces. The ships remaining at Malta consisted of *El Nil*, a passenger liner belonging to the Khedivial Mail Line, caught in Malta on her way between Marseilles and Egypt, *Knight of Malta*, and *Rodi*, an interned Italian prize. These were to form the faster convoy, MF1. A further five slower cargo vessels, loaded with naval stores stockpiled at Malta and badly needed at Alexandria, would make up the slower MS1; they were *Zeeland*, the 1,300-ton *Kirkland* owned by the Currie Line, *Masirah*, *Novasli* and *Tweed*, a 2,700-ton freighter owned by Transitus Shipping. Greater importance was attached to the fast convoy, because of its passengers, and the whole Fleet was to sortie to cover the movements of the merchantmen in a parallel operation code-named MA5. It was to bring on the first, long-awaited brush with the Italian battle-fleet.

Cunningham sailed in *Warspite* on the evening of 7 July, and by midnight *Malaya* and *Royal Sovereign*, the carrier *Eagle*, Tovey's cruisers *Orion, Liverpool, Gloucester, Neptune* and *Sydney,* with numerous destroyers, had cleared Alexandria harbour; the destroyer *Hasty* attacked two enemy submarines lying off the port, with inconclusive results. The fleet formed up into Tovey's Force A, the Australian destroyer *Stuart* joining the 7th Cruiser Squadron, with the C-in-C as Force B in *Warspite* with the destroyers *Mohawk, Nubian, Hero, Hereward* and *Decoy.* Forming Force C under Vice-Admiral Pridham-Wippell were *Malaya, Royal Sovereign* and *Eagle,* these being screened by the destroyers *Dainty, Defender, Hyperion, Hostile, Hasty, Ilex, Juno, Janus,* and the elderly Australians *Vampire* and *Voyager.* A further group of four destroyers intended to act as escorts to MS1 and MF1 proceeded as Force D. Meanwhile at Malta three more destroyers, including HMS *Jervis,* were enduring bombing raids and awaiting the order to sail.[5] Cunningham informed Somerville, who had just returned to Gibraltar from operations against Oran, that he also intended using the sortie to carry out an air attack and possibly a bombardment of Augusta on the east coast of Sicily.

Twenty-four hours earlier an Italian military convoy carrying 16,000 tons of stores, 300 armoured vehicles and 2,200 troops had sailed from Naples bound for Benghazi. It comprised the passenger liner *Esperia,* of 11,398 grt, and the freighters *Calitea* (4,013 grt), *Marco Foscarini* (6,342 grt) and *Vettor Pisani* (6,339 grt). Next day the 6,430-ton *Francesco Barbero* joined, arriving from Catania under the escort of *Abba* and *Pilo.* These reinforced the escort of *Orione, Orsa, Pegaso* and *Procione,* all light destroyers known misleadingly as 'torpedo-boats'. The convoy was given heavy cover by Ammiraglio di Divisione Casardi with the cruisers *Giovanni delle Bande Nere* and *Bartolomeo Colleoni,* and the 10th Destroyer Division (*Maestrale, Libeccio, Grecale* and *Scirocco*).

The Italian Admiralty, Supermarina, learning of a 'cruiser force' arriving at Malta,[6] ordered further cover to sea in the form of the 2nd Squadron commanded by Ammiraglio di Squadra Paladini in the heavy cruiser *Pola,* supported by the destroyers *Lanciere, Carabiniere, Corazziere* and *Ascari.* The squadron was additionally made up of the 1st Division under Ammiraglio di Divisione Matteucci with the heavy cruisers *Zara, Fiume* and *Gorizia* and the destroyers *Alfieri, Carducci, Gioberti* and *Oriani;* the 2nd Division under Ammiraglio di Divisione Cattaneo with the heavy-cruisers *Bolzano* and *Trento* and the destroyers

Artigliere, Camicia Nera, Aviere and *Geniere*; and the 7th Division under Ammiraglio di Divisione Sansonetti with the light cruisers *Eugenio di Savoia, Duca d'Aosta, Muzio Attendolo* and *Raimondo Montecuccoli* and the destroyers *Alpino, Bersagliere, Fuciliere* and *Granatiere*.

Supermarina then added to this powerful force the 1st Squadron under the fleet commander Ammiraglio di Squadra Campioni, flying his flag in the battleship *Giulio Cesare*, with Ammiraglio di Divisione Brivonesi in the battleship *Cavour*, which with the destroyers *Dardo, Freccia, Saetta* and *Strale* formed the 5th Division; the 8th Division under Ammiraglio di Divisione Legnani with the destroyers *Folgore, Baleno, Fulmine* and *Lampo*; the 4th Division under Ammiraglio di Divisione Marenco di Moriondo with the light cruisers *Da Barbiano, Luigi Cadorna, Di Giussano* and *Diaz*, and the destroyers *Vivaldi, Da Noli, Pancaldo, Pigafetta, Zeno, Da Recco, Pessagno* and *Usodimare*.

Clearly, given the paucity of oil reserves held by the Italians, this formidable concentration of the Regia Marina was dispatched to some purpose. Ostensibly it was to cover the troop convoy, but it cannot be supposed that so large a fleet, mustered from several bases, was not intended if possible to achieve something against British naval forces which were currently vulnerable after the loss of their French ally. Clearly Supermarina thought in terms of overwhelming at least the putative cruiser squadron at Malta, for Mussolini had laid down the role of the Regia Marina as being to take 'the offensive at all points in the Mediterranean', adding optimistically, 'and outside'.

Both enemies had active submarine patrols at sea; and one, the Italian *Beilul*, stationed off Derna, caught sight of Cunningham's fleet heading west during the night.[7] At 08.00 next morning the British submarine *Phoenix*, some two hundred miles east of Malta, spotted and reported the presence of two Italian 'battleships' and four destroyers steering south, which Cunningham correctly interpreted as covering a convoy to Libya. Instructing Ford at Malta to send up a Sunderland to locate and shadow them, Cunningham continued north-west at 20 knots.

That same morning, 8 July, Somerville left Gibraltar, somewhat against his will, for he was acutely conscious that the disparate elements forming Force H needed training as a group. But, having been ordered to operate simultaneously in support of

Cunningham, Force H headed east. Somerville, flying his flag in
Hood, had under his command *Resolution* and *Valiant*, with the
aircraft carrier *Ark Royal* and the cruisers *Arethusa*, *Delhi* and
Enterprise. His screen of destroyers consisted of *Faulknor*,
Forester, *Foresight*, *Foxhound*, *Fearless*, *Keppel*, *Douglas*, *Vortigern*,
Wishart and *Watchman*. Although he was allowed discretion as to
the nature of his diversion, Admiralty suggestions indicated that
he might launch *Ark Royal*'s torpedo-bombers at Italian warships
at Taranto or Augusta. Knowing Cunningham's intention to
carry out a raid on the latter and having his own misgivings
about attacking the former, Somerville cautiously ordered an
attack on Cagliari, on the south coast of Sardinia. Matters were
proceeding rather too fast for the commander of Force H's taste.
Several of his destroyers were old and lacked range, and he was
concerned about the strike capability of *Ark Royal*'s aircraft, and
the lack of surprise. Somerville, due in part to his personal experience at Dunkirk, had a better appreciation of the realities of fleet
operation in seas where the enemy had a superiority of air-
power than either Pound at the Admiralty, or Cunningham to
the east.[8]

It was not long before the expected reconnoitring aircraft
found Force H. For three hours in the late afternoon of 8 July,
Somerville's ships were heavily bombed by Savoia Marchetti
79s. Cunningham's fleet had been similarly located and bombed
as it steamed towards the toe of Italy, attempting to make contact
with the Italian fleet, Cunningham in the process developing a
healthy respect for the Regia Aeronautica which soon led him to
concur with Somerville's appreciation of air-power over the
Mediterranean. Although high-level bombing against ships was
generally ineffective, there was little doubt that the Italians were
better at it than the Germans. Somerville escaped any direct hits
but was concerned about the concussive damage caused by near-
misses, and reported that the air 'attacks were pressed home
most determinedly' from 10,000 to 13,000 feet. He considered
that 'As a result of this … it appeared to me that the prospects of
Ark Royal escaping damage whilst operating within 100 miles of
the Sardinia[n] coast the following morning were small.'
Somerville rubbed this danger in, dryly concluding that 'it was
highly improbable that Their Lordships would wish to have *Ark
Royal* put out of action, with the possible loss of … aircraft, for a
minor operation which was intended to act as a diversion'.

Consequently, Somerville 'decided that at 22.15 the Force should withdraw at its highest speed (20 knots).'

But Force H was not yet out of the fire. Anticipating some attack from the west, Supermarina had deployed several of their submarines in the western basin, and during the small hours of 11 July *Guglielmo Marconi*, lying on the surface, torpedoed the destroyer *Escort*. Although *Forester* counter-attacked, Capitano di Fregata Chialamberto crash-dived and escaped. Attempts to tow *Escort* into Gibraltar failed, and she sank at 11.15, by which time Force H was safe inside the mole. *Foxhound*, *Keppel* and *Foresight* were sent back to the scene to attempt to nail Chialamberto. The destroyers combed the area until the following day, enduring an attack by two Italian bombers on the 11th, but in spite of the assistance of aircraft patrols, Chialamberto escaped. Somerville admitted his squadron's lack of training, describing his abortive foray as 'an unsatisfactory outing'.

Far to the eastward, matters had fallen out rather differently. Although *Esperia* and the four freighters arrived at Benghazi unmolested, in the next few hours Campioni's fleet was spread out in some disorder. Italian SM79s from the Dodecanese had struck *Gloucester*, and a bomb exploding on her compass platform instantly killed Captain F.R. Garside, his commander and sixteen others. The reduction in the effectiveness of his cruisers caused by this single bomb was to cause Cunningham concern later that day.

As the British squadron steamed north-west towards the distant Strait of Messina, Campioni attempted to concentrate his fleet. At 15.15 a Malta-based Sunderland reported seeing 'three battleships, six cruisers and seven destroyers' about one hundred miles north-west of Benghazi. They were heading north, having completed their mission. Cunningham continued to steer north and west, intending to cut the enemy off from Taranto.

At dawn on 9 July, a beautiful morning of blue sky and sunshine, *Eagle* swung into the wind to launch three aircraft on a reconnoitring flight. During the succeeding hours these and Malta-based flying-boats informed Cunningham that two battleships, twelve cruisers and numerous destroyers were roughly fifty miles south of Cape Spartivento, the toe of Calabria, some ninety miles west of the British. At the same time Campioni was told of the location of the British by an Italian aeroplane. It was now about midday and Cunningham steered to intercept the Italian fleet, hampered by the slow speed of the ageing *Royal Sovereign*[9] and the limited capability of *Gloucester*, which could steer from her wheelhouse, but had had her gun-control reduced to the auxiliary position aft. Unaware of the exact strength of the Italian forces at sea and apprehensive about the power of his 6-inch-gun cruisers if matched against the heavier Italians, Cunningham nevertheless wanted a crack at the enemy. To achieve this, he knew he had to slow them down; accordingly, he ordered *Eagle* to fly off her strike force of Swordfish. These were frustrated by the thin cloud, which caused the spotting aircraft to lose sight of the Italians at a critical moment, but Tovey's cruisers were stretching out, steaming at full tilt into the light north-westerly breeze ten miles ahead of *Warspite*. Visibility at sea level was up to 20 miles, and a few minutes before 15.00 *Orion* and *Neptune* reported enemy destroyers and cruisers. *Gloucester* was ordered to fall back to join *Eagle* and her screen. Then, at 15.08, Captain R.C. O'Conor's *Neptune* saw the Italian capital ships and signalled 'Enemy battle-fleet in sight'.[10] At 15.14 the first Italian 8-inch shells plunged into the water among Tovey's 7th Cruiser Squadron, subjecting them to heavy fire as they strove to get in range and reply. The Italian heavy cruisers were now, at 26,400 yards, just in range of *Warspite*, and she opened up with her 15-inch guns.

Italian decrypts of British signals traffic had betrayed Cunningham's broad intentions, and Campioni had had instructions from Rome to avoid battle until noon, by which time the British would have been lured well within range of the Regia Aeronautica units operating from Calabria. Four divisions of the Italian fleet had concentrated in four columns, heading north-north-east.The nearest two to the British approaching from the east were composed of 8-inch cruisers, the third of cruisers and the two battleships *Cavour* and *Giulio Cesare*, and the farthest of cruisers. Each had its screen of destroyers.

Warspite's shells induced the cruisers in the nearer two columns to turn sharply away onto a north-westerly heading, afterwards turning to the south-west. The two distant columns also swung to port, though less far, maintaining a course west of north for some time. The battleships stood on as the cruisers retired behind them, and the Italian destroyers swung half-heartedly towards the British and began making smoke.

Meanwhile *Eagle*'s Swordfish took off again and flew incessant sorties against the enemy, the first time carrier-borne aircraft had operated with a fleet in battle. They scored no hits with their torpedoes,[11] but *Warspite*'s Walrus aircraft was catapulted off to maintain contact with the Italian battleships and, to Cunningham's delight, flew above the Italian battleships and acted as artillery spotter.

Seeing the enemy's retrograde movement and fearing the turning cruisers would dash back east and attack *Eagle*, Cunningham checked *Warspite*'s fire at 15.30, and at 24.5 knots a round turn was taken in her course to allow *Malaya*, which had been keeping *Royal Sovereign* company, to catch up and support *Warspite*. Then, with *Malaya* on *Warspite*'s port quarter and *Royal Sovereign* directly astern, all three battleships headed north-west. At 15.53 'the great moment came' and *Warspite* re-engaged at 26,000 yards, receiving fire from the *Cavour* and *Giulio Cesare*. 'They shot well and straddled' *Warspite*.

Meanwhile Tovey's cruisers had turned under *Warspite*'s stern, giving her a clear field of fire, and the 7th Cruiser Squadron with the destroyers from Tovey's and Cunningham's screens moved forward to counter-attack from '*Warspite*'s disengaged bow [, the destroyers] moving joyously ahead at full speed, dodging the overs from the Italian battleships …' Even as the destroyers and cruisers engaged the enemy light forces while they laid smoke, 'the culminating point of the engagement arrived'. Watching the fall of *Warspite*'s shot, Cunningham 'saw the great orange-coloured flash of a heavy explosion at the base of the enemy's flagship's funnels. It was followed by an upheaval of smoke, and I knew she had been heavily hit at the prodigious range of thirteen miles.'[12] Immediately the *Cavour* and *Giulio Cesare* turned away, and at 16.04 *Warspite* ceased fire. Tovey's cruisers continued in action, and the destroyers endured fire from the Italian cruisers while jockeying with their Italian counterparts. Campioni ordered five destroyer flotillas[13] to cover the withdrawal of the damaged *Giulio Cesare*, and they loosed torpedoes and then quickly retired behind the growing smoke screen. *Warspite*'s Walrus reported a degree of confusion in the Italian fleet, which had by now entirely swung away to the south-west to enter the Strait of Messina.

Cunningham 'had no intention of plunging straight into the enemy's smoke screen' and began to work to the north of it. But, although some of the destroyers had cleared the Italian smoke by 17.00, such was the superior speed of the Italian ships, including the damaged *Giulio Cesare* and the heavy cruiser *Bolzano*, which had been hit by Tovey's cruisers, that 'the enemy was out of sight'.[14]

Cunningham was apprehensive of running into a submarine trap as he closed to within twenty-five miles of the coast of Calabria, and although he followed the retreating Italians he soon afterwards broke off the chase, for the Regia Aeronautica had finally turned up again, some four hours after an infuriated Campioni had been told to expect them. As he recalled his own Walrus, Cunningham learned that the Italian bombers were attacking their own fleet in the mistaken belief it was himself.

Cunningham was allowed little time to enjoy this intelligence, for from 16.40 onwards his own ships were again subject to the intense bombing of the SM79s. While they failed to score direct hits, they were accurate enough to be highly disquieting, and near-misses shook even the great *Warspite* as she swung to the southward. About one hundred bombers made nine attacks, concentrating on the flagship and *Eagle* but including the other vessels. 'It was most frightening,' Cunningham candidly admitted. All who witnessed it were filled with apprehension, and only luck, it was felt, preserved the British ships from a disaster. Fortunately the attacks ceased after dark, at 19.25, as the British fleet steamed south, altering course at 21.15 for Malta, where next morning the C-in-C was obliged to send *Royal Sovereign* and the destroyers to refuel.

Meanwhile Vice-Admiral Ford, in addition to sending his Sunderlands out to reconnoitre for Cunningham, had decided to ignore the instruction to hold the merchant ships at Malta. As soon as he knew the outcome of the action off Calabria, he ordered the fast convoy, MF1, to sail at 21.00 on the 9th. The escort was composed of the two 'Malta group' destroyers from Alexandria, plus the new *Jervis* which had been at Malta since 2 July and endured several air raids, including a deliberate attack on her by three Italian seaplanes.

With the remainder of the fleet Cunningham cruised to the southward of Malta until 08.00 on 11 July, when the refuelled *Royal Sovereign* and the destroyers rejoined his flag. He then ordered Pridham-Wippell in *Royal Sovereign*, with *Malaya*, *Eagle*, *Gloucester* and their destroyers, to cover the slow convoy MS1. Cunningham had to attend a conference at Cairo so *Warspite*, with her four screening destroyers, headed for Alexandria at 19 knots, returning by a more southerly route to avoid attack by aircraft from the Dodecanese. This proved a sad misjudgement, for by hugging the African coast he attracted the attention of bombers from the Libyan airfields, 'and on July 11th we were heartily bombed until sunset'. On the 12th, Tovey's force was split. *Orion* and *Neptune* pushed on ahead to catch up with and cover convoy MF1, while *Liverpool* and *Sydney* joined *Warspite*. More bombing raids occurred, and bomb splinter damage from near-misses caused casualties aboard *Liverpool*. Cunningham's ships overtook the fast convoy and steamed into Alexandria at 06.00 on 13 July, just three hours before MF1.

Convoy MF1 had left Valletta late on the evening of 9 July under the escort of *Diamond* (Lieutenant-Commander P.A. Cartwright, Senior Officer), *Jervis*, and HMAS *Vendetta*. Cartwright found to his frustration that *Knight of Malta* was unable to exceed 10.5 knots, reduced to 9.5 when zigzagging. The three merchantmen, *Knight of Malta*, *El Nil* and *Rodi*, steamed in line abreast. *Diamond* was deployed out ahead on the port wing, *Jervis* on the starboard, and *Vendetta* astern. All three escorts zigzagged independently at 15 knots. At 16.35 on Wednesday 10 July, when they were approaching the Cyrenaican coast, a Cant Z501 flying-boat was driven off to the westward by high-angle fire from *Diamond*'s 3-inch anti-aircraft gun, and an enemy report that a convoy had been seen was intercepted. Cartwright consequently ordered *Jervis* and *Vendetta* to exchange stations, to improve the AA defence.[15] At 05.00 on the 11th Captain J.W.A. Waller, RAN, detaching from Tovey's force, arrived in HMAS *Stuart* with *Havock* and *Imperial*. Waller relieved Cartwright, beefing up the escort considerably. *Knight of Malta* continued to cause considerable anxiety because of engine problems and, as MF1 approached Alexandria, Waller left *Imperial* and *Havock* to cover the ailing vessel and increased the speeds of *Rodi* and *El Nil* to the 15 knots of the destroyers, entering the swept approach channel with some dash.[16]

Pridham-Wippell had been far from idle as he waited for the slow convoy to emerge from Valletta. On 10 July *Eagle* had flown

off a strike-force of Swordfish which attacked Augusta roads
with aerial torpedoes and sent the destroyer *Pancaldo* to the
bottom. Though she was afterwards salvaged this was a further
humiliation for Campioni, fulminating at the failure of the Regia
Aeronautica to arrive as intended at noon on 9 July, to which
injury the air force had added the insult of bombing the Regia
Marina *for six hours*. In Rome Ammiraglio di Armada Cavagnari
was of similar mind to Campioni, and sought to counter the vain-
glorious claims of his colleagues on the air staff, which Ciano at
least did not believe. Mussolini preferred his own conclusions,
that 'in three days the Italian Navy has annihilated fifty per cent
of the British naval potential in the Mediterranean'. 'Perhaps', his
son-in-law cautiously added, 'this is somewhat exaggerated.'[17]

The wrangles over its performance did not prevent the Regia
Aeronautica locating and bombing the combined force of
Pridham-Wippell's squadron and the slow convoy, concentrating their efforts on the warships. Although she carried no fighters officially, *Eagle* had embarked three spare Gladiator biplanes
while at Alexandria; these could not be struck below and had to
be kept on the flight-deck. Nor among the pilots of the Fleet Air
Arm Squadrons 813 and 824 embarked in *Eagle* were there any
fighter-pilots, but the Commander (Flying), whose role was not
normally airborne but who had trained in fighters, headed a trio
of volunteers. Commander Charles Keighly-Peach was shot
through the thigh in his first combat, but he and his colleagues
destroyed a shadowing reconnaissance aircraft and two Savoia
Marchetti bombers: 'Not bad', Cunningham commented, 'for a
man of thirty-eight.' Pridham-Wippell endured a more concentrated attack than Cunningham, but nevertheless brought
Convoy MS1 intact into Alexandria, on 15 July.

5

'The door-keepers'

(Operations HURRY *and* HATS, *and Convoy MF2)*

HIS CAIRO CONFERENCE notwithstanding, on his arrival at
Alexandria Cunningham was compelled to review the performance of his fleet. Set against the strategic objective of dealing
decisively with Italy, it had been a humbling experience, for he
had received a very practical and worrying demonstration of
enemy air-power, he had observed at first hand the deficiencies
of both *Malaya* and *Royal Sovereign* in terms of speed and main
armament range, and he had felt the lack of heavy cruisers and
carrier-borne fighters, all of which compromised his earlier
assertion that 'the route to Malta could be opened when
required'.

Cunningham was further hampered by many other difficulties, not least that of his base at Alexandria. This was hardly an
ideal place for a naval fleet and relied heavily upon its vulnerable floating dock, the depot ship *Medway* and repair ship
Resource; it was also exposed to aerial reconnaissance and to
attack from seaward, particularly by submarine craft. As the
C-in-C wrote to Pound at the beginning of August, 'They send
planes over Alex every day and no force in the last three weeks
has been at sea, without being discovered and bombed, in some
cases very heavily.' Moreover, this reconnaissance permitted the
Italians to tranship large quantities of military stores to Libya in
the succeeding months.[1] Reciprocal British air reconnaissance
was, in Cunningham's own word, 'fitful', relying as it did on a
handful of Sunderlands which, though they possessed the great

merit of range, were slow and vulnerable for inshore work. Finally, although the Royal Air Force 'did their best' to cover the fleet, the limited number of fighters available in Egypt lacked range and 'did not like operating over the sea'.[2]

Andrew Browne Cunningham, known throughout the Royal Navy as 'A.B.C.', was not a man to bemoan his fate. He had joined the navy in 1898 and had served extensively in destroyers. Even at the age of 57 he possessed all the energy expected of the breed. 'Big ship time is said to be necessary to us all,' he said, adding, 'I have never found it to be so.' Ruddy-faced with a grim mouth and blue eyes which were also 'red and watery', Cunningham had an explosive temper which could disguise a natural kindliness and was combined with an engaging and 'almost boyish sense of humour'. He believed 'duty' to be 'the first business of a sea officer', and was a convinced anti-bureaucrat. Fortunately he had at his right hand a very able chief-of-staff in Rear-Admiral Algernon Willis, to whom he left the interminable detail of administering his fleet.

Cunningham rightly concerned himself with the grand strategy in which his fleet was to play a vital part. He was acutely aware of the importance of holding Egypt and the Suez Canal, and convinced that maintaining Malta was equally crucial. He referred to himself and Somerville at Gibraltar as 'the door-keepers', for the two were to carry out operations in concert, evidence that if Britain did not 'own' the Mediterranean, neither did the Italians, and the Royal Navy could, when it wished, seize the tenancy.

Cunningham's ascendancy in the Eastern Mediterranean was based upon frequent sweeps by surface units of his fleet, often covering the convoy routes to the Aegean which were run from Port Said and the Suez Canal. He also sent out submarine patrols from both Malta and Alexandria. Those submarines based at Malta were almost as vulnerable in port as at sea, for they could only avoid damage during air raids by submerging to lie doggo on the harbour bottom. During July *Olympus* was damaged in one such raid, while *Phoenix* was lost during an attack on an enemy tanker off Augusta when she was sunk by the escorting torpedo boat *Albatros*. On the other hand, an Italian supply ship of 3,900 tons was sunk in a mine barrage laid by *Rorqual* off Tolmeta, midway between Derna and Benghazi, and another enemy freighter, *Sereno*, of 2,333 tons, was sunk off Tobruk together with the destroyers *Nembo* and *Ostro*, struck by Swordfish of No. 824 Squadron flown off *Eagle* on 20 July.[3]

This air strike was a consequence of an engagement fought the previous day off Cape Spada, following the location of the Italian light cruisers *Giovanni delle Bande Nere* and *Bartolomeo Colleoni*. The two cruisers, on passage from Tripoli to Leros, encountered the British destroyers *Hyperion, Hasty, Hero* and *Ilex*, under Commander H. Nicolson, at ten miles' range on the misty morning of 19 July. Nicolson was engaged on a submarine hunt to the north of Crete but, aware that HMAS *Sydney* and the destroyer *Havock* were forty-five miles away in the Aegean, he bore away to the northward in an attempt to induce Ammiraglio di Divisione Casardi to follow. Casardi took the bait, shelling the destroyers as they made off in line ahead. At 08.30 Nicolson's flotilla came in sight of *Sydney* and Captain J.A. Collins, RAN, ordered *Sydney*'s main armament to open fire, releasing the destroyers from their role as decoys. Nicolson, now joined by *Havock*, at once put about to attack the Italian ships with torpedoes in the classic manner. Casardi, discovering the deception, immediately turned away under full helm. The hunters were now the hunted, and the rearmost cruiser, *Bartolomeo Colleoni*, was battered to a standstill. Collins ordered the destroyers to administer the *coup de grâce* while *Sydney* continued the pursuit of *Giovanni delle Banda Nere*.

With her bows blown off, *Colleoni* was a 'raging furnace' as *Hyperion* and *Ilex* fired torpedoes into her at close range, and she sank with her ensign flying. *Havock* closed to pick up survivors, enduring bombing attacks from the Savoia Marchettis[4] which had now arrived overhead. Meanwhile the remaining destroyers made after *Sydney* in her pursuit of *Banda Nere*. Though hit, the Italian cruiser began to increase her lead, fading into the haze, and Collins, running short of shells, regretfully broke off the chase. As the British headed back towards Alexandria with more than 525 survivors from the *Colleoni*, including her captain, Novaro,[5] they were vigorously bombed by SM79s of the Regia Aeronautica, who succeeded in holing *Havock*, laden with her prisoners, by means of fragments from near-misses.

On receiving intelligence of the action the fleet put to sea and swept to the westwards in the hope of cutting off *Banda Nere* from Tobruk, but failed to locate her; instead, *Eagle*'s Swordfish contented themselves with the raid described above.

During the remainder of July, Cunningham's ships covered convoys to Greece. Again the Italian air force made their presence felt in a frightening but not fatal manner. These movements were ostensibly covered by the capital ships moving to the west of Crete, while the cruisers and destroyers ran from the Aegean through the Kithera Channel, and the ocean boarding vessels *Chakla* and *Fiona* made a feint landing on the small Dodecanese island of Kastellorizo, off the Turkish coast. The true purpose of these manoeuvres was to distract the Italian high command, for as the strength of the Italian army was being built up in Libya attention was increasingly focused on Malta, beleaguered and besieged, urgently in need of reinforcements, and distant midway between the two door-keepers.

Six months older than Cunningham, Vice-Admiral Sir James Somerville was also known for having a short fuse, a robust command of Anglo-Saxon, and a great deal of energy. Some thought his foul language excessive, but it often bridged the social barriers the peacetime navy erected in such profusion, and gave him an accessible image on the lower deck. He was more technologically inclined than Cunningham, had been instrumental in the development of radar, and flew with his air crews to better understand their task. His analytical mind was sharp, he was less willing to take risks than the destroyer-educated A.B.C., and profoundly disliked 'wild adventures'. His reputation lacked the standing of Cunningham's, and he was vulnerable to criticism by the Prime Minister. But above all, and like Cunningham, he was his own man, and knew his business.[6]

On 1 August 1940 it was Somerville's business to inaugurate what the participants variously nicknamed 'Club Runs' or 'Milk Runs', operations to reinforce Malta's air defences by flying in fighter aircraft from carriers which would launch them within range of their destination. Such operations were complicated by a number of factors, the first of which was an understandable resistance to stripping the home front of available fighter aircraft at a critical moment, when the air-battle for Britain was at its height. But Churchill, presciently anxious to buttress Malta before German air-intervention could complete what the Italians had begun, would have none of it. Dismissing a reassessment of the Chiefs of Staff not yet two months old that 'there is nothing practicable we can do to increase the powers of resistance of

Malta', he wrote to the Admiralty on 12 July urging the possibility of flying in Hurricanes, 'As we have a number ... surplus at the moment.' The bombing capability of the Italian air force was a consideration which worried Somerville, but not Churchill, who complained to Pound that while pre-war Boards of Admiralty had made 'sweeping statements to Parliament' about the ability of ships to withstand air attack, the situation had now changed to 'a tendency to ... consider it wrong to endanger His Majesty's ships by bringing them under air attack'. A further problem for naval operations east of Gibraltar was posed by the presence of Italian submarines in the Western Mediterranean; and the fighters themselves, once airborne and committed to the transit from carrier to Malta, possessed insufficient fuel to engage in aerial combat. Nevertheless, the decision to reinforce Malta in this way was urged on the Admiralty by the Prime Minister. 'This will have to be done under the fire of the enemy,' Churchill wrote uncompromisingly on 15 July. A 'small consignment' of Hurricane fighters was available and 'should reach Malta at the earliest moment'. Furthermore, the Prime Minister added, 'stores may be divided between several ships, so as to avoid losing it all if one is hit'. Moreover, the Gibraltar to Malta route was preferable, not only because it avoided the unacceptable delay of a detour round the Cape of Good Hope, but because 'the voyage from Alexandria to Malta ... [is] ... if anything, more dangerous than the voyage from Gibraltar to Malta'.

Cunningham's assertion that 'it should be possible to pass reinforcements through the Mediterranean ...' led Sir Dudley Pound to report back to the War Cabinet on 23 July that, while 'additional fighting ships' could be sent directly from Gibraltar to Alexandria, the passage of 'merchant vessels containing spare ammunition for the Fleet, high-angle guns for Malta, and aircraft for Malta' was 'unsound'.

Churchill's intention was to try to bring about a decisive action with the Italian fleet. His faith in the Royal Navy was such that he was sure the elimination of the Regia Marina wanted only opportunity, which must occur before the appearance of the Germans in the Mediterranean. Thus the reinforcement of Malta would exclude merchant ships, and as a prelude to a major naval operation the available 'small consignment' was to be despatched forthwith.[7]

The Air Ministry were informed that the ageing carrier *Argus* would be made available, and to mask what was to be code-named Operation HURRY, Cunningham was to carry out the operations in the Eastern Mediterranean described above. To Cunningham's diversions, which were given an extra and confusing fillip by the *Malaya* having to return to Alexandria covered by *Eagle*,[8] Somerville added his own. These were an integral part of Operation HURRY, which began with the arrival at Gibraltar early on the morning of 30 July of *Argus*, escorted by the destroyers *Greyhound, Gallant, Encounter* and *Hotspur*. Aboard the carrier were twelve Mark 1 Hurricanes, a pair of Fleet Air Arm Skuas to act as guides, some RAF personnel, and a quantity of air force stores for Malta. Twenty-six hours later, at 08.00 on the 31st, covered by an initial air search for submarines by No. 200 Squadron based at Gibraltar, Somerville's combined force sailed east at 17 knots. It consisted of *Hood, Valiant, Resolution*, the two carriers *Ark Royal* and *Argus*, the cruisers *Arethusa* and *Enterprise*, the destroyers *Faulknor, Foxhound, Forester, Foresight, Escapade* and *Velox*, and *Argus*'s flotilla of four.

Ark Royal flew off anti-submarine air patrols during the day and the weather freshened during the afternoon, a head-sea inhibiting the destroyers' sonars as the small ships started to pitch. During the hours of darkness the fleet pressed on east, flying off air patrols at dawn on 1 August. Radar contacts coming in from *Valiant* 'imposed an unnecessary strain' on personnel since the lack of identification between friendly and enemy aircraft 'gave rise to many false alarms', but by 12.30 the fleet was awaiting air attack in open order. Additional Skuas were flown off from *Ark Royal* at 17.10 to maintain combat air patrols overhead, and were ready to drive off eight enemy bombers forty minutes later, at 17.49. After a few minutes nine more SM79s were seen approaching from the north-west and Somerville swung the fleet 40 degrees to port, opening arcs of fire for the ships' guns. The barrage hit one plane, which turned away trailing smoke, but about eighty bombs were dropped; one SM79 was shot down by a Skua. The attacks lacked the vigour of those experienced during his last foray, a fact Somerville attributed, with some satisfaction, to the improved anti-aircraft fire of his fleet.

Well after dark, at 20.45, Somerville detached in *Hood*, with *Ark Royal, Enterprise, Faulknor, Foxhound, Foresight* and *Forester*, leaving the battleship *Valiant, Argus*, and the destroyers *Hotspur, Greyhound, Gallant, Escapade, Encounter* and *Velox* to continue east towards Malta. A little later *Enterprise* swung away on her own to transmit blind radio signals (coded Operation SPARK) intended to confuse enemy interceptors; thereafter she was to conform to a signal received earlier, ordering Somerville to try to intercept the French merchant ship *Gouverneur-Général de Gueydon*, thought to be on passage from Algiers to Marseilles with Édouard Daladier on board.[9]

Somerville also learned that Italian cruisers and destroyers had been observed passing north through the Strait of Messina by the submarine *Oswald*, from her patrol station at the southern end of the strait, and he had to consider the possibility of encountering these during the coming hours. Nevertheless, he stuck to his operational plan and at 02.00 on 2 August, by pre-arrangement and without signal, *Ark Royal* proceeded ahead of *Hood* to a position suitable for flying off her aircraft against the southern Sardinian air-base of Cagliari. Somerville watched anxiously, acutely conscious that he was 'mucking about only 100 miles' off the enemy coast. At 03.20 he saw 'in the pitch dark ... a small shadow detach itself from the great shadow of the *Ark*. The first Swordfish taking off. And then I thought of those incredibly gallant chaps taking off ... to fly 140 miles ...'; adding, with the true humility of a great commander, 'Well, that shook me up and I realised how small were my personal difficulties compared to theirs.'

As the dozen Swordfish armed with bombs and mines lifted off the carrier's deck, one crashed into the sea. Despite a search by the accompanying destroyers, the aircrew was lost. The strike was also hampered by an ill-timed change in the wind, from south to west, which wrecked the flight plan, setting the biplanes too far to the southward, so that they made their final approach to their targets not at dawn, but in the bright daylight of morning.

Having dispatched her unlucky chicks, *Ark Royal* swung to the south, towards the position of *Valiant* and *Argus*, 'in the van', as Somerville wrote, as he followed in *Hood* with the rest of Force H. At 04.45 more Swordfish were dispatched, eastwards to maintain a watch for the Italian warships and to the south-south-east to locate *Valiant* and *Argus*, while nine Skuas were airborne to provide air cover for the fleet and the returning strike force.

The strike force itself, now in full daylight, had flown in over Cagliari through heavy gunfire, set two hangars at Elmas aerodrome on fire, hit two more, destroyed four exposed aircraft ranged on the aprons, damaged adjacent buildings, and dropped three mines in the harbour. A second Swordfish had been lost, compelled to land at Elmas as the remainder turned back towards the fleet.

All this had been but a diversion. Captain H.C. Bovell in *Argus* had reached his take-off position at 04.45,[10] but the departure of the Hurricanes was delayed by the tardy starting of one of the guiding Skuas. Eventually, half an hour late, the twelve Hurricanes droned skywards and, in the wake of the Skuas, headed east for Malta. Further cover, beyond the range of the Skuas, was provided by two Sunderlands from Gibraltar, but there were no problems encountered. The Hurricanes and their pilots all arrived safely at Malta, a welcome augmentation of Air Commodore Maynard's meagre forces, but no more than a stop-gap measure.

Having sighted *Argus* shortly after the departure of her Hurricanes, Somerville's ships took station, leaving *Ark Royal* room for manoeuvre, as they awaited the returning Swordfish, which the fresh westerly breeze would hamper as they struggled to windward from Cagliari. Visibility had deteriorated and the cloud ceiling had dropped to about 4,000 feet when, at 06.30, the first of the returning sortie landed on *Ark Royal*. The last arrived at 07.20, and with the Swordfish came news of at least one Italian submarine on the surface within striking distance of the fleet. This was the only sighting either navy had of the other, although Supermarina had disposed the submarines *Argo*, *Axum*, *Diaspro*, *Manara*, *Medusa*, *Neghelli*, *Scirè* and *Turchese* in two waiting lines off Cape Bougaroni, where they remained until 9 August.

Several aircraft of the Regia Aeronautica were seen by Skuas flying overhead; one of them was forced down, but they maintained a prudent distance, and by 08.15 Somerville's force was steaming westwards at 18 knots. At 12.50 a Cant Z506 was shot down by the Skuas of No. 800 Squadron belonging to *Ark Royal* and patrolling astern of the fleet.

During the forenoon *Valiant*'s radar had picked up a formation of bombers to the north which came within ten miles before turning away, presumably frustrated in their search. *Ark Royal* also flew off Swordfish on anti-submarine patrols, sending an additional four to assist *Arethusa* which, at 09.30, Somerville dispatched to search for the *Gouverneur-Général de Gueydon*. She was no more successful than *Enterprise*, which at 10.00 from a position north of Minorca reported that she had two aircraft overhead, thus proving the efficacy of Operation SPARK in at least distracting the enemy. Somerville, concerned about her exposure, ordered *Enterprise* direct to Gibraltar where she arrived safely.[11]

Another picket, the submarine *Oswald*, which had earlier reported the northward movement of units of the Regia Marina, was not so fortunate. The day before, 1 August, not long after transmitting her warning, she was located, rammed and sunk off Calabria by the Italian destroyer *Vivaldi*. 'Too large, too old and with auxiliary machinery that was too noisy', the 'O', 'P' and 'R' classes of submarines which had been sent from China were proving highly vulnerable in the Mediterranean, in the clear waters of which, unlike the silt-laden waters of the Chinese coast, they were more easily detected.

Somerville's ships arrived back at Gibraltar on the morning of 4 August, where they immediately refuelled and took aboard ammunition. A number sailed that evening for Britain, including Somerville himself in the ill-fated *Hood*, together with *Valiant*, *Argus* and several of the destroyers.[12] To his wife, to whom he had unburdened himself after the shameful business at Oran, Somerville wrote that he felt 'in a better temper than when I last wrote'. In a coy code, and using an obvious synonym for the fighters, he described HURRY as 'what promised to be a sticky party ... to give old Ma [Vice-Admiral] Ford some gales of wind.' A day or so later he wrote again: 'We got back all right ... I received Their Lordships' congratulations ... and Andrew B. came up with "Nice work" to which I replied as a fellow door-keeper: "To Gog from Magog: Thank you."' He mourned the loss of the two Swordfish crews, without which 'we should have got away with a clean sheet'.

Somerville arrived at Scapa Flow very early on 10 August, transferred his flag to the modernised battlecruiser *Renown*, which 'had first-class AA equipment', and the following day met Sir Dudley Pound at the Admiralty. This was to discuss Operation HATS, desired by Churchill to bring on a battle with the Italians, and to send reinforcements to Cunningham directly through the Mediterranean. Force H would escort these to a position southeast of Sardinia, short of the mine barrage laid by the Italians in what was called the Sicilian Channel or the Narrows; here, between Sicily and Cape Bon, the depth of water was also reduced by the Skerki Bank.

The reinforcements would run the gauntlet until met by Cunningham on the far side, off Malta. At the same time, the opportunity would be taken to ship military stores into Malta. Churchill now wanted a further task accomplished. It was clear that matters were coming to a head in Libya, where by means of the trans-Mediterranean Axis supply route the Italian forces were preparing to attack the British in Egypt. At Cairo General Wavell was reporting the likelihood of a major attack, and his shortage of armoured vehicles, especially tanks, was acute. On 11 August Churchill refused to accept the Admiralty's veto on using merchant ships, fearing the transit time via the Cape would not merely delay the delivery of the fifty tanks destined for Wavell but deliver them too late, possibly in the wake of a defeat. The Chiefs of Staff were directed to re-examine the difficulties and the Admiralty was specifically instructed to 'overcome' them. The tank crews, composed of the 3rd Hussars, could go by the Cape route, since Wavell had manpower already to hand, but Churchill wrote impatiently that he was 'prepared to risk the fifty Infantry tanks in the Mediterranean'. Two days later he sent a withering assessment to the Admiralty in which sarcasm, only lightly veiled, was underpinned by his fear, even as the Battle of Britain raged undecided above his head, that 'if the Germans are frustrated in an invasion of Great Britain or do not choose to attempt it they will have great need to press and aid the Italians to the attack of Egypt.'

But Pound was unusually intractable, causing Churchill grief and vexation. Wavell considered the Italian threat had yet to mature, and the Chiefs of Staff compromised by preparing a plan for two transports loaded with the tanks to sail with the ships from Britain bound for Gibraltar and Operation HATS. They would accompany the force through the Mediterranean only if a deteriorating situation in Egypt warranted it; in the event, it did not, and the transports sailed round the Cape.

Although frustrated in their efforts to locate Force H in early August, the Italians continued what was to be their most aggressive policy, extensive mining operations. Ammiraglio di Divisione Marenco di Moriondo, flying his flag in the cruiser *Da*

Barbiano, accompanied by the cruiser *Alberto di Giussano* and the destroyers *Pigafetta* and *Zeno* and escorted by the torpedo-boats *Cassiopea, Cigno, Pleiadi* and *Aldebaran*, laid 394 mines to the south of Pantelleria during the night of 6/7 August. During the two following nights the minelayer *Scilla*, escorted by the torpedo-boats *Antares* and *Sagittario*, laid two barrages to the west of the island, totalling over 400 mines. Simultaneously, the destroyers *Maestrale, Grecale, Libeccio* and *Scirocco* laid 216 mines on each night.[13]

The absence of Force H from Gibraltar during Somerville's brief return to Britain, reported by agents in Algeciras across the bay, doubtless encouraged Supermarina to carry out these operations. Italian submarines were also on patrol in considerable numbers, but suffered from lack of targets; *Delfino* torpedoed the Greek cruiser *Helle* off Tinos on 15 August, only to have Rome repudiate responsibility the following day. But there was little lull in the eastern basin, where Cunningham, aware of the forthcoming operation, was busy with his own plans and in occupying the enemy's attention.

His submarines were variously employed. *Osiris* was in the Adriatic, where she sank a small ship on 16 August. *Rorqual* laid mines off Tolmeta on the same day, which accounted for a freighter of 3,300 tons and later, in December, the destroyers *Calipso* and *Fratelli Cairoli; Rorqual* was fortunate in escaping a counter-attack by the torpedo-boat *Generale Achille Papa*. Most innovative was an extension of the submarine's cloak-and-dagger role: the *Pandora* and *Proteus* were dispatched to Malta, each loaded with a small quantity of essential supplies.[14]

Having received the much-needed reinforcement of a heavy cruiser in the form of *Kent*, Cunningham himself sailed from Alexandria on 16 August in *Warspite*, with *Malaya, Ramillies, Kent* and the 2nd, 10th and 14th Destroyer Flotillas. Steaming west, Cunningham carried out a short but intensive bombardment of the Italian positions at Bardia and Fort Capuzzo, returning to base under a 'considerable force' of SM79s, twelve of which were shot down, giving the fleet 'a heartening sight' and inflicting 'a nasty reversal of fortune' upon the enemy air force.

A week later, on the night of 22/23 August, three of *Eagle*'s Swordfish of No. 824 Squadron, operating from an advanced airstrip, made a torpedo attack on the Italian sea-plane base at Bomba, west of Tobruk. Led by Captain O. Patch of the Royal

Marines, they launched their torpedoes at the depot ship *Monte Gargano*, alongside which lay the submarine *Iride*. Both vessels were sunk, thereby unwittingly delaying a bold Italian attack by manned torpedoes on the capital ships at Alexandria for which *Iride* was even then preparing. That same night, in the early hours of the 23rd, four of Cunningham's destroyers[15] raced along the coast to throw shells at the port, while the gunboat *Ladybird* supported by the destroyer *Waterhen* attacked Bardia.

The deliberations which Somerville had attended in London were now to bear fruit. He had returned to his new flagship, HMS *Renown*, and sailed from Scapa Flow on the afternoon of 13 August with a screen of four Tribal-class destroyers.[16] Met by the rest of Force H in the Atlantic, Somerville exercised his newly constituted squadron as they steamed back to Gibraltar, arriving at 20.00 on the 20th. Here the preparations for Operation HATS were reaching culmination, and Somerville again took his ships out into the Atlantic 'in order to allow *Ark Royal* some much needed flying practice'. Here too he met both the two tank-laden transports and the ships destined for Cunningham's fleet in the Eastern Mediterranean, all of which had left Britain on 22 August. The transports continued south for Egypt via the Cape, the reinforcing warships joined Somerville's flag. Designated Force F, they were principally the new aircraft-carrier *Illustrious*, which possessed an armoured flight deck and radar, the battle-ship *Valiant*, which was also radar-equipped, and two former light cruisers refitted with anti-aircraft armament, *Calcutta* and *Coventry*. In addition to these ships, the destroyers *Nubian*, *Mohawk*, *Hero*, *Janus*, *Gallant*, *Griffin*, *Greyhound* and *Hotspur* were attached to Force F. The first four were bound for Alexandria, the last only to run through the Narrows to Malta.

Having made his Atlantic rendezvous and taken all the war-ships under his command, Somerville returned to Gibraltar, to sail again at 08.45 on 30 August, this time zigzagging eastwards with a speed of advance of 15.5 knots.[17] Force H, comprising *Renown*, *Ark Royal*, the cruiser *Sheffield* and the destroyers *Faulknor*, *Fortune*, *Fury*, *Foresight*, *Firedrake*, *Forester*, *Encounter*, *Wishart* and *Velox*, was to cover Force F as far as the Sicilian Narrows and then carry out a second raid on Cagliari. Somerville posted his radar-equipped cruisers *Sheffield* and *Coventry* to maintain aerial surveillance ahead and astern, backed up by

Valiant, with the carriers independently acting as their own fighter directors. Inter-ship radio transmissions enabled the fleet's fighter defences to be 'directed on to shadowers with the minimum delay'.

At the opposite end of the Mediterranean, on the evening of 29 August, Cunningham's fleet began to move out of Alexandria. The C-in-C sailed in *Warspite* with *Eagle*, *Malaya*, the 3rd Cruiser Squadron, consisting of *Gloucester*, *Kent* and *Liverpool*, the 7th, *Orion* and *Sydney*, and thirteen destroyers of the 2nd, 10th and 14th Flotillas. Under the wing of Cunningham's fleet went the destroyers *Jervis* (Captain P.J. Mack), *Juno*, *Dainty* and *Diamond*, which were directed to escort to Malta the Royal Fleet Auxiliary *Plumleaf* and two merchantmen, *Volo* and *Cornwall*.

Mack's charges constituted convoy MF2. The masters of the two merchant ships had been summoned to a conference aboard *Warspite* on 27 August, where an outline of the intended operation was given to them. It was made clear to Captain F.S. Pretty of *Cornwall* that Admiral Cunningham expected the Italian fleet to appear and that he and his colleagues represented the bait – hence their escort would be light. Pretty had sailed from Bombay with a cargo consisting of grain and coal, some cotton-seed and five hundred tons of refrigerated Australian beef. Bound for Liverpool via the Cape, he had received orders to divert to Mombasa, discharge part of his cargo and replace it with anti-aircraft ammunition and, for some apparently inexplicable reason, several thousand boxes of matches.

The steamship *Cornwall* was a 10,600-grt cargo-liner belonging to the Federal Steam Navigation Company of London and capable of 13 knots, a fact which recommended her for fast convoy work. Leaving Mombasa, Pretty proceeded north to Suez, transited the canal and steamed out of Port Said to the west. Arriving at Alexandria, still unaware of his destination, he learned from the Egyptian bum-boats swarming about his ship that he was bound for Malta. The news seemed equally well known to the Italians, whose radio broadcasts on the 28th confirmed the fact and indicated that, if they had yet to swallow it, they had seen the bait. While at Alexandria, *Cornwall* embarked two army sergeants and some Maltese, all passengers for Valletta.

Of similar speed to *Cornwall* were the RFA *Plumleaf*, whose capacious tanks held gallons of the boiler fuel oil needed in Malta,[18] and the *Volo*, a much smaller cargo ship of 1,587 tons, owned by Ellerman's Wilson Line and usually employed on short-sea trades. Late on 28 August the three laden vessels sailed to make their rendezvous with Mack's destroyers off Great Pass Beacon and at about midnight, at a speed of 12 knots, set a course to the north-west, well clear of the Italian-occupied coast of Cyrenaica, heading for Gavdo, a small island off the Cretan coast.

Somerville's ships steamed east, the carriers flying off aircraft on exercise and on patrol, searching ahead of the warships. During the forenoon of the 31st, intercepted Italian radio traffic indicated that three Italian cruisers and a trio of destroyers were at sea. Slowing at mid morning to stream paravanes as a mine counter-measure, Somerville prepared his fleet for heavy air attack, and just after midday a Skua dispatched on a radar bearing chased and shot down a Cant Z506B. A second shadower, a Cant Z501,[19] was similarly destroyed two hours later, after the fleet's clocks had been advanced by two hours to conform with the zone-time kept in Cunningham's ships. Well after dark, at 21.50, the destroyers *Velox* and *Wishart*, detached as Force W, raced off into the night to a position north of the Balearic Islands to make extensive and deceptive radio transmissions. This, Operation SQUAWK, was intended not merely to mislead the Italians as to the position of the British fleet, but also to mask low-power transmissions from *Ark Royal* as she manoeuvred to operate her aircraft.

At 03.00 the following morning, 1 September 1940, *Ark Royal* once more steamed ahead into the van and prepared her nine Swordfish with bombs, incendiaries and flares, flying them off into the clear, starlit night a few minutes later from a position a little south of west, and some 155 miles distant from Cagliari.[20] The fleet then followed *Ark Royal* round onto a course which would close the Sicilian Narrows to a position 120 miles south-west of the target area.

The Swordfish again attacked through heavy flak to drop their bombs, sighting some forty aircraft on the ground and a further thirty seaplanes and flying-boats moored in the adjacent harbour. All returned safely to land about 08.00, having seen a small Italian coastal convoy and a surfaced submarine, which was attacked with machine-guns and forced to dive. *Greyhound* and *Hotspur* were sent off to try to locate the submarine but were unable to do so, and rejoined the fleet later. The enemy convoy was ignored, partly on the grounds that it might not be Italian.

Somerville's squadron now turned back to the west, a ruse intended to persuade any aerial observer that the main business of the sortie was over. At the same time two fighter patrols, each of six aircraft, were maintained aloft to see off any shadowers. In the late afternoon *Illustrious* launched seven reconnoitring Swordfish to the eastward and, in an unfortunate incident, one of her patrolling Fulmars hit a patrolling British Hudson.

At 22.00 that evening, when north-east of the Skerki Bank, Force F detached without signal, vanishing into the darkness to the south-eastwards. Somerville's force cruised north for a little longer, then sped west at 24 knots to get into a position to make a second attack on Cagliari, flying off *Ark Royal*'s nine Swordfish at 03.30. The conditions – dark, hazy and with no horizon – were ideal for obscuring the passage of Force F through the Sicilian Narrows, but not for the young Swordfish pilots, whose attacks on Elmas aerodrome and Cagliari power station were foiled by low cloud and the thick mist lying in the Sardinian valleys. Four bombed searchlights, two hit a field, and the remainder jettisoned their bombs in the sea, but all returned safely to *Ark Royal*, and Force H steamed to the west, arriving at Gibraltar without incident at 11.00 on 3 September.[21]

As Mack steamed convoy MF2 north-west towards Malta, Cunningham's division followed in his wake at 16 knots, not having left Alexandria until the early forenoon. At 14.30 a Cant Z501 was sighted and subsequently shot down, while some two hours later a second shadower was heard high above the cloud, but no aerial attack materialised. It was not surprising. The Regia Aeronautica were busy elsewhere.

The early hours of 30 August were calm and clear. At 01.45 *Jervis*, on the starboard bow of the convoy, gained a 'doubtful [submarine] contact which was immediately counter-attacked ... The echo persisted and was subsequently attacked with a full pattern without visible results.' Whether or not this was an Italian submarine remains doubtful. The remainder of the day passed quietly, and that evening the ships of MF2 closed the coast of Crete, passing inside Gavdo and along the southern shore of the main island. At 11.30 the following morning a course of west-north-west was set for Malta. Twenty-five minutes later, when the convoy was six miles clear of Elphonisi Island and pitching in a moderate to rough sea and fresh wind, bombs dropped out of the sky from 'a formation of 4 or 5 enemy aircraft who approached unseen at a height of between 12,000 and 15,000 feet. In all, about 16 or 20 bombs were dropped. One clump fell close to *Dainty* [on the convoy's port bow] and the other close to SS *Cornwall*, three of which hit: two aft, which destroyed both guns and set the ship on fire, and one amidships ... which destroyed the W/T office killing the junior operator ... One man was trapped in the crew's quarters aft, but when the magazine exploded subsequently it blew a hole through which he escaped unhurt.' Such was Captain Mack's laconic report of a remarkably successful attack.

Cornwall, in common with all British merchant ships, mounted an old 4-inch gun aft on her poop, a defensive measure against submarines, along with a 12-pounder. The first bomb burst between them, sending fragments among the gun crews, while the blast threw them bodily through the canvas awning onto the deck below. All were injured or suffered flesh-wounds, but no one was killed. The bomb wrecked *Cornwall*'s steering engine below her poop, however, jammed the rudder, knocked the after lifeboats out of their chocks, and started a fire near the 4-inch ammunition locker. This spread rapidly.

The second bomb detonated amidships and killed Junior Radio Officer Chamberlain.[22] McNeill, the senior 'sparks', was also in the radio office, but while it was blown apart round him, he was only stunned. The explosion caused major structural damage amidships, started several fires, and sent fragments ricocheting down ventilation trunking to cause about a dozen casualties to men below decks. None proved fatal. The third bomb passed through the port deck rail and burst alongside the ship, splitting the shell-plating and blowing the cooling-water injection valves off the ship's side, whereupon the engines were stopped. Water started to flood *Cornwall*'s engine room and she began to heel to port. The list alarmed Pretty, on the bridge, who at first considered his ship lost. Aft of the bridge *Cornwall* was certainly a shambles, but the relatively light bombs had exploded on impact, mainly damaging the superstructure. Although the shell-plating was pierced, it soon became clear that the ingress of water could be coped with. In fact, Pretty's main problem was his loss of steering – difficult to deal with at the best of times, but critical when in company with other ships.

All hands were turned-to. The chief officer, Mr N.A. Thomas, was ordered to muster the deck crew and extinguish the fires and the chief engineer, Mr A. Drummond, to see what he could do to stem the influx of water and restart the engines. Thomas was hampered by a lack of pressure on the fire main, and the fact that most of the hoses near the seats of the fires had been punctured by bomb fragments. Several men, including Able Seaman Dabner, an Australian naval reservist and gunner whose ankle had been broken by blast and who was burnt, returned aft and began to throw shells overboard. About half of the shells and charges had been jettisoned 'over the wall' when the heat drove the men back, and a second or two later the ammunition locker blew up. The sheet of flame mostly dissipated upwards, but searing heat penetrated No. 5 'Tween-Deck and ignited the cotton-seed loaded at Bombay.

It was now twelve minutes since *Cornwall* had been bombed and the convoy had passed on, though *Juno* had dropped back to stand by the stricken merchantman. The destroyer's officers, as they observed the listing and burning *Cornwall*, were astonished when 'she suddenly got under way, and after a couple of erratic circles came lurching after the convoy at quite a surprising pace.'

Although his rudder had jammed almost amidships, by dint of quick experimentation once Drummond had restarted the engines, Captain Pretty discovered that with his starboard engine turning at full power and his port at half, and variations of this, he could steer a reasonably straight course. In less than half an hour he and his crew had their ship under command again and were hurrying to resume their station in the convoy formation. Although the fires continued to burn and ready-use ammunition to explode, *Plumleaf* and *Volo* took station on either side of *Cornwall* and zigzagged as the burning ship lumbered along her almost steady rhumb-line. Thus did MF2, though down to 9.5 knots, resume its course for Malta.

At 13.20 Pretty reported to Mack that his crew were having some success in extinguishing the fires and had successfully reduced the inflow of water. By 16.30, after a prodigious effort by the crew led by Thomas and the carpenter, J. Frater, the fires were finally out, but the water in the engine and boiler rooms, augmented by the enthusiasm of the hose-parties and not helped by the lack of proper ship's side valves, was rising fast. In the boiler room the level was within inches of the fires, and the saturated cotton-seed in No. 5 Hold aft had swelled with retained water, the weight of which increased *Cornwall*'s port list to about 10 degrees. This greatly hampered Pretty's steering, but by 17.00, as the wind and sea dropped, so too did the water in the boiler room. Moreover, Drummond reported that he could increase the ship's speed to 11 knots, which partly compensated for Captain Pretty's difficulties with the list by improving the steering. But if *Cornwall* was now out of immediate danger, her crew were not.

At 19.00 Captain Mack ordered MF2 to abandon its planned route, 'owing to the time that had been lost', and proceed directly towards Malta. Earlier he had refused to stop to transfer his surgeon to *Cornwall*, where the nine wounded were in the hands of Mr J. Jesse, the chief steward; instead, symptoms were flashed by aldis lamp and instructions passed back. The steward's boy had a femoral artery cut and a lump of shell in his thigh, an able seaman had a crushed foot, and a greaser's chest was perforated deeply by three splinters. All were in desperate need of morphia, and at 20.00, under cover of darkness, the convoy stopped while *Juno* transferred Surgeon-Lieutenant Adnams, RNVR. He saved all three, and treated the lesser wounded. He was impressed by the orderly state of the makeshift hospital in the officers' saloon and, of the wounded, wrote that 'Their conduct ... was of the best and never a murmur of complaint was to be heard.' He also reported that 'the officers took their extra labours very lightly, quite as though it was the usual procedure. The ship's company all showed excellent spirits and a cheerful and helpful manner ... All difficulties were minimised. The Captain was particularly impressive, as also was the Chief Officer. Their extraordinary good fortune in so few of the ship's company having been injured is difficult to appreciate without having seen the damage to the ship and realising how close many of the men were to the explosions.' To Adnams' report might be appended similar plaudits to Chief Engineer Drummond, whose unobserved maintenance of power was no less admirable.

During the 31st Tovey's 3rd Cruiser Squadron had joined the C-in-C off Cape Matapan, and that day a Swordfish from *Eagle* sighted the Italian battle-fleet. This had sortied from Taranto and Messina, emerging in a force consisting of five battleships, including the new *Littorio* and *Vittorio Veneto*, thirteen cruisers and thirty-nine destroyers. But it had made little real effort to search for the British fleet, and darkness obscured it from Cunningham's aircraft which, aloft again next morning, saw nothing of the enemy. As for the Italians, neither of their two submarines off Crete, *Corallo* and *Sirena*, spotted the passage of the British ships, nor did the trio of *Berillo*, *Capponi* and *Durbo* on patrol off Malta.

At 08.30 on 1 September Mack's destroyers came in sight of Tovey's cruisers, then of the main body of the fleet beyond. Cunningham ordered Mack to send *Volo* and *Plumleaf* directly into Valletta under the escort of *Dainty* and *Diamond*, while *Jervis* and *Juno* accompanied the crippled *Cornwall* into port.

Aboard *Cornwall* things were deteriorating once more. The heavy list was inducing the cargo of coal to shift and the engines to overheat. Speed had dropped again to 9 knots and Pretty, who had been on the bridge for a day and a night, was finding it increasingly difficult to hold a course. But *Cornwall* was approaching St Elmo's lighthouse, and the bluff bows of the dockyard tugs *Ancient* and *Jaunty* shoved great white waves aside as they hurried out to her assistance. The heavily-listing ship was towed into Grand Harbour at 09.00 on 2 September, only two hours behind her consorts. In his report, Mack was highly complimentary to Pretty and his ship's company. In particular, the master's achievement in 'keeping an accurate course with no steering gear at all' justifiably earned Mack's approbation as 'a most seamanlike performance'.[23]

As *Jervis*, *Juno* and *Cornwall* entered Valletta, Cunningham's fleet saw the ships of Force F approaching from the west along the southern coast of Malta. Most welcome was the carrier *Illustrious* with her Fulmar fighters. She and *Valiant*, the two cruisers *Coventry* and *Calcutta* and four destroyers, swung into the swept channel round the island's easternmost point and turned towards Grand Harbour; there, the first attempt to enter being postponed until after an air raid, they were welcomed by cheering crowds. Aboard *Valiant*, guard and Marine band were paraded; 'a touch', noted Midshipman Lewin, 'which must have impressed the Maltese considerably. They saw us at sea, being bombed and firing at aircraft; half an hour later we were entering harbour with band playing.' Here, breaking off during further air raids, the warships discharged army and RAF personnel, replacement gun barrels, ranging instruments, eight 3.7-inch AA gun mountings, 100 Bren guns, and 10,000 rounds of 40-mm Bofors ammunition.

At 16.45 that same eventful evening the destroyers *Gallant*, *Greyhound*, *Griffin* and *Hotspur*, which had entered that morning with *Valiant* and the cruisers, taken on fuel and joined the AA barrage, left Grand Harbour to return to Gibraltar. The *Gallant* had sustained damage from bombing on the 31st. After carrying out an anti-submarine search off Malta, they arrived safely under the shadow of The Rock on 5 September.

Meanwhile, throughout 2 September, *Warspite* and her consorts had cruised some thirty miles south of the island, waiting for *Valiant* and the AA cruisers to discharge their cargoes. Tovey had been holding a watchful position to the north of Valletta, and as he ran back towards the Commander-in-Chief with his cruiser squadron he was tailed by a pair of shadowing aeroplanes. *Illustrious* homed her Fulmars onto the enemy and 'quickly tumbled both of them into the sea to the loud cheers of the ships' companies, who had had just about as much as they could stand of being bombed without retaliation. The tremendous effect of this incident upon everyone in the fleet, and upon the Commander-in-Chief as much as anyone,' Cunningham candidly and enthusiastically admitted, 'was indescribable. From that moment, whenever an armoured carrier was in company, we had command of the air over the fleet.'[24]

Cunningham now divided his fleet. Tovey's cruiser squadron of *Gloucester*, *Kent* and *Liverpool*, with the destroyers *Nubian* and *Mohawk*, was sent to patrol to the northwards into the Gulf of Nauplia and meet a south-bound convoy; Pridham-Wippell, commanding Force E in *Malaya*, with *Eagle*, *Coventry* and eight destroyers, was ordered to head east, towards Alexandria but passing south of Crete. Cunningham himself in *Warspite*, with *Valiant*, *Illustrious*, *Calcutta* and seven destroyers as Force I, would pass north of Crete.

The unloading of the warships' supplies was delayed by a raid by Junkers Ju87B Stukas of the Regia Aeronautica. These also attacked *Eagle* and the destroyers *Janus* and *Imperial*, but without success. Radio silence was breached to inform Cunningham, who had turned east at 19.45. In the event *Valiant* did not join the Commander-in-Chief's flag until two hours before midnight, but she and the two AA cruisers were soon in the thick of things as

Cunningham now carried out an air strike from each of the carriers attached to Forces I and E. Their targets were the airfields on Rhodes, 'from which came the aircraft that gave us sleepless nights at Alexandria'. The C-in-C ordered every available Swordfish except an anti-submarine patrol of four to be armed as dive-bombers, with the Fulmars forming two flights of six aircraft to give fighter protection to the biplanes. Both carriers launched their aircraft shortly before 04.00, timed to arrive over their respective target areas at dawn. Unfortunately the ninth Swordfish to take off from *Illustrious* struck the ship's superstructure with a wing-tip, blocking the after part of the deck and trapping the flight leader. Nevertheless, once airborne, *Eagle's* aircraft headed for Maritza, *Illustrious's* for Callato. Meanwhile HMAS *Sydney* and HMS *Orion* shelled Scarpanto airfield during the dark hours, and their escorts, the destroyers *Decoy* and *Ilex*, engaged two fast attack craft, *MAS536* and *MAS537*, sinking the latter in the Kaso Strait on 4 September.

Both strike forces 'beat-up' the airfields, setting fire to ammunition and fuel installations and damaging hangars, but the cost was four Swordfish, each with their crew of two officers. 'The Navy could ill-afford to lose them,' Cunningham mourned. 'They were the cream of the Fleet Air Arm.' Having given the enemy 'a good basting', Cunningham headed for Alexandria, arriving on the morning of 5 September with a vastly reinforced fleet possessing both an effective, modern carrier with moderately capable fighters, an enhanced anti-aircraft defence in *Coventry* and *Calcutta*, and the advantage of long-range warning by virtue of their primitive radar.[25]

Operation HATS had, withal, also run some 250 tons of military stores and spares, including 28 anti-tank guns, to the army and air force in Egypt. As for the replenishment of Malta, whatever the Admiralty's doubts about entrusting tanks to merchantmen, *Cornwall*, as only the second British ship to be hit by Italian bombing, had proved that the 'civilians' manning her had the ability and resourcefulness to withstand the rigours of the passage.

It was a fact that did not escape Churchill.

6

'Mare Nostrum is … an established fact'

(Operations MB5, MB6 and Convoys MF3 and MF4, Operation MB8 and Convoys MW3 and ME3, Operations COAT, JUDGEMENT *and* WHITE*)*

OPERATION HATS HAD proved a success, disappointing Cunningham only in that he missed the opportunity to bring the Italian fleet to battle. But the Regia Marina had also lost an opportunity, the best they were to have of catching the British Mediterranean Fleet at a numerical and technological disadvantage. Although Cunningham's reinforcements were an impressive augmentation of his fleet, most notably in the provision of radar, they did not offset the problems associated with his difficult supply lines and the unsatisfactory nature of Alexandria as a fleet base. Three times the distance of Sicily from Tripoli and still, despite the bombing of Scarpanto, under regular and effective aerial reconnaissance, Alexandria remained remote from the cockpit of Mediterranean affairs. Knowing when the British battle fleet was in port enabled the Italians to hasten men and *matériel* into Libya virtually unopposed.

In London, Churchill took a more sanguine view. Reviewing HATS, he brushed aside the damage to *Cornwall* and reasserted his faith in the route through the Mediterranean in a note to Pound of 7 September, ignoring the reality of the risks involved. Two days later Churchill sent Cunningham what the admiral called a 'prodding' signal, urging him to do more against the Italian fleet. Cunningham replied 'in a strong letter to the First Sea Lord', pointing out again that the necessary dispersal of destroyers on convoy escort to the Aegean and Levant and the consequent need for them to undergo frequent boiler cleans, resulted from the reluctance of the Admiralty to send out any of the more appropriate corvettes to carry out this essential duty. This not only squandered resources, but hampered the freedom of movement of the battle fleet. Moreover, Cunningham added trenchantly, Malta would soon require stores at a rate of 'something like two convoys a month', which would need major fleet support and thus offer 'good opportunities for operations against the Italians'.

Churchill's remote detachment, and his impatience to strike the Italians before Germany intervened in the theatre, put unnecessary pressure on Cunningham, and had the appearance of questioning his judgement as the man-on-the-spot. This was unfair, since Cunningham himself wanted nothing more than an opportunity to strike hard at the Italians. For his part, Cunningham failed to appreciate the dearth of escorts in the North Atlantic. But matters in the Mediterranean were far from static; the Italian high command was bestirring itself and, among other things, the Duce was urging Marshal Graziani to administer the '*coup de grâce*' to Great Britain by seizing Egypt.

Accordingly the Italian fleet sortied in strength between 6 and 9 September in anticipation of an encounter with Force H, which had indeed left Gibraltar but was bound for Dakar and Operation MENACE.[1] The Italian capital ships and their screen returned disappointed to port, though the torpedo-boats *Altair*, *Alcione*, *Ariel* and *Aretusa* had, on the night of 5/6 September, added to the minefields off Malta. Furthermore, and with serious consequences for British fortunes in the Eastern Mediterranean, Italian reinforcements of more than 40,000 men, 700 vehicles and 34,000 tons of military stores were conveyed from Brindisi to Albania, preparatory to an offensive against Greece.[2]

The Italian army too was on the move, in the Western Desert, where the long-awaited offensive against Egypt now began. Graziani advanced rapidly with overwhelming numbers, occupying Sidi Barani on 16 September. Cunningham harried the enemy from the sea, sending various units of his fleet to strike at Benghazi, Bardia, Sidi Barani and Sollum, actions in which *Illustrious* figured prominently. The cruiser *Kent* was torpedoed in the stern during a moonlit night air attack. Her screws were damaged, and towing her back to Alexandria proved very difficult. Nevertheless, as one commanding officer reported, 'all targets [were] driven inland, leaving practically nothing to be engaged from seaward'.

Graziani halted his advance in order to fortify his positions and build up his supplies, intending to move forward again as the weather cooled. It was to prove a fatal delay amounting to a blunder, for by the end of September Wavell had received his reinforcing armour and artillery, and on 9 December Major-General O'Connor's Anglo-Indian divisions struck back, exploiting the gaps in Graziani's defences, cutting off Italian units by encirclement and seizing prisoners in vast numbers.

In addition to operations against Graziani's army, the plight of Malta was rarely out of Cunningham's thoughts. The island's limited supplies were again running low, but the most pressing obligation in late September was to transport some 1,500 men to stiffen the garrison against anticipated invasion. The repaired *Gloucester* and *Liverpool* were prepared for this task, embarking the soldiers and sailing from Alexandria on 28 September, escorted by Cunningham's 'first eleven' of *Warspite*, *Valiant* and *Illustrious*, together with the cruisers *Orion*, *Sydney* and *York* and eleven destroyers of the 2nd and 14th Flotillas. The operation, code-named MB5, was spotted by Italian aircraft, and although *Illustrious*'s Fulmars attacked the shadowing planes they 'did not', the Commander-in-Chief remarked ruefully afterwards, 'prevent some heavy bombing'.[3] Worse was to come.

Knowing of the British presence, Supermarina ordered the capital ships at Messina and Taranto to intercept; *Vittorio Veneto* and *Littorio* once more put to sea, with the *Conte di Cavour*, *Giulio Cesare* and *Caio Duilio*, the heavy cruisers *Pola*, *Zara*, *Gorizia* and *Fiume*, which constituted the 1st Division; the 3rd, comprising the *Bolzano*, *Trento* and *Trieste*; and the 7th and 8th, consisting of the light cruisers *Eugenia di Savoia* and *Duca d'Aosta*, and *Duca degli Abruzzi* and *Giuseppe Garibaldi*. These were screened by twenty-three destroyers. With a large number of SM79s already harassing Cunningham's ships, Campioni, the overall commander, seemed set to enjoy some success.

Although the Italian bombers failed to hit a British ship, their superiority overhead, despite *Illustrious*'s presence with the fleet, prevented the flying-off of the few Swordfish available to strike at the Italian fleet, the position of which was known to Cunningham from a report by one of the carrier's fighters. Campioni was no more than eighty miles away to the north, but the nine Swordfish remained impotently on *Illustrious*'s flight deck and the Italians, demoralised in turn by the Aeronautica's failure to weaken the enemy, once again refused battle. 'After some thought,' Cunningham afterwards wrote somewhat disingenuously, 'we decided to press on with the main object of landing troops in Malta.'

As Campioni reached port on 30 September, *Gloucester* and *Liverpool* detached from the main force and made for Malta at speed to disembark their troops. They rejoined Cunningham's flag on the following day, and the whole fleet headed east again.

This episode, subsequently made light of, must privately have stung Cunningham, for on his return, learning that 'a very old and inoffensive Italian torpedo-boat had sailed from Taranto for Tobruk', he gave orders that a division of destroyers should be sent to sea to sink her. His staff urged the necessity of boiler-cleaning the destroyers, but the Commander-in-Chief responded that 'We must never let the enemy think it is safe to go to sea; we must make him realise he is only safe when in harbour. Contrariwise, our Fleet must feel that it is natural for them to be at sea. Go on, send the destroyers and sink the poor inoffensive bugger!'[4]

At Alexandria Cunningham received the heartening news that a further battleship, HMS *Barham*, would be sent out to him, together with the destroyer depot ship *Woolwich* and a reinforcement of four destroyers. He also learned that HMAS *Stuart* and a Sunderland of No. 230 Squadron had sunk the Italian submarine *Gondar* on 30 September, though her mission, which was to launch a manned torpedo at the British capital ships at Alexandria, remained a secret. On 2 October *Hasty* and *Havock* sank the *Berillo* off the Cyrenaican coast, further damaging Italian morale.

While British cruisers bombarded positions in the Dodecanese and British submarines enjoyed some success against the Italian military supply lines off Durazzo, the Italians persistently laid mines off Malta in depths of up to 200 fathoms. With the Regia Aeronautica continuing to dominate the contested air above Malta and this additional ring of offensive weaponry around it, the situation of the island was becoming increasingly acute. Following the action off Calabria, radio broadcasts from Rome and Berlin had boasted of a decisive Italian naval victory.[5] '*Mare Nostrum* is no longer a rhetorical expression, but an established fact', listeners in Europe were informed. 'British dominion of the Mediterranean is at an end.'

This was obvious braggadocio, but from Cunningham's perspective there was a disquieting grain of truth in the broadcast claim. The reality confronting him was that although no one dominated the central Mediterranean, it was an inescapable fact that the Italians currently experienced far less trouble reinforcing Graziani in Libya than did the British resupplying Dobbie in Malta. Regular and immense efforts would be required if Malta were to survive. While his spirit of aggression was undimmed, Cunningham's practical seaman's mind concerned itself with weighing the combination of Italian air and sea forces. The failure of *Illustrious* to do more than defend the fleet on 30 September had given him food for thought; he was less cock-a-hoop than he had been on her first joining the fleet. Having told his staff that the Italian fleet should feel safe only in their harbours, however, he had already begun to meditate a means of nullifying even that comfort, and had put in hand the planning of a punitive raid on the Regia Marina's base at Taranto for 21 October, the anniversary of Trafalgar. In the meanwhile there remained the problem of Malta.

By 8 October 1940 four merchantmen had arrived at Alexandria from Britain by way of the Cape, loaded with stores, food and fuel for Malta. Two Clan Line steamers, *Clan Macaulay* and *Clan Ferguson*, usually employed on the United Kingdom to India service, were joined by *Lanarkshire,* of the Scottish Shire Line, and the Blue Funnel liner *Memnon*.[6] All were of comparable tonnage and speed, *Clan Ferguson* grossing 7,347 tons and *Memnon* 7,506, with a speed of 13 to 14 knots. Loaded to a co-ordinated plan orchestrated by the Sea Transport Division of the Ministry of War Transport (who had Sea Transport officers stationed in the ports of Great Britain and who worked with the cargo-liners' own officers), such vessels each carried a portion of the various commodities and equipment destined for Malta. The loss of one ship would not therefore mean a disastrous shortage of a single vital component of the varied necessary defensive *matériel*, whether it was shells for the ack-ack gunners or sugar for their tea.

The four cargo-liners sailed from Alexandria on 9 October in convoy MF3 under the close escort of the anti-aircraft cruisers *Calcutta* and *Coventry,* and four destroyers. Their passage was covered by Cunningham in *Warspite*, with *Malaya* and *Ramillies*, both carriers (*Ark Royal* and *Illustrious*) under Rear-Admiral A.L. St G. Lyster, the reorganised 3rd Cruiser Squadron of *York*, *Gloucester* and *Liverpool*, the 7th of *Ajax*, *Orion* and *Sydney*, and a cloud of destroyers. The opportunity was also to be taken to bring the discharged *Volo* and *Plumleaf*, together with the gunboat *Aphis*, back to Alexandria in convoy MF4. The whole operation was code-named MB6.[7]

Poor weather, including heavy thunderstorms, prevented the ships being spotted from the air, and MF3 reached Malta safely on 11 October, though the destroyer *Imperial*, having detonated a mine laid in 180 fathoms and suffered some damage, was towed into Malta by *Decoy*. On the return passage, which began immediately, MF4 was spotted from the air by the crew of an Italian civil aircraft. Supermarina decided to attempt an ambush, directing Capitano di Fregata Banfi, commanding the 1st Torpedo Boat Flotilla, to make an attack on the moonlit night of 11/12 October. This was to be supported by Capitano di Vascello Margottini's 11th Destroyer Flotilla.

Although Banfi achieved a degree of surprise as he launched *Airone*, *Alcione* and *Ariel* at the *Ajax*, the northernmost of a line of British cruisers, his approach was not undetected and his ships were received by a devastating fire at 4,000 yards. This destroyed both *Airone* and *Ariel*. *Alcione* made smoke, recovered survivors from the *Airone* and retired, as *Ajax*, commanded by Captain E.D.B. McCarthy, shifted her gunfire to the second wave of attackers. Margottini's leading ships were equally mauled, *Artigliere* receiving heavy punishment and her consort *Aviere* less severe treatment, while their sister ships *Geniere* and *Camicia Nera* appear to have broken off the attack and retired behind a smoke screen. The Italians, using flashless cordite with tracers, inflicted damage on *Ajax*, hitting her seven times and starting a small fire which caused damage to her precious radar. McCarthy's ship did not have the benefit of flashless charges and her gunnery control was hampered by the 'blinding effect' caused by her own guns. Nevertheless, she left *Artigliere* ablaze.

The *Artigliere* was taken in tow early the following morning by *Camicia Nera* and the two ships were discovered struggling back to Sicily by a questing flying-boat from Malta, whereupon the cruiser *York* was sent in pursuit. Swordfish from *Illustrious* were also homed onto the hapless Italians. That same morning, at

Messina, the 3rd Cruiser Division of *Trieste*, *Trento* and *Bolzano* was ordered to the assistance of Margottini's shattered flotilla. They were too late, for although the Swordfish failed to hit their target, Captain R.H. Portal arrived in *York* to find *Artigliere* alone, *Camicia Nera* having abandoned her tow to her fate. Greeted with waving sheets and towels, Portal, reluctant to expose *York* to the bombing which had devastated *Havock* as she rescued the ship's company of *Bartolomeo Colleoni*, ordered Carley floats to be dropped close to *Artigliere*. As soon as her crew had taken the hint, Portal sank the stricken destroyer by gunfire. Some two hundred and twenty-five survivors were afterwards recovered by the hospital ship *Aquileja* after Cunningham had made a plain-language signal to the Italians giving their position. After a gallant and classic destroyer action by the Regia Marina it was the least he could do, but he was reprimanded by London, then under the intense blitz of the Luftwaffe.

The Italians had engaged in desultory and largely ineffective bombing attacks on the dispersed fleet as it made its way back to the eastward. As was now the custom, the carriers were them-selves mounting air raids on an Italian airfield in the Dodecanese: ninety-two bombs were dropped on Leros, hitting hangars, workshops and fuel facilities. Then, in the twilit evening of 14 October, as the Mediterranean Fleet headed home, Italian torpedo-bombers made a reprisal attack, sheering away from the battleships' barrage but successfully penetrating the cruisers' defences and hitting *Liverpool*'s bow. Had the explosion not started a fire, the damage would have been slight, confined to a part of the ship well subdivided for damage-control; but the fire reached a petrol tank and possibly the forward magazine, causing an explosion that blew *Liverpool*'s bows off. The twisted wreckage hung down into the sea, hampering *Orion*'s efforts to tow her by the stern, and after about a hundred miles the drag was such that the tow parted. When they had reconnected and got under way again the whole mass finally tore away and sank, greatly easing *Orion*'s burden.

The main section of the fleet entered the Great Pass at 01.00 on 15 October, harried to the end of its passage by the Regia Aeronautica and firing what the Commander-in-Chief called 'a blind barrage on both sides with our guns flashing and the sparkle of bursting shell all over the horizon'. Cunningham remained impressed with the Regia Aeronautica's persistence,

recalling afterwards that such night attacks 'were nerve-wrack-
ing and dangerous ... thrown in at dusk after our aircraft-carrier
[sic] had flown on all her fighters for the night'. The lack of night-
fighters was to some extent mitigated by the early warning provided by radar and the C-in-C enjoyed the consolation of this
heavy barrage being thrown up by his ships, but he was not
insensible of the advantage the Italians continued to enjoy.

Cunningham was now to be confronted with a rapidly changing
situation in the Eastern Mediterranean. Mussolini and Hitler had
met at the Brenner Pass on 4 October, when a jubilant Führer had
told the Duce that 'the war is won' and 'the rest is just a matter
of time'. Mussolini concealed his own imminent plans; a few
weeks later, however, when they met again in Florence,
Mussolini greeted Hitler in German, announcing 'Führer, we are
on the march!' On the 21st, the day the British had planned to
attack Taranto, Supermarina formed a new command at Brindisi,
Maritrafalba, under Capitano di Vascello Polacchini. Its function
was to protect military convoys passing across the Strait of
Otranto to Valona and Durazzo while building up the Italian
army in Albania.[8]

At 03.00 on 28 October the Italian minister in Athens, Count
Grazzi, woke the Greek prime minister Ioannis Metaxas with an
ultimatum. Mussolini accused Greece of harbouring and suc-
couring British ships and demanded unhindered occupation of
certain strategic locations. Metaxas refused with a famous negative and Mussolini, too impatient to wait for the period of his
ultimatum to expire a mere three hours later, ordered his legions
over the Albanian border into Greece.

Hitler was furious when he learned of the invasion. With his
own plans for the northern Balkans and the Romanian oil fields,
he was fully supportive of an Italian attack on the British in
Egypt. But he could see no logic in stirring up Greece, whose then
government was Fascist in complexion. Moreover, he feared that
an unsuccessful outcome would compromise his own long-
matured plans for the eastwards expansion of the Reich to the
Caspian Sea and the acquisition of the oil fields of Baku and
lebensraum for the *Herrenvolk*.

In the event, Hitler's apprehensions were to be proved
right. The Italian advance across the mountains, hampered by
heavy and freezing rain, was soon suffering at the hands of the

defending Greek army under the command of Alexandros Papagos. With little more than mountain infantry Papagos inflicted a severe defeat on the Italian Julia Division in the Pindus Mountains between 8 and 10 November. Mussolini replaced Generale Visconti Prasca but his troops continued to be driven back into Albania and the Ninth Army, on the northern flank, was trapped in Koritsa. By mid January 1941 a quarter of Albania was in Greek hands, and although Generale Soddu, the new Italian field-commander, mounted another attack on Greece in early March, it too ground to a halt with heavy casualties.

Committed as she was by treaty obligations to preserve Greek independence, Britain gave limited but immediate support to the Greeks. In the coming months this was to alter the whole character of the war in the Mediterranean, requiring as it did an immense commitment of men and ships to military operations, thus further imperilling Malta as priorities competed for attention. As the army Commander-in-Chief, General Wavell, and the Air Officer Commanding-in-Chief, Sir Arthur Longmore, began a reinforcement of the Greeks on their own initiative, Cunningham seized the opportunity to use Suda Bay, on the north coast of Crete, as an advanced base for operations in the Aegean.

He was at sea with the whole Mediterranean fleet at 01.30 on 29 October, and although there were no bombing raids that day, by 1 November 'there were heavy raids on Suda Bay and Canea, the first of many. From now until the end of December', recalled Cunningham, summarising the remainder of 1940 in the Eastern Mediterranean, 'our cruisers and destroyers were hard at it covering and escorting the convoys to the Piraeus and Suda Bay. They had no rest.'

Cunningham had been compelled to postpone the meditated attack on Taranto because of a fire in *Illustrious*'s hangar. Rear-Admiral Lyster had been charged with preparing the battle-plan, using both *Eagle* and *Illustrious*, but two days before the revised departure date *Eagle*'s aircraft fuelling system, much shaken by frequent near-misses, was found to be unserviceable; this meant her dropping out of the order of battle, to the chagrin of her company.

In preparing his attack, which was to be code-named Operation JUDGEMENT, Lyster relied heavily upon aerial photo-reconnaissance of Taranto from Malta. Since September the

British had had in Malta three American-built, twin-engined Glenn Martin Maryland aircraft[9] which relieved the vulnerable Sunderlands of much of this vital work. Initially denominated Flight 431, the Marylands operated out of Luqa; in due course, as their numbers were increased, they became No. 69 Squadron. Among the flight's pilots was 'an irresponsible young officer' named Adrian Warburton.[10] Flight 431 made several sorties over Taranto in early November, but those made on the 10th and 11th were critical. On the 11th, cloud cover was low and total; Warburton and his crew, by now familiar with the naval base, flew low and fast across the Italian anchorage. As the observer plotted the positions of the ships and booms, the gunner tried to identify each vessel. A discrepancy resulted in a repeat flight, which attracted heavy flak as Warburton boldly made his second pass, so low that his Maryland's tail wheel tore off a length of ship's radio aerial. But Warburton returned to Malta with the news Lyster was waiting for in *Illustrious* offshore. The British Mediterranean Fleet was soon at sea again, along with the convoy bound for Malta.

Churchill in London had been locked in debate with the Admiralty. In a note to Anthony Eden, the Secretary of State for War, on the eve of his departure for a fact-finding tour of the Middle East, Churchill wrote: 'Do you realise there is no command of the sea at Malta?' Twelve days later, on 6 October, he was urging the Chiefs of Staff in London to ensure that 'whenever the Fleet is moving from Alexandria to the Central Mediterranean reinforcements should be carried into Malta, which I consider to be in grievous danger at the present time.' Fear of an invasion of the island backed by the Italian fleet preyed on Churchill's mind, and he went on a few days later to raise the reinforcement of Malta to the first priority. More Hurricanes were to be flown there 'as can best be managed', and the next convoy ' should carry the largest anti-aircraft outfit possible …' Troops were also to be sent, 'released from police duty on the Canal or in Palestine', together with 'even three infantry tanks'.

In fact Cunningham already had a further convoy in hand, and on 4 October as part of a complex operation, MB8, convoy MW3 left Alexandria simultaneously with the departure of an Aegean-bound convoy from Port Said, AN6. Escorted by *Calcutta* and

Coventry and the destroyers *Dainty*, *Vampire*, *Voyager* and *Waterhen*, the two convoys steamed towards Crete, and while *Voyager* accompanied AN6 into Suda Bay, the rest headed westwards. The following day the cruisers *Ajax* and *Sydney* left Alexandria for Suda Bay loaded with stores and, having discharged at Suda, sailed again on the 6th to join the Commander-in-Chief the same day. Cunningham, with the might of the Mediterranean Fleet, had sailed to supply cover to MW3 and the strike on Taranto.

With these twin ends in view, Cunningham's force was potent. He now had with him the battleships *Warspite*, *Valiant*, *Malaya* and *Ramillies*, Lyster's flagship *Illustrious*, the 3rd Cruiser Squadron of *Gloucester* and *York*, Pridham-Wippell's 7th Cruiser Squadron of *Orion*, *Ajax* and *Sydney*, and the 14th and 2nd Destroyer Flotillas.[11] In addition the convoy's close escort was composed of anti-aircraft cruisers and destroyers. Convoy MW3 was itself formed by the fleet auxiliary *Plumleaf*, the merchantmen *Volo* and *Rodi*, all making their second passage to Malta, together with Shaw, Savill and Albion's passenger-cargo-liner *Waiwera* of 12,435 grt, and Lamport and Holt's *Devis* (6,054 grt).

While deployed upon this operation Cunningham was expecting to receive the promised reinforcements of *Warspite*'s sistership *Barham*, the two cruisers *Berwick* and *Glasgow*, and three destroyers, *Greyhound*, *Gallant* and *Griffin*. These ships were to be passed through the Mediterranean as Force F, loaded with stores and troops for Malta, and covered from the west by Somerville's Force H in the simultaneously planned Operation COAT. Three of Somerville's destroyers, *Faulknor*, *Fortune* and *Fury*, would accompany Force F as far as Malta, since they each carried fifty of the 2,150 soldiers bound to join the island's garrison.[12]

In accordance with an impressively orchestrated series of movements from the opposite ends of the Middle Sea, Somerville left Gibraltar at 18.00 on the evening of 7 October. He flew his flag in the carrier *Ark Royal* and, in addition to the ships named, had under his command the cruiser *Sheffield* and the destroyers *Foxhound*, *Forester*, *Firedrake*, *Duncan* and *Isis*. *Renown* was to take part, together with *Argus* and the elderly light cruiser *Despatch*, in Operation WHITE, the next Club Run with Hurricanes for Malta.

In fine clear weather at 15.30 on 8 October Somerville increased speed from 18 to 26.5 knots and diverged with *Ark*

Royal, Glasgow, Sheffield and six destroyers to bomb Cagliari aerodrome. On their way the carrier's fighters shot down a lone SM79, and at 04.30 the following morning nine Swordfish took off on their air raid. Three hours later, as well as air and anti-submarine patrols, *Ark Royal* launched three Fulmar fighters for onward flight to join *Illustrious*. These reached Malta at 10.30.

Despite the beautiful weather, the Swordfish attacking Cagliari suffered no loss as they bombed hangars, moored seaplanes, AA-gun batteries and a factory nearby. They all returned safely to land on *Ark Royal*, and by mid morning Somerville had reunited his forces. Soon afterwards the fighters shot down a Cant, but the enemy air force was already approaching, located at a range of fifty miles by radar, and Fulmars and Skuas were flown off to intercept. The Italians pressed home high-level attacks from 13,000 feet, dropping a single carpet of bombs on Somerville's ships steaming in two open, staggered columns a mile apart. There were no hits, although they were shaken by near-misses; but Somerville was critical of his fleet's anti-aircraft fire which, the airborne British fighters reported, burst 2,000 feet below their targets, enabling the Italian aircraft to maintain their formation. Neither the two sections of Skuas nor the single section of Fulmars claimed a direct success. Several SM79s were hit and one was thought to have crashed as it tried to fly away, but it was a drawn action rather than a spectacular success for the British, a fact Somerville was acutely aware of. The failure to break up the Savoia Marchettis' formations was largely a result of the inadequate speed advantage of the Skuas and the inexperience of their pilots. Somerville turned back to Gibraltar just after dark, at 19.15 that evening, using the otherwise uneventful passage to train and exercise his continually changing command.[13]

During the launch of the air strike against Cagliari the holding of a steady course head to wind, while the Swordfish took off, had agitated Somerville. The lack of freedom to manoeuvre during this commitment was compounded by the biplanes' propensity 'to give out beastly sparks and flashes' as they started up. These, Somerville agonised, would be visible to an observant enemy. Fortunately the Italian submarine patrol line maintained off the south-west corner of Sardinia, consisting of *Alagi, Axum, Aradam, Diaspro* and *Medusa*, failed to sight the British squadron in the darkness, igniting Swordfish notwithstanding.

As Somerville turned to head west again, his three destroyers and Cunningham's reinforcements, all under the command of Captain G.L. Warren in *Berwick*, continued east, passing into the Sicilian Channel and running through The Narrows during the night of 9/10 November. They were not alone; also in the channel was the Italian 14th Destroyer Squadron. The forces passed each other, unknowingly and undetected, in the darkness.[14]

By the morning of the 10th Cunningham was off the south-east coast of Malta, in the vicinity of a patrol of Italian submarines. The previous evening *Ramillies* and the destroyers had been sent in to Malta to refuel, and the battleship had been missed by a torpedo from the *Capponi*, Capitano di Fregata Romei.[15] The merchant ships also entered Grand Harbour unscathed. By noon the Mediterranean Fleet had received its reinforcements from the westwards, which had followed MW3 into port to discharge their troops and cargoes, sailing later with the refuelled warships. In due course *Faulknor*, *Fortune* and *Fury* headed back to Gibraltar while the remainder, with the exception of *Coventry*, *Dainty*, *Vampire* and *Waterhen*, rejoined the C-in-C. The *Coventry* and her destroyers now formed escort to the eastbound convoy ME3, made up of the discharged ships of MF3, *Memnon*, *Lanarkshire*, *Clan Ferguson* and *Clan Macaulay*. Also re-emerging were the damaged destroyer *Vendetta* (which had been repaired in the dockyard), and the monitor *Terror*, which had augmented the air defences of the city since the outbreak of war and was now bound for Suda Bay. Finally, *Illustrious* received her additional three Fulmars from *Ark Royal*.

As convoy ME3 steamed east, Cunningham's fleet at first followed suit, *Illustrious*'s Fulmars vigorously attacking the shadowing aircraft of the Aeronautica; but at about 13.10 on the afternoon of the 11th Pridham-Wippell diverged with *Orion*, *Ajax* and *Sydney*, together with *Mohawk* and *Nubian*, bound on a raid on the Italian trans-Adriatic military route. With this diversion to the Straits of Otranto, Cunningham's plan to raid Taranto and remove from the Regia Marina any sense of comfort at being in a home port now began to unfold, as Operation JUDGEMENT got under way.

It was particularly important that *Illustrious* should reach the flying-off position 170 miles south-east of Taranto unobserved. Her Fulmars therefore had to annihilate the Italian shadowing operation, which was accomplished that afternoon. The daylight

detachment of Pridham-Wippell served to divert enemy attention, while at the same time masking any fleet movements being
made to the north. One of *Illustrious*'s planes flew to Malta to pick
up the report of Warburton's reconnaissance flight over Taranto,
which revealed five battleships to be in the port. A subsequent
Maryland flight, in better weather than Warburton's, revealed
that a sixth had entered the anchorage. 'The pheasants',
Cunningham wrote later, 'had gone home to roost.'

At 18.00, as darkness fell, the Commander-in-Chief initiated
the central part of Operation JUDGEMENT, ordering Rear-
Admiral Lyster to detach in his carrier and proceed to the flying-
off position. Supported and screened by *Gloucester*, *Berwick*,
Glasgow and *York*, and the destroyers *Hasty, Havock, Hyperion* and
Ilex, *Illustrious* turned away. Cunningham sent Lyster and his
'lads' a good-luck signal, then settled down to spend the night
'on tenterhooks'.

Taranto consists of a wide bay lying between Cape Rondinella in
the north-west and Cape San Vito to the south-east, some four
miles away. The bight of the bay, open to the south-west, is
broken by the island of San Pietro, which was connected to Cape
Rondinella by a submerged breakwater. A similar breakwater
linked San Pietro to the islet of San Paolo. Between San Paolo and
Cape San Vito, a distance of about 1.8 miles, a further submerged
breakwater obstructed about half that distance, extending seawards from the cape. The intervening gap formed the entrance.
This huge enclosed anchorage constituted the Mar' Grande,
which was subdivided by an extensive boom of steel nets as protection against submarine attack. Behind these nets, at the head
of the bight from north to south, lay the battleships *Caio Diulio*
and *Giulio Cesare*, to seaward of which were anchored the *Littorio*,
then *Vittorio Veneto*, *Andrea Doria* and *Conte di Cavour*. The cruisers *Fiume*, *Zara* and *Gorizia* were penned to the north-west, and
destroyers were anchored among both the cruisers and the
capital ships. A floating dock was moored close to the oiling pier.
The booms behind which the ships lay at anchor were strung
with balloon barrages, and the entire place was heavily fortified
with anti-aircraft batteries.

At the head of the bay lay a small mercantile port, adjacent to
which a narrow neck of land was pierced by a cut leading into
the inner anchorage of the Mar' Piccolo. Upon the shores of the

Mar' Piccolo lay the town of Taranto. Between Taranto and Cape
San Vito lay an oil storage depot, protected by a heavy barrage of
balloons. In the Mar' Piccolo lay some destroyers and the cruisers *Bolzano* and *Trento*, along with a seaplane base.

The notion of a carrier-borne attack on Taranto was not new. It
had been mooted during the Abyssinian crisis five years earlier
and Lyster himself had raised it again when in command of the
Glorious, serving with the Mediterranean Fleet under the then
C-in-C, Dudley Pound. Pound, a traditional gunnery man, had
pooh-poohed the idea, but at his first meeting with Cunningham
Lyster revived it, only to find that Cunningham had already
mentioned it to the First Sea Lord. Again Pound poured cold
water on the project, but he could not veto it. Cunningham and
Lyster were of one mind, and Lyster was charged with the task.

Now, on the evening of 11 November, as the gibbous moon
rose and *Illustrious*, Captain D.W. Boyd, reached the flying-off
position, the Swordfish ranged upon the carrier's long grey deck
rattled into life, emitting their 'beastly sparks and flashes'. At
20.40 a dozen of the ageing biplanes, led by Lieutenant-
Commander K. Williamson, commanding officer of No. 815
Squadron, and composed of elements from Nos 813, 815 and 824
Squadrons, droned down the deck and lifted cumbrously into
the air. By 21.00 they were all airborne, formed up, and heading
for Taranto. Meanwhile the second wave of only nine machines
under Lieutenant-Commander J.W. Hale, in command of No.
819 Squadron, began to follow. All were airborne by 21.30, except
for one which tore her wing fabric in taxiing and was struck
down to the hangar deck for emergency repairs. Captain Boyd,
inclined to cancel this last, was persuaded otherwise by her eager
and supplicating observer, Lieutenant Going; shortly afterwards
he watched Going scramble in behind the pilot, Lieutenant E.W.
Clifford, and the slow and ungainly biplane lifted off half an
hour late.

Once aloft, the cold struck the aircrews in their primitive open
cockpits, numbing them and rendering the performance of
simple tasks difficult. Each Swordfish bore a tank containing 60
gallons of extra fuel. Williamson's dozen aircraft carried a mixed
armament: six had 18-inch torpedoes slung under their bellies,
four carried bombs, and two were additionally tasked to drop
flares. One of the torpedo-bombers made good speed and
arrived ahead of the majority, alerting the anti-aircraft defences;

as the remainder of Williamson's flight followed twenty minutes later, they were met by an intense barrage of flak. It had been intended that the bombers should lead, diving on targets in and along the shore of the Mar' Piccolo with its cruisers, and the dockyard at Taranto. A line of twelve flares was to be dropped along the shore of the Mar' Grande behind the barrage between Cape San Vito and Taranto, thus providing a vivid backdrop against which the capital ships would stand out to the torpedo-bombers flying in from the north-west a few moments later. The flare-dropper was also to bomb the oil depot.

In addition to the early arrival, Williamson had lost contact with three other Swordfish in the cloud. Thus reduced in strength, he led the depleted torpedo section in to the attack as the flares appeared at about 23.00. The slow speed of the Swordfish attracted a devastating fire from the ships and the flak batteries. Dropping to thirty feet, Williamson's planes achieved three successful hits, one on the bow of *Conte di Cavour* and two on *Littorio*, one forward and one aft. The other torpedoes, all loosed at short range, either missed their targets, exploded prematurely, or failed to detonate. Williamson and his observer were taken prisoner after their Swordfish crashed, but the remainder of the first wave returned safely to *Illustrious*.

Hale's planes, reduced by one which had lost its extra fuel tank, approached the now fully alert target area, bound for 'a solid curtain of bursting shell ... [which] ... looked absolutely terrifying' to one observer.[16] Again, both bombers and flare-droppers illuminated the outer anchorage as Hale's four torpedo-armed Swordfish dropped almost to sea level and droned in over the Mar' Grande to press home their attack. Two more torpedoes hit *Littorio*, though one failed to detonate, while *Caio Duilio* was struck on her starboard side; one torpedo, destined for *Vittorio Veneto*, ran wide. Hale's flight lost one aircraft, shot down by fire from *Gorizia* with the loss of her crew. Finally, as Hale's planes broke away, 'jinking' (with limited effect) to avoid the flak, Clifford's solitary, late Swordfish dove on the Mar' Piccolo before flying after its leader, finally landing on *Illustrious* in Hale's wake at 03.30, the last to return.

Illustrious and her escort turned away to rejoin Cunningham at dawn. The jubilant aircrews begged for a repeat the following night, to which Cunningham at first agreed; but, on reflection, he was glad when poor weather prevented it. Pridham-Wippell also rejoined the C-in-C, having attacked a convoy off Valona, sunk one merchantman, set two on fire, and left a fourth in a sinking condition.[17] The escorting auxiliary cruiser *Ramb III* and the elderly torpedo-boat *Fabrizi* appear to have steamed away, after one was hit by a shell. The British raiders also struck shore targets at Durazzo, where they left the Agijo refinery aflame.[18]

The Regia Aeronautica pursued the British as they set course for Alexandria, but three Cant flying-boats were shot down by *Illustrious*'s fighters, no bombing attack matured, and the fleet returned to Alexandria in high spirits. The destruction wrought by a score of obsolescent Swordfish exceeded anything the might of the Grand Fleet had achieved at Jutland a quarter-century earlier, confounding the big-gun theorists. Taranto established the aircraft-carrier as the primary capital ship of the future and, moreover, became a template for the Japanese attack on Pearl Harbor thirteen months later.[19] The *Conte di Cavour* lay beached in the shallows, her decks awash. She was afterwards refloated, but the torpedo which had exploded under her keel had so damaged her that she never went to sea again. The *Littorio* was thought to have been sunk, but was only partially filled with water, and spent four months in dock; the *Caio Duilio* was rendered *hors de combat* for six months. The cruiser *Trento* and destroyer *Libeccio* had both been penetrated by bombs, but these failed to explode. When it was all over, the remaining serviceable ships made for the comfort of Naples, La Spezia and Genoa.

The effect upon Italian morale was considerable. Ciano complained of the attack having been made without warning and called 12 November 'a black day', but recorded that Mussolini, in the grip of his disease, 'took the blow quite well', adding that he did not 'at the moment, seem to have fully realised its gravity'.

Oddly enough, Cunningham too appears not to have fully appreciated quite what the very young men of the Fleet Air Arm had achieved, despite his recognition of the economy of force used. This is the only possible explanation of the otherwise grudging honours which followed what was a fine achievement. Williamson and Hale were expected to receive the Victoria Cross, but in the event only two Distinguished Service Orders and four Distinguished Service Crosses were awarded, with Rear-Admiral Lyster and Captains Boyd and Bridge picking up decorations. No one in the essential maintenance teams received a thing. Six months later a few more DSOs and DSCs were given out, but the gilt was by then long off the gingerbread, for on the night following the attack the BBC's nine o'clock news, announcing a victory at Taranto, had attributed the success to the Royal Air Force.

The practical effect of the damage inflicted on the Regia Marina by knocking out capital ships was to enable the number of British battleships in the Mediterranean to be reduced. *Malaya* and *Ramillies* were in due course sent home, and this had the knock-on effect of releasing destroyers from the battle-fleet's screen for escort duties. Meanwhile, congratulations 'streamed in', not least from King George VI, who had served at Jutland; and from Sir Arthur Longmore, whose flying career had begun in the Royal Naval Air Service and who had dropped the first aerial torpedo in July 1914. Cunningham also received the good wishes of the unfortunate Godfroy, still cooped up in his flagship. As was customary at such times, somewhat facetious and scatological signals were passed between Somerville and Cunningham. From the First Sea Lord, who had not favoured the attack, came the news that Taranto had bucked up a War Cabinet 'rather down in the dumps'.

Notwithstanding these plaudits, Italian air raids on Alexandria continued, hitting the destroyer *Decoy* on 13 November, dropping delayed-action bombs which endangered the only floating dock capable of taking large men-of-war, and damaging a destroyer in the act of undocking. Air defence with the fleet in harbour 'was imposing enough', but without the presence of the warships it was poor. Moreover, Cunningham wanted the burden taken off the shoulders of his weary men, particularly the exhausted crews of his overworked destroyers, for the emphasis was now on building up forces in Greece and Crete, and they were very busy little ships.

As Cunningham's fleet picked up its moorings at Alexandria, Somerville's Force H was preparing to slip its own at Gibraltar and proceed on the second Club Run, known officially as Operation WHITE. The air defence of Malta remained a constant problem as the Regia Aeronautica continued to enjoy the advantage of access to their target despite the gradual build-up of resources on the island to contest the airspace overhead. Reinforcement of the island's air assets therefore continued.

Argus had again arrived at Gibraltar, with a dozen Hurricanes and two Skuas. She anchored under the shadow of The Rock late on 14 November and fuelled, unloading her mails into the oiler to avoid direct contact with the shore and thus preserve a degree of security – 'always', Somerville reported, 'a difficult matter at Gibraltar', with the Spanish port of Algeciras close by. *Argus* was ready to sail again within hours. Somerville had returned to *Renown*, which had in the interim been operating in the Atlantic, and Force H sailed in bright moonlight before dawn the following morning. In addition to *Ark Royal*, whose aircraft provided anti-submarine patrols, Somerville also had with him the cruisers *Despatch* and *Sheffield* and the destroyers *Faulknor*, *Fury*, *Fortune*, *Forester*, *Firedrake*, *Foxhound*, *Duncan* and *Wishart*. The westerly wind, blowing from astern, compelled a reversal of course to fly off and land *Ark Royal*'s aircraft, but by noon on the 16th the weather had deteriorated and Somerville was obliged to cancel flying, maintaining a few fighters ranged in readiness upon *Ark Royal*'s deck; he also had to abort a planned air raid on the aerodrome at Alghero in north-west Sardinia. He now received intelligence that an Italian naval force was concentrating south of Naples, probably meditating an attack on Force H. With the continuing strong westerly breeze and reports in the Malta area of south-westerly winds, he decided to send off the Hurricanes as soon as possible.

As *Argus*, *Despatch* and three destroyers diverged to fly off the fighters, the squadron took station on *Renown* while *Ark Royal* prepared fighter cover, anti-submarine patrols and a long-distance reconnaissance flight to the eastwards. The first sub-flight of Hurricanes was airborne at 06.15 and levelled off at 2,000 feet; the second followed an hour later. Both were accompanied by Fleet Air Arm Skuas acting as navigation guides. They had almost exactly 420 miles to fly and the first wave was to be met off Galita Island by a Sunderland from Malta, the second by a Maryland. As soon as he had dispatched the sub-flights, Somerville executed a full turn and set off for Gibraltar, where he arrived on the 19th, to bad news.

The leading pilot of the first wave of Hurricanes flown off *Argus* was Flying Officer J.A.F. Maclachlan, a decorated veteran of the Battle of Britain. He flew with his eye on his assigned Skua, whose navigator soon realised that an unforecast and unforeseen change of wind was occurring. Soon the Hurricanes were

battling a headwind which brought cloud drifting off the
Tunisian coast. Nevertheless, the rendezvous was made with the
Sunderland, the Skua detached, and the Hurricanes pressed on,
each solitary fighter pilot now subject to a creeping realisation
that he would be lucky to make his goal. The first Hurricane ran
out of fuel 45 miles short of Malta, and Maclachlan followed it in
a dive until it ditched. His action drew the Sunderland down to
land on the sea and rescue the floating pilot, but as they rejoined
the rest of the sub-flight Maclachlan realised that in their absence
a further fighter had fallen out of the sky.

Cloud now completely obscured their destination, but by
radio bearings of Luqa the sub-flight homed in directly, and
landed without ceremony. So fine were the margins that the
engine of one Hurricane cut out before the machine reached the
end of the runway, while the remaining three were reduced to
their last few gallons of fuel.

The second sub-flight never met the Maryland. The Skua navigator was out in his reckoning, in ever-thickening weather and
the strengthening headwind. His pilot cast about desperately for
a landmark as the Hurricanes fell away one by one, their fuel
exhausted. When at last land was sighted, the Skua was met by
flak and shot down. Seventy-five miles off course, the plane
crashed on the coast of Sicily. The subsequent enquiry largely
blamed the pilots' unfamiliarity with the tropicalised Mark II
Hurricane (which was fitted with constant-speed propellers
rather than the variable pitch air screw of the earlier mark) and
the bad navigation of the Skua, but these findings were a bureau-
cratically competent fudge. In fact the range of the Hurricane,
reckoned to be 510 miles, was calculated for an altitude of 10,000
feet, while the two sub-flights were under orders to fly at 2,000
feet: they were flying in far denser air, and in a contrary wind, for
which no allowance had been made. Somerville privately
anguished over his own culpability. Operation WHITE had been,
as he confessed to his wife in a letter written a few days later, 'a
frightful failure'. The causes emerged slowly, but Somerville was
furious that the Skua navigator should have been a volunteer
reserve officer on his first operational flight. 'That', he raged, was
'a positive scandal.'

A subsidiary element of the operation was the fast solo
passage of the cruiser *Newcastle*, which had left Gibraltar on 17
November with some two hundred RAF ground crew, a few

relief pilots, and spare parts for the Hurricanes. She arrived safely on the 19th and after discharging passed on to Alexandria. Here she was caught up in yet another complex operation, involving the transit of ships the length of the Mediterranean and the forces of both Cunningham and Somerville, whose ships had less and less rest. Somerville's Atlantic responsibilities, where heavy German ships had been at sea, were as demanding as the increasing burden on Cunningham, committed as the C-in-C was to the build-up of British forces in Greece. Somerville had, moreover, the complication of acting against the Vichy French, who in retaliation for the raid on Dakar had already bombed Gibraltar.[20] Like Cunningham he also worried about the over-worked state of his destroyers. Both admirals, however, were now involved with the integration of Operation COLLAR and the associated Operation MB9.

7

'The usual crowded programme'

(Operations COLLAR *and MB9, Convoys MW4 and ME4; Operation MC2, Convoys MW5(A) and (B), and ME5(A); Operation* HIDE *and Convoy MG1; Operation* SEEK*)*

THE COMPLEXITY AND integration of the joint operations carried out in the Mediterranean by its two door-keepers bespeak fine staff-work, excellent communications, and the benefits of discipline within the combined sea-services which undertook them. Such admirable arrangements generally underlay British naval achievements world-wide, but the nature of war in the Mediterranean was to turn crucially upon the close conformity of the various ships' movements to the intentions of the door-keepers' staff. The desired smoothness of such operations was easily confounded by the intervention of the enemy, the weather, or mechanical failure. Human misjudgements, made under the fierce imperatives of war, were equally liable to fail the ideal, as demonstrated by the disastrous shambles of Operation WHITE.

The purpose of Operation COLLAR, sartorially coded at the suggestion of Cunningham, was to enable the slow battleship *Ramillies*, the high-sided and capacious heavy cruiser *Berwick*, which was suffering from problems with her turbine propulsion, and the light cruiser *Newcastle*, which was experiencing boiler defects, to make their way west. Four laden merchantmen were at Alexandria awaiting convoy to Malta and would be escorted there, recovering the patched-up Federal steamship *Cornwall* and the empty ships from convoy MW3. In addition, the fleet's carriers would be used simultaneously to strike at enemy airfields in the Dodecanese and Tripoli. At the other extremity of the Mediterranean, three more merchant ships, two loaded for Malta and one for Alexandria, were on their way from the United Kingdom to Gibraltar, where Cunningham's long-awaited corvettes and destroyers and two light cruisers, *Manchester* and *Southampton*, were assembling.

While preparations were finalised for the operation, Cunningham's fleet was busy. The escorting of supply convoys for Greece and Crete continued unabated, and convoys moved between Port Said and Haifa, Cyprus and the Piraeus, with others, bearing oil, from Haifa to Greek ports; meanwhile the large cruisers, including *Berwick*, ferried troops to the Aegean; and all this continued under persistent bombing by the Italians, particularly of Alexandria. Operation MB9, the eastern component, kicked off with the departure of convoy MW4, consisting of *Memnon*, *Clan Macaulay* and *Clan Ferguson*, plus HMS *Breconshire*. The latter was one of the *Glenearn*-class of very fine, fast cargo-liners recently completed for Alfred Holt's Glen and Shire Lines. Propelled by twin diesel-powered screws, they were capable of speeds in excess of 18 knots, and several had been taken up as naval auxiliaries, manned by naval crews in which many of Holt's own men, particularly the ships' engineers, served as reservists. Close escort was provided by the British destroyers *Hyperion*, *Hero*, *Hasty*, *Havock* and *Ilex*, and the Australians *Vampire*, *Voyager* and *Vendetta*. Heavy cover was provided by Force E, the 3rd Cruiser Squadron of *Glasgow*, *Gloucester* and *York*.

Force D, of *Ramillies*, *Berwick* and *Newcastle*, left Alexandria next day, 24 November 1940, followed on the 25th by Force C, the battleships *Barham* and *Malaya*, the carrier *Eagle*, the cruisers *Calcutta* and *Coventry*, and several destroyers.[1] On the 26th, as *Eagle*'s aircraft carried out the planned raid on Tripoli, the destroyers of Force C, led by *Coventry*, continued on to the westwards. Meanwhile, on the 25th, Cunningham's Force A had sailed north in *Warspite* with *Valiant* and the carrier *Illustrious*, screened by more destroyers. Also in company were Force E, the 7th Cruiser Squadron of *Ajax*, *Orion* and HMAS *Sydney*, and a convoy to Suda Bay.

As MW4 arrived unmolested at Malta, ME4 had already departed eastwards. The empty merchantmen consisted of the temporarily repaired *Cornwall* and the *Waiwera*, *Devis*, *Volo* and

Rodi, which had assembled in Grand Harbour and Marsaxlokk. The close escort was provided by *Calcutta* and the Australian destroyers *Vendetta*, *Voyager* and *Vampire*, and the convoy formed up in the swept channel leading south from Marsaxlokk at 17.45 on 26 November. At 16.00 on the 29th, *Vendetta* and *Voyager* parted company with the cruiser and *Vampire*, who took *Waiwera* and *Devis* into Alexandria, continuing with *Cornwall*, *Volo* and *Rodi* to Port Said, where they arrived twenty-four hours later.[2]

Now steaming west from a raid on Rhodes, Cunningham's Force A anticipated the arrival of the warships and merchantmen sent on by Somerville. From Cunningham's point of view all had gone smoothly, and as he waited off Malta on 27 November he heard intercepted radio traffic indicating that Somerville was in contact with the enemy. Cunningham and his staff listened 'with envy', but Somerville's situation was in fact far from enviable.

The intention of Operation COLLAR was to transport 1,400 soldiers and airmen through the Mediterranean to Alexandria in the cruisers *Manchester* and *Southampton*, to strike Alghero airfield, to pass two merchantmen into Valletta and one to Suda Bay, and to forward Cunningham's replacement cruisers, reinforcing destroyers and corvettes. In his usual way Somerville assessed the opposition he was likely to meet, concluding that, after Taranto, 'it appeared to me the obvious strategy for the Italians to adopt was to reinforce the Western basin where they could achieve a considerable superiority over Forces B and F'.

For the purposes of the joint COLLAR/MB9 operation, Force B was to consist of Somerville's covering ships of Force H, while Force F was intended to be composed of *Manchester* and *Southampton*, the destroyers *Hotspur* and *Vidette*, which latter would arrive with the merchantmen, and the corvettes *Gloxinia*, *Hyacinth*, *Peony* and *Salvia*. Also to be included were the two new 7,530-grt Clan liners *Clan Forbes* and *Clan Fraser*, both loaded for Malta, and Vestey's Blue Star liner *New Zealand Star*, of 10,740 grt, all of which were capable of maintaining service speeds of 15 knots and were already on their way towards Gibraltar under the escort of the destroyers *Velox*, *Vidette* and *Wrestler*.

Force F was to be placed under Vice-Admiral L.E. Holland, commanding the 18th Cruiser Squadron and flying his flag in

Manchester.[3] Holland, arriving on the evening of 21 November, had objected to his cruisers being tied to the slow merchantmen and corvettes, partly because, 'with so many men on board, the ships were not in a fit condition to fight', and also because 'extreme importance was attached to the safe and timely arrival of the RAF personnel at Alexandria'. Somerville, balancing the pros and cons attaching to the whole operation, rather than to a single cruiser squadron, thought that Force F should constitute an impressive show, 'since this was more likely than anything else to deter the Italians ...'

Holland, however, wanted Admiralty clarification; and Somerville, his equal in rank, was obliged to query which should be given priority, convoy or RAF personnel. The Admiralty signalled back 'Personnel', but later informed both vice-admirals that the action taken by Holland's cruisers 'must be the same as if personnel were not on board'. Initially Holland would sail in company with Somerville, detaching later to join Force F.[4]

Force B, with Somerville's flag in *Renown*, was made up of *Ark Royal*, the cruisers *Despatch* and *Sheffield*, and the destroyers *Faulknor*, *Firedrake*, *Forester*, *Fury*, *Duncan*, *Encounter*, *Wishart*, *Kelvin* and *Jaguar*, the last two named having just arrived from Britain specifically for the task in hand. Despite her antiquity Somerville wished to include the additional battleship *Royal Sovereign*, in anticipation of the strong probability of an encounter with Italian battleships whose post-Taranto location was in doubt, but two of which were thought to be at La Spezia. Cunningham 'considered [Somerville's] appreciation unduly pessimistic' and thought that *Royal Sovereign*'s inclusion was unnecessary, since three Mediterranean fleet battleships would be within range, but Somerville 'interpreted this as moral rather than material support'. Like *Ramillies*, *Royal Sovereign* was required for duty in the Atlantic, but the Admiralty approved her use if essential; her boilers, however, were in such poor condition as to render her unfit.

Captain G.F. Stevens-Guille, commanding the 13th Destroyer Flotilla in *Duncan*, left Gibraltar with *Hotspur* and the four corvettes at midnight on 24 November, making a rendezvous with the three merchantmen early on the morning of the 25th. These, with *Velox*, *Wrestler* and *Vidette*, had passed Gibraltar, and Stevens-Guille's ships released *Velox* and *Wrestler*.

At about 04.00, the cruisers *Manchester* and *Southampton* began to embark the army and RAF personnel, 660 and 760 men respectively, from the Cunard liner *Franconia*, completing this just before dawn on 25 November. Then, at 07.00, they slipped their moorings with the remaining destroyers of Force F and sailed together with Somerville's main squadron, Force B.

Somerville's and Holland's combined forces sailed east, and at dawn on 26 November the usual anti-submarine patrols lifted off *Ark Royal*'s flight deck, along with reconnaissance aircraft which soon afterwards located the convoy ahead. *Despatch* was sent to join Stevens-Guille as his charges closed the Vichy coast of North Africa. In the mid afternoon Somerville's whole fleet inclined their course southwards, the better to protect the passage of the merchant ships, and two hours later Holland in *Manchester*, with *Wishart*, *Encounter* and *Fury*, transferred to join the convoy and provide heavy cover. By darkness Force B had overtaken the convoy and was stationed some twenty-five miles ahead and to port of it; speed was reduced to 15.5 knots to maintain this station.

Although Somerville did not think he had been seen by Italian reconnaissance, Supermarina knew of his departure from Gibraltar, while Force D, *Ramillies*, *Newcastle* and *Berwick*, hastening westwards, had been seen south of Malta by an Italian civil aircraft. Italian submarines off Sardinia and Malta were alerted.[5] Unknown to Somerville, that same day, 26 November, the Regia Marina were putting to sea once again in some force, fully justifying his caution. Campioni had left Naples with the battleships *Vittorio Veneto* and *Giulio Cesare*, screened by two destroyer flotillas.[6] With Campioni was Iachino leading the 1st Cruiser Division in the *Pola*, with *Fiume*, flying the flag of Matteucci, and *Gorizia*. The cruisers were also screened by destroyers.[7]

The 3rd Cruiser Division and 12th Destroyer Flotilla, under Ammiraglio di Divisione Sansonetti, sailed the same day from Messina in support of Campioni and Iachino.[8] Later the 10th Torpedo Boat Flotilla sortied from Trapani on the eastern extremity of Sicily. In the quiet darkness of the night of 26/27 November the *Alcione*, *Vega*, *Sagittario* and *Sirio* entered the Sicilian Narrows, intending to attack the westbound ships of Force D. The torpedo-boats spotted the British ships and *Sirio* loosed torpedoes, but the attack does not appear to have been pressed home with much energy and the British ships remained unaware of the presence of the enemy, let alone of the passing torpedoes.

During the early forenoon of the 27th, when Somerville was approximately a hundred and twenty miles south-west of the Sardinian Cape Spartivento, *Ark Royal* sent up her reconnoitring aircraft and anti-submarine patrols. Somerville reversed his fleet's course to regain contact with the convoy, only to discover that the corvettes had been unable to keep up and had fallen astern. *Southampton* and the destroyer *Firedrake* now joined Force F as Somerville put about again, some fifteen miles ahead of Holland and the convoy. Then, at 10.05, *Ark Royal*'s signalling projector flashed into life, passing on a report from one of her questing aircraft that five cruisers and five destroyers had been spotted 45 miles to the north-east. Because of a defect in her radio equipment *Renown* had been unable to monitor the air reconnaissance reports, but *Ark Royal*'s tactical plot had been building up an alarming picture for over half an hour. Ordering all his ships to have steam ready for full speed, Somerville requested clarification, thinking the sighting might have been Force D and the covering *Coventry* and her destroyers approaching from the eastwards.[9]

A few moments later a second report of two battleships and seven destroyers heading south-west came in. Somerville immediately ordered *Despatch*, *Duncan* and *Hotspur* to make the convoy's best speed south-east. *Kelvin* and *Jaguar* were assigned to screen *Ark Royal*, and the carrier was ordered to act independently and prepare a strike force. Somerville then ordered all ships under his command to increase speed and work ahead to rendezvous with Force D. These ships now included Holland's two cruisers and destroyers, which were recalled from covering the convoy once *Despatch*, *Duncan* and *Hotspur* were on their way. As soon as contact had been achieved, the vice-admiral ordered the anti-aircraft cruiser *Coventry* to detach from Force D and further augment the defences of the convoy. Force D and Holland's ships now steamed to join Somerville.

A further reconnaissance report which now came in via *Ark Royal*, of six cruisers and eight destroyers, confused the *Renown*'s plot until a Malta-based Sunderland lumbered out of the sky to confirm the position of Force D as being east-north-east of *Renown*, distant 34 miles. Somerville had already ordered *Ark Royal* to fly off her strike force and attack the ships detected to the north-eastwards, and he now instructed the Sunderland 'to shadow and report the composition of the enemy'.

Renown and her consorts reduced speed from 28 to 24 knots and Somerville threw his destroyer screen out to the north and east. He awaited the arrival of Force D, receiving more reports from the carrier that a group of warships consisting of a battleship, one cruiser and six destroyers was steering east-north-east, while a second of two battleships, three cruisers and four destroyers was heading north-north-east. They were about forty-five miles away and their slow speed, some 14 or 15 knots, suggested to Somerville and his staff that they were not running away, but awaiting their own aerial reconnaissance reports.

By 11.30 the masts of Force D were seen breaking the distant horizon and Somerville ordered all ships to increase to 28 knots, instructing *Ramillies* to alter to a course of north-east 'in order that she should not lose ground in the chase that appeared likely to develop'. A few minutes later Somerville signalled Holland to take all the cruisers under his orders (except *Despatch* and *Coventry*, which remained with the convoy), and *Ramillies* to close his flag by converging, in order that she should not be prematurely exposed to superior enemy gunfire.

It was at this point that Cunningham, waiting off Malta, found himself envying Somerville and the action he anticipated. Somerville, however, achieved his dispositions for battle only to be informed that *Duncan*'s boilers had lost water and the destroyer lay stopped (she was later taken under tow). With the loss of the corvettes the convoy escort now had no anti-submarine defence, since no other escorting ship had sonar. Fortunately the ageing *Wishart* was so fitted, and as she was having trouble keeping up the punishing 28 knots the vice-admiral had again ordered, and was also short of fuel, Somerville now transferred her back to cover the convoy.

A few minutes after noon smoke was seen on the northern horizon, and Somerville's fleet altered course towards it. Then, at 12.08, the masts of Matteucci's three cruisers were identified from *Berwick*. At the same time, *Renown*'s engineer commander reported that one of the battlecruiser's shafts was overheating and speed had to drop to 27 knots. Aerial sightings had now confirmed that beyond Matteucci lay two battleships, Campioni's 15-inch-gun *Vittorio Veneto*, and *Giulio Cesare* with her 12.6-inch guns.

Somerville now had, on his own admission, 'to show a bold front and attack the enemy as soon as possible'. But his situation was far from ideal. *Renown*, although bearing six heavy guns of 15-inch calibre, was nevertheless a battlecruiser, and lightly armoured. Despite her overheating shaft she was already dropping the slower *Ramillies* astern, while her supporting cruisers *Berwick* and *Newcastle* both reported flaws, and Holland's *Manchester* and *Southampton* were overcrowded. The light cruiser *Sheffield* was unhampered by defects and in good trim, but scarcely a match for the mounting opposition of the Regia Marina ahead. In *Ark Royal* Somerville possessed his most useful asset, but she had recently received drafts of new aircrew, few of whom were adequately trained in the tactics of attacking with torpedoes. It was clear that Campioni enjoyed a great advantage with his two battleships and Matteucci's heavy cruisers, particularly if he could summon up the air support he should have been able to rely upon. A decisive action might well result in an Italian victory.

Campioni, who had passed south of Sardinia during the previous night, knew from the 10th Torpedo Boat Flotilla of Force D's passage of the Sicilian Narrows. At 10.15 the *Bolzano*'s seaplane sighted *Renown* and reported one 'battleship', two cruisers and four destroyers to be some hundred and thirty miles to the south and west of Cape Teulada, confirmed by *Gorizia*'s seaplane at 11.44. Unaware of the combination of Force B and D or the presence of *Ark Royal*, the departure of which from Gibraltar was nevertheless known by Supermarina, Campioni was sanguine of victory: 'I had in mind the English forces were inferior to the Italian', he afterwards wrote.[10] But just before noon, moments before the two fleets came in sight of each other, Campioni learned the true composition of the British force from a shore-based aircraft of the Regia Aeronautica. As he digested this intelligence with his staff, at 12.21 Matteucci's 8-inch guns opened fire, to be answered by those of *Renown* a minute later, firing at a range of 27,000 yards. Unaware as he was of the slowness of *Ramillies*, the overcrowding of Holland's ships or the mechanical defects of the other cruisers, Campioni now declined action. The 'state of affairs was ... unfavourable to us numerically and qualitatively', he reported. He was not quite right – two 8-inch shells had disabled Y-turret of *Berwick*, killed seven and wounded nine men – but 'in conformity with the spirit and letter of the orders received and with what at the moment I deemed to be my duty, I decided not to become involved in a battle.' 'Almost immediately after opening fire', Somerville wrote afterwards, 'the enemy cruisers and destroyers commenced to emit dense smoke and retired behind it.' A few shots were fired from the Italian battleships, persuading Holland's now pursuing cruisers to sheer briefly out of the line of fire, but by 13.10 Somerville's bold front had won him the day. He asked Holland if he thought they would catch the enemy but Holland flashed back in the negative, afterwards informing Somerville that Campioni enjoyed a speed advantage of 3 knots. Nor could *Ark Royal*'s strike force rob the retreating Italians of their speed. Somerville rightly 'presumed the [air] attack had been unsuccessful, which was not unexpected'.

With his ships extended and rapidly approaching the Sardinian coast and the airfield of Elmas at Cagliari just thirty miles away, a second torpedo strike was not likely to succeed and would probably be destroyed by enemy fighters. Somerville therefore had no option but to fall back and concentrate on his prime duty of covering the now distant convoy as it headed for the Sicilian Narrows. Holland was sent off at 13.45 with *Manchester*, *Southampton* and his destroyers to rejoin it. Twenty minutes later radar located incoming aircraft, which began to bomb from 13,000 feet at 14.35, undeterred by *Ark Royal*'s Fulmars, one of which was lost in the counter-attack. The inaccuracy of the Italian bombing was matched by the poor anti-aircraft gunnery of the British, described graphically by Somerville in a letter to his wife as 'bum'. During this period, at 14.10, *Ark Royal* flew off a strike force of nine Swordfish to attempt to torpedo the enemy battleships, and seven Skuas to dive-bomb an enemy cruiser reportedly stopped in the water. At 17.05 *Ark Royal* signalled that the torpedo strike force had achieved one hit, but this later proved false. A further three high-level bombing raids, each by five SM79s, were endured during the afternoon. The Regia Aeronautica concentrated upon *Ark Royal*, which survived some thirty bombs, some of which were near-misses but none of which hit her. By 16.40 all enemy air activity had petered out, as Somerville and Holland fell back towards Sicily and the convoy. By 18.10 the Skuas reported that though they had failed to locate the stationary cruiser they had attacked three enemy cruisers and shot down a Meridionali Ro43 seaplane (probably one of Matteucci's cruiser's aircraft).[11]

At dusk, with Campioni retiring north along the east coast of Sardinia, Somerville left Holland's Force F and headed west, burying the dead from *Berwick*'s quarterdeck after sunset. By the late afternoon of 29 November Somerville had returned to his moorings at Gibraltar, where cheers and bands welcomed him and his ships. But beyond this fulsome greeting lurked a rather vengeful Admiralty Board already hunting a scapegoat for the loss of the Hurricanes during Operation WHITE and now, critical of Somerville's conduct off Cape Teulada, bent on a second enquiry. This dragged on until 7 December under the chairmanship of Admiral of the Fleet the Earl of Cork and Orrery. Somerville and his captains were furious at the prospect of falling victims to an outdated and distant appreciation of affairs rooted in the prejudices of old men. The First Sea Lord, Sir Dudley Pound, a big-gun enthusiast, nursed the idea that Somerville should have forced a gunnery duel on Campioni; Lord Cork asked why he had not handed over the convoy to Cunningham and pursued Campioni, seemingly insensible of the distances separating the two admirals, the importance of the convoy, or the high speed of the Italian ships. But in the end the earl and his board upheld Somerville's actions, judging his conduct of affairs to have been 'correct and spirited', and that he had achieved 'the primary object ... the safe and timely arrival of the convoy at its destination, and this in the face of a superior Force.'

Lord Cork wrote privately to Somerville in exculpation of his part in an invidious task, alluding to 'people, impatient for results, [who] exist both in and out of the Admiralty and in high quarters'.[12] His reference to the vindictiveness of Churchill was softened by his explanation of why an enquiry had been ordered even before the Admiralty had received Somerville's Report of Proceedings: 'The most expeditious way of silencing them', the old admiral wrote, 'has in this case been adopted.' Let Cunningham close this unhappy episode in which it seemed to Somerville, who had 'no ambition ... and unlike Nelson [didn't] crave for glory',[13] that the hands of the Admiralty Board were against him: referring to the First Sea Lord, Sir Dudley Pound, Cunningham wrote soothingly, 'I don't believe he is at the bottom of it but he allows himself to be talked into these things, by W.C. and others.'[14]

In fact, Cunningham well knew that Pound was after Somerville's skin, and that Somerville had escaped replacement only because of his action with the Italians. Pound had written to inform Cunningham that the Admiralty Board was not satisfied with Somerville's 'outlook' and that a letter had been approved relieving him of his command; fortunately for Somerville it was delayed when Pound 'got the news that he was chasing the Italians'. Somerville was judged to have been over-anxious about his convoy, and avoided supercession only because the Admiralty had no other suitable flag officer to hand.

Yet Somerville's anxiety was fully justified. Two attacks had been attempted by the submarines *Dessiè* and *Tembien* on the British cruisers *Glasgow*, *Gloucester* and *York* which were in the Narrows awaiting the convoy on the night of 27/28 November, but they had failed. As Somerville returned to Gibraltar, the two Clan Line cargo-liners entered Grand Harbour while Holland and his cruiser squadron joined Cunningham. Holland himself shortly afterwards returned to Gibraltar, but Cunningham's fleet had received his reinforcements, the *New Zealand Star* with her cargo of tanks and munitions arrived at Suda, and the four corvettes reached the Eastern Mediterranean.

The consequence of Taranto and the action off Cape Teulada was a reorganisation of the Regia Marina. Iachino replaced Campioni as the fleet's commander, with Riccardi displacing Cavagnari at Supermarina. The remaining serviceable ships were similarly reshuffled under a revised command structure.[15]

In early December *Glasgow* was badly damaged by an aerial torpedo while in Suda Bay, but struggled back to Alexandria. Cunningham also lost two of his submarines stationed in the Strait of Otranto, *Triton* and *Regulus*, thought to have struck mines. As O'Connor counter-attacked Graziani in the Western Desert, Rear-Admiral Rawlings took command of a supporting force[16] and harried the Italians along the coast of Cyrenaica. Italian submarines were deployed against Rawlings' ships and the main Mediterranean Fleet. On 13 December *Neghelli* torpedoed *Coventry*, but *Naiade* was lost to the destroyers *Hyperion* and *Hereward* the next day.

With O'Connor's Anglo-Indian army pushing west, Cunningham undertook the further replenishment of Malta, to be combined with an air attack on targets in the Dodecanese, a raid on the Strait of Otranto, and a bombardment of Valona, to 'give our Greek friends a helping hand'.[17]

Cunningham sailed from Alexandria at 01.00 on 16 December 1940 in *Warspite* with *Valiant*, *Illustrious*, *Gloucester*, *York* and twelve destroyers.[18] Early on the 17th, aircraft from *Illustrious* bombed Rhodes and Stampalia before refuelling at Suda Bay. Pridham-Wippell, who had been operating in the Aegean with the 7th Cruiser Squadron, *Ajax*, *Orion* and HMAS *Sydney*, screened by *Janus*, *Jervis* and *Juno*, joined Cunningham as the weather deteriorated during the 18th. 'High and variable winds, strong squalls and heavy rain' decided Cunningham to leave *Illustrious* astern as he pushed north towards the strait to attack Valona. By the time they arrived off the Albanian port, however, it was clear and cold, with snow on the hills. Pridham-Wippell's cruisers swept up the channel while Cunningham bombarded Valona with the 15-inch guns of *Warspite* and *Valiant*. On completion Cunningham withdrew, steaming south and west, bound for Malta.

While this was in progress the battleship *Malaya*, cruisers *Calcutta* and *Coventry*, and a mixed force of destroyers and corvettes, which also included the armed boarding vessel *Chakla*, covered the passage of two convoys to Malta, MW5(A) and MW5(B). The first consisted of the *Lanarkshire* and *Waiwera*, reloaded with stores and munitions; the second, a larger group, consisted of the veterans *Volo*, *Rodi* and *Devis*, and the 8,290-ton tanker *Pontfield* belonging to the Field Tank Steamship Company, Leif Hoegh's Norwegian merchantman *Hoegh Hood* of 9,351 grt, and *Ulster Prince*, a requisitioned Irish Sea ferry. They all arrived safely on the 20th.

On 22 December, with her band playing and her guard paraded, *Warspite* herself entered Grand Harbour in the grand manner. 'The Barracas [sic] and other points of vantage were black with wildly-cheering Maltese. Our reception was touchingly overwhelming,' Cunningham recalled afterwards, adding, 'It was good to know that they realised that though the fleet could not use Malta for the time being, we had them well in mind.' Apart from boosting morale – and he was almost mobbed by the population – Cunningham wanted to confer with Dobbie and Ford, to see for himself how Malta was bearing up under her ordeal, and what her requirements and priorities were. *Warspite* remained in Grand Harbour for about forty hours, unmolested by air attack.

Meanwhile, offshore, Rear-Admiral Lyster had taken *Illustrious* and the fleet towards Pantelleria, and on the afternoon of the 21st his Swordfish had located two Italian convoys off the Tunisian coast. They successfully torpedoed two supply vessels of the second without intervention by the escorting torpedo-boat *Vega*.

As Cunningham conferred in Valletta on the 22nd, reassured as to the state of Malta's collective morale, *Malaya* continued into the Sicilian Narrows, heading west with the destroyers *Hasty*, *Hereward*, *Hero*, *Hyperion* and *Ilex*, and the now-emptied *Clan Forbes* and *Clan Fraser*, which had joined them from Malta as convoy MG1.

Part of what Cunningham later described as 'the usual crowded programme' was Operation HIDE, Force H's operations from Gibraltar. Vice-Admiral Somerville had sailed from there in daylight at 18.00 on 20 December, taking Force H west into the Atlantic to deceive, or at least raise doubts in the minds of, the observers at Algeciras who reported his movements. After dark he turned back, heading east to pass The Rock and re-enter the Mediterranean, in a manoeuvre which was to become his almost invariable practice. Nevertheless, at 09.30 on the morning of the 20th he had dispatched *Duncan* and four other destroyers[19] directly eastwards at economical speed.

Somerville's Force H consisted of his flagship *Renown*, *Ark Royal*, *Sheffield* and the destroyers *Faulknor*, *Forester*, *Fury*, *Firedrake*, *Fortune* and *Foxhound*. As dawn broke on the 21st, Force H overhauled *Duncan* and her group, which then joined it. *Ark Royal* flew air patrols ahead of the ships and maintained a flight of fighters warming up on her flight deck. That evening, at 18.00, *Duncan*, *Encounter*, *Isis* and *Jaguar* increased speed to 26 knots and ran ahead to carry out the subsidiary Operation SEEK, designed to flush out or keep down enemy submarines and ensure that the Skerki Channel was clear by the time *Malaya*, her accompanying destroyer screen and the two Clan Line cargoliners approached from the eastward.

Unfortunately the enemy had already struck, in the early hours of the 22nd. Once in the Sicilian Narrows *Hyperion* was torpedoed by the Italian submarine *Serpente*; she was taken in tow by her sister-ship *Ilex* but they drew too close to Pantelleria, exposing *Ilex*, whereupon Cunningham ordered *Janus* to sink *Hyperion* and relieve *Ilex*.

By 09.40 *Malaya*'s group from the east had joined Somerville's flag and the combined forces proceeded westward. At 17.00 the next day, 23 December, the vice-admiral left *Sheffield* and five destroyers to escort *Clan Forbes* and *Clan Fraser* at 13 knots, proceeding himself with Force H, *Malaya* and nine destroyers towards Gibraltar at 18 knots. He arrived by 10.00 on the 24th and was followed by the remainder at 14.00.

Retiring to Alexandria, Cunningham's Mediterranean Fleet covered convoy ME5(A), the withdrawal of the empty transports *Breconshire*, *Memnon*, *Clan Macaulay* and *Clan Ferguson* from Malta to Alexandria. On his arrival, Cunningham travelled to Cairo to meet Wavell and Longmore on Boxing Day. Discussing the situation in the Middle East, they agreed that, as the year drew to its close and the counter-offensive against Graziani proceeded, there was a faint glimmer of light illuminating the fortunes of the British. Although they were dissatisfied because a decisive naval victory over the Italian fleet had eluded them, Malta was unsubdued and it seemed that the Italian vision of dominating the Middle Sea could be prevented. 'Compared with ... our situation six months before,' Cunningham recollected in his autobiography, 'we had cause for satisfaction.'

But this optimism was to prove sadly premature. Hitler, concerned about the Italian position in Albania and the central Mediterranean, and about the potential threat to the Romanian oil fields posed by the Royal Air Force operating from Crete or Greece, had begun his own sinister involvement in the Mediterranean War. On 10 December 1940, OKW issued a directive to transfer Fliegerkorps X to air bases in southern Italy and Sicily. Kesselring's air army included Junkers Ju87B Stuka dive-bombers, and their target was Malta.

8

'Things started to go wrong'

(Operations EXCESS *and MC4, and Convoys MW5½, ME5½ and MW6)*

CUNNINGHAM HAD BEEN heartened by his brief visit to Malta. The imperturbable and resourceful Dobbie was ably seconded by Ford and Maynard, and the recent deliveries of fighters, stores, oil, food and munitions had put new heart into the population, who turned out to cheer Cunningham as he made his formal inspections of the dockyard. Helped by their shelters, which at Birzebbuga also concealed quantities of aircraft fuel, the Maltese had learned to live with the high-level Italian air raids, and these had now slackened off somewhat. Inconveniences like petrol rationing and the limitation of buses to certain fixed times, though irksome, were tolerable. Losses had not yet reached tragic proportions, and the spectre of invasion seems not to have unduly troubled the Maltese at this time.

Thanks to replenishment by sea the island's anti-aircraft defences were now in better shape, with increased anti-aircraft batteries of high-angle 4.5-inch, 3.7-inch and 40-mm Bofors guns. No. 261 Squadron of Hurricanes now operated from Ta' Qali, with Hal Far turned over largely to Swordfish of the Fleet Air Arm. In addition to its long-range reconnaissance flying-boats, Malta also now possessed the means of striking back, with No. 37 Squadron of Wellington medium bombers based at Luqa, and sorties by the large submarines of Captain Raw's 1st Flotilla which paid occasional visits to Valletta during their patrols against the Italian supply lines to Libya. However, it was clear to all the senior officers concerned that such a state of affairs increasingly relied upon constant rearmament and resupply, and that this must be maintained at the regular routine level Cunningham was already considering.

As *Warspite* returned to her mooring at Alexandria, the opening shots of the next round of the battle for Malta were being fired in the Atlantic, as the German heavy cruiser *Admiral Hipper* attacked the twenty merchantmen in convoy WS5A. Kapitän-zur-See Wilhelm Meisel had been dispatched from Kiel by Grossadmiral Raeder to attack the British convoys coming from Halifax, then to relocate to Brest. As he passed south through the Denmark Strait heavy weather prevented Meisel from seeing a single British merchantman, and *Hipper* was proceeding discon-solately towards her new base when, on Christmas Eve, her primitive radar picked up the surface echoes of WS5A. The mer-chantmen were about seven hundred miles to the west of Cape Finisterre, laden with tanks, guns, ammunition and troop rein-forcements for the British Eighth Army in North Africa. The convoy also included five ships due to take part in the next series of movements in the Mediterranean from Gibraltar designed to reinforce Greece and Malta, code-named Operation EXCESS. Meisel shadowed them overnight, a delay which robbed him of his advantage, for on Christmas morning he was promptly engaged by the heavy cruiser *Berwick* and the light cruisers *Dunedin* and *Bonaventure*. Nevertheless, before *Hipper* turned away her shells had hit *Berwick*, the troopship *Empire Trooper* and one other merchant ship in the scattering convoy.[1]

Operation EXCESS was again designed to coincide with convoy movements between Alexandria and Malta. HMS *Breconshire* and *Clan Macaulay* were to proceed to Malta as convoy MW5½, while *Lanarkshire* and *Waiwera*, forming convoy ME5½, and *Volo*, *Rodi*, *Pontfield*, *Devis*, *Hoegh Hood*, *Trocas* (a tanker which had been at Malta since the outbreak of war as a fuel store) and the RFA *Plumleaf* returned in ballast to Alexandria as convoy ME6. This subsidiary operation, covered by the Mediterranean Fleet, was code-named MC4.

Somerville's Force H had left Gibraltar on Christmas Day in response to the news of *Hipper*'s attack on WS5A, and after an anxious period in poor weather had rounded up the scattered vessels of WS5A, which proceeded on their way. *Empire Trooper* had been holed in Nos 1 and 4 Holds, so two cruisers and four corvettes were directed to stand by her to take off the 2,500 troops on board if she should sink before reaching Ponta Delgada in the Azores. It had proved 'a hell of a job to sweep up this mess', Somerville confided to his wife, and *Renown* had suffered heavy-weather damage to her starboard anti-torpedo bulge, which necessitated her immediate drydocking when she returned to Gibraltar on the forenoon of New Year's Eve.

Gibraltar was stuffed with ships, for the Admiralty was insisting on operations against the French at the same time as the muster of both men-of-war and merchant transports for EXCESS was in hand. The weather continued stormy, and on New Year's Day 1941 two of the five eastbound merchantmen were in trouble. *Northern Prince* dragged her anchor and drove ashore, while *Clan MacDonald*'s cable parted, such was the violence of the wind, though her master skilfully worked her through the crowd of shipping and re-anchored her outside the harbour.[2]

Somerville's warships were divided into two groups. One, consisting of the EXCESS convoy and its heavy escort, operationally designated Force F, sailed on the evening of 6 January 1941 and headed west, turning back and running through the Strait after dark, though the moon was up. Force F, formed on the four merchant ships at the core of the whole operation, was made up of the light cruiser *Bonaventure*, Captain H.J. Egerton, and the destroyers *Duncan*, *Hereward*, *Hasty* and *Hero*. The merchantmen *Clan Cumming*, *Clan MacDonald* and *Empire Song* were bound for the Piraeus loaded with tanks, while the Federal Steam Navigation Company's *Essex*, of 11,063 gross tons, was bound for Malta. In her holds *Essex* carried what Cunningham described as 'an even more important cargo', some 4,000 tons of ammunition, 3,000 seed-potatoes, and a dozen crated Hurricane fighters. Somerville himself finally got away with the second group, Force H, just after eight o'clock in the morning of the 7th. Force H comprised *Renown*, *Malaya*, *Ark Royal*, *Sheffield*, *Faulknor*, *Firedrake*, *Forester*, *Fury*, *Foxhound*, *Fortune* and *Jaguar*.

As Force H left Gibraltar the convoy was in loose formation, steaming east-north-east within sight of the Spanish coast, but at the onset of darkness the ships turned south and increased speed, until some thirty miles north of the African coast they swung east-north-east again, with Somerville's overtaking battlegroup to seaward of them. Covered by *Ark Royal*'s anti-submarine

Swordfish on their aerial patrols, Somerville's forces reached a position some 350 miles west of Malta at 05.00 on the morning of the 9th and flew off five Swordfish of No. 821 Squadron, which reached Malta unharmed. Somerville then steamed to join the convoy. Just after he had done so, at about 09.00, *Ark Royal*'s aircraft, having driven off a shadowing Italian aeroplane, reported the approach of two cruisers and a destroyer from the east.

This was Rear-Admiral Renouf's 3rd Cruiser Squadron, which had sailed from Alexandria on 6 January and disembarked 500 soldiers at Valletta on the 8th. As Renouf berthed in Grand Harbour the Australian cruiser *Sydney* and her fellow destroyer HMAS *Stuart* left to return to the eastward and join the approaching Cunningham, some 210 miles to the east-south-east of Malta. Renouf meanwhile left within hours, to rendezvous with Somerville at 10.20 the next morning. Operationally designated Force B, Renouf flew his flag in *Gloucester*, Captain H.A. Rowley, and had with him *Southampton* and the destroyer *Ilex*. His squadron was seen passing Pantelleria in bright moonlight and challenged by a signal station there, but he safely negotiated the extensive minefields laid by the Italians, although his cruisers' paravanes cut mines adrift as they did so. At 09.00 on the 9th, shortly before meeting Somerville and the EXCESS convoy, Renouf's ships had driven off a reconnoitring Italian plane by gunfire. His task was to augment the convoy's close escort through the Skerki Channel and the Sicilian Narrows, and finally meet Cunningham coming up from the east.

At 13.20 *Sheffield*'s radar picked up the echoes of aircraft approaching at a range of 43 miles. Soon in sight in the clear skies and estimated at 11,000 feet, the ten Italian SM79 bombers flew round the fleet and then swung into the attack with the sun behind them. Usually in despair over his ship's anti-aircraft gunnery, Somerville was able to report on this occasion that its accuracy 'showed a marked improvement on previous encounters', and no hits were scored by the enemy. Two enemy planes were shot down by *Ark Royal*'s Fulmars, and three airmen were rescued from the sea. Six hours later, handing the convoy and Force F over to Renouf, Somerville's ships turned back for Gibraltar, where they picked up their moorings at 19.20 on 11 January. His last aerial patrols, which had run a hundred miles ahead of the convoy and as far north as Sardinia, reported nothing in sight, and this was confirmed by long-range RAF

Sunderland patrols flying to the north and west of Sicily. Although the Italian submarines *Bandiera* and *Santarosa* were both in the vicinity, they lay low; as for the Regia Marina, it remained in port.

By the evening of 9 January 1941, Renouf and his charges had passed the Galita Bank and were approaching the Skerki Channel. The night passed peacefully, the convoy hugging the African coast, rounding Cape Bon and heading so as to pass south of Pantelleria. Off the island, as a windless dawn broke over a calm sea, two Italian torpedo-boats, *Vega* and *Circe*, dashed in to the attack. Sighted by *Jaguar* and engaged by *Bonaventure*, Capitano di Fregata Fontana's *Vega* rushed in firing her 4-inch guns and loosing her torpedoes, which *Bonaventure* avoided as Captain Egerton put his ship's helm over and combed their approach. *Vega* was brought to a standstill as Renouf turned the convoy away while *Jaguar*, *Southampton* and *Hereward* made towards the attackers. All four ships now opened fire on *Vega*, *Bonaventure* alone firing 600 rounds (75 per cent of her low-angle ammunition), but this failed to sink her, and she was finally dispatched by a torpedo from *Hereward*. *Circe* had long since withdrawn. *Bonaventure* lost one man killed and had four wounded. The salvo of torpedoes loosed by the patrolling Italian submarine *Settimo* was similarly unsuccessful – the British ships seem indeed to have been unaware of this attack. To Admiral Cunningham,[3] approaching from the eastward in time to witness the closing moments of the forty-minute action, British ascendancy in the Mediterranean seemed assured.

A little later Renouf's Forces B and F, with the EXCESS convoy, effected their juncture with the Commander-in-Chief. The Mediterranean Fleet manoeuvred to take station astern of the merchantmen and Renouf, but as Cunningham's destroyers swung into their new screening positions, the carefully-laid plan began to unravel. *Gallant* struck a mine, and the flagships' signal projectors began to flash in the sunny morning. The combined squadrons and convoy were within a mere hundred miles of Malta but it was the point, Cunningham afterwards remembered, at which 'things started to go wrong'.

Three days earlier, on 7 January, *Warspite* had once again led the Mediterranean Fleet out of Alexandria to cover the new operation, described by Cunningham afterwards as 'rather more intricate than usual, with, of course, every movement and alteration of course prearranged and carefully synchronized'.[4] Cunningham's movement of his fleet was in response to Somerville's anxiety over interdiction by the Regia Marina, though he thought his fellow door-keeper was unduly concerned. Nevertheless he had sent Renouf to take over the close escort through the dangerous Sicilian Channel after disembarking his troops at Valletta, agreed to take his capital ships well to the westward of the usual rendezvous point and, as an additional guard against fast cruiser attack, ordered three submarines onto patrol lines off Sardinia.[5]

Accompanying *Warspite*, as Force A, were *Valiant* and *Illustrious* and the destroyers *Jervis*, *Juno*, *Nubian*, *Mohawk*, *Dainty*, *Gallant*, *Greyhound* and *Griffin*. All left on 7 January, sweeping aside the watching but otherwise harmless Italian submarines *Aradam* and *Axum*, though they were soon located by Italian aerial reconnaissance, which as always was good. A few hours after Cunningham's departure, convoy MW5½, *Breconshire* and *Clan Macaulay*, sailed from Alexandria under the covering support of Force D, Pridham-Wippell's cruisers *Orion*, *Perth*, *Ajax* and *York*. Close escort was provided by Captain D.M. Lees, in the anti-aircraft cruiser *Calcutta*, and the destroyers *Defender* and *Diamond*. The convoy, limited by *Clan Macaulay*'s speed, made 15 knots, arriving safely at Valletta on the forenoon of the 10th, at about the same time that Cunningham was effecting his junction with Renouf and the EXCESS transports some one hundred miles to the west.

Lees, leaving *Diamond* at Valletta, now transferred his attention to the eastbound ME6, a six-ship, 11-knot convoy which he escorted out of the swept channel until they came up with Pridham-Wippell's cruisers. These had been stationed to the northwards of MW5½ and now took over the cover of ME6, sending Lees's *Calcutta* in the wake of *Defender* to join the main fleet and the EXCESS convoy. ME6 set a course parallel to but to the southwards of the intended track of the main EXCESS ships. Pridham-Wippell now covered ME6 until dark on the 10th, when he departed with *Orion*, *Ajax* and HMAS *Perth*, leaving *York* escorting the convoy with four corvettes arriving from Suda Bay, whence they had gone to cover the passage of the auxiliary tanker *Brambleleaf*; *Gloxinia*, *Hyacinth*, *Peony* and *Salvia* now provided close escort to ME6.[6]

Debouching from Grand Harbour that morning in the wake of the merchant vessels, the destroyer *Janus*, which had been dry-docked at Malta, raced off to join Cunningham. Also coming out of Valletta was the faster convoy ME5½, *Waiwera* and *Lanarkshire*, which proceeded under the escort of *Diamond*, Lieutenant-Commander P.A. Cartwright, to meet and join the EXCESS ships. Very shortly afterwards, however, *Diamond* was ordered west-wards to the support of Cunningham's fleet, whose troubles had only begun with the mining of *Gallant*.

Cunningham had been watching the destroyer screen take up its new stations, 'always a fascinating sight to an old destroyer officer … [, when] I suddenly saw a heavy explosion under *Gallant*'s bows. She had been mined, and in water through which the battle-fleet had passed only a short time before.' Sixty men lay dead in her mangled bow, and a further twenty-five were wounded.

Swiftly Cunningham began the redisposition of his ships, ordering *Mohawk* to take *Gallant* in tow with *Bonaventure* (aboard which were passengers transferred from *Northern Prince*, grounded at Gibraltar) and *Griffin* standing by. Renouf was later directed to cover 'what remained of *Gallant* into Malta' with *Gloucester* and *Southampton*.[7] *Mohawk* was bombed by two SM79s as she manoeuvred, but the guns of *Bonaventure* and *Griffin* forced the Italians to drop their torpedoes prematurely and retreat. The fire of the escorts kept high-level bombers at bay all day as *Mohawk* painfully dragged the stricken *Gallant* along at some 5 knots, with the escort zigzagging about them at 20 knots. At 13.00 one HeIII bomber succeeded in damaging *Southampton* with a near-miss, but that evening the defence was augmented by the arrival of *Diamond* and later by Renouf's two cruisers. By 05.00 on the 11th, when they were within fifteen miles of Malta, Renouf, with *Gloucester*, *Southampton* and *Diamond*, detached with orders to proceed to Suda Bay. *Bonaventure* and *Griffin* covered *Mohawk* and *Gallant* until they all arrived safely at Malta just before noon. In the meantime the main body of the fleet had steamed south-east, following the convoy, and into major trouble.

Admiral Cunningham was inordinately proud of his armoured carrier *Illustrious*, and ignored Lyster's protests that he risked the ship by working her closely with the other capital ships. Her presence in the main body of the fleet, Cunningham claimed, acted like a tonic. One of his staff commanders, Power, had protested that the plan for EXCESS required the capital ships to work too far to the westwards, but Cunningham waved his objections aside with one of his infamous sarcasms. Thus it was that at 10.06 on 10 January 1941, as the Mediterranean Fleet steamed in the wake of Forces B and F surrounding the merchantmen *Essex*, *Clan Cumming*, *Clan MacDonald* and *Empire Song*, five Fulmars lifted off the carrier's flight deck and climbed to 14,000 feet, to provide fighter protection for this formidable force. An hour later they were engaged in driving off a few Italian aircraft which appeared to approach the convoy in a half-hearted manner. The Fleet Air Arm pilots shot two down, expending their ammunition and fuel as they buzzed after the enemy. By noon one of the Fulmars had returned to *Illustrious* with combat damage, two more had run out of ammunition, and the remaining pair had expended half their magazines. Twenty minutes later a pair of SM79s flew in very low over the sea from the south, heading directly for *Illustrious* and causing Captain Boyd to order the carrier to be swung out of line in order to comb the torpedo-tracks. The two Italian planes drew down the vengeance of the remaining pair of Fulmars, which dived on them as they jinked away to the north, towards the coast of Sicily over the horizon. The Fulmars pursued, flattening out as their altitude reduced. On the bridge of *Illustrious* Captain Boyd looked at the empty sky and then at his watch. It was 12.28. Below him on the deck a sub-flight of Fulmars was ranged, their engines fired up, waiting to take off. They were due to go at 12.35. Momentarily Boyd considered getting them airborne immediately, but dismissed the thought. He had standing orders from Cunningham expressly forbidding him to turn into the wind on his own initiative. The prior permission of the C-in-C was necessary, and it would be automatically forthcoming at 12.35. Two minutes later radar reports of an enemy air formation reached Boyd, Lyster and Cunningham. At 12.34 Cunningham ordered *Illustrious* to alter course and fly off her aircraft, and half a minute later the first Fulmar was airborne. At 12.36 a large group of enemy aircraft was sighted on the starboard quarter and *Illustrious*'s anti-aircraft armament opened up in concert with that of the rest of the fleet as the last of the Fulmars roared down the flight deck. Two minutes later the air was full of the shrieking crescendo of diving Stukas.

The Luftwaffe had arrived.

The German High Command, OKW, had had its first meeting with Marshal Badoglio, the Italian Supreme Commander, in early November 1940. As a consequence of Italian appeals, Hitler had written to Mussolini suggesting that German aircraft should attack British shipping. The Duce agreed and Hitler ordered Luftwaffe units south on 10 December 1940, sending Erhard Milch, the Secretary for Air, to arrange for the deployment of German units in southern Italy and Sicily. In accordance with Operation MITTELMEER, numbers of aircraft flew across Italy over Christmas, chief among which was Fliegerkorps X, an anti-shipping unit armed with Junkers Ju87B dive-bombers. Commanded by General Hans Geisler, Fliegerkorps X stationed itself at Catania and Comiso in Sicily, and began at once to practise dive-bombing a floating mock-up of an aircraft-carrier, for Geisler's primary order was a model of military brevity: '*Illustrious* müssen sinken'. The staff of Fliegerkorps X had calculated that four direct hits would carry out this imperative task. Almost immediately, on 10 January 1941, they had their opportunity, and it came with the priceless advantage of complete surprise.

From their Enigma decrypts the British had received some indication of the transfer of Fliegerkorps X to southern bases from which it could operate against the Mediterranean Fleet. Such a thing had long been feared, but air reconnaissance of Sicilian airfields on 5 January showed the situation to be normal. Then, on the 9th, the Air Ministry reported the presence of the Luftwaffe in Sicily to the Chiefs of Staff; but no attempt was made to forward this intelligence to either Cunningham or Somerville, it being supposed that the Luftwaffe would pose no greater problem for the door-keepers than the Regia Aeronautica, which they appeared to have well in hand.[8]

The transfer of the aircraft of Fliegerkorps X, their establishment on Italian airfields and their training programmes were carried out with impressive speed. By 8 January Geisler had ninety-six Junkers dive-bombers, both Ju87Bs and Ju88s, operational from Catania and Comiso. Italian reconnaissance had provided daily reports of Cunningham's whereabouts, and by the 10th Geisler was ready to attack the specified target: *Illustrious*.

Cunningham had an hour's warning. The unwitting victim's intelligence officer intercepted German wireless traffic, but this conveyed no sense of the scale, ferocity or intent of the air raid. That came as a complete surprise, and in the aftermath of *Gallant*'s mining, the shock was profound. A day which had begun with an easy victory over two Italian torpedo-boats was, as Cunningham conceded, going badly wrong.[9] Backed up by Italian high-level bombers and a pair of torpedo-bombers, some forty German aircraft were diving on the *Illustrious* from 12,000 feet before the carrier's own Fulmars could climb to intercept them. The fleet, already at action stations, sent up a ferocious anti-aircraft barrage, but Geisler's training, based on Italian debriefs of British air defence, divided the fire of the fleet in a masterly fashion.

Thirty Stukas were ordered to concentrate on *Illustrious*, the remaining ten to carry out distracting attacks on *Warspite* and *Valiant*. The Stukas striking at *Illustrious* broke into three groups, constantly changing height and relative formation, confusing the range-finding of the defence, peeling off from different groups and diving from different directions, further frustrating the ack-ack gunners. The Stukas descended, some directly from 12,000 feet, some dropping first to 7,000 and checking their descent before plunging again, at angles between 65° and 80°. Their intimidating screeching devices added to the crescendo of their engines and the rattle and bang of all-calibre gunfire. Nor did they arrest their descent after releasing their single bombs but followed them down, flattening out and strafing the flight deck of the carrier as they flew below the level of her island. Watching, Cunningham was as fascinated as he was appalled. *Illustrious* disappeared 'in a forest of great bomb splashes ... there was no doubt we were watching complete experts ... We could not but admire the skill and precision of it all.'[10]

The attack was made by I and II Stukageschwader, commanded by Kapitän Hozzel and Major Enneccerus respectively. Six aircraft were engaged in diving at the same time, with no single Stuka pilot impeding his colleagues. 'Severe, brilliantly executed, and pressed home with the utmost skill and determination' was how Boyd later described the attempt to destroy his ship.[11] Cunningham 'saw her hit early on, just before the bridge, and in all, in something like ten minutes, she was hit by six 1,000-lb bombs, to leave the line badly on fire, her steering gear crippled, her [aircraft] lifts out of action and with heavy casualties.'

It actually took the Stukas six and a half minutes to reduce *Illustrious* to an impotent liability. The first bomb struck at 12.38, passing through the loading platform of the forward port pom-pom gun without exploding. Wounding two of the gun's crew, it passed out through the ship's side, to explode on impact with the sea and pepper the carrier with shrapnel. Within seconds the next bomb struck the armoured plating at the bow, passed through the flight deck and exploded in the paint-store. A serious fire started at once, variegated smoke pouring across the deck to choke the anti-aircraft guns' crews exposed there. The store was quickly sealed off and flooded by the forward damage-control party, and although smoke continued to eddy from the gash in the deck, neither of the first pair of bombs seriously threatened the life of the great ship. The third, armed with an impact fuse, missed the island by less than two feet and fell on No. 2 starboard pom-pom, which was dismounted by the explosion. The spread of steel splinters wiped out the pom-pom's crew, struck four men of the adjacent No. 1 pom-pom and threw the ammunition supply parties off their feet. The bombs of the first trio were probably not of the weight Cunningham assumed, but lighter, anti-personnel devices, intended to have a profound effect upon the morale of the carrier's exposed anti-aircraft gunnery personnel. Although Cunningham's heart sank as he watched the attack on his carrier developing he nevertheless was gratified to see 'every gun ... flash into action, a grand and inspiring sight'. The next wave of Stukas, already descending in their carefully prearranged sequence, bore 500-kg armour-piercing bombs, and the fourth of these struck the after aircraft lift at 12.40 as it rose bearing a fully kitted-up Fulmar and its pilot, a young midshipman. The lift twisted upwards as the Fulmar erupted in a ball of fire, then the mass dropped into the hangar deck below. Bomb fragments and wreckage flew outwards, scything through the heavier 4.5-inch turrets and setting fire to the nine Swordfish and four Fulmars parked there. The Swordfish were loaded variously with depth-charges and torpedoes, the Fulmars were armed and fuelled. Men in the attending maintenance crews were severely burnt, or struck by splinters and debris. The damage-control parties rushed to the scene; fire screens were dropped and the aircraft fires were attacked with such vigour that within a few minutes the damage had been contained and the flames were dying under the onslaught of the hoses.

At this point another bomb hit the wreckage of the after lift, but failed to detonate on impact, deflected by the lift's crazy angle, and burst with shattering effect in the hangar below. The explosion blew out the steel fire screens and they disintegrated. Bomb splinters and steel shards lanced through the crowded hangar, the debris and fireball igniting ammunition and exploding the assembled aircrafts' fuel tanks.

A few seconds later, yet another 500-kg bomb burst further forward, under the bow of *Illustrious*. The blast damage was transmitted upwards and arched the forward lift, already distorted by the impact of the previous bomb. The carrier, proceeding at speed to fly off her Fulmars, was generating considerable ship's wind and this now roared into the hangar deck under the curve of the distorted forward lift, fanning the fire and producing a huge flame and column of smoke which rose into the sky from the gaping hole in the flight deck where, only a moment earlier, the ascending Fulmar and its young pilot had been.

The last group of Stukas now came in for the kill. What anti-aircraft armament remained to *Illustrious* was aft, the gun crews blinded and choked by eddies of smoke and the heat waves pouring up from the inferno below. It was now that *Ilustrious*'s own aircraft came to her aid. The Fulmars ranged on the deck, at which Captain Boyd had been idly looking less than twenty minutes earlier, had climbed into the sky through the first bomb splashes. The slow climb-rate of the Fulmars placed them still below the last wave of Stukas, but their pilots drove their machines against the Ju87s, disrupting the precision of the final part of the German assault so that several Stukas released their bombs prematurely and some were shot down. However, one of the final ten Stuka pilots pressed home his attack, and his bomb landed about six metres forward of the after lift. The stressed flight-deck fractured and the bomb penetrated the hangar deck below before exploding, with devastating effect, on the ammunition conveyor. The ship's electric power failed on detonation, and as the electric pumps stopped the fire parties lost all control of the fires which now took hold of the after part of the ship. A broken aviation fuel pipe sprayed gasoline into the inferno and smoke and flames roared through the alleyways, to which steam, venting from the damaged fire-main, added heat and further impeded visibility. Numberless men were dead or dying of burns, shrapnel wounds and suffocation.

Illustrious slowed and lay askew the line of the Mediterranean Fleet, her whole after part engulfed in black smoke beneath which the ominous flicker of a raging conflagration and the white feathering of escaping steam could be seen from the other ships. She listed to starboard and steamed round in a circle; the international signal for being not under command, above her bridge, was hidden in the obscuring smoke. On her bridge Boyd and Lyster assessed the situation. Even if the ship could be got under control, they were ninety miles from the partial refuge of Malta; and whether *Illustrious* was at sea or in Grand Harbour, both officers knew the Stukas would be back once they had been rearmed.

Warspite and *Valiant* had also been hit and suffered minor damage, the former by a bomb on her starboard anchor, the latter losing one man killed and two wounded; but this was trifling compared with the agony of *Illustrious*. In addition to the six direct hits, other bombs had exploded as near-misses, effecting lesser damage through their shock waves. As the Stukas withdrew to the north towards their bases in Sicily, the carrier's Fulmars broke off their pursuit and flew towards Malta. Fortunately, although she still burned furiously, *Illustrious*'s steam turbines were undamaged and she was capable of 17 knots. However, her electrically-controlled steam steering presented a problem, and three attempts to complete the control circuitry failed. Finally, however, the steering engine was induced to bring the rudder amidships, allowing Boyd to use his engines to steer, an advantage of multiple screws, and he steadied the wounded ship on a course for Malta, his turbines now giving him a gratifying 21 knots.

Then, at 13.20, *Valiant*'s radar located another wave of airborne echoes. There was no air defence cover at all, so Cunningham ordered the fleet to close on the carrier, and as the enemy formation approached at 14,000 feet the barrage was thrown up. The seven SM79s of the Regia Aeronautica lacked the aggression of their Teutonic allies. Dropping their bombs wide, they withdrew. But the relief of Lyster and Boyd was brief, for *Illustrious*'s rudder now became unmanageable and the ship began an erratic turn, endangering the adjacent escorting war ships. For half an hour her engineering staff, with fire raging above their heads in the hangar deck, strove to regain control, and by 14.00, at the reduced speed of 15 knots, she had again steadied for Malta.

The reduced speed was the result of the fires below. The boiler-room staff had been ordered to maintain steam 'whatever the cost', and that cost was mounting. The huge ventilator fans were drawing toxic fumes and smoke into the boiler-rooms, where the temperature was rising all the time. The boiler-room staff fainted as the bulkheads began to glow. Breathing through wet rags and forming chains to report water levels and pressures from almost invisible gauge glasses, these men battled asphyxiation and overheating by drinking and wetting themselves with water from the feed pumps.

Much of this magnificent effort was directed to provide *Illustrious* with motive power, but water pressure was required to fight the fires forward and in the hangar deck. A spray system which had been coaxed into action was proving ineffective against the continuing explosions and burning of ammunition, gasoline and aircraft as the intense heat welded steel pipes and melted bronze valves. The fires in the forward part of the ship were gradually doused, and more canvas hoses were run aft, but neither water, foamite nor asbestos sheeting quenched the blaze in the hangar. By 15.00 this was threatening the ship's main magazines and upper fuel tanks, but just as it seemed their luck was running out, the ship's company made a significant discovery. The senior engineer officer found that an oil line feeding the steam steering gear was leaking and fuelling the fire. The steam steering was suspended, and immediately the fire fighters began to gain ground. By 16.00 the ship was steaming a straight course for Malta at 18 knots, when Fliegerkorps X struck again. Fifteen Stukas escorted by five Messerschmitt Me110s took advantage of the pall of smoke drifting astern of *Illustrious* and flew in under its cover. *Illustrious*'s own Fulmars, however, returning rearmed to the fray from Malta, succeeded in breaking up the attacks and shot down more Stukas. Only one of the dive-bombers managed to break through, but with devastating effect, her 500-kg bomb hitting the after flight deck, within feet of the gaping after lift well. Penetrating the armour, it burst below, where a temporary sick-bay had been rigged up, incinerating some thirty men instantaneously. The flash reignited the dying fires in the hangar, and after a further hour's desperate effort the exhausted fire-fighting and damage-control parties despaired of success.

On the bridge, at 17.30, Boyd received the report that the fire was out of control and the pumps burnt out. Urged to flood his magazines, he refused: it would be an act almost akin to surrender, leaving the carrier utterly bereft of defence. There was nothing to do but continue to contain the fire. They were approaching Malta all the time, and something might yet be achieved.

Suddenly *Illustrious* lolled further over to starboard, the free-surface effect of the copious amounts of water sloshing about within her; vents and scuppers were laboriously cleared, men squeezing through wreckage to find the causes of blockage. Soon *Illustrious* was nearing the channel which, approaching Valletta from the south, was swept regularly to preserve it clear of mines. The carrier's grey form remained shrouded in smoke and steam as darkness fell, and the low bulk of the island loomed on the horizon in the light of a rising moon. As they drew closer to Malta, Lyster and Boyd received a message that aircraft were approaching. Half a dozen SM79s armed with torpedoes were driven off by the remaining operational guns aboard *Illustrious* and fire from her close escorts, *Hasty* and *Jaguar*; a moment later *Hasty* gained a sonar contact and dropped depth charges. At 21.45 tugs from the dockyard arrived, and at 22.15 the listing carrier edged alongside Parlatorio Wharf. Crowds welcomed her and, incongruously, a band played 'Roll out the barrel'.

In Malta that day General Dobbie, his aide, a civil servant and his daughter Sybil had been playing tennis in the grounds of the beautiful white palace of San Anton, built for Grand Master Anthony de Paula in 1623. It was a chilly but bright January day, the oranges gleamed on the trees, their silver-green leaves ruffled by a light south-westerly breeze. The game was not being taken very seriously and the players stopped when their attention was caught by 'a very distant noise of firing'. As there had been no air raid warning, indeed a lull in air raids generally, and there were no aircraft above them, they realised this was something out of the ordinary. It was the first intimation on Malta of *Illustrious*'s plight, but within hours Dobbie and his senior officer had rallied all possible aid to meet the requirements of the carrier when, and if, she made Grand Harbour. As she berthed, 'lines of ambulances were waiting ... and doctors, nurses, VADs and orderlies were standing by in the Service hospitals.

'They were needed. Numbers and numbers of men, mostly horribly burnt, were hurried in, and all that night and most of the next day the fight for their lives went on.' The fight for *Illustrious* was not over either, for she was now a static target, and in the succeeding days as the dockyard workers tried to patch her up, the Luftwaffe's two Stukageschwaders struck again and again, 'plane after plane drop[ping] like a hawk on to its prey', devastating the neighbouring dockyard installations. As the attacking Stuka pilots flattened out after their dives they flew so low over Grand Harbour as to be below the level of the Maltese-manned anti-aircraft gun emplacements – 'safe from the guns which could not be depressed to fire at them from the bastions'. Irritated by the cool waves and grins of the German pilots, one Bofors battery commander, a Maltese territorial officer, Lieutenant Micallef Trigona, took matters into his own hands. His guns on the ravelin of the Lower Barrakka Gardens were prevented from depressing by a rail, and he had this removed. Standing conspicuously next to his weapon, Trigona met a wave of escaping Stukas with gunfire and the unmistakably obscene Latin gesture of crossing his right arm over his left.[12]

Just as *Illustrious* was being prepared to make a run for it, an attack on the 16th again succeeded in hitting her after lift well. Three days later, on Sunday 19 January, two near-misses exploded so close to the great hull that it was driven against the dock wall, holing the shell plating, fracturing her port turbine and flooding a boiler-room. Shifts of men worked in unremitting sequence to repair the damage while the Hurricanes of the RAF and the Fleet Air Arm's Fulmars struck back, destroying fifteen bombers and two fighters the same day, while the air defence gunnery also shot down several. Such losses could not be sustained, even though Fliegerkorps X was daily being reinforced from Germany.[13] The towns about Grand Harbour received fresh damage,[14] while the Luftwaffe also attempted to neutralise Malta's air assets, beginning on the 17th, when fifty-one Stukas and a dozen Ju88s, covered by seventeen Me110s and some Macchi 200 fighters, attacked the island's airfields.

Also in port with the carrier during the latter part of this period, known in Malta as 'the *Illustrious* blitz', were HMAS *Perth*, sent to provide additional anti-aircraft fire for the wounded carrier, and the Federal Steam Navigation Company's cargo-liner *Essex*.

In the drama of the fight to preserve *Illustrious*, it is easy to forget that the purpose of the huge naval presence was to ensure the safe arrival of the laden merchant transports at their several destinations. The twin-screw motor vessel *Essex*, built in 1936 by John Brown of Clydebank, was capable of 19.5 knots, but she was to spend a long time in Grand Harbour as a result of the attack on the 16th, when a bomb passed through her boat-deck just to port of the funnel, descended through into the engine room and burst in the upper part, level with the crew's accommodation. Sixteen members of her crew were killed, and twenty-three were wounded. Mercifully, however, the explosion dissipated itself in the central superstructure and failed to detonate the hundreds of tons of ammunition which still lay in her partly discharged holds. Among the Maltese dockers there was some talk of refusing to continue work on the ship, and drafts of soldiers and airmen were brought in to assist in completing the unloading. As soon as this was finished, the ship was towed clear of her berth and shifted to moorings in Frenchman's Creek, where her fourth engineer, Mr J. Lynch, was killed in an air raid on 1 March. On 7 March she sustained further heavy bomb damage which wrecked all her electrical circuitry and flooded the engine room to a depth of thirty feet. She was again moved, this time to the obscurity of Rinella Creek, where she was to remain for two years; only her chief engineer, Mr W. Reddington, and chief electrician, Mr C. Kidd, were left in her, while her master, Captain F.N. Wyatt, and the remains of his ship's company were repatriated. In Rinella Creek she received further bomb damage on 12 April 1942.[15]

As *Illustrious* had detached from Cunningham's flag and headed towards Malta escorted by *Hasty* and *Jaguar*, the C-in-C had pressed on after the EXCESS convoy and its heavy escort, still steaming eastwards towards Crete, zigzagging at 15 knots and, with the enemy air forces concentrating on *Illustrious*, relatively unmolested. Just before the initial bombing raid struck the unsuspecting carrier, it will be recalled, the cruiser *Calcutta* had left ME6. She was to join the close escort of the EXCESS convoy and supplement the three destroyers, replacing *Bonaventure*, which had been sent in to Malta. The battle-squadron, Force A, was stationed on the convoy's port quarter, but fell astern as the attack on *Illustrious* developed. At roughly the same time as the second attack on the carrier, about 13.30, a high-level bombing raid was made on the convoy by Savoia Marchettis. Fire from *Calcutta*, stationed in the rear of the convoy, accounted for one SM79. As the Italian air attack faltered and faded, the ships stood on towards the entrance to the swept channel into Valletta where, later that afternoon, they were joined by the two fast merchant ships of ME5½, *Lanarkshire* and *Waiwera*. These two ships were to accompany them to the point off Crete where they would alter to the southward for Alexandria, while the Piraeus-bound vessels would stand on to the north and east. It was at this point, as convoy ME5½ joined the EXCESS vessels, that Captain F.N. Wyatt swung *Essex* away towards Malta, escorted into port by *Defender*, which immediately afterwards rejoined the convoy.

Ahead of them the slower ME6 was proceeding east, escorted until dark, as noted earlier, by Pridham-Wippell's two cruisers, *Orion* and *Perth*, and the destroyers *Jervis* and *Janus*. The vice-admiral then detached to make for a prearranged rendez-vous with the C-in-C to the eastwards the following day. Cunningham, however, had been considerably held up by the necessity to cover *Illustrious*, and ordered Pridham-Wippell to steer not east but north, to head off or give warning of any possible raid by the Regia Marina from either Taranto or Brindisi. Overnight Force A then made east at full speed, reaching a position some twenty-five miles north of the combined ships of ME5½ and the EXCESS convoys by daylight. Here Pridham-Wippell's four ships rejoined Cunningham's flag and the warships covered the eastbound track of the convoy until the afternoon, when they diverted on hearing news of an attack on the slower convoy ME6, some sixty miles to the southward.

Cunningham left the combined fast convoys to continue under the escort of *Calcutta* and her three destroyers. That evening *Lanarkshire* and *Waiwera* headed south for Alexandria, *Calcutta* ran on ahead to oil at Suda Bay, while *Clan Cumming*, *Clan MacDonald* and *Empire Song* stood on for the Piraeus, where they arrived on the morning of the 12th.[16]

Having escorted *Gallant* into Grand Harbour, Rear-Admiral Renouf, with *Gloucester*, *Southampton* and *Diamond*, left Malta at 05.00 on 11 January to rejoin the fleet. However, just after noon, in response to a revised order from Cunningham flown in by *Warspite*'s Walrus aircraft, Renouf diverted to cover ME6.

Steaming at 24 knots, *Gloucester* launched her own Walrus to locate the slow convoy which, it will be recalled, had only the cruiser *York* and the corvettes *Hyacinth, Gloxinia, Peony* and *Salvia* as escort, the latter, being designed for anti-submarine work, almost devoid of anti-aircraft defence. Neither of Renouf's cruisers was fitted with radar and at 15.22, when thirty miles astern of ME6, they were surprised by a dozen Ju87s of II Stukageschwader. Unaware of the attack 'until the whistle of the first bomb was heard',[17] each cruiser was picked upon by six aircraft which dived out of the sun and did not release their bombs until they were down to 1,000 feet. The cruisers and *Diamond* opened fire with their 4-inch armament, increased speed and put their helms over, but it was too late. Two or three bombs hit *Southampton* and a further hit with two near-misses shook *Gloucester*. Half an hour later, seven high-level Italian bombers were driven off by gunfire, though a single aircraft flew ahead and dropped two bombs between the columns of convoy ME6.

Cunningham, turning towards Renouf, ordered Pridham-Wippell to race ahead with his squadron, and himself swung east again when he learned that *Southampton* was so badly damaged that she would have to be abandoned. The cruiser, on fire, had been kept on course and at speed for almost two hours after the attack, but the fire began to spread rapidly, and it was found that her magazines could not be flooded. After four hours the case was deemed to be hopeless. Transferring the ship's company to *Diamond* and then *Gloucester*, Renouf ordered his flagship to sink her sister; but the single torpedo failed to dispatch *Southampton*, and upon his arrival a little later Pridham-Wippell ordered his flag-captain, Captain G. Back, to torpedo her. It took three torpedoes before, as Lieutenant Hugh Mulleneux of *Jervis* wrote in his diary, 'she blew up with a simply gigantic explosion'.[18]

Pridham-Wippell and Renouf then turned east again to rejoin the C-in-C, who was himself intending to join Rear-Admiral Rawlings[19] for further operations; the loss of *Illustrious* curtailed these, however, while Rawlings' alternative plan to raid the Dodecanese, referred to earlier, was aborted due to bad weather. Cunningham therefore proceeded directly to Alexandria with *Warspite, Valiant, Gloucester* and their destroyer screen. Pridham-Wippell was ordered to the Piraeus where, taking over a task previously allocated to *Southampton*, he embarked troops destined for Malta and carried in some of the EXCESS transports. HMAS

Perth was left at Malta to cover *Illustrious*'s departure with the destroyers *Hasty* and *Jaguar*. In the aftermath of the affair *Bonaventure*, instead of returning west, had instead to proceed to Alexandria and replenish her wantonly expended ammunition. Here Cunningham retained her for her anti-aircraft capability. The emptied *Volo*, *Rodi*, *Pontfield*, *Devis*, *Hoegh Hood*, *Trocas* and the RFA *Plumleaf* of ME6 were the last ships to reach their destinations, arriving safely at Alexandria on 13 January.

Back in Malta, *Illustrious* enjoyed a few days of peace after the intense raids on her and *Essex*, sufficient for jury repairs to be completed. To deter the Luftwaffe further, Wellington bombers flew from Malta and struck at Catania, Augusta and Comiso on the night of 23 January. The following night, in conditions of secrecy, the great ship slipped quietly from Parlatorio Wharf, repair stages still dangling from her topsides, gliding out of French Creek to swing and steam seawards. The islanders awoke to find her gone. Escorted by HMAS *Perth* and the two destroyers she gradually increased speed to 25 knots, though water in her fuel caused her to belch smoke. In the early afternoon of 25 January she entered Alexandria, afterwards proceeding via Durban to the United States. Here, at Norfolk in Virginia, she was repaired, her armoured flight deck arousing much interest in United States Navy circles. In his report, Captain Boyd drew attention and paid tribute to 'the sound construction of the ship, which enabled her to withstand such heavy punishment'. She was recommissioned on 29 November 1941.

She was a significant loss to the Mediterranean Fleet, although her aircraft were dispersed: a squadron of Swordfish and a dozen Fulmars were left at Malta, and the remaining Swordfish were sent to Crete and the Western Desert. The disablement of *Illustrious* and the sinking of *Southampton* were a direct result of the appearance of the Luftwaffe in the Mediterranean skies. 'From that day,' the Admiralty's Battle Summary states, 'a heavy menace hung over the Sicilian route, and the voyage to Malta became one of perilous hazard.'

'Even a gunnery officer cannot miss'

(Operations MC8 and MC9, Convoy MW6 and the Battle of Matapan)

CUNNINGHAM RETURNED TO Egypt with much to occupy his mind. The appearance of the Luftwaffe on the shores of the Mediterranean coincided with increased calls coming from Greece, where the military situation was deteriorating, for equipment, supplies, and material support from the RAF. The Luftwaffe had taken over airbases in the Dodecanese and mounted a bombing raid on the Suez Canal on the night of 18/19 January 1941. Shipping was held up while unexploded bombs were cleared, and Cunningham's anxiety for his back-door supply route became acute. The presence of units of the Italian navy east of Suez was no serious threat,[1] but bombing of the canal by the Germans was potentially catastrophic. Thus it proved; magnetic mines were dropped in a raid by seven He111s of Kapitän Kühl's II Kampfgeschwader on 29 January, and soon three ships had been mined, one of which blocked the canal for some time.[2] Cunningham, under orders to send the unarmoured *Eagle* home for a refit, was anxious to have the canal clear by 5 March, when he expected the arrival of his replacement aircraft-carrier *Formidable*. In the event, she was delayed in the Red Sea.

The Chiefs of Staff in London had vetoed Cunningham's initial plans to raid the Dodecanese island of Kásos, but approved the occupation of Rhodes; *Breconshire*'s sister ships *Glenearn*, *Glenroy* and *Glengyle*, all of which had been converted to assault ships, were prepared for this service. Meanwhile, the campaigns in the

Sudan, Abyssinia and the Western Desert were going well. Bardia fell on 6 January, when 30,000 Italian prisoners were taken. On the 22nd the Italian garrison in Tobruk surrendered, and on the 30th Derna fell. The Australians stormed into Benghazi on 6 February and the next day, following the battle of Beda Fomm, Agedabia and a further 20,000 Italian soldiers were in British hands. Two days later El Agheila was taken.

As O'Connor's forces advanced the length of the Cyrenaican coastline, Cunningham's ships assisted. The five-hundred-mile advance had secured 130,000 prisoners, 400 tanks and 800 guns, at a cost of fewer than 2,000 dead and wounded. Having destroyed the Italian 10th Army, O'Connor and Wavell wished to sweep further west, into Tripolitania; but Churchill, concerned about the fate of Greece, ordered Wavell to reduce the strength of the army in Cyrenaica to a minimum and to prepare to send military help to the Greeks. German intervention was now imminent, and not only in Greece, as Churchill feared. On the same day as Wavell received his instructions, General Erwin Rommel landed at Tripoli.

Cunningham had continued to worry about Malta, aware that the dockyard had taken a thrashing during 'the *Illustrious* blitz'; but 'there seemed to be no limit to the degree to which a damaged dockyard could rehabilitate itself', and the drydock could already accommodate a cruiser. 'The indefatigable and undefeated Ford' and his men had done wonders, though labour and electric power remained in short supply.

As to his fleet, Cunningham fretted over the lack of a modern aircraft-carrier, worried that *Bonaventure* would not be able to replenish her low-angle ammunition until *Formidable* arrived with more in early March, and had to organise coastal convoys to Tobruk and Benghazi while increasing those to the Aegean in response to Churchill's diktat.[3] He was losing ships, too: the destroyer *Dainty* was dive-bombed by Ju88s and sunk off Tobruk and the monitor *Terror*, the early defender of Valletta, was similarly dispatched off Derna, both in February.

Despite this, 'the really critical business was getting *Formidable*, *Illustrious* and *Eagle* past the wreck of one ship which lay across the Suez Canal. However, by dredging and pulling the obstructing vessel to one side, a passage was eventually cleared.'[4] But all this took time, and while Cunningham awaited the arrival of *Formidable* it was necessary to make a further fast run to Malta with two infantry battalions, vehicles and military stores.

Operation MC8 was covered by Rear-Admiral Rawlings in *Barham*, accompanied by *Valiant*, *Eagle*, *Coventry*, *Decoy*, *Hotspur*, *Havock*, *Hereward*, *Hero*, *Hasty*, *Ilex*, *Jervis*, *Janus* and *Jaguar*. The troops, small vehicles and stores were embarked in Pridham-Wippell's cruisers *Orion*, *Ajax* and *Gloucester* and the Tribal-class destroyers *Nubian* and *Mohawk*, which left Alexandria on 19 February and arrived at Valletta on the 21st. The warships, steaming at speed, were unmolested, the patrolling Italian submarine *Dagabur* failing to see them. The discharged *Breconshire* and *Clan Macaulay* were picked up, and all the ships were back in Alexandria by the 23rd.

The route of MC8 crossed that of the Axis route to North Africa in use since 8 February to transport the first elements of the Afrika Korps to Tripoli. Three German cargo-vessels, *Alicante*, *Arcturus* and *Ankara*, escorted by the Italian destroyer *Turbine* and torpedo-boats *Orsa*, *Cantore* and *Missori*, had been delayed at Palermo by an offensive operation against Genoa carried out by Force H, and their return was hampered by a Swordfish attack from Malta on 14 February; by then a second convoy consisting of the German freighters *Adana*, *Aegina*, *Kybfels* and *Ruhr*, escorted by *Camicia Nera* and *Procione*, was on its way, initiating a wholesale movement of troops. These reinforcements were a considerable success and in due course proved fatal to British arms, but the dangers of their continuation were already appreciated.

Early in the new year, Malta-based Wellingtons had struck at shipping at Naples. In addition to aircraft, however, there was building up at Malta another force capable of attacking the Axis supply route. A new submarine flotilla, the 10th, which under the command of Commander G. Simpson was soon to establish a reputation in the theatre, had begun to form in the last weeks of 1940. Smaller and more effective than the larger submarines hitherto employed in the Mediterranean, *Upright* and *Ursula* were the first U-class boats to be based at Marsamxett, *Upright* having arrived on 4 December 1940.[5] Their first missions astride the Trapani to Tripoli route were unsuccessful, but at the beginning of February, when four boats were on station, Lieutenant-Commander David Wanklyn of *Upholder* sank a 4,000-ton freighter on passage to Tripoli. At the end of February *Unique* and *Upright* both missed convoys, and a large troop convoy from Naples to Tripoli, consisting of the former passenger liners *Esperia*, *Conte Rosso*, *Marco Polo* and *Victoria*, with a close escort of *Baleno*, *Camicia Nera* and *Aldebaran*, went unmolested.[6] But the supporting cover provided by the cruisers *Giovanni delle Bande Nere* and *Armando Diaz* and the destroyers *Ascari* and *Corazziere* was intercepted by Lieutenant E. Norman's *Upright*, and he succeeded in torpedoing the *Armando Diaz* on 25 February. Further military convoys during March got through and returned without loss, however, allowing Rommel's Afrika Korps to be built up rapidly to operational strength. Limited successes were scored by *Utmost* and *Unique*, which each sunk a freighter on 10 March, and again on the 28th when Lieutenant-Commander R. Cayley of *Utmost* sank two ships in a Naples to Tripoli convoy escorted by *Folgore*, *Strale* and *Dardo*.

The death of Prime Minister Metaxas on 29 February shook the intransigence of the Greek government, who now required full military support from Great Britain. After the failure of a raid on the island of Castelorizzo, Cunningham was now ferrying British troops under General Maitland Wilson across to Greece. Hitler, who on 31 January had given OKW orders to prepare Operation BARBAROSSA, the invasion of Soviet Russia, had been strengthening the Fascist position in the Balkans by means of a Tripartite Pact which enmeshed Romania, Hungary and Bulgaria in the Axis net. It also enabled him to deploy troops up to the Greek frontier in Macedonia, and although the Yugoslavs resisted, this only drew down Hitler's wrath. In a twelve-day Blitzkrieg in April 1941 Yugoslavia was occupied. The invasion of Greece was also under way.

The events thus set in train were to dominate the eastern Mediterranean and the employment of the British fleet for some weeks, but in the interim Cunningham intended to force another convoy through to Malta, well aware that his 'commitments', as he signalled to the Admiralty, 'exceed available resources'.[7] Malta was now under a continual round of raids, with 'the Germans coming over in droves and machine-gunning people in St Paul's Bay and other outlying villages.' The island was 'down to eight serviceable Hurricanes', and six were to be sent from Egypt, where they were equally badly needed. 'I am really seriously concerned about Malta,' Cunningham reported to the First Sea Lord, Dudley Pound. 'I am running a convoy there ... but ... I am quite expecting some of the ships to be damaged. The Grand Harbour and the creeks are also being mined whenever the enemy cares to come.'[8] Poor Cunningham received a 'tart' rebuke from Pound – 'I am not sure you fully appreciate events outside the Mediterranean ... ' – who went on to say: 'I hope you will disabuse Longmore that the reinforcement of Malta with Hurricanes will become a routine affair.' There were more acerbic exchanges in this grim game of battledore, but Cunningham, as was his wont, buckled down to the task in hand. On 19 March the four merchantmen of convoy MW6 left Alexandria after their long haul round the Cape, escorted by Waller's Australian destroyers *Stuart*, *Vampire*, *Vendetta*, *Voyager* and *Waterhen*, with the anti-aircraft cruisers *Coventry*, *Calcutta* and *Carlisle*. *Coventry* had been torpedoed some weeks earlier and lacked half her bow, while *Carlisle* was running on only one screw, her damaged tail shaft having been sent to Malta for repair, strapped to the casing of a submarine.

Operation MC9, the naval component in support of convoy MW6, sailed the following day. It again required the cover of the Mediterranean Fleet, now including *Formidable*, which had been 'squeezed through the canal' on 10 March. Neither she nor the Royal Air Force could provide an adequate number of fighters to combat the Luftwaffe, while Cunningham continued to lack adequate aerial reconnaissance assets and was consistently at a disadvantage thereby, for this was one area where the Regia Aeronautica excelled. Astonishingly, however, the Italians on this occasion remained ignorant of the fleet's movement.

Warspite, *Valiant*, *Barham*, *Formidable*, *Gloucester*, *York*, *Bonaventure*, *Orion*, *Ajax* and *Perth*, screened by the destroyers *Defender*, *Decoy*, *Greyhound*, *Griffin*, *Hasty*, *Hero*, *Hereward*, *Hotspur*, *Havock*, *Ilex*, *Jervis*, *Janus*, *Jaguar*, *Mohawk* and *Nubian*, steamed west, providing cover until the night of 22 March, when the fleet turned back. Convoy MW6 consisted of *Lanarkshire*'s sister ship, *Perthshire*, owned by the Scottish Shire Line and managed by Turnbull, Martin and Company, another Clan liner, *Clan Ferguson* (7,347 grt), and Ellerman's two ships, the *City of Manchester* (8,917 grt), managed by Ellerman's Hall Line, and the *City of Lincoln*, managed by the Ellerman Bucknall Steamship Company.[9] All arrived safely at Malta, though two were bombed after their arrival in port and near-misses shook *Bonaventure* and *Griffin* on the return passage. There were no empty merchant ships to bring home, *Essex* being too badly damaged, and the fleet returned to Alexandria on 26 March.

Convoy MW6 took place in the middle of Operation LUSTRE, the protracted conveyance to Greece of 68,000 troops, their vehicles and stores which also preoccupied the Mediterranean Fleet between 4 March and 24 April. At the same time Cunningham's command structure was undergoing a number of changes. Renouf's nerve had cracked in the fiasco of Castelorizzo, and Cunningham had written to Pound that he was 'not quite happy about' him; he was relieved by Rear-Admiral Glennie, who became Rear-Admiral, Destroyers (RAD). Vice-Admiral Lyster's valuable expertise in naval air warfare, 'unshaken by his experience in *Illustrious*', was required at home, and he was appointed Fifth Sea Lord; he was replaced by Boyd, who 'was a bit shaken but has bobbed up again splendidly' and was given acting rank as rear-admiral. Willis, Cunningham's superbly able Chief of Staff, was exhausted, and Cunningham let him go with reluctance and kind words. Fortunately in his relief, Captain J. Edelsten, Cunningham had found another officer of administrative ability, whom he had first known at the Admiralty as Deputy Director of Plans.[10] It was with this team that Cunningham and the combined service chiefs of the Middle East became embroiled in the disasters of Greece and Crete set in train by a meeting with Anthony Eden, General Dill, Wavell and Longmore at Cairo on 19 February.[11] Convinced that 'the authorities at home were living in a land of optimistic dreams', Cunningham's staff began preparing for the evacuation of the very troops the ships were then carrying to Greece. The German threat to Greece was becoming increasingly obvious, with a stepping-up of aerial reconnaissance flights over the eastern Mediterranean persuading Cunningham that the Italian fleet would sortie in support of German operations. In order to disrupt whatever the Axis intended and avoid the danger of being driven back to port for lack of fuel at a critical moment, Cunningham needed to secure intelligence of the enemy fleet's movements without betraying any hint that the British anticipated an attack. Convoys to Greece went on as normal while the British air reconnaissance units, never very adequate, kept up their watch. In the forenoon of 26 March Cunningham received his first of several warnings derived from decrypts by the Government Code and Cypher School at Bletchley Park.[12] These, some in the Italian 'Alfa' code and others to Fliegerkorps X in the German 'light-blue' Enigma code, indicated a combined Luftwaffe/Regia Marina operation. The Admiralty appreciation indicated the most likely location to be the Aegean. On this assumption Cunningham prepared his capital ships for action, and ordered Pridham-Wippell, then in the Piraeus refuelling as part of the continuing support of Operation LUSTRE, to a rendezvous thirty miles west of Gavdo. Finally, No. 815 Squadron's Swordfish at Maleme in Crete were alerted, and ordered airborne at dawn on the 27th. The wisdom of these measures was confirmed when, in poor visibility on the morning of 27 March, a Sunderland flying from Malta briefly spotted a squadron of Italian cruisers some eighty miles east of Sicily, heading towards Crete.

Supermarina had been prodded into action by the German Naval Liaison Officer in Rome who, aware that for the first time since Taranto three Italian battleships were operational, determined that they should be sent to sea. The German strategic appreciation which precipitated Supermarina's move was based on a false claim made after a torpedo attack by two Heinkel HeIIIs on the Mediterranean Fleet when it was making a sweep west of Crete in support of Operation LUSTRE on 16 March. Two battleships having supposedly been torpedoed, it was assumed that only *Valiant* was serviceable. The German Naval Staff, who wanted both to arrest British reinforcement in Greece and to stop the interdiction of supplies to Libya, where Rommel was already complaining of losses, therefore considered 'that the appearance of Italian units in the area south of Crete [would] seriously interfere with British shipping, and [might] even lead to the complete interruption of the transport of troops, especially as these transports are at the moment inadequately protected'.[13]

Cunningham received the Sunderland's report at 12.20. The previous day *York*, his only heavy cruiser, had been badly damaged, and the tanker *Pericles* sunk, by Italian explosive boats sent into Suda Bay from the destroyers *Quintino Sella* and *Francesco Crispi*. Anxious as ever to nail the Regia Marina, though he bet Commander Power ten shillings that they would see nothing of the Italians, Cunningham sprung his trap. The single northbound convoy then at sea, AG9, was ordered to steam on until darkness, then reverse its course, while a southbound convoy, GA9, was halted at the point of departure and ordered to wait at the Piraeus. Orders were also passed to the fleet to prepare for sea, though not until after dark. In the meantime staff officers were sent away by air, dinner invitations were issued, and awnings remained stretched over the fleet's quarterdecks against the torrid sunshine. This deceived Italian reconnaissance flights over Alexandria that afternoon, convincing the Italians that three battleships and one aircraft carrier would still be in port at 19.00 (the very hour appointed for their departure). To perfect the ruse Cunningham decided to play golf that afternoon, and conspicuously carried an overnight bag ashore. He was observed, as was usual, by the Japanese consul, also a keen golfer, who was suspected of passing information of British naval movements to the enemy.

All deception ended at sunset: officers returned, dinner invitations were scrapped, and the awnings were taken down. Force A slipped its moorings as decreed at 19.00, *Warspite* grazing a muddy shoal, which partially choked her condenser intakes and limited the speed of advance to 20 knots. With the flagship were *Barham*, Captain G. Cooke, flying Rawlings' flag; *Valiant*, Captain C. Morgan; and *Formidable*, Captain A. Bisset, flying Boyd's flag and with her own Nos 803 (Fulmar), 826 and 829 (both Albacore) Squadrons embarked. The capital ships formed Force A and were escorted by Force C, Captain Mack's 14th Destroyer Flotilla, Captain Waller's 10th and *Hotspur* and *Havock* from the 2nd. Pridham-Wippell's cruisers, *Orion*, *Ajax*, HMAS *Perth* and *Gloucester*, already at sea, were screened by the rest of the 2nd Flotilla, *Ilex*, *Hasty* and *Hereward*, along with HMAS *Vendetta*.[14] *Jaguar*, *Juno* and *Defender* remained at immediate notice at the Piraeus. Finally, Cunningham had deployed HM Submarine *Rover* on a patrol line off Suda Bay, with *Triumph* south of Milos in the southern Cyclades.

Formidable flew off an air search at dawn, her Albacore 5B locating four cruisers and some destroyers ahead at 07.28. A second Albacore, 5F, sent in a similar report, but gave a slightly different position. Both Cunningham and Pridham-Wippell assumed the two aircraft had located the cruisers of Force B. Earlier Pridham-Wippell had been informed that an Italian reconnaissance plane had spotted them and he had altered course slightly away from the bearing and towards Cunningham, so as to discourage further investigation in that direction. As the vice-admiral was used to Italian air-reconnaissance sorties this aircraft raised no especial alarm, although 'somebody said [it was of a type that] could only have come from an Italian cruiser'. Then, at 07.45, *Orion's* lookouts spotted smoke astern, and a few minutes later Sansonetti's 3rd Division came in sight. Pridham-Wippell immediately reported an eastbound force to the north of him and, turning away, headed south-east at 28 knots, drawing the heavier and faster Italian cruisers towards Cunningham, some hundred miles distant. On receipt of this news Cunningham 'cheerfully' paid up to Power; where there were Italian cruisers, there might also be battleships. 'At intervals', the fleet gunnery officer wrote afterwards, 'a smile could be seen on the face of the tiger.' In fact, neither Cunningham nor his vice-admiral yet realised that another force, that which had been spotted through the clouds by *Formidable's* Albacores, was also on the scene: Ammiraglios di Divisione Legnani's 8th and Cattaneo's 1st Divisions of light and heavy cruisers, with their six destroyers, were to the east of Sansonetti and steaming south-east, parallel to and abeam of Pridham-Wippell, though out of sight over the eastern horizon. Moreover, astern of Sansonetti came Iachino's flagship, *Vittorio Veneto*. All the Italian squadrons were steaming at 30 knots, two knots faster than Pridham-Wippell.

The numbers and dispositions of the Italian fleet were far from clear to Cunningham but, in order to meet up with Force B, Force A increased speed to *Warspite's* current maximum of 22 knots – a limitation which was to cause Cunningham 'much annoyance' in the ensuing hours, for Pridham-Wippell was now reporting the enemy ships with which he was in contact as heavy cruisers. At 08.12, at a range of 13 miles, the Italians' 8-inch guns opened fire.

Devoid of capital ships of their own in the Mediterranean, the German Naval Staff had for some time been planning a major strike with the Italian navy in the Aegean. Iachino, discussing matters in Rome on 15 March, had been made fully aware of German impatience. As a result of the prod, by the 25th plans had been formulated for the operation to be undertaken on the 28th, when it was anticipated that the British would be refuelling after the passages of GA9 and AG9 and preoccupied by the strike at Suda Bay by *Francesco Crispi* and *Quintino Sella*. It was a tight schedule but the plan had the advantage of full support from the

Luftwaffe, who had removed units from Libya to Palermo in anticipation of its role of maintaining full aerial reconnaissance over the whole area, and carrying out air strikes against Crete.

The Regia Marina sailed on 26 March 1941. Iachino left Naples flying his flag in the battleship *Vittorio Veneto*, Capitano di Vascello Sparzani, with the 13th Destroyer Flotilla. The 1st Division of heavy cruisers, *Zara*, *Pola* and *Fiume*, left Taranto under Cattaneo with the 9th Destroyer Flotilla. The light cruisers *Duca degli Abruzzi* and *Giuseppe Garibaldi* of the 8th Division under Legnani, with the 16th Destroyer Flotilla, sailed from Brindisi, and Sansonetti's 3rd Division, the heavy cruisers *Trieste*, *Trento* and *Bolzano*, with the 12th Destroyer Flotilla, emerged from Messina.[15]

Iachino's[16] forces met at their rendezvous east of Sicily and formed up to steam eastwards, but at 12.25 on the 27th the Italian C-in-C was told about the questing Sunderland. The flying-boat's transmission was intercepted and Iachino was slightly reassured by the fact that the Sunderland had obviously not seen the entire fleet, but there was no sign of the promised German air cover so he decided to alter from his reported course, abandon the idea of a strike into the Aegean, and head towards Cyrenaica. Once his location had been reported, he concluded, convoy traffic would be stopped and Cunningham would leave Alexandria, possibly boxing him into the Aegean; Iachino therefore turned south-eastwards, heading to the south of Crete. The aerial reconnaissance report he received later, stating the British Fleet to have been at Alexandria with awnings spread at 14.00 that afternoon, persuaded him to swing back towards the east, onto a course of south-east, and to increase speed to 23 knots. At first light the following day he flew off an aeroplane from *Vittorio Veneto* to sweep east in search of any convoy, and then land at Leros. *Bolzano*'s aircraft was sent over the Aegean on the same task. If neither aircraft reported a target, the admiral decided, he would cancel his mission. At 06.43, however, *Vittorio Veneto*'s IMAM Ro43 floatplane spotted Pridham-Wippell's inferior force only fifty miles away and steaming at 18 knots. Reasoning that a convoy was in the vicinity, and that his own force was overwhelming since Cunningham, still in Alexandria at 19.00 the previous evening, had no prospect of interfering, Iachino ordered speed increased to 30 knots: he intended to annihilate the British cruisers.

Pridham-Wippell was sighted from *Trento* just before 08.00 and reported to Iachino as 'evidently bound for Alexandria'. A few minutes later, at 08.12, Sansonetti opened fire.

These salvoes missed their apparent target, *Gloucester*; Captain Rowley 'snaked the line', his helm full over one way and then the other as his ship evaded punishment. Unsurprisingly, *Gloucester*'s lighter-calibre response, fired at 08.29 as the range reduced to 23,500 yards, fell short. Rowley next catapulted his Walrus and it droned off to spot his fall of shot. Sansonetti swung away for a few moments, then at 08.37 resumed his course, continuing to fire, though his shells failed to reach their target. At this point, Pridham-Wippell's 'four cruisers [were] in line abreast, zig-zagging and making smoke and the four Australian V and W destroyers [*sic*] scattered round us. We were shot at', recalled Commander R. Fisher, 'for quite a long time and lots of salvoes came close – close enough for us to get some splashes on deck – but nobody hit.'[17] At this moment *Vendetta* developed engine trouble and was ordered to proceed independently to Alexandria. Fortunately the Italians did not spot this casualty, and at 08.55 Sansonetti inexplicably turned to port and retired to the west-north-west.

For several minutes the British cruisers ran on, and Iachino was surprised, 'considering the equality of force', that Pridham-Wippell 'had refused to fight'; but the British vice-admiral now hauled round and began to pursue. Meanwhile Rowley had received a report that his Walrus had spotted the combined divisions of Cattaneo and Legnani also heading west-north-west. This report was not made on the correct frequency and was therefore known only to Rowley, though he assumed Pridham-Wippell had heard it. Instead, the vice-admiral was pooh-poohing, as manifestly incorrect, a sighting of three Italian battleships made by Albacore 5F a few minutes earlier. At 09.36 Pridham-Wippell told Cunningham he was chasing Sansonetti's force, steering north-west at 28 knots and 18 miles ahead of the C-in-C.

Iachino still believed the Mediterranean Fleet's capital ships to be at their moorings. Now, at about 09.00, he received a report from Rhodes, derived from aerial reconnaissance, that a carrier, two battleships, nine cruisers and fourteen destroyers had been seen at 07.45 in a position which approximated to his own. As these were also reported as steaming south-south-east Iachino, believing the ships to be his own fleet, informed Rhodes of their blunder and resolved to trap Pridham-Wippell, who persisted in his pursuit. At 10.30 Iachino ordered Sparzani to alter course and *Vittorio Veneto* and her destroyers steamed to the eastward, intending to work unseen to a position north of Pridham-Wippell, on his starboard quarter. At the right moment Sansonetti would turn and drive the British cruisers back on Iachino's heavy guns: it was the boldest manoeuvre undertaken by the Regia Marina during the Mediterranean war.

Pridham-Wippell, meanwhile, deceived by the similarity of *Cavour*-class battleships to the *Garibaldi*-class cruisers, had had no problem in discounting reports of any enemy 'battleships', and thus had no idea of Iachino's meditated aggression. Cunningham was still plodding north-west at 22 knots, but at 08.32 ordered his fastest battleship, *Valiant*, with *Nubian* and *Mohawk*, to push on ahead to Pridham-Wippell's assistance. *Formidable* was also ordered to prepare a torpedo strike force. *Warspite*'s engineering staff had by now partially cleared the blocked condenser intakes and she increased speed so that *Valiant* was unable to overtake the flagship. Hearing that Sansonetti had broken off the action, Cunningham accordingly cancelled his orders and all the capital ships resumed a speed of 22 knots, to allow *Barham* to keep up. Unaware of the force he was in reality opposed to, Cunningham was nevertheless frustrated by his fleet's inability to steam faster. The tiger was not smiling quite so frequently.

Cunningham had already sent a message via the beached *York* at Suda for No. 815 Squadron's aircraft from Maleme to attack enemy cruisers, giving the chasing position of Sansonetti at 08.49; but the message did not reach Maleme until 10.05. Having flown an abortive mission that morning, the Swordfish biplanes took off again at 10.50 and succeeded in locating Sansonetti at noon. They worked round to the south-east and made a down-sun torpedo-attack at 12.05. The Italian ships took evasive action and all torpedoes missed – as did the defensive anti-aircraft fire, so the Swordfish returned safely to Maleme. In the meantime Cunningham had ordered *Formidable*'s strike force airborne, and at 09.56 the carrier turned into the wind to fly off six Albacores, two escorting Fulmars and an observing Swordfish, all led by Lieutenant-Commander G. Saunt.

Unfortunately, Cunningham's informative signal that a torpedo striking force was on its way was assumed by Pridham-

Wippell to indicate that an attack on his own squadron was imminent. At 10.45 the British cruisers, as Saunt's planes over-hauled them steaming in line ahead, opened 'friendly' fire, keeping up 'a steady barrage ... [on the Albacores] until [they] eventually passed out of range ahead'.[18]

In pursuit Pridham-Wippell, with his staff 'feeling braver and braver as we recovered from our first plastering', was blithely entering Iachino's trap. 'It was sunny,' recalled Commander Fisher, 'and the sea was void of enemy; the [gun] turret crews were sitting on the roofs of their turrets, and action bully beef sandwiches arrived ... The commander (T. Wynne) came on the bridge and, with his mouth full of sandwich, nudged me and said, "What battleship is that over on the starboard beam? I thought ours were miles to the east of us." As I took my binocu-lars to examine a vessel hull-down to the northward there was a whistling noise and the first salvo of 15-inch from the *Vittorio Veneto* landed somewhere around. We made a very hurried turn to the south (I think without waiting for our turn signal to be answered [by the other ships in company]), and did another hurried retreat making smoke.' It was 10.58.[19]

This candid admission is eloquent of the circumstances of battle. Iachino was sixteen miles away and Pridham-Wippell ordered speed increased to 30 knots, course altered to due south and smoke made 'by all available means'. Hearing this in *Warspite*, Cunningham was 'electrified'. Geoffrey Barnard, the fleet gunnery officer, recalls the C-in-C stopping the chatter of junior staff officers engaged in wondering 'what on earth' Pridham-Wippell was up to. '"Don't be so damn silly,"' the tiger snapped. '"He's sighted the enemy battlefleet,"' adding for good measure, '"and if you'd ever done any reasonable time in destroyers, you'd know it without waiting for the amplifying report."' Then, pointing at the plotting table, Cunningham ordered, '"Put the enemy battlefleet in at visibility distance to the northward of him."'[20]

As the first 15-inch shells plunged into the water astern of the British cruisers, Sansonetti turned to fall upon Pridham-Wippell's starboard quarter. In the following half-hour the Italian ships closed the range, reducing it to 12 miles and straddling the fleeing British cruisers with their gunfire. Fifteen-inch shells burst around *Orion*, causing some damage, though the Italian gunnery was frustrated by the cruisers' smoke screen which, with a light north-easterly breeze, rolled along astern of them. Only *Gloucester* was visible, and Sparzani's guns shifted onto her until Lieutenant-Commander L. Tyrwhitt steamed *Hasty* across her stern, belching black smoke. As Sansonetti moved in for the kill at 11.27, *Formidable*'s striking force arrived on the scene.

The enemy had been in sight from the air for some time as Saunt's attack, flying at about 90 knots, curved round in pursuit of the Italians to attack them from astern. Lieutnant F. H. E. Hopkins, Saunt's observer, had seen the *Vittorio Veneto* open fire and, 'Since the battleship was steaming at 30 knots, it was clear that our cruisers were in for trouble, and they could expect no help from the main fleet which was more than eighty miles away.' It was now that the tardy Luftwaffe appeared, as 'two German Ju88 fighter bombers dived out of the sun into our formation. They were at once spotted by our two Fulmars. One was shot down in flames, and the other fled.'

But Saunt's flight was still astern of Iachino. With a strong headwind at 9,000 feet, Saunt was taking valuable minutes to catch up with a relative advantage of speed of only 30 knots. 'I think', Hopkins wrote, 'it took the best part of twenty minutes to creep up to a suitable attacking position ahead of *Vittorio* [*sic*]. Throughout … she and her four destroyers kept up a spirited but fortunately inaccurate bombardment with their AA guns.' Hopkins also noted that the battleship was frequently straddling her targets, and that 'the only reason they did not score any direct hits was that the spread of their individual salvoes was too large.'[21]

By now Saunt's Albacores were closing their attack positions. Iachino, who had been almost as surprised as the British to locate Pridham-Wippell, thinking him some miles to the south, had assumed the aircraft coming up astern to be air support from Rhodes, until advised that they were British aircraft. As the Albacores, having finally worked ahead of the battleship, broke into sub-flights and attacked, the first coming in on the starboard bow, Sparzani turned his ship and combed the torpedo tracks. The second group, coming in on the other bow, thought they had hit the *Vittorio Veneto*, as the great ship swung and exposed her entire port side, but they were to be disappointed. At a target speed of 30 knots all torpedoes missed, most passing astern of the speeding Italian battleship, but their effect was deterrent, for they snatched victory from Iachino at the point at which, had he pressed on after the Albacores disengaged, he might well have scored a singular success against Pridham-Wippell.

The British vice-admiral was as unaware of the air attack behind the smoke screen astern of him as he was of the turning-away of both Iachino and Sansonetti. After the Italian shells ceased to fall and the smoke finally cleared, the horizon astern was empty. Relieved, Pridham-Wippell altered course to the north-east intending to join Cunningham, and at 12.24 *Gloucester* reported the British battle squadron in sight.

As for Iachino, despite having fired ninety-four 15-inch shells, he had failed to achieve anything more than a near-miss, and was withdrawing to the north-west at 28 knots, consoling himself with the thought that he had at least made the British Royal Navy run for it.

Cunningham was deeply frustrated not only by the slow speed of his battleships, but by the further requirement of *Formidable* to reverse her course into the easterly breeze to handle her aircraft. Aware that he needed to come quickly to grips with the Italian fleet, he was boiling with impatience. *Formidable*'s pilots having claimed that *Vittorio Veneto* must have slowed because of a torpedo hit, he anticipated battle. Now he learned from a recon-noitring RAF Sunderland that a further force of 'two *Cavour*-class battleships' and some heavy cruisers was also retiring westwards. These were, of course, the cruiser divisions of Cattaneo and Legnani, but with the *Vittorio Veneto* actually 65 miles ahead and steaming at 30 knots, the 'chase' the Mediterranean Fleet was then engaged upon was something of a farce. Even to Cunningham, then in possession of only part of the overall tactical situation, 'it was clear enough [the chase] would be a long one and without reward unless the *Vittorio Veneto* was damaged and slowed up by our aircraft.' An air strike was Cunningham's only option. He had already attempted it and it had failed, but he must perforce try again. *Formidable* was ordered to fly off a second strike. About this time the easterly wind dropped and 'it became a flat calm with occasional light airs from the westward, which meant that *Formidable* could carry out all her flying operations from her station in the line.'[22]

Three Albacores and two Swordfish of No. 829 Squadron were prepared on *Formidable*'s flight deck. They would be led by the squadron commander, Lieutenant-Commander Dalyell-Stead, and supported by two Fulmars of No. 803 Squadron. The weakness of this force is eloquent of the parlous state to which British naval aviation had been reduced by neglect. Cunningham, in anticipation that Pridham-Wippell would draw the Italian fleet onto his heavy guns, now flew off *Warspite*'s two seaplanes for gunnery spotting. At the same time he broke the security of his destroyer screen, assigned two destroyers to Boyd, and ordered *Formidable* to act independently. He then ordered the destroyers to form on their leaders in preparation for their torpedo-attack on the enemy. The three battleships, remnants of the Grand Fleet of 1916, trained their guns to starboard, lumbering on after Iachino, 'their white ensigns contrasted with the cobalt of the sky and the ultramarine of the sea'.[23] The sun was now shining brightly, accentuating 'the black, white and grey camouflage of the great forms of *Warspite*, *Barham* and *Valiant*.' Overhead Saunt's returned aircraft were stacked, waiting to land on the detached *Formidable*. At about 12.30 Dalyell-Stead's strike force took off, allowing Saunt to land and the carrier's crew to eat a hurried meal of tea and sandwiches, while *Formidable* herself charged off at 30 knots in pursuit of the three battleships. Suddenly Captain Bisset roared an alarm: a single SM79 was approaching low over the wavetops. Leaning over the bridge front, Bisset pointed to starboard, bellowing at the unseeing pom-pom crews below him: 'Wake up! Over there! Fire at the buggers!' The Savoia Marchetti was half a mile away when the barrage erupted along the carrier's side; it dropped its torpedo and swung sharply away. 'Hard a starboard!' Bisset ordered, and *Formidable* had leaned to her full helm when he shouted his second warning – another SM79 was approaching on the starboard bow. The forward guns shifted target and the Italian aircraft released its torpedo, banking sharply away. Again *Formidable* swung to starboard, and her officers anxiously counted the few seconds for the torpedo to run; but Bisset had saved his ship and, with relieved smiles all round, *Formidable* swung back to port and resumed her course.

It was at about 12.30, too, that the cracks in the tactical appreciations began to appear. At 12.24, as noted, Pridham-Wippell's cruisers had sighted the British battle squadron, and the two British forces closed. Now, as the moments dragged by, the extent of the distance to Iachino's ships became clear. Cunningham's welcome to Pridham-Wippell was sharp: 'Where is the enemy?' he flashed, to which Pridham-Wippell lamely responded: 'Sorry don't know. Haven't seen them for some time.' 'We were back in the normal ... situation', wrote Barnard ruefully, 'of attempting to catch a much faster enemy with a good start ... It was a bitter anti-climax, and no prudent staff officer approached the "caged tiger" without good cause ...'[24]

At 13.05 Cunningham sent Pridham-Wippell and his cruisers out ahead of the capital ships, at maximum visual signalling distance. 'All afternoon we padded away to the westward,' recalled Fisher wryly, 'once again feeling braver and braver as we recovered.'[25] An hour later *Formidable* caught up with them.

Meanwhile Dalyell-Stead's aircraft flew towards their target, Iachino's flagship. Aware that he was outrunning the British ships, the Italian admiral reduced *Vittorio Veneto*'s speed slightly to conserve fuel in the accompanying destroyers. At noon, informed that *Formidable* had left Alexandria, he had made the incredibly naïve assumption that the British battleships had remained behind. At 12.25 a signal from Rhodes stated that a battlegroup had been located from the air, and Iachino's staff put it about eighty miles to his east. A second message from Supermarina at 13.15 gave the position of an enemy force, obtained by high-frequency radio direction-finding as 170 miles to the south-east. Iachino chose to favour the greater accuracy of the second report, dismissing the first as inaccurate and unreliable, a faulty conclusion influenced by his understanding that *Formidable* had sailed later than she in fact had, which would indeed have put her south-east of him, not east. At 14.20 three RAF Blenheim light bombers from Greece had made the first of a series of unsuccessful high-altitude attacks on *Vittorio Veneto*. Blenheims also attempted to bomb Sansonetti's cruiser division at 15.20 and 17.00, and Cattaneo and Legnani were repeatedly bombed between 15.15 and 16.45.

By 15.00, therefore, the Italian commander-in-chief assumed that, in addition to Pridham-Wippell, a carrier with escorting destroyers was at sea in pursuit, but more than a hundred and fifty miles away. The only real danger to his fleet therefore lay in aerial torpedo-attacks, and he had already endured one of these, which *might* have come from *Formidable* but could equally have originated in Crete or Greece. Iachino felt 'deceived' by the lack of the expected and planned German air cover. Then, at 15.20, as Blenheims again dropped bombs from high altitude, Dalyell-Stead struck.

Preoccupied as Iachino was with the Blenheims, the three torpedo-laden Albacores, *5F*, *5G* and *5H*, 'approached without being sighted until very close' in an attack conducted 'with particular ability and bravery in aircraft which had evidently come from an aircraft-carrier'. The Albacores attacked from ahead as one of the escorting destroyers opened fire on them and turned away. *Vittorio Veneto*'s helm went over in a turn to starboard, as the Albacores loosed their torpedoes at her port side. Seeing the turn the second sub-flight of *5K* and *4B* dived immediately from 8,000 feet on *Vittorio Veneto*'s starboard side, while the Fulmars machine-gunned the battleship's two bridges and upper superstructure. The leading Albacore, flown by Dalyell-Stead himself, was hit and dropped into the sea with the loss of its three-man crew, but within seconds its torpedo struck the *Vittorio Veneto* aft, fifteen feet below the waterline and close to the outer port screw. The ship's side was ripped open, and at 15.30 the engines stopped as the battleship settled by the stern. At this moment a near-miss from a Blenheim made the ship shudder even more, raising another great plume of water alongside her. Iachino and his escorting destroyers slowed so that, to a watching air observer, 'the destroyers made no noticeable wake'.

At 16.30, having been airborne for more than four hours, the surviving Albacores returned to *Formidable*. Boyd signalled to Cunningham that the carrier's planes had scored three possible hits, to which the C-in-C replied: 'Well done. Give him another nudge at dusk.' Anxious to regain contact with his now disabled foe, Cunningham ordered Pridham-Wippell to increase his speed, with *Nubian* and *Mohawk* stretching out ahead of Cunningham to keep a visual link in the clear light. At 17.35 six Albacores of No. 826 Squadron and two Swordfish of No. 829 Squadron under Saunt lifted off *Formidable* with orders to fly back to Maleme after completing a further attack after dark. The flight time would eat up the last hour of daylight, and surprise was anticipated. Unfortunately, as the sun westered two Swordfish from Maleme also made an approach, attracting the anti-aircraft fire of the Italians and removing the element of surprise from Saunt's force, which now arrived on the scene. It was five minutes to sunset.

The damage inflicted by Dalyell-Stead on *Vittorio Veneto* as he died was severe, but her two starboard shafts were soon

revolving again, and by 17.00 the battleship had worked steadily up to a sustainable 19 knots. Iachino now drew his fleet
about him, with his own four destroyers *Alpino*, *Bersagliere*,
Fuciliere and *Granatiere* in a close screen. Cattaneo's 1st Division
of cruisers, *Zara*, *Fiume* and *Pola*, were disposed in line ahead to
starboard of him, with Sansonetti's 3rd Division, *Trieste*, *Trento*
and *Bolzano*, to port. Legnani's *Duca degli Abruzzi* and *Giuseppe
Garibaldi*, with the 8th Flotilla, were sent directly to Brindisi, the
remaining destroyers forming in two lines on the outer wings.
As the Italian warships worked into their new stations, heading
into the sunset, Iachino saw approaching him from the east 'the
planes whose job it was to give us the *coup de grâce* at nightfall'.[26]

Despite the numerous aircraft airborne, the excitement and stress
under which they were operating resulted in a confusing degree
of conflict in their positional reports. There was also the unre-
solved matter of the second *Cavour*-class battle-group reported
earlier. To Commander Power at the tactical plot in *Warspite*, and
to Cunningham preparing for the night ahead, it became essential to establish the true state of affairs. The experienced observer
of *Warspite*'s recovered spotting plane, Lieutenant-Commander
A. Bolt, was carefully briefed, and the Walrus was refuelled and
catapulted again at 17.45. Bolt overflew the area, sighting *Vittorio
Veneto* at 18.20 and observing the Italian concentration of their
forces into five columns: *Vittorio Veneto* was in the centre of a box
guarded at the corners by destroyers; three cruisers were disposed on either flank, with a further line of destroyers outside
this on either wing. Bolt sent his reports direct to Alexandria:
'These signals, repeated by Alexandria W/T to Malta and
Gibraltar [as well as *Warspite*,] were received immediately in
Whitehall ... and the Admiralty had them nearly as soon as the
Commander-in-Chief in *Warspite*.'
    As far as Cunningham was concerned, Bolt's report was not
encouraging. Iachino's position was only 400 miles from Taranto,
and the reported speed of 12 to 15 knots was still too fast for his
liking (and, incidentally, a lower estimate than the 19 knots the
wounded enemy ship was actually making). It gave the British
little advantage in speed and the course, north-west by west, was
not only homeward for the Italians but towards the airbases of
Sicily and Calabria where lay the Luftwaffe's Stukageschwaders.

Moreover, the disposition of the Italian fleet was skilfully defensive, particularly against Cunningham's next option, for the fastest vessels he had were his cruisers and his destroyers. It was to the latter than he now turned his mind. His staff urged caution on all points: the fleet had had no night gunnery practice for months, a night action was always confused and might prove disastrous. With a warning look in his watery blue eyes, Cunningham glared round. 'You're a pack of yellow-livered skunks,' he said. 'I'll go and have my supper now and see after supper if my morale isn't higher than yours.'[27]

Saunt's aircraft, seen by Iachino high astern of him, were waiting for the favourable moments when the Italian battleship would be silhouetted against the afterglow of sunset and they themselves would be almost invisible against the creeping darkness of the eastern sky. High above Saunt's jinking biplanes, Bolt continued to watch, first as Iachino altered course to due west, then as Saunt went in to the attack. It was 19.30 and almost completely dark. At *Alpino*'s first alert all the Italian ships made smoke, the outer destroyers switching on their searchlights in an attempt to blind the incoming British pilots. The anti-aircraft barrage was impassable and the aircraft withdrew, to divide up into individual attacks from different angles. These were unsuccessful, and *Vittorio Veneto* continued to retreat at 19 knots while Saunt's planes, forbidden to return to the darkened *Formidable*, retired towards Maleme. Only three made the distance, the remainder ditching, but all the aircrews survived. Bolt's Walrus was ordered to Suda Bay at 19.50, being relieved by a last Swordfish flown off from the carrier. By 22.00 that evening, Bolt had reported to Captain Portal aboard the damaged cruiser *York*.[28]

For half an hour after the departure of the British aircraft Iachino thought that his luck had held and his anti-aircraft fire had completely frustrated the British air strike. But then he received a report that in almost the last attack *Pola* had been hit. Albacore *5A*, flown through a withering barrage by Sub-Lieutenant C. Williams, had attacked 'a large warship' at wave height, believing her to be *Vittorio Veneto*. Williams's torpedo had struck the cruiser *Pola* amidships, plunging the ship into darkness, stopping her engines and flooding three compartments. *Pola* fell out of the starboard line and dropped astern. When Iachino learned of *Pola*'s predicament he ordered Cattaneo to reverse course and assist her, for her commanding officer had formerly been Iachino's flag-captain. It never occurred to Iachino, he afterwards admitted, that he had the Mediterranean Fleet in his rear. At 21.00, as Cattaneo turned back, Iachino altered course directly for Taranto.

Having eaten his supper, at 20.37 Cunningham unleashed his destroyers, signalling Captain Mack to take the 14th and 2nd Flotillas and 'attack enemy battlefleet with torpedoes'. Forming into two columns, *Jervis*, *Janus*, *Mohawk* and *Nubian*, and *Ilex*, *Hasty*, *Hereward* and *Defender* rapidly worked up to full power and sped away in the darkness to the westward. Both the distance and the speed of the enemy passed to Mack from the tactical plot were inaccurate. The Italian admiral's alteration of course for Cape Colonne, moreover, was to frustrate Mack as he signalled his intentions to Nicholson, leading the 2nd Flotilla, and to Pridham-Wippell, out ahead of the accelerating destroyers. At 21.55 one of Pridham-Wippell's cruisers, *Ajax*, reported that her new radar had located three unknown vessels to the south-west. Mack assumed this report was of an imperfect radar location of his own force, and this mistake was compounded by errors in the actual positions of the respective forces, which confused the relative relationship of all the various units on the plots running in the ships engaged. In fact it seems probable that at this time Mack was actually passing Pridham-Wippell on the vice-admiral's *north-eastern* flank: the strange ships were therefore Cattaneo's force returning on a roughly reciprocal course to succour *Pola*.

Mack pressed on under the delusion that he was working past *Vittorio Veneto*'s starboard beam, and intended in due course to swing round and attack from ahead: at the time Iachino was 28 miles to the north of him, well out of harm's way. Mack now received a signal from Cunningham ordering a retirement to the north-east of all ships not engaged in sinking the enemy. Understandably Mack queried the order even as his ships obeyed it, asking if it applied to him – to be told at 23.37 that it did, but only *after* his attack. Mack therefore resumed his chase until midnight, when he slowed and turned to port, fully expecting to intercept the *Vittorio Veneto* in the coming minutes.

Pridham-Wippell had chased as ordered in line abreast to the west-north-west, spreading his cruisers out at darkness the better to locate an enemy. A report of ships ahead of him led him to reform in line ahead, and the presence of the enemy was confirmed by the flashes and glow of tracer and searchlights low on the horizon which arose from Saunt's Swordfish attack. Night fell with a low mist, reducing visibility. At 20.15 *Orion's* first-generation radar had picked up an echo which, after careful plotting, proved stationary. Pridham-Wippell slowed and reported it to Cunningham in the belief that it was the damaged *Vittorio Veneto*, and that Mack would be directed towards it. It was his job to keep touch with both Cunningham and the remainder of the Italian fleet, and he prudently turned north-east for eight minutes to work round the stationary vessel, anxious not to confuse Mack's plot, and to avoid 'an all-British battle'. The cruisers then headed north-west again, increasing to 20 knots.

Mack did not intercept *Orion's* report, only the later one made by *Ajax* which he thought referred to himself. Pridham-Wippell assumed the same, and it seemed to confirm his appreciation that Mack was making an attack, from ahead, on the disabled *Vittorio Veneto*. Pridham-Wippell, content that Mack had the matter in hand, altered course a little further to the north, to give Mack a clear field, and sped away, intending to turn back and cut off from Messina the remaining cruisers and destroyers of the Italian fleet. As he headed north-north-west, lookouts aboard *Orion* and *Gloucester* saw a red flare on their port sides at 22.43; this was also spotted from *Hasty*. At the time it seemed of little significance, though Pridham-Wippell transmitted a general alarm signal and concentrated his line ahead. Nothing materialised, and at 23.32 the cruisers of Force B swung to the north-east in conformity with Cunningham's signal to do so. As the vice-admiral had left Mack to attend to his business, Mack now left Pridham-Wippell to his; the destroyers continued their attack to the south, still confident of raising the black bulk of *Vittorio Veneto* at any moment.

In fact, at 22.32 Iachino's flagship was 35 miles west-north-west of Pridham-Wippell and 30 miles north-north-west of Mack.

Cunningham's signal to retire to the north-east, received by both Mack and Pridham-Wippell, followed a series of gunflashes seen from both the cruisers and the destroyers. Cunningham's appreciation of the 'stopped ship' report coincided with Pridham-Wippell's: it *must* be the wounded Italian flagship. The

Commander-in-Chief crowded with his staff onto the *Warspite*'s compass platform, the better to see in the darkness. Astern of *Warspite*, in line ahead, came *Valiant*, *Formidable* and *Barham*. HMAS *Stuart* and *Havock* maintained a screen to starboard, *Greyhound* and *Griffin* to port. Speed of advance was again 20 knots on a course of west by north. At 22.03 *Valiant*'s radar had also picked up the 'stopped ship', and at 22.10 Cunningham received the report of a large vessel only six miles away. The battle-fleet altered to port, in quarter-line, *en échelon*, to open the arcs of the battleships' great 15-inch guns as they turned in their turrets onto the enemy's bearing. It was an unprecedented act in naval war, for in a night action it was orthodox to turn away; but Cunningham's views on gunnery were unorthodox. He bemoaned the inaccuracy of his guns, and had earlier written that 'the right range ... to engage an enemy is point-blank ... at which range even a gunnery officer cannot miss!'[29] He had meant it only half as a joke; the other half he reserved for such an event as he was now embarked upon.

At 22.20 *Valiant* reported the target 'S by W at 4.5 miles' and the port-side destroyers were ordered out of the line of fire, to move quickly across the battle-fleet's line and join their consorts on the starboard side. But at that moment Waller of *Stuart* gave the night alarm: ships were in sight bearing west-south-west, passing across the line of advance from starboard to port at a distance of only a little more than two miles!

Led by *Alfieri*, Cattaneo's two heavy cruisers *Zara* and *Fiume* were followed by the remaining three destroyers *Gioberti*, *Carducci* and *Oriani*, which were actually 'crossing the T' of Cunningham's line, unlocated by *Valiant*'s radar. After months of anxious longing to engage the enemy, Cunningham had now stumbled across them in the obscurity of darkness.

Before Waller's alarm had been verbally passed to Cunningham, Edelsten, the new chief of staff, who had sailed with the fleet for the experience before relieving Willis at Alexandria, saw the Italians through his binoculars. Power, a submariner and an expert at instant recognition of silhouettes, immediately identified the heavy cruisers and, in a few tense moments, the big guns swung ominously in their turrets, grey shapes in the greyer darkness, to be laid upon the new targets. The range was to be as Cunningham desired, point-blank.

The order was passed for line ahead again, as the hushed

voices of the gun director floated down to the tense knot of officers crowded on the compass platform; and, as the British battleships swung onto an almost reciprocal course to the Italians, Barnard ordered 'Shoot!', the gongs rang, and the gun muzzles punched the night with gouts of flame and filled the air with the reek of cordite. *Warspite* shuddered throughout her massive fabric at her own discharge, and searchlights from the destroyers and battleships suddenly lit up the target, *Fiume*, 'a silvery-blue shape in the darkness'. The Italians 'were quite unprepared. Their guns were trained fore and aft. They were helplessly shattered before they could put up any resistance.'

Formidable swung hurriedly out of the line as *Warspite*, *Valiant* and *Barham* opened fire. The speed of *Valiant*'s 15-inch gunfire astonished Cunningham, for whom it was a sublime but horrifying moment. 'The plight of the Italian cruisers was indescribable ...', he recalled; 'in a short time the ships ... were nothing but glowing torches and on fire from stem to stern. The whole action lasted no more than a few minutes.'[30]

Rapid fire from the lighter 6- and 4.5-inch guns added to the destruction, and *Fiume* began to fall over to starboard. In just over three minutes *Valiant* fired five 15-inch broadsides into *Zara*. *Fiume* blazed from end to end, the incandescence abruptly extinguished at 23.15 as she sank.

Barham, the rear ship behind *Formidable*, had not quite swung into line ahead as the carrier turned away. She had trained her guns on red lights to port, the flare seen by the lookouts on Pridham-Wippell's cruisers and *Hasty*. These had been thrown up by *Pola*, either as an identification signal or as a warning to the approaching Cattaneo. As *Barham* swung to starboard to get in line she shifted her guns onto the leading Italian ship, the destroyer *Alfieri*, reducing her to a wreck at 3,100-yard range. Caught in *Greyhound*'s searchlight beam by the sudden change of target, the destroyer *Griffin* was straddled by *Warspite*'s 6-inch shells in passing across her bow to clear her field of fire. *Griffin*'s commanding officer, Lieutenant-Commander J. Lee-Barber, recalled being told to 'get out of the way, you bloody fool!' Similarly at risk was *Formidable,* off the starboard side of the battleships. For a moment there was a danger of the carrier receiving fire from *Warspite*'s secondary armament as her searchlight beam swept across the disengaged side to guard against surprise attack from more of the enemy, but the 6-inch broadside was stopped in time. Cunningham now swung the four capital ships through a wide turn to starboard, by fixed-light manoeuvring signal, 'as he would a division of destroyers'. His intention was to avoid any torpedoes fired by the Italian destroyers which were astern of the wrecked cruisers. At 22.38 Cunningham ordered Waller, Lee-Barber, Marshall-A'Deane and Watkins to complete the night's work, and *Stuart, Griffin, Greyhound* and *Havock* moved away from the capital ships.

It was now that Cunningham received the sighting reports of Pridham-Wippell and Mack, of the red flare upon which *Barham*'s guns had been laid. Under the impression that the elusive *Vittorio Veneto* was not far away, Cunningham made the signal for all ships not engaged 'in sinking the enemy' to retire to the north-east on parallel tracks to avoid confusing those committed to tasks. The signal had 'the unfortunate effect' of causing Pridham-Wippell to cease his efforts to gain touch with *Vittorio Veneto*.

In a night of confusions this was just one more, and Pridham-Wippell, though in the eyes of some guilty of breaking the cardinal rule that cruisers should never lose touch with the enemy, was as misled as his chief. It had been a long day, and the night was not yet over.

For the British destroyers left on the field of battle, *Fiume* was in the last of her death agonies, *Alfieri* was limping away to the south and *Zara* was still moving forward, but out of control, ablaze and listing to port. Having threatened the battleships, *Gioberti, Carducci* and *Oriani* completed a full turn to port and withdrew rapidly away to the south, making smoke, while *Griffin* and *Greyhound* gave chase, shot at them, and hit *Oriani*.

Stuart and *Havock* harried *Fiume* and *Zara* in misty darkness lit by the burning ships, aboard which explosions were constantly taking place. Two of the retreating trio of Italian destroyers passed Waller closely and he fired into one, thought to be *Carducci*. Later *Havock* engaged *Carducci*, hitting her with torpedoes and gunfire. The Italian destroyer blew up and sank at about 23.30. A few minutes earlier, *Alfieri* had been seen to capsize and sink.

Within forty minutes *Oriani* and *Gioberti* had disappeared over the horizon and *Griffin* and *Greyhound* abandoned their pursuit, dropping back to *Havock*'s assistance. *Havock* had engaged the burning *Zara*, which was just able to make steam, but now turned her attention on the stopped cruiser *Pola*, which she had just encountered and which her commander, Lieutenant G. Watkins, assumed was *Vittorio Veneto* – an assumption which was passed to Mack, *Warspite* and the other destroyers. Mack was sixty miles away to the west-north-west and turned back to the east-south-east at 00.30 on 29 March. A few minutes later Watkins revised his identification and signalled that he was shadowing, but Mack did not learn of this until 01.34. It was too late for recriminations, though Watkins, as the most junior commander in the engagement, might have expected some rebuke; fortunately, he was far from being the only officer to have made a mistake that night in the confusion of action, darkness, mist, inaccurate tactical information, poor positional data, and faulty judgements.

At 02.00 Mack's destroyers steamed through the wreckage of the action and shortly thereafter came upon the still burning but abandoned *Zara*. Leaving his colleagues to pick up survivors, Mack manoeuvred *Jervis* to fire a spread of five torpedoes, three of which appeared to hit: *Zara* exploded, splitting the night and illuminating the scene of horror and devastation. After the fireball had died away a great cloud of smoke climbed out of the stricken ship, and at about 02.45 she finally gave up the ghost, rolled slowly over, and disappeared.

A few miles away, *Griffin* and *Greyhound* had come up with *Havock* at about 01.40, to find *Pola* 'stopped and longing to surrender'.[31] *Havock* had expended all her torpedoes and requested instructions from Mack as to whether to blow the *Pola*'s stern off with her depth charges. Mack ordered Watkins to 'get clear' and closed the dead ship to take off the 257 remaining crew members.[32] Other destroyers also took up this task, after which *Jervis* and *Nubian* torpedoed the Italian cruiser.

By dawn Mack had rejoined Cunningham. The C-in-C watched his beloved destroyers approach, counting them anxiously, 'feeling fairly certain in our minds that the *Warspite* had sunk a destroyer [Lee-Barber's *Griffin*] in the mêlée the night before.' But the 'bloody fool' had survived and, counting his dozen, Cunningham's heart 'was glad again'.[33]

The annihilation of Cattaneo's squadron had cost not only the Italian admiral's life but those of some 2,400 of his fellow countrymen, yet Cunningham, like the dying Nelson at Trafalgar, had hoped for more. Nevertheless, although he was cheated of his chief objective, the *Vittorio Veneto*, the battle of Cape Matapan had a far more profound effect upon the morale of the Regia Marina than even Taranto, and one which was to help the British in the weeks ahead.

Cunningham steamed back to the scene of the action and recovered a few more survivors, taking the number recovered to 55 officers and 850 men. Sixteen Ju88s now made a belated if vigorous attack; they were driven off by *Formidable*'s fighters, but Cunningham did not wish to expose his ships unnecessarily to Stukas and sent a plain-language signal to the Italians, leaving the recovery of further survivors to them. The hospital ship *Gradisca* later saved another 13 officers and 147 ratings, and yet more were recovered by a squadron of Greek warships which might have taken part in the action had they arrived earlier. Astonishingly, British losses were confined to Dalyell-Stead and his aircrew. A Fulmar was lost when, after engaging the Luftwaffe on the 29th, her engine cut out as she was approaching *Formidable*'s round-down. The aeroplane ditched astern of the carrier, but the crew were picked up by *Hasty*.[34]

For the retreating Iachino there was only the bitterness of defeat. It was no consolation that the Regia Marina were untrained and ill-equipped for night fighting. In the British ships, prisoners were telling their delighted captors that their guns had been trained fore and aft to show they had no intention of fighting! Watching the destruction from *Formidable* in the darkness, a British sailor had remarked to the carrier's chaplain, 'Poor devils, they never had a chance'.

The British Mediterranean Fleet picked up its moorings in Alexandria on the early evening of Sunday, 30 March 1941. As they approached Great Pass, one of the observing Italian submarines was located by sonar. 'Clear the area ahead of the fleet with depth charges,' Cunningham ordered, and the eventful three days ended to the roar of high explosives.

10

'A memorable achievement'

(Operation WINCH, *Convoy ME7, Operations* DUNLOP, SALIENT, TEMPLE, TIGER, *Convoys MW7A and B, and Operations* SPLICE, ROCKET, TRACER *and* RAILWAY*)*

IN THE FIRST few days of April 1941 an escorted Axis troop convoy consisting of the Italian passenger liners *Esperia*, *Conte Rosso* and *Victoria* ran unmolested between Naples and Tripoli, and this was followed by a second convoy of five cargo vessels. Five more freighters followed on 8 April, when the emptied ships of the earlier convoys returned to Italy and further troops and supplies were run to Tripoli. Although a British submarine, Wanklyn's *Upholder*, located one convoy and unsuccessfully attacked it, it was the 11th before a small tanker of 2,474 tons was sunk by the submarine *Tetrarch*, Lieutenant-Commander Greenway. These operations failed to hinder the flow of supplies to the rapidly advancing Afrika Korps.

The British, meanwhile, concentrated on flying a dozen more Hurricanes into Malta during Operation WINCH. Brought out to Gibraltar in *Argus*, the aeroplanes were transferred to *Ark Royal* before she sailed, covered by Somerville in *Renown*, with *Sheffield* and the destroyers *Faulknor*, *Fearless*, *Foresight*, *Fury* and *Fortune* making up the balance of Force H. Somerville's ships were sighted by a reconnoitring Cant aeroplane, but this was shot down by a Fulmar from *Ark Royal* at the eastward extremity of the sortie on 3rd April. The same day the Hurricanes, which 'took off easily and in most cases were airborne between the island and the bows of *Ark Royal*', all arrived safely. Having left

Gibraltar very early on the 2nd, Force H was back at its moorings under The Rock by noon on the 4th, unobserved by the Italian submarines intended to report any such incursion.[1]

Despite the success of this Club Run it became clear, as military disaster overtook the British in Egypt and Greece, that command of the central Mediterranean had been dashed from Cunningham's hands. Yet it is a measure of the man that despite this fading of Malta from the immediate forefront of events, he was still mindful of the whole spectrum of his fleet's responsibilities and, although he came perilously close to it, never quite lost the initiative.

In North Africa Rommel pushed east, took Agedabia and launched an attack on Benghazi, which fell the following day, 3 April 1941. Four days later the Afrika Korps had taken Msus and Mechili, and captured Generals O'Connor and Neame, together with troops and tanks. By the 11th, Rommel's forces had taken Bardia and laid siege to Tobruk. This was bad enough, but the British and Commonwealth forces withdrawn from Egypt to reinforce the Greeks were in trouble too. On 6 April the Wehrmacht had invaded Yugoslavia and Greece. Belgrade was bombed and on the 12th the Yugoslav capital fell, the entire country capitulating five days later. Meanwhile the German assault on Greece was made with heavy air support and overwhelming numbers of troops and armour. The Greek army fell back under pressure from the Italians in Albania, and Maitland Wilson's British, Australian and New Zealand forces, attempting to hold the Germans, were outflanked and compelled to retreat through the mountains. Metaxas's successor, Koryzis, committed suicide, and on the 20th the First Greek Army surrendered. The remaining Greek forces capitulated next day, and British and Anzac forces began to withdraw towards the sea.

Although the British were successful in Eritrea and the Red Sea, revolt in Iraq and the prospect of defeat in the Western Desert made the collapse of the Balkans seem like the final blow. Already committed to acting on the army's flank along the North African shore, Cunningham now had the additional demanding duty of withdrawing the remnants of Wilson's troops from Greece: Operation DEMON was entrusted to Pridham-Wippell. With six cruisers, a score of destroyers, three sloops, two corvettes, the assault ships *Glengyle*, *Glenroy* and *Glenearn*, nineteen transports and many smaller craft, Pridham-Wippell succeeded in evacuating 50,672 men to Crete and Egypt between 24 and 29 April.[2] The operation was not without losses, particularly among the vital and versatile destroyers. *Wryneck* and *Diamond* were bombed by Stukas of Fliegerkorps VIII off Cape Malea. Both ships were loaded with survivors from the transport *Slamat* which, with other British and Greek merchant ships, had been bombed in Greek ports.[3] While in the water the survivors were machine-gunned by enemy aircraft, and only one officer, fourteen ratings and eight soldiers were rescued.

The Germans entered Athens on 27 April, but in North Africa Tobruk resisted their assaults and the long siege of that port began. Supplied by sea, Tobruk was to hold out until December, a constant drain on Cunningham's slender and diminishing resources. He had already been deprived of the elderly carrier *Eagle*, which had been ordered home, and worse was to come.

The deteriorating situation in Greece and a sense of impending disaster in the Balkans notwithstanding, Cunningham's fleet had been active throughout April, both on Rommel's flank and in the central Mediterranean. In order to harry the otherwise largely unmolested Axis supply route between Italy and Libya, he had sent a small force of destroyers to Malta to supplement the 10th Submarine Flotilla. These destroyers, *Jervis*, *Janus*, *Mohawk* and *Nubian*, under Captain P. Mack, initially called the Malta Strike Force, were later better known as Force K. They began a series of nocturnal sorties which, after several frustrated attempts to locate the enemy, yielded their first fruit on 16 April. An Axis convoy of five transports under the close escort of three destroyers was spotted by aerial reconnaissance off Cape Bon at 16.00 on the afternoon of the 15th. Four German merchant ships, *Adana*, *Arta*, *Aegina* and *Iserlohn*, carried between them 3,000 troops, 3,500 tons of military stores and 300 vehicles. The fifth ship, a small Italian cargo ship named *Sabaudia*, was fully laden with ammunition. The escort was provided by three destroyers, *Luca Tarigo*, commanded by the senior officer, Capitano di Fregata de Cristofaro, *Lampo* and *Baleno*. Mack sailed to arrive on the convoy's track off the Kerkenah Bank at night. Turning north to intercept, he was unable to locate the convoy, so he swung inshore and headed south, his destroyers in line ahead following *Jervis*. At about 02.00 the enemy came in sight, silhouetted against the rising moon to seaward. The British crept up, to open fire at point blank on the *Baleno*, nearest escort on the convoy's starboard quarter. *Janus*'s first shells instantly killed Capitano di Corvetta Arnaud and his officers. The other British destroyers laid their guns on the merchantmen as Cristofaro turned *Luca Tarigo* and *Lampo* back from the head of the convoy to engage its assailants. *Jervis*'s gunnery officer recovered his weapons from over-enthusiastic local control just in time to co-ordinate them and discharge a broadside into *Lampo* as *Jervis* raced past at full speed, launching her torpedoes as the British shells tore *Lampo* apart. *Mohawk* delivered a broadside into *Luca Tarigo* which mauled one of Cristofaro's legs, mortally wounding him, but he gallantly continued to direct his ship, loosing torpedoes at *Jervis* and *Mohawk*. One passed beneath the former, another hit *Mohawk*'s stern, disabling her after gun and magazine. Still under fire from the British destroyers, the merchant ships in the convoy took matters into their own hands, boldly attempting to ram the British warships. Both *Jervis* and *Nubian* only narrowly avoided being struck, using rapid acceleration and violent helm movements.

Despite the wreckage aft, *Mohawk*'s shafts continued to turn until a second torpedo from *Luca Tarigo*, fired a few moments before the Italian destroyer sank, struck her in the boiler-room. Slowly the British destroyer rolled over and *Nubian* moved in to pick up survivors as the action died away, guided in the darkness by the familiar strains of the popular song 'Roll out the barrel'! With *Luca Tarigo* sunk, *Baleno* wrecked (she foundered the next day), and *Lampo* aground along with several of the merchant ships, not one of the enemy remained unscathed. Those ships still afloat were on fire, and *Sabaudia*'s cargo now blew up. At 04.00, having recovered as many of *Mohawk*'s men as he could, Mack withdrew, leaving the shattered remnants of the convoy behind him.

The following day seven Italian destroyers, two torpedo-boats and two hospital ships succeeded in rescuing 1,248 men, and while *Lampo* was salvaged a few weeks later, to be afterwards recommissioned, the value of a strike force at Malta had been demonstrated to such telling effect that, despite the loss of *Mohawk*, Churchill's somewhat euphoric reaction to the action off Sfax was to order the complete interdiction of the Tripoli supply route. The Prime Minister's flight of fancy went further, for he suggested that *Barham* should be scuttled as a blockship to close the port itself – a suggestion that an alarmed Cunningham swiftly scotched with counter-plans to bombard Tripoli and pass further supplies through to Malta.

Mack, meanwhile, had returned to Valletta during the forenoon of 16 April with battle ensigns flying. In retaliation, German air raids intensified, and on the night of 18/19 Stukas dive-bombed all the ships in the moonlit port, paying particular attention to Mack's destroyers.

The aerial bombardment of Malta had been steadily intensifying since February when, five weeks after the raids on *Illustrious*, Stukas again appeared over the island. Mixed forces of bombers with a fighter escort of Me109s 'generally came three times a day, with small reconnaissance raids in between to survey the damage'. High-level and dive-bombing attacks were made systematically on specific targets, one after the other. The interim was filled with 'blood-curdling threats' issued over Italian radio which, playing on the religious susceptibilities of the Maltese, promised retribution during the festival of Easter. This intimidation was followed by a heavy raid. Two days later matters worsened. Up to this time the bombing targets had been generally military or naval, though numerous misses had already caused considerable damage to domestic and public buildings; but among the raids following Easter Day was 'a deliberate attack on Valletta itself'. The enemy force consisted of a hundred bombers, and their bombs fell squarely upon the city. Seen from the governor's residence at San Anton, 'The whole of the town and the two harbours were soon completely hidden, lost in white clouds of dust from the stone of Valetta's [*sic*] homes and churches and historic buildings.'[4] The damage was heavy; several of the old *auberges* of the Knights were hit, as were churches and one hospital, not to mention numerous dwellings. In addition, the offices of the civilian government in Valletta Palace were wrecked, water and power were cut off, telephone lines were cut and streets were blocked; but the limestone tunnels protected an uncowed population, to whom the unwelcome enemy propaganda had at least given a timely warning.

Night raids became increasingly frequent, and despite Somerville's recent delivery of Mark II Hurricanes for No. 261 Squadron, RAF, and the stores and ammunition run into the island during Operations MC8 and MC9, Malta remained hard pressed. New anti-aircraft gun emplacements had been erected as the weapons arrived and the defences had steadily increased in potence, but it had become necessary to reorganise their personnel. The Dockyard Defence Battery was disbanded and incorporated into the Royal Malta Artillery, while the Volunteer Defence Force became the Home Guard, enrolling younger men and being rearmed with better equipment than its predecessor.

In the weeks that followed, No. 261 Squadron was reconstituted. The available Hurricanes were to be flown by No. 185 Squadron, stationed at Hal Far, and Nos 126 and 249 Squadrons at Ta' Qali. Luqa remained the bomber station, with additional Blenheims flown in from the west. In due course, on 1 June, Air Commodore Maynard was replaced by Air Vice-Marshal Hugh P. Lloyd, a change of command which coincided with a lull in enemy air activity over Malta.

But the end of April, as well as marking an intense period of bombing, also saw the Regia Marina active in the disputed waters off Cape Bon. Casardi's 7th Cruiser Division, *Eugenio di Savoia*, *Duca d'Aosta*, *Raimondo Montecuccoli* and *Muzio Attendolo*, with a screen of six destroyers, laid two minefields consisting of more than a thousand mines and just under five hundred explosive floats. A further convoy of five troop transports, with a close escort of four destroyers and distant cover from the cruisers *Giovanni delle Bande Nere* and *Conte di Cadorna* and two destroyers, safely crossed from Naples and Palermo to Tripoli, missed by Mack's destroyers though sighted by aircraft from Malta.[5]

It was not merely enemy air raids that placed demands upon Cunningham's planning staff. Although ammunition, petrol, oil and other materials directly related to the war effort were constantly consumed by the defenders of Malta, so too were more mundane commodities. Food was the primary concern: without it, not only would the garrison falter, but the Maltese themselves would lose heart. Nor could the spectre of starvation be ignored; though distant, it was to loom throughout the coming months, a clear indication that the island of Malta was in a very real state of siege. It was at this point that Cunningham countered Churchill's plan to scuttle *Barham* in the entrance to Tripoli, though he bent to the government's imperative 'that every possible step must be taken by the Navy to prevent supplies reaching Libya from Italy . . . even if this results in serious loss or damage to H.M. ships.' Mack's skirmish off Sfax had somewhat mollified London's demands, and other units of the Mediterranean Fleet kept up pressure on Rommel's coastal flank. Then, early on 18 April, *Warspite, Barham, Valiant* and *Formidable*, the cruisers *Phoebe* and *Calcutta*, with a destroyer screen of *Jaguar, Juno, Hasty, Hotspur, Havock* and *Hero*, sailed north from Alexandria to refuel in Suda Bay, the usual route taken to Malta. With them went the fast transport *Breconshire*, laden with boiler oil for the destroyers and also with 'much needed oil and aviation spirit for Malta'. On the evening of the following day, after hours of air attacks on Grand Harbour, Mack in *Jervis*, with *Janus, Nubian* (bearing *Mohawk*'s survivors), and the ill-fated *Diamond*, left Malta to escort convoy ME7, made up of the emptied cargo liners *Clan Ferguson, Perthshire, City of Lincoln* and *City of Manchester*. At dawn on the 20th, *Calcutta* and *Phoebe* joined the eastbound convoy escort, exchanging places with *Jervis* and *Janus*. In addition to these two destroyers, *Gloucester* also attached herself to Cunningham's main body later that evening, as *Warspite* led south to bombard Tripoli.

Cunningham detached *Formidable* and the four H-class destroyers and, with the three battleships, *Gloucester* and the J-class destroyers, located the submarine *Truant*, on station offshore, as a mark. He began his bombardment of Tripoli at 05.00 from a position seven miles off the coast; after a mere forty minutes and the delivery of 530 tons of shells, he withdrew. This colossal expenditure of ammunition, though spectacular, failed to do any permanent damage to the dock installations, though the warehouses were severely hit and oil installations set on fire. Only one cargo ship loaded with ammunition was sunk; five others were hit and the torpedo-boat *Partenope* was damaged, but not disabled. On completion Captain Mack, his strike force now consisting of *Jervis* and *Janus*, with *Juno* and *Jaguar* added, returned to Malta, where the *Breconshire* had meanwhile arrived. Cunningham returned to Alexandria, meeting Pridham-Wippell's cruisers off the Cyrenaican coast where they too had been engaged in shore bombardment. *Formidable*'s Fulmars scored some successes against Ju88s, but the enemy was largely unresponsive.

Cunningham was at pains to point out in his report of the action against Tripoli that the might of the fleet had accomplished, at some risk, little more than what a squadron of Egypt-based bombers could have done with equal facility and at considerably less cost. But the Royal Air Force had begun its distracting bombing offensive against Germany, hitting Kiel and Berlin, and the Royal Navy did not receive the air support it required in either the Mediterranean or the Atlantic theatres while this misguided offensive dominated the minds of Churchill and the Chiefs of Staff. Cunningham wanted a Coastal Command set up for the Mediterranean, and bemoaned the refusal to send Beaufighters to augment the strike capability of the Royal Air Force on Malta. He also wanted a fast tanker, comparable in speed to *Breconshire* (whose actual deep-tank capacity was limited), to speed up fuel deliveries to the island, a requirement which was to echo down the succeeding weeks as Cunningham fought his war at sea on two fronts. Instead of tankers and Beaufighters, he received gratuitous advice which 'seriously annoyed' him, compounding his real problems with an additional 'source of worry'. He cannot have been unmindful of the knives being sharpened in London for Somerville's back, but refused nevertheless to send one of his battleships to reinforce the Malta Strike Force, because of the dubious benefits of such a move as against the certain weakening of the main battle squadron and the considerable drain of so large a vessel on Malta's oil reserves. Instead he compromised, sending *Gloucester*, which as a cruiser possessed a long range. He remained in want of the more economic and effective weapon of strike aircraft like the Beaufighter, which could react quickly, a want underlined by Mack's failure to intercept the enemy convoy referred to above, which slipped south even as Cunningham retired to Alexandria after the bombardment of Tripoli.

Mack's destroyers, continuing their fruitless hunt for the elusive Axis convoy, did however run into the solitary 3,300-ton Italian auxiliary *Egeo*, which was hit by one of a salvo of four torpedoes fired by *Juno* and 4.7-inch shells from *Jervis*; the convoy, it seems, saw the star shell used in the sinking of the *Egeo* and thus evaded interception. Only 26 of the *Egeo*'s crew were picked up next day by an Italian hospital ship; a hundred perished in her wreck.

Mack returned to Grand Harbour, to find *Gloucester* waiting to join his force. The cruiser attracted the Luftwaffe, and for two days heavy bombing took place. With the exception of air defence gunners and fire parties, the crews of the warships were withdrawn into the deep shelters until, to rest his men, Mack took the entire force to sea to cruise east of Malta during the hours of darkness. This routine was repeated the following night. Then, shortly after the strike force's return on the forenoon of 28 April, Grand Harbour was seen to be surprisingly full of ships: the 5th Destroyer Flotilla commanded by Captain Lord Louis Mountbatten in *Kelly* had arrived. With *Kelly* came *Kashmir*, *Kelvin*, *Kipling*, *Jersey* and *Jackal*, the light cruiser *Dido* and the fast minelayer *Abdiel*, all carrying cargoes of *matériel* for Malta.[6]

The presence of Mountbatten's ships as reinforcements for Cunningham highlighted both the problem and the value of Malta. Lying in Grand Harbour busily guzzling fuel, *Kelly* and her sisters underlined both the utility of the island as a strategic oiling port, and also the importance of sustaining that facility. Too much emphasis cannot be put upon the simple fact that victory in the Mediterranean relied on the maintenance of a supply train which extended for hundreds of miles beyond the southern end of the Suez Canal. From fuel oil originating in the Persian Gulf to the bars of confectionery known as 'nutty' which came from Britain and were enjoyed as a small comfort by the crews of the warships, the disparate and diverse sinews of war were, collectively, fundamental to British achievements in the Mediterranean, as elsewhere. The laden merchant ships that left Alexandria under the escort of Cunningham's battle squadron either carried transhipped cargoes brought to Egypt in other vessels, or had made long hauls from world-wide ports of departure. Malta convoys were, in fact, simply the culmination of a far greater convoy system which, with the integrated supply organisation behind it, made it possible for the Royal Navy to prosecute its business.

This business was to reach a critical importance in the next few weeks, as the Battle for Crete began, in which the 5th Destroyer Flotilla was to play its part. Mountbatten's destroyers were originally intended to relieve the Malta Strike Force, but they were subsequently diverted to Crete, and their brief presence at Valletta merely attracted heavier bombing raids.

The 5th Flotilla had left Gibraltar at 22.00 on 24 April as part of Operations DUNLOP and SALIENT. While Cunningham bombarded Tripoli, Somerville, previously operating in the Atlantic, had been unable to mount a diversion in the western Mediterranean because of mechanical defects in his squadron. At dawn on the 24th *Argus* had arrived with twenty-two more Hurricanes, and these had been transferred to *Ark Royal*. Operations DUNLOP and SALIENT then got under way. *Dido*, *Abdiel* and the 5th Destroyer Flotilla, coded Force S, were followed out of Gibraltar Bay an hour later by Force H, which headed directly east. Somerville had only the sketchiest idea of what was happening in Greece, where the defeat of the British and Anzac troops was then in progress.

Force H reached the flying-off position at 05.15 on 27 April, and within an hour all the fighters were airborne. Having then flown off an anti-submarine patrol and a fighter air patrol Force H withdrew to the west, though remaining in a position to assist Force S as it raced eastwards, to arrive safely at Malta on the following day.[7]

Captain Mack left *Janus* in Grand Harbour with Mountbatten's ships for essential repairs, and pushed on to the eastwards on the evening of 28 April; with him went *Dido*, *Abdiel*, and the discharged *Breconshire*. Astern of them, Mack's departing ships' companies saw the sky lit up with enemy bomb flashes and tracer from the shore-based island air defences and the guns of the 5th Destroyer Flotilla. These air raids resulted in serious damage to the port and to shipping lying in it.

As April ended and the Wehrmacht completed their occupation of the Greek mainland, a single merchant ship on Admiralty service, the Pyman Brothers' *Parracombe*, was run unescorted through the Western Mediterranean towards Malta. She had sailed from Leith and proceeded via Methil and Oban, where she embarked a Spanish national, one Luis Diaz, as 'navigator'. The *Parracombe* finally left Britain as part of the outward convoy OG59, but detached under the special escort of the corvettes *Columbine* and *Gardenia* to pass through the Strait of Gibraltar during the night of 28/29 April. When off Europa Point the escort was ordered to detach, and patrol vessels were under strict instructions to let the solitary merchantman pass unchallenged so that nothing might draw attention to her. As the *Parracombe* passed Gibraltar, Captain D. Hook mustered all hands and told them they were bound for Malta. The crew then turned to and under Diaz's direction transformed the ship, painting the neutral Spanish flag on her bow as they hung precariously over the side on stages.

The ship had been volunteered by her owner, a Mr J. Bilmeir, who seems to have been addicted to such schemes. Under the provisions of Operation TEMPLE the *Parracombe* sailed through coastal waters under false colours, first flying the Spanish national colours and later hoisting the tricolour as a Vichy French merchantman, having painted the French ensign on her bow over the Spanish. At this point she assumed the identity of a French merchant ship, the *Oued-Kroum*, which name now adorned her hull. It was intended that she should hug the French North African coast, as though bound for Sfax, until she was past Cape Bon, when she would make a dash for Malta, receiving fighter cover when fifty miles off the island. As *Parracombe* steamed east, she was infected with premonitions. Her master, Captain Hook, a veteran blockade-runner of the Spanish Civil War, was aware that his vessel would have to cross enemy mine-fields, in the dark. The risks were appalling, the odds heavily stacked against success.

East of Cape Bon, in the early hours of 2 May, the *Parracombe* struck a mine which detonated ammunition in her forward holds. The explosion destroyed the fore part of the ship, includ-ing her bridge and boat deck, killing many of her crew. As the survivors jumped over her side she went down by the head, taking more men with her, so that thirty of her company were either killed by the explosion, or drowned; a large amount of debris rising from the wreck enabled the remainder to stay afloat. An Arab fireman subsequently died of exposure, while the remaining eighteen survivors were picked up by a French sea-plane and landed at Bizerta. Here they were questioned before being moved on to Tunis, where they were marched through the streets barefoot and insulted and spat upon by the crowds. In due course *Parracombe*'s survivors were interned in a Vichy camp at El Kef, near Sfax. They were a Glasgow 'crowd', and some, singled out as trouble-makers, were separated from the rest and sent to Bordj-le Boeuf; from here they later broke out, stole a train, and eventually met up with American troops landed as part of Operation TORCH.

Nothing was heard of *Parracombe* after the corvettes left her and the British authorities remained in ignorance of her fate for many months, though it was correctly assumed that she had hit a mine. She took with her to the bottom twenty-one crated Hurricanes with all their spares, rocket projectors, ammunition, and a quantity of military stores. It is difficult to justify the wisdom of such an operation, if such it can be called, yet the ruse was to be repeated several times. As elsewhere, the running of single ships, unless they possessed the high speeds of passenger liners, was a folly that cost the loss of valuable lives, ships, and *matériel*.[8]

In the wake of Cunningham's raid on Tripoli, Casardi's 7th Cruiser Division again put to sea and successfully laid a minefield north of the port, a movement unopposed by the British although Mountbatten was at sea on the night of 1/2 May in quest of Axis shipping. He had sailed to intercept a supply convoy bound to Tripoli from Augusta and Messina which had been reported and attacked by Malta-based aircraft and submarines. Three German and two Italian merchant ships, with a heavy escort, had assembled in Sicilian waters on 30 April, to be run simultaneously with a returning empty convoy of one Italian and four German cargo ships.[9] Two of the unladen northbound vessels were sunk by Wanklyn's *Upholder*, but Mountbatten had no luck. The frustrated Malta Strike Force, returning to Grand Harbour on 2 May, fell victim to an aerial mine dropped in the approaches. *Jersey*, following *Kelly*, *Jackal* and *Kelvin* through the entrance, was blown up; thirty-six of her company were killed, and her wreck sank across the entrance, effectively blocking it. Mountbatten and his three leading destroyers were thus mewed up, while *Kipling*, *Kashmir* and *Gloucester*, left outside, were compelled to proceed to Gibraltar.[10] Admiral Ford now mobilised the resources of the dockyard, and the stern of the wrecked *Jersey* was blown off to clear the fairway – an operation of intense significance, because approaching Malta at the time were a number of ships with a critical role to play in the events then unfolding in the Middle East theatre. Had the entrance to Grand Harbour remained blocked, it would have compromised the huge effort then being made by the major operation designated TIGER.

Operation TIGER was a direct result of Churchill's insistence on the situation in the Western Desert being 'stabilised'. The regular supplies reaching Rommel's Afrika Korps had ensured that the tide of German victory rolled inexorably eastwards. Tobruk was beleaguered, its fighters lost, its air defences reduced to anti-aircraft batteries, and ships engaged in its replenishment were constantly sunk.[11] Meanwhile the German occupation of Greece raised the disturbing likelihood of an air assault on Crete, which Churchill and the Chiefs of Staff considered to be impending.

On Sunday, 20 April, Churchill received an intelligence appreciation from Wavell emphasising his weakness in tanks, despite the fact that he had on the ground sufficient trained personnel for six tank regiments. Knowing that WS7, a large convoy of munitions including tanks, was on the point of departing from the Clyde and Liverpool, bound for Suez round the Cape of Good Hope, Churchill 'resolved not to be governed any longer by … Admiralty reluctance …' and insisted that instead of proceeding round the Cape the fast cargo liners containing the tanks should detach from WS7 near Gibraltar and form convoy WS8, which would then pass straight through the Mediterranean to Alexandria. Moreover, the entire might of the Royal Navy in that sea was to be mobilised to cover its passage, simultaneously pushing additional reinforcements and supplies through to Malta from both Gibraltar and Alexandria. Churchill's personal minute to General Ismay and the Chiefs of Staff bore his absolute imperative command: *Action this day*.

Operation TIGER was aptly named.

The Chiefs of Staff were not optimistic, but Pound bowed to Churchill's forcefulness; in addition, Air Marshal Portal finally agreed to send a squadron of Beaufighters to Malta, and these passed through Gibraltar on 3 May. Meanwhile an attempt was made to load an extra sixty-seven Mark VI tanks into a sixth ship in time, but delays in the docks prevented her from joining WS7. All this hurried preparation was made in the knowledge that Axis reinforcements were in train, with the German 15th Armoured Division on its way to Libya.

On 4 May what Somerville called 'a proper jig-saw of destroyer exchanges and refuelling', necessary to initiate TIGER, got under way at Gibraltar. In the late afternoon the battleship *Queen Elizabeth*, on her way from Britain to join Cunningham's fleet, left Gibraltar with the destroyers *Foresight*, *Fortune*, *Fearless* and *Velox* to relieve the battlecruiser *Repulse* and the destroyers *Havelock*, *Harvester* and *Hesperus* from the escort of convoy WS8 – which had now broken away from WS7 and was headed for the Mediterranean – so that they could run ahead and bunker at Gibraltar. Having been so dramatically excluded from Grand Harbour, *Gloucester*, *Kipling* and *Kashmir* arrived at Gibraltar that evening. *Gloucester*'s run of bad luck had continued: when passing the Sicilian Narrows she had entangled and exploded a mine in her paravane wires, and shortly afterwards was hit by a bomb. She was sent straight into drydock as a matter of urgency.

During the forenoon of 5 May Somerville left Gibraltar in *Renown*, with *Ark Royal* and the cruisers *Fiji* and *Sheffield*, following *Kashmir* and *Kipling* out as the destroyers swept ahead hunting for submarines, in the usual 'westward blind' intended to deceive the watching spies in Algeciras. To the west of Gibraltar Somerville made his rendezvous with WS8, supported now by the cruiser *Naiad* flying the flag of Rear-Admiral E. King, the battleship *Queen Elizabeth*, and her four destroyers.

The five ships of WS8 contained 238 tanks, the majority of which were the 'cruiser' type required by Wavell, as well as guns and forty-three crated Hurricane fighter aircraft. The speed and secrecy considered so vital had led to the route for the merchantmen being kept from them until almost the last moment. As Churchill instructed, 'Everyone on board the convoys must think they are going round the Cape'. However, on the night of 5/6 May the convoy, made up of the *Clan Lamont*, *Clan Chattan*, *Clan Campbell*, the *New Zealand Star* and the *Empire Song*, together with its heavy escort, passed the Strait. As it did so *Faulknor*, *Forester*, *Fury*, *Havelock*, *Hesperus* and *Harvester* joined, the last three tagging on having slipped out of Gibraltar Bay as late as 03.30. Less than an hour later a hastily patched-up *Gloucester* raced after the mass of eastward-bound shipping, while *Repulse*, for lack of adequate anti-aircraft armament, and (it appears) *Velox* were left at Gibraltar. Somerville's Force H and King's convoy and escort followed diverging tracks, the latter making a series of feints off Cape da Gata, but converged as they approached the Sicilian Narrows.

Although German radio broadcast the fact that Force H was at sea (for the ships had passed through a concentration of Spanish fishing boats as they made their westward feint), Somerville's destination remained secret. The element of surprise was maintained until the forenoon of 8 May, when a shadowing aircraft sighted the convoy. In the afternoon, the first torpedo-bombers appeared: 'eight or nine wicked looking brutes' skimmed in shortly after 14.00. *Renown* was the first to open fire and Captain McGrigor handled the great ship with consummate skill until, to Somerville's horror, as the battlecruiser combed the track of an approaching torpedo the weapon suddenly altered course through a right-angle and headed straight for Renown's bow. Providentially, however, the torpedo had ended its run and slowed to a stop, sinking ten yards from the passing warship as Somerville and his officers watched in relief.

The wide spacing of the heavy warships that allowed this freedom of movement 'also permitted Ark Royal to operate her aircraft with greater ease, and it was fascinating to watch the way in which she hauled out of line to fly on or fly off her machines constantly patrolling overhead ...' The attack was fierce, and the attackers split up into small groups which 'swooped upon the ships from different directions, some coming low and others straightening out at a few thousand feet; twisting, turning and diving, at one moment catching the glint of sun on their wings, at the next appearing black against the background of blue ... Every ... ship including the merchant ships in convoy [opened fire] ... until the sky was full of bursting projectiles and the air around was stabbed by the tracers of short-range weapons.'[12] Ark Royal was straddled and Queen Elizabeth was near-missed on her port bow.

The torpedo-carrying Heinkel IIIs, accompanied by SM79s, Junkers Ju88 dive-bombers and Fiat CR42s, were engaged by fighters from No. 808 Squadron, embarked in Ark Royal. The squadron commander, Lieutenant-Commander Tilliard, and his observer, Somerville's nephew, were shot down and killed in the action. With unseasonal cloud cover at 5,000 feet, the bombing attacks were driven down to an altitude at which, for once, the fleet's gunnery proved capable of satisfying Somerville. This was as well, for Ark Royal had sailed with only a dozen Fulmars available to provide air cover; but one of these, piloted by Lieutenant R. Hay, succeeded in shooting down a shadowing Savoia Marchetti at 17.10.

Further attacks followed towards twilight, with Stukas and Ju88s of the Luftwaffe, escorted by a dozen Me110s, flying in to attack. Sadly, a failure of interceptor release gear in Renown's port 4.5-inch battery resulted in No. 3 gun firing two rounds into the adjacent mounting, killing five men, wounding five more, one mortally, and injuring a further twenty-two. The air attacks were finally driven off with no further casualties. Seven enemy aircraft had been shot down, four by anti-aircraft fire, three by fighters, at a cost of two Fulmars, the crew of one of which had been recovered. Hard-pressed, *Ark Royal*'s Fulmars had been reduced to seven serviceable machines; at times there had only been two airborne, while the others were refuelled, repaired and rearmed.

At 19.00, as the convoy approached the Skerki Channel, the merchantmen, hitherto disposed in two columns, formed a single line to minimise mine damage. Force H was turning away when three low-level Italian torpedo-bombers made a sudden attack on *Ark Royal*. 'It was', recalled *Queen Elizabeth*'s navigating officer, 'the most spectacular incident yet … Shells burst all around them, tracer bullets were seen to enter their fuselage[s], but still they came on. At length one was seen to crumble and crash, but not before it had dropped its torpedo at a range which must have been less than 200 yards. The other two released their torpedoes at about the same distance; then, banking sharply, made straight towards *Queen Elizabeth*, passing so close to her port side, and only just above the level of the sea, that hardly any guns could be depressed sufficiently to bear.' Fortunately, caught in the very act of turning, *Ark Royal* successfully combed the torpedo tracks, but the attack was one of those claimed by the German propaganda broadcaster William Joyce, known to the British population as Lord Haw-Haw, to have sunk *Ark Royal*.

In the wake of the attack, Force H completed its planned turn back to the westwards. Somerville intended to hover off Algiers and await the return of the destroyers, under Captain De Salis in *Faulknor*, which were to escort convoy WS8 to Malta, to fuel at Valletta and then rejoin his flag prior to the whole force returning to Gibraltar.

The sun was now setting and the full moon rose. Convoy WS8[13] and its close escort of the K- and the F-class destroyers of the 8th Destroyer Flotilla, with the *Queen Elizabeth*, *Fiji*, *Gloucester* and *Naiad*, pressed on eastwards, all hands remaining at action stations. The sea was mirror-smooth, the ships drew luminous phosphorescence in their wakes, and moonlight gleamed dully on the steel superstructures of every vessel. But a low mist limited visibility and succeeded in shrouding them from surface attack.

The convoy had escaped the Axis air forces and predatory torpedo-boats, but the minefields in the Sicilian Narrows now took their toll, despite the paravanes streamed from A-frames over both the merchant ships' bows and those of the destroyers. The *New Zealand Star* detonated a mine, but although she sustained damage was able to carry on. The fourth merchantman in the line, *Empire Song*, was less fortunate: she struck two mines and, slowing the line astern of her, began to sink. As the following ships bunched up and reduced speed, so that the huge *Queen Elizabeth* was down to six knots, a torpedo-bomber made an attack on the battleship. Desperately Captain C. Barry increased speed and flung his helm over, sounding his alarms, hauling *Queen Elizabeth* out of line, in a reaction that saved his ship by a margin of some twenty feet. The torpedo, churning its own arrow of bioluminescence through the dark sea, was clearly visible to those fearfully watching its passage.

The battleship drew past the sinking *Empire Song*, her decks 'crammed with tanks and aircraft ... the crew quietly making preparations to lower boats ...' Commander Salter was ordered to embark survivors in *Forester*. He thought the salvage of the freighter was a possibility and summoned the master to the bridge, but found him drunk and incapable. Instead he persuaded the *Empire Song*'s rather reluctant chief officer to go back, with some of his own and some of *Foresight*'s men. The destroyer's whaler was on its way when 'there was a sudden terrific explosion ... lifting tanks, guns, aircraft and motor vehicles high into the air where they seemed to hang grotesquely before they fell into the sea ... It was a terrifying spectacle ... as the air was filled with flying debris,' much of which showered *Foresight*. A large steel plate killed a man on deck, in the whaler one man was killed and another had a foot blown off, and the destroyer's deck-plating was penetrated.

Empire Song disintegrated. Eighteen of her crew were killed, and in addition fifty-seven tanks, ten Hurricanes, munitions and equipment were lost with her.[14]

During these events, Cunningham's fleet was steaming west from Alexandria. The first ships to sail, on 6 May, were those of the 'slow' 10-knot convoy MW7B, consisting of the Norwegian tankers *Hoegh Hood* and *Svenor*, bearing a total of 24,000 tons of desperately needed oil fuel.[15] These were followed by the 'fast' 15-knot convoy MW7A, made up of the cargo-liners *Settler*, *Amerika* and two other Norwegian ships, the freighters *Talabot* and *Thermopylae*. These were escorted by the cruisers *Dido*, *Phoebe*, *Calcutta*, *Coventry* and *Carlisle*, three destroyers and two corvettes. The remaining available destroyers screened Cunningham's main fleet.[16] Flying his flag in *Warspite*, the C-in-C was accompanied by *Valiant* and *Barham*, the carrier *Formidable*, and Pridham-Wippell's cruisers *Orion*, *Ajax* and HMAS *Perth*, and by the *Abdiel* and *Breconshire*, both loaded with supplies for Malta. The latter was fitted for refuelling the destroyers, which she accomplished on 7 and 8 May. Because of aerial mines, each capital ship was swept out of Alexandria individually, a time-consuming business which was further hampered by a dust-storm. Cunningham's departure coincided with Somerville's from Gibraltar.

Until the following day, however, Cunningham remained ignorant of the state of the channel into Grand Harbour. Ford had succeeded in clearing most of the impediment of *Jersey*, but expressed grave concern to Cunningham over the intensity of enemy air attacks, which were known to have seeded the approach to Grand Harbour with mines, leaving Mountbatten boxed up and fuming inside. Cunningham directed his staff torpedo officer to give the matter some thought, and Commander W. Carne came up with the idea that every available motor torpedo-boat or harbour defence motor launch in Malta should drop depth charges to detonate the mechanisms of the magnetic mines on the sea-bed. This was done, resulting in numerous explosions, and the channel thus 'cleared' was buoyed. Even so, on the morning of 9 May the corvette *Gloxinia*, fitted for minesweeping and streaming her gear, detonated about a dozen more mines as she led the ships of MW7 A and B, plus *Abdiel* and *Breconshire*, into Grand Harbour. Mountbatten slipped out to sea on 9 May, intending (but too late) to join *Orion*, *Perth*, *Dido* and *Phoebe* in meeting the TIGER convoy coming through from the Narrows, while Captain De Salis and the destroyers of the 8th Flotilla entered Valletta, refuelled and then hurried away to the west to rejoin Force H. *Foresight* overheated a shaft bearing and this slowed the flotilla until she was compelled to turn back. The delay compromised De Salis, who by dawn the following morning was not as far west as had been planned, and the flotilla was attacked in the Skerki Channel by aircraft eager to make up for their failure the previous day. *Fortune* was ringed by bombs and these near-misses affected her steam turbines; her speed rapidly fell off and she received bomb damage aft. Hearing of this, Somerville ordered Force H to full speed, in defiance of the advice of his staff. Afterwards, James Somerville firmly repudiated criticism of this action: 'I couldn't leave my little boats unprotected, though in cold blood I ought to have. If Dad does not take a chance in helping the Boys, the latter will inevitably lose confidence.' Ever cautious and unwilling to take on unacceptable risks Somerville may have been, but he was not one to dodge the responsibilities of his rank. As the shapes of Force H loomed out of the sea har to the west, the destroyers' companies cheered their approach. 'Dad' was clearly appreciated, and notwithstanding the damage to *Fortune* Lieutenant-Commander Sinclair was able to work her up to about ten knots, despite being heavily awash aft.

As Force H returned to Gibraltar, Somerville continued to exercise his ships ruthlessly. *Ark Royal*'s Fulmars carried out dummy torpedo attacks using the Italian tactics so recently experienced; *Sheffield*'s Walrus was sent out on a reconnaissance; a destroyer was detailed to tow a target for *Ark Royal*'s Swordfish to dive-bomb, while a second wave of Swordfish exercised with dummy torpedoes afterwards recovered by a destroyer. Not for a moment were the ships' companies of Force H to be allowed to feel complacent, or that they had earned a respite. It was another way in which 'Dad' looked after 'the Boys'.

Mountbatten joined Cunningham in time to take part in the second bombardment of Benghazi. The first took place during the night of 7/8 May, when Captain McCarthy in the cruiser *Ajax* detached from Cunningham's westward-bound fleet with the destroyers *Imperial*, *Hotspur* and *Havock* to shell the port. On completion of this task McCarthy ran into and engaged two enemy transports, one of which exploded after suffering gunfire while the other ran aground and caught fire.

Meanwhile, just as Somerville was engaged by both the Luftwaffe and the Regia Aeronautica on 8 May, so too was Cunningham, with similar negative results. Intervention of the Regia Marina failed to materialise, although a division of Italian cruisers and destroyers sailed from Palermo. The sortie was too late and too half-hearted ever to have had any prospect of success against so formidable a force as Cunningham's, and seems in retrospect to have been little more than a token gesture.[17]

Hearing that Pridham-Wippell's cruisers had met the merchantmen of convoy WS8 and were now heading with them for Alexandria, Cunningham turned east again, redeploying his fleet as it steamed through fog. He left Mountbatten in *Kelly*, with *Jackal*, *Kashmir*, *Kelvin* and *Kipling*, to shell Benghazi again on the night of 10/11 May. More than 850 rounds of 4.7-inch shells fell onto the port, then Mountbatten detached to sweep up the Axis convoy route between Tripoli and Messina. Having so clearly advertised its presence, Mountbatten's flotilla was duly attacked by Ju87s of II Stukageschwader under Leutnant Rieger. These, the first night attacks by dive-bombers, scored no direct hits but shook both *Kelly* and *Kelvin* with near-misses.

The Alexandria-bound merchantmen of convoy WS8 arrived safely on 12 May to begin discharging their tanks. In London, Operation TIGER was considered 'a memorable achievement', but Cunningham countered the First Sea Lord's congratulatory telegram with an expression of his own dissatisfactions. The merchantmen of WS8 in Egypt discharged speedily, but it was discovered that neither the tanks nor the Hurricanes had the sand filters necessary for desert warfare: as a consequence, not only did they have to spend some time 'under one roof, a few hundred yards from *Warspite*', vulnerable to the nightly German air raids, but the delay in fitting the filters consumed a third of the saving of time in getting them to the front gained by passing them directly through the Mediterranean. Furthermore, Cunningham deplored the fact that the assessment of TIGER as 'a memorable achievement' gave the impression that he had exaggerated the difficulties: the 'apparent ease with which a convoy was brought through from end to end of the Mediterranean, caused many false conclusions to be drawn at home'; in fact, 'the success of the operation must be ascribed to the thick and cloudy weather, which for that time of the year … was unprecedented.'[18]

By 12 May, at the conclusion of TIGER, all British naval units had returned to their respective bases – Cunningham to Alexandria, Somerville to Gibraltar, and Mountbatten to Malta where, lacking any intelligence of enemy convoys, he remained until the 21st, when he was ordered to Crete. Malta, safe for the moment, was now to recede from the list of priorities facing the Mediterranean Fleet. Between 11 and 14 May, almost immediately upon the opportune withdrawal of the British from the central Mediterranean, Axis convoys resumed. Six loaded southbound ships and two convoys of emptied freighters were escorted to Tripoli by the destroyers *Aviere, Geniere, Grecale, Dardo* and *Camicia Nera*, covered by the cruisers *Giovanni delle Bande Nere, Conte di Cadorna, Duca degli Abruzzi* and *Giuseppe Garibaldi*, and nine destroyers.[19] Seven Axis supply ships were run south between 19 and 21 May, escorted by *Euro, Folgore, Fulmine, Strale* and *Turbine*, with cover from *Duca degli Abruzzi, Giuseppe Garibaldi, Granatiere, Alpino* and *Bersagliere*. These were attacked by HM Submarine *Urge*, unsuccessfully, though Lieutenant-Commander Tomkinson caused sufficient confusion to precipitate a collision between two of them. He sank a ship of 4,856 tons off Tunis the next day but missed the cruiser *Duca degli Abruzzi*, while *Upholder*'s attack on two northbound convoys failed.

Minor successes were scored by the British submarines *Taku*, which sank a small cargo vessel off Calabria, and *Tetrarch*, which sank a ship of 2,300 tons off Benghazi on the 18th, but these were offset by several losses. On the 13th the *Undaunted* was sunk by depth charges thrown by the torpedo-boat *Pleiadi* off Tripoli, adding to the loss of *Usk*, believed to have been blown up by a mine off Cape Bon on the 3rd. Also on the coast of North Africa, the gallant little gunboat *Ladybird* was finally bombed and sunk, while in Tobruk the hospital ship *Karapara* was bombed.

If Mountbatten's Strike Force achieved little during its brief sojourn at Malta, British submarines continued to harry the Axis supply lines with increasing success. Wanklyn may have failed in his attack on the northbound convoys, but sank a ship of 4,854 tons off Messina on the 24th, and later the same day earned himself a Victoria Cross when *Upholder* attacked a troop convoy composed of the liners *Conte Rosso, Esperia, Marco Polo* and *Victoria* shortly after its departure from Messina at sunset. His submarine's hydrophones were defective, but Wanklyn torpedoed *Conte Rosso*, 17,879 tons, in defiance of the close escort of the destroyers *Camicia Nera* and *Freccia* and the torpedo-boats *Procione, Orsa* and *Pegaso*. Some 1,680 of the 2,500 troops on board *Conte Rosso* were picked up while *Upholder* endured a spirited counter-attack.

At the western end of the Mediterranean, Somerville continued the Club Runs towards Malta. Operation SPLICE, between 19 and 22 May, saw forty-eight Hurricanes flown off *Ark Royal* and *Furious* on the 21st, all of which arrived safely. Force H provided the cover and the Italian submarines *Corallo* and *Diaspro* did not interfere.[20] The next Club Run, Operation ROCKET (5–7 June), was a virtual re-run of SPLICE. Thirty-five Hurricanes were flown into Malta, led by eight Blenheim bombers from Gibraltar. On 13 June, Force H sallied again for Operation TRACER, covering *Ark Royal* and *Victorious*, which on the 14th flew off forty-seven Hurricanes, led this time by four Hudson bombers.[21]

Operation RAILWAY was mounted in two phases, and was less successful. The first, with twenty-two Hurricanes transferred aboard *Ark Royal* from *Furious*, which was acting as a ferry from Britain, sailed from Gibraltar on 26 June. Led by Blenheims, the Hurricanes took off in bad weather, and all arrived safely but one, which crashed on landing. Force H returned to Gibraltar on the 28th, to turn round and sail again the following day after *Furious*, fresh from a dash home for more aircraft, had transferred further Hurricanes to *Ark Royal*. The remaining crated aircraft were then assembled on board *Furious* as she joined for phase two of RAILWAY. From the flying-off position south of the Balearics at 06.00 on 30 June twenty-six Hurricanes left *Ark Royal*. The first Hurricane took off from *Furious* at 05.00 but the second fighter slewed across the flight deck and struck the port navigating position. A long-range fuel tank was knocked off and caught fire, and although the Hurricane fell overboard the fire spread rapidly, killing nine men and burning four more before the ship was turned off the wind and stopped. The fire was eventually doused and in due course the operation resumed, so that by 12.45 some thirty-five Hurricanes and six Blenheims had landed on Malta.[22]

These successes were however overshadowed by the disaster which had occurred in Crete and the waters surrounding the island, where the Royal Navy had endured heavy losses.

11

'On the verge of disaster'

(Magic Carpets and Operation SUBSTANCE, *with Convoy GM1)*

ON 20 MAY 1941 the German high command launched Operation MERKUR, the invasion of Crete. The primary assault was made by airborne forces under General Student, backed up by a seaborne assault largely frustrated by the Royal Navy, but at terrible cost, for the enemy enjoyed air supremacy. German paratroops, swiftly reinforced by the 5th Mountain Division, landed by gliders and frustrated the defence of General Freyberg which, covering likely landing-points, was quickly isolated as the enemy seized Canea and Maleme in the west of the island and Heraklion and Retimo in its centre. The British and Anzac defenders inflicted very heavy casualties on the paratroops and there was fierce fighting for possession of Maleme airfield, vital for the landing of the gliders, but a decision to regroup for a counter-attack permitted the Germans to take it. Their seizure of Maleme, under the umbrella of the Luftwaffe, opened the door to Student's reserves, and Freyberg's hard-pressed troops, already short of equipment, were compelled to retreat across the island's mountainous spine.

Meanwhile a furious battle was taking place between the Royal Navy, intercepting further seaborne reinforcements, and the Luftwaffe, hell-bent on achieving overwhelming superiority in the sea area north of Crete. As Freyberg withdrew the remnants of his forces to Sfakia, on the south coast, Cunningham's fleet was receiving terrible punishment. Freyberg's decision to evacuate the island, taken on the 27th, switched the task of the

Royal Navy from that of preventing the enemy reinforcing their forces by sea to that of evacuating Freyberg's troops.

The unfortunate *Gloucester*, crippled by a shortage of anti-air-craft ammunition, was sunk on the 22nd, the same day that another cruiser, *Fiji*, was also lost to German aircraft, defending herself in her final moments with practice ammunition. Later, on 1 June, a third cruiser, *Calcutta*, was sunk as she proceeded north to provide anti-aircraft fire-power to the evacuation. Six destroy-ers, *Juno, Greyhound, Kashmir, Kelly, Imperial* and *Hereward*, were also lost; *Warspite, Barham, Formidable, Naiad, Carlisle, Ajax, Dido, Orion, Perth* and six destroyers suffered damage, several seri-ously. Two thousand naval personnel were killed in extricating some 15,000 troops, and half of Freyberg's soldiers were left behind. The defeat coincided with the advance of Rommel and the Afrika Korps to the Egyptian border and, insofar as the Royal Navy was concerned, with the highly emotive loss of *Hood* to the guns of *Bismarck* in the North Atlantic.

Before the débâcle Cunningham had written to the First Lord, repeating his concern over the lack of aerial reconnaissance, pleading for more fleet fighter aircraft, and requesting help over a shortage of 5.25- and 4.5-inch anti-aircraft ammunition. Malta too was in difficulties, for Ford had reported serious losses of Hurricanes to the superior German machines now engaging them in the skies overhead. 'I feel great anxiety for the future,'[1] Cunningham wrote on 18 May, the day on which the contest for mastery of Crete opened with a heavy air attack on *Coventry* as she patrolled south of the island.[2]

Cunningham received little encouragement from home, beyond some additional flag-officers. Their arrival proved timely, however, for Cunningham had decided that he person-ally would be better employed ashore, in an office near the Gabbari Docks at Alexandria. He therefore appointed Pridham-Wippell to command the battle-fleet in his absence, and the vice-admiral hoisted his flag in *Queen Elizabeth*. The 15th Cruiser Squadron was now commanded by Rear-Admiral King in *Naiad*, the 7th by Rear-Admiral Rawlings in *Orion*, and Rear-Admiral Glennie was in command of the destroyers, his flag in either *Dido* or the depot ship *Woolwich*. Thus the burden of the active sea fighting around Crete was borne by Cunningham's subordinate admirals. Despite numerous acts of gallantry performed by men of his fleet, Cunningham remained analytically critical, attributing one reason for the ensuing losses to 'the disregard of a golden rule ... never to detach ships for any particular tasks. The fleet should remain concentrated ...' The impact of the battle for Crete was best summed up by Cunningham himself, as he received news of his fleet's mounting succession of losses: 'Sea control of the Eastern Mediterranean', he reported to the Chiefs of Staff in London, 'could not be retained after another such experience.' In the event, the experience was not yet over, and Churchill was cabling General Wavell in Cairo that 'Victory in Crete [was] essential ... Keep hurling in all you can', even as Freyberg's exhausted men were being overwhelmed.

The loss of Crete had two important impacts upon strategy in the Eastern Mediterranean. Although Suda Bay had proved inadequate as a logistical base, the presence of an oiler at anchor there had greatly helped British operations both in the Aegean and on the convoy route to Malta. To this loss of such a useful facility was now added the presence of the Luftwaffe in Crete, 'on the flank of our convoy route to Malta', making the replenishment of the island from the east 'costly and hazardous'.[3] Moreover, the advance of Axis airbases to Crete also provided an air umbrella for Axis ship movements in and about the Aegean.

On the other hand, the tying-down of German troops in the Balkans and the delay the campaign ultimately caused Hitler's invasion of Russia are now known to have been critical. Similarly, the losses among Student's paratroops dissuaded OKW from an air assault on Malta. But the consequences of these events lay in the long term; the immediate future faced by Cunningham and his fleet was bleak. Not only was Alexandria now even more vulnerable to enemy air attack, but the arm of the Luftwaffe extended to Port Said and Ismailia on the Suez Canal and even to the anchorage of Suez Bay itself. The threat to the unloading and transhipment of war supplies was explicit, and on 14 July Ju88s operating from Crete bombed and ignited the 27,750-ton Cunard–White Star liner *Georgic*. Fortunately the transport had discharged her troops at Port Tewfik, but she burned for two days before sinking.[4]

The continuing supply of Tobruk, although 'more or less a matter of routine', resulted in a string of serious losses among the smaller vessels in the fleet and remained a 'costly undertaking'.

The ships of the 10th Destroyer Flotilla, an Anglo-Australian force consisting of *Stuart*, *Vendetta*, *Waterhen*, *Voyager*, *Vampire*, *Defender*, *Decoy* and *Dainty*, augmented by the sloops *Flamingo*, *Auckland* and *Parramatta*, were frequently engaged by enemy aircraft, and by the end of June both *Waterhen* and *Auckland* had been lost off Bardia; the first, damaged by dive-bombers, was under tow by *Defender* when she sank. Then, on 11 July, *Defender* herself was bombed, and sank off Sidi Barani the following day when under tow by *Vendetta*.

As for the sea-route to Malta, it was now effectively enfiladed by enemy air bases in both Crete and North Africa. 'To send convoys to Malta from the east was to court disaster ...,' Cunningham recalled. 'The best we could do ... was to get out two of our minelaying submarines, the *Cachalot* and *Rorqual*, and to start them off on regular trips with what petrol and essential supplies they could carry. It was not very much. As regards petrol, each submarine took sufficient to keep the ... aircraft in Malta in operation for about three days.' In a detailed situation report sent to London, Cunningham emphasised that 'We are on the verge of disaster here for we stand to lose [the] fleet and thus Malta, Cyprus and Egypt unless we act at once (repeat) at once.'[5]

Complications with the Vichy French in Syria which necessitated the diversion of surface and submarine forces to the Levant further burdened Cunningham, while an attempt to turn the tide in the Western Desert, Operation BATTLEAXE, failed lamentably, and with it any hope of wresting air power from the Axis by means of the capture of the airfields along the Cyrenaican coast. German bombers dropped mines on Alexandria harbour during the night of 7/8 June, most of which landed on the Arab population of the great city, causing panic and a suspension of work in the dockyard. Although many of the men returned within a few days, Cunningham was now forced to send his badly damaged warships through the Suez Canal to repair yards in Britain, South Africa and the United States. Thus *Warspite* and *Barham*, among others, left the Mediterranean for the time being, as did *Formidable* a month later. Cunningham received a few reinforcements. Among these, some minesweeping vessels and the fast minelayer *Latona* arrived in thirty-six days from Britain, laden with a cargo of Oerlikon guns for the fleet, anti-tank guns for the army, and other essential supplies, including ammunition.

*

During British preoccupations with Crete and Syria in June and the first half of July, the Italians had bestirred themselves, laying further minefields in the Sicilian Channel and off Malta[6] and Tripoli.[7] Italian submarine patrols were not particularly effective; of the four off Cyrenaica, only *Malachite* fired torpedoes and these missed their target, the cruiser *Phoebe*. Those hoping to intercept Force H in the Western basin were also disappointed, for after phase two of Operation RAILWAY Somerville made no Club Runs during the first three weeks of July. In the matter of reinforcing Rommel, the Axis were much more successful. A six-ship convoy was passed across to Tripoli at the end of May, despite an attack by British aircraft from Malta. These enjoyed more success a few days later when, off Tunisia on 3 June, Blenheims sank two 6,000-ton cargo vessels, the *Beatrice C* and the *Montello*, out of a six-ship convoy. A returning Axis convoy in late June, though frequently attacked by British aeroplanes, reached Trapani and Naples without major loss, though two ships were damaged. Similarly, four large Italian troop transports moved from Naples to Tripoli by way of Taranto, and though the *Esperia* sustained slight damage from marauding British aircraft, the convoy, its escort and heavier distant cover all escaped harm. Hit by an aerial torpedo delivered by a Malta-based Swordfish from No. 830 Squadron flown by Lieutenant Osborn, the Italian tanker *Panuco* survived, and although she was compelled to return to Italy with 6,000 tons of petrol undischarged, she did so unscathed, living to fight another day. These virtually unimpeded movements of supplies, often routed eastwards first, under the Luftwaffe's extended umbrella, greatly increased the strength of the Afrika Korps.

British and Allied submarines operating throughout the Mediterranean in late May, June and July did however deny the Italians the overwhelming initiative they ought to have been able to seize. *Triumph*, based on Alexandria as part of the 1st Submarine Flotilla, torpedoed the auxiliary cruiser *Ramb III* off Benghazi on 30 May and sank the Italian submarine *Salpa* off Sollum at the end of June; she was in action again on 6 July off Benghazi, when Lieutenant-Commander Woods sank the Italian coaster *Ninfea* and her escort, the gunboat *De Lutti*, in a surface engagement. Operating out of Gibraltar, Commander Ingram in the submarine *Clyde*, Lieutenant-Commander Campbell in *Severn*, and Luitnants ter Zee 1e Klasse De Booy and Van Erkel of the Dutch submarines *O24* and *O23* sank between them seven enemy vessels. In the central Mediterranean *Unique*, *Utmost*, *Urge*, *Upholder* and *Union* accounted for a further seven. Making an attack on an Italian convoy off Cape Bon, *Union* was sunk by the *Circe* on 20 July, but on the 28th Lieutenant-Commander Cayley in *Utmost* sank an Italian troopship of 11,500 tons, and a torpedo from *Upholder* damaged the Italian cruiser *Giussepe Garibaldi* as she returned from providing cover to an Axis convoy from North Africa. In addition to successes in the Aegean and Adriatic, on 5 June *Taku* unsuccessfully engaged the Italian anti-submarine trawler *Valoroso* and a tug and tow she was escorting, following up this success by sinking two more Italian merchant-men a few days later. Similarly, on 5 July *Torbay*, commanded by Lieutenant-Commander Miers, sank the Italian submarine *Jantina* and several coasters.

By the end of July the British offensive was beginning to bite. Axis convoys continued to make the passage, but the loss of the 7,000-ton former Norwegian tanker *Brarena* and the 8,000-ton German ammunition ship *Preussen* impacted upon the Axis supply route, and Berlin approached the Vichy French for assist-ance. Thanks to prevarication on the part of Admiral Darlan, nothing came of this initiative.

British efforts to sustain Malta through this difficult period never let up, however apparently small and insignificant each individual consignment appeared. Submarines bound for the Mediterranean called at Gibraltar to load whatever they had capacity for. Many managed no more than a few hundred gallons of kerosene, but *Talisman*, bound for Alexandria, dropped off 5,000 gallons of high-octane aviation spirit for the aerial defend-ers of Malta.[8]

Meanwhile the so-called Magic Carpet shuttle runs by *Cachalot* and *Rorqual* from Alexandria to Malta carried on. *Cachalot* escaped detection despite surfacing off the Great Pass (from the trim dive made by every submarine as she left harbour) amid a slick of heavy boiler oil: unknowingly she then leaked her own trail across the eastern Mediterranean, which the enemy fortu-nately failed to see. On the misty night of 30 July 1941, however, her luck ran out. Proceeding on the surface having delivered sup-plies and personnel, she sighted and prepared to attack an escorted enemy tanker making for Benghazi. The tanker made smoke as Lieutenant-Commander Newton engaged, then out of the smoke and mist patches dashed the torpedo-boat *Generale Achille Papa*. Flashless cordite was not supplied to the Mediterranean fleet until September of the following year: Newton, already hampered by the mist and the smoke screen, therefore failed to see the approaching warship until she was about half a mile away. Tenente di Vascello Rosica was approaching at full speed with the obvious intention of ramming *Cachalot*. Ordering his gun crew below, Newton was unable to dive quickly because of a jammed hatch.

Realising that a ramming was inevitable and his boat was defenceless, Newton now ordered *Cachalot* abandoned, in the hope of saving as many men as possible. The *Achille Papa* struck the *Cachalot*, ripping open a ballast tank but failing to rupture the pressure hull. Newton increased speed to make a run on the surface, but Rosica swept the *Cachalot* with gunfire and he was compelled to scuttle, his crew scrambling out onto the casing. Rosica picked up his surrendering enemies and remained on the scene for some time in a vain attempt to find the one man who failed to escape, a Maltese steward.[9]

Notwithstanding this loss, the Magic Carpet runs to Malta during July 1941 alone carried 84,280 gallons of petrol, 83,000 gallons of kerosene, 6 tons of munitions including aircraft ammunition and submarine torpedoes, 30 tons of general stores, 126 service passengers, and 12 tons of all-important mail. Remarkable though this was, a submarine was no substitute for a merchant ship with her capacious holds.

It is a measure of the quiet organisation that united British merchant and naval shipping that, despite the disaster of Crete, early June marked the first planning of the next major operation to relieve Malta. Code-named SUBSTANCE, it began in conditions of utmost secrecy, initiated by Cunningham, who on 2 June 1941 pointed out to Pound, the First Sea Lord, that as the Mediterranean Fleet was 'absorbing most of the attention of the Luftwaffe ... it would be a good idea if a convoy were run in to Malta from the west.'[10] In this the British were fortuitously aided by the withdrawal of a substantial part of Fliegerkorps X for redeployment on the Polish border prior to the surprise attack on Soviet Russia which began on 22 June.

Cunningham was incapable of supporting Malta directly, but his battle-fleet was to make a conspicuous sortie between 23 and

24 July while two of his submarines radioed manoeuvring signals from positions west of Crete to simulate the continuing westwards progress of *Queen Elizabeth* and her consorts as they quietly slipped back to Alexandria under cover of darkness. These two operations, ME2 and ME3, were at least partially successful in hoodwinking the enemy, small but vital components in the greater movement of shipping now under way from the westward and code-named Operation SUBSTANCE.

The masters of the merchantmen nominated for Operation SUBSTANCE had no idea of their destination, nor initially of the convoy organisation that would subsequently unite them. There was a deliberately vague air about their assembly. On 27 June the *Port Chalmers*, discharging a cargo of frozen mutton from New Zealand in Avonmouth, was taken over by the MoWT for special service and ordered to Newport, across the Bristol Channel, but nothing more was imparted to her master, Captain W. Higgs. On arrival at Newport, however, the loading of a mixed cargo began at once. Quantities of cement, wheat and maize, cigarettes, corned beef, cloth, guns, ammunition, vehicles and aircraft parts filled the ship, and No. 4 Hold was entirely taken up with 2,000 tons of cased petrol in four-gallon cans. That matters were far from routine was confirmed for Higgs when, on the eve of departure, 250 officers and men of the Royal Artillery embarked, along with a regular naval liaison officer, Lieutenant-Commander Stirling. Moreover, six Bofors guns were fitted to the ship to supplement her seven Lewis guns and the old 4.7-inch gun on her poop. On 11 July, still ignorant of her destination but escorted by the Dutch destroyer *Jacob van Heemskerck*, *Port Chalmers* left Barry Roads and, joined by the Blue Funnel liner *Deucalion* from Swansea, proceeded north towards the Mersey.

The following morning the fast cargo-liners *Sydney Star* (12,696 grt) and Ellerman's *City of Pretoria* (8,049 grt) emerged in fog from the Mersey, escorted by destroyers. The two portions of the convoy proceeded for some time on parallel courses, unaware (such was the secrecy prevailing) of who was commodore. After a while a brief exchange of signals resolved the matter, and Captain T. Horn of the *Sydney Star* ordered the ships to fall into line abreast with his own ship. So ingrained had the habits of convoy discipline become that his fellow masters immediately conformed.[11]

At 06.00 on Sunday, 13 July 1941, a further group of ships from the Clyde joined off the Mull of Kintyre; these were the former French liner *Pasteur*, two more Blue Star cargo-liners, the *Melbourne Star* (12,806 grt) and the *Avila Star*, the Federal Steam Navigation Company's 10,893-grt *Durham*, and the Irish Sea ferry *Leinster*. The merchantmen formed up and steamed south, bound for Gibraltar, becoming convoy WS9c, one of 'Winston's Specials'. The convoy commodore responsible for the command and control of the merchantmen was Captain D. MacFarlane, master of the *Melbourne Star*, and joining them was a powerful escort: out of the Atlantic fret loomed the battleship *Nelson* and the cruisers *Arethusa*, *Manchester* and *Edinburgh*, the latter flying the flag of Rear-Admiral E. Syfret, together with a screen of destroyers. It was only now that the masters were informed by their naval liaison officers that they were bound for Malta.

During the passage south, Syfret exercised his disparate command. As Higgs afterwards wrote, 'The random collection of merchant ships, each normally accustomed to going its own way alone, gradually became a unit ... ready to [act] simultaneously.' It was as well, for at one point the cruiser *Manchester*'s steering gear failed and she sheered wildly toward *Port Chalmers*, hoisting the 'not-under-command' signal.

A few alarms disturbed their passage and *Avila Star* detached, not being a part of the operation; then on 20 July, as the convoy and escort approached the Strait, a destroyer from Gibraltar, HMAS *Nestor*, arrived, shooting a line aboard each merchant ship in turn and sending over orders to be opened when instructed.

The convoy spent the daylight hours west of the Strait undergoing strenuous exercises, had a brief break until 20.20 and then, after a final flourish of manoeuvres, steadied on course for the passage into the Mediterranean. Fog and squalls accompanied them, causing great anxiety on the bridges of the merchant ships, which had no radar and whose lookouts stared into the white blindness, trying to keep their eyes on the fog buoy towed by the ship ahead (these were small devices which threw up a plume of water by which the next ship astern could keep station); but in the end they switched on their navigation lights, and *Port Chalmers* kept station on a cargo hatch light thoughtfully hung over *Deucalion*'s stern.

Suddenly the merchantmen cleared the fog; lights were

hurriedly doused and speed was increased to close formation, but not quickly enough to avoid a rebuke from *Edinburgh* to *Port Chalmers*: 'You were a long way astern even before the fog came down. It is vital that close station be kept both by day and night.' It was a reproof Higgs took 'meekly'.

As WS9c made the transit of the Strait that night it metamorphosed into convoy GM1. Revolving about its steady progress at 14 knots, the warships dashed ahead to top up their fuel and effect troop transfers at Gibraltar. At about 03.30 the wind had dropped and the fog cleared sufficiently for Somerville to order some of the supporting warships to sail from Gibraltar. With them went the troop-carrying ferry *Leinster*. Unfortunately the fog patches persisted and the *Leinster*, without benefit of radar, ran aground off Carnero Point and was left behind, there being no time to transfer her passengers, air force personnel intended to maintain the Beaufighter squadrons now stationed at Malta. This misfortune was compounded by the difficulties experienced in transferring troops into several of the warships. Soldiers had been brought out to Gibraltar in the *Pasteur* (which proceeded no further), but the organisation for moving them into the warships was woefully inadequate. The commanding officer of the troops had embarked with his adjutant in *Edinburgh* 'leaving another officer to take over the administration ... for which considerable naval help eventually proved necessary', the Admiralty complained to the War Office. 'The military officers responsible' had 'insufficient knowledge of the numbers of troops concerned and the quantities and stowage position of gear and equipment.'[12]

Convoy GM1 debouched into the Mediterranean at dawn in tolerable order and the masters were told to open their secret orders. They were from Somerville, who wrote: 'For over twelve months Malta has held out most gallantly against all assaults of the enemy. Until Crete fell we were able to supply Malta from both ends of the Mediterranean, but since [then] ... the situation has changed. For the present Malta can only be supplied from the west and this is the task with which we have been entrusted ...' There followed the customary exhortations to avoid making smoke and showing lights, to keep station and a good lookout. Somerville warned the masters of the enemy's technique of occupying their attention with high-level bombing, then attacking at sea level with aerial torpedoes, and of the long periods they would have to remain at varying states of readiness. He concluded with the simple order: 'THE CONVOY MUST GO THROUGH!'

In addition to *Nelson*, *Manchester* and *Arethusa*, the fast minelayer *Manxman*, the fleet destroyers *Cossack*, *Maori*, *Sikh*, *Lightning* and HMAS *Nestor*, and the Hunts *Eridge*, *Avon Vale* and *Farndale* had arrived from the Home Fleet as escort to the merchantmen of GM1. With the exception of *Nelson*, which joined Force H as Somerville followed them, these vessels formed Force X, commanded by Syfret. Force H consisted of Somerville's flagship, the battlecruiser *Renown*, *Nelson*, the carrier *Ark Royal*, the cruiser *Hermione* and the destroyers *Faulknor*, *Fearless*, *Foxhound*, *Firedrake*, *Foresight*, *Fury*, *Forester* and *Duncan*.[13]

The movements of shipping in and about Gibraltar had been complex. Between them the two 'door-keepers' had made substantial deployments of submarines, with two off Naples, one off Palermo, a second off Marittimo and a third off Cagliari. Two more guarded the southern end of the Messina Strait, another the northern.[14] The usual complications of refuelling destroyers and cruisers had passed off well, only the troop transfers from *Pasteur* and the temporary loss of *Leinster* marring the smooth running of the arrangements. Somerville's force had dispersed among it about 5,500 troops, some in the warships *Manchester*, *Arethusa*, *Cossack*, *Maori* and *Sikh*, which had dashed in to Gibraltar to embark them, others already aboard the merchantmen.[15]

The departure of the warships had been delayed by wind and fog, and the latter persisted intermittently until daylight was well established, causing some confusion as the various groups of ships took up their stations.[16] Initially air reconnaissance was carried out by Sunderlands from Gibraltar, *Ark Royal* keeping her fighters ranged on deck but otherwise not advertising her presence at sea by flying her Swordfish. In the event no enemy submarines were detected, but two neutral or Vichy French merchant ships were sighted during the 21st.

The additional reinforcement of Force H by the ships from the Home Fleet indicates the commitment behind this operation, hence Somerville's imperative that the convoy must succeed, for intervention by the Regia Marina was expected. Additional fuel was to be made available by means of the oiler *Brown Ranger*, sailing in company escorted by the Town-class destroyer *Beverley*. In the mist *Brown Ranger* had been mistaken by the over-flying Sunderlands for *Leinster*, a report that led to a degree of confusion in *Renown* but was soon cleared up once it became known what had happened to the 'personnel vessel'.

In addition to the reinforcements moving from the west, the opportunity was to be taken to pass a westward convoy, MG1 (not to be confused with the later naval operation so designated), of emptied merchant ships from Malta. As well as the Commissioned Supply Ship *Breconshire* there were several Norwegian ships, the *Talabot* and *Thermopylae*, both owned by Wilhelm Wilhelmsen of Trondheim, the tanker *Hoegh Hood*, owned by Leif Hoegh, and S. Ugelstad's *Svenor*. The *Settler*, originally a French ship belonging to the Charente S.S. Company which was now under the management of T. and J. Harrison of Liverpool, and *Amerika*, run by the United Baltic Corporation on behalf of the MoWT, made up the rest of MG1. Vice-Admiral Ford thought these vessels should for preference be sent to Alexandria, where cargoes were already waiting for some of them; but the impassable nature of the eastern Mediterranean and the importance of getting them away from Malta, where they were little better than magnets drawing the attention of enemy bombs, over-rode this desideratum. *Breconshire* and *Talabot* were capable of 17 knots, *Thermopylae* and *Amerika* of 14 and the remainder of 12, a fact which complicated their withdrawal as only a single destroyer, *Encounter*, was available to escort them.

On the afternoon of the 21st Somerville's Force H overtook the Malta-bound convoy, altered course further to the north-east-wards and, at about thirty miles' distance, reduced speed to 18 knots. A single Italian aircraft sighted it next day, but failed to detect the convoy with its close escort and Force X beyond. Syfret's destroyers spent the 22nd refuelling from *Brown Ranger*, whereupon the oiler and *Beverley* turned back for Gibraltar.

Meanwhile, at noon Force H swung to the west for two hours and, having reduced the distance from the convoy, at 14.00 resumed an easterly course. Enemy aircraft were sighted in the distance, but *Ark Royal*'s fighters failed to intercept them due to high-altitude cloud. To maintain all possible secrecy, Somerville and Syfret communicated via a Gibraltar-based Sunderland, which used Morse code to flash the news that Somerville would close with the convoy next morning.

During that afternoon radar indicated the presence of enemy aircraft, but again the Fleet Air Arm Fulmars failed to locate these. Then, at twilight, *Hermione's* radar staff vectored the Fulmars onto an improperly identified target which turned out to be a patrolling Catalina from Gibraltar. The flying-boat was holed and her gunner had both legs wounded by this friendly fire.[17] While this unfortunate incident was taking place the ships of Force H streamed their paravanes and later turned west for ninety minutes, reducing to twenty miles the distance between themselves and the convoy and Force X.

The first serious contact with the enemy occurred shortly before midnight when the Italian submarine *Diaspro*, lying on the surface, fired a salvo of torpedoes; these were detected by Sub-Lieutenant P. Colclough, RANVR, of HMAS *Nestor* stationed on the starboard wing, and the force took avoiding action. Four torpedoes exploded at the ends of their runs, and lookouts on *Nestor* saw two of the tracks pass ahead of and under their ship. Commander A. Rosenthal immediately counter-attacked, and made three passes before contact was lost. Although shale oil was smelt on the night air, 'there was no material evidence of . . . destruction'; in fact, Capitano di Corvetta Dotta had escaped, and claimed to have sunk an unspecified ship.[18]

Early the next morning, the 23rd, Fulmars flew off from *Ark Royal*, but although two enemy reconnaissance aircraft were sighted from the ships, the attempt to vector the Fulmars onto the shadowers was frustrated by low sun, mist and the failure of radar to pick up low and distant targets. By 07.00, however, radio intercepts of Italian air-to-ground traffic had revealed the enemy to be aware of the presence of both groups of ships as they now met.

By 07.45, as the convoy approached the sector most easily reached by aircraft from Cagliari, Force H joined Force X and the convoy, Somerville's flagship and *Hermione* protecting *Ark Royal* as a 'flexible port column of the convoy, with the object of providing anti-aircraft protection whilst still remaining free to manoeuvre for flying.'[19] *Nelson, Manchester, Edinburgh, Arethusa* and *Manxman* were stationed closer to the convoy as, zigzagging, it pursued a mean course of due east, at a speed of advance of 13.5 knots. Ahead of the large ships a crescent of destroyers was spread across the van of the entire formation. The sky had been blown clear of cloud by a light north-easterly breeze and the sea state was slight, conditions which soon revealed the combatant forces to one another.

At 09.15 *Port Chalmers* was two cables astern of her station, though increasing speed to catch up; *Manchester*'s captain flashed 'S stands for Straggler and Sunk'.[20] Sixty miles away to the north-east small formations of enemy aircraft had now been located on radar. Half an hour later eight high-level SM79 bombers, flying overhead from south to north, dropped their payload on the convoy itself. Up went the barrage, the Bofors guns aboard *Port Chalmers* 'pointed to the zenith' and Stirling, the naval liaison officer, called out 'Hit the bastards! Hit one of them, for God's sake!'[21] But the Italian planes were too high, and it was time for Somerville's warning to be recalled as, simultaneously, six torpedo-armed SM79 bombers flew in from right ahead, splitting into two groups of three and sheering off as the crescent of destroyers in the van of the formation opened a barrage of anti-aircraft fire. Nevertheless, 'it took some seconds to depress the guns' as a well-planned attack developed, one aircraft from each group banking and crossing the ships' line of advance, flying in to concentrate upon the destroyer *Fearless* stationed on the extreme starboard wing of the screen. The two remaining torpedo-bombers on the port side of the convoy then attacked the merchantmen, as did their opposite numbers on the starboard side. Within minutes, as the convoy took avoiding action, the attack from the port side had succeeded in hitting *Manchester* with one torpedo, and 'the two aircraft which attacked *Fearless* released their torpedoes from a height of 70 feet and a range of about 1500 and 800 yards respectively. Avoiding action was taken and the first torpedo passed about 90 yards ahead. The torpedo from the second aircraft ran shallow. Course was shaped to comb the track but when abreast the stem on the port side, at a distance of about 30 feet, the torpedo broke surface, altered course to port, and hit the ship …' This consequence followed what Commander Pugsley of *Fearless* called 'a most resolute attack in the face of good shooting'.[22]

Fearless was entirely disabled, her engines out of action, her rudder jammed over to port, her switchboard wrecked, and all power gone. Her after fuel tanks and stern were ablaze, and twenty-five men were dead or dying. Exploding ready-use

ammunition in the vicinity was partially jettisoned by
Lieutenant S. Wright, *Fearless*'s first lieutenant, and Sub-
Lieutenant F. Fowler of the RCNVR. Receiving Commander
Pugsley's report, Somerville promptly ordered Lieutenant-
Commander Tancock to take off survivors and then sink *Fearless*;
Forester accordingly ran alongside her stricken sister and, having
removed her survivors, including those who had been com-
pelled to jump into the water to avoid being burned, she drew
off, shot a single torpedo into *Fearless* at 10.55, and resumed her
position in the screen.

Manchester had been in the act of combing torpedoes, but the
turn to port had brought her close to *Port Chalmers* and Captain
Drew was then obliged to swing to starboard. At this moment
another aircraft, which was passing between *Durham* and
Deucalion, in the port column ahead of *Port Chalmers*, saw the
cruiser expose her side as she turned and dropped its torpedo.
Drew reversed his helm again but it was too late, and *Manchester*
was hit on the port quarter. Water poured into her, slowing her
and causing an immediate list to port as her steering failed,
though hand gear was swiftly instituted. The explosion had travelled upwards, forcing oil fuel and water into the after engine
room, two magazines, the after wireless office and other compartments in the cruiser's after hull. Oil fumes sent many men
choking in search of fresh air as *Manchester* slowed down. Only
her starboard outer shaft was still turning, but she was found to
be capable of 8 knots, and this was cautiously raised to 12. By
dint of great exertions, emergency power cables were led to the
steering, and powered control of the rudder was resumed by
13.15. Three naval and five military officers had been killed,
along with twenty ratings and seven soldiers; three ratings were
missing, and six other men were wounded. Somerville's concern
for the convoy was paramount: he ordered Drew to take
Manchester back to Gibraltar, escorted by the Hunt-class *Avon
Vale* to provide additional anti-aircraft support and, if the worst
came to the worst, evacuate her complement and the 750 military
personnel she had on board.

The high-level bombs had fallen harmlessly among the
convoy, which now steamed on 'over a sunlit, rippled sea
beneath a cloudless sky', surviving a second attack at 10.11 when
five Fiat BR20s dumped their bombs from 17,000 feet in a 'rather
half-hearted attack … The presence of five Fulmars 1,000 feet

below and astern, endeavouring to overtake the bombers, may have induced them to get rid of their bomb loads as soon as possible.'[23] The Fulmars had engaged the first high-level Savoia Marchettis and shot two down, scoring hits on two others, while the combined fire of the ships had accounted for two of the low-level SM79s making the attack with torpedoes. Six aircrew were picked up by *Avon Vale*, but in the mêlée three Fulmars were shot down, though all the Fleet Air Arm personnel were recovered from the sea by the industrious destroyers.

A respite followed for the convoy as it passed north of Galita Island, but at 14.23 an enemy signal revealed that the retiring *Manchester* and her escort had been spotted. Then at 16.43 radar reports indicated aircraft in the north-west quarter more than forty miles away. Led by a Cant seaplane, five SM79s were spotted low on the port quarter. The Fulmars pounced on them, shot down two of the torpedo-bombers and damaged the Cant. 'The remainder retired without attacking.'

Half an hour later, as the ships approached the Skerki Channel, Somerville ordered Force H to put about, hoping to cover the damaged *Manchester* but assigning *Hermione* to the battered cruiser's place in Force X; he was also waiting for the westward-bound and empty merchant ships of MG1 coming from Malta under the solitary escort of *Encounter*. As *Ark Royal* turned in *Renown*'s wake, a section of her Fulmars remained patrolling over the convoy, to be relieved at 18.30 by Beaufighters from Malta. After fifty minutes they landed on the carrier, and a few minutes later, just before sunset, Force H encountered four Italian airmen sitting on the wreckage of their SM79, shot down two hours earlier.

At 18.05, one hundred miles west of Force H, *Manchester* and *Avon Vale* were located by a group of SM79s. Having worked round up-sun, the torpedo-bombers attacked *Manchester*. Lieutenant Dreyer had taken *Avon Vale* two miles ahead, in the direction of the sun, however, and her gunfire, together with that of *Manchester*'s forward turrets and starboard secondary battery, deterred the Italians from pressing home their attack.

As Force H detached, Syfret redisposed his own ships to present a narrower front as they entered the Skerki Channel. The main convoy and heavy ships steamed in two columns, each led by a destroyer with minesweeping gear streamed. *Firedrake* led the port column, which consisted of *Edinburgh*, *Durham*, *Port Chalmers*, *Deucalion* and *Arethusa*. *Foxhound* led the starboard, followed by *Manxman*, *Melbourne Star*, *Sydney Star*, *City of Pretoria* and *Hermione*. The columns were five cables apart, each ship three cables from her next ahead. Five cables on either side, the destroyers *Cossack*, *Maori*, *Sikh*, *Nestor*, *Foxhound*, *Firedrake*, *Farndale* and *Eridge* flanked the formation, so that the four columns of the whole force occupied a narrow front of no more than one and a half miles.

At 19.00 four torpedo-bombers raced in low from the south and were met by a heavy barrage from the ships which sent one crashing into the sea, apparently before it loosed its weapon. As the other torpedoes sped towards their targets two passed close to *Edinburgh* and one close to *Hermione*, but avoiding helm movements averted disaster. It was disappointing that the Malta-based Beaufighters had 'failed to intercept this raid', but worse occurred forty-five minutes later, when radar detected a formation approaching from the east-north-east at 12,000 feet. Syfret ordered the Beaufighters, then flying at 8,000 feet, to climb to 10,000 and circle some five miles to the east-north-east of the convoy 'in a position to intercept the incoming aircraft. They failed to do this and approached from the same direction as the enemy without identifying themselves and were engaged by the gunfire of the fleet. They then withdrew as the enemy approached 3,000 feet above them.'[24]

This poor showing by the Beaufighters exposed the leading destroyer of the port column to high-level bombs, about twenty of which were seen in the gloom to splash into the sea. Caught with her minesweeping gear streamed, *Firedrake* was 'either hit or very near missed' and holed in both boiler rooms, with her steering gear disabled. There were no casualties and Lieutenant-Commander Norris reported that he hoped to be able to resume steaming on one boiler very soon, so Syfret ordered *Eridge* to take her under tow towards Gibraltar, which was accomplished by 20.38. Until repairs to it had been effected *Firedrake*'s jammed rudder caused the disabled destroyer to sheer about, but by midnight she was steering docilely in *Eridge*'s wake at 10 knots. Norris's optimism about his boiler proved false, however, and *Eridge* towed *Firedrake* until 09.30 on the 25th, when she slipped her tow and secured alongside, continuing to make way as she transferred 10.5 tons of feed water and two tons of drinking water into *Firedrake*. Just before noon *Firedrake* finally raised steam, let go, and at 9 knots edged ahead under her own power. Lieutenant-Commander Gregory-Smith of *Eridge* earned Somerville's commendation for this fine piece of work. Gregory-Smith afterwards reported that it was inexplicable why they were not attacked when the *Settler* (a westbound merchant ship of MG1; see below) was being bombed by three aircraft within visual distance.

Syfret's forces stood on to the east. Deprived of *Firedrake*'s mine-sweeping capability, the rear-admiral ordered *Cossack* into the van of the port column, considering the delay involved in *Nestor*, the only other destroyer fitted for sweeping, shifting station and getting out her gear to be unacceptable. When it had cleared the Skerki Bank and was in a position some twenty-five miles north of Cape Bon, the force altered course to the north-east before working round to pass close to the north of Pantelleria. This route 'had been selected solely from the point of view of safety from enemy mines, but the alteration … had another and unexpected advantage, for just over an hour later [at about 21.05] enemy aircraft … made an abortive attempt lasting half an hour to locate the convoy.' Their certainty that the convoy would pursue a direct track between the Skerki Channel and Pantelleria had led to there being 'no attempt [by the Italians] to keep the convoy under air observation during the critical period before and just after sunset, and in consequence … the anticipated attack at dusk, which was most to be feared, never materialised.'[25]

The convoy's course had edged round to south-east by 23.00, when enemy aircraft were seen for an hour dropping flares to the southward. Syfret was grateful for this circumstance, as he picked his way through the minefields so assiduously laid by the Italians on the flank of their own convoy route, which ran along a north–south axis from Marittimo, past Pantelleria and down to Lampedusa. The port column was particularly exposed: not only did *Cossack* have no sweeping gear out, neither did *Durham*, *Port Chalmers*, nor *Deucalion*. It was therefore 'with considerable relief' that at 00.13 on the 24th Syfret turned to the south-south-east, 'into the Italian convoy route.'

The night was to spring further surprises. At 00.46 *Foxhound*, leading the starboard column, fouled a mine and had to clear it; *Nestor* had earlier been thought to have bumped a mine without detonating it; but these were the only encounters with this deadly and impersonal weapon. Two hours later, however, as the convoy approached Pantelleria, the radar of *Cossack*, now leading the port column, picked up three small and unidentified objects, raising the alarm among the ships. At about 02.50, 'short flashes of light followed by the sound of motor engine [*sic*] starting up indicated to *Cossack* and *Edinburgh*', immediately astern of her, the presence of Italian fast-attack or *MAS*-boats. The British destroyer and cruiser promptly lit up one of the craft in their searchlights and opened fire. *Manxman*, second in the starboard column, finding 'the target perfectly illuminated by cross searchlights', also opened fire. Loosing a torpedo, which passed close astern of *Cossack*, the *MAS*-boat 'retired at high speed but not before she had been repeatedly hit'. Two more torpedoes, whose exact origin was uncertain, passed close to *Edinburgh*. One of the Italian boats lay doggo between the port column and the destroyer screen, allowing the convoy to pass, until she was seen from *Farndale* and *Arethusa*, both of which engaged her before they lost sight of her in the pitch darkness astern.

The defensive fire of the British ships had destroyed one and disabled a second Italian torpedo-boat, but four or five remained unscathed to press the attack further. At 03.05 a wake was seen from *Edinburgh*, accompanied by engine noise. Once again the target was illuminated by searchlight 'and raked with Pom-Pom, 0.5-inch and Oerlikon fire at 1500 to 2000 yards range, the target appearing to be enveloped in a hail of tracers. The E-boat [*sic*] stopped out of control, and at this moment ... [*Edinburgh*'s] main armament fired a broadside of 12 guns ... When the splashes subsided, nothing was seen.' During the excitement 'one North Country gunlayer so far forgot his ... training as to report "There's the bastard" instead of the more orthodox "Gunlayer on".'[26]

The noise of the second torpedo-boat was heard as a hydrophonic effect on *Cossack*'s sonar a few seconds before the boat herself was sighted from the bridge. Captain Berthon ordered an immediate increase in speed and alteration of course, intending to ram the boat, just under his port bow. The enemy craft fired a torpedo as it 'passed across *Cossack*'s bows too close for [her] searchlight to follow. Fire was opened and sounds of splintering wood [were] heard', but the force commander remained uncertain of the fates of his assailants because 'for the next 20 minutes further sounds of motor engines were heard by *Cossack* and

Edinburgh, but no further contacts were made, other than a fleeting glimpse from *Cossack* of a boat withdrawing under cover of smoke.'

The action seems to have come as a surprise to both parties engaged, for the *MAS*-boats do not appear to have been lying in ambush, yet their stationary state discounts any suggestion that they were on a routine patrol. *MAS532* and *533* were lost, but the remainder made it home: 'discretion ... was apparently allowed to suppress their valour.' Despite radar and hydrophonic warning it was their wakes, once they made way, that betrayed them to the watching British. Syfret mentioned the frequent Italian radio transmissions being intercepted aboard *Maori* during the preceding five hours, in which 'clear deliberate speech by three voices was heard' and in the course of which 'excitement rose to an almost hysterical pitch'. He added that 'an Italian interpreter might have proved most useful ...', and also complained trenchantly 'of not having a flashless propellant for starshell'.

The brief action upon the port flank of GM1 had caused a degree of confusion within the convoy. Searchlight beams traversing the darkness and lines of low tracer skimming the sea had all but destroyed the night vision of the officers on the bridges of the unengaged ships. One such was Captain Horn, master of the *Sydney Star*, half-way down the starboard column. Horn had not left the bridge since his ship left the Mersey, even abandoning his cat-naps on the chart-room settee once the convoy had passed Gibraltar. By the time of the *MAS*-boat attack he had had no sleep for sixty hours. As the action developed his ship was savaged by friendly machine-gun fire from an adjacent vessel, which holed his starboard lifeboats.

Suddenly Horn saw the wake of a *MAS*-boat 'running parallel to the *Sydney Star*, less than fifty yards to port'.[27] It was too late for him to do anything: he was in the act of ordering an alteration of course when the torpedo struck amidships, exploding into No. 3 Hold with a great flash which was apparently unseen by the neighbouring escort, HMAS *Nestor*, doused as it was a second later by a huge column of water. Listing immediately, slowing as her engines stopped and swinging out of line, *Sydney Star* seemed doomed. Horn's first thought was for the 464 officers and men, mostly of the 32nd Light Anti-Aircraft Regiment, who in addition to grain, ammunition and naval stores formed his 'cargo'. He ordered abandon ship and the soldiers began to muster at their lifeboat stations, even as the ship's officers, in lowering the boats, made the discovery that they were punctured.

Meanwhile Commander Rosenthal, unaware of the presence of the *MAS*-boat, was investigating why 'one ship of the starboard column was dropping astern', initially unaware that the dark shape was *Sydney Star*. 'On closer approach it was observed that the starboard boats were being lowered, the ship however appeared undamaged, with no list and at normal trim ... Some time elapsed', the report continues somewhat testily, 'before *Nestor* could obtain a reply to repeated requests for information, but eventually *Sydney Star* reported that she had been torpedoed in No. 3 Hold, and that she had 30 feet of water in that hold and appeared to be sinking.'[28]

Four miles from the hostile Italian island of Pantelleria, with the convoy passing on and *MAS*-boat engine noises still to be heard in the darkness, Rosenthal laid his destroyer alongside the *Sydney Star*, somewhat inconvenienced by one of two lifeboats launched from her port davits; it had come round to the starboard side, from where it was ordered off to enable the destroyer to manoeuvre alongside. Secured by wires, for fifty minutes the two ships ground together uneasily in the low swell. Planks, pilot and cargo ladders were rigged from *Sydney Star*'s starboard bulwark to *Nestor*'s forecastle, down which precarious escape route the soldiers made their way. By the time the transfer had been completed, *Nestor* had 774 souls on board – her own complement of 231, her own quota of army personnel (56), and 487 officers and men from the Blue Star liner, including 23 of her crew. While the transfer was in progress, three *MAS*-boats were spotted in the offing.

During this operation Rosenthal 'formed the impression that the Master of *Sydney Star* was unduly pessimistic concerning the state of his ship'. He reported that Horn had 'remarked that he did not like the feel of her [the *Sydney Star*]' and that he 'thought he would have to leave her'. Rosenthal 'impressed on him the importance [the 'absolute necessity', in Somerville's own report] of keeping the ship afloat and getting her under way, and that drastic measures must be taken without delay to further this end.' As *Nestor* drew away Rosenthal 'had the satisfaction of seeing *Sydney Star* go ahead on her engines and follow at 12 knots: by 07.00 she had worked up to 14½.' Somerville's report attributes this to Rosenthal's 'salutary admonition', a most infamous, if only implied, imputation of lack of resolve on Horn's part.

According to Horn's account, matters were rather different. While the troops were disembarking, Horn's chief engineer, Mr G. Haig, and chief officer, Mr J. Mackie, were still carrying out their damage assessment. The exchange with Rosenthal probably occurred while he was still awaiting the outcome of his officers' exertions in the holds and engine room. Horn afterwards claimed that he had declined to be taken off, saying that he and his crew would stay and that they 'weren't finished yet'.[29]

In fact the water was rising inexorably in all three forward holds and 'at 05.56, *Sydney Star* informed *Nestor* that the ship had 12 feet of water in No. 1 Hold and 7 feet in No. 2 Hold, in addition to the 30 feet in No. 3 Hold. This was the first intimation that *Nestor* had received of the presence of water in … [*Sydney Star*] other than in No. 3 Hold. It subsequently transpired that the ship had been holed by a projectile fired by one of the escorts during the E-boat [*sic*] mêlée.'[30]

With dawn close upon them, Horn realised that their proximity to Pantelleria exposed them to certain destruction at daylight. According to his report to his owners, he 'informed the Commander of the destroyer that I would make an attempt to reach our destination, some 130 miles off, under our own power'.[31] He ordered Haig to give him steam for 12 knots and, with an overloaded *Nestor* circling about him, he set a course of 116 degrees. The report to *Nestor*, flashed by lamp at dawn, ends with the sentence, 'Have hopes I will make it.'[32]

An incident had occurred during the transfer of soldiers and crew which may have coloured Rosenthal's attitude. A few men of *Sydney Star*'s crew, mainly seamen who doubled as gunners, had found their way aboard *Nestor* in circumstances which gave some colour to the destroyer commander's attitude and resulted in a dearth of gunners in *Sydney Star* in the succeeding hours. What happened was that upon Horn's orders to abandon ship, the four lifeboats were lowered under the direction of the third officer. As has been noted, those on the starboard side were found to be useless; those on the port side, having been worked round under oars to the starboard side, where the rope ladders were already being rigged, found *Nestor* edging alongside. One

of them obstructed Rosenthal's approach, so that he had to order
it off: Acting Leading Seaman Anderson (of *Nestor*) 'jumped
down and got [the boat] ... clear from between the ships when
delay was unacceptable'. The men in *Sydney' Star's* lifeboat, one
of them plaintively recalled, 'were ordered to board ... [*Nestor*, by
which] ... time she was under way moving away from MV
Sydney [*Star* and] the gap between the two ships (20 feet) was too
great to get across. We had to stay on HMAS *Nestor* for the next
12 hours ... It was really a foul up ...'[33]

In the confusion of the incident, such events and the discrepancies in the accounts thereof are unsurprising. The safe transfer of the troops was completed without interruption, despite
prowling *MAS*-boats, betrayed by their noise and the occasional
glimpse of a wake or a low grey hull. As daylight grew it
revealed a low mist, the presumed reason for the lack of further
interference by the Italians. However, as the two ships followed
the convoy they were subjected to attack from the air: at 06.15
two torpedo-bombers were seen from *Nestor* on the port
quarter. Driven off by barrage fire, they flew towards the main
convoy. At 06.50 a pair of torpedo-armed SM79s made another
approach which was driven off in similar fashion. Convinced
that further intervention would occur, Rosenthal 'made a
"Help" signal' to Syfret, who responded by detaching *Hermione*
to his assistance.

At the time *Hermione* turned back towards the isolated ships,
Syfret's main force was only thirty miles west of Gozo and well
under air cover from Malta – a mixed blessing, as the approaching Beaufighters persistently failed to identify themselves and
thus caused great anxiety as they flew in at low altitude, inviting
and receiving anti-aircraft fire. Syfret complained in addition,
afterwards, of the Beaufighters' failure to submit to direction,
despite attempts made aboard his flagship *Edinburgh*, the fighter-
director for the operation, to take control of them. This had necessitated handing over the Fulmar direction to the reserve ship
Hermione and Lieutenant C. Joy, *Edinburgh's* Fighter Direction
Officer, strove to impose some order on the Beaufighters. During
this anxious time 'a half-hearted attack was carried out' by three
Italian torpedo-bombers which dropped their weapons as the
outer screen of destroyers opened fire. All the 'ships took avoiding action, but no [torpedo] tracks were seen.'

Syfret's plan to proceed ahead with his cruisers and destroyers at speed, to refuel and land service personnel and stores while the merchant ships followed at 14 or 15 knots safe under the air umbrella, was now put into motion: *Edinburgh*, *Arethusa* and *Manxman* raced ahead, entering Grand Harbour at 11.30 'with ships' companies fallen in and bands playing', and crowds turning out to greet them from the ramparts.

During the forenoon *Sydney Star* was enduring high-altitude bombing raids. 'Several bombs dropped in close proximity each side of vessel,' Horn reported of an attack at 09.30. 'Helm [was] manoeuvred to best advantage', he reported, while the combined gunfire of the three ships drove off the enemy, one being 'hit and seen to lose height with black smoke pouring from his tail.' But *Sydney Star* was slowly sinking, the water now up to 'tween-deck level, so that violent helm orders only made matters worse, causing the ship to loll even further. The decision had been made to pass close north of Malta to shorten the distance to Grand Harbour, risking further attacks but allowing Horn to reduce speed and ease the pressure on his ship's straining bulkheads. As it was, Rosenthal signalled to Horn, 'Would hate to lose you now. Am considering alternative sites for beaching in case flooding progresses to a dangerous extent.' As the blue silhouette of Malta hardened into a recognisable coastline, Rosenthal and Horn made arrangements for tugs to meet them.

An hour later, at about 10.30, a concerted attempt was made by high-level SM79s, torpedo-armed Savoias and Italian Stukas to destroy the wounded ship. Two Beaufighters intercepted the torpedo-armed SM79s, but in pursuing part of the formation almost out of sight they exposed the *Sydney Star* to the assault of the remainder. Horn swung his wallowing and sluggish ship to try to comb the oncoming low-level attack as the temporary gunners, largely off-duty engine room greasers and firemen, opened a barrage to complement that of *Nestor* and *Hermione*. Two Savoia Marchettis passed spectacularly close to their target and one torpedo exploded as it hit the water, showering the forward part of the cargo-liner with splinters. Simultaneously, Captain Oliver had ordered *Hermione*'s anti-aircraft fire to break up the high-level formation. This was partially successful, though bombs near-missed *Sydney Star* and, for a second time, her engines were stopped. At this critical moment the Stukas dived, one on the cargo-liner, the other on *Nestor*. Their attack failed and, as they withdrew, Haig restarted *Sydney Star*'s engines. With 18 miles to go and his ship foundering under his feet, Horn took his final gamble and threw caution to the winds. Doubtless Rosenthal would have agreed with him. *Sydney Star* worked up to her best speed and, under a cloudless sky and over a smooth sea, made her final approach to Grand Harbour. Three tugs, *West Dean*, *Robust* and *Ancient*, awaited her arrival, together with huge crowds, and at about 14.00 she passed the forts and was gingerly edged alongside. Divers afterwards reported that, in addition to much collateral damage, the main rent in her shell plating caused by the primary torpedo impact was some 40 feet by 16 feet. A later survey by her owners reported that *Sydney Star* would not have floated for much longer, and attributed the ship's survival to the decision to ignore 'all routine instructions' and to make 'a bee line for Malta, taking all risks of minefields, etc., in doing so.'

The remainder of the convoy, having covered a much greater distance routed south of Malta, then slowed while, to the delight of those watching from the bridges of the waiting merchantmen, *Sydney Star* was brought safely in. These ships had beaten off an attack by Italian torpedo-bombers since Syfret had left them, but entered port unscathed at 15.30, escorted by *Cossack*, *Maori*, *Sikh*, *Foxhound* and *Farndale*. *Deucalion* led, followed by *Port Chalmers*, *City of Pretoria*, *Melbourne Star* and *Durham*. The damage to *Sydney Star* and the spoiling of a large part of her cargo notwithstanding, convoy GM1 had got through.

Somerville's formal report attributes much to Rosenthal, without mention of Horn. 'The safe arrival of *Sydney Star* reflects great credit to the Commanding Officer of *Nestor* … who showed great … initiative and good seamanship on handling a delicate situation so close to the enemy's coast.' Horn was not ignored, however, nor were his key staff, Chief Engineer Haig in particular. With her pumps running continuously and quite unable to stem, let alone reverse, the inflow of water, they had also to keep the main engines and boilers running. Reporting to Blue Star, Horn acknowledged his debt elsewhere: 'We were extremely lucky to reach our destination, and [you] will also appreciate the good work done by the crew who remained on board with me.'[34]

Syfret paid due tribute to Horn, as did Ford and Dobbie, sending his ship a message from the signal station at Valletta: 'The Royal Navy offer you their congratulations on a very fine piece of seamanship.' Horn and Haig received the OBE, Mackie an MBE. In the House of Lords, Lord Marchwood afterwards quoted the ordeal of the *Sydney Star* as evidence that the risks undertaken by the civilian merchant service were in certain cases equal to those of the armed services, and that equal awards should therefore be made, a practice which was adopted in due course.

After her cargo had been discharged the *Sydney Star* languished at Malta until December, undergoing repairs. For Syfret's warships however, there was little respite. Once they had disembarked their army personnel and the quantities of stores they had tucked away – especially *Manxman*, whose mine deck was stuffed with supplies – they prepared to sail again.

Many miles to the west, Vice-Admiral Somerville had early that same morning, 24 July, located the crippled *Manchester* ahead of Force H as she limped at 11 knots towards Gibraltar with *Avon Vale* in company. At 08.16 a questing Cant, sighted east of Force H as it steamed west at 18 knots, was intercepted and shot down by the carrier's Fulmars. Further astern came *Firedrake* and her escort *Eridge*. By 10.00 they were steaming west at 8 knots to the south of Galita.

On the previous morning, as convoy GM1 was approaching the Sicilian Narrows and its action with the *MAS*-boats, six of the seven westbound ships of MG1 had left Valletta. Empty of cargo, they carried instead a number of British women and children whose evacuation was desirable both for safety reasons and to reduce, even by a small amount, the number of civilians on the island to be fed.

At dusk, when still a few miles east of Pantelleria, the six ships had divided into groups, aiming to run twenty miles to the south of this Italian island; they would then enter Vichy French territorial waters to round Cape Bon, pass south of Zembra Island and within ten miles of Cani Rocks, hugging the coast of Tunisia. From the point of this dispersal, MG1 could not be described as a convoy; indeed, with only *Encounter* to 'escort' them, it was more a game of hazard. The faster vessels took advantage of their speed, so that by 10.00 on 24 July the six merchant ships were strung out in positions varying from forty miles west to twenty miles east of Galita Island. The leading group, the motor ships *Breconshire* (commanded by Captain C. Hutchinson) and *Talabot*, were logging 17 knots; the second, *Thermopylae* and *Amerika*, escorted by *Encounter*, were making 14 knots; and the third, *Settler* and *Hoegh Hood*, 12 knots. Far astern the seventh, the *Svenor*, delayed by an accident, had only just left Malta.

Concerned with the safety of these valuable if empty ships, Somerville nevertheless resolved to continue west until he was reasonably certain that *Manchester* was out of danger. By the time the cruiser was passing out of range of aircraft from Cagliari she would have been joined by the two old destroyers *Vidette* and *Vimy*, sent out to assist from Gibraltar. Somerville would then turn east again, fly off six of his Swordfish as additional reinforcements for Malta, and meet the ships of both MG1 and Force X, under Syfret, returning from Grand Harbour.

During the forenoon of the 24th units of the Regia Aeronautica struck again from Cagliari, roughly where they had hit *Fearless* and *Manchester* the day before. Four torpedo-bombers attacked *Encounter*, *Thermopylae* and *Amerika* at 12.30, followed up by four high-level bombers at 12.50. Lieutenant-Commander E. Morgan had ordered a 'Help' signal sent the moment his lookouts spotted the reconnoitring Italian Cant which soon afterwards called in the SM79s, but in the event all torpedoes missed. The high-level attack resulted in about thirty bombs falling between *Amerika* and *Thermopylae*, but the merchantmen were unaffected. It was now the turn of *Breconshire* and *Talabot*, which at 13.40 were north of Annaba. A high-level attack resulted in bombs dropping between the two ships, and half an hour later *Breconshire* was near-missed by some small bombs dropped from a Caproni. At 14.30 Morgan increased speed to 28 knots to catch up with these two ships, fearing a more determined attack on the invaluable *Breconshire*. *Encounter* herself fought off an unsuccessful high-level bombing attack at 17.40, and four hours later she joined up with *Breconshire* and *Talabot*; the three ships thereafter enjoyed an uneventful passage to Gibraltar, arriving at dawn on 26 July 1941.

Meanwhile, astern of the destroyer the Italians had located *Settler* and *Hoegh Hood*, attacking at 17.11 and again at 18.15. The Norwegian tanker was hit by a torpedo and her speed fell, but the greater subdivision inherent in a tanker, in contrast to the capacious holds of a general-cargo vessel, averted the consequences endured by *Sydney Star*. *Hoegh Hood*, though she had dropped astern of *Settler*, entered Gibraltar at 09.15 on the 27th, seven hours behind her consort. *Thermopylae* and *Amerika* had already arrived at 15.30 the previous afternoon; and *Svenor*, proceeding alone and at daylight through The Narrows, arrived under the protection of The Rock at 05.00 on the 28th, having been untouched by the enemy.

Behind this extended gaggle of merchant ships, Syfret's cruisers and *Manxman* had sailed from Grand Harbour at 18.00 on the 24th, followed three-quarters of an hour later by the refuelled destroyers. As they left, they received 'a fine send-off from the Maltese and in particular from the crews of the M.T. [merchant transports, i.e. merchant ships] and the troops who had taken passage'.[35] *Farndale*, which had developed condenser troubles, remained behind. The speed of Syfret's turnaround was a tribute to Ford's organisation at Valletta; while this activity had been taking place, Syfret had made representations to Air Chief Marshal Longmore regarding the disappointing performance of his Beaufighters. No delay occurred in passing the rear-admiral's disapprobation to the aircrews, for 'better support from [the] Beaufighters' ensured that no air attacks developed from formations of high-level Savoia Marchettis as Force X set off that evening to follow MG1 to Gibraltar.

Somerville's Force H finally turned back to meet Syfret's Force X at 03.30 on 25 July. Two hours earlier *Ark Royal* had flown off the six Swordfish for Malta;[36] fitted with long-range fuel tanks, they reached their destination safely. Shortly before dawn a flashing light was seen to the north-east and a Swordfish was launched, armed with depth-charges in anticipation of discovering a surfaced Italian submarine homing aircraft onto the British fleet; in fact the biplane discovered the Italian hospital ship *Sorrento* vainly searching for aircrew of the Regia Aeronautica shot down after the action of the 23rd. Somerville left her unharmed to attend to her dismal and fruitless task. More Swordfish flew off at twilight to search for enemy submarines between Forces H and X, with a fighter patrol airborne at sunrise.

Ark Royal's aircraft reported Syfret's cruisers in sight 22 miles east of Force H at 07.48 on the 25th with the destroyers a few miles astern of them. Less than half an hour later, 26 miles to the north-west of Galita Island, Syfret and Somerville joined forces and shaped their course to the west. Progress was limited by

Nelson's top speed of 23 knots, and by the necessity to turn into the south-easterly breeze every time *Ark Royal* handled her aircraft.

The combined squadrons were located by a Cant seaplane at 07.15, but poor aerial visibility prevented its destruction until an hour later when 'in full view of the fleet. Unfortunately one of the attacking Fulmars ... was shot down in the encounter and crashed heavily leaving no survivors.[37] Four Italians out of a crew of six were rescued from the Cant by *Foxhound*.' The spotters had had time to call up reinforcements, and just as British radar observers were reporting them approaching at a range of 69 miles, *Maori* lost feed water to her boilers and was obliged to stop; *Sikh* was left to patrol round her while Fulmars circled overhead. An hour later she got under way, reporting a failure of her No. 2 boiler but able to make 17 knots, which she slowly increased to 27. Meanwhile *Ark Royal*'s Fulmars were vectored to intercept the enemy air formations coming from the east, and 'at 11.00 the first "Tally-Ho" was received'. High-level and torpedo-bombers were attacked 'with great dash' by the Fulmars; the Italians were forced to jettison bombs, while 'three S79 [sic] high level bombers were shot down for certain, one [more] was probably destroyed and two others were damaged'.[38] The cost, however, was the loss of two more Fulmars, the crew of one of which was rescued unhurt by *Nestor*, while the second was lost.[39]

This was the last actual attempt by the enemy to interfere with Operation SUBSTANCE, although the destroyers subsequently reacted to some spurious sonar contacts. Somerville sent *Forester* ahead with the survivors and wounded from *Fearless*[40] and cancelled the planned rendezvous with the fleet oiler *Brown Ranger* and her escort *Beverley*, in the knowledge that all his ships had sufficient fuel to make Gibraltar. He now turned his mind to other matters, ordering *Maori* up to collect copy from press reporters embarked in *Hermione* and *Ark Royal*, to be passed to *Renown* for censoring before being transferred back to *Ark Royal* and then flown on to Britain by way of Gibraltar. During that afternoon Somerville swung the whole force east again 'for a few hours to avoid reaching harbour before daylight', and during this eastwards leg, at 16.40, 'the fleet was manoeuvred to pass on opposite courses to *Firedrake* and her escort of *Eridge* and *Avon Vale* who were in position [due east] 88 miles from Cape de Gata proceeding at 9 knots.' As Forces H and X passed the three destroyers on a reciprocal heading their ships' companies cheered, and a pair of Swordfish continued to overfly the fleet on anti-submarine patrol. Dad was still looking after the Boys.

Though they manned the sides in acknowledgement of *Firedrake*'s survival, the fleet was not suffered to remain idle; Somerville ordered eight Swordfish to carry out a dummy attack on the fleet, to ward off complacency. But at 03.00 the next morning he relented sufficiently to order *Hermione*, *Manxman* and *Arethusa* to make for Gibraltar at 24 knots, followed at 06.00 by *Ark Royal*, *Edinburgh* and four of the destroyers. The remaining seven stayed with *Renown* and *Nelson*: in the light of his poor opinion of The Rock's heavy defensive guns, Somerville had ordered an exercise. The practice proved 'deplorably bad and once more demonstrated the lamentable inefficiency of the Fortress long range artillery'. The two capital ships entered Gibraltar harbour at 09.00, Somerville having sent *Foxhound* back to beef up the anti-submarine cover as *Firedrake* limped along the coast of Granada.

Relentless in his pursuit for efficiency, even in his summing-up of Operation SUBSTANCE, Somerville spared no one, complaining, *inter alia*, that 'it was unfortunate that the instructions for exercising the convoy whilst on passage forwarded to the Admiralty for transmission to *Nelson* failed to reach their destination. This imposed on the Rear-Admiral Commanding, 18th Cruiser Squadron [Syfret], the necessity to exercise certain manoeuvres during the first day's passage of the convoy through the Western Mediterranean.'[41] Syfret himself entertained fewer misgivings about this particular shortcoming, and reported that the success of the eastbound GM1 was 'due in no small measure to the behaviour of the merchant ships in convoy. Their manoeuvring and general conduct was excellent and caused me no anxiety whatever. I had complete confidence that orders given to them by me would be understood and promptly carried out. Their steadfast and resolute behaviour during . . . attacks was most impressive and encouraging to us all. Particular credit is due to [Captain MacFarlane of the] SS *Melbourne Star*, Commodore of the convoy, who set a high standard and never failed to appreciate directly what he should do.' Syfret went on to single out the *Durham* for additional praise, since she had experienced trouble with her port engine but managed to maintain the required 14 knots despite the fact that this was only one knot less than her designed maximum speed. Of his own ship's company Captain P. Pycraft of the Blue Funnel liner *Deucalion* reported to his owners, 'I ... cannot adequately express my admiration for the steady and efficient manner in which all my orders were carried out, making it possible for me to get my ship through safely.' To Somerville he was more restrained, expressing himself merely as being 'well satisfied with the behaviour of my men under the concentrated attacks to which the convoy was subjected'.[42]

Of the westbound convoy, MG1, Somerville expressed his horror at discovering on arrival at Gibraltar that the merchant ships had had aboard women and children. Had he 'known this earlier', he wrote, 'I should have sent a destroyer to escort each group.' He also pursued Syfret's complaints about the poor performance of the Beaufighters, and in September the Admiralty informed the Air Staff 'that much remains to be done in the way of establishing an accepted general procedure for the conduct of RAF fighters in escorting ships.'[43] The Beaufighter pilots' apparent lack of appreciation of the difficulties of identification experienced by the ships' crews is partly offset by a remark in the report of Captain R. Dickson of *Manxman*: 'The need for better aircraft recognition from ships was well proved ... A few minutes before, our Beaufighters were patrolling just where the attack developed and were driven off by the deliberate fire of our destroyers'[44] – a situation arising from the fact that the Beaufighter was unfamiliar to the ships' gunners.

Privately Somerville admitted to his colleague Dudley North at Gibraltar, in a letter of 30 July, that he had not expected to get all the ships through 'or [,] even more miraculous [, to] get the seven empty ones back. And the latter were all damn good ships.' He was pleased too with Rear-Admiral Syfret, who (he told Cunningham) he had thought 'might be a bit rusty after nearly two years ashore but ... proved to be very much on the spot.' The lack of action by surface units of the Italian fleet had been partly due to Cunningham's feint from Alexandria, referred to earlier, helped by the offensive operations of the patrolling submarines, which had made their deterrent presence felt by attacking at least one coastal convoy.

As for Malta herself, despite the difficulties Operation SUBSTANCE had passed to the island about 65,000 tons of stores and supplies of all kinds, including three months' food for the inhabitants (among which were coffee, tea, edible oils and sugar), spare Hurricane engines, 10,000 tons of ammunition for the defence and the restocking of warships, and torpedoes for the 10th Submarine Flotilla. For the time being, at least, disaster had been averted, and as the slings of cargo were lifted out of the holds of their ships in Grand Harbour, Higgs and his fellow masters could laugh at the Italians' broadcast claims that 70,000 tons of British merchant shipping had been sunk.

12

'A most hectic afternoon'

(Operations STYLE, MINCEMEAT, STATUS *1 and 2,* PROPELLER, *MD6 and* HALBERD, *with Convoys GM2 and MG2)*

ITALIAN RADIO CLAIMED that the 'remaining ships' of convoy GM1, 'which had been attacked for three days and three nights', were now taking 'refuge in the Malta Harbour of Valletta, and were detected there.'[1] While they were thus vulnerable in port, Supermarina had decided to attack them 'with those tiny but powerful craft on which the designers had worked in silence for many years to perfect one of the most precious secrets of the Italian war machine. The men chosen for this task knew that retreat was impossible – knew that they must either be taken prisoner or killed – but despite the formidable nature of the British defences, none flinched before this task.' Notwithstanding the rodomontade, it was an attack exactly suited to the courageous *élan* of the Italian character at its most martial. On the evening of 25 July 1941 the 10th Light Flotilla, commanded by Capitano di Fregata Moccagatta, left Augusta led by the sloop *Diana*, carrying nine small explosive motor-boats, the bow of each one of which bore an awesome charge. In tow was a barge bearing two manned *Siluro a Lenta Corsas*, or slow-running torpedoes. These, known colloquially to the Italians as *maiali*, literally 'pigs', were manned human torpedoes. The *Diana* was escorted by *MAS451* and *452*, carrying the gallant crews of the *maiali* and commanded by Teseo Tesei, the inventor of the human torpedo, who had been working on the device since 1929.[2] When the flotilla was about fifteen miles from the entrance to Grand

Harbour, the explosive craft and *maiali* were launched and towed in by the two *MAS*-boats to within five miles of Malta before proceeding independently. Their first objective was to blast an entry into Grand Harbour, enabling the remaining boats and human torpedoes to attack the merchant ships lying inside while their defenders were distracted by an air raid. The entrance to the port was closed by a movable boom, but the mole across the entrance to Grand Harbour itself was connected to the foot of the ramparts of Fort St Elmo by a steel viaduct. The two spans of this normally allowed the passage of small craft between Grand and Marsamxett Harbours, but were closed for the duration of the war by heavy steel wire nets. The two human torpedoes had been worked near the viaduct, ready to enter Grand Harbour once the obstructing net had been cleared away, which was to be achieved by the explosive boats. But the first of these rammed into the outermost net and blew up with such violence that it defeated its intended purpose: the steel span above was dislodged and fell, completely blocking the boat-passage. As the concussion died away the searchlights at St Elmo went on, illuminating the Italian craft waiting offshore. Within a very few minutes the withering fire of depressed anti-aircraft guns had destroyed the would-be attackers, one of the *MAS*-boats being sunk by a shell ricocheting at extreme range and finding its target. In the first light of dawn Hurricanes flew low over the sea and pitilessly picked off the second wave, although *Diana* escaped. The bold Italian plan had entirely and literally misfired: not only had they rendered the already obstructed entrance completely impassable, but their approach had been detected and monitored by radar. While this had not prevented the Italians' initial approach, the result of it was abject failure.

Defence against such attacks and against the regular air raids was a constant drain on ammunition. Moreover, the 1,750 troops and RAF support personnel now in Gibraltar as a result of the grounding of *Leinster* were not only urgently required on Malta but an embarrassment where they were. To maintain stocks of munitions between major convoys and to push through the stranded soldiers and airmen, Operation STYLE was run from the west, the designated ships sailing from Gibraltar after dark on 31 July. This was an all-naval operation, a fast passage made by *Arethusa*, *Hermione* and *Manxman*, each of which embarked her quota of passengers and cases of aviation spirit, ammunition and foodstuffs. *Manxman's* mine decks were capacious compared with the available space on the two cruisers, where every water-closet and bathroom was stacked with cases, drums, and cartons of tinned food. The ships, designated Force X, were screened by two destroyers, *Sikh* and *Lightning*, and covered by Somerville and Force H, which also mounted an air raid and shore bombard-ment on Alghero on the night of 31 July/1 August. The shelling was carried out by the destroyers *Cossack* and *Maori* while the remaining destroyers, *Faulknor*, *Fury*, *Foresight*, *Forester*, *Foxhound*, *Encounter*, *Lightning* and HMAS *Nestor*, remained well off the Sardinian coast as a screen to *Renown*, *Nelson* and *Ark Royal*. As Force X sped east, *Hermione* ran down the Italian sub-marine *Tembien*. She had been lying on the surface in the moon-less darkness off Tunis recharging her batteries when the British cruiser rammed her. Both *Arethusa* and *Manxman*, steaming at speed in *Hermione's* wake, felt their ships roll the wrecked sub-marine under their hulls.[3]

The turnaround in Grand Harbour was very fast and Force X was soon at sea again, leaving Malta at 16.00. The ships raced west, rejoining Force H off Bône next morning, their crews short on sleep – so much so that when they arrived at Gibraltar on 4 July, their decks were littered with dozing bodies. Coming aboard *Manxman* to confer with Captain Dickson, Somerville dis-turbed some of the recumbent forms; apologies were mutual, for Somerville's genuine solicitude for his men endeared him to them.

There next arose the problem of recovering the now emptied merchant ships of GM1, the SUBSTANCE convoy. This operation, code-named MINCEMEAT, was to be covered by an incendiary bombing raid on cork-oak woods in the north of Sardinia by air-craft flown off *Ark Royal*, and by the laying of a minefield off Livorno by *Manxman* – movements to be carried out partly in the hope, too, of drawing the Italian fleet out to action while 'a minor but important operation' took place 'elsewhere'.[4] *Renown* having been sent back to Britain for a refit, Somerville hoisted his flag in *Nelson* and left Gibraltar on 21 August. The rest of Force H con-sisted of *Ark Royal*, *Hermione*, *Manxman*, *Encounter*, *Foresight*, *Fury* and *Forester*.

The 'minor operation' Somerville referred to was the passage of *Durham* and *Deucalion* from Malta to Gibraltar without close escort. They were the only ships ready, for *Port Chalmers*, *City of Pretoria* and *Melbourne Star* had yet to complete their discharge, while *Sydney Star*, having been so badly damaged, was destined to languish in Malta for some weeks yet.

In the lull after SUBSTANCE the Italians had again been active laying minefields, the converted ferries *Aspromonte* and *Reggio* and the destroyers *Zeno*, *Pigafetta*, *Da Noli*, *Da Verazzano*, *Da Mosto* and *Pessagno* having been at sea on this task during the middle of the month. Supplies continued to be sent by submarines, *Atropo*, *Corridoni* and *Zoea* running 200 tons of fuel and supplies to Bardia, and convoys were maintained to Tripoli. British submarines operating from Malta sought to interdict these, but *P32* was lost in one such attack when she struck a mine, and *P33* was sunk by the torpedo-boat *Partenope* off Pantelleria. However, the 11,398-grt liner *Esperia* was sent to the bottom by Hezlet in *Unique* while acting as a troopship, although the liners *Marco Polo*, *Neptunia* and *Oceania* reached North Africa, escorted by the destroyers *Vivaldi*, *Gioberti*, *Da Recco*, *Oriani*, *Scirocco*, *Grecale* and *Maestrale*. With more than a thousand Italian soldiers swimming in the water, the escorts did not counter-attack with depth-charges, and the retiring British submarine commanders were later upbraided by Captain Simpson for not renewing their assault upon the remaining ships. The Italians continued to send small convoys across to Libya, and although Wanklyn's *Upholder* sank a 4,000-ton Italian merchant ship on the 22nd and a 5,000-ton freighter was sunk by Lieutenant-Commander Tomkinson in *Urge*, aircraft from Malta attacking a convoy on 23 and 24 August succeeded in sinking only one ship.

As for the Italian fleet itself, the 9th Division of *Littorio* and *Vittorio Veneto*, with five destroyers, sortied on the 22nd under Iachino. The following day, off Cagliari, he joined forces with the 3rd Division from Messina, consisting of the cruisers *Trieste*, *Bolzano*, *Trento* and *Gorizia*, with four destroyers, and a further ten destroyers in the offing. Iachino's objective, based on the assumption that Force H was conducting its normal cover of a supply convoy to Malta, was to lure Somerville within range of the Regia Aeronautica, stiffened by units of the Luftwaffe, the reduction in Somerville's force due to the return of *Renown* to Britain having been reported to Rome by agents in Algeciras. In the same locality as Iachino lay the submarines *Alagi*, *Aradam*,

Diaspro and *Serpente*, while in the Sicilian Channel, supplementing the minefields, lay the *Bandiera*, *Squalo*, *Tricheco*, *Topazio* and
Zaffiro, with several *MAS*-boats. A surface force of the 8th
Division, intended to intercept the British and Allied merchantmen off the Tunisian coast, left Palermo on the 23rd, consisting
of the cruisers *Duca degli Abruzzi*, *Muzio Attendolo* and *Raimondo
Montecuccioli*, screened by five destroyers.

Somerville was discovered on the 22nd by a pair of Cants
which proved impossible to shoot down, he complained afterwards, suggesting that they might have received armour plating
and requesting that his Fulmars be rearmed with cannon. But the
Italians lost contact with Force H as it ducked to the west of the
Balearics to cover *Manxman*'s approach to Livorno, where
during darkness on the 24th she laid 140 mines. *Ark Royal*'s
Swordfish attacked the airfield at Tempio and set fire to extensive tracts of cork-woods, as planned, but by the time Somerville
was free to pursue Iachino he was in the now all-too-familiar situation of being unable to catch up with him as the Italians fell
back towards the Tyrrhenian Sea. Wanklyn had observed units
of the Regia Marina and reported them to Ford at Malta, but
Iachino's initially bold move ended when Lieutenant-
Commander Woods in the submarine *Triumph* succeeded in
hitting *Bolzano* with a torpedo as she retired towards her base at
Messina.

The two merchant ships which left Malta did so unaware that
Supermarina had prepared so comprehensive an ambush for
them. They had been harried by bombing raids during their stay
discharging in Malta, but neither had been more than superfi-
cially damaged. The first to leave was *Durham*, and as she had
made the outward passage with one cylinder of her port diesel
blanked off, her master, Captain Pilcher, was confident that his
ship was capable of 14 knots and that she could cover the distance through The Narrows during darkness. But off Tunisia,
despite having her paravanes streamed, *Durham* struck a mine
which tore a hole in her shell plating, admitting water to No. 1
Hold; it was the following day before it was realised that her paravanes had entangled a second mine, and that she had had the
thing in her gear for twenty hours. The ship was stopped and 'the
two paravanes, the mine and the tangle of wire ... were cut adrift'
by the ship's carpenter, Mr J. Newlyn.

With the ship again proceeding at her best speed, it was now found that water was entering the engine room, where the diesel engine flywheels picked it up from the bilge below and threw it across onto the electric generators. The port engine was stopped, and an investigation by Mr G. MacDougall, the chief engineer, revealed the flooding to be water from the breached hold forward which, running aft under pressure along the duct keel, had dislodged the cofferdam manhole in the engine room. 'Mr MacDougall immediately jumped on the manhole,' Pilcher reported to his owners, 'and by the sheer weight of his body, which is considerable, forced the manhole back into position, enabling the Seventh Engineer to secure the manhole nuts and caulk the lid with wooden wedges. When Mr MacDougall was sitting on the lid he was up to his chest in oil and water.'[5]

Durham was now overdue at Gibraltar, and a Sunderland was flown out to search for her. The pilot was a New Zealander, and having located the ship, which he knew to have regularly visited his homeland, he flashed by lamp the Maori greeting 'Kiaora'.[6] Arriving safely at Gibraltar the following day, *Durham* made for the commercial anchorage, where her damage was assessed.

Following *Durham*, Holt's Blue Funnel liner *Deucalion* sailed on 26 August. Running along the Tunisian coast with her paravanes streamed very early the following morning, she was briefly shelled by a Vichy French shore battery before 'a terrific explosion' occurred abreast of her foremast. Clearly her mine-sweeping gear had, like that of *Durham*, caught a mine. The detonation caused only the flooding of *Deucalion*'s forepeak, however, thanks to the immensely strong hull, for which Holt's ships were renowned. On the bridge an anxious Captain Pycraft, urging the chief engineer Mr Urquhart to 'keep her going', was relieved 'to hear the continued steady pounding of the engines'.[7] A British destroyer appeared briefly at daylight, asked by lamp if they had had a quiet night and, receiving an appropriate reply, sheered off and disappeared. Her presence would have been a comfort later that day when, just after noon, two Italian SM79s attacked *Deucalion*. Pycraft combed the tracks of the torpedoes, while his guns' crews retaliated. By 16.30, however, well within range of Cagliari-based planes, a second attack arrived. Pycraft ordered his gunners to hold their fire and, as the torpedo planes approached, tense silence reigned on the bridge. 'The Bofors gunners on the starboard side of the fo'c's'le head withheld their fire until the leading plane faltered and fell slightly away. From the bridge came the order ... and a well-timed vicious burst sent the first attacker crashing into the sea.' The dropped torpedo 'streaked along the starboard side of the ship only a few feet away ...', while the second 'actually grazed the side of the ship ... [but] almost miraculously' failed to detonate. *Deucalion* was then left alone until shortly before dusk, when a submarine periscope was sighted. But nothing occurred, and *Deucalion*'s 'weary but cheerful ship's company' arrived out of the mist and passed under the shadow of The Rock on 29 August, after a 'short but exciting passage'.

Italian attempts to disrupt the passages of *Durham* and *Deucalion* or to bring the British squadron to battle were a complete failure, for the three Italian cruisers sent to search the area off Cape Bon had done so in the brief interval between the passage of the two British merchantmen. British attempts to disrupt Italian troop convoys were slightly more successful. At the end of August 1941 the trooping liners *Neptunia*, *Oceania* and *Victoria* made the crossing safely from Naples to Tripoli, while a northbound convoy of five freighters and a minelaying vessel heading for Naples also eluded the British.[8] In early September, however, the returning freighters were not so lucky, and Malta-based aircraft sank a ship of 6,300 tons and damaged a second, which had to be towed back to Naples by the destroyer *Dardo*.[9]

September marked an increase in British successes against Italian supply convoys, modest at first but gradually increasing, so that by the end of the month Admiral Weichold, German Naval Staff Liaison Officer in Rome, was reporting the state of affairs to Berlin, emphasising Malta's significance in interrupting Rommel's supplies. He had already deplored the failure of Italian escorts to counter-attack after the sinking of *Esperia* on 20 August, but worse was to come when the submarine *Thunderbolt* sank three small ships in a coastal convoy in the Gulf of Sirte, despite an escort of two torpedo-boats.[10] British aircraft then attacked a heavily escorted Tripoli-bound six-ship convoy on both 12 and 13 September, sinking three ships totalling over 15,500 tons.[11] Weichold's gloomy forebodings were further justified on 17 September. Ultra decrypts passed to Malta had revealed that a major Axis troop convoy was to leave Taranto bound for Tripoli, made up of the liners *Vulcania*, *Neptunia* and *Oceania*, escorted by the destroyers *Da Recco*, *Da Noli*, *Pessagno*,

Usodimare, and *Gioberti*. The submarines *Upright, Upholder* and *Unbeaten* were dispatched to patrol lines off Tripoli, with *Ursula* closer inshore. Located off the Calabrian coast by British aircraft, the Italian ships fell into the trap. Although *Upright* was driven off by the escort and *Ursula's* salvo of torpedoes aimed at *Vulcania* was out-manoeuvred, Wanklyn sank the *Neptunia* (19,475 grt) and *Oceania* (19,507 tons). Only 384 soldiers drowned, some 6,500 being rescued, but the loss of two large trooping ships was a bad blow, following as it did torpedo damage to a further trooping liner, *Diulio*. Destroyers were subsequently used for troop reinforcements, and the Axis supply route was badly compromised. As a result of Weichold's report, represented to Hitler by Raeder, the Führer ordered the reduced Fliegerkorps X based in Italy to concentrate on the defence of convoys to Libya. Minesweeping boats and fast attack craft, the *Schnellboote*, or E-boats, as they were known to the Allies, were to be transferred to the Mediterranean via the French canal system. Ominously, too, six U-boats were to run the gauntlet through the Strait of Gibraltar to operate in the Mediterranean. This reduction in force in the Atlantic was to compromise Dönitz's operations in the Western Ocean but have a contrary impact in the Mediterranean.[12] The U-boats had arrived at their new base at Salamis by 5 October, but an unforeseen and unintended by-product of Hitler's order was to ease Malta's burden: Goering, uncooperatively punctilious as was his wont, forbade the Luftwaffe to operate against shipping.

As for Italian perceptions, the loss of three large and formerly prestigious passenger liners, despite the relatively small loss of life in the benign waters of the Mediterranean, had its own effect upon Supermarina. Ciano considered that 'In reality the Mediterranean situation is dark, and will become more so because of the continued loss of merchant ships ... in responsible quarters they are seriously beginning to wonder whether we shouldn't give up Libya voluntarily, rather than wait until we are forced to do so by the total lack of shipping.'[13]

Following MINCEMEAT, the destroyers *Encounter* and *Nestor* were returned to the eastern Mediterranean via the Cape, assisting with the escort of convoy WS11 south to Freetown in Sierra Leone, while *Farndale*, having been left in Malta with condenser trouble, made her own way back to Gibraltar. Somerville himself had meanwhile returned briefly to London with Lord Gort, the Governor of Gibraltar, 'to dispose of some of the wet ideas about Gib. that were in active circulation and emanating chiefly from Chequers' (i.e., Churchill himself). Operation SUBSTANCE was also discussed, and the groundwork was laid for another major convoy operation, to be called HALBERD.[14]

Somerville and Gort flew back to Gibraltar by Sunderland on 5 September. Also arriving at that time was *Furious*, ferrying out more fighters bound for Malta. Under the cover of darkness the old carrier was warped alongside *Ark Royal* to transfer by ramp some twenty-six Hurricanes and one Swordfish of No. 812 Squadron. The ships designated to support *Ark Royal* in Operation STATUS 1, the next Club Run, sailed on the 8th. The need to launch aircraft patrols from the crowded carrier was avoided by relying upon anti-submarine sweeps by a Catalina from Gibraltar, and early the next morning Blenheims from Malta appeared overhead as guides. By noon all the Hurricanes had arrived safely on the distant island. *Nelson*, *Hermione*, the carriers and the destroyers *Gurkha*, *Lively*, *Lance* and *Forester* returned to Gibraltar, where a further transfer of Hurricanes took place between *Furious* and *Ark Royal*. That evening, 10 September, room now being available to fly off from *Furious* as well as *Ark Royal*, Operation STATUS 2 took place. *Furious* sailed at 19.00, screened by *Legion*, *Foresight* and *Forester*, followed at 21.50 by *Nelson*, *Hermione*, *Lively*, *Lance*, *Zulu* and *Gurkha* with *Ark Royal*. Both forces adopted the usual ruse of steaming west before doubling back through the Strait, but on this occasion, once Somerville's ships were well into the Mediterranean, Italian reconnaissance aircraft sighted them without themselves being detected, either by radar or visually – which only became known to the British from intercepted radio traffic, as they reported the presence of Force H at sea.[15]

All the Hurricanes had been flown off by 08.00 on the 12th and, forming on *Nelson*, the two groups of ships combined to steam westwards at *Furious*'s best speed of 20 knots. The enemy failed to make an attack but, as usual, Somerville kept up the pressure by carrying out a series of taxing exercises on his way home. After returning to Gibraltar at the end of the operation, *Furious* then left on 18 September for a refit in the United States.

The insatiable demands from Malta for supplies of all kinds reached a curious crisis at this time. The islanders relied heavily upon horses and donkeys for transport and work on the land (the animals also provided an emergency reserve of meat) and were running drastically short of fodder. Even in times of peace this was largely imported from Sicily, but with all available land now given over to the cultivation of vegetables, home-grown animal feed supplies were negligible. Accordingly the *Empire Guillemot*, a standard ship built in the United States in 1919 as *West Caddoa* and part of a laid-up fleet of war-reserve merchantmen chartered or sold to Great Britain, was loaded with fodder. The cargo was topped out with a small amount of additional military stores and the ship was dispatched from Britain as part of the outward Gibraltar-bound convoy OG73. Following the precedent of *Parracombe* in Operation TEMPLE, *Empire Guillemot* detached from her convoy under the escort of the corvettes *Gentian* and *Jasmine* and passed the Strait during the dark hours of 13/14 September. Having shed her escort by daylight, she headed west under Spanish colours and markings, maintaining this fiction until the 15th, when the rising sun found her to have switched to Vichy French nationality. Off Bizerta she became Italian, and appeared to be heading for Sicily. Swinging towards Malta in the early hours of the 19th, however, she approached the island wearing her proper red ensign, in sight of an Italian convoy actually under attack by Malta-based Swordfish. The Fleet Air Arm pilots strictly obeyed their orders not to attempt to identify or attack any single ships they might encounter and, undetected by the enemy in the darkness, *Empire Guillemot* therefore arrived safely that morning after her lonely passage, the only single merchant ship to do so during the entire period.

During his meeting with Churchill at Chequers, Somerville had been at pains to let the Prime Minister know the risk that all ships engaged in the supply of Malta were running. 'I trust our luck will hold good but the tune has been played so often now that any variations are most difficult ...' As one such variation, Operation PROPELLER was a success, and saved Malta's quadrupeds from starvation; but the sending of single, unescorted merchant ships was fundamentally unsound and, as noted earlier, usually disastrous.[16] 'We ... must always take a lot of chances,' Somerville went on, emphasising to Churchill and the Chiefs of Staff that 'they must be prepared for a set-back sooner or later'.[17] It was inconceivable to Somerville that the Italians would not eventually attack a major convoy with the might of their fleet, and matters were so finely balanced that the defeat of a single British supply operation would achieve at a stroke what the Axis now most wanted in the Mediterranean, the defeat of Malta.

The war cabinet in London were bolder than their enemy; all the inherent risks of such a major operation as was now being mooted as HALBERD were accepted unequivocally. Nevertheless, Somerville was to be strongly reinforced, in anticipation that the luck which had so far presided over British exertions might evaporate. The new battleship *Prince of Wales*, flying the flag of Vice-Admiral A. Curteis, second-in-command of the Home Fleet, with *Nelson*'s sister ship *Rodney*, would provide Somerville with a battle squadron of considerable gun-power, if limited by the slow speed of the two ageing battleships. Cruiser reinforcements were also sent out, *Sheffield* returning to Gibraltar in company with *Kenya*, flagship of Rear-Admiral H. Burrough, commanding the 10th Cruiser Squadron. The Admiralty insisted that Burrough should take Syfret's place, overriding Somerville, who considered him inexperienced. Syfret nevertheless sailed in *Edinburgh* as Rear-Admiral commanding the 2nd Cruiser Squadron, and they were joined by *Euryalus*. In addition to the destroyers already at Gibraltar (namely *Gurkha*,[18] *Legion*, *Lance*, *Lively*, *Lightning*, *Fury*, *Cossack*, *Zulu*, *Foresight*, *Forester* and *Farndale*), the old flotilla leader *Duncan*, the fleet destroyers *Laforey* and *Oribi*, the Hunt-class *Heythrop*, the Dutch *Isaac Sweers*, and the two Polish destroyers *Garland* and *Piorun* made the total assigned to HALBERD eighteen. To maintain them in fuel, the fleet oiler *Brown Ranger* escorted by the corvette *Fleur-de-Lys* was to operate in support. Immediately on completion of the operation the Home Fleet ships were to return to British waters, with the exception of *Euryalus* and the two Hunt-class destroyers, which were to join Cunningham's flag. (In the event it was considered too dangerous for them to steam directly the 900 miles from Malta to Alexandria, because of overwhelming German air power – a profound comment on British assessments of Axis command of the eastern Mediterranean at the time. Instead they returned to Gibraltar and sailed round the Cape, delaying their arrival by weeks.) Cunningham himself had dispatched his submarines from Malta and Alexandria to cover Somerville's movements, with one off Palermo, two off San Vito, two off Messina, and two to extend the patrol line at fifteen-mile intervals.

The laden merchant ships intended for HALBERD sailed with

the units of the Home Fleet as convoy WS11x under Captain Hutchinson as convoy commodore in *Breconshire*. With her were Alfred Holt's *Ajax* (7,539 grt), built in 1931 and the oldest ship in the convoy; Clan Line's *Clan MacDonald* (9,653 grt) and *Clan Ferguson* (7,347 grt); the Blue Star liners *Dunedin Star* (11,168 grt) and *Imperial Star* (10,733 grt); the Ellerman and Bucknall's *City of Lincoln* (8,039 grt); Ellerman's City liner *City of Calcutta* (8,063 grt); and the Union Castle's *Rowallan Castle* (7,798 grt). All were capable of 16 to 17 knots, and to expedite communications each carried a small naval signals staff under a liaison officer. Borne in the holds and 'tween-decks of these modest cargo and cargo-passenger liners were 85,000 tons of food, ammunition, aircraft, spares and supplies. All bore a quantity of each, so that the loss of one ship did not mean a dearth of a particular commodity or resource. Also divided among all the ships were a large number of service personnel, more than three hundred in the cruisers *Kenya* and *Euryalus*, more than four hundred in *Imperial Star* – altogether a total of 1,882 in the merchant vessels plus 790 in the men-of-war. All the merchant ships were 'to be prepared to abandon personnel to a rescue destroyer and to scuttle the ship', but 'no ship is to be scuttled if she is capable of steaming and there is no immediate risk of capture'. The operational orders concluded that 'so long as a ship is afloat a rescue destroyer is to stand by her.' To this end, however, only two destroyers were actually assigned the duties of rescue ships, *Oribi* and *Heythrop*.

On passage, convoy WS11x was joined by *Foresight*, *Forester*, *Fury* and *Legion*, which had escorted *Furious* some distance to the westward on her way to America and then made for a rendez-vous with WS11x. The convoy would become GM2 as it passed Gibraltar and Operation HALBERD got under way.

However, as the British men-of-war and merchantmen were approaching Gibraltar or preparing for the coming operation, the Italian submarine *Scirè*, commanded by Capitano di Fregata the Prince Borghese, entered Gibraltar Bay and launched three *maiali* at 01.00 on the morning of 20 September. It was intended that one human torpedo should enter the harbour through the northern entrance and attack *Ark Royal*. The other two would pass through the southern entrance and make for *Nelson*, lying on the South Mole. One of the latter, commanded by Tenente Vesco, shaken by the explosive charges randomly dropped as a deterrent by patrolling motor launches, turned back and, locating the old oil storage hulk *Fiona Shell* of 2,444 tons, attached his warhead and retired. Driven off by the charges from the north entrance, Tenente Catalano placed a limpet on the after body of the *Durham*, still in the outer harbour, before making for the Spanish shore. Finally, Tenente Visentini, undeterred by the explosives, penetrated the inner harbour, only to be confronted by numerous patrols. He therefore selected the 17,000-ton fleet oiler *Denbydale*, lying at the Detached Mole. Swimming across to her with his warhead, he and his chariot crew then made their escape through the southern entrance. At 07.43 the charge blew a huge hole in the oiler's side. Almost simultaneously the other mines exploded; *Fiona Shell* sank on the bottom and *Durham* began to settle in the water but, being a motor vessel, she quickly got her anchor aweigh and beached before she sank.[19]

The explosions alerted all the warships; water-tight doors were shut and steam raised. Motor launches with depth charges were immediately ordered to sweep the bay with sonar and to patrol the booms. *Cossack* and *Heythrop* were also sent out, to see if they could locate the source of the attack, but Borghese withdrew unharmed, leaving as evidence of his passing the wreckage of three ships and a breathing apparatus, picked up near *Durham*. Somerville rightly concluded that this proved the incursion of 'two-men submarines', afterwards giving the Italians 'credit for great initiative and daring in these sort of adventures ...'[20] Nor was this the only enemy activity on the area; by an odd coincidence, on the same night that HALBERD was set to commence, German U-boats began to pass through the Strait of Gibraltar bound for their new base of Salamis.[21] A more immediate threat was posed by Capitano di Vascello Melodia, leading the Regia Marina's 12th Destroyer Flotilla in *Corazziere* on the night of 22/23 September. With *Ascari*, *Carabiniere*, *Lanciere*, *Aviere* and *Camicia Nera*, Melodia laid two mine barrages to the south-east of Malta.

Undaunted by Borghese's raid, Somerville ordered *Sheffield* to sea to join the incoming WS11x as planned, though she was to leave Gibraltar 'at high speed for a short period' to avoid any further ambush by Italian submarines. Meanwhile the remainder of the fleet relaxed to four hours' notice for steam. As a result of the combined pleas of both Cunningham and Somerville for greater and more effective air support from the Royal Air Force, particularly the Beaufighters at Malta, the Officer Commanding the latter flew in by Sunderland from Malta. Somerville stressed to him the importance of receiving early warning of Italian warship movements, particularly on the fourth day of the operation, when the convoy would be most vulnerable. That same day, Somerville exhibited his *sang-froid* by entertaining the military governor of Algeciras to a convivial lunch, the relaxed attitude of the admiral and his staff suggesting that nothing unusual was in train. Two days later Somerville concluded his final arrangements with Cunningham, who was to provide a powerful diversion if reports were intercepted that enemy air reconnaissance had located HALBERD; Cunningham did in fact mount Operation MD6 in support of his colleague, a sortie by *Queen Elizabeth*, *Barham* and *Valiant*, with cruisers and destroyers, which sailed from Alexandria on 25 September and returned two days later.

Convoy WS11x was to metamorphose into GM2 during the hours of darkness of the night of 24/25 September. The endurance of the merchant ships allowed them to steam directly through the Straits but, as on former occasions and despite a more direct route being taken by WS11x than was usual in order to conserve the destroyers' fuel, each of the escorting warships was to detach after dark, race ahead into Gibraltar and top up their bunkers, rejoining before daylight. As they passed the Strait or lay in Gibraltar all army personnel were kept below decks, and no shore leave was given during the brief stops alongside for fuel. Signals to the dockyard tower were forbidden, although transmissions of an urgent nature directly to Somerville's flagship were permitted. On completion of bunkering, all departing warships from Gibraltar proceeded west for a while, as had now become customary.

In the case of *Rodney*, which unavoidably arrived at Gibraltar to refuel during daylight, an extra ruse was employed to confound the watching agents in Algeciras. Somerville boarded her at 18.00 on 24 September. Shortly after his flag had been hoisted aboard *Rodney*, *Nelson* sailed with her marine band playing 'Rolling Home', the traditional tune signifying the end of a ship's time on station and her return to Britain. The great grey man-of-war was accompanied by the Polish destroyers *Garland* and *Piorun*, and the Dutch *Isaac Sweers*, all from the Home Fleet, adding to the illusion. *Nelson* headed west, her mainmasthead denuded of Somerville's flag, though he had in fact slipped back aboard her.[22]

Following *Nelson* and her three destroyers, *Brown Ranger* and *Fleur-de-Lys* were next to go, at 20.00, in readiness to top up the destroyers closely escorting the convoy on the operation's second day. Finally, well after dark, Somerville's spurious flagship *Rodney* set out for the rendezvous in company with *Ark Royal, Hermione, Duncan, Foresight, Forester, Gurkha, Zulu, Lance, Lively* and *Legion*. *Hermione* had on board some RAF personnel and a quantity of aircraft torpedoes; *Foresight* had loaded RAF stores.

The plans carefully concerted by Somerville, his staff, the Admiralty and the Ministry of War Transport began to take shape as daylight spread over the western Mediterranean on 25 September 1941. Forming on the convoy was the close escort of destroyers, each catching up to join the screen after refuelling. The nine cargo-liners led by *Breconshire* were closely escorted by Curteis in *Prince of Wales*, with *Rodney, Kenya, Edinburgh, Sheffield, Euryalus, Duncan* (commanded by Captain (D) 13th Destroyer Flotilla, Captain H. Williams), *Gurkha, Legion, Lance, Lively, Oribi, Isaac Sweers, Piorun, Garland, Fury, Farndale* and *Heythrop*.

Somerville's covering Force H, proceeding closer to the North African shore, comprised his flagship *Nelson, Ark Royal, Hermione, Cossack* (commanded by Captain (D) 4th Destroyer Flotilla, Captain E. Berthon), *Zulu, Foresight, Laforey* (commanded by Captain, 19th Destroyer Flotilla, Captain R. Hutton) and *Lightning*. *Ark Royal* provided a Swordfish on anti-submarine patrol ahead of the two groups and flew air patrols overhead from dawn to dusk. The 26th passed quietly, despite the sighting of a distant Cant seaplane and the failure of the Fulmars to be vectored onto it due to a radio fault; however, the Italian report was intercepted, as was the rebroadcast to dispersed Italian units at sea. These consisted of eleven submarines: *Adua, Dandolo* and *Turchese* off Cape Ferrat; *Axum, Serpente, Aradam* and *Diaspro* off Cape Bougaroni; *Squalo, Bandiera* and *Delfino* off Cape de Fer; and *Narvalo* stationed off Cape Bon. In addition to the minefields in the Narrows, *MAS*-boats were to be made ready in the vicinity of Pantelleria.

During the morning Force H came in sight of the Swiss

merchantman *Tunisian*, and at 15.37 two aircraft were sighted, at first thought to have been Hudsons. Somerville afterwards admitted his error in not intercepting them, for they too reported the progress of the British ships. Meanwhile, the programme to refuel the destroyers from *Brown Ranger* was delayed, for the oiler had trouble catching up with the convoy and failed to make the rendezvous on time. This meant the destroyers had to be withdrawn individually in order to steam towards *Brown Ranger*, and it was dark before *Fury* and *Heythrop* returned to their stations. Last to complete this task was *Oribi*; Lieutenant-Commander McBeath subsequently failed to locate the convoy by night and tagged onto Force H until daylight on the 27th, when the two groups joined forces. During the 26th a Spanish civil aircraft was seen in a cloud gap and was thought to have added to the reports locating HALBERD, while at 18.30 a Vichy French merchantman passed the convoy.[23]

That evening Iachino put to sea from Naples with the two battleships *Littorio* and *Vittorio Veneto*, the 8-inch-gun cruisers *Trento*, *Trieste* and *Gorizia*, the 6-inch-gun light cruisers *Muzio Attendolo* and *Duca degli Abruzzi*, with fourteen destroyers. Other units of the Italian fleet failed to sail because of a shortage of oil fuel. Italian intelligence had underestimated the British strength, and it remained Iachino's intention to cruise to the south of Sardinia, under the air umbrella provided by Cagliari, and intercept Somerville.

Somerville had no idea Iachino was at sea.

At noon that same day, *Melbourne Star* had left Grand Harbour for a dash to the west. As she departed Ford, annoyed, signalled Somerville, expressing his indignation and anxiety that she had on board army and air force personnel, including wives who, although they had gone aboard understanding the risks and at the request of General Dobbie, had done so without his own knowledge. 'I feel I should have been consulted,' he agonised, 'since a moral obligation arose to give [... her] some degree of close protection ...' In the event *Melbourne Star* arrived safely at Gibraltar at 07.00 on 29 September 'after an uneventful passage'.

At daylight on 27 September *Ark Royal*'s Fulmars were airborne, and the first radar contact with Italian reconnaissance planes occurred at 07.20. Italian signals were received during the forenoon indicating increasing interest, and just before noon, when sixteen Fulmars were overhead, one of them made an abortive chase after a shadowing Cant. The tardiness of the expected Italian attack was the result of a bombing raid made on Cagliari the previous evening: Malta-based bombers had inflicted serious damage and numerous aircraft had been destroyed, but after a morning's repair work the Regia Aeronautica were capable of retaliation that afternoon.

By 12.55 radar was indicating to the watching and waiting British naval officers that an air attack was in the offing, with two enemy formations thirty miles away, one to the north, the second to the east. The Fulmars were vectored to intercept but the numerous planes airborne made the primitive radar plot unmanageable and fighter direction was abandoned. In the confusion of this first air action one Cant 1007 torpedo-bomber was shot down at about 13.00 by *Ark Royal*'s Fulmars. Coming in from the north, six Fiat BR20 torpedo-bombers were 'engaged by the port wing of the screen and the ships on the port side of the fleet and two were lost to this barrage fire as the fleet altered course to avoid the torpedoes, dropped at 5,000 yards range'. Several of the ships, including *Lance*, *Isaac Sweers* and *Rodney*, had to take sudden avoiding action. One of the attackers was shot down by the destroyers' barrage, another by an attacking Fulmar, but in the confusion a damaged Fulmar was hit by fire from the *Prince of Wales* at 13.10. In this 'unfortunate accident', which was 'deeply regretted', Lieutenant M. Watson and Sub-Lieutenant P. Couch were killed. Twenty minutes later a second Fulmar was shot down, but her crew was rescued. 'Both fighters approached low-down straight towards the convoy during a T/B [torpedo bomber] attack and appeared menacing. The considerable amount of smoke from bursting shell added to the difficulties of identification', which were compounded through what Somerville afterwards reported was 'a phonetic misunderstanding'. This intense action lasted less than half an hour, then there was a brief respite until a second wave of about seven Fiat BR20s was seen approaching very low from the east at 13.27. These divided, coming in on the starboard bow and starboard beam of the convoy, three of them penetrating the barrage to attack *Nelson*. Captain Troubridge swung the battleship to comb the anticipated torpedo tracks as one Italian aeroplane flew down *Nelson*'s starboard side, to be cut into three pieces by pom-pom shells. But another BR20 let her torpedo go right ahead, at 400 yards distance. 'The chances of a hit seemed remote', Somerville later wrote to Cunningham, 'until the bloody bubbles appeared about 120 yards ahead … coming straight for us. Possibly helm hard over or keeping her swinging to starboard *might* have let us take it on the bulge but I doubt it. Anyhow there was always the danger of a hit right aft which would have been worse.' As the torpedo struck *Nelson*, 'there was a large "crump" [and] the ship whipped considerably …' The aircraft flew low over *Nelson*, only to be shot down by the combined fire of the ships astern. The battleship had been hit on the port bow and her speed rapidly dropped to 18 knots as water poured into her forward hull and she settled by the head. The full extent of the damage was not of course known until later, but it proved serious. A second torpedo, dropped presumably by the plane shot into three pieces, missed narrowly, and the third BR20 heading for the flagship was shot out of the sky by *Laforey*'s guns. Another made for *Rowallan Castle* dropping its torpedo, which passed under the ship's stern, and 'as it rose to turn away was hit by our Bofors gun and disintegrated into a shower of matchwood'. One survivor from this attack, a wireless operator with a broken leg, was picked up by *Forester*, while *Duncan* rescued the crew of a Fulmar shot down by *Rodney*'s anti-aircraft fire. The remaining torpedo-bombers were kept at bay largely by the destroyers' barrage, though one was shot down by a Fulmar.

This second attack was over by 13.37, but at 13.45 the third arrived, consisting of 'ten or eleven' SM79s in two groups approaching very low. Some dropped their torpedoes at long range and one was destroyed by a Fulmar before they swung away. Two of the enemy aircraft returned, only to be driven off, while one persisted until, before it could release its torpedo, it was shot down by the combined fire of *Ark Royal* and *Nelson*. *Cossack* evaded a torpedo dropped outside the screen while her consorts were engaging a CR42 which was 'seen diving on the starboard wing destroyers and performing aerobatics over them, evidently to make a diversion' for the others. 'Insofar as the destroyers expended a large amount of ammunition … [the Italian aircraft] succeeded, but after six minutes [the CR42] was either shot down or failed to pull out of a dive', for it crashed into the sea. Captain Hutton of *Laforey* afterwards described the pilot as 'a very brave man'.

As the enemy withdrew there was relief that the aerial torpedo attack had not been accompanied by high-level bombers. Two casualties had been sustained in *Oribi*, caused by shell splinters from friendly fire, and *Nelson* had been very severely damaged. As Somerville afterwards wrote to his wife, it had been 'a most hectic afternoon' but, importantly, 'no aircraft were able to reach a good position to torpedo a ship of the convoy during day attacks.' There was no remedy for friendly fighters which 'approach the fleet in the same manner as an enemy T/B whilst an attack is in progress.'

But it was in these critical few moments that Somerville received a report that Iachino was at sea; moreover, the Italian battle squadron was only 74 miles away.

The Italian admiral had been misled by aerial reconnaissance into thinking only a single British battleship was with Somerville. As the afternoon passed, confusing reports reached him; he was also apprehensive about an attack by *Ark Royal*'s Swordfish torpedo-bombers, and the overhead cover from the Regia Aeronautica (which he not only expected, but which was a fundamental tenet of Italian naval thinking) had yet again failed to materialise. His seaman's instincts were further alerted by the presence of a mist, limiting visibility to five miles. Without either radar or reliable air intelligence, the visible horizon was the extent of Iachino's strategic certainty; consequently, at 15.00 he turned nervously to the north and began to retire.

He might have derived some small comfort from the plight of *Nelson*, had he known of it. When at 14.04 Somerville received the report of a scouting Maryland from Malta, that at 13.40 'two battleships and eight destroyers ... [were] steering 190° [south by west] at 20 knots', it was thought that *Nelson* was not badly hurt and that she could keep up 18 knots and thus continue to cover the convoy. Somerville therefore immediately decided to form a battle squadron with *Nelson*, *Rodney*, *Prince of Wales* and six destroyers, and head for an engagement with the Italians. He would leave Burrough in *Kenya* with *Edinburgh*, *Sheffield* and ten destroyers, as escort to the convoy, while *Ark Royal*, with *Hermione* as fighter director, *Euryalus*, *Piorun* and *Legion* would continue to act close to but independently of it. Two Swordfish would take off 'to take over shadowing duties' from the RAF, while an air striking force was prepared. At 14.25 an updated and

1. Grand Harbour, Malta: an anti-aircraft Bofors gun maintains the air defence of Valletta and the Three Cities. Such weapons required a steady supply of ammunition

2. Sir James Somerville, shown here as an Admiral of the Fleet in August 1945. As the 'door-keeper' at Gibraltar, Somerville often frustrated Churchill in his assessments of risk, but he was a keen advocate of technology

3. Admiral Cunningham, the burden of high command clearly evident in his oddly bloodshot eyes. His duties as 'door-keeper' at Alexandria involved 'A.B.C.' in the débâcle of Crete as well as the supply of Malta

4. Force H, Somerville's principal weapon: the battlecruiser *Renown*, with the aircraft-carrier *Ark Royal* and cruiser *Sheffield* in the background

5. The Hunt-class destroyer *Bramham*, a distinguished participant of Malta convoys. Slower than the fleet destroyers, the Hunts were intended as fast convoy escorts with an effective anti-aircraft capability

6. HM Cruiser *Euryalus* passes north through the Suez Canal on her way to join Cunningham's Mediterranean Fleet in November 1941. One of the *Dido* class, she too was designed for anti-aircraft defence with a 5.25-inch main armament

7. Operation HALBERD: Force H escorts the convoy eastwards through the Western Mediterranean in September 1941

8. HM Destroyer *Forester* alongside her stricken sister-ship *Fearless*, removing survivors, 23 July 1941

9. The very fast minelayer HMS *Welshman* arrives in Grand Harbour after her dash from Gibraltar, 15 June 1942. *Welshman*, bearing a small but essential cargo, is wearing the disguise of a *Léopard*-class French man-of-war

10. More satisfactory to the authorities at Malta was the safe arrival of laden merchant ships

11. Lying as a bombed-out wreck in No. 2 Dock amid the wholesale destruction surrounding Grand Harbour, the destroyer *Lance* represented the cost to Great Britain in men and *matériel* of the support of Malta

12. Admiral Sir Wilbraham Ford, Vice-Admiral, Malta, the man responsible for co-ordinating the arrival, fuelling, discharge, loading and departure of the men-of-war and merchantmen participating in Malta convoys

13. The British Blue Funnel liner *Deucalion*, seen here with the destroyer *Bramham*, was typical of the fast 15–16-knot cargo-liners required to make supply convoys to Malta

14. Not quite as bad as it looks. On arrival at Malta in mid June 1942, the ships of Operation HARPOON were caught in enemy air-raids. Although debris from the buildings surrounding No. 4 Dry Dock covered her decks, *Troilus* successfully discharged her cargo

15. The cargo-liner *Breconshire*, fitted out as a military transport, arrives at Malta on 19 December 1941. Vital to the supply of the island, *Breconshire* made several successful runs from Alexandria

16. *Breconshire*'s luck finally runs out. She is here on fire, shortly before she capsized in Marsaxlokk Harbour

17. The aircraft-carriers attached to Operation PEDESTAL: *Eagle* (nearest camera), *Indomitable* and *Victorious* in line abreast in the Western Mediterranean

18. Operation PEDESTAL: the convoy forms up east of Gibraltar in perfect Mediterranean weather

19. Operation PEDESTAL: aboard the cruiser *Nigeria* in the Clyde, the convoy conference breaks up prior to departure. The masters of the merchant ships, still in their civilian suits, leave with their naval liaison officers. Here, Rear-Admiral Burrough shakes hands with Captain Dudley Mason of the tanker *Ohio*

20. Operation PEDESTAL: *Victorious* leads *Indomitable* and *Eagle* as they form into line ahead. The aircraft in the foreground is a Sea Hurricane

21. Additional armaments were fitted to the merchant ships assigned to Operation PEDESTAL. This mobile Bofors gun is aboard *Melbourne Star*. Note the spare barrel on the deck alongside, and the fact that it has no protection

22. A flag signal is hauled down on *Melbourne Star*'s bridge during Operation PEDESTAL. Note the mixture of Merchant Naval and Royal Naval personnel, the extensive flag locker, the PAC rockets on the wheelhouse top, the stopwatch hung on the shuttered wheelhouse side and the engine telegraph set at full speed ahead

23. Captain R. Wren, DSO, Master of the *Rochester Castle*

24. Captain F. N. Riley, DSO, Master of the *Brisbane Star*

25. Captain D. R. McFarlane, OBE, Master of the *Melbourne Star*

26. Apprentice F. Treves, survivor of the *Waimarama*, received the British Empire Medal and Lloyd's War Medal

27. Operation PEDESTAL: the damaged flight-deck of the aircraft-carrier
HMS *Indomitable*

28. Operation PEDESTAL: as the cargo-liner *Deucalion* settles in the water and her crew
make for the attending destroyer, the convoy stands on to the east

29. *(above)* The cost: the loss of the American ship *Chant* during Operation HARPOON sent a dense column of smoke into the sky for many hours

30. *(left)* Captain Riley's *Brisbane Star* displays the wreckage of her bow as she arrives in Grand Harbour

31. *(below)* The tanker *Ohio* is finally manoeuvred into Grand Harbour, concluding Operation PEDESTAL The warship nearest the camera is HMS *Penn*

32. *Melbourne Star* discharges her cargo at Canteen Wharf, next to No. 3 Dock, Grand Harbour, August 1942. The tug *Robust* is on hand as preparations are made for repairs

33. *Brisbane Star*, her stem damaged, discharges her cargo into lighters during Operation CERES, August 1942

accurate report of the composition of Iachino's force was received from Malta and shortly afterwards, with *Nelson*'s speed now dropping significantly, Somerville sadly ordered Curteis to take over in *Prince of Wales*. Although within the next few minutes the reconnoitring Swordfish discovered that Iachino had reversed his course, Somerville nevertheless urged Curteis on ahead and sent a dozen Swordfish escorted by four Fulmars after the retreating Italians in an attempt to nail them. Forty minutes after their departure, at 16.20, Fulmars maintaining overhead patrols broke up a formation of Italian bombers to the north and shot down a Cant seaplane shadowing astern.

Once more the mist and the speed of the Italian ships confounded the Swordfish, while Somerville was again anxious about his primary concern, the convoy. At 16.58, with Curteis drawing away from him in pursuit of an elusive quarry, Somerville recalled the battle squadron. He needed the cruisers to reinforce the convoy escort as it approached the Skerki Bank, and the destroyers to screen his damaged flagship and *Ark Royal* as nightfall approached. The wisdom of this decision was clear when at 17.40 the air striking force reported themselves unable to locate Iachino's ships. They were ordered to return to *Ark Royal*.

It was now necessary for Somerville to detach and turn back into a blazing sunset towards Gibraltar with the three battle-ships, the carrier and their screen of destroyers, leaving Burrough and Force X to continue east with the convoy, above which a crescent moon was rising. The question being put to him by Somerville, Burrough decided to route the convoy north, close to the Sicilian shore, on the grounds that it was the bolder route and less likely to attract attention from the *MAS*-boats operating off Pantelleria. This brief exchange holds a key to both Burrough's ability and Somerville's attitude to his subordinate admirals, for the choice was the lesser of two evils and, in view of Somerville's earlier misgivings about Burrough, showed his willingness to change his mind when evidence as to the wisdom of so doing confronted him.

Burrough's forces were now reorganised for the passage of the mine-strewn Narrows astern of the destroyers *Foresight*, *Fury* and *Forester*, which streamed their minesweeping gear. His flag-ship *Kenya* led the port column, followed by the cargo-liners *Ajax*, *Clan MacDonald*, *Imperial Star*, *Rowallan Castle* and *City of*

Calcutta, the cruiser *Euryalus* bringing up the rear. *Cossack* was out on *Kenya*'s port bow, under the protection of *Foresight*'s paravane, and behind her were *Zulu* and *Heythrop* providing air and anti-submarine defence on the port wing. Syfret led the starboard column in *Edinburgh*, followed by *Clan Ferguson*, *Dunedin Star*, *Breconshire* and *City of Lincoln* with the cruisers *Sheffield* and *Hermione* as rear guard. *Laforey* was out on the starboard wing, tucked behind *Forester*'s paravane, with *Lightning* and *Farndale* following to form the starboard flank. In the rear came *Oribi*, ready to pick up survivors.

This neat cruising disposition was broken up shortly after 19.55 when *Cossack* detected an incoming aircraft on her radar and at 20.00 caught sight of an aeroplane on her port side. The night was clear, the day's mists having dispersed. In the wan moonlight, the grey shapes of the ships stood out to the incoming Italian torpedo-bombers. Burrough ordered an emergency turn of 40 degrees to port, sounded two blasts on *Kenya*'s siren and was followed 'belatedly' by the ships astern of her. *Edinburgh* received the order as a starboard alteration and the two columns diverged, adding in the dark to the coming confusion. Aircraft were now detected racing in from the south and east, crossing the convoy to locate targets and then turning and attacking from the port side. While the whole force attempted to regain station, the night began to light up with tracer as the destroyers on the port wing, with the merchantmen and cruisers of the port column, began to throw up a barrage: Captain A. Clarke of *Sheffield* reported several ships 'continually and grossly out of position' as the merchant vessels ahead of him, not designed for the quick helm response expected of men-of-war, yawed wildly to dodge torpedoes.[24] In the confusion, at about 20.30, as they strove to avoid the same torpedo, *Rowallan Castle* struck *City of Calcutta*, raking her 'with a glancing blow along her midships section, which left most of … [*City of Calcutta*'s] port boats in pieces on our foredeck, and left … [*Rowallan Castle*] with a badly bent bow and making some water in the forepeak.'[25] As *Rowallan Castle* rolled, many of her crew thought she had been torpedoed, and something tripped her PAC rockets, so that she fired these conspicuously into the night sky, attracting an admonishment from Hutchinson in *Breconshire*.

One torpedo exploded at the end of its run on the port quarter of the convoy, and other torpedoes were seen to be dropped by the aircraft, one of which *Sheffield* avoided only by using full helm herself. *Oribi* opened fire on aircraft engine noises to port, seeing nothing but the splashes of two torpedoes half a mile away. McBeath swung to starboard, turning his stern to the approaching weapons, and increased to full speed, a manoeuvre which allowed his Oerlikon and pom-pom gunners to destroy their assailant as it flew past, suddenly revealed in the pale moonlight. But even as *Oribi* took avoiding action, her sonar operators picked up the sound of an explosion: the Italian torpedo-bombers had succeeded in reaching a target. At 20.32, *Imperial Star* was struck on the port side near her stern.

It was thought that the ship had lost both her screws as No. 6 Hold, the double-bottom tank below it, and her engine room began to flood. Seeing her drop out of line as both her engines stopped, Captain Bush of *Euryalus* ordered *Oribi* to stand by, but as McBeath approached the stricken ship he found that Lieutenant-Commander Stafford had anticipated him, and *Heythrop* was already taking off about three hundred of the 420 servicemen who were embarked in *Imperial Star*. McBeath laid *Oribi* alongside *Imperial Star* and held a brief conversation through his megaphone with her master, Captain S. Phillips, and his naval liaison officer. Both men thought it best that the ship be towed back to Gibraltar, but McBeath, mindful of her mixed general cargo (500 tons of frozen meat, 500 tons of kerosene, crates of light and heavy bombs, grain, flour and ammunition), considered the only real chance of saving the ship was to attempt the much shorter distance of 220 miles to Malta. At 22.00 *Heythrop* departed to catch up with the convoy while the companies of *Imperial Star* and *Oribi* strove to complete connection of the destroyer's ninety-fathom 5-inch towing wire to an unshackled anchor cable on *Imperial Star* and get the cargo-liner under way. This they had succeeded in doing by 20.35, achieving 8 knots, but the dead weight of the larger ship proved impossible to tow in a straight line. *Imperial Star* was heavily down by the stern and incapable of steering herself owing to the destruction of her electric steering gear and, though it was not known at the time, her rudder. Furthermore, a section of her keel had been torn and folded back, which constantly compelled her to swing perversely to starboard. 'Nothing', McBeath complained, 'would prevent her steering in circles', and as *Imperial Star* sheered about, drawing 38 feet aft as she slowly sank, she dragged *Oribi*'s stern in a perfect example of the tail wagging the dog. McBeath, a determined man, persisted until at 01.20 on 28 September *Imperial Star* took a sudden, heavy sheer and dragged *Oribi* bodily astern. McBeath was 'forced to slip the tow'. Having recovered her wire, *Oribi* ran back alongside to consult Phillips and his naval colleague. Consequently 'it was reluctantly decided that the remaining 141 persons aboard should be taken off by *Oribi* and the ship scuttled.'[26]

To achieve this, three depth charges were lashed just below the waterline, abreast a bulkhead in the engine room, and the naval liaison officer dumped the confidential books. At 03.40 *Oribi* cast off, having disembarked all hands. The charges exploded at 03.51, failing to counter-mine the ammunition in *Imperial Star*'s cargo but starting a large fire. This, however, did not spread: *Imperial Star* refused to sink. McBeath ordered semi-armour-piercing shells fired from his 4.7-inch guns and for half an hour *Oribi*'s gunners blazed away, until the cargo-liner was on fire from stem to stern and listing heavily. At 04.52 *Oribi* withdrew, increasing speed to 32 knots. She caught up with the convoy at 12.15 on the 29th as it approached the swept channel into Grand Harbour, 'having passed unmolested within seven miles of the Sicilian coast in daylight'.

During *Oribi*'s absence, the decision to pass the convoy close along the Sicilian shore proved to have been inspired. *MAS*-boats waited fruitlessly to the south of Pantelleria, and at 20.30 on the evening of the 27th *Hermione* detached from the convoy to approach Pantelleria from the north at 25 knots. Captain G. Oliver's targets were the barracks, harbour and warehouses on the north-west tip of the island, set behind Punta Santa Leonardo. At 01.35 on the 28th *Hermione* swung to port and fired a salvo of star shell before discharging thirty rapid-fire salvoes to the south-west at a range of 12,000 yards. Shore batteries on the headland replied, but the shells fell to seaward of *Hermione* as she steamed east, finally dropping decoys off Punta Spadillo and turning away at 28 knots as the 'enemy hotly engaged smoke floats'. The after gunnery control officer claimed that the majority of *Hermione*'s shells fell in the target area, reported Oliver, though he wisely added the caveat that 'he may have been an optimist'. This proved to be correct, for *Hermione* caused no serious damage, though she did shake up the garrison. Oliver, along with his superiors, again requested flashless cordite for night operations,[27] *Hermione*'s bombardment being 'clearly visible from the convoy and escort, then distant 50 miles'.

By daylight, Malta-based aircraft were flying above the convoy. A pair of Fulmars appeared first, at 06.15, quickly followed by six Beaufighters and subsequently a number of Hurricanes. Enemy air formations in the offing dispersed, and the news that no enemy surface forces were in sight allowed Burrough to break away. His cruisers entered port first, to oil and start off on the homeward run to Gibraltar. It seemed that the entire population of Valletta had turned out to greet the inward-bound vessels as they swung slowly round the narrow bend between Ricasoli Point and Fort St Elmo mole. The cruisers paraded their guards, their bands playing, their white ensigns languidly lifting in the warm afternoon air, while the crowds waved and cheered from the Barrakka Gardens and the ramparts. Two hours later, led by *Breconshire* with her naval colours, grimly grey in their own war paint and flying the red ensign above their sterns, the laden merchant ships of GM2 followed, receiving an equally warm welcome. All but one had made it. As for *Imperial Star*, her cargo of ammunition had finally exploded and taken her to the bottom, so that no aircraft could find a trace of her the following day.

In Malta's congested harbours, complained Vice-Admiral Ford, the arrival of the cruisers and the necessary priority afforded them was unhelpful; Ford considered they should have been detached as soon as the convoy was under the Malta air-umbrella, to prevent overcrowding in the port. He added that *Kenya* had relaxed to four hours' notice to steam without his permission, and that neither the composition of the escort nor its fuel requirements had been made known to him in advance. Perhaps most telling was Ford's irritation that, as a consequence, the damaged *Rowallan Castle*, which required the urgent attention of the Dockyard, had to be kept waiting for seven hours before she could be taken in hand. Burrough's poor staff work and lack of experience in this respect were cruelly exposed by Ford, whose efficiency in running the turnaround and accommodation of laden inward-bound ships, irrespective of ensign, had become legendary.[28]

For Somerville, the separation of the convoy at sunset on 27 September marked the end of the first phase of the operation.

As he turned Force H south, opening his distance from Cagliari, he was now preoccupied by worries over the state of *Nelson*. Underlying these was his ignorance of Iachino's movements, for the sortie of *Ark Royal*'s air striking force had been frustrated. RAF reconnaissance, moreover, had ended as soon as Iachino's turn to the north had been reported, while nothing had been forthcoming from his own aerial reconnoitring. One of the two Swordfish sent out in advance of the strike force had been mauled by seven Italian fighters and limped back to *Ark Royal*, while the second had searched in the wrong area, hampered by cloud and faulty navigation.

Italian claims arising from the hit on *Nelson* led Supermarina to expand pilots' reports that the Regia Aeronautica had sunk one cruiser and possibly a battleship, and damaged two other cruisers. Iachino therefore turned south again, but after sunset, at about 19.45, he was ordered east into the Tyrrhenian Sea. Here the Italian warships had to run the gauntlet of British and Polish submarine patrols, but only *Utmost* managed to catch sight of them, and failed to score any hits when she made an attack on the three heavy cruisers. Once again Iachino had failed to seize an opportunity, hampered by a dearth of air support, poor visibility, and a fatal and fundamental lack of resolution. 'They could have eaten up the convoy without the slightest difficulty,' Somerville wrote, dismally contemplating his water-logged flagship. 'This ship feels like a real wounded thing. She's ten feet down by the head and sluggish ...' Slowly *Nelson*'s speed dropped off as Captain Troubridge sought to prevent the seas from washing over her bows and straining her bulkheads, for it was estimated that by this time some 3,500 tons of water had entered her. Somerville decided to retain all his destroyers and not detach any to the support of the merchant ships of MG2, now steaming west from Malta in two batches.

Next morning, the 28th, a Cant was seen 'very low down and fighters were vectored. After a chase to the SE, the Cant was shot down near Cape de Fer, 55 miles from the Fleet and only 200 yards from the Algerian shore. This was a fine example of fighter control and relentless pursuit.'[29] At 21.00 Somerville handed over to Curteis the duty of waiting for the return of Burrough, and with three destroyers as screen *Nelson* crawled westwards. Anxious not to give away either to enemy aerial reconnaissance or to the eyes that would watch her in Gibraltar the impotent state to which *Nelson* had been reduced, Somerville and Troubridge caused her to be retrimmed. Her wretched seamen had to shift her massive anchor cables aft, reducing her forward draught and realigning her on an even keel.[30] In this deep but less revealing state, she arrived at Gibraltar at 11.00 on 30 September, to be docked a few days later. Somewhat regretfully, and much moved by a gift from Troubridge and *Nelson's* company, Somerville transferred his flag to *Rodney*.

Meanwhile, as Curteis turned east again to rendezvous with Burrough, the two remaining merchantmen of MG2 were on their way to Gibraltar in the wake of *Melbourne Star*. *Port Chalmers*[31] and *City of Pretoria*, both with service personnel aboard, left Valletta at 10.30 on 27 September, escorted until sunset by the corvette *Gloxinia*. The departure of the three vessels was reported by Italian aircraft at noon. Once *Gloxinia* had turned back they proceeded in line ahead, the Ellerman liner leading, their intended route south of Pantelleria and close along the Tunisian coast. That evening, at 23.30 when they were some fifteen miles to the south-south-west of the Italian island, look-outs on *Port Chalmers* thought they spotted the dark shape of a *MAS*-boat lying stopped ahead of them, about 350 yards on the port beam of the *City of Pretoria*. Captain Higgs sheered *Port Chalmers* to starboard and sent a few rounds in the general direction of the supposed torpedo-boat. A few minutes later the unmistakable sound of powerful engines roared up astern and *Port Chalmers* made a second turn to starboard. Laying the poop-mounted 4-inch gun on the approaching bow wave, the gun crew opened fire. The *MAS*-boat retaliated with her machine-gun and, after enduring six rounds, crossed astern of *Port Chalmers* and vanished into the darkness. Captain Higgs then resumed his station astern of the *City of Pretoria*.

At 05.35 next morning the two ships hoisted French colours and parted company on slightly diverging courses, the *City of Pretoria* edging ahead thanks to a small advantage in speed. At 09.15 an Italian Cant 506 seaplane flew towards them from the direction of the coast of French North Africa and investigated the two ships, neither of which interrupted this scrutiny by opening fire. With all service personnel hidden away neither ship drew attention to herself, and the Cant flew off. Then an hour later the *City of Pretoria* was circled by a 'large 3-engined seaplane with distinct French markings and from Bizerta' and, as she approached Galita, a twin-engined Italian seaplane was sighted lying on the sea some five miles away.

Now out of sight, *Port Chalmers* was unaware of either of these last two encounters by her late consort and saw little until 15.55, when she was circled by an Italian Breda 20 which, Higgs reported, 'could not have been deceived by the French colours'.

At 17.25, however, their disguise was positively penetrated and three torpedo-bombers swooped on the *City of Pretoria*. She immediately hoisted British colours and sent up an anti-aircraft barrage, her master skilfully avoiding the dropped torpedoes. As one of the aircraft was machine-gunning them, two lookouts spotted a periscope on the starboard quarter. Smoke floats were dropped and a depth charge set at 150 feet was launched, the *City of Pretoria* turning away under the partial cover of the smoke. She had her last encounter with the enemy in the small hours of the 30th, when at 02.00 as she was approaching Cape de Gata she observed in the darkness the presence of a shadowing craft. This was assumed to be a submarine, and 'two or three shots, followed by a dull explosion' were heard. Once again smoke floats were dropped and the ship made smoke, turning into the bight of Almeria Bay and Spanish territorial waters as she escaped.

Taking a more direct route, *Port Chalmers* made her numbers to Europa Point that morning and at 09.00 anchored off Gibraltar, followed a few hours later by the *City of Pretoria*. The two ships had maintained an almost perfect radio silence, transmitting only two short, coded signals to indicate that they had been under attack on the afternoon of the 28th.[32]

As Somerville was to record, 'The able and resolute handling of both *Port Chalmers* and *City of Pretoria* in successfully driving off enemy attacks deserves high praise. Both Masters showed excellent restraint in withholding fire at enemy aircraft while there was a chance of their false colours being effective ...'

Following the merchantmen of MG2, Burrough's returning warships began to leave Grand Harbour on the afternoon of 28 September. At 16.15 *Kenya, Edinburgh* and *Oribi* departed, with the remainder of the destroyers, *Sheffield* and *Hermione* following at 18.30. They were to take the southern route along the Tunisian shore, in the wake of MG2. Cunningham's reinforcements, *Euryalus, Heythrop* and *Farndale*, awaited a final decision whether they were to continue east or, as ultimately happened, to return to Gibraltar and proceed by way of the Cape of Good Hope.

Meanwhile, as Vice-Admiral Curteis steamed back to the east prior to his rendezvous with the returning Burrough, one of his screening destroyers, *Gurkha*, obtained a sonar contact on the morning of 29 September. Commander C. Lentaigne made an attack and dropped a pattern of fourteen depth charges which was followed after six minutes by an underwater explosion, but in the event, no enemy submarine was destroyed.

Burrough joined Curteis at 10.30, about forty miles off the African coast. The warships steamed west, spotting the conning tower of a submarine that afternoon. This was quickly followed by two torpedo tracks which were evaded by *Lively*, the destroyer then counter-attacking with a fourteen-charge pattern set for shallow detonation. A moment earlier *Legion* had dashed in and Commander R. Jessel had fired a five-charge pattern. Jessel then stationed *Lively* on his starboard beam and the two destroyers hunted the enemy for an hour, but *Diaspro* and *Serpente*, both of which had been in the vicinity, escaped destruction. Shortly after this incident Curteis in *Prince of Wales*, with *Kenya*, *Sheffield*, *Laforey*, *Lightning*, *Oribi*, *Foresight*, *Forester* and *Fury*, increased speed to arrive at Gibraltar late on the 30th.

The remaining ships followed, and at 09.38 on the morning of the 30th *Gurkha* made another sonar contact and Lentaigne attacked as his operator held the echo until they were only 100 yards away. As *Gurkha* passed overhead, she fired a fourteen-charge pattern on shallow setting. A black circular buoy attached to a length of electrical cable surfaced, to be followed by a loud underwater explosion accompanied by oil. Attacking in support of *Gurkha*, Jessel's *Legion* now picked up the dodging echo and dropped a similar charge, also set shallow, regaining contact immediately afterwards and dropping a second pattern set deep. After this, oil and wreckage surfaced. Among the latter 'were an Italian dictionary, a mattress, pillow, numerous pieces of wood, some with bright screws, and a piece of human scalp attached to a piece of wood by a splinter of metal. The interiors of the dictionary, pillow and mattress were dry.'[33] These gruesome remains were evidence of the destruction of the Italian submarine *Adua* and her complement.

Between 07.00 and 09.00 on 1 October 1941 Burrough's ships returned to Gibraltar. It was the end of Operation HALBERD. The

matériel conveyed to Malta in the ships of GM2 would, it was calculated, sustain both defensive and offensive operations for
about four months. There were the usual post-mortems, of
course, Ford's among them. Syfret considered the two-column
cruising disposition to be too close for comfort when ships were
dodging torpedoes; many commanding officers bemoaned the
devastation caused by so-called friendly fire; others thought the
destroyer screen should be at a greater distance from the convoy,
even if this was at the expense of anti-submarine defences. Even
a crescent moon provided too much light, revealing the convoy
and exposing it to night attack; and the chorus of cries for flashless cordite increased. Such reviews were standard practice,
meant to adduce lessons and thus enable better planning of
future operations. Blame was laid where blame was due without
the hunting of scapegoats, unless inefficiency had compromised
matters. Among the thousands of words written afterwards, as
each commanding officer submitted his report up the chain of
command to be carefully drafted into Somerville's final Report
of Proceedings, there were those of encouragement. Somerville
praised Captain Maund of *Ark Royal* and the conduct of the
masters of several merchant ships. Captain Williams in *Duncan*
spoke highly of the 'Allied division of destroyers' he had commanded, which included the two Polish and a single Dutch
warship; McBeath commended Able Seaman Robert Clark, gunlayer of *Oribi's* port, foremost Oerlikon. And increasingly there
were the reports of technical advantage, especially of radar.
Kenya claimed to have shot down the aircraft which torpedoed
Imperial Star 'with 6-inch barrage fire timed and controlled for
line by Type 271' radar. Significantly, too, integration with the
RAF had improved, and although it was still not without its limitations, Somerville placed on record his 'high appreciation of the
excellent co-operation furnished by the RAF throughout this
operation.'

13

'The blackest of days'

(Operations CALLBOY, PERPETUAL and ASTROLOGER)

MALTA, RELIEVED BY the cargoes of convoy GM2 in Operation HALBERD, now also experienced fewer air raids by the Regia Aeronautica. Throughout the whole of September, Dobbie reported only twelve nights of raids, resulting in the deaths of three men and one woman, a remarkable reduction from the spring of 1941. It was but a temporary easement, however, for the consolidating hold of the Germans on Greece, the presence of their U-boats and the return of the Luftwaffe from the Russian front during the winter months were to alter the strategic balance in the Mediterranean.

The increase in Malta's fighter force, particularly in the numbers of Hurricanes now available, had done much to blunt the Fascist axe, and it was decided to reinstate the Malta Strike Force, diverted and largely dissipated by the disaster of Crete and the losses among Mountbatten's ships. While this was possible because of the island's improved air defences, it was also necessary, because despite all their efforts the submarines of the 10th Flotilla and the strike fighters of the RAF based on Malta proved unable to throttle the enemy's communications with North Africa.[1] Axis convoys were now able to proceed eastwards and then south from Crete under an air umbrella provided by friendly fighter cover extending over their whole route. The depleted resources of the Mediterranean Fleet were still concentrating on the supply of Tobruk,[2] and there was little Cunningham could do to prevent enemy stores and supplies arriving at Tripoli other than rely upon air and sub-sea operations from Malta. By the end of August, however, Cunningham and Pound were agreed that a surface strike force should again be based at Malta, although Cunningham worried about the increased consumption of the 30,000 tons of fuel reserves that would inevitably follow, and the fact that he could spare none of his own destroyers.[3] In the event the light cruisers *Aurora* and *Penelope* were dispatched from home waters, and together with two destroyers, *Lance* and *Lively*, 'borrowed' from Force H, were sent out to make their name as Force K. A further powerful argument for the presence of these ships at Malta arose from the Italians' switch, under German pressure, to the use of the C38m cypher machine. The crypt-analysts at Bletchley Park, who had made virtually no inroads into Italian codes, now gained immediate access to information about Axis shipping movements, with 'advance notice of virtually every convoy ... that sailed with troops or supplies across the Mediterranean'. British Intelligence were careful to disguise their possession of this 'most valuable acquisition': aerial reconnaissance was always sent out to 'find', in as conspicuous a manner as possible, any revealed Italian convoy bound from Naples to North Africa – as, for example, on 10 October, when four freighters and one tanker, escorted by three destroyers, were 'discovered' south of Pantelleria. Malta-based bombers then struck the following evening, sinking two of the freighters, the *Zena* (5,219 grt) and *Casaregis* (6,485 grt). A third ship, the *Bainsizza* (7,933 grt), which had to return to Trapani with engine trouble, was bombed on the 14th during her second attempt to reach Libya, and foundered the next day. British submarine operations were similarly informed. *Ursula* sank a 5,000-ton cargo-vessel off Lampedusa on 18 October despite a heavy escort, *Utmost* sank another of 6,000 tons on the 28th, and other strikes were made in the Adriatic and Aegean. The value of fast surface units in further exploiting this rich and accurate source of intelligence was obvious.

The passage of Force K to Malta was tagged onto Operation CALLBOY, another Club Run intended to fly more Swordfish and Albacores brought out by *Argus* into Malta. Meanwhile Ford, at Malta, anxious to rid the harbours of the emptied ships of Operation HALBERD and also *Empire Guillemot*, prepared 'convoy MG3', which in fact never formed a convoy, but resulted in a succession of unescorted sailings. First to leave, on the 16th,

were *Clan MacDonald* and *Empire Guillemot*, but the latter suffered engine problems and turned back. Force H was at sea occupied with CALLBOY and *Clan MacDonald's* passage was loosely
covered by the Club Run, which proceeded as normal.
Somerville sailed from Gibraltar in *Rodney*, with *Ark Royal*,
Hermione, Cossack, Zulu, Sikh, Legion, Foresight, Forester and *Fury*
at 11.00 on 16 October 1941. With anti-submarine patrols being
flown by *Ark Royal's* Swordfish during daylight, Force H zigzagged east at 18 knots. During the following afternoon a questing Cant 506 was intercepted and shot down after a twenty-mile
chase at sea level. The flying-off position was reached at 01.30 on
the morning of the 17th, and the thirteen biplanes began trun-
dling down *Ark Royal's* flight deck; all were airborne ten minutes
later, whereupon the ships turned about. During the forenoon
signals were received that all eleven Albacores had arrived
safely, but only one Swordfish had made it. As the news was
broken, Fulmars from *Ark Royal* were vectored onto a Fiat BR20,
which was shot down 'about 10 miles from Cape Bengut'.

Force H returned to Gibraltar at 16.17 on 19 October, the same
day that *Clan MacDonald* arrived. She had had a brush with Italian
aircraft on the 17th, but had successfully evaded their torpedoes.
At 22.00 that same evening Captain W. Agnew in *Aurora* led
Penelope into Gibraltar harbour, and the cruisers oiled from the
San Claudio and *Viscol* respectively. Simultaneously, over their offshore sides, dockyard lighters were brought alongside and each
cruiser loaded seventeen aerial torpedoes, along with 200 rounds
of 4-inch semi-armour-piercing ammunition, as a reserve stock
for the two destroyers. They also each hove aboard an Oerlikon
gun and 2,400 rounds of 20-mm ammunition taken out of *Rodney*
and *Hermione*. The destroyers *Lively* and *Lance* had meanwhile
each loaded two torpedoes and 200 rounds of 4-inch ammunition
in addition to their normal stocks.They then sailed at 17.15 to
carry out gunnery exercises to the east of Gibraltar, where on completion they awaited the cruisers. Before dawn on the 20th *Aurora*
and *Penelope* cast off from the oilers and slipped out to sea, making
their rendezvous with the two destroyers at 08.00. The four ships
then steamed east at speed, entering Grand Harbour late the following day, 21 October 1941, the anniversary of Trafalgar.

At Malta, the elderly *Empire Guillemot* had rectified her engine
defect and was ready to leave on 22 October, as the hunter's

moon waned. She followed the *City of Lincoln* and *Dunedin Star* as they slipped out of Grand Harbour at 10.00 on the 21st under a grey, overcast sky and headed westwards, the Ellerman and Blue Star liners at first keeping company but gradually drawing apart as each made her best speed. Both were attacked on passage but beat off and damaged their assailants, to arrive at Gibraltar within hours of each other on 25 October.

The best speed of *Empire Guillemot* was 11 knots – not in fact a particular handicap, since her age and American origin made her far less readily identifiable than either *City of Lincoln* or *Dunedin Star*. It was intended that the long-range Catalinas regularly overflying the Western Mediterranean should keep an eye out for her, as for the other solitary ships, but it was soon clear that she was overdue. Then, on 29 October, an Italian radio broadcast claimed the sinking of 'a large enemy supply ship'. It was suspected that this referred to the *Empire Guillemot*, but her fate remained a mystery until much later.

Captain R. Rouse had kept *Empire Guillemot* close to the Tunisian shore, employing the usual devices of false colours, and rounded Cape Bon at dawn on the 23rd in a moderate sea with a mercifully persistent grey sky. He maintained his fictional nationality by keeping very close inshore, passing south of Galita Island, and by late morning had run well to the westward. Then three Cant seaplanes dropped out of the cloud and machine-gunned *Empire Guillemot*'s bridge. Her single Lewis gun was disabled and her telemotor damaged, so that her helm lodged hard over. The Cants then withdrew to make bombing runs; the first bomb missed but the second fell diagonally, broke through the covers of No. 5 Hatch and burst the bulkhead into the engine room, killing the third engineer, W. MacNeil. The explosion immobilised the ship and ruptured the seams of her shell plating, and she began to settle by the stern. Rouse ordered his ship to be abandoned and the crew lowered the two boats undamaged by the strafing. Once the crew were in the lifeboats the Cants circled, but took no further action, satisfied when the *Empire Guillemot* stood on her stern and sank, some twenty minutes after being hit.

Rouse was in one boat with nineteen of his crew, Halliday the mate in the second with twenty-two. The inhospitable Tunisian shore was close at hand, but Rouse ordered them to start pulling, so the survivors 'rigged up a makeshift sail and set course for Gibraltar', 850 miles away. The boats made painfully slow progress; some men with Halliday began to grumble and several, unused to the motion of small craft in the ground-swell, were debilitatingly sea-sick. The second day they did better. Rouse and Halliday pooled their provisions, which consisted of forty emergency food packs, some raisins and chocolate bars, and four barrels of ship's biscuit. They had a sufficiency of water. However, when the weather worsened next day with a hot levanter blowing off the coast, trouble began to brew in Halliday's boat, and in defiance of his orders the men waved and flashed torches at two aircraft that passed low over the sea to the west. The planes failed to react and the weather deteriorated still further on the 27th, separating the boats by nightfall. During the night the wind reached gale force and the boats began to fill. It was clear that they lacked the resources to carry on, and both Halliday and Rouse individually decided that their only real chance of survival was to attempt to land. But a dangerous surf ran on the shore of La Marsa Bay, and Rouse's boat broached and capsized, breaking up and flinging its occupants up the beach. Here they were found next morning by patrolling coastguards who took them to Bône, and confinement in the barracks of the 3rd Algerian Tirailleurs. Halliday's boat landed farther to the west on an exposed beach west of Cape Fer, striking an offshore bar and capsizing in steep breakers. Beyond the bar a shallow lagoon was made almost impassable by the gale, and only thirteen men struggled ashore. Two of these died of exposure before the coastguard picked them up and eventually found a truck to take them to a cork factory at Philippeville. Here they were put in front of a fire with tea and brandy, a doctor administered camphor injections, and they were taken to a military hospital in Jemmapes. After three days they joined their shipmates in Bône, where they languished until the end of the war.[4]

The attempt to clear one more of the emptied HALBERD ships, *Clan Ferguson*, also misfired, though with less dire consequences. She sailed from Malta about noon on 24 October but was soon spotted by an Italian aircraft and attacked. With her passage betrayed so early to the enemy she was recalled, and compelled to languish in Maltese waters for some time to come.

November opened with the sinking of two Italian freighters in surface engagements by Lieutenant-Commander Cayley in *Utmost*.[5] This was followed by Force K's first success. Ultra decrypts at Bletchley Park of Luftwaffe Enigma signals indicated that an Italian convoy of seven vessels would be leaving Naples and proceeding to Tripoli through the Strait of Messina. As usual, to cover their apparent prescience the British 'undertook air reconnaissance of the targets before acting'[6] and accordingly, on the afternoon of 8 November, a Maryland of No. 69 Squadron at Malta duly 'located' the convoy off the toe of Calabria, heading east across the Ionian Sea. It was heavily escorted by Capitano di Vascello Bisciani in the destroyer *Maestrale*, accompanied by *Euro, Fulmine, Grecale, Libeccio* and *Oriani*. Substantial cover was provided by the heavy cruisers *Trento* and *Trieste*, the former flying the flag of Ammiraglio di Divisione Brivonesi, and by the 13th Destroyer Flotilla, consisting of *Granatiere, Fuciliere, Bersagliere* and *Alpino* under Capitano di Vascello Capponi. In addition, four submarines were deployed to support the convoy.

Force K immediately sailed from Grand Harbour, and at 04.00 on the 9th made contact by radar some hundred and forty miles to the eastward of Syracuse. *Aurora, Penelope, Lively* and *Lance* now worked round to a position up-moon of the convoy, following Captain Agnew's standing orders, rehearsed by his subordinate captains[7] so that signals between the ships should be unnecessary. Count Ciano described how, undetected by the covering force or the escort, Force K fell upon the convoy 'as wolves among the sheep. An engagement occurred, the results of which are inexplicable. All, I mean *all*, our [merchant] ships were sunk, and maybe one, or two or three destroyers. The British returned to their ports [*sic*] after having slaughtered us.'[8] At 6,000 yards range (which provoked Captain Agnew, mindful of the limited stocks at Malta, to send his only signal during the action: 'Do not waste ammunition') the British ships opened a devastating fire of whole salvoes into the unfortunate merchantmen. The cargo vessels *Duisberg* (7,389 grt), *San Marco* (3,113 grt), *Maria* (6,339 grt), *Sagitta* (5,153 grt) and *Rina Corrado* (5,180 grt) and the tankers *Conte de Misurata* (7,599 grt) and *Minatitlan* (7,599 grt) were blown apart. Returning fire, the destroyer *Fulmine* went down with her guns blazing, Bisciani's *Grecale* was shot through and immobilised by six armour-piercing shells which failed to explode, and *Euro* was also damaged. Brivonesi's cruisers, only three miles away, failed to engage Force K, unable to identify hostile targets in the confusion. Not fitted with radar, untrained in night action and fearful of hitting their own ships, they proved useless. Agnew, meanwhile, having achieved his objective, withdrew at high speed, leaving the wreckage behind him. As daylight grew over the scene of devastation *Grecale* was taken in tow and *Libeccio* moved in to pick up survivors, only to be torpedoed by Wanklyn in *Upholder*, waiting and watching in the offing. Taken in tow by the damaged *Euro*, *Libeccio* sank later. The destroyers of the 13th Flotilla rescued 704 men, before the whole force retreated to Messina.

Force K entered Grand Harbour at 13.00, 'completely unscathed'. From North Africa, Rommel complained to Berlin that his supply line had been cut and that, of 60,000 troops promised, only 8,093 had arrived.[9] In the aftermath of the action Mussolini was 'depressed and indignant', Brivonesi and Bisciani lost their commands, and Ciano considered there would be 'profound repercussions ... Under the circumstances we have no right to complain if Hitler sends Kesselring as commander in the South.' The Italian high command had a capacity for self-delusion, 'pulling out their usual inevitable and imaginary sinking of a British cruiser by an Italian torpedo plane; nobody believes it.' Italian reconnaissance photographs taken after Force K had returned to Malta showed a cruiser moored near the dry-dock. This, insisted the Regia Aeronautica's chief of staff, Generale Pricolo, was evidence that one British cruiser had been hit. 'This', commented Ciano despairingly, 'is equivalent to declaring that a man is probably dead because he has gone to live near the cemetery. Clowns, tragic clowns ...'[10]

As Count Ciano was wringing his hands and Supermarina were trying to offset the news by claiming great successes by the submarine *Alessandro Malaspina* (which had actually been missing for a week in the Adriatic), Somerville had sailed from Gibraltar for another Club Run. The vice-admiral, having flown home for a conference at the Admiralty, returned to hoist his flag temporarily in *Malaya*. He was most unhappy about this further change of flagship, disrupting as it did all his hard work in uniting Force H; moreover, *Malaya's* unsuitability irked him. He was also upset about the loss in the North Atlantic on convoy duty of *Cossack*, whose first lieutenant had been the son of a friend, and shaken by the news that in his absence in London his chief of staff, Captain E. Jeffrey, a solitary, sensitive and introverted officer, had hanged himself. Susceptible to criticism, Jeffrey had perhaps made too much of his admiral's fiery outbursts. But for Somerville the panacea was action, and on 10

November Force H departed from Gibraltar on Operation PER-
PETUAL.

A further consignment of Hurricanes had arrived in *Argus* just
before midnight on 7 November, followed next morning by the
aircraft transport *Athene*, a new ship which had been delayed by
engine trouble on her maiden delivery.[11] *Athene*'s cargo having
been transferred to *Ark Royal*, Force H slipped out of Gibraltar at
02.35. By 08.00, with a single Swordfish flown off *Argus* and a
Gibraltar-based Catalina on anti-submarine patrol above, the
large ships *Malaya*, *Ark Royal* and *Argus* were zigzagging east at
18 knots. They were screened by *Hermione*, the fighter director,
and the destroyers *Laforey*, *Lightning*, *Legion*, *Zulu*, *Gurkha*, *Sikh*
and *Isaac Sweers*. The Hurricanes choking *Ark Royal*'s deck precluded the flying-off of Fulmars, so Somerville 'enjoined a very
careful watch for submarines and low flying shadowers'.[12]

Nothing untoward occurred during the 11th, and by 10.21 next
morning thirteen Hurricanes had flown off *Ark Royal*, followed
by six from *Argus*. Led by Blenheims from Malta, they climbed
away to the east. Two more Blenheims were sighted at 10.48 and
a further thirteen Hurricanes took off from *Ark Royal*, five from
Argus. Force H then turned and headed west at 16 knots, 'the
maximum speed which destroyers could maintain without
damage in the short rising sea'. One Swordfish flew ahead on the
lookout for submarines, while four Fulmars were airborne as
fighter patrol until darkness.

At daylight on 13 November Somerville was informed that
Legion had reported an underwater explosion at 04.13. This was
thought to have been a torpedo detonating at the end of its run
and argued the presence of enemy submarines, so at 06.45 a
Swordfish was flown off *Ark Royal* to carry out a search to a distance of seventy miles, but nothing was seen. Nevertheless,
more of the biplanes were sent up to maintain an anti-submarine watch and Somerville alerted Force H to the presence of
submarines, exhorting all ships to great vigilance. In the hope of
avoiding any possible ambush he also varied his usual return
route, but at 09.55 the fleet had to alter course away from a sonar
contact obtained by *Laforey*. Captain Hutton cancelled this as
spurious a few minutes later, and Force H resumed its mean line
of advance.

Captain Maund now sent Somerville a signal requesting permission to carry out deck landing training that afternoon, neces-

sitating a degree of freedom of movement for *Ark Royal*. It was part of Somerville's policy of constant exercising, and he approved, provided Maund kept within the destroyer screen, for he intended to carry out his own gunnery practice from *Malaya*. He and Maund concerted their proposed actions and then, as these manoeuvres were about to take place, Hutton reported another sonar contact; again the fleet altered course. A few minutes later Maund swung *Ark Royal* further to starboard to fly off two Fulmars and six Swordfish, before taking aboard five Swordfish and realigning her course with that of the other ships. Three minutes later she swung to starboard again to land aircraft. While the starboard wing destroyer, *Legion*, was covering the carrier's movements, her sonar operators heard 'hydrophone effect', but as it coincided roughly with the bearing of *Gurkha*, it was discounted on *Legion*'s bridge.

At 15.40 the remainder of the force swung to a course of west-north-west, in accordance with the zigzag. Somerville warned Captain Coppinger of *Malaya* to be aware of *Ark Royal*'s close proximity four cables on *Malaya*'s starboard quarter as the course of the two ships converged slightly, and Maund was committed for a few more minutes to landing aircraft. A moment later *Ark Royal* was struck by a torpedo on her starboard side: *Legion*'s sonar operator had not been deceived.

Somerville himself witnessed the impact, saw the aircraft on *Ark Royal*'s flight deck bounce as she whipped. With several aircraft circling overhead, *Ark Royal* slewed to port, listing to starboard. *Malaya* turned to port, steadying on a course of south-west by west, while *Gurkha* and *Legion* immediately swung outwards to search for the attacking submarine. There was a flurry of activity among the destroyers in the ensuing minutes as signals flashed between *Ark Royal* and *Malaya*, *Laforey* and *Hermione*. The listing carrier dropped astern, gradually slowing to a stop. *Laforey* and *Lightning* were ordered to stand by her, as was *Hermione*. *Malaya* carried on at 18 knots, screened by *Sikh*, *Zulu* and *Isaac Sweers* until, at 16.22, Somerville sent *Zulu* back to join *Hermione* and the destroyers *Laforey*, *Gurkha* and *Lightning*, which were circling *Ark Royal*. *Legion* lay alongside her, beginning the evacuation of her huge complement, but it was not intended to abandon her; only one torpedo had struck her, and every effort was to be made to salvage the carrier. Signals were transmitted to Gibraltar to muster tugs and motor launches to *Ark Royal*'s assistance, and as soon as *Malaya* passed the Mole at 18.30 Somerville transferred to *Sikh* and turned back, racing east at 32 knots.

The night was very dark and the destroyers and harbour patrol motor launches from Gibraltar circled, dropping deterrent depth-charges. The tugs *Thames* and *St Day* had arrived, and although a third, the *St Omer*, failed to locate the carrier and returned to Gibraltar, by 21.00 *Ark Royal* was under tow towards Gibraltar at 2 knots. Anxious about renewed action by the enemy, Somerville ordered *Sikh*, *Isaac Sweers* and *Wishart* (sent from Gibraltar) to redeploy and guard against an up-moon attack after moonrise at 01.30. At about 22.30 Hutton, whose L-class destroyers were removing the crew, reported from *Laforey* that *Ark Royal* was able to make some way under her own power and that the flooding appeared to be under control. Further encouragement came shortly afterwards when the anti-submarine guard was reinforced by the arrival from Gibraltar of the corvettes *Rhododendron*, *Marigold* and *Pentstemon*, which Somerville sent five miles astern of *Ark Royal* with orders to close her at daylight.

At midnight, when they were less than thirty miles from Gibraltar, the situation appeared to be hopeful, for the down-flooding had been contained. Then at 02.21 next morning, Hutton signalled the worst: a fire in the operational boiler-room had caused *Ark Royal* to lose steam and with that her ability to generate electricity, for she had no diesel generators; the pumps therefore failed. A large salvage unit was urgently requested, whereupon *Pentstemon* was ordered alongside with a heavy-duty salvage pump she had taken aboard at Gibraltar. Twenty minutes later Hutton asked for a third tug immediately, and *St Omer* and *Rollicker* were dispatched from Gibraltar. These measures were in vain. Despairing, Somerville ordered Commander Stokes to take *Sikh* closer, but Hutton advised him to transfer to a motor-launch, and by this means Somerville boarded *Laforey*, lying close alongside *Ark Royal*'s port side with the *St Day*.

Hutton had just taken off Captain Maund, the last of those retained on board for steaming and towing purposes. The carrier was now listing 35 degrees to starboard and the *Laforey* let go and lay off, clear of the doomed ship. *Ark Royal* listed further and further, and at 06.00 the *St Day* cast off. Above the watching ships, the Swordfish ranged on *Ark Royal*'s flight deck began to slide across and fall into the sea as the end came. 'It was the blackest of days when I saw my poor *Ark* sink,' Somerville wrote to his wife. 'Just a blur in the dark as she lay on her side for some time and then slowly, slowly she turned over like a tired and wounded ship going to sleep … I am rather cut up about this … and her loss is deeply regretted.' But there was a sting in the tail of his letter which was to be echoed in the subsequent court-martial: 'I can't understand', he concluded, 'how one torpedo should have caused the loss of this fine ship.'[13]

Somerville also expressed concern over the poor performance of the destroyers' sonars, the result of differing density layers in the sea where the complex currents funnelled in both directions between the Atlantic and Mediterranean through the Strait of Gibraltar. The first explosion heard by *Legion*'s operator had in fact been one of a salvo of three torpedoes fired by Korvettenkapitän Reschke from *U205* which detonated in the destroyer's wake. *U205* belonged to the four-strong 'Arnauld' group, named after a First World War ace, which had passed the Strait between 11 and 16 November, Reschke and his colleagues having been informed of the presence of Force H by Italian air reconnaissance. But it was another of the 'Arnauld' group which was responsible for the fatal shot, one of a salvo of four fired by Korvettenkapitän Guggenberger from *U81*, heard as 'hydrophone effect' by *Legion* and thought to have been merely *Gurkha*'s propeller noise. So successful a deployment of German submarines, north of Alboran and closer to Gibraltar than the dispersed patrol lines of the Italians farther eastward, was a nasty shock. Despite this, Somerville's perplexity was justified, for he was never complacent and had taken considerable trouble to warn his force of the dangers, making his dispositions accordingly. His constant drills and exercises were one mark of his cautious competence, but so was his constant, active attention to detail: the reminders to Coppinger to give *Ark Royal* sea room, and to Maund not to stray out of the destroyers' screen. That *Ark Royal* was hit owed much to the boldness of Guggenberger, and while the reduced effectiveness of the then state-of-the-art sonars fitted in Somerville's destroyers had contributed to the carrier's loss, so too had the misinterpretations of the hydrophonic evidence. That *Ark Royal* sank was another matter, one which Admiral of the Fleet Sir Charles Forbes and a board of inquiry were swiftly flown out to Gibraltar to determine.

'It was quite the worst inquiry I have ever attended,' Somerville thought. 'Forbes appeared to be convinced it was

poor asdic [sonar] conditions',[14] but this did not satisfy
Somerville. The extent of the damage to the ship surprised him:
as *Ark Royal* capsized, the men on one motor launch played an
aldis lamp on her, revealing a gash of about 140 feet in length and
30 feet wide under the starboard bilge. The main charge against
Maund, however, centred around the fact that the carrier's
damage-control parties were not properly closed up and ready
to react. The defence pleaded that essential maintenance
required men to be kept at work dealing with the arrears of
defects; *Ark Royal* was not therefore at full action stations, and the
resultant slow response may have been compounded by the
failure of temporary repairs to earlier explosion damage caused
by the detonation of depth charges close to the ship that spring.
Specifically, the defective damage-control organisation in the
ship had failed to shut and secure a manhole in a main hatch
above the switchboard room, and this had led to extensive flooding. Consequently poor Maund was found negligent, and also
reprimanded on the grounds that 'the engine and boiler room
crews and repair parties had been brought up prematurely from
below'.[15] Somerville had some compassion for Maund's order to
evacuate them, commenting that '... when you see that enormous great flying deck canted over at an angle of 20°, you certainly do get the impression that the ship must be going right
over, and with over 1,700 people on board and the difficulty of
getting on deck in a Carrier, I for one don't blame him for his
decision'.[16] In the event only one man died, but that was small
consolation to Somerville and Cunningham, neither of whom
now had an aircraft carrier in his fleet.

The loss of *Ark Royal* enforced upon Somerville a period of
idleness which he found most irksome. Efforts were made to
clear the Straits of U-boats; the corvette *Marigold* sank *U433*,
another of the 'Arnauld' boats, on 16 November, and van Dulm
of the Dutch submarine *O21* sank *U95* on the 28th, but these successes were small compensation for the loss of *Ark Royal*.

Efforts were also being made to run further supplies through to
Malta by single ships even as the drama concluding Operation
PERPETUAL was taking place. Operation ASTROLOGER was a re-
run of TEMPLE and PROPELLER; in view of the fates of *Parracombe*
and *Empire Guillemot* it ought never to have been planned.
Unfortunately, the relative success in returning the empty fast

cargo-liners from Malta and the safe arrival there of *Empire Guillemot* with her cargo of animal fodder encouraged the MoWT and the Admiralty to persist. Two ships were assigned to ASTROLOGER. *Empire Pelican*, originally built in 1919 in America as the *Stanley* of 6,463 gross tons, had been purchased from the United States war reserve fleet and placed under the management of Dene Bros Ltd by the MoWT. *Empire Defender*, of 5,649 tons, was older, built in Germany, at Tecklenborg, in 1910. Having changed owners and flags, she had been captured at Haifa in June the previous year as the Italian *Felce*, and was placed by the MoWT in the hands of the Stanhope Steamship Company.

In October the two vessels loaded military stores and ammunition at Glasgow, where they were painted black with white upperworks and buff funnels. Not content with covering their grey paint, the MoWT ordered their armament removed. At this juncture the *Empire Defender*'s sixty-strong Lascar crew refused to sail and were quietly removed, to be replaced by a pool crew who were offered a £10 bonus for sailing in 'lascar accommodation'.[17]

The two ships sailed in convoy, breaking away in good time to try the fiction of neutral status, hoisting false colours and painting the customary succession of bogus ensigns on their hatch tarpaulins: Spanish, French and (had the ruse worked for long enough) Italian. *Empire Pelican* went first. On 12 November she passed the Strait of Gibraltar close to the Moroccan shore, then hugged the Algerian and Tunisian coasts. At dawn on 14 November she was located by Italian aircraft south of Galita, torpedoed and sunk. On the following day at sunset, in roughly the same locality, *Empire Defender* was similarly dispatched.[18] Although Club Runs recommenced the following spring, the two ships of Operation ASTROLOGER were to be the last merchant ships sent from the west to relieve Malta for six months.

14

'The crisis in our fortunes'

(Operation CHIEFTAIN *and Convoy GM3, Operations* LANDMARK, *MD1 and MF1, with Convoy ME8, and the First Battle of Sirte)*

IN THE FINAL two months of 1941 the war in the Mediterranean reached a critical point. Axis forces in North Africa were running short of supplies and reinforcements, due to interdiction from Malta. But the British in Egypt, reliant upon the long sea-route from the United Kingdom round the Cape of Good Hope to the vulnerable choke-point of the Suez Canal, were under constant threat from Axis air-power. The pressure applied by the Regia Aeronautica had been bad enough, but the situation was far worse under the Luftwaffe, now operating from Crete.

On the ground, the relief of Tobruk and the discomfiture if not the defeat of the Afrika Korps were now essential. The smaller ships of Cunningham's fleet had done prodigious work in keeping Tobruk supplied, and on 18 November his younger brother, Lieutenant-General Sir Alan Cunningham, appointed commander of the newly formed Eighth Army, began a bold thrust towards Tobruk to raise the siege. Operation CRUSADER opened after torrential rain; advancing British armour churned the desert to mud, and the following day the tanks of the 22nd Armoured Brigade were thrown back by those of the Italian Ariete Division at Bir el Gubi. Although the British 7th Armoured Brigade broke the Italians at Sidi Rezegh, the Italians surrounding Tobruk resisted the garrison's attempt to break out. Then Rommel's armour clashed with the 4th Armoured Division at Gabr Saleh in an action claimed as a victory by both sides.

Although the British were left in possession of the field, their tank losses far exceeded those of the enemy, and Rommel quickly counter-attacked before the British could move the 22nd and 4th Armoured Divisions to Sidi Rezegh in support. On 22 November General Crüwell, in the teeth of a bitter resistance, compelled the British and Commonwealth forces to fall back. On the next day General Cunningham faltered and Auchinleck, Wavell's successor as Commander-in-Chief of Middle East Land Forces, arrived on the scene and ordered a stand at Sidi Rezegh, replacing Cunningham with his own chief of staff, Major-General Ritchie. Against Rommel's renewed attack the Allied forces gave ground, only to re-form after the Panzer groups had swept through towards Cairo and savage the reinforcements that sought to consolidate Rommel's advance. Auchinleck also sent the imperturbable Freyberg along the coast with the 2nd New Zealand Division to relieve the beleaguered garrison of Tobruk, part of which now fought its way out of encirclement to meet Freyberg's troops at El Duda. Isolated, Rommel struck back, and a confused few days followed during which the contenders fought themselves to a standstill until, with heavy air support, it was the turn of the Eighth Army to counter-attack. Tobruk was relieved on 10 December.

Rommel was now compelled to fall back, slowly relinquishing his gains, largely because he was receiving no reinforcements or supplies. Though he stubbornly contested every inch of the way, by early 1942 he had lost Derna and Benghazi. Despite Crüwell's action at Beda Fomm, Rommel found himself back at El Agheila, where he laboriously regrouped.

During Operation CRUSADER an attempt was made to draw off enemy aircraft to the west by sending a decoy convoy into the Mediterranean from Gibraltar. This phoney Malta convoy, code-named GM3, was mounted as Operation CHIEFTAIN and consisted of the merchant vessels *Baron Newlands*, *Blair Atholl*, *Cisneros*, *Ottinge* and *Shona*, with the fleet oiler *Brown Ranger*, escorted by the sloop *Deptford*, the destroyer *Wild Swan* and the corvettes *Convolvulus*, *Rhododendron* and *Samphire*. The convoy sailed on the evening of 16 November and the intention was that each merchant ship should break off and return independently under cover of darkness, while the naval vessels remained at sea for two days carrying out an anti-submarine sweep – but it was the corvette *Marigold*, sailing late after rectifying an engine defect, which attacked and sank *U433*.

At the other end of the Middle Sea, Admiral Cunningham's light forces had been more directly involved with CRUSADER, busily supplying both Tobruk and the troops advancing along the coast. At Mersa Matruh, for instance, 600 tons of water had to be delivered daily, but the ships were under constant air attack and were now to face another threat. In mid November the two Australian sloops *Yarra* and *Parramatta* escorted an ammunition convoy to Tobruk, and a few days later *Parramatta* returned with *Avon Vale* as escort to the ammunition transport *Hanne*. On 27 November *Parramatta* was torpedoed by *U559*, one of a mounting number of U-boats at large in the eastern Mediterranean, another of which had already struck a dire blow at Cunningham's battle-fleet as it in turn moved to throttle Rommel.

Ultra decrypts had informed London of the desperation of Rommel's fuel situation. By the same means, London also knew that the enemy were exerting themselves to resupply Rommel, and that a number of ships were preparing to undertake the crossing to Cyrenaica. Churchill insisted, through Pound, that Cunningham sever the supply completely: 'Stopping of these ships may save thousands of lives apart from aiding a victory of cardinal importance.' Cunningham found Churchill's assumption that all enemy air resources were engaged elsewhere than over the sea irritating; he replied accordingly, warning that the proposed operation would be 'a chancy enterprise', relying as it would on imperfect air surveillance and the need for Force K to be at sea in daylight, because of the distances involved. Well aware that no initiative was to be missed, Cunningham agreed to supplement Force K with a second strike group, Force B, but indicated that their sorties might be curtailed by a fuel shortage on the Allied side, particularly at Malta.

Force K had already provided limited support for the Eighth Army, supplementing the decoy Operation CHIEFTAIN from Gibraltar by sailing from Malta on the afternoon of 18 November and heading west, as if for a rendezvous with GM3, then reversing course during the night and re-entering Grand Harbour during the forenoon of the 19th. A second diversionary operation, code-named LANDMARK, left Malta on the morning of the

21st with every appearance of heading for Alexandria, Force K being joined by the mine-sweeping corvette *Gloxinia* as the escort for the patched-up *Sydney Star*, *Breconshire*, *Ajax* and *Clan Ferguson*. Captain Agnew's dummy convoy operation was given added credibility by Cunningham sailing with the battle squadron in pretended support, the whole demonstration being intended to deceive Axis reconnaissance, threaten Tripoli, draw off enemy air forces from the battlefield, and entice the Italian fleet to attack.[1]

Four Italian destroyers and four submarines, *Atropo*, *Ammiraglio Saint Bon*, *Cagni* and *Millo*, had successfully run supplies from Taranto to Bardia between 13 and 26 November, but a far greater effort with essential petrol, ammunition, tanks and artillery was now under way. On 21 November, the same day that Agnew and Cunningham were making their conspicuous decoy manoeuvres, two small Axis convoys, each of two ships escorted by destroyers and torpedo-boats, were dispatched from Naples, covered by the 3rd Division of heavy cruisers commanded by Ammiraglio di Divisione Parona. These cruisers, *Gorizia*, *Trento* and *Trieste*, were in turn joined off Messina by the *Duca degli Abruzzi* and *Giuseppe Garibaldi*. One of the transports developed engine defects and had to turn back, but four further freighters joined, two from Brindisi and two from Taranto, along with the cruiser *Luigi Cadorna*, acting as a fuel carrier, her decks stacked with canned petrol.

The cruisers were located by Wellington bombers carrying airborne radar and operating from Malta. Shortly before midnight on 21/22 November the Wellingtons dropped flares in the vicinity of Parona's cruisers, just as Lieutenant-Commander Cayley was making a silent surface approach under electric power in the submarine *Utmost*. One of Cayley's torpedoes hit and severely damaged the *Trieste*, compelling Capitano di Vascello Rouselle to struggle back to Messina.[2] A little later Swordfish from No. 830 Squadron at Malta attacked Parona's combined squadron and hit the *Duca degli Abruzzi*, though the torpedo did not wound the cruiser fatally.

The German decrypting service, B-Dienst, had for its part learnt from British naval radio traffic that Force K had left Malta. Far from enticing the Italian fleet, this intelligence had the opposite effect: the undamaged heavy cruisers *Gorizia* and *Trento* were ordered back to Taranto with the remaining freighters and transports, while *Giuseppe Garibaldi* and the smaller escorts[3] clustered round the limping *Duca degli Abruzzi*. The *Luigi Cadorna* and the three merchantmen in her company were too far advanced to turn back, and continued on their passage.

But this was only part of the desperate attempt by the Axis to move supplies into Libya. In order to contain the likely effects of a strike by Force K, valuable supplies had been dispersed among other small convoys. Such a measure would, it was hoped, make their destruction disproportionate to the expenditure of effort, while attacking them would dissipate British resources both in the air and at sea and expose the Royal Navy's surface units to the grey wolves now diverted from the Battle of the Atlantic. Two other Italian convoys were at sea, making the by now familiar passage, coasting from port to port in a circuitous route via the Aegean, under the air cover of the Luftwaffe.

Just before dusk on 23 November a Maryland spotted one of these small convoys. Once Ford heard of it he passed the intelligence to Alexandria, and ordered Force K back to sea immediately: with *Aurora*, *Penelope*, *Lively* and *Lance* hurriedly refuelled and a watch of happily roistering sailors recalled from their shore leave, Agnew sailed. Force K was seen by the patrolling Italian submarine *Settembrini*, one of five boats on patrol east of Malta, and at this news all Italian convoys were ordered into the nearest friendly port.[4]

The convoy located by the Maryland consisted of two German ships, the *Maritza* of 2,910 tons and *Procida* of 1,842 tons, escorted by the torpedo-boats *Cassiopea* and *Lupo*, which had left Taranto on 14 November. Bound for Benghazi, they were still on this intermittent passage when radio operators aboard *Lively* and *Lance*, working the Italian frequencies as Agnew sought to intercept the convoy, succeeded in jamming the recall signal.[5]

Force K's pursuit was compromised at daylight when an Italian aeroplane was seen overhead, but again the petty officer telegraphists in *Lively* and *Lance* quickly jammed the Cant's transmissions and the Italian convoy stood on unsuspecting. During the forenoon, however, the first intimation of trouble occurred when a radar-equipped Wellington flew over the enemy convoy. Learning of the Italian position, Agnew continued to head as though for Alexandria before turning upon his quarry, allowing it to extend its distance from help. Agnew was assisted in his deception by thunderstorms which reduced visibility, but when a lone Ju88 suddenly appeared and attacked *Lively*, it seemed that the game was up. Nevertheless, attempts were made with some success to jam the Junkers' radio reports of Force K, and at 13.10 Agnew decided he should wait no longer, for fear of the convoy retreating. He extended his ships into line abreast, each five miles from her neighbour, with the two cruisers on the flanks, *Penelope* being the northernmost. HeIIIs flying south overhead carrying supplies across to Rommel by air assumed the patrolling line of British warships, only about 140 miles west of Crete, to be Italian. In the mid afternoon another Ju88, providing air cover for the convoy, dived on *Penelope*, but it was too late. A few minutes later the masts of merchantmen were seen to the north-west, whereupon Captain Nicholl passed the word and turned towards the hapless Italians.

With *Lively* turning in her wake, Nicholl ordered *Penelope*'s battle ensigns hoisted and increased speed to over 30 knots. *Lance* too was accelerating, coming up from the south with *Aurora* in the rear. At about 15.45 *Penelope*'s 6-inch guns rose in elevation, and with a flash and roar opened fire. The escorting German dive-bombers overhead were now fully alerted to the hostile British warships, and attacked in earnest.

The two freighters turned away to the north-west while Capitano di Fregata Mimbelli's torpedo-boats zigzagged across their line of retreat, making smoke and dodging out of the black cloud to fire at the advancing British. Several of their shells hit *Penelope* as she fired 6-inch broadsides, simultaneously defending herself against the Ju88s with anti-aircraft gunfire and heeling as Nicholl applied violent helm to avoid the falling bombs. But Nicholl had ordered his gunnery controlled by radar, which made light of the obscuring smoke; consequently, at 16.18 Mimbelli broke off the action and disappeared into the grey deluge of a thunderstorm, leaving his two charges to the mercy of the British.

Penelope slowed as she broke through the covering smoke screen. Nicholl used the International Code to order the masters of the two merchantmen to abandon their ships, an order which was quickly complied with. As soon as their lifeboats were clear, *Penelope*'s shells rapidly ignited the immense numbers of cans of petrol stacked upon the freighters' decks and the *Maritza* and *Procida* were soon ablaze. *Lively* moved in to pick up survivors as the burning ships drifted together, both shaking from periodic internal explosions. Coming up in *Aurora* and fighting off a further attack by Ju88s, Agnew decided that with two hours of daylight remaining he should withdraw. Force K headed for Malta at 28 knots. Behind them their burning victims were lost in the rain.

Cunningham received the news of the two Axis convoys heading for Benghazi shortly after midnight on 24 November 1941. Although Force K were already in pursuit of one he was anxious not to miss the other, and ordered Force B to sail at 04.00 in search of the *Luigi Cadorna* and her three laden freighters.

Force B was under the command of Rear-Admiral Rawlings in *Ajax*, with her fellow cruisers *Neptune*, *Naiad*, *Euryalus* and *Galatea*, and four destroyers. Twelve hours later Cunningham also left Alexandria, in *Queen Elizabeth*. The flagship was followed by *Barham* and *Valiant*, the former flying Pridham-Wippell's flag, and the three huge ships were screened by eight destroyers. The C-in-C held the battle squadron ready to bombard the shore if required by General Cunningham, while affording heavy cover within call of the two cruiser squadrons if the Regia Marina decided to force the issue of pushing the two Axis convoys through.

It was not the capital ships of the Italian navy that covered these two small but vital convoys, however. With the withdrawal of Parona's cruisers, Supermarina had to rely upon air cover and the submarines *Beilul*, *Dagabur* and *Zaffiro* lying off the coast of Cyrenaica, while *U79*, *U331* and *U559* patrolled along the supply route.[6]

The afternoon of 25 November 1941 was fine as Cunningham's three great battleships and their screen of destroyers, led by Mack in *Jervis*, steamed in the Gulf of Sollum. Men were idling on deck in the sunshine as the squadron zigzagged, following an east-to-west patrol line, awaiting developments. At 16.17 the sonar operators in *Jervis* reported a contact, but it was indistinct, and when consulted the officers on duty discounted it. Neither *Decoy* nor *Griffin*, on *Jervis*'s quarters, nor the following destroyers of the flanking screen noticed anything amiss.

A few moments later the battle squadron altered course to conform with their zigzag routine, bringing the battleships into shallow echelon. Cunningham was relaxing in his bridge cabin drinking tea when at 16.30 he 'suddenly heard and half-felt the door give three distinct rattles, and thought we had opened fire with our anti-aircraft guns. I went quickly up the one ladder to the bridge, and then I saw the *Barham*, immediately astern of us, stopped and listing heavily over to port.' Unknown to the British, *U331* had penetrated the destroyer screen and Leutnant-sur-Zee von Tiesenhausen had fired a salvo of four torpedoes at short range into Pridham-Wippell's flagship. The *Barham* had rolled over onto her beam ends and some of her crew were visible scrambling out onto her uppermost side when there was 'a terrific explosion as one of her magazines blew up. The ship became completely hidden in a great cloud of yellowish-black smoke, which went wreathing and eddying high into the sky. When it cleared away the *Barham* had disappeared. There was nothing but a bubbling, oily looking patch on the calm surface of the sea, dotted with wreckage and the heads of swimmers. It was ghastly to look at, a horrible and awe-inspiring spectacle ...'[7]

Astern of the exploding ship Captain Morgan, alarmed, ran onto *Valiant*'s bridge to see on his starboard bow the conning tower of *U331* briefly break surface as the submarine was thrown out of trim by the discharge of her torpedoes. He ordered the helm hard over, but *Valiant* was already altering in the opposite direction to avoid the violently heeling *Barham* and he was too late to bring her massive hull into contact with the momentarily vulnerable U-boat. Regaining control, von Tiesenhausen submerged as the battleship swept past only yards away. Slipping under the stern of *Valiant*, *U331* was hidden from the destroyers turning to exact retribution.

At the same terrible moment as *Barham*, still moving ahead, rolled inexorably over, Mack had swung *Jervis* through eight points to counter-attack. Petty Officer Edmunds 'saw [*Barham's*] bottom open up like a tin can followed by a huge explosion and smoke that went up a thousand feet. When the smoke cleared there was nothing left.' Another witness, John Ellis, saw above the smoke 'a 15-inch turret in the sky with the figure of a man above it.'[8] That there were any survivors at all from the multiple counter-mining detonations that tore the massive capital ship apart is incredible, but Pridham-Wippell and 450 officers and men were recovered by *Hotspur* and HMAS *Nizam*. Mack's *Jervis*, with *Jackal* in company, searched the area all night, but there was no trace of *U331*; all they found was a single survivor, floating more than a mile away from where *Barham* had disintegrated.

Having fruitlessly expended numerous depth charges, Mack's destroyers returned to Alexandria on the afternoon of 27 November.

Cunningham had picked up his moorings the previous day. The return passage had been nervous – the C-in-C had to restrain *Queen Elizabeth*'s Captain Barry from opening fire on aircraft that Cunningham thought 'were mostly ours'. Like Somerville, he mourned the loss of his great ship, but unlike his brother door-keeper, whose casualty list had been mercifully small, Andrew Cunningham had witnessed the instantaneous death of Captain G. Cooke and 861 of his ship's company. To Pound he wrote that *Barham* was 'indeed a heavy loss. We blundered straight on to the submarine'; betraying the lonely burden of high command, Cunningham added plaintively, 'There was no necessity for us to be there any more than anywhere else …'[9]

It was all for nothing. Elsewhere, Rawlings' Force B had failed to locate the second convoy and the rear-admiral returned, disappointed, to Alexandria. The *Luigi Cadorna* and her three consorts entered Benghazi on 22 November. The state of the Axis fuel reserves remained parlous, despite the safe arrival of these consignments, and this was soon known in London, as Ultra decrypts of signals referring to the loss of *Maritza* and *Procida* revealed that the quantity of oil in those two relatively small vessels had greatly exceeded the reserves then held in Cyrenaica.

To increase the chances of finally capitalising on this deficiency and delivering a further decisive blow, Cunningham was ordered to send a second strike force to Malta, to act alternately with Force K. Rawlings accordingly left Alexandria with Force B on 27 November, his squadron now consisting of *Ajax* and *Neptune*, with the destroyers *Kingston* and *Kimberley*. With Force B went the 15th Cruiser Squadron, to operate in partial support but with the supplementary objective of sweeping east along the Cyrenaican coast on their own return to Alexandria. Vice-Admiral King had been posted to the Admiralty and was succeeded by Rear-Admiral Vian, who had hoisted his flag aboard *Naiad* on 1 November; he was accompanied by *Euryalus* and the destroyers *Griffin* and *Hotspur*. Rawlings arrived safely at Malta, where the cruisers hurriedly discharged the quantities of stores they had brought from Alexandria.

As they approached their destination the Italian submarine *Tricheco*, lying in wait south-east of Malta, had taken a pot-shot at them, but the Italians were using many of their submarines to carry supplies and few were available for such patrols. During December a dozen made a total of twenty-one runs to Benghazi, Bardia, Derna and Tripoli, carrying in all some 1,800 tons of urgently wanted supplies. One, the *Caracciolo*, was located and sunk by the *Farndale* on 11 December, but she was on her way home, having delivered her cargo of desperately needed petrol.[10]

On 29 November the Axis surface convoys resumed. The freighters *Capo Faro* (3,476 grt), *Iseo* (2,366 grt) and *Sebastiano Venier* (6,300 grt), the troop transport *Adriatico*, and two tankers, the small *Volturno* and the 10,000-tons dead weight *Irido Mantovani*, sailed from several ports. With the exception of the *Irido Mantovani*, which was bound for Tripoli, they were headed for Benghazi via the Ionian Sea. Small close escorts were provided, while two groups of cruisers gave support. One, the 7th Division under Ammiraglio di Divisione de Courten, consisted of the light cruisers *Muzio Attendolo*, *Duca d'Aosta* and *Raimondo Montecuccoli*, with the destroyers *Aviere*, *Camicia Nera* and *Geniere*. The second group, under Ammiraglio di Divisione Giovanola in the battleship *Caio Duilio*, comprised the cruiser *Giuseppe Garibaldi* and the destroyers *Granatiere*, *Alpino*, *Bersagliere*, *Corazziere*, *Carabiniere* and *Fuciliere*. Acting on a string of detailed Ultra decrypts, British air and sea patrols were alerted, and sighting reports of these movements began to arrive at Valletta; the patrolling submarine *Thunderbolt* sent one, and others came in during the succeeding hours. In anticipation, Ford ordered Forces B and K to sea. Agnew sailed at dusk on Sunday, 30 November with *Aurora*, *Penelope* and *Lively* (leaving *Lance* in drydock), followed by Force B. Learning of these departures, Supermarina ordered the Italian cruisers to concentrate, but engine trouble aboard the *Giuseppe Garibaldi* detained Giovanola and delayed the rendezvous, so that Supermarina ordered the two admirals to avoid contact with what they assumed would be Rawlings' combined force. In fact Rawlings had not combined, the better to deal with the multiple Axis ship movements then in train.

During the 30th Blenheims located, bombed and sunk the *Capo Faro* and damaged the *Iseo* so that she made a run for Argostoli in Cephalonia, while the Italian cruisers retreated to Taranto. At the same time Force K was steaming east at speed and at 01.30 the next morning a Wellington located the *Adriatico* proceeding unescorted. Shortly after 03.00 the solitary former passenger ship came in sight and *Aurora* engaged, flashing the international signal to abandon ship as her broadside fell short. There was no response, so two further broadsides followed; the *Adriatico* slowed and appeared to be stopping, so Agnew held his fire until, instead of leaving their ship, the Italians returned fire, thereby sealing their fate. *Aurora* responded, fires broke out on board *Adriatico*, and the hapless Italian soldiers embarked in the troopship began to go over the side. *Lively* moved in to recover survivors and then the two cruisers circled the burning ship, pumping shells into her until she blew up.

Agnew then received a signal from Ford to intercept the Tripoli-bound *Irido Mantovani* and her escort, many miles to the east. The three ships of Force K rapidly worked up to full speed and, as daylight grew, raced across the Gulf of Sirte. They were spotted again, by a questing Cant, but again successfully jammed its report, and the aeroplane flew off, to be lost in rain clouds. Meanwhile Agnew's target had been located and bombed by Blenheims, whose near-misses had brought the tanker to a standstill with her engine room flooded, seventy-odd miles north of her destination. But she remained afloat and Capitano di Corvetta dell'Anno, commanding the escorting destroyer *Alvise da Mosto*, had taken her in tow and was engaged in an attempt to haul her cargo of petrol into Tripoli. A handful of Fiat CR42 biplanes flying an air patrol overhead in support of dell'Anno gave away the location of the crippled tanker to the approaching lookouts of Force K. With the Tripolitanian coast not far away and darkness encroaching, *Aurora* and her two consorts drove over the eastern horizon. They were swooped on by the CR42s but these, having overflown them, turned away 'without taking any offensive action'. At the first report of the British presence dell'Anno cast off, and gallantly prepared to defend his charge by laying a smoke screen. As *Aurora* opened fire from a range of 16,000 yards, Nicholl hauled *Penelope* out on *Aurora*'s quarter and engaged in the gathering gloom. With the eleventh salvo from her forward turrets *Penelope*'s 6-inch guns hit the destroyer's stern, blowing up her after magazine. A second later shells from *Aurora* also hit her, and she vanished with a bright flash and an awful concussion. Eight minutes after engaging, the Italian destroyer and her ship's company had ceased to exist. Turning their guns on *Irido Mantovani* the cruisers set her ablaze, leaving *Lively* to embark the tanker's survivors from their boats and administer the *coup de grâce* with a torpedo. At 19.53, as the British ships headed for Malta, the *Irido Mantovani* exploded astern of them.

Alone of the merchantmen which had set out, the *Sebastiano Venier* and her escort of the destroyer *Da Verazzano* reached Benghazi. As for Rawlings' Force B, it had missed the Italian cruisers and returned to Malta, leaving the laurels to Force K. After its long series of high-speed chases, Agnew's three ships entered Valletta to cheering crowds. Unusually, due compliments were paid to the squadron's engineering branch, as well as to Flight-Lieutenant Spooner, whose Wellington had overshot its theoretical endurance in order to maintain contact with the *Adriatico*.

But in refuelling, the cruisers and destroyers depleted the island's stock to a dangerous degree, a fact Ford signalled to Cunningham. Efforts to obtain a fast tanker and ease the constraints imposed by the fuel shortage at Malta had failed, a serious deficiency under the circumstances. Cunningham and Ford therefore concerted a plan consisting of Operations MD1 and MF1. On the late afternoon of 5 December, *Breconshire* left Grand Harbour escorted by *Ajax*, *Neptune*, *Kimberley*, *Kingston* and *Lively*, heading eastwards, the following dawn *Hobart*, *Jaguar* and *Kandahar* left Alexandria, and that evening *Ajax*, *Neptune* and *Lively* turned back for Malta, leaving *Breconshire* with *Kimberley* and *Kingston* until, at dawn on the 7th, the three ships met *Hobart* and her two destroyers. The latter continued west towards Malta to join Force K, while *Hobart* turned in support of *Breconshire*, *Kimberley* and *Kingston*. During the afternoon *Hobart* was detached to the assistance of the sloop *Flamingo*, immobilised off Tobruk after an air attack; meanwhile the fast transport and her two destroyers reached Alexandria on 8 December.

During her conversion to a naval auxiliary *Breconshire* had had her deep-tank capacity enlarged to take 5,000 tons, less than a tanker could have carried but the best that could be done in the circumstances. She was now filled to capacity with a precious cargo of boiler oil, and in the next few days the orlop and 'tweendecks under her six hatches were loaded with military supplies.

But if Ford and Cunningham were worried about their fuel stocks, there were few immediate consolations for the Italians. Ciano bemoaned their merchant shipping losses, especially that of the *Irido Mantovani*, which 'it cannot be denied is a hard blow'. However, the news from the Japanese ambassador that a rupture with the United States was imminent raised spirits in Rome, while in Berlin the devastation being caused to Axis communications was reviving plans for the invasion of Malta.

Meanwhile, as the dozen Italian submarines continued the carriage of small consignments, the light cruiser *Luigi Cadorna* successfully eluded detection in bad weather and again reached Benghazi with a cargo of canned petrol on 10 December, the day on which Rommel, under pressure from his enemies, signalled he had a single day's fuel left for his tanks. Returning with 900 prisoners-of-war, the cruiser made another successful run a few days later. The *Sebastiano Venier* was not so lucky, however, being damaged by a torpedo from the British submarine *Porpoise* when she was heading home with more than two thousand prisoners on board.[11] A few days later, on the 15th, *Torbay* finished the job. Despite heavy weather the Italian hospital ship *Arno* succeeded in rescuing about 1,800 men, but 320 were lost, 309 of whom were British. Another Italian supply ship, the *Calitea*, of 4,013 tons, was sunk by the submarine *Talisman* off Cape Matapan, inflicting further damage on Axis communications.

In Malta, Vice-Admiral Ford conserved his meagre stock of boiler oil with a strict hand. A quantity had to be reserved for a group of destroyers expected shortly on passage from Gibraltar to Alexandria, and constraints were therefore laid upon the units of Force K.[12] Thus, when Ultra decrypts revealed the intended running of two cruisers as fuel transports from Palermo, the news that they would pass Cape Bon within air strike range of Malta came as a relief. Instead of Force K, the Fleet Air Arm's Fairey Swordfish of No. 830 Squadron and Albacores of No. 828 based at Hal Far were prepared for the strike.

Rommel's fuel situation made this Italian operation supremely important and the officer entrusted with its execution, Ammiraglio di Divisione Toscano, was ordered not to risk losing his cargo. The cruisers *Alberico da Barbiano* and *Alberto di Giussano* sailed from Palermo on 9 December and were intercepted and bombed that night by the Fleet Air Arm. Although undamaged Toscano retired, and sailed again the following night, to be attacked and driven back a second time by the Swordfish and Albacores. By now Rommel's situation was even worse, but on the third sally matters looked better for Toscano. To avoid the

British torpedo-bombers the two cruisers, joined now by the torpedo-boat *Cigno*, had swept well to the westwards before doubling Cape Bon and turning south, close inshore. Then the rumble of aero-engines was heard overhead, and Toscano decided that his mission was again compromised: at 02.00 on 13 December he turned back for Palermo.

At Hal Far the Swordfish and Albacores were ready to attack, and awaited only the locating signal from the searching Wellington which had found Toscano's ships. But Toscano's Nemesis was approaching from an entirely different direction.

Commander G. Stokes had left Gibraltar in *Sikh* with the destroyers intended to reinforce Cunningham's fleet, for which Ford was holding fuel at Malta. Stokes had been informed by signal that an Italian cruiser force was operating west of Malta, and at 02.30 that morning, as his destroyers approached Cape Bon from the west, their lookouts caught sight of Toscano's squadron to seaward. Completely unobserved by the Italians, who were engaged in signalling to each other by lamp, *Sikh* increased speed and led *Legion*, *Maori* and the Dutch destroyer *Isaac Sweers* close inshore. Racing along the mine-free territorial waters of Tunisia, the Allied destroyers rapidly closed the range, suddenly emerging unseen from the black backdrop of the coast. Stokes attacked with torpedoes. As the night erupted with explosions and the canned petrol congesting the decks of the Italian cruisers caught fire, the Italian guns trained on and extinguished the lighthouse on neutral Cape Bon. It was the only target they could locate before their ships were engulfed in the insufferable heat of fatal conflagration. *Cigno* made off in the darkness, later returning to embark the 645 survivors from the combined companies of the two lost cruisers.

Like Toscano, Stokes had had orders not to engage superior forces, for he had RAF personnel on board bound for Malta; but unlike Toscano (who perished in the action), Stokes had seized the opportunity offered. Such initiative was expected of a Royal Naval officer, especially of a commander of destroyers: the strand of legitimate and justifiable disobedience had been woven into the fabric of the Royal Navy long since.

The destruction of Italian supply ships went on unabated. Despite their losses, and under urgent prodding from Berlin, the Italians continued to attempt Rommel's relief. On 13 December eight transports in a trio of convoys were to set out under the cover of the Regia Marina. But that morning *Upright*, one of three British submarines patrolling off the toe of Calabria,[13] sank the *Fabio Filzi* and *Carlo del Greco*; both loaded with tanks, the two ships were on passage to the rendezvous at Taranto and escorted by the destroyers *Nicoloso da Recco* and *Antoniotto Usodimare*.

Undaunted by this, that same afternoon the three Italian freighters *Monginevro, Napoli* and *Vettor Pisani* left Taranto under the escort of three destroyers. Two more sailed separately as escort to the German freighter *Ankara*, and a further two-ship convoy left Argostoli accompanied by two destroyers. In the wake of these departures from Taranto, Ammiraglio di Squadra Bergamini, his flag in the battleship *Caio Duilio*, sailed with the cruisers *Giuseppe Garibaldi, Raimondo Montecuccoli* and *Gorizia*, screened by three destroyers. Bergamini was supported by de Courten in the cruiser *Duca d'Aosta*, the battleship *Andrea Doria*, the cruiser *Muzio Attendolo* and three destroyers. In addition, a further seven destroyers sailed, four of them speeding off to the south-west to meet Iachino coming from Naples with the two battleships *Littorio* and *Vittorio Veneto* and four more destroyers. This wholesale departure, which constituted virtually the entire operational strength of the Italian navy, was known to the British in Alexandria from both Ultra decrypts and reports from their submarines lying in the Strait of Messina and off Cape Spartivento. It was one of these that knocked the whole enterprise awry when Iachino passed the Strait on the following evening: Lieutenant-Commander Tomkinson torpedoed the *Vittorio Veneto*, and Iachino turned immediately and made for Taranto, cancelling the entire operation and recalling the convoys. Off Argostoli the freighters *Capo Orsam* and *Iseo* collided and further frustrated matters by returning damaged to port.

That the operation would collapse so easily had not been anticipated in Alexandria, from where Rear-Admiral Vian had departed on the 13th with *Naiad, Euryalus, Galatea* and a destroyer screen. The minelayer *Abdiel* had been sent out to transmit confusing radio messages indicating fleet manoeuvres, while the cruisers in Malta, mindful of the fuel situation, waited there, ready to join forces with Vian when he drew closer. The news that the whole operation had been cancelled by the Italians caused Vian to be recalled, and he turned back. Then, a few minutes after midnight on 14/15 December, as Vian's squadron approached the searched channel to Alexandria, *Galatea* was hit by a torpedo.

Early December had seen a further five U-boats arrive in the eastern Mediterranean, almost tripling the number operational there.[14] Apart from their success in sinking *Barham* they enjoyed mixed fortunes, missing several targets, including Cunningham's flagship *Queen Elizabeth*. But *U431* had sunk the water-tanker *Myriel* on 13 December, and now *U557* had wrecked *Galatea*. It was a bad blow, coming as it did only a few days after *Jackal* had been severely damaged by bombs when Mack's destroyers were operating with Vian off Derna. Yet other dire events lay ahead, in the Mediterranean and elsewhere, in which the Royal Navy were to sustain losses to which those of *Barham* and *Galatea* were but the overture.

Galatea sank so quickly that only about a hundred and fifty of her crew were saved; the rest, including Captain E. Sim, were lost. Korvettenkapitän Paulshen did not long enjoy his elation, however. As she returned to her Greek base the following day, *U557* was accidentally rammed and sunk by the Italian submarine *Orione*.

By this time Vian was already back at sea, having sailed at 22.00 on the 15th in *Naiad* with *Euryalus* and *Carlisle*, the destroyers *Jervis*, *Kimberley*, *Kingston*, *Kipling*, *Hasty*, *Havock*, *Decoy* and HMAS *Nizam*. He was bound for Malta, covering the all-important transport *Breconshire* with her 5,000 tons of urgently needed boiler oil, a movement designated as Operation MD1. It was an impressive escort for a single cargo-carrying naval auxiliary. During the night *Breconshire* had to repair a defect, and the delay meant that Vian headed west during the daylight hours of the 16th without zigzagging, 'in order to make the westing by nightfall essential to the plan'. Although provided with 'good fighter cover', his ships were observed by Ju52s on supply runs to Rommel, and *Jervis* investigated two sonar contacts. After dark Vian detached the slower *Carlisle* and the destroyers *Kingston* and *Hasty*. *Carlisle* made further spurious radio transmissions intended to mislead the enemy into supposing the main battle-fleet to be at sea.[15]

Stokes's refuelled destroyers left Malta on 16 December, followed by Force K. At 18.00 that evening *Aurora*, *Penelope*, *Lively* and *Lance* slipped out of Grand Harbour to head east and take over the escort of *Breconshire* from Vian. But that afternoon

Supermarina had resuscitated their own convoy operation, M42, and *Monginevro, Napoli* and *Vettor Pisani* left Taranto under the escort of the destroyers *Vivaldi, Da Noli, Da Recco, Malocello, Pessagno, Vivaldi,* and *Zeno.* They were to be followed by the German freighter *Ankara,* escorted by *Saetta* and the torpedo-boat *Pegaso.* Heavy cover was provided by Bergamini in the battleship *Caio Duilio* and by de Courten's cruisers *Duca d'Aosta, Muzio Attendolo* and *Raimondo Montecuccoli,* screened by the destroyers *Ascari, Aviere* and *Camicia Nera.* Iachino followed with the battleships *Andrea Doria, Giulio Cesare* and *Littorio,* plus Parona's 3rd Division of heavy cruisers, *Gorizia* and *Trento.* The destroyers *Granatiere, Bersagliere, Alpino, Fuciliere, Corazziere, Carabiniere, Antoniotto Usodimare, Maestrale, Alfredo Oriani* and *Vincenzo Gioberti* provided Iachino's *Vincenzo* screen.

This impressive armada headed for North Africa, massively outnumbering the British warships strung out to the south of them. At 23.30 that night the Italians were first seen and reported by the patrolling submarines of the 10th Flotilla. As this 'placed Vian in rather a serious predicament' Cunningham, anxious, ordered Ford to dispatch every warship available at Malta: *Breconshire* must be brought safely into Grand Harbour. With *Ajax* defective and out of action, it was *Neptune* that led *Jaguar* and *Kandahar* out of Grand Harbour to meet the incoming transport in the early hours of the 17th. Cunningham went further, instructing Vian to continue in company with *Breconshire* until met by the ships from Malta, whereupon he was 'to attack the enemy with torpedoes'.[16] He could do no more but wait 'fretting and fuming at Alexandria', for his battleships were 'immobilized ... through lack of a destroyer screen'. The situation was 'galling in the extreme' for the Commander-in-Chief.

Far to the west, as dawn broke on the scene, Vian met Force K, which had made a rendezvous with Stokes's destroyers an hour or so earlier, and the combined force of cruisers and destroyers steamed westwards, clustered round *Breconshire,* which was reported by one German aircraft as a battleship. Throughout the afternoon, from 13.00 to 18.20 and the onset of darkness, the British were harried by high-level bombing and torpedo attacks. The Savoia Marchetti SM79s of the Regia Aeronautica were accompanied by Junkers Ju88s, returned to Italy from the Russian front, and they maintained a relentless attack which, while it achieved little damage, kept the ships on constant alert and at action stations. Only 'one torpedo-bomber penetrated the screen, and it was shot down'. Meanwhile, with Vian now exposed to the north-west of Benghazi, the Regia Marina were approaching from the north and estimated at 15.30 to be 60 miles distant. Lacking proper air reconnaissance, Vian was receiving sketchy reports of enemy warship groups and disinclined to consider the situation grave, arguing that neither of the reported forces would be within sixty miles of him by darkness. Then, at 17.30, a capital ship's seaplanes were seen, the torpedo-bombers held off attacking and signal flares were released over the British ships. 'It appeared ...', Vian noted, 'that our reconnaissance had been at fault.' At 17.42, 'shortly before sunset', the upperworks of capital ships and cruisers were seen, breaking the line of the northern horizon. It was Iachino, his three battleships, two cruisers and ten destroyers. When 14 miles distant, Iachino 'deployed to the eastward and opened fire. The fire was accurate.'

Thanks to Axis air superiority the Italian admiral had known of the presence of Vian for some time, but was unaware of his priorities or the nature of his task. He knew his enemy lacked an aircraft-carrier, and despite the reported presence of 'a battleship' in the British force had increased his squadron's speed to 24 knots and altered course towards the British, intending to bring them to battle before dark. Vian responded by immediately detaching *Breconshire* with *Decoy* and *Havock* to the south-west, then turning the rest of the force towards the Italians. This was 'hampered by a well executed attack delivered by the torpedo-bombers' and two torpedoes were dropped. Neither found a target, and Vian claimed that his destroyers shot down one of the attacking aircraft.

Smoke and gunfire covered the retreat of *Breconshire*. Meanwhile the British cruisers made smoke and, in the gathering dusk, proved difficult targets for the optically controlled Italian guns. Vian's destroyers stretched out on either flank, threatening the Italian capital ships with their torpedoes. But 'it was no part of [Vian's] plan to offer the enemy battle, unless ... [compelled to do so,] under conditions which ... were favourable to him'; he therefore restrained the destroyers from actually attacking and, maintaining his posture between *Breconshire* and Iachino, was able to hand the escort of the transport over to Agnew as Force K arrived and made smoke.[17]

At 18.04 Iachino turned away, fearful of a torpedo attack. Vian believed him to have turned north 'between dusk and dark', adding that by nightfall he had also 'lost touch ... with the majority of the forces acting with me. This is a disadvantage of diversionary tactics.' This inconclusive encounter which lasted barely eleven minutes is known to history as the First Battle of Sirte, though it was no more than an imperfect skirmish. But in conforming to Cunningham's orders and retiring to Alexandria after sending Force K west after *Breconshire*, Vian allowed the Italians to pass their transports through to Cyrenaica, supplying Rommel with a portion at least of what he so earnestly desired. Thus it was claimed by the Italians that, having 'taken the offensive for a whole day against a British group', Iachino 'had forced it to retire'.[18]

As Vian returned to Alexandria, Force K reinforced *Decoy* and *Havock* escorting *Breconshire*. Agnew's *Aurora* took station ahead of her with *Penelope* astern, the destroyers flanking her as night fell. At 07.00 on the 18th, Force K met *Neptune* and her two destroyers, and the ships spent the day dodging the attacks of Ju88s. By the early afternoon Malta-based Hurricanes had begun to break up the Luftwaffe units, and at 15.00 the ships entered Grand Harbour. Hardly had *Breconshire* berthed before pipelines and pumps began to extract her precious cargo of oil, while Force K thirstily drew much of it straight into their own bunker tanks. In all, it took two days to discharge *Breconshire*'s entire cargo.

Just before midnight the same evening the rear-admiral arrived back at Alexandria, having been joined by Stokes and his reinforcing destroyers. Unbeknown to Vian, he had been unsuccessfully attacked by *U371*, though *Jervis* had hunted a submarine contact which Mack wrongly thought he had damaged. Vian was also ignorant of an even more sinister event, for into Alexandria through the open boom defences he had been accompanied by three Italian *maiali*, launched a little earlier from Prince Borghese's submarine *Scirè*. Entirely undetected, the three human torpedo teams attached their warheads to Cunningham's flagship *Queen Elizabeth*, the battleship *Valiant* and the Norwegian tanker *Sagona*, alongside which Mack's *Jervis* lay.

Flushed with his 'victory', Iachino remained at sea on the 18th to cover the final arrival of his transports at Benghazi and Tripoli. It was known in Valletta that a portion of the Italian shipping had not yet reached its destination of Tripoli, so despite Iachino's

continuing presence, which was reported by an aircraft reconnoitring from Malta, Force K was sent in pursuit while Fleet Air
Arm Swordfish and Albacores were armed with torpedoes and
made ready at Hal Far to assist the warships. Wellingtons had
already taken off to lay acoustic mines in the approaches to
Tripoli in the hope of preventing the entry of the convoy. The
speed with which these dispositions were made was the very
stuff of naval strategy and reflected Cunningham's relentless
policy, which stiffened the responses of all senior officers in his
wide-ranging command and found a perfect echo in Wilbraham
Ford and his colleagues at Valletta. But Force K, now under the
command of Captain R. O'Conor, was unknowingly sailing on
its last sortie. Working up to 30 knots, *Neptune, Aurora, Penelope,
Lively, Lance, Havock* and *Kandahar* steamed south-east with a
gale on their port quarters, in windy but hot pursuit.

As O'Conor's warships closed the Libyan coast at around midnight and in heavy seas, the Italian men-of-war and merchant
vessels were off Tripoli. But here they were compelled to anchor,
unable to enter the port because of the risk to them from the
mines dropped earlier by the British Wellingtons. One attack was
made on them by the Fleet Air Arm biplanes, without significant
results in the blustery darkness, and they lay exposed to O'Conor
as he approached.

It was now Force K's fate to receive a mauling, for only a few
miles away from Tripoli, at 00.40 on 19 December, O'Conor's
ships ran into the enemy's coastal mine barrage. First *Neptune*
fouled and detonated a mine in her paravanes and then, when
O'Conor went astern, she ran into a second which destroyed her
screws and steering gear.[19] *Aurora* and *Penelope*, following in her
wake, steered to pass her, but within seconds they too both detonated mines. Seriously damaged, *Aurora* pulled clear and
Agnew began to limp off towards Malta escorted by *Lance* and
Havock, while the lesser-affected *Penelope* stood by, preparing to
get *Neptune* under tow once the wind had blown her clear of the
minefield. At 01.00, however, *Neptune* detonated a third mine,
and Commander Robson of *Kandahar* eased ahead to take off survivors, whereupon his destroyer had her stern blown off. Finally
O'Conor signalled Nicholl to stand away and not bring *Penelope*
any closer. But his agony was not yet over. At 04.00 a fourth mine
exploded under *Neptune*'s bridge, and she began to capsize and
sink as water poured into her shattered hull.

With sunrise looming over an enemy coast and the sea littered with mines, Nicholl had to withdraw *Penelope*, refusing permission to Hussey to take *Lively* in closer to rescue *Kandahar's* people. However, he broke radio silence to send a cypher signal to Ford, requesting that a Sunderland or submarine be sent to try to pick up the survivors from the two ships. *Kandahar* remained afloat, drifting away from the single Carley raft that bore all that was left of *Neptune's* crew.

Catching up with *Aurora*, *Havock* and *Lance*, *Penelope* and *Lively* struggled into Grand Harbour at noon. The damage to Force K was serious: *Penelope* was to move from Parlatorio Wharf into No. 2 Drydock at the head of Dockyard Creek over Christmas for repairs; *Aurora*, more grievously wounded, remained in No. 5 Dock until 28 March 1942.

Kandahar had meanwhile continued to drift helplessly. She lay low in the water, unmolested by the enemy and sending out signals to Malta. Ford determined to save her company and ordered Lieutenant-Commander Tyrwhitt to sea in *Jaguar*. At 16.20 *Jaguar* sailed, after an inexplicable delay, and aided by a radar-equipped Wellington located *Kandahar* at 04.00 on 20 December. Heavy weather prevailed and it was necessary for *Kandahar's* survivors to swim across to *Jaguar*, but 164 of them were thereby brought to safety.

The handful left from *Neptune's* ship's company clung through the night to their single Carley raft. The cruiser had been intended for transfer to the Royal New Zealand Navy, and among her lost company were 160 young New Zealanders. By daylight only the unfortunate O'Conor and fifteen men were left on the raft. They died during the succeeding days, so that by 23 December only Leading Seaman J. Walters remained alive, to be taken prisoner by an Italian torpedo-boat, the *Calliope*, that ranged up alongside him.

At about the time that the fourth and fatal mine detonated under *Neptune's* bridge, Cunningham was woken from sleep in his cabin aboard *Queen Elizabeth* to hear that two Italians had been found clinging miserably to the mooring buoy to which *Valiant's* bow was shackled. In Alexandria, as at Gibraltar, patrolling motor launches dropped random detonating charges to deter acts of sabotage, and in addition to the main boom across the harbour entrance each battleship, when at her moorings, was surrounded by heavy curtains of wire netting. Cunningham had the two prisoners brought back from the shore and confined in a forward compartment aboard *Valiant*, 'well below the waterline'. All hands were called in the fleet and men were turned-to to keel haul their ships with light drag chains. While this was going on Cunningham paced his flagship's quarterdeck, and at about 06.00 the warhead attached to the *Sagona* detonated. The tanker's stern was destroyed, while alongside her *Jervis* sustained sufficient damage to detain her in dock for a month.

Twenty minutes later an explosion abreast and below A-turret of *Valiant* betrayed the presence of a second device. Four minutes later, when Cunningham was right aft by the ensign staff of *Queen Elizabeth*, he 'felt a dull thud and was tossed about five feet into the air by the whip of the ship and was lucky not to come down sprawling … *Valiant* was already down by the bows. The *Queen Elizabeth* took a heavy list to starboard'.[20] Though the ship was out of action, the list was corrected by counter-flooding, and until generators could be got to work again the flagship's power was provided by a submarine moored on either side. Cunningham then employed a famous ruse, maintaining all routines, remaining on board himself and parading the marine bands, ostentatiously performing the ceremonies of morning colours and sunset as though nothing was amiss. *Valiant* was docked, eighty feet of her bottom, including her keel, having been badly damaged, but only temporary repair work could be carried out in Alexandria. It was clear that six audacious Italians had succeeded where the might of the Regia Marina had failed: the British Mediterranean Fleet was effectively emasculated.

It was, Cunningham confessed to Pound, 'a disaster'. He was driven to fretting over how to protect the ships from future attacks, until a junior engineering officer came up with the simple suggestion that if the ships were to keep their screws turning slowly astern, they would generate a sufficiently strong current along their bottoms to defeat even a powerful swimmer: 'Thereafter we adopted this procedure …', Cunningham recorded. 'It is a pity we did not think of it before.'

There was one small triumph to mark Christmas for the British – the passing of reinforcements through to Cunningham from Gibraltar by way of Malta, where the warships dropped off quantities of stores and supplies. Led by the cruiser *Dido*, which

had aboard Rear-Admiral H. Diesen, senior officer of the Royal
Norwegian Navy, the destroyers *Gurkha, Zulu, Nestor, Foxhound*
and *Arrow* sailed at 05.30 on 22 December and arrived at Malta
on Christmas Eve. They left the island in company with the operational remnants of Force K, the destroyers *Lively* and *Lance*, with
the cruiser *Ajax*, and this combined force escorted the emptied
merchant ships of convoy ME8 on Operation MF1. *Clan Ferguson,
City of Calcutta, Ajax* and the repaired *Sydney Star* had been languishing in Malta for far too long, constantly shifting their moorings to fool Italian air reconnaissance and frustrate their
bombing, their crews unable to understand why they were left
idle during a period when only a trickle of supplies was being
maintained by the submarines *Clyde, Olympus* and *Porpoise*. The
Blue Funnel liner *Ajax*, for instance, was equipped with such
superb cargo-handling gear that she had discharged her lading
within forty-eight hours of her arrival, only to spend three
months dodging about Grand Harbour, ending up moored at the
head of Marsa Creek. Here, surrounded by the heights of Marsa,
the ship's company sheltered in an adjacent tunnel during air
raids, leaving one watch on duty to man the ship. As they were
forbidden to use their anti-aircraft armament because of the
shortage of ammunition, it was a profoundly frustrating experience. The crew, predominantly Liverpool men, fielded a good
football team and were much in demand to play naval crews; on
one occasion, both teams and the spectators were subject to strafing during an air raid. On Christmas Eve *Ajax* received a bomb
hit which fortunately passed through her stern without exploding, and entirely missed the telemotor steering gear. It did,
however, take a crate of chickens that *Ajax*'s Chinese greasers
were fattening up for their New Year celebrations. 'I have never
seen an angrier man than our Number One greaser,' Third
Officer Sibly afterwards recalled; he was 'literally dancing up
and down with rage when he found they were gone.' *Ajax* sailed
with the hole in her stern.

The Luftwaffe arrived overhead the next day and subjected
convoy ME8 to constant attack. *Ajax* 'was only saved from disaster by the superb seamanship of the Master, John Scott, who time
after time prevented the ship from being hit by watching astern
and as the bomber lined up, swung her on one side or the other
by a hard-over helm order and stopping one engine. We were
near-missed on numerous occasions, one such was so close

astern, the column of water [thrown up by the bomb-burst] washed the 4-inch gun crew [on the poop] off their feet. They got their revenge, however, by shooting the tail off a dive bomber and watching it crash, which cheered us all up.'[21] The convoy and its escort, although hard-pressed, lost no vessels and the men-of-war entered Alexandria on 29 December while the merchantmen ran on to the eastwards, arriving at Port Said on the penultimate day of the year.

As 1941 drew to its close, the gradually increasing activity of German units made itself felt. On four nights during the latter half of December, German *Schnellboote* laid seventy-three mines off Malta in the approaches to Grand Harbour, while the U-boat force at Salamis was steadily augmented. By the end of December there were fourteen, all available for patrols along the coasts of Egypt, Libya and Cyrenaica where the British maintained the supply of the Eighth Army by sea. On 23 December a group attacked an Alexandria-bound convoy from Tobruk, escorted by *Hasty* and *Hotspur*. Korvettenkapitän Heidtmann of *U559* torpedoed the China Navigation Company's 3,059-ton steamer *Shuntien*, engaged as a war transport on Admiralty service, but in the counter-attack the two destroyers succeeded in sinking *U79*. The next day, Christmas Eve, the corvette *Salvia* was torpedoed and sunk on convoy duty by *U568*, and on Boxing Day Heidtmann struck again, sinking another ship in convoy of 3,059 tons. He was less lucky on the 28th in an attack on a Tobruk convoy, missing his target, but his colleague Korvettenkapitän Ringelmann in *U75* torpedoed the *Volo*, an early participant in Malta convoys. As the *Volo* sank, the escorting destroyer *Kipling* exacted revenge, sinking Ringelmann and *U75*.

The Japanese attack on Pearl Harbor on 7 December 1941 had the effect, by the middle of the month, of further reducing the strength of the Mediterranean Fleet. The minelayer *Abdiel* and the Australian cruiser *Hobart* were ordered east, deficiencies which could not be made good despite the return of the repaired *Dido*, for off Malaya the *Prince of Wales*, so lately in the Mediterranean, and *Renown*'s sister ship *Repulse* had been bombed to destruction by the air arm of the Japanese navy. The British capital ships had had no carrier to provide local air cover, for *Indomitable* had run aground on her way to join Force Z.

Though the entry of the United States into the war ended the isolation of Great Britain and the free forces sided with her, and was ultimately to prove the most decisive factor in the subsequent attrition, it was many months before this influence tipped the balance in the Allies' favour. Insofar as the Mediterranean was concerned, no sight of it was perceptible. The situation had merely grown blacker with the year's end.

As early as October Hitler had decided to step up German support for Italy by the diversion of an entire Air Fleet. On 2 December he appointed Kesselring with orders, *inter alia*, 'to secure mastery of the air and sea in the area between Southern Italy and North Africa in order to secure communications with Libya and Cyrenaica and, in particular to keep Malta in subjection.' The field marshal was also charged to 'paralyse enemy traffic through the Mediterranean and British supplies to Tobruk and Malta ...'[22] Kesselring was sent to Rome as joint commander with Rommel of the campaign in North Africa; nominally he was to take orders from Mussolini through the Italian high command, the Comando Supremo, but his real master lay farther north, in the concrete Führer Headquarters in the dark pine forests of east Prussia.

Kesselring brought massive reinforcements by way of Luftwaffe units withdrawn for the winter months from the Russian front, to be consolidated in the succeeding spring. His orders clearly prioritised Malta, and, after the fall of Tobruk on 21 June the following year the island received his full attention. Reluctant to invade, however, the Axis high commands renewed their faith in 'siege' by air power. The full implications of the German intervention in the Mediterranean and its impact upon Malta and the war in the Western Desert now revealed themselves. In the last weeks of 1941 the Axis powers surpassed their previous efforts to supply Rommel. Slender as the advantage they gained was, these exertions were to delay the outcome of the desert war for a full year, a year in which Malta was to be both the lynchpin, as Cunningham called it, and the Achilles' heel of British strategy in the Mediterranean theatre. In London the First Sea Lord, Sir Dudley Pound, described the situation as nothing less than 'the crisis in our fortunes'.

15

'At very great hazard'

(Operations MF2, 3, 4 and 5, with Convoys MW8, ME9, MW9, and ME10; Operations SPOTTER, PICKET *and MG1 with Convoy MW10 and the Second Battle of Sirte)*

———————

THE TOTAL LOSS of *Barham* and the disablement of *Queen Elizabeth* and *Valiant* combined with the lack of a carrier in the Mediterranean Fleet to render Cunningham's situation in January 1942 'depressing in the extreme'. Despite the reinforcements received from Gibraltar in the last few days of the old year it was the Italians, not the British, who now possessed a viable battle squadron and held the dominant position, particularly in the central Mediterranean. This superiority enabled the Italians to run Operation M43, a convoy to which they 'entrusted … [their] arms and hopes for the resistance in Libya'.[1] On 3 January six transports left Messina and Taranto, escorted by the destroyers *Vivaldi, Da Recco, Usodimare, Bersagliere, Fuciliere* and *Freccia*, and the torpedo-boats *Antares, Aretusa, Castore, Orsa* and *Procione*. Combining on the following day they made a rendezvous with Bergamini, flying his flag in the battleship *Caio Duilio*. The admiral was accompanied by the cruisers *Giuseppe Garibaldi, Raimondo Montecuccoli, Duca d'Aosta* and *Muzio Attendolo*, and his force was screened by the destroyers *Maestrale, Scirocco, Vincenzo Gioberti, Alfredo Oriani* and *Lanzerotto Malocello*. Distant cover was provided by a battle squadron commanded by Iachino and consisting of three battleships, *Littorio, Giulio Cesare* and *Andrea Doria*, the cruisers *Gorizia* and *Trento*, and a screen of eight destroyers.[2] This powerful fleet was flanked to the east of Malta by a cordon of seven patrolling submarines,[3] with a further four deployed between Crete and Cyrenaica.[4]

Although sighted by the patrolling British submarines *Ultimatum* and *Unique* of the 10th Submarine Flotilla and by aircraft, all operating from Malta, Iachino and Bergamini were unimpeded and the merchant transports arrived at Tripoli on 5 January, successfully discharging their cargoes. Having demonstrated to the east of Malta, Iachino reached home the same day, Bergamini's force returning on the 6th.

If Cunningham's battle-fleet had ceased to exist, his anti-submarine forces were too 'attenuated' to combat the menace of the Axis submarine threat. Meanwhile Malta's ordeal continued; Kesselring's bombing disrupted both air reconnaissance by the Royal Air Force and offensive air operations, thus largely negating the advantages of Ultra decrypts.[5] Captain Simpson's submarines continued to enjoy minor successes in the Aegean, however, and Wanklyn's *Upholder* had, on 5 January, sunk the large Italian submarine *Saint Bon* which was carrying a cargo of petrol to Tripoli. On the 12th, lying off the toe of Calabria, Lieutenant Woodward of *Unbeaten* discovered a U-boat proceeding on the surface and fired a salvo of three torpedoes at a range of 1,300 yards, sinking *U374* and recovering a single survivor.[6] But both *Upholder* and *Unbeaten* were harassed by German aircraft when approaching Marsamxett Harbour on the surface; *Triumph* was lost on or about the 14th, probably to a mine off the Greek coast; and *Uproar* was damaged that day while lying in Lazaretto Creek during an air attack. Although a trickle of submarine reinforcements was arriving in Marsamxett to join Simpson, Malta's situation was worsening. The welcome arrival on 5 January of the laden British submarine *Talisman* from Alexandria with service personnel and a cargo of kerosene,[7] welcome though it was, was insufficient to ease Ford's mind. Preparing to relinquish command to his successor, Vice-Admiral Sir Ralph Leatham, former C-in-C, East Indies, who was himself being relieved by Somerville, Ford had written to Cunningham on 3 January that Malta had been bombed seven times between 09.00 and 16.00 that day. The enemy, he reported, was 'trying to neutralize [sic] Malta's effort and, I hate to say, is gradually doing so ... Malta must', he continued, emphasising the imperative, 'be made stiff with *modern* fighters, Mosquitoes and Spitfires ... Guns and stores must come in a submarine beforehand ... The powers at home must ... send out the latest if they want to hold Malta ... Minesweeping is now difficult, and ... [the enemy] seem to be laying them everywhere ... ' Repair work in the dockyard was hampered by the raids, and the submarines in Lazaretto Creek were vulnerable. Ford bemoaned the failure to build underground submarine pens, which he had advocated months earlier, pleading that 'something must be done at once. How I can unload convoys I cannot think ... '

The recipient of this letter was also at his wits' end, despite the army's advance along the Cyrenaican coast to Al Agheila and the regaining of several air strips. Signalling his appreciation to Ford for his sterling service, Cunningham was unstinting in his praise. In an unglamorous shore-posting, Wilbraham Ford had kept Malta up and running as a naval base, repairing, refuelling and restoring ships despite all the manifold difficulties, not least of which was the co-ordination and prioritising of competing demands. In this his touch had been masterly; 'most of his bricks', the official history records, 'had to be made with little or no straw'. Ford remains one of those uncelebrated men whose contribution to the war effort, obscured by the battle-honours of others, has passed unrecognised.[8]

Cunningham was, of course, as acutely aware of Malta's position as Ford himself. Mercifully, the supply route round the Cape ensured that a reasonable flow of basic stores and ammunition was available in Egypt, but the passage to Malta from the east was still full of hazard. Nevertheless, that of *Talisman* had been successful, and on the same day that she arrived in Grand Harbour and the Italian supplies reached Tripoli, 5 January, the British initiated Operation MF2, an exchange of fast transports. The two former merchant vessels involved were the sister-ships *Breconshire* and *Glengyle*, the former to be withdrawn from Malta, the latter, her tanks filled with oil fuel, her 'tween-decks stuffed with food and ammunition, forwarded from Alexandria. *Glengyle* was escorted by the cruisers *Naiad* and *Euryalus* and the destroyers *Foxhound*, *Gurkha*, *Sikh*, *Kipling* and *Kingston*, which constituted Force B, under the command of Vian. Sailing from Malta the next day, *Breconshire* was escorted by Force C, the destroyers *Lance*, *Lively*, *Jaguar* and *Havock*. On the 7th the two forces met and *Havock* joined Force B, exchanging with *Sikh* which went to Malta with *Glengyle* and Force C, while *Breconshire* continued east with Vian's warships. No enemy intervention occurred and *Glengyle* and Force C arrived at Malta on the 8th, Vian's Force B and *Breconshire* at Alexandria on the 9th.

The arrival of *Glengyle*'s cargo was no more than a stop-gap measure. Malta needed regular replenishment, and Cunningham had the burden laid upon him. He was also once again supplying the advancing Eighth Army through Tobruk, and lost the operational use of another of his precious destroyers on 12 January, when *U77* disabled *Kimberley* by blowing her stern off; she was towed to Alexandria. This more than offset the success of Sunderland X of No. 230 Squadron, which had sunk *U577* a few days earlier.

At the other end of the Mediterranean, Somerville had gone home for leave and promotion prior to taking command in the Far East. He left in *Hermione*, handing over to Syfret with few regrets. His reputation has been overshadowed by his famous feud with Mountbatten, but as he passes from the war in the Mediterranean it should be noted that it was with Force H and its operations in support of Malta that the warmth and humanity of the man were shown most brightly. He was no glory-hunter, but his strenuous and unremitting efforts maintained that transient collection of ships known as Force H as a fighting unit capable of the many tasks with which it was faced, not least of which were the Club Runs and operations in support of Malta convoys. A modern admiral in every sense of the word, he was a very different man from his fellow 'door-keeper'. Yet they were of one mind, operating in close concert, always exerting themselves as much as the ships for which they were responsible, for the Royal Navy's command of the Middle Sea during the fall of 1941 was a tooth-and-nail business.

Cunningham's work at Alexandria went on a little longer. Operation MF3 was to consist of two heavily escorted groups of merchantmen sailing for Malta from Alexandria. Holt's *Ajax* and Wilhelmsen's *Thermopylae* were to form convoy MW8A, with *Clan Ferguson* and the *City of Calcutta* forming MW8B. The naval participation was to consist of the now familiar exchange of escorts to the south-west of Crete, with the ships of Force K coming from Malta and ships from Alexandria covering the eastern sector. Three submarines, *Torbay*, *Unique* and *Upholder*, were deployed on picket duty to give warning of any Italian fleet movements. Convoy MW8A departed from Alexandria early on 16 January 1942, escorted by the cruiser *Carlisle* and the

destroyers *Arrow, Griffin, Hasty* and *Hero.* MW8B followed later
in the day escorted by the destroyers *Gurkha, Maori* and *Legion*
and the Dutch *Isaac Sweers.* Force B, the cruisers *Naiad, Dido* and
Euryalus, with the destroyers *Foxhound, Havock, Hotspur, Kelvin*
and *Kipling,* left to provide cover and assistance under Vian's
command late the same evening. By dividing the convoy, it was
hoped, the attentions of the enemy would at worst be similarly
divided, while at best one section at least might avoid detection
altogether.

Ahead of the convoys, in the eastern approaches to Valletta,
German E-boats of the 3rd Flotilla had laid another mine barrage
on 15 January, and in addition to the Axis air forces, U-boats also
lay in wait. Early on 17 January, as MW8B passed north of Bardia,
Fregattenkapitän Hesse attacked in *U133* and succeeded in torpedoing *Gurkha.* Oil leaking from the sinking destroyer caught
fire, but before she sank Commander J. Houstmuller gallantly
manoeuvred *Isaac Sweers* in close, passed a wire across to *Gurkha*
and dragged her clear of the burning slick. By this means most of
Gurkha's people were saved.

Early on 18 January the two convoys merged and Vian's Force
B closed up, but at noon *Thermopylae* developed engine trouble
and had to be detached towards Benghazi, escorted by *Carlisle,*
Foxhound and *Hotspur.* Unfortunately, when they were approaching Benghazi the orders were changed, and *Thermopylae* was re-
routed to Alexandria. Although her escort was augmented by
the arrival of the corvette *Gloxinia,* her slow speed made her an
easy target for the Luftwaffe, which caught her off Derna on the
19th and bombed her so severely that she had, perforce, to be
abandoned and sunk. *Gloxinia* returned to Tobruk, *Carlisle* and
the two destroyers to Alexandria, arriving there on 21 January.

Meanwhile MW8 was harassed by German aircraft, but in
addition to the ships' own air defences, RAF aircraft from No.
201 Naval Co-operation Group flying from Cyrenaica again
assisted in countering the enemy's attacks. Then, by the early
afternoon, Force K arrived to relieve Vian. *Legion* and *Maori*
joined Force K and *Jaguar* left, coming under Vian's direct
command and continuing east as the rear-admiral retired. As the
convoy approached Malta Hurricanes from the island drove off
the last of the German aeroplanes, and on the afternoon of
19 January convoy MW8, *Ajax, Clan Ferguson* and *City of Calcutta,*
steamed round Ricasoli Point and under the ramparts of St Elmo,

bringing in about 30,000 tons of supplies. This was the last convoy arrival at Malta witnessed by Ford, who flew out of the island shortly afterwards.

Vian's squadron returned to Alexandria the following day. Almost immediately another convoy operation was mounted, designated MF4. *Breconshire* was to be sent west, with convoy ME9 withdrawing *Glengyle* and *Rowallan Castle* from Malta to Alexandria. Like the crews of other merchant ships, the men of *Rowallan Castle* had spent much time in the limestone shelters surrounding Grand Harbour; orders to sail meant not only their own evacuation of the Corrodino tunnel, but that 'of some forty women and children (service families) who were put into our temporary accommodation in No. 3 Hold'.[9] The *Rowallan Castle* and *Glengyle* sailed after dark on 25 January, escorted by Force K, the cruiser *Penelope* (Captain Nicholl) with the destroyers *Lance, Lively, Legion, Maori* and *Zulu*.

Breconshire had left Alexandria the previous day under the protection of Vian's Force B (*Naiad, Dido, Euryalus, Carlisle, Griffin, Kelvin, Kipling, Kingston, Jaguar, Hasty, Arrow* and *Isaac Sweers*). Air attacks were again countered by British planes from Cyrenaica and the two British naval forces met off Derna, exchanging escorts on the afternoon of 26 January. *Kingston*, bound for a dry-docking in Malta, changed places with *Lance*, and Force K arrived back in Grand Harbour with the welcome sight of a deeply laden *Breconshire* next day. Vian turned back to Alexandria with the two merchantmen, and picked up his moorings on the 28th. The comparative ease with which these last operations had been carried out was not to last.

A week earlier, the Italians had themselves succeeded in running four transports from Taranto and Messina. Operation T18 had been escorted by the destroyers *Malocello, Vivaldi, Da Noli, Aviere, Camicia Nera* and *Geniere* with the torpedo-boats *Orsa* and *Castore*. De Courten had provided close cover with the cruisers *Duca d'Aosta, Muzio Attendolo* and *Raimondo Montecuccoli*, screened by *Alpino, Bersagliere, Carabiniere* and *Fuciliere*, while Bergamini had taken the battleship *Caio Duilio* to sea as distant support, screened by *Ascari, Pigafetta, Oriani* and *Scirocco*. On this occasion air cover *was* provided to the Regia Marina, though by Ju88s of the Luftwaffe, not by the Regia Aeronautica. Despite this, four Malta-based Swordfish of No. 830 Squadron succeeded in penetrating the defence and sinking a fifth transport, the

13,000-ton liner *Victoria*, in the approaches to Tripoli. Two further Italian transports were sunk by the British submarines *Ultimatum* and *Umbra* in the closing days of January, but such had been the success of the Axis replenishment that on 21 January Rommel went onto the offensive – an offensive that was to last until he was halted at El Alamein, on the very threshold of Cairo, in the following June. By 1 February the British had once more lost Derna and fallen back almost as far as Tobruk. The loss of the Cyrenaican airfields again had a dire effect upon convoys to Malta, emphasising the continuing lack of an aircraft-carrier with the Mediterranean Fleet.

British fortunes now reached a new nadir in the Mediterranean. From February until August of 1942 the plight of Malta was acute. Surgeon-Commander Tozer at Fort St Angelo warned of the dangers of scurvy, asking that in the absence of sufficient fresh vegetables, vitamin C tablets should be flown in, while fish livers and rabbit meat were restricted to the use of hospitals. Dobbie's regular enumeration of food, fuel and ammunition stocks established a date beyond which the island could not hold out. It became known as the 'Target Date', but this was a euphemism. Both London and Valletta knew this date was that upon which Malta would be surrendered; the implementation of such a capitulation was entirely conditional upon the vulnerable abilities of the sea-services of Britain to postpone it.

For the crew of *Rowallan Castle*, arrival at Alexandria failed to produce the hoped-for onward passage east to Port Said and a voyage home via the Cape. Instead the ship loaded another cargo for Malta, while her crew enjoyed a pantomime put on by the ship's company of *Queen Elizabeth*. It was considered 'a first rate show', though it was supposed by the merchant seamen that the naval personnel 'had plenty of scope for this sort of thing as at the time the [damaged] *Q.E.* was lying on the bottom'. *Rowallan Castle* took on board 'a great deal of ammunition as well as other supplies, some motor transport secured on deck and another Bofors gun at No. 3 Hatch. We sailed early evening [on] Thursday 12 February an hour or two behind *Clan Chattan* and *Clan Campbell*', the other two merchantmen in convoy MW9. The *Clan Campbell* had arrived back in the Mediterranean after assisting in the tow of the liner *Georgic* and like her sister ship was carrying a mixed cargo which included cased petrol. The Clan liners forming MW9A sailed with *Carlisle, Lance, Avon Vale, Heythrop* and *Eridge* that morning. *Rowallan Castle*, as MW9B, left in the evening with *Beaufort, Dulverton, Hurworth* and *Southwold*. At dawn next morning Vian followed in *Naiad* with *Dido, Euryalus, Griffin, Hasty, Havock, Jaguar, Jervis, Kelvin* and *Kipling*.

That evening Nicholl left Malta with Force K (*Penelope, Decoy, Fortune, Legion, Lively, Sikh* and *Zulu*).[10] An attempt had been made to reinforce him with *Cleopatra* and *Fortune*, arriving from Gibraltar on 11 February. Both brought supplies, the destroyer's decks being so encumbered with aero-engines that her stability was compromised as she consumed fuel and reached neutral metacentric height during the passage, so that she lolled alarmingly in bad weather. The *Cleopatra* had received a bomb hit on her forecastle, so she was not able to join Force K immediately. Nicholl was escorting the emptied transports *Breconshire, Clan Ferguson, City of Calcutta* and *Ajax*, which made up convoy ME10. Prior to leaving Grand Harbour he had lost the destroyer *Maori*: moored alongside the Blue Funnel liner *Ajax*, she had succumbed to a bomb on 12 February. Fortunately most of the crew had been withdrawn ashore, and *Ajax* lowered her boats to rescue the surviving watchkeepers.

That same afternoon, the 13th, while the three westbound cargo-liners from Alexandria and their escorts were combining as MW9, the submarine *Porpoise* entered Marsamxett, delivering a cargo of petrol, kerosene and stores from Alexandria.[11]

In support of convoy MW9 and as part of the overall operation coded MF5, three of Simpson's submarines, *Una, Upright* and *Tempest*, were patrolling the Gulf of Taranto. These patrols were intended to both watch and prey upon Italian shipping, and in early February *Upholder, Una* and *P38* sank a further three Italian transports. One of these was the tanker *Lucania*, sunk by *Una*. Not for the first time, *Lucania* had been granted immunity from attack, since her cargo was allegedly to be used as fuel for ships repatriating civilians from East Africa. *Upright* had let her pass, but Lieutenant Martin failed to identify her, and sank her.[12] The Italians were subsequently out for revenge, and in the early hours of Friday, 13 February Capitano di Fregata Palmas detected a submarine from his torpedo-boat, the *Circe*. Making repeated attacks, he forced Lieutenant-Commander Cavaye, but newly arrived at Malta, to bring *Tempest* to the surface. As Palmas tried to tow the captured British submarine into Taranto she sank, taking with her thirty-nine members of her crew.

Friday, 13 February continued ominous for the British; that afternoon Axis air reconnaissance located MW9 and in the evening a bombing attack by Lehrgeschwader 1 damaged *Clan Campbell* so severely that she had to be detached towards Tobruk, escorted by two of the Hunt-class destroyers. Early the next morning LG 1 relocated MW9 and bombed *Clan Chattan*. Catching fire, the Clan liner had to be abandoned. Shortly after noon, the east- and westbound ships met. *Decoy* and *Fortune* joined Vian's flag, while *Lance* continued west, rejoining Force K and Captain Nicholl. Vian came across the still-burning hulk of *Clan Chattan* a couple of hours later, and *Decoy* was ordered to torpedo her.

To the west, Ju88s now pounced on *Rowallan Castle*. 'It was', as one crew member recalls, 'one thing to be in a large convoy and a target for random or opportunist attack: it's quite another to be alone and therefore *the* target for any attack. Our turn came at about 15.00 … several Ju88s coming from different directions, dropping their loads all around until one put a stick of bombs right along our port side.' An 'enormous wall of water' rose, then swamped the boats and deluged the Oerlikon gunners on the boat deck. 'It felt as though the ship had taken a leap in the water.' *Rowallan Castle* slowed to a stop, her fuel lines fractured, until emergency repairs allowed her to creep along at 4 knots. Nicholl ordered *Zulu* to take her in tow, 'but that wasn't done in five minutes' although almost the entire ship's company turned-to to haul the insurance-wire from its stowage aft, all the way forward to the forecastle. As the work was begun, the welcome appearance overhead of Malta-based Beaufighters allowed the tow to be connected in peace. Their endurance was severely limited, however, and it was not long before they departed, leaving the *Rowallan Castle* to the returning Junkers Ju88s, which repeatedly attempted to finish her off until gunfire and finally darkness drove them away.

It was clear that they would be back at dawn, when both *Rowallan Castle* and *Zulu* would be sitting targets. Moreover, Italian fleet movements were in hand, with Bergamini leaving Taranto in *Caio Duilio*, with *Duca d'Aosta* and *Raimondo Montecuccoli, Folgore, Fulmine, Saetta, Alpino, Carabiniere, Fuciliere* and *Bersagliere;* Parona had also left Messina, with *Gorizia, Trento,*

Aviere, Geniere, Camicia Nera and *Ascari*. Warned of this new threat, Nicholl ordered *Zulu* to let go the tow and *Lance* to run alongside and remove the Union-Castle crew. The *Lance*'s armourer boarded the doomed cargo-liner and stripped her of her Oerlikon gun barrels, which were much in demand throughout the fleet. As *Lance* drew away, *Lively* torpedoed *Rowallan Castle*, denying the enemy the satisfaction of sinking her, but also depriving Malta of her cargo. As she went down, Nicholl in *Penelope*, with *Lance* and *Legion*, withdrew towards Malta at speed, arriving on the forenoon of 15 February. *Lively*, *Sikh* and *Zulu* turned east after Force B, which late on the 14th was unsuccessfully attacked by the Italian submarine *Topazio*.

The British retaliated as Bergamini and Parona retired frustrated to their bases. Lieutenant Edmonds, patrolling south of the Strait of Messina in *P36*, attempted to torpedo the heavy Italian warships, but was subjected to a ruthless counter-attack. He scored a hit on the destroyer *Carabiniere* with a torpedo, though he failed to sink her and she was towed into Taranto.

Lively, *Sikh* and *Zulu* caught up with Vian, and Force B entered Alexandria with *Breconshire* during the evening of 15 February. *Clan Ferguson*, *City of Calcutta* and *Ajax* steamed on to Port Said. In the air attacks, Vian's cruisers alone had fired 3,700 rounds of 5.25-inch ammunition.

Clan Campbell and her escort, detached from MW9 on the 13th, had arrived safely in Tobruk. The Clan liner had been hit by a bomb which had pierced the boat deck and the cadets' accommodation and actually passed through the engine room shell plating, before exploding outside the ship. But her port boats were wrecked and the hole in her topside was about twenty feet in diameter. The naval surveyors who boarded her on arrival told her master, Captain Vooght, that they would weld plates over the damage without discharging the ship. Since the bomb blast had caused quantities of the cased petrol to burst its cans and fill the adjacent hold bilges, Vooght went 'through the roof' and, refusing to endanger the ship in this foolish fashion, insisted that *Clan Campbell*'s cargo be unloaded. It was a demand that caused the hard-pressed naval authorities at Tobruk a great deal of inconvenience, but Vooght had his way. The ship was discharged, replacement plating was furnished from the wreck of an Italian warship lying in Tobruk, and much of the patchwork was carried out by the ship's own engineers. But when Vooght protested that his lifeboats were now inadequate for his large crew, the naval authorities had had enough: the ship's Lascars were ordered ashore and Vooght was provided with a scratch crew of naval ratings. On completion of the work, *Clan Campbell* reloaded her cargo and left for Alexandria. Her safe arrival marked the only consolation in this dismal enterprise, for although her cargo had not reached Malta it remained largely intact, as did the ship herself. Her chief officer was most unhappy about the imposition of a naval crew who, being largely 'hostilities-only' ratings led by petty officers with at best a jaundiced view of the merchant service, were far from ideal and gave little satisfaction to *Clan Campbell*'s master and mates.

The situation in Malta was now grave. Since early December 1941 the Luftwaffe had steadily increased their air-raids on Grand and Marsamxett Harbours. The surrounding cities had received and continued to receive a terrible hammering. Kesselring's airmen attacked specific targets until they got the result they sought, effecting much collateral damage in and around the port. Nor did Kesselring neglect the airfields of Ta' Qali, Luqa and Hal Far, pursuing the neutralisation of the island with Nazi thoroughness. It had long been clear to General Dobbie that the inhabitants should be prepared for the worst, and in the New Year the assistant to the lieutenant-governor had broadcast to the Maltese, telling them what was to be done in the event of invasion.

'Life had become like a continuous air attack ... the intensity [of] which was constantly increasing with the obvious determination with which the enemy pilots seemed to be imbued in pressing their attacks home, notwithstanding the punishment they were receiving.'[13] Shortages of everything necessary to life, let alone defence, were now acute, and every possible means was taken by the Maltese government to reduce demand. A party of Maltese internees sympathetic to the Italian cause, for instance, had been evacuated aboard the Egypt-bound merchant vessels of ME10. Leatham, Ford's successor, issued a secret memorandum to his departments: 'The non arrival of convoy MW9 makes it most necessary that each one of us should drastically reduce his consumption of stores of every kind ... the individual must make what he has got last longer and wherever possible manage without asking for more.' This stricture did not however prevent him requesting an investigation into 'the possibility of shipping rum in bulk in a submarine tank if there is no other means of transport' – only two months' supply remained on Malta, and consumption was 1,600 gallons a month! To help ease the situation, every warship arriving at Malta was ordered to land 'certain naval stores'. *Cleopatra* was asked to put ashore from her own resources – such were the necessities of the naval establishment – rum, chocolate, pickles, oatmeal, tinned vegetables, bacon, sausages, steel pins, steel wire rope, copper sheathing, electrodes, taps and dies, drills, methyl chloride, sulphuric acid, glycerine, grease, wicks, linseed oil, water-finding paste, and solder.

Not only were the stocks of such supplies running low, but so too were those of ammunition of all calibres. Bigger items were also in demand: the Hurricanes on Malta were now being outclassed by the Messerschmitt Me109 fighters, and Air Vice-Marshal Lloyd was urgently requesting reinforcement with Spitfires. Meanwhile the hated Stukas kept up their persistently noisy, vicious and demoralising attacks, while the Ju88s delivered their less conspicuous through equally dreadful bomb-loads. 'The population continued with its fast, dug in debris to retrieve things … cried over its dead and injured and hoped for something to happen.' Local food supplies were fast being depleted. Even the fishing boats crossing from Gozo were strafed.

Gallant efforts were made by the Royal Navy's submarines, but the quantities they brought in were pitifully small. The most capacious was HM Submarine *Clyde*, one of the River-class, the largest in the world at the time of her building in 1934. One of her three battery tanks was emptied, reducing her submerged endurance but providing valuable stowage capacity for anti-aircraft ammunition on the outward passage from Gibraltar to Malta. On the return run it provided accommodation, usually for merchant service personnel who, stranded in Malta through the loss of their ships, represented an unwelcome additional victualling burden on the authorities there. About 600 tons of aviation spirit were loaded in *Clyde*'s ballast tanks, while her torpedo tubes were filled with smaller aerial torpedoes for the Fleet Air Arm, powdered milk, and tinned ham. In all, about 1,000 tons could be carried, although it made the submarine difficult to trim, the density of aviation spirit being somewhat different from that of sea-water.

The passage from Gibraltar took eleven days, running through the Italian minefields in The Narrows at 110 feet, and discharge occupied a further four. This was undertaken largely at night, the only time the submarines could lie in Marsaxlokk on the surface. They, and their colleagues in Lazaretto Creek, Marsamxett Harbour, spent most days sitting on the bottom in 160 feet of water, still at risk from random bombs but partially concealed from the enemy.[14] A regular schedule of three submarines worked this run, *Clyde*, *Pandora* and *Olympus*, one outward bound, one at Malta and one on the homeward passage; though all submarines transiting between Gibraltar and Malta were obliged to carry cargo, it was usually no more than 200 tons.

Despite these endeavours, Malta was rapidly becoming a liability. Churchill, ever pugnacious, was aware that Kesselring's assault had already broken down Britain's ability to obstruct Axis convoys to Tripoli. Recapture of North African airfields offered the opportunity of better air cover to naval operations, but Auchinleck proposed to delay his own offensive against Rommel. Churchill put increased pressure upon him not to do so, since thereby 'Malta itself was threatened with starvation unless a steady monthly flow of supplies could be maintained', pressure which culminated 'in positive and formal orders to attack the enemy and fight a main battle rather than see Malta fall.' But Auchinleck had already lost the initiative. 'The supreme struggle for Malta now began,' Churchill afterwards wrote, 'and grew in intensity during the whole spring and summer.'[15]

Rommel's successes in North Africa had coincided with a remarkable event, the escape from Brest of a heavy German squadron which passed unmolested the length of the Channel, an incident which, *The Times* recorded, marked a British humiliation such as had not been known since the Spanish Armada entered the English Channel in 1588. Its consequence was to put Hitler into a mood receptive to Grossadmiral Raeder's plans for the Mediterranean, a revival of General Jodl's strategy of defeating Britain by destroying her prestige with the seizure of Gibraltar, Malta and the Suez Canal. In the Middle East, Japanese penetration west of India, already planned, was increasingly felt to be possible. 'Suez and Basra are the western pillars of the British position in the East,' Raeder urged, insisting that Malta was the key to the prosecution of this grand plan. If the island was not actually to be invaded, then it was imperative that the Luftwaffe should continue its ruthless air offensive, since 'such attacks alone will prevent the enemy from building Malta's offensive and defensive capacity.'

On 7 February 1942 Cunningham had given Pound his assessment of Malta's situation 'in all its grim bleakness'. The further Auchinleck pulled his defensive line back and the longer he deferred a counter-attack, the more difficult Cunningham's task of replenishment became. While Malta's stocks of aviation spirit might last until 1 August, other stores would be sufficient only until the beginning of June. As for the critical matter of boiler oil for the navy, only 5,000 tons remained. Nor were Cunningham's problems confined to Malta. Vian's 'colossal expenditure' of ammunition during MF5 had reduced reserves to no more than one and a third outfits for each cruiser; and while Cunningham did his best to push stores through to Malta, with the submarines *Porpoise* and *Thunderbolt* complementing the efforts from Gibraltar, finding the requisite merchant ships for a new convoy was a problem.[16] They needed to be cargo-liners possessing a minimum speed of 15 knots, 'and these were scarce. Some merchant vessels, all honour to the gallant men who served in them, made the highly hazardous voyage again and again; but their good luck could not hold out for ever.' Nor did it. Convoy MW9 had not merely failed: its failure had underlined the apparent impossibility of the task. Any future convoy could only be attempted 'at very great hazard'.[17]

At the end of February the Chiefs of Staff advised Cunningham that they were unable to replenish Malta from Gibraltar. Club Runs were to be carried out, however, and one was attempted by Syfret on 27/28 February when *Argus* and *Eagle* left with Force H, Syfret's flag flying in *Malaya*, and escorted by *Hermione, Laforey, Lightning, Active, Anthony, Duncan, Whitehall, Wishart, Blankney* and *Croome*. The run was then aborted because the long-range tanks dispatched were found to be incompatible with the aircraft, an error the news of which was suppressed because the aircraft ranged pointlessly upon the carriers' flight decks were Spitfires.

Governor Dobbie was disappointed, but it made little difference: without food, fuel and ammunition, Malta's situation would be in crisis by May. A 'substantial convoy' was needed to build up stocks well above the critical level, and plans were put in train to run one in March, London insisting that 'no consideration of risk to the ships themselves need deter' Cunningham. 'The operation was to be regarded as ... [his] primary military commitment.'[18]

While these deliberations were taking place, two further Italian convoys were run to Tripoli, one from Corfu and one from Messina – six transports in all, escorted by ten destroyers and two torpedo-boats.[19] Heavy cover was provided by the battleship *Caio Duilio* and the cruisers *Banda Nere*, *Gorizia*, and *Trento*, which were themselves screened by seven destroyers.[20]

Ultra decrypts revealed these movements and British planes took off, only to be driven off by the German aircraft escorting the Regia Marina. Further disaster occurred as *P38* attacked the convoy but was detected by the vigilant Palmas in *Circe*, who caught her 32 miles north of Misurata on 23 February. Depth-charging the British submarine, he forced her to the surface where she was attacked by gunfire from the destroyer *Antoniotto Usodimare*. Palmas lowered a boat, having seen 'small bits of wood, a canvas bag and human remains'. In the canvas bag were 'two black flags and three Union jacks ... '[21]

Wanklyn in *Upholder* struck back, sinking an escorted Axis transport off Tripoli on the 27th, and *Torbay*, *Unbeaten* and *Uproar* also sank enemy tonnage; in early March Malta-based Wellingtons raided Palermo, blowing up the ammunition ship *Cuma* and damaging several others. But the balance of power in the central Mediterranean had tipped in favour of the Axis. Smarting from the disaster of his previous attempt at a Club Run, Syfret sallied on a revived Operation SPOTTER on 6 March. His force was identical except that *Duncan* had exchanged with *Exmoor*. South of the Balearics the fifteen Supermarine Spitfire fighters were launched, properly fitted with compatible fuel tanks, and reached Malta with seven Blenheims flown directly from Gibraltar. News of the Spitfires' arrival passed through Malta like wildfire. They were in action on 10 March against a force of Ju88s escorted by Me109Bs, and had a noticeable impact upon the attackers.

As Force H fell back to Gibraltar a more confident Regia Marina, clearly stiffened by the presence of Luftwaffe air cover, continued its vigorous reinforcement of Rommel. Between 7 and 18 March a series of Axis convoys left Brindisi, Messina and

Naples for Tripoli, with northbound convoys of empty vessels returning to Italy escorted by destroyers and torpedo-boats and covered by submarines.[22]

Cunningham was not the man to concede control of the central Mediterranean to the Axis under any circumstances, but the essential concealment of Ultra decrypts necessitated the fiction of 'discovery' by aerial reconnaissance, which the Axis bombing raids on Maltese airfields were particularly effective in frustrating, thereby limiting British offensives against these movements. Wanklyn in *Upholder* did however dispatch one of the covering submarines, *Millo*, and on 9 March a Wellington spotted a homeward-bound Italian convoy south-east of Malta. A little later an outbound convoy was seen and aircraft were sent in pursuit, but the results of these attacks were unsatisfactory. Nevertheless, a report of a damaged cruiser decided Cunningham to send out Vian, who sailed at 04.00 on 10 March to pass Tobruk under cover of darkness and fall upon the wounded enemy next day. Vian's flagship *Naiad* was accompanied by *Euryalus, Jervis, Kipling, Kelvin, Lively, Sikh, Zulu, Hasty, Havock* and *Hero*. The report proved false, but the opportunity was taken to extract the cruiser *Cleopatra* and the destroyer *Kingston* from Grand Harbour, and they joined Vian for the return passage.

Vian's ships were subjected to an almost continuous harrying by Italian torpedo-planes and German bombers. Once again they threw up a profligate barrage which kept the enemy from pressing home a successful attack, but just as darkness closed down on 11 March *U565*, commanded by Leutnant-sur-Zee Jebsen, sent a torpedo into *Naiad*.[23] The cruiser took a severe list and sank in twenty minutes. Captain Mack turned back and brought *Jervis, Kipling* and *Lively* in to pick up survivors.[24] Seventy-seven of *Naiad*'s company were lost, but Vian and his flag-captain, Guy Grantham, were among the rescued, the latter almost exhausted after helping several men in the water. Vian's flag was hoisted aboard *Dido* for the run back to Alexandria, and on their return Vian took Grantham with him to *Cleopatra*, his new flagship.

Having filled Vian up 'with all the stout he can take', Cunningham shrewdly sent the 15th Cruiser Squadron to bombard Rhodes on 15 March, an operation more cathartic than effective in which the memory of *Naiad*'s death was drowned in the restorative thunder of the guns. 'It was good to keep us busy,'

Bush of *Euryalus* wrote, 'with no time to dwell upon the loss of *Naiad*.'[25]

Among the reinforcements Cunningham had received by way of the Cape were the 5th Destroyer Flotilla, consisting of Hunt-class ships. These were added to the Hunts already operating with the Mediterranean Fleet, one of which, *Farndale*, had already been damaged. On 20 March the remainder were sent out on an anti-submarine sweep intended as a prelude to the next convoy.[26] During the operation, when the Hunts were north of Sollum, *U652* (Leutnant Fraatz) torpedoed *Heythrop*, which had to be dispatched by *Dulverton*. Fifteen men were killed or missing.

Resources were not available to make this convoy, MW10, as substantial as London wished. Once again *Breconshire* was to be included, as was the patched-up *Clan Campbell* with her naval crew and Clan Line officers. Wilhemsen's *Talabot* of 6,798 grt and the Royal Mail Line's 5,415-grt *Pampas* completed the quartet of merchantmen. *Breconshire*'s tanks were refilled with 5,000 tons of boiler oil, while her 'tween-decks were stuffed with 150 tons of rifle and machine-gun ammunition, one hundred crates of AA ammunition, one hundred crates of 500-pound armour-piercing bombs, crates of depth charge detonators, 176 tons of kerosene, 650 tons of grain, 690 tons of coal, and miscellaneous military stores. With the exception of the oil, these commodities were repeated in greater quantities in the other cargo-liners. Captain Hutchinson aboard *Breconshire* was again convoy commodore, and each merchant ship bore a naval liaison officer with a small signals staff of four ratings in addition to their quota of DEMS (Defensively Equipped Merchant Ships) naval gunners. All were well-armed, *Pampas* having a 4-inch LA (low-angle) gun, a 12-pounder and four Marline machine-guns aft, four Oerlikons (two forward on the forecastle and two aft), two Harvey machine-guns above the bridge wings and two Lewis guns abaft her funnel. Her forty army passengers manned additional Bren guns, and by supplementing the DEMS and merchant marine gunners with soldiers to operate the bridge and boat deck guns, *Pampas*'s armament could be ready day and night. Similar arrangements pertained in the other vessels. *Talabot* bore sixty service personnel from the army and the Royal Air Force, and these assisted with her light armament.

Convoy MW10 sailed at 07.00 on the morning of 20 March

under the close escort of the cruiser *Carlisle*, Captain D. Neame, and the 22nd Destroyer Flotilla, *Sikh* (Captain (D) St J. Micklethwait), *Lively*, *Hasty*, *Havock*, *Hero* and *Zulu*. Almost immediately Hutchinson was rebuking Captain Vooght of *Clan Campbell* for being 35 minutes late in passing the boom defences. In fact *Clan Campbell*'s tardiness was due to her anchor having been fouled on the sea-bed, but as Hutchinson put the merchant ships through their paces with a series of exercises, it soon became clear that the Clan-liner would have trouble maintaining the convoy speed. Aboard *Talabot* the Breda guns failed, but the fault was rectified thanks to the expertise of her naval liaison officer.[27] Cover was provided by Force B, Vian's 15th Cruiser Squadron of *Cleopatra*, *Dido* and *Euryalus*, and the 5th Destroyer Flotilla, *Jervis* (Captain (D) A. Poland), *Kipling*, *Kelvin* and *Kingston*. Vian followed the convoy at 18.00 that evening.

As the convoy passed 70 miles north of Tobruk, the refuelled six remaining Hunt-class ships of the 5th Destroyer Flotilla, led by Commander C. Jellicoe in *Southwold*, left Tobruk to join forces. With Vian's cruisers, *Carlisle* and the Hunts, the escort was well provided with anti-aircraft firepower as the entire force united on the morning of 21 March. The mean speed of advance of 12 knots was already proving hard to achieve because of *Clan Campbell*'s badly shaken engines. Aboard the 18-knot *Breconshire*, leading *Talabot* in the starboard column, Captain Hutchinson was experiencing extreme anxiety as the carefully planned timetable became unavoidably and cumulatively compromised. At 09.45 he ordered Vooght to steam a straight mean course as the remaining ships maintained their zigzag, ordering *Pampas* to exchange places and lead the port column. The station-keeping of the merchant ships earned the usual disapprobation, Lieutenant MacFarlane reporting it as 'poor' on the 20th, but it 'improved considerably as the ships' officers gained practice and one felt by Saturday night that all the Watchkeeping Officers could be trusted to keep as good station as might be expected'. It was as well, for that evening the ships saw enemy troop-carrying planes flying overhead, and knew the convoy would be reported.

The whole operation, code-named MG1, included help from others. The submarines *Ultimatum* and *Unbeaten* were stationed in the southern approaches to Messina, with *P36*, *Upholder* and *Proteus* deployed in the Gulf of Taranto to give the usual warnings of possible attack. The Long Range Desert Group were to mount a diversionary raid upon enemy airfields at Martuba and Tmimi while the RAF and land-based Fleet Air Arm aircraft from Egypt bombed them, with the intention of keeping grounded the Ju88s which would otherwise harry MW10 as it passed between the German-held airfields of Cyrenaica and Crete. Finally, air cover and reconnaissance ahead of the ships was to be provided by the RAF's Naval Co-operation Group, No. 201. Operation MG1 had been carefully planned to maximise hours of darkness, since the new moon set early and the proximity of the spring equinox would give almost equal periods of day and night.

At this time two other movements of British warships were taking place in the Mediterranean. The nearer to Vian's ships was the departure of the remnant of Force K, *Penelope* and *Legion*, which joined his flag at 08.00 on the morning of the 22nd. At the other end of the Mediterranean, and in part to divert the attentions of Supermarina, Syfret had left Gibraltar with Force H for a Club Run. He was spotted by two Italian submarines and one, *Mocenigo*, attacked *Argus*, but without success. Unfortunately, Operation PICKET went off at half-cock: still thwarted by defective long-range fuel tanks, Syfret was again unable to fly Spitfires off *Argus* and *Eagle*. It was an inglorious moment.

Prior to their departure from Alexandria Vian had convened a conference aboard *Cleopatra*, present at which were all the commanding officers of His Majesty's ships and all the masters of the merchant vessels in MW10. Vian explained what he thought would happen, and what he intended all ships should do in the event of a surface attack. 'In the event his forecast was correct,' Grantham recalled, 'and the only signals he had to make to start the action were *Enemy in Sight* and *Engage the Enemy* ... ' Immediately upon sailing Vian put theory into practice and carried out a series of exercises with his cruisers, following which they hurried after the convoy.

At 05.18 on 22 March news was received aboard *Cleopatra* that an Italian battle squadron was at sea. This derived from Lieutenant Edmonds, commanding the submarine *P36* lying at periscope depth at the head of the Gulf of Taranto. With MW10 already working clear of the first area of potential damage, the 'bomb alley' between Crete and Cyrenaica, Cunningham instructed Vian to remain with the convoy until sunset. Air cover was now withdrawn, and owing to the damage at Malta little more could be expected from air reconnaissance.

Matters were now in the hands of one of the most obdurate of all British admirals, Philip Vian. A destroyer man, like Cunningham, he had fought at Jutland and first achieved fame in the attack on the German auxiliary *Altmark* in a Norwegian fiord when commanding *Cossack*.[28] Fast-tracked to flag rank under a scheme introduced by Pound, he was a ruthless, complex and generally disliked officer who terrorised his staff, causing them to cringe in his presence. Officers and ratings working or passing in the vicinity of his quarters had to observe absolute silence. Yet if he was hard on others, he could be harsh on himself, and he was totally committed to the fighting ability of the ships he commanded. He was, in Admiral Ramsay's words, 'damned temperamental' and 'not quite normal at times', qualities that made him 'an annoyance to his superiors' and resulted in inexcusable arrogance towards his subordinates.[29] Insensitive, incapable of garnering hearts and minds, Vian demanded, and got, responsive respect. It did not matter to him that it was derived from fear rather than fondness; only that it was manifest. One of his cruiser captains afterwards summed him up: 'He was extremely efficient; merciless with the incompetent; and inclined to remain aloof.' But 'he had the 15th Cruiser Squadron so well trained that it was hardly ever necessary to make a signal: the Nelson touch. We all knew what to do.'[30] Similarly, a gunnery officer in his squadron recalled that 'in spite of his traits, we all felt that we could not go into battle with a better man in command'. Addicted to operating independently, Vian was withal possessed of great courage and tenacity, and far from foolhardy, as his conduct in the First Battle of Sirte had shown. At the right moment he excelled in being what Cunningham described as 'a superb fighting sailor', and such a moment was now to hand.

Convoy MW10 was spotted by the German troop-carrying aircraft at 17.05 on 21 March when it lay about the mid-point of a line roughly between Derna and Gavdo. The Italian submarine *Onice* caught sight of MW10 less than an hour later, and the convoy was also reported by *Platino*. British efforts to subdue Axis aircraft during the 21st had been successful, but British aircraft were similarly pinned down at Malta, and the Regia Marina were thus able to concentrate without interference. The main Italian battle squadron had sailed from Taranto at 00.30 under the command of Iachino, whose flag was hoisted in the *Littorio*, and headed south into a freshening head wind from the south-east. Iachino's flagship was screened by the destroyers *Ascari*, *Aviere*, *Grecale* and *Oriani*. Completely undetected by the British, the ships of Ammiraglio di Divisione Parona left Messina at 01.00, consisting of the heavy cruisers *Gorizia* and *Trento* and the light cruiser *Giovanni delle Banda Nere*, screened by the destroyers *Alpino*, *Fuciliere*, *Bersagliere* and *Lanciere*. In addition to the surface warships Supermarina had dispatched the submarines *Perla*, *Acciao*, *Galatea*, *U73*, *U205* and *U431*, while air superiority was to be exploited by the close co-operation of Fliegerkorps II and the Italian 4th Air Fleet.

As daylight broke over the mouth of the Gulf of Sirte that Sunday morning, 22 March 1942, visibility was good with clear skies, but the south-east wind was rising and the visibility soon began to shut in slowly. Far to the north the Italian destroyers plunged and pitched into the head sea, having trouble keeping up the speed essential to intercept the British. Iachino was making 22 knots and Parona slightly more, but during the forenoon *Grecale* developed engine trouble and was ordered back to Taranto, *Geniere* and *Scirocco* sailing to reinforce *Littorio*.

Meanwhile, by mid morning Italian aircraft had located MW10, and at 10.35 occurred the first of five torpedo-bombing attacks made on the convoy during the forenoon. The first two were made by a trio of SM79s acting in concert, the remainder, the last of which was over by 12.09, by single aircraft. The experienced Nicholl thought them futile, the torpedo-bombers dropping their weapons too early, and the naval liaison officer on *Pampas* reported them as 'half-hearted'. Vian had thrown an outer, anti-submarine screen of his fleet destroyers two miles ahead of the main body while an inner, anti-aircraft defensive cordon was provided by his three cruisers, *Carlisle* and the Hunts. At 14.20 fire was opened by the convoy on a lone Ju88, and half an hour later the main attack developed. The combined Italo-German air assault began intermittently but intensified, reinforcing the high-level bombing with low, fast torpedo runs. Hutchinson opened out the merchant ships' formation 'so that each ship could safely take avoiding action independently: whilst during the torpedo attacks I manoeuvred the convoy as a whole to avoid the torpedoes; no ship was hit or even damaged by near misses.' Some sixteen attacks were made, predominantly by Ju88s, five of which made a simultaneous attack on *Breconshire* at 17.30. These near-missed her, but her gunners claimed to have at least damaged two aircraft. A further torpedo-bombing run was made on *Breconshire* at 18.10, but when the enemy aircraft withdrew at 18.50 the convoy was unscathed.

Bereft of any further intelligence of the Italian fleet movements after that received from *P36* many hours earlier, Vian calculated on the likelihood of an Italian surface force manifesting itself early that afternoon. At 12.30, as the first series of air attacks died away, he prepared his force: *Carlisle* and the Hunts were to remain with the convoy, the old cruiser and *Avon Vale* laying smoke across its rear as it retired; the remaining ships were to form five striking groups, the cruisers to engage with gunfire, the destroyers to use the potent threat of their torpedoes. These five detachments were to be made up of Poland in *Jervis* with *Kipling*, *Kelvin* and *Kingston*; McCall in *Dido* with *Penelope* and *Legion*; Graham in *Zulu* with *Hasty*; Vian with Grantham in *Cleopatra* supported by *Euryalus*; and Micklethwait in *Sikh* with *Lively*, *Hero* and *Havock*.

Anticipating confrontation by heavy ships, Vian intended to use diversionary tactics employing smoke, the strong breeze favouring the British, who were upwind and therefore held that old advantage of naval warfare, the weather gauge. Within an hour, at 13.22, an Italian seaplane dropped flares to indicate the British presence to the gunnery officers of the distant Italian warships peering through their optical rangefinders. The seaplane was clearly from a large warship, another firm indication that the Regia Marina were in the vicinity. At this stage the British also relied upon eyesight, for although almost all the ships engaged were fitted with radar, the primitive sets were much hampered by 'sea-clutter', returns from wave crests, which were considerable in the near gale-force conditions prevailing. Nor was a tactical appraisal possible, since plan position indicators or screens on which the surface situation could be assessed were non-existent at this time.[31]

It was Captain Bush of *Euryalus* with his acute eyesight who claimed the first spotting of the Italians. At 14.10 Vian was informed of smoke to the north and then, at 14.27, just after the lone Ju88 appeared over the convoy as a prelude to the main air assault, of enemy ships. His prearranged executive signal rose on *Cleopatra*'s flag halliards and streamed out in the strong wind. He had to drive off the enemy before dark, both to preserve fuel (for there was none available to him in Malta) and to ensure that the convoy diversion was not excessive, which would delay its arrival under Malta's air umbrella and expose the merchantmen to air attack next day. As Captain Hutchinson in *Breconshire* turned the other three cargo-liners of MW10 and their close escort of *Southwold*, *Dulverton*, *Beaufort*, *Eridge* and *Hurworth* away to the south-west at 14.30, Vian led off to the north, the cruisers and the destroyers swinging into their five divisions in line ahead. Only Nicholl in *Penelope* was in some doubt as to what to do, not having received the orders Vian had had flown to him in Malta; but, as he wrote afterwards, there was 'a well tried course of action I had learned in my time in destroyers: "When in doubt, follow father." So I tacked on to Vian's cruisers and *Legion* joined the nearest destroyer division ... I had no difficulty in sensing what Vian wanted the cruisers to do.'[32] As they scended in the following sea, the battle ensigns breaking out at their mastheads, the first wisps of dense black smoke began to uncoil from their funnels.

To the south, across the convoy's wake, Neame in *Carlisle* with *Avon Vale* in company turned east and also made smoke, which the two ships continued to do until about 15.15; like the convoy they too came under air attack, and in dodging bombs had a glancing collision in the swirling murk. Meanwhile Vian's ships turned east at about 14.33, by now all belching black smoke which, propelled to the north-west by the 25-knots wind, formed a dense curtain. Parona's cruisers, approaching in line abreast, swung south-east to open their gunnery arcs and opened fire. None of the shells landed near Vian's ships, and after nine minutes Parona turned away to the north-west, not – as was the first thought of the British – through pusillanimity, but to draw Vian down upon the heavy guns of *Littorio* astern of him. Seeing his opponents were cruisers Vian led *Euryalus* after them, opening fire at extreme range at 14.56, with *Dido* and *Penelope* still getting into station. This engagement lasted until 15.08, when Parona altered course to the north. However, a few moments later the *Giovanni delle Bande Nere* swung back and her shells straddled *Cleopatra* in 'a sharp exchange of fire' until she turned away at 15.15 after her consorts. But Vian was not to be thus seduced from the convoy. At about the same time that Neame ceased making smoke and set out to catch up with MW10, which had now turned due west, Vian also broke off the action, heading to overhaul the convoy. At 15.35 he signalled Cunningham that the enemy had been driven off.

During the action McCall of *Dido* had sent a crisp signal to Nicholl, who had been working *Penelope* up astern of *Cleopatra*, enquiring 'What is seniority of captain?', to which Nicholl promptly replied 'July 1939', only to be told to 'take station astern [of *Dido*]' – which, as Nicholl wryly conceded, was 'a great help'.

By 16.00 *Carlisle* and *Avon Vale* had regained the convoy screen and Vian's cruisers and fleet destroyers, rapidly catching up, were about eight miles away to the north-east, steering to intercept. Thus ended the first phase of the surface action known as the Second Battle of Sirte. Although a few bombs had been dropped among the striking force and *Carlisle* had been near-missed, the Axis aircraft had concentrated on the convoy and its close escort, subjecting it to repeated assaults. 'The whole sky above it [… was] pock-marked by the black bursts of a tremendous barrage' and several aircraft were shot down.[33] No merchant ship had been hit, thanks to Hutchinson's able handling and the masters' obedient responses, but there was a cost: as Jellicoe in *Southwold*, the senior officer commanding the Hunts, reported to Vian, they had endured 'nine attacks so far; [and had only] forty per cent 4-inch ammunition remaining.' *Carlisle* for her part had shot off a third of her outfit of anti-aircraft shells. It was the same old story.

As a consequence, Vian ordered Poland's destroyers and *Legion* to join the close escort and ease the burden on Jellicoe's little Hunts, which were not only short of ammunition but had had trouble serving their forward, open-breeched guns in the rough seas. As the afternoon drew on, Vian was increasingly anxious about his ships' fuel and meditated withdrawing to Alexandria.

But Parona had not been driven off. At 15.15 he had made contact with Iachino and turned south-south-west on a course to rendezvous with the Italian Commander-in-Chief. The two forces united at 16.18, about twelve miles north of Vian and eighteen miles north-east of MW10. Iachino now headed south-west, to bar the convoy's route to Malta; and although he had again been misinformed about the presence of a battleship with the convoy, he was a more confident commander with the Luftwaffe over-head. His main problems on this occasion were the strong wind, force 6 on the Beaufort scale, and a slight mist which might hamper optical gunlaying.

The mist was, however, insufficient to obscure him from Vian when at 16.37 lookouts in *Zulu* and then *Euryalus* reported a rein-forced and formidable enemy squadron ten miles away on their starboard quarters. Iachino, in pursuit, had seen Vian beyond the clearing smoke some six minutes earlier, and the heavy guns of his flagship, supplemented by the 8-inch weapons in *Gorizia* and *Trento*, ought to have picked off the British cruisers with ease. Vian's force immediately belched smoke again, however, and began a series of complex dashings hither and thither which the Italians took for confusion but which the irrepressible Vian intended should head off either the obvious Italian move – to work east and then south round the smokescreen – or any shorter but less advantageous attempt to outrun the smokescreen to the west. Iachino chose the latter course of action, and although the superior speed of his big ships enabled him to draw ahead he lacked the nerve to penetrate the smoke, which 'lay well in the prevailing conditions'. As this became apparent, MW10 edged away to the south-west behind its own smokescreen, still under air attack but still intact. While Vian's three excursions to the east compromised the safety of the convoy, taking away as they did not merely his own division of *Cleopatra* and *Euryalus* but McCall's of *Dido* and *Penelope*, dutifully followed by Graham's *Zulu* and *Hasty*, Micklethwait's 5th Division of *Sikh*, *Lively*, *Hero* and *Havock* filled the breach. At one point Micklethwait forced the Italian squadron away as his destroyers emerged from the smoke, their torpedo tubes aligned with the enemy battle squadron.

At 16.43 *Cleopatra* and *Euryalus* opened fire at extreme ten-mile range, with *Dido* and *Penelope* following in echelon on Vian's starboard quarter. The British cruisers were within range of the heavier Italian guns and *Giovanni delle Banda Nere* hit *Cleopatra* with her second salvo, wrecking radar and radio installations and causing a score of casualties. A moment later a shell frag-ment from one of *Littorio*'s bursting 15-inch shells hit *Euryalus* as the Italian battleship straddled her. Bush manoeuvred to alter the range before the next salvo, his main armament divided: the cruiser's three forward turrets, each with its twin dual purpose 5.25-inch guns, were occupied engaging *Littorio*, the after pair with attacking aircraft.

The cruisers dodged into the smokescreen as *Cleopatra* led round to port, with McCall following. As his own ships were obscured in smoke, Vian was unable to account for all the enemy, and was constantly preoccupied lest Iachino should detach a part of his force to double the smoke to the eastwards, hence his movements in that direction. But Iachino was staying out of range, edging round to port in an attempt to get ahead of the convoy as it fell away from him. As they gained ground on the convoy the Italian ships were now receiving assistance from aircraft acting as artillery spotters.

Vian first moved east at about 17.00; Micklethwait was then to the westward of him, and had been in action himself for six minutes before he dodged back into the swirling smokescreen. At about 17.15 Vian turned back to the west for five minutes, still uncertain of the exact position of all Italian units while the spray thrown up by the turbulent movements of the cruisers and destroyers in the near-gale was tossed high over the director towers. At 17.20 Vian led round to the east again, a second retrograde move which might have had serious consequences, since he was unable to support Micklethwait's exposed destroyers. A 15-inch shell burst alongside *Havock*, killing or wounding fifteen men, putting one boiler-room out of action and reducing her speed to 16 knots; she was ordered to proceed to join the convoy.

By this time Vian was drawing out his distance from the Italians to 14 miles while they in turn were closing the convoy, which now lay in range of *Littorio*'s primary armament. Micklethwait, having disengaged, made smoke and then, steering south-west and roughly parallel to Iachino, edged out to starboard to engage again. *Sikh*, *Hero* and *Lively* were rolling and plunging through the heavy seas, their long iron decks periodically swept by green water, firing at the battleship, though the range was too great for them to observe their fall of shot; in fact they straddled the *Littorio*, which returned fire from her secondary batteries. At 17.48 *Sikh* was herself straddled and Micklethwait responded by firing two torpedoes, resolved not to be sunk with all his torpedoes remaining in their tubes. Range and conditions were inauspicious for such weapons, but the threat of them caused Iachino to turn away.

Even so small a delay was crucial, for although Vian had turned back to the west at 17.35, the Italian squadron was now on a rapidly converging course with MW10, which was in turn effectively pinned down by the attacking enemy aircraft. Should the smokescreen shred to reveal the precise position of the merchantmen to the gunnery directors on *Littorio*, destruction of the convoy would inevitably follow.

Vian, McCall and Graham now sped west again. At 17.42 *Cleopatra* fired her 5.25-inch main armament at a fleeting glimpse of *Littorio*, but Vian was now frustrated by his own smoke, and lack of radio. He tried to edge out to starboard, but the wind carried the smoke with him. His crew eventually managed to rig a jury radio aerial, and at 17.59 he broadcast an order to McCall and Graham to 'prepare to fire torpedoes under cover of smoke'. Astern of the flagship, *Euryalus*'s Type 284 radar had enabled her to open fire on a bearing, keeping up pressure on *Littorio*. Three minutes later *Cleopatra* burst out of the smoke and, slewing to port, opened fire with all turrets. With a menacing hiss of compressed air she discharged her starboard torpedoes, which leapt from the tubes and slid away into the sea. A moment later the smoke blew over Vian and obscured his distant target as *Littorio* turned away to starboard.

Partially seeing Micklethwait's isolation, Captain Poland had diverged from the convoy and was running parallel to the Italians' mean line of advance on his colleague's port beam. But Vian was still worried by his windward quarter and, fearing the Italians had continued their starboard turn and reversed their course, once more led round to the east. In fact Iachino had only swerved, and at 18.17, reassured, Vian finally abandoned this near-fatal preoccupation and turned west again, racing to support Micklethwait. The latter had now turned a full circle to port and was proceeding north, laying a new smoke screen to obscure the increasingly vulnerable convoy, which he had signalled to head south.

In Micklethwait's wake, Poland prepared to launch torpedoes. At about 17.10 he had caught a quick glimpse of *Cleopatra* as she emerged from and then disappeared again into the billowing clouds of dark oil vapour, receiving the incomplete flashed lamp signal 'Feint at ... ' At 17.14 he had seen heavy gun flashes

through the murk, realised that Micklethwait was under extreme
pressure and guessed that Vian required him to relinquish direct
cover of the convoy and move against the enemy. At 18.08 he
received a radio signal from Micklethwait with the alarming
news that the Italian squadron was no more than eight miles
from MW10: *Jervis* was immediately headed to the north-west to
close the enemy, then south and west again as she searched for a
glimpse of the Italian ships, simultaneously avoiding an attack
by torpedo-bombers.

Then, quite suddenly at 18.34, as he led his destroyers north
again, Poland saw the enemy battleship leading the three cruisers, no more than six miles away on his port beam as Iachino
turned further south towards the convoy. Immediately Poland
ordered an alteration of course to west and an increase of speed
to 28 knots, which had the effect of turning *Jervis*, *Kipling*, *Kelvin*,
Kingston and *Legion* into a rough line abreast. As they did so they
had to manoeuvre to comb the tracks of torpedoes dropped by
SM79s, but then steadied and headed west. *Jervis* and the three
K-class ships were armed with 4.7-inch guns and opened a vigorous fire on *Littorio*. *Legion*, slightly astern of her consorts and
with only 4-inch weapons, held her fire until the range closed.

As Poland's destroyers made their turn to attack, Vian caught a
glimpse of the enemy and exchanged salvoes until Micklethwait's
smoke once again hid the Italians, now some ten miles from him.
Then Vian's cruisers suddenly emerged from the murk to engage
the Italians for about twenty minutes, providing Poland's attacking destroyers with useful if somewhat fortuitous covering fire.
This confused the Italian gunnery officers, confronted by a dual
threat. Confusion also reigned in the British ranks as in the remnants of smoke and the flying spray kicked up by wind and the
violent manoeuvres of the destroyers, Commander St Clair-Ford
on *Kipling*'s bridge wondered 'what we were going to see' when
they cleared the smoke. 'As we emerged, we sighted the *Littorio*
... two 8-inch cruisers and one 6-inch cruiser in line ahead six miles
away. I must admit ... it looked a sticky proposition closing the
range whilst under fire from the main armament of these four
large ships.'[34] 'The range', Poland himself reported, 'seemed to
take an unconscionably long time to shorten. When ... the nearest
enemy from *Jervis* was about 3.5 miles it was grand to see the
second ship in the enemy line lose her nerve. She turned away
from us, making volumes of black smoke. Eventually the range

was down ... to two and [*sic*] three miles ... [At 18.41] We turned, and some 25 torpedoes started off towards the enemy line.'[35]

The leading destroyers now turned to starboard to fire their torpedoes. *Legion*, unable to see Poland's executive signal, which was obscured by shell splashes, swung to port, but discharged all eight of her torpedoes. *Kelvin* discharged two of her four too early, misled by the conditions, but *Jervis* and *Kipling* each fired five, the latter by hand. Just as she was turning, *Kingston* was hit by a 15-inch shell which passed right through the ship and burst outside her; despite this, she fired three torpedoes. As the destroyers turned away to reverse their course into the seas, their forecastles were deluged by green water and they were compelled to slow down. Damaged, the stricken *Kingston* came to a stop. She was able to get under way a little later, and Poland ordered her to join the convoy.

It was now Micklethwait's turn, but Iachino was already retiring and smoke was obscuring the field of view. Nevertheless, eight torpedoes were fired from Micklethwait's destroyers, though none from either his or Poland's attack actually hit an enemy vessel. It was at this point that a bursting 15-inch shell from *Littorio* sent a heavy splinter into *Lively*; though she took on some water there were no casualties, and she was able to keep pace with her consorts.

None of the destroyer officers thought the action over, yet they had driven the enemy from the field. Iachino had swung to starboard at 18.40; at 18.51 he ordered a course of north-west, and at 18.56 his ships fired their last salvoes. It was sunset and as the darkness 'was rapidly deepening, Admiral Iachino realised that the action had to be considered ended.'[36]

The Italians were virtually untouched, whereas the British had had two destroyers badly damaged and had expended 36 torpedoes; the cruisers had fired 1,600 and the destroyers 1,300 rounds. But the convoy was safe and Vian, collecting his warships, began to run down towards it.

The convoy was unscathed, although the afternoon air attacks had gradually mounted in ferocity. As noted above, they had begun about 14.20, and lasted throughout the battle. At about the same time as *Euryalus* reported her first sighting of enemy warships, a brief glimpse of the Italians had been seen from *Talabot*, but once the convoy had turned away under cover of the

smoke laid by *Carlisle* and *Avon Vale* this proved to be so efficient
that the merchantmen 'were completely in the dark as to what
was happening the other side of it.' They were relieved to see the
cruisers rejoin and receive the signal 'Enemy Battle Fleet driven
off', but it was not long before Vian detached again for the second
phase of the engagement. By now the wind was south-south-
east, Force 7, and as *Carlisle* took station astern again 'she was
washing down for'd [though] the guns' crews were sticking to
their posts'.[37]

The Junkers Ju88s 'were now diving much lower before releasing their bombs' and *Clan Campbell* seemed to be a particular
target, for 'a stick of bombs came down apparently on [her]
bows,' wrote Captain Edkins of the Hampshire Regiment, taking
passage in *Talabot* and manning a Bren gun in the action.

> She emerged undamaged through great gouts of water … bombs
> were fairly whistling down, audible above the din of the
> barrage … I saw one stick of bombs pitch almost certainly on the
> stern of the unfortunate Clan boat; but once again she reappeared
> from a curtain of water all in one piece. By 15.30 the weather had
> turned really foul and we were bouncing all over the place. A
> stick of four came crashing down to starboard … The 15-inch
> splashes were all over the place … the wind rolling the smoke
> towards the Italians. It was blowing like hell and with the smoke
> and gun flashes … one sight I shall never forget: a cruiser belting
> along, parallel to the smoke, every detail etched out in silver by
> the sun before she disappeared into the murk. Only a flash, but
> unmistakably the *Penelope* with the seas going right over her quar-
> terdeck. Then directly above us at about 12,000 feet we saw six
> Ju88s. They peeled off and we had our first dive bombing attack.
> My Brens were loaded with part tracer and I got rid of four mag-
> azines … I saw one stick [of bombs] … actually spreading out
> before it was obscured by the funnel. I followed the [Ju]88 down
> the length of the ship. One of our Bredas got him – our first kill.
> Within minutes two more 88s came in but their aim was pretty
> wild. Finally a single 88 came down in a vertical dive; smoke was
> pouring out from one engine as he pulled out just in time … At
> about 17.00 the light began to fade and what looked like a possible
> torpedo-attack came in out of the sun. Ju88s and Savoias, very
> low. We couldn't see any 'fish' but a Savoia came straight at us,
> only a couple of hundred feet above the sea. He began to wobble,
> banked round our bows and went straight into the sea. Shortly
> afterwards a Ju88 was shot down to end the party.[38]

When the *Littorio*'s heavy shells began to appear between the convoy and the *Carlisle*, the ship's company of *Pampas* 'seemed less worried by the fall of 15-inch shells (which by this time had been joined by smaller-calibre splashes) than by the dive-bombing. My own feelings', Wright, the naval liaison officer, reported, 'were exactly the reverse. Now another, and more determined, torpedo-bombing attack developed, one plane coming straight for us. Our Oerlikon fire, which had been accurate all day, continued to hit the machine and we had the satisfaction of seeing the plane come down in the sea just astern of us … At the same time we were constantly altering course to avoid bombing attacks and also on orders from the Commodore.'

Aboard *Talabot* the 'occasional glimpses of a cruiser or a destroyer coming through the smoke' were alarming. 'One was never sure at first whether it was one of our own or an enemy ship.' They could also see gunflashes on the horizon *west* of the smokescreen. Combined with the columns of water thrown up by the plunging 15-inch shells this suggested they were 'for it, until miraculously the battle, which seemed to be coming at one time unpleasantly close to us, receded. All we could see at dusk was a few of our own destroyers well away to the north-westward still apparently firing at something.' Although they had been ordered to monitor certain radio frequencies the merchantmen had no idea what had occurred, and 'one was apt to take a very pessimistic view of our prospects of reaching Malta.'[39]

In Alexandria Cunningham had held his peace and his hand, watching the developing tactical situation as best he could, making occasional approbatory comments as the action progressed. It was only when Vian announced the enemy had been driven off again and that he intended to withdraw that Cunningham intervened. He insisted that Vian leave the *Carlisle* and her anti-aircraft guns to cover the convoy; he also tactfully 'suggested' that doubtless Vian had considered dispersing the convoy to enable the merchant ships to make their individual best speeds to Malta. In fact Vian was already heading home, as the fuel situation in all his warships was approaching an acute state. Force K, *Penelope* and *Legion*, with the damaged *Kingston* and *Havock*, began the last phase of the passage to Malta. As for convoy MW10, at 19.00 Hutchinson, acting in light of the discretionary nature of his own operational orders, had on his own initiative dispersed it.

Dispersal involved divergence at speed, not a wild scattering, and Hutchinson had so arranged matters that *Clan Campbell*, with her slow speed, was to make a direct track to the entrance to the swept channel into Grand Harbour, while *Talabot, Pampas* and *Breconshire* 'were to make legs to the southward, the amount of the diversion depending upon the speed of the ships, and the idea was that at daylight on Monday 23 March, the convoy would again be concentrated and in the swept channel with *Carlisle* and the close escort to look after them.'[40] This was not what Cunningham intended, and it was an illogical use of dispersal since, as the ships were to reunite at daylight, the advantage of speed was lost. By proceeding alone, *Breconshire* at the very least might have made Malta; at 19.00 she had already increased to 17 knots in the company of *Southwold* and *Beaufort*, but her heading of 255 degrees was not directly towards Malta and it was 21.00 before her head was swung to the north-west. The detour was to prove fatal.

In fact Hutchinson's dispersal plan seems to have required each ship to diverge five degrees more to port than her neighbour, *Clan Campbell*'s 'direct course' being somewhat north of west.[41] At 21.45 that evening *Carlisle* joined *Breconshire* and her escorts, Neame taking over as senior officer. *Talabot*'s course was 260 degrees and she was joined by the damaged *Havock*, which took station ahead of her, with *Dulverton* astern. At 21.00 she too had turned to the north-west, uncertain of her exact position from having been 'driven well down into the Gulf of Sidra [Sirte] during the action'. The course she steered was 'in the nature of a guess "aimed" at the centre of the island. Apart from the two Hunts, no other ships were in sight. A very heavy sea was running by this time with a strong easterly wind blowing, making it very uncomfortable for the destroyers in company.'

Escorted by *Hurworth, Pampas* made off on the most southerly course. She too was uncertain of her exact position, but at 21.00 altered to the north-west and, at 15 knots on a direct course, hoped to clear the defensive, known minefield. Just before the alteration of course she developed a steering fault, and before it was rectified *Hurworth* had disappeared in the windy darkness. Shortly before midnight, *Clan Campbell* and a destroyer were briefly sighted. After that, the night was quiet 'and most ... were able to get a few hours sleep.'

At dawn next morning the officers aboard *Pampas* felt the psychological impact of dispersal, observing 'with a certain amount of trepidation' that they were alone. Taking a stellar fix which confirmed the reliability of their dead-reckoning, they anticipated making land at 08.30. It was still blowing quite hard from the south-east, with a heavy swell running: surface visibility was limited by a low haze, but above the sky was clear and blue. At 07.15 a Ju88 attacked low, out of the haze. One 500-pound bomb damaged the forward derricks before bursting over the side, the second dented the funnel and, stripped of its fins, shot overboard unexploded. From then on *Pampas* was continuously harried by Ju88s 'which finding us alone, often came down to below 1,000 feet and sprayed us with machine-gun fire.' One of three Junkers came in from the port side and released a bomb 'not more than ten yards from the ship's side with a deep slant on it'. It exploded under No. 4 Hold and shook the ship but she continued to steam and steer, though taking water aft. At 08.30 *Talabot* was sighted in company with her two destroyers, and 'our spirits soared'.[42]

The Norwegian ship had had an eventful night. She had closed *Havock* at one point, when the destroyer stopped, but then she had moved ahead again and the officer of the watch had seen nothing more of any destroyers until the grey light of dawn revealed them still in company. The Luftwaffe found them at 07.00, but although the Ju88s circled, sporadic fire from *Havock* and *Dulverton* prevented an attack on *Talabot* developing until one flew in at about three hundred feet. Her bombs 'just missed ahead'. At 08.15 land was sighted and 'two Hurricanes appeared over us – a most welcome sight. Despite this fighter escort, which continued most of the way into harbour, two or three Ju88s continued to circle round us, occasionally being sighted and driven off by the fighters [which] ... seemed to have difficulty seeing the enemy aircraft despite frequent "indicating salvoes" from the destroyers and an occasional burst of tracer ... from our Bredas.'

Talabot passed up the swept channel and was off Ricasoli Point, within half a mile of the mole, when she was attacked by a Messerschmitt Me109, which dropped small bombs on her without effect. 'Grand Harbour was entered without difficulty at about 09.15, the Captain handling the single screw ship in a heavy following sea very skilfully' as the ship negotiated the tight port turn. She was boarded inside the mole by 'a rather frightened and very talkative Maltese' pilot and was secured to No. 6 mooring trot off Floriana.

Pampas followed her in, also being attacked by an Me109 fighter-bomber. The single bomb missed, but the Me109 'came back and sprayed us with machine-guns [*sic*], wounding four of our guns' crew, none, however, seriously'. The ship passed inwards at 09.30, and the pilot boarded. 'The terraces were lined with cheering Maltese and I felt', Lieutenant-Commander Wright wrote, 'a lump in my throat at our reception. I was not alone in this as the captain left the bridge, telling me later that it was for this reason.'

The damaged destroyers *Havock* and *Kingston* entered Grand Harbour with the two cargo-liners, passing 'up harbour to the cheers of the populace'.[43] But things had not gone as well for the other two transports, and the remaining destroyers were still required at sea. Neither of the masters or liaison officers aboard *Pampas* or *Talabot* seems to have had any intention of reforming the convoy. The dispersal plan left them to their own devices, and they had made the best of it, but it is clear from their experiences that its value was negative.

Clan Campbell's poor speed was to cost her dearly, for when *Pampas* sighted her she was already falling astern. At daylight she was about fifty miles from Malta in company with *Eridge*, and by 10.30 was only twenty miles offshore. But now she was attacked and successfully bombed from a height of only fifty feet. She sank quickly, taking Vooght and five others with her. One survivor was wounded, the remaining 112 of her crew and passengers being hauled from the water during the next two and a half hours by *Eridge*.[44] Ordered to join *Clan Campbell* and *Eridge*, *Legion* was severely damaged by a near miss in the same attack and had to withdraw, to be beached at Marsaxlokk.

By this time *Breconshire* too was in trouble. Like the other ships ahead of her she had had a rough night, and the conditions at daylight did not seem to Hutchinson particularly propitious for air cover; nevertheless, he sent a signal to Malta outlining the situation, and requesting it. It was a Cant, however, not a Spitfire that overflew the ships at 07.50, and at 07.55 a Ju88 dived deeply on *Breconshire*, its bombs exploding in her wake. A second sped in at 08.17 to be met with a hail of fire, and was driven off streaming oily smoke from an engine nacelle. Then, at 09.20, with Delimara Point in sight, three Messerschmitt Me109B fighter-bombers 'flew just over the ship from port to starboard'. *Breconshire's* guns opened fire but the German aircraft 'attacked with bombs and machine guns; [all] the bombs hit and [the] engine room began to flood'. Twenty minutes later a Ju88 dropped a bomb which exploded beneath *Breconshire*, and her engines stopped; she was just 7.6 miles east of Grand Harbour. At 10.00 another Ju88 made a bombing and strafing run, her bombs passing over the ship to detonate close alongside and further damage the transport, while a machine-gun bullet severely wounded an able seaman. Two further if ineffective bombing raids were made on the ship.

Carlisle and two Hunts, *Southwold* and *Dulverton*, were in the vicinity, standing by in the heavy swell, as *Breconshire*, no longer under command, fell into the troughs and began to roll as she drifted down onto the Maltese coast and the Zonker Beacon minefield to leeward. Neame was desperately short of ammunition and, leaving air defence to Jellicoe, manoeuvred to pass a tow wire. He was unsuccessful, but then Nicholl arrived on the scene in *Penelope*, fresh from replenishing with fuel and ammunition, and relieved Neame of this duty. After a struggle aboard *Breconshire*, where there was no power, a wire was eventually passed and secured; it soon parted, however, and Hutchinson was obliged to let go both anchors to prevent *Breconshire* drifting into the minefield, or onto the lee shore. Here the stricken transport lay wallowing all day, and at sunset Nicholl signalled that tugs would arrive at 06.00 the following morning. At that moment a single Beaufighter flew over.

The night was spent trying to restore power and pump out the ship by hand. Despite her two anchors *Breconshire* had dragged inshore, and at daylight mines could be seen breaking the surface nearby in the heavy swell. At daylight the trawler *Beryl* twice tried to get alongside, without success, and at 10.21 the *Southwold*, still standing by to give air defence, struck a mine which 'exploded under the engine room'. The tug *Ancient* had now arrived and, instead of the transport, was diverted to take *Southwold* in tow. Just as *Ancient* secured her wire at 13.00 the destroyer broke her back, though the two halves remained united by the plating of the upper deck. Half an hour later Me109s and Ju88s resumed their bombing, and at 15.45 'one heavy bomb fell only thirty feet to port of *Southwold*, [causing] more underwater damage. [The] ship steadily listed to starboard, [her] bow rose up ... and began to roll over.'[45] At 15.55, *Southwold* sank.

Attempts were now made to take *Breconshire* in tow in spite of continuing German air raids and – such was the simultaneous effectiveness of Luftwaffe raids on Malta itself – an absence of friendly fighters. Mercifully no further bombs hit *Breconshire*, but at darkness *Ancient* withdrew. *Beryl* had made another attempt to get alongside and take off the service personnel, but this had failed. Then, at midnight, *Ancient* reappeared with the tug *Robust*. Aboard the former was Captain Nicholl and the senior harbour pilot, Mr Murphy. After a struggle an exhausted Hutchinson slipped his anchors, and under the tow of the two tugs *Breconshire* was hauled east, clear of the minefield. It had been decided to get her round to Marsaxlokk, but the heavy head trim and the wind and sea made things very difficult for the tugs, and *Robust*'s line parted. Grimly *Ancient* hung on, her master, Mr Bromley, handling her with great skill, and at dawn the escorting *Eridge* ran a line to the yawing transport's stern, to aid steering and to enable *Breconshire* to double Delimara Point. By noon on 25 March *Breconshire* was moored to No. 1 Buoy, Marsaxlokk Harbour.

Hutchinson proceeded at once to Valletta to report to Leatham, and plans were made to move the fleet oiler *Plumleaf*, almost resident at Malta as fleet bunkering facility, to Marsaxlokk next day and tranship *Breconshire*'s 5,000 tons of boiler oil.

In the meantime, the cargoes of *Talabot* and *Pampas* remained unloaded. There was no cargo discharge at night: the Maltese dockers ceased work at 18.30, for the working practices of the dock labour remained unmodified except when stopped altogether during air raids. Nor were military personnel brought in to help. 'I should have thought night work would have been possible at certain periods,' Wright complained from *Pampas*. 'The first night, for instance (the 23/24 March), was completely air raid free.' From *Talabot* MacFarlane added: 'There was a cruiser and one or two small ships in dockyard hands and one felt that all available naval ratings could have been put on the job and that work should have gone on day and night, stopping only when bombing attacks were actually being made ... and accepting the risk of casualties if the ship was hit.'[46]

This tardy breaking of the bulk of the two vessels' cargoes on the morning of the 26th was inexcusable. Twelve valuable hours had been lost, a fact which did not go unnoticed by men debating the wisdom of the convoy's dispersal. Less than a thousand tons of supplies had been discharged from *Pampas* and *Talabot* when the air raid sirens wailed and the red flags were hoisted.[47] Well aware of the arrival of the three ships of MW10, the local Luftwaffe commanders in Sicily ordered a tremendous raid on Malta. Attacks began on the afternoon of the 26th, when the Luftwaffe located and dive-bombed *Breconshire*. Initially they succeeded only in shaking the ship with near misses, but shortly afterwards she was finally set on fire by a stick of bombs from a Ju88. All four hit her, two forward where her special oil tanks were, rupturing No. 2 Tank; a third penetrated No. 4 Hatch and ignited the consignment of coal below; the fourth blew a hole in the ship's shell and admitted the sea to No. 5 Hold. Counter-flooding was tried to correct her list, but her port rail was soon awash and Hutchinson gave the order to abandon her at 20.00 on the 26th.

Things were far worse in Grand Harbour, on which the Germans turned their main attention after first raiding Hal Far. Here they 'achieved a degree of accuracy with their bombing which they had never attained before.'[48] Anchored at Parlatorio wharf before she could move out to Marsaxlokk, *Plumleaf* was bombed and badly holed, her engine room flooded. *Talabot* was hit and set on fire at 12.30, *Pampas* two hours later, despite RAF interceptors and a terrific barrage which accounted for a claimed seven Stukas, four Ju88s and three Me109s. Nor did darkness discourage the attackers; they persisted for some time. *Pampas* settled slowly and a further 950 tons of her cargo were taken out of her, but *Talabot* was burning furiously, work on her hampered by oil which covered everything and made diving operations impossible. 'The shortage and repeated blocking of all fire-fighting and salvage apparatus was another bar to rapid progress.'[49] Meanwhile fire floats manned by parties from *Penelope* and the Maltese crew of *Ancient* made every effort to extinguish the blaze during the next two days, as the German attack persisted. A few tons of cargo were snatched from the ship as the kerosene ignited. In due course, however, the danger that her ammunition would explode and cause immense collateral damage resulted in the decision being made to scuttle her. Lieutenant D.

Copperwheat of *Penelope* fixed and fired the charges, then swam away from the doomed ship; he was afterwards awarded the George Cross for his courage. When *Talabot* finally sat on the bottom, only her gunwhales were above water.

Similar exertions had been going on to empty *Pampas*. Power to operate her electric derrick winches was first provided by the dockyard, and when this failed *Avon Vale* was secured alongside to provide it, and work continued. Pumps were run continuously but the water gained on the salvors, and while 'every endeavour was made to unload ... *Pampas* as quickly as possible ... the heavy and continuous bombing of the harbour area inevitably slowed up the work'. *Pampas* eventually sat on the bottom, 'aground with two holds intact but the remainder flooded'.[50]

Breconshire had neither sunk nor capsized and 'in the night the fire (in the coal in No. 4 Hold) was got under control ... [and] there seemed a chance that she might be saved. In the morning, however, the fire broke out again with great intensity and at 11.07 she slowly sank, turning over on her side as she did so ... with only six feet of her bilge above water ... [*Breconshire*] was now comparatively safe from the evil designs of the enemy and there seemed to be every prospect of recovering in due course a fair quantity of her cargo.'[51] In fact, over a protracted period her bottom was drilled and some 5,000 tons of oil were extracted; but there was no immediate benefit for Malta.

In total, out of the 29,500 tons of stores and munitions that had been borne in the four transports of MW10, only 4,952 tons, mostly from *Pampas*, had been safely landed. It was a dismal result – and bombs had taken their toll of others, too. The refloated *Legion* was blasted into wreckage; the tug *Ancient* was hit and beached; the submarine *P39* had been blown in two by a bomb-hit astonishingly, and almost incredibly the Polish submarine *Sokol* lying alongside was unharmed; the *Avon Vale* was slightly damaged; No. 2 Dock caisson was distorted and jammed; and *Penelope* was persistently attacked, near-missed, flooded forward, and struck by so many splinters that she was christened 'Pepperpot' by her crew.

It was a bad introduction for Leatham as Vice-Admiral, Malta, and he can have taken only small comfort in the arrival of the submarine *Pandora* from Gibraltar on the 31st. She discharged a cargo largely of kerosene at Marsamxett, surrounded by some of the remains of MW10. But it was by no means the end of the story. The intense German air raids continued for days, and it was necessary for Leatham to dispatch all ships not required at Malta. *Carlisle* and the Hunts *Dulverton*, *Hurworth* and *Eridge* had sailed for Alexandria on Wednesday 25 March, as soon as they had consumed the small reserve of fuel held at Malta. On the 29th the slightly damaged *Avon Vale* left with the cruiser *Aurora*, which had been in the dockyard's hands, bound for Gibraltar, followed by the battle-damaged *Havock* on 5 April and *Penelope* on the 8th. Nicholl's cruiser had spent a brief period in dock, and the departure of these three ships was only possible after 'a series of the most determined efforts on the part of the ships themselves and the dockyard authorities in the face of continuous and heavy attack. *Penelope* actually expended her outfit of AA ammunition [in defence of Grand Harbour,] and had to re-ammunition before she could sail', with the gallant Nicholl wounded. Steaming at 27 knots, *Penelope* was attacked off Cape Bon on 9 April by German and Italian high-level and torpedo-bombers, finally arriving at Gibraltar the following day. Unfortunately 'Havock grounded at high speed near Kelibia [near Cape Bon], due to a navigational error probably caused by fatigue. She was destroyed by her ship's company, who were interned by the French authorities.'[52] Her wreck was also torpedoed by the Italian submarine *Aradam*. *Kingston*, finally, too damaged to sail, had been dry-docked, and in a raid on 11 April she was bombed to destruction, her captain, Commander P. Somerville, being among those killed.

As for the forces that had retired from the action known as the Second Battle of Sirte, Iachino had avoided two air groups sent from Egypt and Malta to locate him on Sunday, 22 March.[53] The weather had deteriorated so very badly that the cruisers *Giovanni della Banda Nere* and *Trento* were damaged and the Italian destroyers *Scirocco* (sent as a reinforcement to Iachino) and *Lanciere* both foundered. *Bande Nere* reached Messina on 24 March, but was sunk on 1 April off Stromboli by the British submarine *Urge* when on passage to La Spezia for repairs. Iachino attributed the losses and damage to his ships to poor hull construction and defective pumping systems. The ingress of water even aboard the massive *Littorio* had caused electrical failures affecting the battleship's main armament.

Nor had Vian escaped, the speed of Force B steadily reducing to 15 knots in the ferocious gregale. By dawn on 23 March, *Sikh* was the only destroyer still within sight of Vian's three cruisers. The rest could not keep up in the head sea, and *Kelvin* had already lost a man washed overboard as she turned away from the torpedo attack just before sunset. Vian had to turn back and gather his flock to provide mutual cover as they approached bomb alley, a sensible precaution denied the merchantmen of MW10 as they approached Malta. An attack was mounted by Stukas, which concentrated upon the damaged *Lively*, but she was detached to Tobruk and suffered no further injury. Sporadic attacks by Ju88s and SM79s continued until dark but were futile, and the following day, with the weather moderating, speed was increased. A final attack by two Savoias ended Operation MG1, and Force B arrived back at Alexandria shortly after noon to a 'tremendous reception by the ships in harbour'. Cunningham was 'unnaturally silent at first, but then all his delight burst out, and he cheered with the rest of us,' recalled his chief of staff, Commander Woods.[54]

Whatever the motives for Cunningham's momentary restraint (and he cannot then have known of the outcome), he was too much a professional not to have been moved by the sight of Vian's battle-scarred ships. Although the squadron had achieved a noteworthy tactical victory against considerable odds, as Vian's immediate knighthood attested, Operation MG1 as a whole had been a strategic failure. Iachino could – and should – have destroyed the convoy over Vian's head, using his own cruisers and destroyers to engage the British admiral. Such an action might well have settled Malta's fate. But Vian's dismissal of the Italian squadron from the field had not ensured the safe, let alone the timely, arrival of the convoy. It was, moreover, a fundamental mistake to disperse the merchant ships: they ought to have remained together under escort and thus able to mitigate the total absence of the air umbrella they should have been afforded from Malta. In the event, after all the effort Malta was only marginally better off at the end of MG1 than she had been before convoy MW10 left Alexandria.

Furthermore, three of those scarce, fast cargo-liners had been sacrificed to little avail; and, worst of all, *Breconshire* with her precious oil capacity lay bilge uppermost in the blue waters of Marsaxlokk.

16

'A question of survival'

(Operations PICKET, CALENDAR, BOWERY, LB, STYLE, SALIENT *and*
HARPOON *with Convoy GM4)*

———————

As *AURORA* AND *Avon Vale* made their dash westwards to the
sanctuary of Gibraltar, Syfret was at sea on a Club Run, the repeat
of Operation PICKET. Force H[1] had sailed on 27 March in support
of the carriers *Eagle* and *Argus*, which flew sixteen Spitfires into
Malta; Syfret returned to Gibraltar on the 30th. The fighters were
urgently needed, for Fliegerkorps II were laying waste to Malta
in an orgy of destruction, flying 4,082 bombing sorties in daylight
and a further 256 during the dark hours. Over 7,000 tons of
bombs were dropped on the island – more than the total dropped
on London during the entire course of the Blitz. They fell mostly
in the vicinity of Grand and Marsamxett harbours, damaging
Valletta, Sliema and the Three Cities, as the airborne 'neutralisation' of the island fortress spiralled towards its climax.[2] It was in
these dark days that General Dobbie was able to inform the
people of Malta that King George VI had honoured the island
with the award of the George Cross.

As March turned to April those ships fit for sea departed, as
noted earlier, and those left behind were condemned. Bombs still
fell on *Plumleaf, Talabot* and *Kingston*; damage to the dockyard
was severe; oil lighters, water boats, tugs, fire floats and auxiliary
craft like the drifter *Sunset* were sunk; and on the 6th, the floating crane went down. The crews of the merchant ships suffered
with the islanders, sheltering ashore when not on watch, occasionally provoking complaints from the Maltese, who were

capable of regarding them as a drain on the slender food stocks, or from the Royal Navy. The superintendent of the Victualling Yard had earlier protested vigorously because the officers and most of the crew of the *Talabot* were sleeping in the Naval Flour Mill. Describing them as 'a number of not necessarily cleanly [*sic*] people', this worthy went on to report how, 'when it was brought to my notice that some of their habits were not hygienic, I insisted on their removal'.[3]

A trickle of stores continued to come in by submarine. *Pandora* arrived late on 31 March and immediately discharged a cargo of white oils at Marsamxett. At dawn she moved round to Hamilton Wharf in Grand Harbour to land dry stores, and this continued even when the first air raid of the day began. Nearby her lay the Greek submarine *Glaukos*, and in the adjacent drydock the destroyer *Lance*. The ships received the attention of German dive-bombers, which dropped a stick of bombs on Senglea before hitting *Pandora*. A gout of flame roared out of the submarine's open conning tower, instantly incinerating the twenty-five men on board. Damage and serious casualties were caused on the other ships, the submarine *P36* in Marsamxett being sunk. On 4 April three bombs hit and sank *Glaukos*, while the next day the remains of *Gallant*, still lying in the port after receiving extensive damage in January the previous year, were bombed and the destroyer was reduced to a total wreck. *Penelope* and *Havock* escaped destruction, but on the 9th *Lance* was heavily bombed and declared a total loss. The Polish submarine *Sokol*, which was undergoing repair and escaped damage when *P39* was sunk alongside her, led a charmed life. Karnicki, her commander, moved her every night and hid her under camouflage during daylight. By the middle of the month she could submerge, but lost a propeller on the defensive boom and was ordered to Gibraltar. By this time both *Urge* (Lieutenant-Commander Tomkinson) and *Upholder* (Lieutenant-Commander Wanklyn) were missing, presumed lost, and a few days later the decision was taken for the 10th Submarine Flotilla to evacuate Malta. Captain Ruck-Keene flew in from Alexandria with the news[4] and Captain Simpson, the flotilla commander, who had lost half his boats and men, not all in action, echoed Ford's conclusion that the failure to build submarine pens before the war had been an expensive negligence.

The destruction went on relentlessly. In Grand Harbour the

minesweeper *Abingdon* was bombed, beached and abandoned, the naval trawlers *Coral* and *Jade* were sunk, as were the naval tug *Andromeda* and the harbour tugs *Emily*, *Hellespont*, *West Cocker* and *West Dean*.

Following the loss of *Pandora*, *Clyde* crept in from Gibraltar on 16 April and berthed in Msida Creek to discharge food and aviation spirit. Her departure on the 19th was aborted when she was attacked by an Me109, though she was able to slip out the next day – the day on which, it seemed, Malta's fate was sealed. The Axis build-up of aircraft to more than five hundred machines capable of operating against the island was making itself felt. Iachino's failure to destroy MW10 combined with the effectiveness of the Luftwaffe in the very entrance to Grand Harbour convinced Kesselring and Loerzer, of Fliegerkorps II, that the Luftwaffe was quite capable of achieving Hitler's objective as far as Malta was concerned.[5] In short, the enemy were getting the upper hand; Malta was increasingly indefensible, and the fate of convoy MW10 was eloquent testimony to the fact. The island was now toothless, with 126 of its aircraft destroyed on the ground and a further 20 in air combat; it was unusable as a naval base; and Axis convoys were running south from Italy to Tripoli with impunity.[6] The paucity of *matériel* reaching Malta in MW10 had, along with the need to maintain supplies to Russia with the sailing of PQ16, the May Arctic convoy, persuaded Churchill not to run in any more merchant ships until adequate air defences were in place. The plea for Spitfires had been made in London by Squadron Leader Gracie on behalf of Air Vice-Marshal Sir Hugh Lloyd (who had taken over from Maynard as AOC Malta). Lloyd had written that 'Malta's need is for Spitfires, Spitfires and still more Spitfires. And they must come in bulk, not in dribs and drabs.' This last was a comment on the failure of Syfret's Club Runs, which as has been noted had been subject to several frustrations, not the least of which was the fact that the flight deck of *Argus* was not long enough to fly off Spitfires with long-range tanks in anything like the numbers required. Moreover, *Eagle* was undergoing emergency repairs to her steering gear, and the lifts fitted to other larger carriers could not cope with the wingspan of Spitfires.

Churchill cabled President Roosevelt, outlining the situation. Between 20 and 30 British fighters were ranged against some 600 enemy aircraft. But there was an American carrier in British waters: Churchill asked the President, 'Would you be willing to allow your carrier *Wasp* to do one of these trips ... ?' As Churchill afterwards recorded, 'the response was generous.'[7]

Operation CALENDAR kicked off in the Clyde when *Wasp*, commanded by Captain J. Reeves, USN, and her escorting destroyers, the USSs *Lang* and *Madison*, entered the river. *Wasp* proceeded to Shieldhall and by 14 April had loaded fifty-two Mark 5B Supermarine Spitfires and their pilots, all belonging to Nos 601 and 603 Squadrons. The carrier passed Ailsa Craig that same day, hauled out into the Atlantic north of Malin Head and, with her escort, headed south. Designated Force W, *Wasp* and her destroyers were joined by *Renown* (Commodore C. Daniell, senior officer) and the British destroyers *Inglefield, Ithuriel, Echo* and *Partridge*. The passage of the Strait was made during the night of 18/19 April and from Gibraltar more ships joined, the two cruisers *Charybdis* and *Cairo* and the destroyers *Westcott, Wishart, Vidette, Wrestler* and *Antelope*. Aboard *Wasp* the British air staff briefed the pilots and provided meticulous details for the coming flight, while their planes were fitted with long-range fuel tanks. The first sign of ill-preparedness was the discovery that these, once again, were defective and leaked copiously; it was then also realised that a high proportion of the aircrafts' guns were faulty, and three-quarters of their radios were inoperative.

Notwithstanding these serious deficiencies, at dawn on 20 April, in fine weather and as the task force passed the meridian of 3° 20' East, *Wasp*'s Grumman Wildcats climbed into the clear sky to provide air patrols as the Spitfires were flown off. At 05.18 the first Spitfire took off, piloted by Gracie. As the forty-eight machines deemed serviceable set course towards the east, the sun rose, 'filling the whole of space with light ...' In due course the pilots saw 'two islands, like autumn leaves floating on the water, grow larger and larger ... White walls crinkle a hilltop. The small fields are yellow. Blue water in front of my propeller and, as we cross the channel between the two islands, I can see waves breaking on the sunlit rocks ahead. Then we are leaping inland over the island of Malta.'[8]

The elation was short-lived. Once the Spitfires had landed on the devastated airfield of Ta' Qali, the wrecked bunkers provided no protection from a Luftwaffe attack which followed: well aware of the operation, three hundred German aircraft flew over Malta that day. Within seventy-two hours of their arrival not a single Spitfire was airworthy, the majority having been destroyed on the ground within a few minutes.[9] Those that survived a few hours were, like those flown in earlier, hampered in their operational effectiveness by a lack of spares of all types, and by a lack of ground crew conversant with the machines. That the condition of the Spitfires was anyway poor only exacerbated this situation. Lloyd despaired; he was no better off than he had been, and the whole humiliating shambles had been witnessed by the Americans. As for Dobbie, the similarities of that fatal day to the débâcle of MW10 prompted him to report that the situation in Malta had passed beyond the critical: 'It is obvious that the very worst may happen if we cannot replenish our vital needs, especially flour and ammunition.' All had been reduced to 'a question of survival'; stocks would run out in the middle of June. Such anxiety seemed to Churchill, dauntless as always, evidence of Dobbie's general 'worn-down' condition.

It must have seemed almost a cruel mockery when the submarine *Porpoise* arrived from Alexandria on the 25th with a small consignment of stores, some fuel, and some service personnel. A few days later, having been engaged on the same task, *Olympus* struck a mine off Grand Harbour newly laid by German E-boats, and sank. She was Gibraltar-bound with men of the crews of the submarines sunk in Lazaretto Creek, and the casualty list was large.

The post-mortems that followed the failure of Operations MG1 and CALENDAR concluded, among other things, that Malta's air defences were inadequate, and implicit in this conclusion was the judgement that Dobbie should not have asked for a convoy when he could not give it the umbrella it required. He was quietly replaced and left the island in conditions of secrecy without saying goodbye, officially worn out by the crisis; something of a scapegoat, but really only a man trying to do an impossible job. His successor was Lord Gort, who was flown in from Gibraltar. The two men met at the seaplane base at Kalafrana, in the middle of an air raid on the evening of 7 May. As the Sunderland flew Dobbie west, the following dawn revealed a large naval force steaming east. This was Operation BOWERY.

Also replaced and departing in conditions of great secrecy, though for entirely different reasons, was Admiral Cunningham.

He handed over to Pridham-Wippell on 1 April, until such time as his successor, Admiral Sir Henry Harwood, should arrive. On departing, Cunningham sent the customary signals of farewell, not forgetting the Merchant Navy whose unobtrusive yet sterling work he greatly admired. To his fleet he spoke of his deep sadness in laying down his command, privately regretting that the need to keep his departure secret from the enemy meant he could not visit each ship in turn. His staff were bereft; Alexandria felt like 'Devonport on a wet Sunday afternoon.'[10]

Cunningham was destined first for Washington and then, on the illness of Pound, to become First Sea Lord. He left his beloved Mediterranean Fleet at a bad moment, but was tight-lipped about MG1, preferring to concentrate on Vian's action, which he considered 'one of the most brilliant ... of the war, if not the most brilliant'.[11] He wrote to his former chief of staff, Algernon Willis: 'My heart remains in the Mediterranean. I was told the other day that Nelson once said "Waking or sleeping, Malta is always in my thoughts", and that exactly describes my case.'[12]

On completion of CALENDAR Force W had turned and, after a brief stop at Gibraltar, arrived back in the Clyde on 26 April. The intention was to make a second run, to be code-named Operation BOWERY. Shamed by the appalling outcome of CALENDAR, Gracie, largely responsible for lobbying for the consignment of fighters in the first place, reorganised the reception arrangements, and Lloyd was able to secure the services of an experienced air combat control officer at Malta. In London, plans were made to get spares and experienced ground-crews through to the island by means of a fast minelayer, and Welshman was nominated. 'We may well lose this ship,' Churchill warned Pound, 'but in view of the emergency ... there appears to be no alternative.'

But back in Glasgow the embarkation arrangements remained shambolic. On 30 April Wasp had again moved upstream to King George V Dock at Shieldhall, adjacent to Renfrew airfield. Within a few minutes the first of forty-seven Spitfires was lifted aboard, and it was immediately apparent that the long-range tanks still leaked. Captain Reeves ordered loading to cease, and agreed to its continuation only after some tanks had been rectified. He then undertook 'to carry out such further repairs as were necessary with his own labour.' This recurrence of a previously notified fault, the flag-officer at Glasgow reported with breathtakingly deplorable understatement, 'is unsatisfactory, and has unfortunately created a very bad impression ... '[13]

Having loaded her quota of forty-seven Spitfires, Reeves took *Wasp* to the Tail o' the Bank, anchored, and turned his men to, to render the tanks operational. Then *Wasp* and her escort proceeded to Scapa Flow, finally leaving on 3 May with the American destroyers *Lang* and *Sterett*, acting under the orders of Daniell in *Renown* and accompanied by *Charybdis* and the destroyers *Echo* and *Intrepid*. During the night of 7/8 May Force W was joined by the repaired carrier *Eagle*, which had sailed from Gibraltar screened by *Ithuriel*, *Partridge*, *Westcott*, *Wishart*, *Wrestler*, *Antelope*, *Salisbury*, *Georgetown* and *Vidette*. *Eagle* still had on board seventeen Spitfires which had not been delivered in Syfret's earlier Club Runs.

Discreetly following but proceeding independently from Daniell's Force W was the fast minelayer *Welshman*. Her commanding officer, Captain W. Friedberger, had been given secret orders, and a consignment of strange items. On Thursday 7 May *Welshman* filled her mine decks with 340 tons of medical and other stores, food, and 72 crates of smoke-making compound. She also loaded 100 spare Rolls-Royce Merlin engines and 120 passengers, the majority of whom were RAF ground crews trained to maintain Spitfires. After dark the curious packages were opened, and *Welshman*'s crew fitted plywood bulkheads to her superstructure and smoke cowls atop her three funnels. Work was completed at 03.00 the following morning and *Welshman* stood out to sea, an hour astern of Force W, disguised as the large French 'super-destroyer' *Léopard*.

As Force W steamed east throughout the 8th they were observed by General Dobbie, homeward bound in his Sunderland. At dawn on the following morning the Spitfires took off, forty-seven from *Wasp* and the seventeen from *Eagle*. A few hours later, sixty-one of them arrived to a very different reception from that of their predecessors. With limited resources, Gracie had arranged for the incoming machines to disperse to all three airfields. Their pilots were immediately relieved by experienced men and, refuelled and rearmed, they were ready for scrambling half an hour after their arrival. The German planes sent to repeat their success of 20 April found them airborne and ready. No one could know it at the time, but the arrival of those Spitfires courtesy of USS *Wasp* turned the tide in the air-war over

Malta. And *Wasp* had provided more than mere transport: Reeves and his people had materially rectified the deficiencies of the shameful British embarkation procedure.[14]

The Spitfires engaging the incoming Junkers and Messer-schmitts that day destroyed or damaged thirty-seven enemy air-craft at a cost of three of their own. Although the Luftwaffe laid mines in the approaches to Grand Harbour, 'daylight raiding was brought to an abrupt end',[15] and the air action of 10 May 1942 has justifiably been called 'The Battle of Malta'.

Ironically, it was a victory abetted by Kesselring himself. Flushed with his success of 20 April he triumphantly reported that Malta was finally neutralised: Hitler cancelled Operation HERKULES on 16 June, and the troops being prepared for Malta were diverted to reinforce Rommel instead.

Welshman had been overflown by the Spitfires as she sped east on the morning of 9 May under French colours. At 10.00 a suspicious Junkers Ju88 circled her in a helical approach that brought the aeroplane close enough for Friedberger to see her squadronal markings. Suddenly the plane made a shallow dive, but Friedberger, although apprehensive, had not rung action stations; he kept his guns trained fore and aft, and a couple of his hands loitered in the sunshine and waved. The Ju88 came round again, flew past at masthead height, then rose, waggled his wings, and flew off to the east. A few minutes later a Catalina flew past, and Friedberger flashed her to stand off. Shortly afterwards a second Ju88 appeared, then it too flew away. Relieved, Friedberger passed south of Galita, where he was intercepted by a Vichy seaplane, then called up by a signal station; but *Welshman* pressed on, holding to her bluff all the way and coasting the Tunisian shore.

As the last of the daylight faded out of the sky, the minelayer embarked on a piece of blind pilotage that reflects great credit on her navigating officer, Lieutenant-Commander Gellatly. Friedberger increased to full speed, something approaching forty knots, and Gellatly conned the ship through the shoals south of Cape Bon, skirting west and south of Pantelleria before turning east and hammering towards Malta. Friedberger made his landfall two minutes before sunrise.

Off Delimara Point *Welshman* was met by the trawler *Beryl* and led inshore in shallow waters along a passage used by fishing boats, so great was the fear of mine damage. As she swung round Ricasoli Point her starboard paravane cut loose two mines which passed perilously close to her stern, but the ship pulled clear, and a moment later the bomb-site that was Grand Harbour lay before her. This daylight arrival was promptly obscured by a protective smoke screen initiated from the canisters *Welshman* had brought with her, and Leatham reported it 'effective, though the area was heavily bombed'. Above her raged an air battle in which eighteen enemy aircraft were shot down and a score damaged. *Welshman* was showered with debris and bomb splinters, and four tons of steel girders were dumped by blast on her forward Oerlikon guns; she was holed above the waterline, her boats were wrecked and her deck plating buckled; but under partial cover of the smoke her cargo of 'valuable stores, aircraft spares and ammunition' was safely discharged. Gort called upon Friedberger as *Welshman* hauled across French Creek to oil at Canteen Wharf. Another raid developed but the ship was unscathed, and at 20.00 she prepared to sail in the calm of the night. 'Our departure', Friedberger wrote, 'was most affecting. The … shattered dockyard frontage … a circle of five burnt out or sunken merchant vessels … then a ring of cheers which seemed to come from the bastions of Valletta and Senglea, and the singing of "Roll out the Barrel", a tune which … expresses the spirit of Malta.' Following Leatham's last remaining serviceable minesweeper until she was in deep water, *Welshman* then sped away, reaching Gibraltar on 12 May.

Unfortunately, such consignments of aircraft, personnel and parts, vital though they were, did not address the matter of survival that Dobbie had emphasised. In order to keep the initiative, the British would have to provide more Spitfires, more fuel, more ammunition, more spare engines, more spare tyres, while their air crews and the population as a whole required more food. General Dobbie might have been recalled, but his deadline of mid June remained stubbornly inescapable.

So desperate was the fuel situation in Malta that throughout May attempts were made to recover some of the oil from the wreck of the *Breconshire* at Marsaxlokk, by piercing her bottom and fitting a suction and stand-pipe. On 3 May, 'owing to water seepage only 22 tons' of oil fuel were extracted from her, and the next day one of the oil lighters intended for the transhipment was bombed and sunk. By the end of May a further 47 tons had been recovered but had to be taken off in barrels, because all the oil lighters had been sunk. In the hiatus, the Germans were free to continue laying mines, though at some risk. They lost a *Schnellboot*, *S31*, to a mine off Valletta on 10 May, and a second, *S34*, was sunk by a shore battery a week later.

The Italians also sought to repeat their successful *maiali* attack on Alexandria by launching three human torpedoes from the submarine *Ambra* on 14 May. Their intended targets were the *Queen Elizabeth* again, lying in the only floating drydock available to the British in the Mediterranean, and the depot ship *Medway*, home to those submarines which now constituted the chief threat to the Axis supply route to Cyrenaica. Having released her three *maiali*, *Ambra* grounded in withdrawing, after misjudging the currents in the approach. Though she later returned to La Spezia her three forlorn hopes, equally frustrated by the strong currents and deterred by the activities of the British defences, failed to close their objectives. The two-man crews swam ashore, two to be captured immediately, one to enjoy two months of liberty in Alexandria before being caught. The British had, of course, prior warning of the attack, gleaned from Ultra decrypts on 5 May.

These successes were offset by the annihilation of Poland's destroyers, which had sallied from Alexandria to intercept an Axis convoy known to be bound for Benghazi. Poland's orders required him to turn back if he was spotted from the air and this he did on 11 May, but he was too late. Fourteen Ju88s of I Lehrgeschwader 1 under Kapitän Helbig, specially trained for maritime air operations, struck from Heraklion and sank *Lively*, thus depriving the force of its main anti-aircraft component, for she was equipped with eight high-angle 4-inch guns. A second wave of II Lehrgeschwader 1 from Eleusis, near Athens, was beaten off, but at 20.00 Helbig returned and bombed *Kipling* and *Jackal* from 1,500 feet. The former sank and *Jackal* was taken in tow by *Jervis*, but the attempt to rescue her had to be abandoned in the early hours of 12 May, for the delay involved would have ensured Poland's doom in the daylight. He therefore torpedoed *Jackal* and recovered 630 survivors, many of whom had been bombed while in the water. There were 112 fatalities, and some survivors later died on board *Jervis*, Captain Hussey of *Lively* among them. Many men were in tears, for it had been 'such a bad time', and while Poland conned *Jervis*, Jellicoe of *Kipling* held the burial service on her quarterdeck. At 04.00 *Sikh* and *Hasty* arrived as escort, and *Jervis* finally berthed alongside No. 46 Shed at Alexandria later that same afternoon. Crowds of onlookers were kept at bay by the police, but ambulances and South African nurses were on hand to tend the wounded. The pressure was unremitting, so by that night *Jervis* had hauled off to a buoy under twenty minutes' notice for steam, for she was duty destroyer.[16]

This cruel misfortune to Poland's division, which had done so much in the Gulf of Sirte, was the consequence of operating ships unsupported in waters dominated by the enemy in the air. Pound confronted Churchill with 'unusual force' when the Prime Minister next wanted Axis convoys attacked by the Royal Navy.[17] Some inroads had been made against enemy supply operations by the submarines *Turbulent*, *Thrasher* and *Proteus*, which sank six transports and the destroyer *Pessagno*. The destroyers *Hero*, *Hurworth* and *Eridge* accounted for *U568* on 28 May after a prolonged hunt and British aircraft so damaged *U652* that *U81* had to sink her on 2 June; but the loss of fleet destroyers was grievous. It was an inauspicious start to Harwood's command of the Mediterranean Fleet.

The acting admiral was not to enjoy anything approaching Cunningham's reputation. Passed over for flag rank during peacetime, his victory off the River Plate in December 1939 had attracted Churchill's patronage and now placed him in a post for which he was unsuited. A fine fighting sailor, popular on the lower deck as a kindly and decent senior officer, Harwood seems to have lacked that peculiar quality which combines aggression and charisma with an eye for essential detail and a ruthless ability to overcome problems. His personality was not such as to set his staff on fire, and he walked in Cunningham's long shadow. The kindest assessment is that he was beset by cumulative logistical and administrative difficulties, some deriving from Cunningham's own faults[18] but many of which must be attributed, in view of what happened, to the parlous strategic situation confronting the British in the Middle East in the spring of 1942. In short, Harwood, new to the scene, hardly had his feet under the table before he was faced with a complex operation. Moreover, he had as his principal subordinate admiral Philip Vian.

On 20 May Harwood hoisted his flag aboard the *Queen Elizabeth*, then in drydock, and shortly afterwards reinforcements began to arrive. The cruiser *Birmingham* and four destroyers passed the Suez Canal and entered Alexandria on 7 June, with *Newcastle*, *Arethusa* and *Hermione* following. The latter had come from Gibraltar, from where Syfret was still operating Club Runs.

Force H had left the shadow of The Rock on 17 May, bound on Operation LB. *Charybdis* and six destroyers[19] accompanied the carriers *Argus* and *Eagle*, the former to provide fighter cover, the latter carrying the last of the Spitfires held up at Gibraltar. Seventeen of these were flown off with some Albacores; six of the latter had to return, but the rest of the aircraft landed on Malta and the ships returned safely on the 19th, despite a torpedo attack on *Charybdis* by the Italian submarine *Mocenigo*.

The Spitfires needed supplementary spares and technical support for their maintenance and so, emerging from drydock on the Clyde, *Welshman* loaded her cargo and set out to make a second fast run. Arriving at Gibraltar at midnight on 1 June she unfortunately collided with a dockyard tug on berthing, damaging her bow and her port propeller. Her departure was delayed by the necessary repairs, and in the end she joined Operation JULIUS.

As this huge operation was being initiated by the passage of laden merchantmen from Britain to their respective Mediterranean departure points, Gibraltar and Alexandria, Force H pushed through more aircraft to Malta. Unseen by the patrolling Italian submarines *Brin* and *Malachite*, *Charybdis* and her destroyers[20] left Gibraltar with *Eagle*. Off the Balearic Islands at dawn on 3 June the carrier flew off thirty-one more Spitfires, four of which failed to reach Malta. This operation, code-named STYLE, was followed by SALIENT on the 7th. As Force H and *Eagle* steamed east, Catalina *M* of No. 202 Squadron caught the Italian submarine *Veniero* on the surface and destroyed her. The next day *Eagle* flew off thirty-two Spitfires, all of which arrived safely, whereupon the carrier, *Charybdis*, *Cairo* and their screen of six destroyers put about.[21] Ahead of them a second flying boat from No. 202 Squadron, Catalina *J*, sank the submarine *Zaffiro*.[22]

In Malta the Spitfires were most welcome; so too were the *Porpoise* from Alexandria and the *Clyde*, which arrived on the 1st and 8th respectively; but Leatham and Gort were now anticipating much-needed foodstuffs, medical stores and basic commodities such as boiler oil, kerosene and anti-aircraft ammunition. For his part, Churchill wanted Malta to be returned as quickly as possible to an advanced base from which attacks on Axis communications could be resumed. Only a complete replenishment of war *matériel* would enable the island to recover this status, and such was the purpose of the ships mustering at both ends of the Mediterranean under the code-designation Operation JULIUS. JULIUS was broken down into two naval operations, HARPOON from the west and VIGOROUS from the east, and they were scheduled for the nights of maximum darkness in the middle of June. Although they were to run simultaneously, their command structures were autonomous and their fates distinct.

Operation HARPOON began on 4 June when convoy WS19z left the Clyde. The masters of the merchantmen had orders for Freetown and were led to believe they were bound for Malta via the Cape. The secret was blown in the Blue Funnel liner *Troilus* when her owner's office instructed her chief steward to 'prepare for a short voyage', while the presence of a naval liaison officer and five signals staff on board each merchantmen, in addition to her naval gunners, was clear evidence that they were 'on special service'. That Malta was the destination could scarcely be kept confidential.

Escorted by the cruisers *Kenya* (flying the flag of Vice-Admiral A. Curteis) and *Liverpool*, with ten destroyers,[23] WS19z passed the Strait of Gibraltar under cover of darkness on 11/12 June, becoming convoy GM4. Here it was joined by a powerful naval escort and the American tanker *Kentucky*, whose passage from Philadelphia to Gibraltar had been her maiden voyage. The presence of this large 9,308-ton tanker carrying 14,100 tons of fuel oil and kerosene was a result of further assistance from President Roosevelt. Owned by the Texaco Company, she was on loan to the British Ministry of War Transport and largely British-manned. Two other Allied ships were present, the American-flagged *Chant*, a former Danish ship of 5,601 grt,[24] and the Dutch *Tanimbar* of 8,169 grt, a ship capable of only 13 knots, with a Dutch and Indonesian crew, and American Armed Guard gunners. The other ships in the convoy were the Hain Steamship Company's *Burdwan* (6,069 grt), the large 10,350-ton *Orari* owned by the New Zealand Shipping Company, and Holt's 7,422-ton *Troilus*, aboard which sailed the convoy commodore and his signals staff.

By 08.00 on 12 May, as the ships proceeded eastwards at 12 knots, the augmented escort was divided into several units, each with a prescribed task. Heavy cover as far as the Sicilian Narrows was provided by Force W under Curteis in *Kenya*, and included *Malaya* and *Eagle* with four Fulmars and sixteen Hurricanes, *Argus* with two Fulmars and eighteen Swordfish, *Liverpool*, *Charybdis*, and the destroyers *Onslow*, *Icarus*, *Escapade*, *Wishart*, *Westcott*, *Wrestler*, *Vidette* and *Antelope*.

Force X under Acting Captain C. Hardy in *Cairo*, with *Bedouin*, *Marne*, *Matchless*, *Ithuriel*, *Partridge*, *Blankney*, *Middleton*, *Badsworth*, *Kujawiak* and the minesweepers *Speedy*, *Hebe*, *Rye* and *Hythe*, was to form the close escort. To this were attached six motor launches for service in Malta.[25] Hardy's orders included instructions to avoid excessive fuel consumption or expenditure of ammunition, 'so that no extra ship need enter Malta'.[26] To this force was tacked *Welshman*, repaired and laden, with independent orders.

Additionally, the fleet oiler *Brown Ranger* and two corvettes, *Geranium* and *Coltsfoot*, formed Force Y which had already sailed to top up the short-legged escorts, especially the Hunts, and then cruise off Ibiza in order to refuel the returning ships after their dash through the Narrows. Patrolling to give warning of any approach by the Regia Marina were submarines *Unison*, *Unbroken*, *United* and *Safari*.

The concentration of British shipping in Alexandria and Gibraltar, especially the arrival of a large tanker like the *Kentucky*, left no doubt of British intentions and confirmed intelligence gleaned by the enemy from a source in Cairo, thought to be the American military attaché, whose radio transmissions were intercepted. Rome made a concerted attack to frustrate the replenishment of Malta: nine Italian submarines were sent to patrol off the Algerian coast, a further five took station between Malta and Lampedusa, five more cruised in the Ionian Sea east of Malta,[27] and a group of two Italian and six German torpedo-boats lay between Crete and Cyrenaica in what was intended to be a comprehensive ambush. Furthermore, surface units consisting of cruisers, destroyers and *MAS*-boats, plus a large number of aircraft, were mustered to cover the western basin.

On the evening of 12 June the HARPOON ships sighted a Spanish merchantman, and the following morning their air defences failed to drive off shadowing enemy aircraft which arrived overhead. These and a submarine reported the convoy, and because *Brown Ranger* was off the rendezvous delays occurred in the oiling operation, so that it was not completed until late. To save time, *Cairo* and eleven destroyers took fuel from the oiler, while three destroyers were topped up from *Liverpool*. Reports from their submarines kept the enemy aware of the convoy's progress through the night, and before dawn the *Uarsciek* launched torpedoes. These missed and the surfaced *Otaria*, following astern, was located by a Gibraltar-based Sunderland, depth-charged and damaged.

On the morning of 14 June, well within the range of Cagliari's aircraft, the convoy came under air attack. Radar indicated incoming enemy planes and one Italian SM79 was shot down by a fighter from *Eagle*. A light westerly stern wind blew over an azure sea; overhead a cloudless Mediterranean sky gave high visibility. The wind hampered aircraft taking off, particularly those from *Argus*, which did not possess enough speed to neu-tralise the tail wind. The carriers were acting to port of the convoy, *Eagle* with anti-aircraft support from *Cairo* and screened by *Wishart*, *Argus* astern of her with *Charybdis* and *Vidette*. The Hurricanes were expected to operate as high-level interceptors, the Fulmars to act at lower altitudes.

The convoy itself was deployed in two lines, *Kenya* leading the port and *Liverpool* the starboard column. The remaining destroy-ers and minesweepers formed an outer screen well clear of the merchantmen and carriers, free to fire outwards and inwards, while the motor launches stretched across the rear of the convoy to provide close-range fire support and act as rescue vessels. *Malaya* and *Welshman* brought up the rear.

Air attacks by about ten Italian CR42 fighter-bombers began at 10.30 and concentrated on *Argus* and her close escort. Two aero-planes were shot down by *Eagle*'s Fulmars and the attack fizzled out. The convoy's defences were probed again thirty minutes later when twenty-eight SM79s, escorted by Macchi fighters, carried out an attack combined with high-level bombing by Cants. This had been well planned, the SM79s splitting into groups as they rounded the convoy and coming in from the rear, heading for the starboard column. *Liverpool* was swinging to meet them when she was hit by a torpedo. *Tanimbar*, rear merchant ship in the column, was torpedoed in the same attack, caught fire, burnt furiously for seven minutes, then sank. Fifteen of her crew were picked up by *ML462*, a further sixteen by *Rye*.

Curteis ordered an emergency turn as the second wave of Italian planes made for the port column; they dropped their torpedoes prematurely and scored no hits. Meanwhile the Cants at 10,000 feet dropped their bombs on the carriers and the foundering *Tanimbar*. Between them, the British fighters and the ships shot down three torpedo-bombers and three fighters, but the loss of the Dutch cargo-ship and the disablement of *Liverpool* in the first mature attack prompted Captain Rushbrooke of the *Eagle* to consider the air defence by the combined carriers a 'most inadequate measure', for three British aircraft had been lost, one to 'friendly' fire.

As the attack ended about noon *Liverpool* was listing badly, having been hit in the engine room. Only one shaft was operational and she could make no more than 4 knots, so she was ordered back to Gibraltar, towed by *Anthony* and escorted by *Westcott*. Attacked by air, the ships fought off their tormentors and, although the tow parted and had to be reconnected, the arrival of tugs from Gibraltar on the late afternoon of the 15th allowed *Anthony* to join the anti-submarine screen. This was further helped by the arrival of two corvettes, *Jonquil* and *Spiraea*, on the 16th, and a shadowing Italian submarine was driven off. *Liverpool* arrived in Gibraltar on the evening of 17 June; her station in the convoy was taken by *Welshman*.

The Regia Aeronautica had misguidedly allowed itself to be drawn off into attacks on the damaged cruiser, and the convoy enjoyed a respite until the evening, when it came within range of the Luftwaffe's Sicilian airfields. At 18.20 ten Ju88s dropped from 10,000 to 6,000 feet before attacking out of the sun. 'It was very difficult to see these', reported Curteis, 'till they had reached the bombing position, and gunfire was ineffective.'[28] *Argus* suffered a bomb-burst under her bow, and a Fulmar was shot down, but the Germans had no other successes, although the action was spirited.

As the sun westered Captain Friedberger hauled *Welshman* out of her station and cracked on speed, heading as before for the coast. Gellatly, her navigating officer, repeated his previous display of masterly blind pilotage, and the minelayer entered

Grand Harbour at 07.30 on 15 June. The difference from
Welshman's previous arrival, under smoke and an air battle,
struck Friedberger: 'In spite of a current air-raid warning, the
harbour was alive with steamboats and *dghaisas*, and the tug
Robust was ready to meet us, newly painted in her gay Maltese
colours.' Unloading began at once, the discharge of the Merlin
engines *Welshman* carried being facilitated by special trolleys
built during the ship's repair period in Scotstoun. Calling on
Leatham, Friedberger was asked how long it would be before he
was ready to sail, as the convoy was in trouble and he was
required to help. The discharging was galvanised and, quickly
emptied, the ship was hauled over to Canteen Wharf for bunkering and sailed at 13.30.

The convoy was in trouble almost immediately *Welshman* had
raced off. Shortly after 20.00, heavy air forces arrived. Sixteen
SM79 torpedo-bombers flew in low from the north-east and
crossed astern of the convoy out of range. As they positioned to
attack, ten Ju88s ran in from the east, flying the length of the
convoy and dropping their bomb loads without effect but near-
missing *Troilus*, which shook violently, whereupon Ju87 Stukas
dive-bombed the port flank, narrowly missing *Icarus* and
Wrestler. The arrival of the Stukas entirely distracted the anti-
aircraft gunnery from the torpedo-bombers, reported Armstrong
of the *Onslow*, and these now bore in as Curteis turned the
convoy to comb the anticipated torpedo tracks.

Meanwhile *Malaya*, *Argus*, *Charybdis* and *Vidette* had fallen
astern, partly due to the constraints of operating aircraft, but also
because *Malaya* had sighted a periscope. A submarine, in fact the
Alagi, had been spotted and attacked by *Middleton* and two other
destroyers, but the 'noise' created by the numerous wakes in the
area prevented a sonic contact and the submarine dived, to reap-
pear momentarily close to the bulk of *Malaya*. Captain Waller
turned the battleship under full helm and flashed a signal to
Speedy as she swung towards the little minesweeper. Lieutenant-
Commander Doram had seen *Middleton* dropping depth charges
and he now obtained a sonar contact and attacked while maintaining anti-aircraft fire.[29]

That the convoy survived this co-ordinated onslaught has to
be attributed to Curteis's cool handling of the ships: it was the
manoeuvring rather than the anti-aircraft gunnery or fighter

cover which preserved it. Moreover, the preoccupation of the British fighters with those of the enemy exposed the heart of the operation, the five remaining merchantmen, which maintained station perfectly. It cost the fighters dear, however, for three more aircraft were lost, one in air combat, one to the fire of *Troilus* and *ML135*, and one on landing down-wind.

As the enemy drew off, the convoy, now to the north of Bizerta, approached the Narrows, and at 21.00 Beaufighters from Malta arrived overhead. Half an hour later Curteis detached with Force W and turned to the west, leaving Hardy in *Cairo* with Force X to carry on. Convoy GM4 now formed line ahead. Aboard *Orari*, Captain Nelson Rice viewed Curteis's departure with 'surprise and some apprehension ... We didn't like this a bit, just as we were entering bomb alley, and the enemy took advantage of the changed situation by plastering us as dusk fell ... '

As the upperworks of *Malaya* dropped over the western horizon against the sunset, eight Ju88s flew out of the dusk to the east, dropping bombs on the convoy silhouetted against the afterglow. None of these hit, while a Beaufighter shot one Ju88 down, the ships' gunfire a second. After the Germans withdrew, night fell. During the hours of darkness the convoy passed the Skerki Bank, slipped inside Zembra Island and coasted round Cape Bon as far south as Kelibia, before heading south-east for Malta at a mean speed of 12 knots.

Although *Tanimbar* was lost and *Liverpool* wounded, the enemy's plans had been largely frustrated; the air attacks had borne little comparison with Lehrgeschwader 1's attack on Poland's destroyers, while the performance of the Italian submarines had been, as usual, half-hearted. Comando Supremo in Rome had, however, a further card to play. At 21.00 on the 14th the 7th Division of the Regia Marina had left Palermo under the command of Ammiraglio di Divisione da Zara, while two cruisers and five destroyers which left Cagliari on the evening of the 13th had been reported and unsuccessfully attacked by the watching *Unison*, thereafter passing *Safari*, which was too far off to attack. Wellingtons were sent from Malta and located Da Zara at 02.55 eastward-bound off Cape San Vito, but failed to attack because of a lack of flares. Da Zara was next observed in Palermo, but he was not seen heading west for Marittimo at sunset on the 14th, and Leatham wrongly, if reasonably, concluded that he would head east from Palermo, pass the Strait of Messina and join the main Italian battle-fleet which had left Taranto to intercept the British ships approaching Malta from Alexandria as the VIGOROUS component of the overall operation. Air reconnaissance was stepped up and Albacores prepared to strike as soon as the 7th Division debouched into the Ionian Sea. Curteis, now heading west, was also aware of Da Zara's first movement, and came to the same erroneous conclusion as Leatham. In fact the Italian vice-admiral was intending to intercept the HARPOON ships and *should* have been assisted by Italian *MAS*-boats, though in the event these remained at Pantelleria.

As the Italian ships rounded the westernmost point of Sicily and headed south two of the destroyers, *Zeno* and *Gioberti*, put back with engine trouble. Da Zara's squadron now consisted of the light cruisers *Eugenio di Savoia* and *Raimondo Montecuccoli*, with the destroyers *Ascari*, *Vivaldi*, *Malocello* and *Premuda* (a captured Yugoslav warship).

Dawn broke on 15 June 1942 with a light breeze blowing from the west ruffling the deep-blue sea. Once again visibility was good, and Pantelleria lay almost abeam to port of the convoy. At 06.20 a Beaufighter arriving from Malta to provide air cover overhead sighted the approaching Italians fifteen miles away and signalled their presence to *Cairo*. Hardy reformed the merchantmen into two columns, disposing the fleet destroyers to starboard and the Hunts to port, with the minesweepers and motor launches astern. A little later the superstructures of the Italian cruisers could be seen south of Pantelleria against the dawn. Broad on the convoy's port bow, they were on a converging course but at such a speed as to draw their bearing further ahead.

It was quite clear to Hardy that he was out-gunned, and he turned GM4 away and made smoke, heading for the neutral water of Tunisia. His 'immediate intention was to gain time and to fight a delaying action in the hope that an air striking force could be sent from Malta'. Ten minutes later the 6-inch guns of *Raimondo Montecuccoli* and *Eugenio di Savoia* opened fire at an extreme range of ten miles, straddling *Cairo* and badly shaking her. Meanwhile Commander Scurfield gathered the fleet destroyers astern of *Bedouin* and led them to attack. Racing through the water, *Partridge* followed, then *Ithuriel* and *Marne*, with *Matchless* working up to 32 knots to get into her station.

Though out of range, *Bedouin* and *Partridge* opened fire, their guns at maximum elevation as they dashed at the enemy with the gallantry expected of the Royal Navy's destroyers. *Bedouin* began to take punishment. Her bridge was hit and the mast and radio aerials were shot away. Her signals staff were shot to pieces, while on the iron deck the torpedo-officer preparing his tubes was wounded; his assistant lay dead beside him. Writing later to his wife from prison camp, Scurfield described his situation: 'The splendid *Bedouin* was forging ahead and closing the gap minute by minute ... At 06.50 the [gunnery] director was hit ... and I felt in my bones that she would not go much further. So ... when the range had come down to 5,000 yards – tracer was being fired at us by the enemy's close-range weapons – [I] turned the ship to starboard. During the turn we were hit several times, but the torpedoes were fired when the sights came on. [Then ...] the ship came to a standstill.'

It was 07.00. Both *Bedouin* and *Partridge* had been stopped in their tracks by direct hits, and the attack passed to Lieutenant-Commander D. Maitland-Makgill-Crichton in *Ithuriel*. This officer had held his fire until the range was down to seven miles, and succeeded in hitting one of the cruisers just before *Ithuriel* passed *Bedouin*. Despite his success Da Zara was fearful of the British torpedoes and edged away, making smoke and zigzagging to frustrate the British gunlaying. Though his ships had expended a high proportion of their armour-piercing shells, these often passed undetonated through the light scantlings of the British destroyers. It was some consolation to them. 'We were at least masters of the battlefield,' Scurfield wrote later.[30]

As they approached, *Marne* and *Matchless* also opened fire, exchanging shot with two of the Italian destroyers, *Vivaldi* and *Malocello*. A shell hit the engine room of the *Ugolino Vivaldi*, though she had fired two torpedoes, and this persuaded Da Zara to detach his destroyers, so that they retreated to the north. In due course *Vivaldi* was towed into Pantelleria. Meanwhile, the two British destroyers pressed on after the enemy cruisers.

A little earlier Hardy, who had retired the convoy under smoke, gathered the Hunts *Blankney*, *Middleton*, *Badsworth* and *Kujawiak* and headed after the enemy, exchanging fire with the retiring Italian destroyers as they passed at extreme range. At about 07.00 Hardy was also again under fire. Da Zara's cruisers were now using their forward turrets against *Cairo* and the

Hunts, the after pairs against *Ithuriel*, *Matchless* and *Marne*. As an AA cruiser *Cairo* only possessed 4-inch guns, and Hardy decided that in view of this and the incapacity of *Bedouin* and *Partridge*, he must order *Ithuriel* to join him. Maitland-Makgill-Crichton turned towards Hardy in conformity to this order immediately after hitting one of the cruisers, leaving *Marne* and *Matchless* to engage the enemy for a further half an hour. No more hits were gained by either side and at about 07.45 the Italian cruisers, having slowly turned towards the south, swung round to the north, Da Zara having realised that by attacking, Force X was driving him away from the convoy.

Hardy concentrated all his ships and turned inside the Italians, falling back on the convoy, which was now heading east again, having come under air attack by a skein of Ju88s. Without the anti-aircraft fire of the Hunts, these had soon bombed the *Chant* and near-missed *Kentucky*. *Chant* listed badly and was ablaze as she sheered out of line and headed for *Orari* on her port side – fortunately Captain Rice 'stood not upon the order of our going and thanked the powers for that extra touch of speed *Orari* [could] produce in a tight corner'. However, it was soon clear that *Chant* was sinking and her crew abandoned her, to be picked up by *Rye*, *ML135* and *ML462*.

The tanker *Kentucky*'s main steam supply pipe was fractured and she was thereby immobilised, though otherwise intact. At Gibraltar her master had ordered the starboard anchor hung off in the hawse pipe, so her cable was already cleared for towing and she was soon in the charge of *Hebe*, Mowatt being determined, as were *Kentucky*'s master and his liaison officer, to bring in her vital cargo. *Rye* stood by as air guard. These three were soon left behind the convoy, not far from the 'terrific pall of fire and smoke that was visible for most of the day', arising from *Chant*'s oil fuel, which burned on the surface above her for many hours.

The convoy commodore, Commander Pilditch aboard *Troilus*, now decided that he must head for increased air cover, and at 07.50 turned the ships east again. Although the gunfire of the defending ships had shot down one of the Junkers, without the Hunts and with most of the minesweepers mopping up astern, his situation was unenviable. Beyond the welcome sight of the returning *Cairo* and her consorts were the Italian cruisers, still firing at Hardy's reduced force. At 08.40 Hardy ordered the convoy to execute an eight-point turn and reverse its course, laying smoke across its retreating wake. About ten minutes later Da Zara, having lost a float-plane to *Cairo*'s guns and with a pair of Beaufighters briefly overhead, turned north-east and, still firing at the British ships with his after turrets as he withdrew, succeeded in hitting *Cairo*, though the shell failed to explode.

As Hardy rejoined the convoy he ordered *Ithuriel* to assist the tow of *Kentucky*. It was now 10.30 and GM4 was heading east again, escorted by Spitfires which engaged and shot down a few enemy bombers as they approached. However, this exhausted the fighters' fuel and they withdrew, leaving the exposed convoy to the mercies of the next wave of enemy aircraft. A mixed force of ten Ju88s and Ju87s came in, the former bombing from high altitude as well as dive-bombing alongside the intimidating Stukas. Gunfire dispatched one and the tardy Spitfires arrived and shot down a second, but not before the *Burdwan* was seriously damaged by a near-miss and came slowly to a halt. Hardy was now confronted with a major problem. He was by no means certain he had seen the last of Da Zara and he had insufficient resources to cover *Kentucky*, now occupying three of his remaining serviceable escorts. He was therefore compelled to come to a disagreeable conclusion, and reluctantly ordered *Burdwan* and *Kentucky* sunk, in an attempt to get the two remaining ships into Grand Harbour.

At about 10.00 *Ithuriel* had taken a wire from *Kentucky*'s port quarter to assist steering, but a little later she let go and the naval liaison officer in the tanker, Lieutenant Huntley, RNVR, heard that *Cairo* had 'apparently ordered *Hebe* to sink *Kentucky*'. Mowatt ordered her abandoned and as *Rye* ran alongside to remove her crew, Huntley dumped his confidential books and stripped *Kentucky*'s bridge Oerlikon of its barrel and passed it with some ammunition across to *Rye*.

The consequences of *Kentucky*'s loss and of the fact that she was deliberately abandoned and sunk were significant both for Malta and for Anglo-American relations, but Hardy's decision was one of those brutal choices war presents. He would have been damned either way, and with a force entirely inadequate to defend even half a dozen merchantmen against such odds he had little time to consider matters, and no alternative. On receipt of her instruction *Hebe* began to cast off her tow, joined *Rye* in picking up the tanker's crew, and prepared to torpedo her while *Badsworth* attended *Burdwan*.

A further dive-bombing took place at 13.15. Of the dozen enemy aircraft attacking, one was shot out of the sky and a further two were engaged and sent down by the relieving Spitfires which arrived at the end of the attack. As convoy GM4 approached Malta, increasing numbers of Spitfires appeared, for the air-controllers in the plotting room at Lascaris were acutely aware of its predicament, and *Welshman* was even then singling up to leave Canteen Wharf. The news that Da Zara's division had appeared south of Sicily had long since prompted a response from Leatham. The Fleet Air Arm striking force readied to attack to the north was diverted to the west, and Lieutenant-Commander Roe led his four Albacores with an escort of two RAF Beaufighters to nail the cruisers. He located them at 10.30, twelve miles south of Pantelleria in contact with their destroyers, which were attempting to take the damaged *Vivaldi* in tow. The Albacores' torpedoes missed their targets and it was now the turn of Da Zara to strike back. Learning from air reports of the damaged stragglers astern of GM4, he left *Vivaldi* with *Malocello* and *Premuda* and turned south again.

These stragglers consisted of *Hebe* and *Badsworth*, which were still dealing with *Kentucky* and *Burdwan*, and the *Bedouin* and *Partridge*. At 12.55 the approaching predators were seen from *Hebe*. She had failed to sink *Kentucky* while *Badsworth*, which had not yet completed the sinking of *Burdwan*, was still picking up her crew from their boats. Both ships made off, though the slower *Hebe* was inexorably overtaken. Half an hour later she was engaged by the Italians, who succeeded in hitting her at 13.41. Receiving Mowatt's report, Hardy ordered *Ithuriel*, *Marne* and *Matchless* to join him and led off to engage the Italians a second time. On the appearance of the indefatigable British destroyers Da Zara turned away again, towards two more likely victims to the west. Hardy had to pull back to the convoy, already fifteen miles astern of him, leaving Da Zara to fall first upon *Burdwan*. The transport was finally sunk by gunfire from *Ascari*, after which *Oriani* dispatched *Kentucky* with a torpedo. Da Zara then closed what he thought was a third ship, but he was to be disappointed; *Chant* had sunk long since, and only her fuel remained, burning fiercely as it rose to the surface from the ruptured hull on the seabed below.

It was now the turn of *Bedouin*, which since 10.00 had been under the tow of *Partridge*, to attract the enemy. *Partridge* was under way again less than an hour after being temporarily disabled, although Lieutenant Commander W. Hawkins had had to drive off two of Da Zara's retreating destroyers before proceeding with the tow. The two British ships were making 8 knots to the west, since 'in order not to saddle Malta with another crock' Scurfield hoped to land the wounded in Tunisia and, 'one way or another', make Gibraltar. By 11.45 they had almost fortuitously rejoined the convoy as it made its westward leg, and Scurfield was optimistic about getting one engine going. Shortly afterwards the convoy drew away again to the east and so, with all guns manned and ready, Scurfield's men tried to repair their damaged steering and alleviate the strain on *Partridge*. At 13.00 their luck ran out with the approach of Stukas. Scurfield, about to bury his dead, ordered the tow slipped, and at 13.20 the Italian destroyers reappeared in company with the distant cruisers. Hawkins laid smoke round the helpless *Bedouin*, then gallantly stood away to draw the enemy's fire. In this he was successful, *Partridge* being straddled at long range, but his intention of returning to *Bedouin* was foiled when at 14.25 a Savoia Marchetti torpedoed her, and she started to founder. *Bedouin*'s gunner shot down their assailant, but the ship was doomed, and within a few minutes she had slipped beneath the sea – ironically, for after a struggle, her engineering staff had finally coaxed her into motion. Her company abandoned her and remained, 'an oily huddle', slowly chilling down with hypothermia. At dawn a German aircraft spotted them and dropped a flare, and that evening an Italian seaplane, 'all spotlessly white', rescued ten men. Later a small hospital ship arrived and those who had survived having been dive-bombed by four Cant CR42s were taken aboard, to become prisoners-of-war.

Partridge had remained under fire as Italian aircraft overhead spotted for their cruisers, but Da Zara now left the British destroyer to them and withdrew. In the confusion he had himself come under attack by German aircraft.[31] German bombers also near-missed *Partridge*, jamming her steering gear, so that she circled for an hour while her artificers fought to free it. Hawkins watched with chagrin as Italian destroyers circled *Bedouin*'s last position. 'It is deeply regretted', he reported, 'that even if the ship could not be saved, the *Bedouin*'s commanding officer and her ship's company could not be rescued by a British warship.' Hawkins crept west, hoping to rectify his defects in neutral waters. Leatham ordered him to Gibraltar where, remarkably, he arrived on 17 June.

During this unhappy episode Leatham had prepared a second strike force to attack Da Zara. Having failed to locate him on the outward flight, on the way back to Malta Leatham's force found the Italian squadron off Pantelleria at 17.00. By now Da Zara had an air escort, and although the Albacores attacked, one of the three biplanes was shot down and no torpedoes hit home. The 7th Division and its air support had had the opportunity to destroy GM4; but at 20.45 that evening *Unbroken*, lying northwest of Marittimo, spotted Da Zara retiring ingloriously to Palermo at high speed. Once again the Regia Marina had failed to achieve a complete victory.

Hardy rejoined the shattered remnant of convoy GM4 at 15.30, and two hours later *Welshman* arrived. Two air attacks had been defeated during the afternoon and at 19.10 a third developed, but despite their best endeavours the twelve bombers failed to hit *Troilus*, *Matchless* or *Welshman*. Another attack at 20.40 was driven off by gunfire and the patrolling Spitfires. By now sunset was approaching and the coast of Malta with the off-lying bulk of Filfla was in sight. Spirits in the surviving ships began to rise.

It had not been intended that Hardy's Force X should enter Grand Harbour – *Brown Ranger* was to top the ships up as they cleared the Narrows westbound next day – but such had been the expenditure of ammunition that, in concert with Leatham, a tired Hardy arranged for all ships to enter the harbour and rearm. It was the innocent prelude to further misfortune.

In the preceding months the 3rd *Schnellboote* Flotilla had sown 24 minefields in the approaches to Grand Harbour. The magnetic mines tended to explode spontaneously, and the Germans had had the leisure to replace them with contact mines. The minesweeping forces at Valletta had been all but annihilated in the bombardment, and so it had become customary to sweep individual ships and convoys in and out of the port; even this could not prevent disasters such as the loss of *Olympus*, however, and measures such as *Welshman*'s coasting under the guidance of *Beryl* were not practicable for a convoy. To make up for the losses at Valletta, the 17th Minesweeping Flotilla and motor launches of the 3rd M/L Flotilla had been tagged on to the escort of GM4; but it still remained for them to get the ships inside Grand Harbour on the night of 15/16 June.

As the plan was initially conceived, the minesweepers under Lieutenant-Commander Doram would deploy as the convoy approached. *Speedy, Rye, Hebe* and *Hythe* should have swept ahead of GM4, while launches from Valletta anchored as sea-marks. However, because of *Welshman's* second arrival, and the movements of the supply submarines, a small channel was to be swept by local resources, a proceeding made feasible by the *Schnellboote* squadron's mid May redeployment to North Africa, though compromised by the loss of the auxiliary minesweepers *St Angelo* and *Eddy* in late May. The deficiency was made good in part by fitting the last serviceable motor launch, *ML126,* and the anti-submarine trawler *Beryl* as minesweepers, the swept channel being dan-buoyed by a picket boat. Other small craft – the drifters *Trusty Star* and *Justified,* the whaler *Swona* and the tug *Robust* – were also converted, though *Trusty Star* was soon lost to a mine. By these means a channel half a mile wide had been swept three miles to seaward by 11 June, but it did not reach the outer limit, the 100-fathom isobath off Benghisa Point on Malta's south-east extremity. Instead, in the time available *ML126,* with its attendant picket boat, was to sweep a very narrow channel out to this point, a task she had completed by 14 June. On her arrival on the 15th, *Welshman* again followed the inshore route, while *ML126* carried out another sweep of the narrow extension of the standard channel; this was again cleared by *Beryl, Robust* and *Swona* prior to the departure of *Welshman* when she sailed to Hardy's relief at 14.00. In the late afternoon, as the HARPOON ships approached, *Beryl, Justified* and *Robust* put to sea to act as marks, but because of the action the convoy was late. Moreover, although in giving Hardy permission to enter Grand Harbour Leatham had told him to follow the mine-sweepers, he had overlooked the fact that since it had not origin-ally been intended that Force X should enter the harbour, Hardy had no way of fully understanding the constraints implicit in such permission.

At 21.30, after a prolonged day, Doram's minesweepers moved ahead into echelon and prepared their gear. At 23.39 they began sweeping, but thanks to a coding error in the signal sent to them they actually began work 4.75 miles to the *east* of the entrance to the narrow channel swept by *ML126*, into which the leading and most vulnerable minesweeper, *Speedy*, should now have passed. Moreover, they then headed north, not north-east towards the *Justified*.

Cairo was six miles south of Benghisa Point at the entrance of the narrow channel long after dark and headed north-east, expecting to catch sight of Doram's minesweepers close ahead. Hardy, however, could only see *Rye*, 'steering to starboard of the proper course'. At this time the motor launches from Gibraltar increased speed and overtook the convoy to take station ahead of Doram and stream their own sweeping gear, but failed to locate *Speedy* in the darkness. From their wakes they were taken for enemy torpedo-boats, and ineffectively fired upon by shore batteries. The reports of 'enemy MTBs' compounded an already confusing situation, in which Hardy seems to have located the light of *M126* and led the convoy toward it at 12 knots. This effectively cut the corner of the narrow swept channel along its inshore margin, past Delimara Point and perilously close to the minefield. Hardy's *Cairo* was followed by *Troilus*, *Orari* and *Welshman*, the destroyers in turn following in two flanking columns on their quarters – a formation asking for trouble.

Off the entrance to Marsaxlokk the commanding officers of the motor launches, casting about aimlessly for the minesweepers after being shot at from the shore, saw the wakes of the destroyers and finally tagged on the rear. Seeing the broad approach of large ships, *Justified* and *ML126* moved aside to avoid being run down; the former blew up almost immediately on a mine detonation, with the loss of three of her Maltese crew.

Spotting the entrance ahead, Hardy now turned and led the centre column safely towards the open boom tucked behind the mole, round which a sharp turn had to be made. Suddenly, at 01.10, *Badsworth* detonated a mine, then the Polish-manned Hunt *Kujawiak* blew up a second and *Matchless* a third, in a rapid trio of concussions.

Off the mole *Cairo* pulled aside, allowing *Troilus* to approach the entrance first, a task made difficult for the tired men 'owing to searchlights. It was fortunate that [Pilditch had] ... considerable local knowledge. But even so the lack of knowledge about booms was worrying.'[32] *Troilus*'s master, Captain W. Harrison, trained since his days as a midshipman to value his Blue Funnel liner as if she were his own property, had streamed his ship's paravanes, and *Troilus* consequently entered Grand Harbour unscathed. Astern of her *Orari* began to turn to starboard and round the mole in her wake. Captain Rice did not consider the precaution of streaming paravanes to be necessary, probably because he assumed the channel to have been swept in accordance with the operational plan. Unfortunately *Orari* detonated a mine (thought to have been cut free by *Troilus*'s gear); it blew a hole in No. 4 Hold, the only space in the ship not containing ammunition or inflammable fuel. A quantity of foodstuffs was spoiled as *Orari* rapidly settled until her stern was well down, fouling the boom as she passed it. Nevertheless, she was taken up the harbour and moored astern of the wrecked *Talabot*, Captain Rice skilfully handling his crippled ship without the benefit of a pilot or tugs.[33]

Even at that late hour, people lined the ramparts to cheer the ships in as the rest of Force X entered harbour. Meanwhile the tugs *Robust*, *Carbine*, *Supply* and *Lady Strickland* went to the assistance of the mined destroyers. *Matchless* and *Badsworth* were hauled into the dockyard by morning, but *Kujawiak* sank at 02.10, some three miles east of the mole; Commander Lichodziejewski and his exiled sailors had lost their only home.

Outside, *Rye* had become separated from her sisters. She hit a mine without detonating it and afterwards swept her way into Valletta at 03.00 with one motor launch in company, apparently unaware that the ships she had followed in were destroyers and not, as her commanding officer supposed, her own consorts. By 02.00 the remnants of the convoy were safe and an order was sent to the minesweepers to cease operations. They anchored, it appears, off Delimara Point, to be led in through the narrow channel next morning by *Swona*; on weighing, however, *Hebe* struck a mine and was towed in by the others. Thus ended a unfortunate incident resulting from a miscoded signal.[34]

An inquiry was ordered by Leatham and held in Valletta on Friday, 26 June. It was chaired by Hutchinson, late of *Breconshire*, and the captain's report mentions difficulties in coming to a conclusion arising from the 'loss overboard' of cypher files, the dumping of confidential books, and the lack of experience at sweeping of some of the commanding officers.[35] Evidence as to visibility suggested that 'It was a clear dark night and ...

[Mowlam of *Matchless*] could see the merchant ships the whole time', but Pilditch 'could just see *Cairo* through [his] glasses at about half a mile … ' One of the young volunteer reserve commanders of a minesweeper, who had had two hours' practical training in sweeping at Gibraltar, said 'the visibility was not good', which was quite possible, offshore in a patch of mist. The senior officer of the 17th Minesweeping Flotilla, Lieutenant-Commander Doram, complained of a lack of detailed information at his briefing at Gibraltar, a point of view echoed by his colleagues.

Hutchinson, not then aware of the error in coding, concluded there was some navigational confusion, adding that in the sailing orders issued to sweepers and motor launches there appeared to be no evidence 'of the express purpose for which they were put into the convoy – namely to sweep the convoy in.'

Unacknowledged, but underlying this sorry business, was the fact that all concerned were approaching exhaustion.

Cairo, *Welshman* and the four seaworthy destroyers *Ithuriel*, *Marne*, *Blankney* and *Middleton* left Malta that evening and were shadowed from daylight on the 17th as they skirted Cape Bon, but they were west of Galita before they were attacked by German Ju88s that evening. These concentrated on *Ithuriel*, whose commanding officer reported the period as a 'struggle for existence'. Near-misses caused minor leaks, but *Cairo* dispatched one of their tormentors before the attacks petered out as Hardy rejoined Curteis at 20.17 north of Bône. In the interim Curteis had cruised west of Sardinia and had been shadowed and attacked. *Eagle*'s Hurricanes had driven off the enemy, and in due course Curteis had sent the *Malaya*, the carriers and the destroyers on to Gibraltar, to remain cruising on the rendezvous in *Kenya* with *Charybdis* in company from the forenoon of the 16th until the next noon, when he stood east again to meet Hardy. Thereafter the weary ships steamed west to rendezvous with Force Y and take fuel. The oiler and her two corvettes had cruised 'for some six days or more unmolested across the enemy submarine patrol areas', a fact that appeared to Captain Russell of *Kenya* to be entirely 'the fault of the enemy'; in fact 'the corvettes [had] fired on enemy aircraft at medium range on three occasions and enjoyed themselves'.[36] Moreover, the Italian submarine *Giada* had attempted to torpedo the *Brown Ranger*, but had failed, being driven off by the approach of *Coltsfoot* which had detected her on radar.

Hardy and Curteis entered Gibraltar at dawn on 19 June.

Rigging their cargo gear in Grand Harbour, *Troilus* and *Orari* had begun to discharge their cargoes before daylight on the 16th and were hard at it when Lord Gort and Vice-Admiral Leatham visited them that morning. 'Both [Gort and Leatham] were very profuse with their congratulations and thanks,' Rice reported 'This proved true of everyone we came into contact with and it made us feel that we had done something really worthwhile. When we saw the condition of the island and harbour we realised what they had been through … ' Rice derived his greatest pleasure from Pilditch's praise of *Orari's* station-keeping.

The crew of *Troilus* 'were worn out by the two days' harassing by the enemy … nevertheless, in spite of this they did all they could before turning in.' It was, however, late afternoon before *Troilus's* copious derricks were all topped-up, allowing two gangs of men to work at each hatch. Smoke was raised from the ramparts surrounding the French Creek so that the discharge could continue when under air raid. In five days the two ships were emptied of a total of 13,552 tons. Four hundred tons had been spoiled by the flooding of *Orari*, and some coal was left aboard to trim her for repairs.[37]

Supervised by the ubiquitous Hutchinson, whose experience in *Breconshire* had made him almost as much an expert in cargo work as a Holt's master, the excellence of the discharge on this occasion was a consequence of careful preparations made under the code-name BRASSO, designed for the reception of *all* the ships of both the HARPOON *and* the VIGOROUS operations, and to avoid the fate of the cargoes brought in by *Pampas* and *Talabot*. Operation BRASSO provided 500 servicemen and 400 Maltese for each of two shifts, to 'get the cargo out of the ships and to remove the bulk of it at once to safe dumps' two and half miles away. In the event, because of the paucity of arrivals 'the whole plan was recast'.[38] *Troilus* in No. 5 Dock was discharged by servicemen, starting at 04.15 on the 16th; *Orari*, near No. 5 Berth, began breaking bulk an hour later with Maltese labour, who did 'exceptionally good work.'

Thereafter the two cargo-liners were subjected to the same exposure as their predecessors while they waited for a convoy to return. *Orari* was put in dock, but the caisson was so damaged that the dock could not be emptied, and she had to be careened by ballasting and shifting coal so that a patch could be welded on the hole in No. 4 Hold.

Also at work outside Grand Harbour was the 17th Mine-sweeping Flotilla, clearing a proper channel from the mole out to deep water and enduring machine-gun attacks by Me109s, as on 28 June, for instance, when they swept and destroyed no fewer than nineteen mines.[39] The work was completed by 12 July, ready for *Welshman* to enter again on her third run on the 16th. Ten days later the submarine *Unbroken* arrived to resume offensive operations. Malta was again able to take up her task as a naval base, but only just. She was still desperately in need of food, for the ships of Operation VIGOROUS from Alexandria had failed to materialise.

'An imperial balls-up'

(Operation VIGOROUS and Convoy MW11)

OPERATION VIGOROUS WAS the counter-poising element of Operation JULIUS; mounted from the eastern Mediterranean, it possessed even more strategic complexities than its twin from Gibraltar, Operation HARPOON. It involved most of the Mediterranean Fleet as close or distant escort to the comparatively large convoy of laden merchantmen which had made the long haul round the Cape in answer to the pleas of General Dobbie.[1] The safe arrival of this convoy would not only provide Malta with a significant respite from her travails but score a valuable psychological victory over the enemy, since whoever triumphed in the dispute over its passage would have effective mastery over the eastern Mediterranean.

In contrast with Operation MG1 and the passage of MW10 under cloudy skies, VIGOROUS went through at the height of summer, within a fortnight of the solstice. As if to further mark the difference, the Mediterranean Fleet, already deprived of the guiding genius of Cunningham, was not merely still bereft of a capital ship or carrier but had been beefed up by odd units on loan from the Eastern Fleet, resulting in a collection of ships which inevitably lacked that co-ordination of enterprise that, throughout the centuries-old tradition of the British naval service, had formed the cornerstone of a fighting fleet in an operational theatre.

The appointment of Admiral Harwood as the new naval Commander-in-Chief had coincided with that of a new senior air officer, Air Marshal Tedder. Even had Harwood been of equal ability to Cunningham, common sense ought to have postponed his appointment until after VIGOROUS. However, the die was cast, and the untimely change was made at the insistence of Churchill and A.V. Alexander, the First Lord of the Admiralty, who overrode complaints of Harwood's shortcomings.

In Harwood, Tedder and their staff, the assumption that air superiority over Malta had been achieved with the safe arrival of *Wasp*'s second consignment of Spitfires had bred an opinion that, provided the merchant ships could be delivered within a reasonable distance of Malta and under her air cover, they would be safe. This notion rested comfortably with Harwood, since it neutralised any fears arising from the savage attrition of the ships of MW10 during the final hundred miles of their passage. It may well be that this apparent complacency derived from a genuine belief that British air supremacy over Malta was absolute, but it may also be attributed in part to the apparently greater difficulties it was anticipated the VIGOROUS ships would endure in the first part of the passage, and it was with these Harwood was wrestling. It was sensibly assumed that during this phase of the operation, the enemy would attack the convoy by air and sea; and also, but with less prudence than experience confirmed, that the combined air-defences of the ships would prove adequate to counter such attack. There remained, then, the conundrum of the Regia Marina, of which contemporary opinion varied as to its potence, and to oppose which Harwood concerted a defensive plan with Air Marshal Tedder, using submarines and aircraft. The former were to be pulled back from their usual forward stations into the central basin, between Crete and Malta; they would surface during the convoy's passage and run parallel to the convoy's track to the north, providing a picket line with complete freedom of action to intercept an enemy force. After the safe arrival of the convoy, some would form a similar line to protect the returning ships, others would close up to the Italian ports in order to catch returning Italian warships.[2]

Air strikes were to be made by a force of forty-odd aircraft which would act against any sortie by Italian capital ships attempting to interfere with the passage of the VIGOROUS convoy. Malta-based Beaufighters, Beauforts and Wellingtons, more Beauforts from Egypt, and some American Liberators from the Suez area were detailed for the task. The Beauforts at Malta consisted of aircraft of No. 217 Squadron *en route* for Ceylon but held at Malta to cover VIGOROUS. Fuel for these additional aircraft had been brought in by the submarines on their Magic Carpet runs. Given the dispersal of the air groups involved, it was an ambitious plan, relying heavily upon a high degree of co-ordination, but without the proper resources to guarantee success. Nevertheless, to better handle matters, Harwood and Tedder were headquartered in a special combined operational control room at the Royal Air Force's Naval Co-operation Group base at Alexandria. This somewhat divorced Harwood from his hard-pressed fleet and marked a change of command style driven by perceived necessity, but which probably resonated among the staff as something less than satisfactory. Operational command of the increasingly exiguous collection of ships involved was therefore left to Vian, who, despite a paper strength greater than he had had under him during MG1, afterwards claimed to have had no confidence in the plan. Among the ships assembling under Vian's flag was one representing a singular stratagem: Admiral Lord Jellicoe's *ci-devant* Grand Fleet flagship *Centurion*, stripped and converted to a target-vessel between the wars, had been unconvincingly disguised as a battleship of the *King George V*-class and was brought from Bombay, lightly armed with Oerlikons, to masquerade as a capital ship. It was a desperate measure.

On the day Operations HARPOON and VIGOROUS sailed, 11 June 1942, Rommel broke out of the area known as 'the Cauldron' south of Gazala and began to harry the Eighth Army back towards Tobruk. The successes of his renewed offensive eastwards along the coast preoccupied the Royal Air Force, and it was not long before he had once again deprived the RAF and the Fleet Air Arm of those western desert airfields which in part compensated for the absence of a fleet aircraft carrier. The nickname for the stretch of water between Derna and Crete, 'bomb alley', became ever more apt as time passed.

As for the merchant ships which would form convoy MW11, to deceive the enemy they were loaded at Alexandria, Port Said, Suez, Haifa and Beirut. Most were below their marks, a circumstance which, with the long wait, had depressed their anti-fouling and caused sea-grass to accumulate on the hulls. This was to slow some of them significantly. After loading they concentrated at Port Said and Haifa, but the supposed secrecy surrounding the operation prevented any practice with the guns, practice that would have revealed such serious defects as those in *Potaro*'s Breda gun, for instance, as well as any deficiencies in gun-laying. Each of the vessels carried a naval liaison officer and his small signals staff, plus a transport officer and military stevedores to expedite the discharge. The drafts of soldiers each ship bore as passengers were organised into fire-fighting and damage-control parties.

The first group to move was MW11c, which left Port Said on the afternoon of 11 June. The transports were *Aagtekirk*, a 6,800-ton Dutch cargo vessel, Hain's 6,100-ton *Bhutan*, the *City of Calcutta* and the Bolton Steamship Company's *Rembrandt* of 5,560 grt, each of which towed a motor-torpedo-boat.[3] Escorted by *Coventry* and eight Hunt-class destroyers, what was called Operation REMBRANDT headed west along the coast.[4] Operation REMBRANDT was intended to give the impression of being the whole reinforcement bound for Malta, in the hope that this would draw out the Italian fleet prematurely, exposing it to submarine attack and wasting its precious fuel. Instead of the Italian fleet, on the evening of the 12th MW11c was attacked by fifteen Ju88s of I Kampfgeschwader 54 from Crete, which near-missed the *City of Calcutta*. The shaking damaged her engines and she stopped with a list as water entered No. 5 Hold, but soon afterwards she was under way again, though she signalled that her speed was down to 11 knots. She had already caused Captain Dendy of *Coventry* some anxiety because of her poor compass equipment, and *Bhutan* had replaced her as guide, the merchant ship upon which the others maintained station. At 23.00 that evening further damage reports persuaded Dendy to detach the Ellerman liner to Tobruk, so she left towing her MTB, escorted by *Exmoor* and *Croome*.

Meanwhile, early that morning convoy MW11a had left Haifa. Escorted by the 7th Destroyer Flotilla of *Napier*, *Norman*, *Nizam*, *Inconstant* and *Hotspur* and the fleet minesweepers *Boston* and *Seaham*, the cargo ships were *Ajax*, *City of Edinburgh*, *City of Pretoria*, *City of Lincoln* and Knutsen's Norwegian *Elizabeth Bakke* of 5,450 tons. After her last appearance in the Mediterranean *Ajax* had shuttled between Bombay and Port Said with military supplies, but since the end of March had been 'loafing in Suez, Port

Said, the Bitter Lakes and an anchorage on the western side of the
Red Sea south of the Gulf of Suez, called Safarga.' She had then
been sent to Haifa, where her naval liaison staff joined.
Lieutenant P. Aylwin mustered the deck officers in the chief
officer's cabin 'before supper on Thursday 11 June ... with the
idea of finding out ... how far the rumours had got as to the destination of the ship. [The Chief Officer] produced three possibil-
ities, Odessa, a landing in the Gulf of Sirte, and Malta. The
Second Mate informed me that there were cases on board
marked "Saccone and Speed – Malta" and "Wembley Stores –
Malta", so I do not think there was much doubt in any of their
minds as to their future movements ... Later on during the
voyage more than one officer said to me, "Once a ship loads with
Grain, Ammunition, Petrol and Coal you know she is bound for
Malta."'

The departure from Haifa was rather slower than the commander of the escort would have liked, one reason being the
fouling of the starboard anchor of *City of Lincoln* by another
vessel. Aylwin remarked: 'This was no fault of the Masters of
Ships, but because of the rather cramped space in Haifa harbour.
One must not expect six merchant ships to weigh two anchors
and manoeuvre in the same fashion as destroyers can.'[5]

Under cover of the short summer night of 12/13 June, MW11c
reversed course to make the rendezvous with the remaining two-
thirds of the convoy. As it approached Alexandria the escorting
Hunts were sent in for fuel, to be joined by their sister ship
Exmoor for their return. Accompanying MW11a, Captain Arliss
in *Napier* signalled to Poland in *Jervis* that *Elizabeth Bakke* 'was to
be sent into Alexandria as she did not appear to know her way
and was seen to be steaming to the northward'. This exaggera-
tion of a ridiculous situation was caused by a badly fouled
bottom, overloading, and a consequent failure to maintain the
convoy speed of 13 knots; *Elizabeth Bakke* was accordingly
detached under the escort of *Zulu*.

At roughly the same time, MW11b left Alexandria. It consisted
of the Royal Mail Line's *Potaro* (5,410 grt) and an 8,000-ton tanker,
the Anglo-American Oil Company's *Bulkoil*, manned and
managed by the MoWT, which carried the convoy's commodore,
Rear-Admiral H. England. To these two merchantmen were
attached the 'unarmed special service vessel' *Centurion* which
was loaded with supplies, two rescue ships, the former cross-

Channel ferries *Malines* and *Antwerp*, and an escort of five destroyers and four corvettes.[6] The three components of MW11 met to the north of Mersa Matruh on the afternoon of 13 June and formed up, heading west for Malta. Meanwhile a complex series of escort exchanges took place as the 7th Flotilla went into Alexandria to refuel, the remainder of the destroyers sailing under the command of Captain Poland in *Jervis*, or leaving soon afterwards with Vian's main body.

Flying his flag in *Cleopatra*, Vian had with him a cruiser squadron drawn from several sources. *Euryalus* and *Dido* had been with him in March; *Arethusa* had come from Gibraltar; *Hermione* joined the 15th Cruiser Squadron from Madagascar, whither much of the British naval forces from Gibraltar had been diverted for Operation IRONCLAD, the first Allied invasion of the war. *Birmingham* and *Newcastle* formed the 4th Cruiser Squadron, under Rear-Admiral W. Tennant, whose flag flew in the latter ship, which had been diverted from the Indian Ocean. With them sailed numerous destroyers.

That afternoon, as the weather worsened, it became impossible to tow the MTBs astern of the merchantmen, and they were ordered to slip their lines and return to Alexandria. *MTB259* was so heavily damaged that she foundered, though the others reached port on the 14th. During that night a raiding party of four Free French soldiers led by a British commando officer, Captain Lord Jellicoe, landed from the Greek submarines *Papanicolis* and *Triton* and destroyed or disabled about a score of aircraft of Lehrgeschwader 1 on the ground at Maleme. One of three raiding parties of British commandos from the Special Boat Service landed the week before on the coast of Crete from the same Greek submarines[7] had tried to attack the aircraft which had inflicted such damage on Poland's flotilla but found Maleme too heavily defended, and the operation had to be repeated by Jellicoe.[8] Unfortunately, the earlier attacks merely added to the intelligence derived from intercepted radio traffic emanating from the United States embassy at Cairo in alerting the Axis in Rome that a large British operation from both ends of the Mediterranean was under way. Having disdained to be lured by Operation REMBRANDT, the combined Axis commanders in Rome were preparing as large a reception for VIGOROUS as had met HARPOON.

*

From sunset on the 13th a series of desultory but demoralising air attacks kept up the pressure on MW11. Flares were continuously dropped and a few bombs occupied the energies of the escort until, at about 04.30, the German aeroplanes transferred their attention to Vian's main covering force coming up from the east. They continued to drop flares and small bombs near *Cleopatra* until Vian's large squadron joined the convoy at dawn on 14 June. The enemy air attacks petered out as British fighters arrived and drove the Junkers bombers away. The escorts to the convoys were now redeployed. In addition to the four corvettes, two minesweepers and the 5th Destroyer Flotilla of nine Hunts, Vian now had the 7th, 14th, 12th, 22nd and 2nd Destroyer Flotillas to hand,[9] a total of seventeen fleet destroyers, including the two previously detached to escort the *City of Calcutta* which rejoined at this time, after hunting an enemy submarine on their return passage.

The convoy itself was now further depleted by the detachment of *Aagtekirk*, *Erica* and *Primula*, which had all developed engine problems and were unable to sustain the planned operational speed. *Erica* was ordered to Mersa Matruh, the *Aagtekirk* and *Primula* were sent into Tobruk, escorted by the Hunt-class destroyer *Tetcott* to provide anti-aircraft cover. This proved inadequate, for at 12.20, when the ships were a mere twelve miles from Tobruk, they came under air attack. Having fallen astern, *Primula* was bombed first and severely shaken by near-misses. The German pilots then turned upon the other two ships. Lieutenant Rycroft, commanding *Tetcott*, reported the assault by 'between 30 and 40 aircraft, mixed Ju 87s, and 88s. About nine to twelve dived … in "hosepipe" formation, the remainder attacking *Aagtekirk*.' Three of the attacking aircraft were shot down but the Dutch ship was 'hit on the bridge and caught fire, flames spreading rapidly due to a ready-use diesel oil tank by the funnel catching fire. She turned round and round in circles with her wheel jammed to starboard and did not stop for about an hour by which time she was on fire from the 2nd to the 3rd masts.' Ryecroft asked the Naval Officer in Charge at Tobruk for assistance, and MTBs, launches and the minesweeping sloop *Aberdare* were sent to sea, but there 'was little to do other than pick up the survivors which was completed by 1430/14, when the last men were taken off by MTBs'. Other accounts mention the fire spreading rapidly, the fire pumps having been disabled by a bomb hit

on the main switchboard which isolated those forward from
those aft. Several soldiers jumped over the side before ordered
to, though the ship was still steaming at speed as she swung
round. Second Officer Bos, commanding the after gun, made
valiant efforts to connect the after emergency hand-steering gear,
but eight near-misses had distorted the stern frame and jammed
the rudder. Orders were now passed to release the lashings on
the lighters being carried as deck cargo, to provide extra lifesav-
ing facilities. By this time 'the men were very restless and were
slipping over the side on their own' as the ship came to a standstill. The engines had been stopped by the two junior engineers,
Mynheers Van der Vlugt and Pruin, who had returned to the
engine room through the shaft tunnel escape. With a deck cargo
of coal on No. 3 Hatch just forward of the bridge burning fiercely,
the order was passed to abandon the ship. 'Whilst lowering the
wounded over the ship's side, the Senior 3rd Officer, Mr Mak,
swam from aft to enquire if any of the ship's officers were
forward and from him it was learned that the captain was safe
aft, though badly burned, but there was no sign of the Chief
[Engineer] ... ' or two other engineers. Mak 'cheered everybody
by his presence and behaviour', reported the *Aagtekirk*'s naval
liaison officer.

In due course the *Aagtekirk* grounded near Tobruk and became
a total loss, 'a good ship burnt out'.

During this forenoon the convoy itself was unmolested, a large
enemy formation of bombers being driven back by two squadrons of Hurricanes and Kittyhawks diverted 'at a moment's
notice from the land battle' then raging on the mainland to the
south.[10] This timely interception by Tedder's squadrons must
have given the combined commanders-in-chief a feeling of satisfaction, for such co-operation could scarcely be bettered, and it
was noticeable that the pilots of Lehrgeschwader 1 were less
aggressive in the attacks mounted that afternoon. Nevertheless,
that they reappeared at all boded ill for MW11, and at about 16.30
they began a series of seven attacks involving about sixty aircraft,
which lasted for almost five hours and resulted in further
material damage to the convoy.

The eight remaining merchantmen and *Centurion* were disposed in four shallow columns with the two rescue ships in the
centre. The eight cruisers were formed as a screen some 1,200

yards outside MW11, with a further air defence screen of Hunts and minesweepers a mile beyond the cruisers. Anti-submarine cover was provided by the fleet destroyers, 2,500 yards beyond the Hunts. The formation, although able to put up a barrage, and formidable to torpedo-bombers, was relatively weak when confronted by dive-bombers. Despite the presence of an occasional British fighter overhead, the Luftwaffe chose to make their attacks with groups of ten or twelve Stukas or Ju88s which dived from 10,000 feet from astern or on the quarters of the spread of ships. These groups would break up into pairs or trios before releasing their bombs at low altitude and this, although unsuccessful, began to draw considerable fire from the ships below. At 17.30 a large group of some twenty aircraft attacked from the beam, splitting into groups of three, to bomb the *Bulkoil*, *Potaro* and *Bhutan*. The tanker *Bulkoil* 'zigzagged throughout this attack and was missed by a stick [of bombs] which fell about 50 and 100 feet on [her] port quarter. This threw the dynamos off and [the] ship lost speed slightly but was able to regain station after a short while', reported her master, Captain E. Tyrell, later. Near-misses badly shook the *Potaro*, but she too was able to keep going, though her Nos 2 and 3 Holds were flooded to a depth of nine feet; that the ingress of water was kept under control was largely due to the ship's engineers, led by the chief engineer, Mr J. McWirther. The *Bhutan*, in the rear of the port wing column, received a direct hit. The ship's close-range weapons fought off two Stukas, but 'the third pressed home his attack and the ship was hit by three bombs', the naval liaison officer, Lieutenant Fanshawe, reported. 'The first burst in No. 1 Hold and split open the starboard side. The second and third struck in No. 2 and the engine room, both of which filled up at once. It was seen after five minutes that the ship was sinking fast and I [sic] gave the order to abandon ship.' The sea transport officer on board, Lieutenant Patrick, stated that Captain Champion gave the order, as was more probable. Four of the ship's five boats were lowered, though one 'was overloaded by Lascars [and] the remainder of the personnel went over the side. The ship sank in twenty minutes ... '

One hundred and fifty-three men survived, with eight engine room staff missing and only eight other men unaccounted for, thanks to the presence of the rescue ships *Antwerp* and *Malines* and the destroyer *Griffin*. The two former cross-Channel ferries had been thoroughly prepared, with recovery lines, scrambling nets, rafts and lifebuoys. Their crews had been told off and trained as net-men, inhaul parties, boats' crews and mooring parties, and special reception facilities for oiled survivors had been made ready. When the *Bhutan* was hit, she caught fire and began to settle by the head. In a rough sea kicked up by the fresh north-westerly wind Lieutenant Freeman, RNR, took *Malines* close, as several boats were lowered from the stricken ship. A handful of men were observed on the *Bhutan*'s poop and *Malines* was edged alongside to remove them, receiving two near-misses at the same time. These, in the words of the two surgeon-lieutenants, 'did much to enhance fear, concussion, and [were] instrumental in the swallowing and inhaling of fuel oil'. At 18.05 the *Bhutan* sank; two underwater explosions which occurred as she foundered were believed to have been part of her cargo of bombs. Freeman then sent his whaler after men in the water, as '*Malines* appeared to be in the middle of a sea of oil fuel and bobbing heads'.

Freeman rescued seventy-three men, including Captain Champion, Fanshawe the naval liaison officer, and most of the ship's officers. Two RAF airmen died from drowning as they were hauled aboard and were 'later buried at sea in accordance with custom'. Two cases of hysteria were added to the sprains and injuries, and there were nine burns cases, three of which were serious. The majority of 'the fit survivors covered in fuel oil were able to wash in a canvas bath erected on the Quarter Deck', while those more seriously affected were tended by first-aid parties who 'worked excellently, and the average casualty was dry in a blanket, and drinking a cup of tea within ten minutes of coming on board'. The assiduous young surgeons added to their report: 'It is interesting to note that one case of recurrent malaria suffered an exacerbation due to chilling.'

The two rescue ships were detached for Tobruk, *Antwerp* being straddled by a stick of bombs on the way. At the time Tobruk was under shellfire from German artillery, but here serious cases were transferred to the hospital ship *Aba* before *Malines* and *Antwerp* returned to Alexandria, sailing at 21.15 on the following day. This was a somewhat premature retirement of these useful and morale-boosting vessels, for they were not yet at capacity.[11]

Two hours after the loss of the *Bhutan*, as the air attacks continued, draining the anti-aircraft ammunition magazines, the periscope of *U77* was seen on the surface as she made an attack on *Pakenham* in the outermost screen. The torpedo missed, but Captain Stevens's counter-attack failed to locate the U-boat and was broken off a few minutes later when a British fighter over-head reported fast craft approaching from the north-westwards.

The fighters were directed to attack the approaching torpedo-boats, but such was their preoccupation with the German bombers that only one complied, to find that Me109 fighters were flying above the enemy boats. The German air attack partially ended with the onset of nightfall. As on the previous night, flares and a few bombs were dropped. Vian ordered all ships into night formation, which brought the fleet destroyers into an anti-submarine screen across the head of the convoy, a special night-screen of two cruisers and four destroyers on the quarters, and single destroyers some five miles out on the four corners of the formation which, thus tightened, made any possible torpedo-boat attack an 'unattractive proposition'. The enemy flares, although they distracted the defenders (Rear-Admiral Tennant reported that they gave 'everyone a very naked feeling'), also deterred *Schnellboote* attacks by exposing them: thus illuminated, five were driven off at about midnight by gunfire from both *Airedale* and *Aldenham*, on point duty on the quarters. However, although the reported *Schnellboote* had failed to press home their attack, Vian was concerned that fatigue and the heavy expendi-ture of ammunition were slowly eroding the capability of his command. Air support had been disappointing, ships' defects and the enemy had materially reduced the size of the convoy, and a question as to the continuing viability of the operation must have begun to arise in Vian's mind. It had certainly done so by 23.15 when, having learned from Harwood that an Italian battle-fleet had left Taranto and was heading south with an esti-mated time of interception of 07.00, Vian signalled an interroga-tive: 'Do you wish me to retire?'

He argued that with good weather it would prove impossible to hold off a fleet throughout the whole of the morrow. Afterwards he was to say, with great candour, that the force might have got through had it been commanded by an officer of greater determination. This seems as much disingenuous as candid, however, a bitter reflection upon the inevitable, for Vian was not a man to accept defeat easily, even if it could be dis-guised as a tactical withdrawal. Perhaps he had hoped that air strikes against the Italian battle fleet might succeed, though it seems that, realistically, he considered this possibility to be a chimera from the start. If Harwood had originally been sanguine, his reply to Vian's interrogative betrayed his current indecision: he ordered Vian to continue west until 02.00 on the 15th, before turning back along the same track. It was an order with no discernible strategic value. The reasoning that he 'intended the convoy to make as much westing as possible' becomes fatuous if, having done so, it had then to retrace the miles already steamed. To what end was it to continue westwards, beyond that of appeasing London by the making of an effort? Sacrifice was as much a tenet of the Royal Navy as close engagement of the enemy, but the resources in those few cargo-ships were finite and once lost would, like the ships themselves, be gone forever. At this moment poor Harwood exhibited a Micawberish tendency in his postponement of the inevitable, with a touching faith that something might turn up as a result of the activities of his submarines and Tedder's aeroplanes. His floundering at this critical moment is the vindication of those who criticised his appointment to high command.

It was a reconnoitring Wellington from Malta that first sighted the Italian fleet at 18.45 on the 14th, and accurately reported its strength. Two battleships with four destroyers were seen steaming south in the Gulf of Taranto, with a second group of four cruisers and four destroyers ahead of them. Harwood received the news at 22.30, prompting the exchange of signals with Vian. Subsequent photo-reconnaissance of Taranto at 20.00 had revealed the absence of the *Littorio* and *Vittorio Veneto*, four cruisers and eleven destroyers, but this news did not reach Harwood until 03.00, although he had received a report of a sighting of the capital ships steaming south at 20 knots at 02.24. By this time Vian had reversed his course.

The order to turn about was sent from *Cleopatra* at 01.45 on 15 June 1942. There was considerable risk inherent in so large a group of vessels executing a sixteen-point turn after a day of battle, with ships slightly out of station, conned by tired officers, and an eager enemy prowling about its skirts. Delaying the manoeuvre for a further two and a half hours had served only to increase the fatigue of those to whom the graveyard hours might otherwise have given a little respite.

The bulk of the ships swung in tolerable order, but Tennant's cruisers dropped astern, exposing themselves to Leutnant-sur-Zee Wuppermann's 3rd *Schnellboote* Flotilla as they strove to regain station. Having laid the mines which entrapped the HARPOON ships outside Grand Harbour Wupperman had moved on to Derna, and was now placed to strike at VIGOROUS. Leading in *S56*, he fired a torpedo at about 03.50 and hit *Newcastle*, Tennant's flagship. Attacked from ahead, Captain P.B.R.W. William-Powlett succeeded in dodging one torpedo and had the small consolation of receiving the other well forward, so that by swift damage-control *Newcastle* was soon able to steam at 24 knots. In the meantime, the rear-admiral sent *Birmingham* and one destroyer to catch up with the convoy, retaining a screen of three to tend *Newcastle* while the work of shoring-up bulkheads was undertaken. But before he could rejoin the convoy the *Schnellbootes* scored again: Leutnant Weber of *S55* torpedoed the destroyer *Hasty* at 05.25, and disabled her so completely that, after her crew had been taken off by *Hotspur*, Lieutenant Herrick was obliged to torpedo her. Of his ship's company, Lieutenant-Commander Austen lost only twelve men.[12]

When daylight broke, convoy MW11 was headed back towards 'bomb alley'.

Meanwhile, to the north-west, Iachino was racing south, flying his flag in *Littorio* and accompanied by Ammiraglio di Divisione Fioravanzo in *Vittorio Veneto*. In support were Parona's two heavy cruisers *Gorizia* and *Trento*, de Courten's two light cruisers *Giuseppe Garibaldi* and *Duca d'Aosta*, and twelve destroyers of the 7th, 11th and 13th Flotillas.[13] At midnight a small striking force of torpedo-armed Wellingtons had been sent out from Malta by Leatham and Lloyd. The four planes located the Italian battleships at 03.40, dropping flares to illuminate their target. Iachino turned away and made smoke, confusing his attackers, so that only one Wellington dropped its torpedoes. These were ineffective.

As the Wellingtons broke off their attack at 04.00, the nine Beauforts of No. 217 Squadron took off from Malta. By dawn they were approaching the Italian fleet. At this time Iachino had concentrated his capital ships and light cruisers behind a screen of six destroyers, with the heavy cruisers and remaining destroyers removed some miles to the west. At 06.10 three Beauforts headed for the aftermost heavy cruiser, the *Trento*, and succeeded in scoring a torpedo hit on her, so that she was driven out of line and broke away to the westwards with two destroyers accompanying her. The other Beauforts pressed home fierce attacks on the two battleships beyond, passing low over them, later certain they had scored two strikes against each; in fact they had not, though whether because of weapon failure or lack of accuracy is unknown. In any event, the Italian ships reacted under violent helm movements to avoid the torpedoes.

These evasive actions also saved them from submarine attack since, by an ironic coincidence, No. 217 Squadron struck as Iachino was passing close over the British submarines of the 10th Flotilla. These were in the act of returning to their earlier patrol positions, having received the cancellation of the order to take station along the patrol line to the north of the convoy's assumed track, sent to them as soon as it was known that the Italians had sailed, and the convoy had been turned back. Aboard *Umbra*, Lieutenant Maydon had taken a stellar fix and dived; shortly afterwards he heard the noise of approaching ships on *Umbra*'s hydrophones. At periscope depth he saw the flares dropped by the first air attack, and steered to intercept. He then found his submarine 'in the unenviable position of being in the centre of a fantastic circus of wildly careering capital ships, cruisers and destroyers ... of tracer-shell streaks and anti-aircraft bursts ... there was not a quadrant of the compass unoccupied by enemy vessels weaving to and fro ... [yet] It was essential to remain at periscope depth, for an opportunity to fire might come at any moment.'[14] With the Beauforts withdrawing, Maydon watched as Iachino's heavy squadron steamed west to circle *Trento* and then, leaving the cruiser astern, shaped a course for the south again in two groups. The battleships moved out to the east and, as they passed him at 06.46, Maydon fired a salvo at the *Vittorio Veneto*, but missed.

Iachino's ships had also been spotted by Lieutenant Harrison through the periscope of *Ultimatum* at 06.15 and, as they detached from *Trento*, he found the three cruisers, now in one group to the westwards of the capital ships, heading towards him. He commenced an attack at 06.22 and penetrated the screen but was frustrated as the cruisers abruptly zigzagged and, as he dived deep, passed above him. He caught a brief glimpse of the Italian battleships, but by then he had lost his chance. An equally distant sighting was made by Lieutenant Kershaw in *Uproar*.

Thrasher, *Taku* and *Thorn* had also received the early sighting report as they reverted to their former positions and, since they were faster than the U-class, their commanders surfaced and steered to intercept as best they could. The first two abandoned the attempt on receiving a report that the Italians were steering south-west and were therefore beyond their reach. The most westerly was the *Thorn*; Lieutenant-Commander Norfolk had submerged when east of the Italian line of advance, and at 07.00 he saw a column of smoke rising in the north-west. Shortly afterwards he sighted the upperworks of Iachino's ships as they passed to the westwards, again out of range.

The column of smoke was from the disabled *Trento*, about which Harrison, Maydon and Kershaw now gathered as she lay 'burning gloriously' while her attendant destroyers laid a smoke screen round her. As *Trento* was so clearly out of action Harrison withdrew to apprise Alexandria of the situation, intending to return and torpedo the Italian cruiser; but Maydon forestalled him: at 10.06 *Umbra* fired two torpedoes which both hit the *Trento*, and an hour later she had sunk.

Iachino continued south, retaining his formation of two groups, and at about 09.00 eight Liberators of the United States Army Air Corps arrived on the scene. Nine of these had taken off at 04.30; one had returned to their base near Suez, but skilful navigation brought the others 14,000 feet overhead, and they dropped their bombs with considerable accuracy through an erratic anti-aircraft barrage. Many of the bombs near-missed but did little damage to the heavy ships, while the one direct hit of a 500-pound bomb on the *Littorio* had little effect (though this did not prevent some wild claims on the part of the jubilant aircrews). As the Liberators turned for home five Beauforts from No. 39 Squadron arrived, flying far below the Americans. These aircraft had left Bir Amud, just behind the front line in the Western Desert, at 06.25. They should have been escorted by Beaufighters until beyond the range of Me109s and Macchi MC202 Folgores based near Gazala, but the Beaufighters were diverted to attack Rommel. The Me109s had therefore been able to ravage the formation; two Beauforts were shot down and five turned back after sustaining damage, one of which was lost. Thus it was that only five approached their assigned targets at 09.40, to be met by a heavy long-range fire that damaged a further two machines.

In turning away to open their firing arcs, Iachino's ships exposed their flanks, and the Beauforts released their torpedoes, claiming a hit on one of the battleships, while high above the observing American airmen excitably claimed seeing hits on a cruiser and a destroyer. In fact, 'all the gallantry of the airmen, all the skilful leading that enabled the little striking forces to find their targets on each occasion, had not availed; the Italian fleet stood on.'[15] As for the wreckage of No. 39 Squadron, this was led into Luqa by Squadron-Leader Gibbs, who believed he had hit an Italian battleship. His Beaufort was so damaged that he crash-landed her on arrival, to receive the sardonic reproof that crash-landings were usually done off the runway.[16]

At Alexandria, Harwood and Tedder had only the vaguest notion of the progress of events. Indeed, until 11.15 on the 15th, Harwood was ignorant of the fact that Malta-based aircraft had attacked Iachino. But by dawn he grew increasingly anxious as the convoy was about to run the gauntlet of 'bomb alley'. Caught thus between frying pan and fire, and confronted with abject failure, Harwood turned the convoy again, and at 07.00 Vian's entire force executed another sixteen-point turn. A few moments later, Harwood transmitted revised instructions: 'Avoid contact until aircraft have attacked, which should be by 10.30. If air attack fails, every effort must be made to get convoy through to Malta by adopting offensive attitude. Should this fail, and convoy be cornered, it is to be sacrificed, and you are to extricate your forces, proceeding to the eastward or westward.'

An hour and a half later, at 08.30, air reconnaissance informed Harwood that, far from being obstructed, the Italian fleet were still headed south-east in strength and, although deprived of one cruiser, were only 150 miles from MW11. Thoroughly alarmed, Harwood turned Vian about yet again, and at 09.40 all the ships hauled wearily round to a course of 105 degrees, east-south-east. A little later, at 11.15, Harwood received the jubilant reports of the Beauforts' debriefings at Malta. In addition to the disabling of *Trento*, it seemed certain that the Italian battleships had been hit; Vian was therefore ordered to turn back towards Malta. The time was 11.51, and Harwood followed this instruction with a repeat of his order to sacrifice the convoy and extricate the war-ships if Iachino came within range. Finally, at 12.45, Harwood added: 'I must leave the decision to you whether to comply with my 0705/15, or whether to again retire with hope of carrying out a night destroyer attack, if enemy stands on.'[17]

Mercifully, implementation of this last order proved unnecessary. At 13.45 Vian had received Harwood's order of 11.51 to turn west again. He was then under an intense air attack in bomb alley which had begun at 11.50 with a score of Stukas pouncing on the quarters of the convoy and escort. The enemy tended to ignore the merchantmen, it being 'apparent' to Lieutenant Field aboard *Rembrandt* 'that the pilots had been instructed to concentrate upon units of the fleet', and to the master of *Bulkoil* that 'this attack [was] definitely against cruisers and escort'. Several of the merchant transports were set upon, nevertheless, and the gunners of the near-missed *City of Edinburgh*, who 'behaved magnificently', claimed one bomber certainly and one probably destroyed. Aboard the *City of Pretoria* a near-miss briefly stopped the main engines, but the ship was soon under command again. *Ajax* fought off five bombers which dived upon her at 13.00: 'Extremely accurate gunfire ... ', reported Lieutenant Tate, RNR, the sea transport officer, 'diverted the attack and all bombs missed the ship, one bursting in mid-air about 50 feet on the starboard beam.' The main onslaught of six Ju87s fell upon the cruiser *Birmingham*, stationed out on the port bow of the convoy itself. Thunderous near-misses shook the cruiser to such an extent that one of her forward turrets was disabled. Although one Stuka was shot down and no other damage was sustained, Vian was now in receipt of a further air reconnaissance report that confirmed the proximity of Iachino's battle-group, and this settled the matter in his own mind: he must withdraw. He 'held on to the eastward awaiting [Harwood's] reactions to Aircraft T's report', receiving the C-in-C's discretionary signal of 12.45 at 14.20.

His decision confirmed, Vian continued eastwards, and an hour later his ships endured a further air attack as the cumulative delay in retiring now exposed the ships to the full evils of bomb alley. Again the Germans directed their main effort upon the men-of-war. About a dozen Stukas, a third of the attacking force, fell upon *Airedale*. The destroyer, stationed in the air-defence screen on the starboard quarter of the convoy, was 'smothered with hits and near-misses, and completely disabled'. Eager to avoid further delay, Vian was compelled to order Lieutenant Stuart-Menteth of *Aldenham* to sink her. The remaining Stukas dived on the merchant ships without success, and on the *Centurion*, inflicting damage on the ancient battleship, which nevertheless shot down one of her opponents as she reappeared from a straddle 'belching forth clouds of smoke'. They were, Captain Tyrell of *Bulkoil* recorded, 'a hectic two hours'.

It was now that Supermarina chose to intervene, and snatched victory out of Iachino's grasp: he was ordered not to proceed further east. At 15.15, when he was about 110 miles from Vian, Iachino accordingly turned away to the north-west. His orders were to cruise west of Greece, ready to head south again if the British made another attempt to cross the central basin. The news that he had broken off his pursuit was reported to Alexandria by the shadowing British aircraft at 16.05, and twenty minutes later Harwood sent another signal to Vian: 'Now is golden opportunity to get convoy to Malta. Have Hunts, *Coventry*, minesweepers, and corvettes enough fuel for one-way trip? If so, I would like to turn convoy now, cruisers and destroyers parting company after dark and returning to Alexandria.'

Vian received *this* signal during another air attack. Harwood waited two hours for Vian's acknowledgement and then changed his mind, intending to send on to Malta only the four fastest merchant ships, escorted by *Arethusa* and two destroyers. Vian, for his part, was unable to manoeuvre until after the air attack, which had begun at 17.20 and lasted for two hours, and would only be able to assess fuel and ammunition states some time after it had ended. 'All known forms of attack were employed,' Vian reported, 'the fire of the fleet being fully extended.' German high-level and dive-bombing attacks were carried out by about forty Stukas and Ju88s, combined with Italian torpedo-bombing runs by ten SM79s. The high-level attacks were made at 16,000 feet from the western sky, lit by the sunset. Three ships were closely near-missed, but blind, radar-controlled gunnery deterred the attackers. At 18.00, shallow-diving Ju88s attacked both the screen and the merchantmen. Light, near-miss damage was caused to *Arethusa* and *Centurion*, with HMAS *Nestor* badly holed. Finally, SM79s made a half-hearted attack after two patrolling Beaufighters had knocked one out of the sky. Three further Savoia Marchettis and two bombers were brought down by the ships' guns.

As the torpedo-bombers flew off, Vian forwarded his assessment to Harwood. His ships were, he had estimated quickly, down to less than one-third of their ammunition stocks. This was insufficient to continue, and Harwood cancelled his second plan. At 20.53 he ordered Vian to 'Return to Alexandria with your whole force.'

Meanwhile Iachino was retiring to await events. The British aircraft reconnoitring the Italian squadron was lost, and her relief was intercepted and engaged by German fighters, so that it never located the Italian fleet; contact was broken off about 16.30. Captain Ruck-Keene, commanding the combined 1st and 10th Submarine Flotillas, now tried to move his boats into position to intercept Iachino, but signals were taking some four hours to get through and thus were quickly out of date. Several submarine commanders surfaced, both to intercept signals and to keep a sharp lookout, and Lieutenant Bennington, learning at 15.35 that the Italians were steering north again, hurried to meet them in *Porpoise*. But at 19.35 he was spotted and bombed by an aircraft escorting the Italian ships, thereby losing his opportunity. Lieutenant Mackenzie, having been too far to the east that morning, was now too far to the west, and headed east. Then, at 20.00, he too had to dive to avoid air attack and, through his periscope, had the mortification of sighting the enemy out of range to the south-eastwards.

At Malta, Leatham and Lloyd prepared their own response. A reconnoitring air patrol took off and located the Italians at 22.55, calling up the five torpedo-armed Wellingtons of No. 38 Squadron readied to sortie. Locating their targets at about 00.30 on 16 June, the bombers were once again met by smoke and violent manoeuvring, which disrupted their attack. Nevertheless, Pilot Officer Hawes persisted and was rewarded by a torpedo hit on the bow of *Littorio*. The damage was not serious, however, and Iachino's flagship was able to maintain her speed.

Vian was similarly assaulted during his return to Alexandria in the early hours of 16 June. At dusk, the last enemy air attack was driven off without damage, and in night stations the convoy zig-zagged east at 13 knots, leaving *Nestor* astern. Commander Rosenthal's badly damaged destroyer was by now under the tow of *Javelin*, with *Eridge* and *Beaufort* as escort. Down by the bow, *Nestor* towed awkwardly and provided a target for two air attacks, both of which were driven off with losses inflicted on the enemy. Rosenthal must have recalled the ordeal of towing *Sydney Star* as he now struggled to save his own ship.

At 01.27, Korvettenkapitän Reschke in *U205* approached the main convoy and, penetrating the screen undetected, fired a salvo at *Hermione* (Captain G. Oliver). Suddenly, on the starboard quarter of the convoy, the night was filled with the roar of exploding warheads, and *Hermione* fell over onto her side and sank very quickly, still making way. The speed with which this fine cruiser sank Harwood found 'disquieting', reporting that 'the behaviour of her company in adversity was exemplary' as *Exmoor*, *Beaufort* and *Aldenham* rescued about four hundred of them.

Aboard *Javelin*, Lieutenant-Commander Simms was having great difficulty towing *Nestor*. At 04.30 the tow parted for the second time and, while Simms manoeuvred to reconnect, fast attack craft were observed. With daylight not far off and the long hours of a summer day to endure, exposed to aircraft, motor-torpedo-boats and submarines, Rosenthal decided that the additional risk he posed to *Javelin* was unacceptable. At 07.00, her Australian crew having been evacuated, *Nestor* was scuttled and the three destroyers, *Javelin*, *Eridge* and *Beaufort*, raced after Vian, rejoining his flag late that afternoon.

That same day, 16 June, the *City of Calcutta* set out from Tobruk for Alexandria, escorted by *Tetcott* and *Primula*. Reschke's triumph proved to be the last, for the numerous enemy submarines stationed along Vian's route failed to hit any of his force, though his destroyers were kept busy dropping depth-charges on the flanks of the convoy.[18] Vian approached Alexandria that evening with the greater number of the ships. The *Centurion* had been partially flooded and lay too deep to enter the port, so she was anchored outside the Great Pass; but the remaining five ships of convoy MW11, *Potaro*, *City of Lincoln*, *City of Edinburgh*, *City of Pretoria* and *Rembrandt*, entered Alexandria with Vian. Captain Stevens in *Pakenham*, with *Griffin*, *Fortune* and *Inconstant*, escorted *Bulkoil* and *Ajax* on to Port Said.[19]

It was a bleak moment. Operation VIGOROUS had been a disaster, 'an imperial balls-up', the gunnery officer of one cruiser described it, and the retreat of MW11 was a defeat for Britain. Dominated by the Axis, the central Mediterranean was impassable to British forces. In a 'Most Secret' appreciation made that same day to the Admiralty, Harwood stated: 'We are outnumbered both in surface ships and Air Force [*sic*] and very gallant endeavour of all concerned cannot make up for the ... deficiency.'[20] His later report damned the inadequacy of the Royal Air Force in failing to provide real muscle against capital ships: 'Events proved with painful clarity that our air striking force had nothing like the weight required to stop a fast and powerful enemy force, and in no way compensated for our lack of heavy ships.'[21]

Malta was truly besieged, her isolation complete. The sole mitigation was not that of any lessons learned but the cargoes of *Troilus* and *Orari*, conveyed during the HARPOON component of Operation JULIUS. These gave Malta a slender breathing space of one week, and the 'Target Date' broadcast by Lieutenant-Governor Jackson to the Maltese people was thereby deferred. In view of what was happening elsewhere, it seemed but the postponement of the inevitable. Within four days of Vian's dismal return to Alexandria Rommel had taken Tobruk, the garrison having surrendered. Wuppermann's *Schnellbootes* and Dönitz's U-boats operated against shipping fleeing east from Tobruk. By the end of June Auchinleck, having taken over in the field from Ritchie, had pulled back to El Alamein, sixty miles from Alexandria. The British were facing defeat in the Middle East.

18

'The largest possible convoy'

(Operations PINPOINT, INSECT, BERSERK, ASCENDANT, MG3 and PEDESTAL, with Convoys WS21s and MW12)

THE AXIS DOMINATION of the central Mediterranean was due principally to the command of the air achieved by General Loerzer's Fliegerkorps II operating under Kesselring who, as noted earlier, regarded his objective of removing Malta from any strategic consequence as having been achieved by 10 May 1942, despite the simultaneous arrival there of the first Spitfires. Although German and Italian units continued to train for an invasion of the island, Hitler, whose attention was upon the opening offensive in Russia, accepted Kesselring's assessment. Given the abject failure of VIGOROUS and the limited achievement of HARPOON to push through more than a trifling quantity of stores, Kesselring may be forgiven his conceit, underpinned as it seemed to be by the successes of Rommel in the Western Desert. The British were surely on the threshold of a final defeat in the Mediterranean and the Middle East.

The disasters which had reduced the strength of the Royal Navy both in the Mediterranean and elsewhere stretched its remaining men-of-war to the limit. Political imperatives to supply Soviet Russia resulted in the diversion of ships to the Barents Sea where, on 4 July, there occurred a convoy defeat greater than that of MW11. Convoy PQ17 was scattered and thereafter systematically destroyed, an event of rumbling consequence, not least because both British merchant seamen and Joseph Stalin formed the opinion that the Royal Navy had run away.[1]

Though the perceptions of the merchant seamen subsequently gave serious grounds for concern in respect of their morale, Stalin's were of far greater importance to Churchill, confronted as he was by defeat. Despite these preoccupations, however, the decision not to attempt a convoy to Malta during the July new moon stopped neither the Magic Carpet submarine passages nor the Club Runs, by which means Malta was steadily reinforced with Spitfires, absolute necessities, medicines, ammunition and some foodstuffs, much of the latter being carried in the gallant *Welshman*. Such slender replenishments did not extend the deadline of Malta's final collapse, for they were inadequate in quantitative terms, but they eked out her viability as a fortress.

After HARPOON, *Welshman* had returned to the Clyde for drydocking and a boiler clean, following which she loaded 350 tons of powdered milk, edible oils, fats and flour, with 98 tons of soap, 30 tons of minesweeping stores, and mail. Sailing on 9 July, her passage through the Bay of Biscay was rough, damaging her cargo and covering her minedeck with a viscous mixture of oil and milk. Loading ammunition, mostly 20-mm Oerlikon shells, *Welshman* left Gibraltar on 14 July in company with the carrier *Eagle*, the cruisers *Charybdis* and *Cairo*, and five destroyers. The operation was designated PINPOINT.

The next morning, as *Eagle* flew off thirty-one Spitfires, *Welshman* detached to speed along the coast of Algeria hidden by a heat haze. The clear blue sky overhead was blemished on the 16th by a Ju88, joined about noon by a Cant 506B. Four hours later another Cant and Junkers arrived, the pairs circling in contrary directions, just out of range, as *Welshman* continued her progress with her crew closed up at action stations. Mesmerised as they were by these distant shadowers, the attack by single-engined CR42 fighter-bombers coming in low out of the sun was a surprise. The Italian pilots side-slipped and twisted as they approached, attacking independently in rapid succession from the quarters, so that *Welshman*'s forward guns were impotent. Despite such *brio* only one bomb caused concern, bursting close under the speeding minelayer's transom so that, as her stern was lifted, she dipped her bow and sluiced her entire upper deck with green water. The CR42s buzzed away, whereupon the next onslaught was from a small group of SM79s dropping high-level bombs from 14,000 feet. *Welshman* emerged unscathed from the near-miss explosions and was left alone for an hour, though still attended by her quartet of shadowers. At about 18.50, as the shimmering ball of the Mediterranean sun began to set, eight Ju88s dived upon the ship but were driven off by a furious barrage, achieving nothing. A few moments later eight Stukas descended on the ship; again, anti-aircraft fire burst about the screaming machines, disrupting the attack. One had its under-carriage shot off and one broke away spewing smoke, but several near-misses shook *Welshman* as Captain Friedberger manoeu-vred her at a speed approaching 40 knots. One Stuka penetrated the defence and dropped a stick of bombs which again exploded under her stern. The ship was heeled over and drove her bow under, sending a second wall of water the length of her deck, but although there was damage to some electrical circuitry she was still making 35 knots, heading into the approaching night. At twilight a gliding Ju88 coasted down with engines cut, to drop a single bomb in the swirling, marbled wake.

Three Italian destroyers sent out to intercept *Welshman* failed to catch her, although advised of her position from the air. The submarine *Axum* sighted her and fired torpedoes, but the speed of the minelayer was too great, and they missed. Under cover of darkness Lieutenant-Commander Gellatly repeated his previ-ous feats of pilotage, and by 06.00 *Welshman* was speeding towards Filfla, to enter the swept channel and berth in Grand Harbour an hour later. The safe arrival of Spitfires from *Eagle* enabled *Welshman* to discharge unhampered, and Freidberger left Malta at twilight on 18 July. The Italians had mobilised a patrol line of six submarines off Cape Bon and a torpedo-boat flotilla at Pantelleria. A cruiser squadron of the *Muzio Attendolo* and *Raimondo Montecuccoli* with escorting destroyers also sallied to ambush her, but bad weather concealed the British ship until the late forenoon of 19 July, when she was off Bougie. That afternoon *Welshman* survived a further air attack by a combined force of twenty SM79s and Ju88s, to arrive safely at Gibraltar on 21 July.

This homeward passage coincided with Operation INSECT: *Eagle*, *Charybdis* and *Cairo* with their five destroyers *Antelope*, *Ithuriel*, *Vansittart*, *Westcott* and *Wrestler* left Gibraltar again on 20 July. During the day *Eagle* was ineffectively attacked by a salvo of four torpedoes from the Italian submarine *Dandolo*, and at dawn the following day twenty-eight Spitfires took off from the carrier, arriving safely on Malta later that morning as the task force returned to Gibraltar.

During July, Magic Carpet supply runs were made to Malta by the submarines *Parthian* and *Clyde*. The *Clyde*'s arrival on 1 August was of particular significance, for instead of powdered milk she brought a quantity of smoke-making devices, ready to cover the discharge of the merchant ships of the next convoy when they reached Malta.

During the same period, however, Italian submarines made fifteen passages to North Africa, conveying 1,105 tons of stores to enable Rommel to build up his forces for the final assault on the Canal Zone.[2] Italian surface communications were less secure, *Unbeaten* sinking a 6,400-ton transport, *Vettor Pisani*, off Argostoli, and *Thorn* the 5,300-ton *Monviso* off Cyrenaica. In the eastern basin of the Mediterranean, the war of attrition went on. British destroyers regularly shelled German positions at Mersa Matruh, engaging the enemy *Schnellboote* and hunting Axis submarines; both *U372* and *Scirè* were lost to British destroyers and aircraft. This credit balance was offset, however, by damage to the submarine *Thrasher* inflicted by shore-based Fleet Air Arm aircraft in an unfortunate attack off Port Said, the Swordfish taking her for an enemy laying mines, and of *Thorn*, sunk by the torpedo-boat *Pegaso* a few days later.

But it was the western Mediterranean that was to become the crucible for the climactic stage of the war in the Middle Sea. As Malta edged inexorably towards starvation and surrender, a major naval offensive was being put in train to avert this. The operation became famous – too famous, claim many veterans of other attempts to replenish Malta, for it did not on its own raise the siege. It did, however, further postpone the fatal and euphemistic 'Target Date', and the purchase of this respite ultimately proved crucial.

For the Maltese, the entry of the last surviving ship conferred upon this convoy the name of the day's saint, Santa Marija; to the British it was known as Operation PEDESTAL.

The preparations for Operation PEDESTAL were extensive, thorough, and complex. At the highest levels the arrangements, though not without their problems, went well; at the lowest they were beset by difficulties, inefficiencies, and downright stupidities. In the summer of 1942 the British position overall was dire, and in early July the Chiefs of Staff were planning for the very worst, the loss of Egypt and the Suez Canal.[3] The Admiralty's general assessment was stark: 'We are now approaching a crisis in the war and we must face the facts. We have lost control of sea communications over very wide areas, and wherever we have lost this ... we have also lost all that depends upon it ... Our merchant ship losses are immense; the tanker situation is grave; and the supplies reaching this country are much less than we require ... Thus slowly we are being forced into a position such as we have never faced before whilst our enemies have gained where we have lost.'

In formulating future strategy, Their Lordships were succinct: 'Sea and air power must be used in conjunction. It is of course axiomatic that aircraft carriers now play a vital part in naval operations on the wide ocean ... Ships alone are now unable to maintain command at sea ... '[4] These lessons had been learned from British experience world-wide, and their official recognition amounted to an acknowledgement of the imminence of probable defeat.

It was against this bleak background that Operation PEDESTAL was planned and executed. Essentially a repeat of HARPOON, it recognised the necessity of adequate carrier-borne air forces and, less easy to achieve, sufficient tanker capacity. The abject failure of JULIUS to replenish Malta, flagged months earlier, only made Dobbie's final plea after the failure of MW10 the more poignant.[5] His replacement, Lord Gort, was repeatedly reassured by Churchill that 'you may be sure we shall do everything to help you'.[6]

In expectation of the fulfilment of this promise, Gort reported in detail on 27 July, outlining the state of Malta's morale, and her dietary deficiencies. Mindful of the island's ability to help herself, he stated that 'arrangements to receive the next convoy are well in hand, and when the ships arrive unloading will begin at once. The two ships of the last convoy which arrived [Troilus and Orari] were unloaded in record time for Malta. The salvage operations to get such cargo as we can from the ships of the March convoy [MW10] are proceeding. Every little bit we can collect is a welcome addition.'[7]

PEDESTAL's inception had begun even as JULIUS was collapsing in ruins, when the Chiefs of Staff met late on the night of 15 June. Churchill argued that American success at Midway

Island had relieved the pressure on Somerville's Eastern Fleet, so that one of the battleships destined for him could be recalled. Sir Dudley Pound acquiesced. The committee therefore 'invited the Admiralty to put up proposals for the largest possible convoy to be run into Malta from the west during the July dark period'.[8] It was then postponed for a month, but the delay enabled arrangements to be better made. As the decisions at Cabinet and Chiefs of Staff level percolated the British war machine, sub-committees were formed; requests and enquiries for information became transmuted into instructions, requisitions, signals and orders. These began to draw together the ships, men and vast quantities of war materials necessary, not merely to replenish Malta but to make possible the achievement of the objective itself.

The suspension of Arctic convoys until the shortening days of autumn fortuitously released a number of warships from the Home Fleet for service in support of PEDESTAL, but it was not so much men-of-war the Admiralty needed as suitable merchant ships, especially a minimum of one tanker. There was nothing fast enough available under the British flag in home waters, and while a proposal to use *Glengyle* was mooted, her tank capacity of 4,000 tons was far less than envisaged and could only bear a single type of the oil products required. On 18 June Churchill was with General Ismay in Washington, where the Chiefs of Staff cabled him, urging him to request the loan of the tanker *Ohio*, on the same basis as *Kentucky*. The *Ohio* was expected in the Clyde two days later and *Glengyle*, fitted as an infantry assault vessel, was offered in exchange.

The original enquiries for *Kentucky* had been made by Sir Arthur Salter, head of the British Merchant Shipping Mission in Washington. The tanker's owners, the Texas Oil Company, had been reluctant to release so new a ship to a weak and faltering ally, and were supported in their objection by the United States Navy Department and the American Director of Shipping; it was Roosevelt's personal intervention that ensured *Kentucky*'s availability, with *Ohio* in reserve if required. Fortunately, while the sinking of *Kentucky* was perceived in some quarters as a cavalier act, especially as it was witnessed by American crew members who had been retained on board in the tanker's engine room, these objections had had little time to surface. On Churchill's asking again, Roosevelt sanctioned *Ohio*'s release, and Texaco were advised by the US War Shipping Administration on 21 June

that their tanker was being requisitioned forthwith. Captain
Peterson was cabled not to leave the Clyde, and *Ohio*'s unfortunate master found his ship transferred to the British register on 25
June. A fortnight later he was visited by the Texaco agent and an
official of the British MoWT, who instructed him to turn *Ohio* over
to a British master; soon afterwards he was superseded by
Captain D. Mason, of the Eagle Oil Company. A British crew and
two dozen DEMS gunners were soon aboard, and *Ohio* moved
up-river and into King George V Dock for the fitting of supplementary anti-aircraft armament, increased fire-fighting equipment, sprung supports to vital pipework, and rubber mountings
to the ship's main steam turbines. On completion, *Ohio* proceeded
to Dunglass and loaded 11,500 tons of kerosene and diesel oil.

She was a particularly appropriate acquisition, for she had
only been built in 1940, a welded ship with a system of framing
that combined the traditional technique of transverse ribs in her
long sides with longitudinal framing in her double bottoms and
under her decks. This combination was intended to make tank
cleaning easy but, with the subdivision necessary to provide
multiple tanks, also made her immensely strong. That her powerful Westinghouse turbines gave her a service speed of 16 knots
was what chiefly recommended her to the British Admiralty, but
it was her strength which was to pull the chestnuts out of the fire
for Their Lordships.[9]

The *Ohio* was not the only new American ship in the convoy.
Also requested from the American administration were *Santa
Elisa* and *Almeria Lykes*, and these were among the selected merchantmen mustering in British waters. Built in 1941, *Santa Elisa*
was owned by the Grace Line of New York. Her master, Captain
T. Thomson, had sailed as the ship's mate and been promoted
before the ship left Boston when her master fell sick. She was a
standard C2 cargo ship of 8,300 grt and capable of the intended
convoy speed of 16 knots. The *Almeria Lykes* (Captain W.
Henderson) was owned by Lykes Brothers of New Orleans and
had been built in 1940. She registered 7,773 grt and, like *Santa
Elisa*, carried an Armed Guard of American naval personnel to
man her armament. Having discharged their transatlantic
cargoes, *Almeria Lykes* was sent to Belfast and *Santa Elisa* to
Newport, where the two freighters lay for over a month while
additional armaments were fitted, including Oerlikon and
Bofors mountings. Here too, drafts of British gunners from the

Maritime Regiment of the Royal Artillery joined the United States Naval Armed Guards already on board.

The remaining merchant ships were British, several of them already veterans of the Malta run, and with the exception of the *Empire Hope* were all fine, fast cargo-passenger liners, many with refrigerated space. *Empire Hope* (Captain G. Williams) was a war-built standard refrigerated ship of 12,688 grt, capable of 17 knots. She had been constructed to a Shaw, Savill and Albion design, and was manned and managed by that company on behalf of the MoWT. Two more large Shaw, Savill ships of similar tonnage joined the assembling convoy, *Waimarama* (Captain R. Pearce) and *Wairangi* (Captain H. Gordon). There were two 13,000-ton Blue Star liners, *Brisbane Star* (Captain F. Riley) and *Melbourne Star* (Captain D. MacFarlane), along with two of Alfred Holt's vessels, the 7,500-ton Blue Funnel liner *Deucalion* (Captain R. Brown), and Glen Line's 9,000-ton *Glenorchy* (Captain G. Leslie). Clan Line provided *Clan Ferguson*, 7,400 tons (Captain A. Cossar); the Federal Steam Navigation Company the 10,600-ton *Dorset* (Captain J. Tuckett); the Union Castle Line the 7,700-ton *Rochester Castle* (Captain R. Wren); and Port Line the 8,500-ton *Port Chalmers* (Captain H. G. Pinkney). It was a formidable muster, as formidable as the organisation behind it.

Like the American vessels, most of the British ships required modifications in the form of extra anti-aircraft guns, additional fire-fighting gear and improved paravane rigs. *Empire Hope*, for instance, had arrived at Avonmouth with a single 4.7-inch gun mounted on her poop. By the time she was equipped for PEDESTAL, she carried an additional eight 20-mm Oerlikons and four 40-mm Bofors anti-aircraft guns in gunpits, twin Browning machine-guns on each bridge wing, sixteen depth charges on the poop, and two aerial mine throwers.[10]

Security was clearly paramount, yet although officially the merchant crews, from masters to galley boys, were ignorant of their vessels' destination, once again cases and bales swung up off the dockside and into the ships' holds were clearly marked 'Malta', in some cases disguised as 'Latia'. Joining *Port Chalmers*, Commander A. Venables, the convoy commodore, was astonished to be told by the stevedores that he was bound for Malta; one engine room hand, signing on *Empire Hope* shortly before she was due to sail, was also told where he was going by the dockers.[11] On joining *Deucalion* young Dr Murphy was met by

the chief officer, who advised him with an air of 'realistic pessimism' that *Deucalion* would be sunk.[12] Folios of Mediterranean
charts delivered to the warships returning from the Arctic
prompted scuttlebutt on the messdecks which informed open
discussion in pubs ashore. It was an aspect of PEDESTAL which
deserved the adverse criticism it received, provoking an MoWT
enquiry after a statement made in the House of Lords by
Admiral of the Fleet the Earl of Cork and Orrery on 29
September 1942.

Lord Cork had received a letter from a father whose son, an
engineering officer in one of the merchant ships, had complained
of the clearly-marked cargo betraying their destination. Visiting
his son, the earl's informant had found the entire ship's company
incensed, convinced the lack of secrecy meant they were bound
for a death-trap. They were openly discussing whether they
should refuse to sail, but in the end obeyed orders. The ship was
lost, and Lord Cork's informant did not see his only son again. In
making his statement the earl was able to quote corroborative
evidence from another source, having lately found himself a
fellow house guest at Froyle Place in Hampshire with a well-con-
nected young apprentice who had just returned from Malta.
Frederick Treves, who had clearly survived a harrowing experience, mentioned that when he joined *Waimarama* he saw cases on
the dockside marked 'Malta'.[13] It was a serious and unforgivable
breach of security, and following the MoWT enquiry all destinations were encoded and cargoes marked accordingly.

The loading of the ships was otherwise in accordance with the
standard procedure for 'military cargoes' – that is, an even
spread of commodities throughout the convoy. *Empire Hope*'s six
holds were all filled to the same plan, the lower holds with petrol
and kerosene in cased 4-gallon cans, topped off with foodstuffs
and flour. The 'tween-decks were packed with bombs and
ammunition of all calibres; on deck, cargoes of coal sacks were
lashed over the hatches and trucks filled with more cans of kerosene and full tanker wagons were secured on the side decks
until 'there was hardly room to move'. Small consignments of
chocolate, biscuits, cigarettes, wines, spirits and mailbags were
stowed in strong-rooms and cargo lockers. The deck cargoes of
cased petrol were greater in some ships, and this flimsy method
of carriage of so inflammable a commodity was inferior to the
German 'jerry can'. Not only did it expose the ships to a huge

risk, but its presence worked adversely upon the imaginations of predominantly young crews. *Ohio*'s cargo of diesel oil and kerosene was clearly the exception to the loading rule, and made her preservation uniquely important.

Loaded at different ports in the Bristol Channel, Belfast, Liverpool and Glasgow, the merchant ships made the rendezvous at the Tail o' the Bank anchorage in the Clyde estuary, where they were largely cut off from the shore. The last drafts of army and navy gunners joined their ships, astonished at being welcomed by a party of senior officers, and the guns' crews, British and American, were given special supplementary training in the crypt of a bombed out-church. The simulated air attacks were chiefly designed to train the young gunners in aircraft recognition, in an attempt to minimise damage to friendly aircraft. Here too the ships' naval liaison officers with their small signals and coding staffs joined. On 1 August a signal was read to the crews of all the ships: the mission upon which they were about to depart was extremely dangerous, and anyone wishing to leave was free to do so. Despite all their fears and misgivings, not one man did. The following day all the merchant shipmasters, some of their second officers, senior radio officers, and naval liaison officers were summoned to the convoy conference aboard the cruiser *Nigeria*, flagship of Rear-Admiral Burrough. Since his last sorties into the Mediterranean, Burrough had been commanding the cruiser-covering forces of Arctic convoys; now he was to command the through-escort of PEDESTAL. The briefing was complex, carried out by Burrough himself, members of his staff, and the convoy commodore, Commander Venables. The old admonition that the convoy must get through was duly emphasised, and it was particularly impressed upon the masters that under no circumstances whatsoever were they to stop to pick up survivors; that duty would be assigned to the escorts. Not long after their return to their ships the cat was finally out of the bag, and the crews of all the merchantmen in company officially knew the worst: they were going to Malta.

It was a dull day, but at about 17.00 the weather cleared, and a fine evening promised when at 20.00 *Nigeria* weighed anchor. As the escort got under way the destroyer *Lamerton* collided with a passing merchant ship, the *Almenara*, and was so severely damaged that she dropped out of the operation. Meanwhile Commodore Venables aboard *Port Chalmers* gave the order, the flag hoists ran aloft and the windlasses of the fourteen fast cargo-ships and the single tanker began to weigh their anchors.[14]

Convoy WS21s headed out through the North Channel towards the Atlantic, and after daybreak next morning it gathered about it a steadily increasing number of warships. Watching from *Deucalion*, Dr Murphy was 'impressed by the escort. All the pessimism seemed unjustified.' To Cadet Andrews aboard *Empire Hope* it was a 'fantastically wonderful sight'. Warships were 'everywhere, with Coastal Command Sunderland flying boats overhead'.

The naval force accompanying WS21s was indeed formidable, with additional groups of ships assigned distinct tasks within the overall operation. The limited bunker capacity of the destroyers necessitated complex refuelling arrangements which were to continue unabated throughout the passage to Gibraltar, during the transit of the Strait, and until well into the Mediterranean.

The escorting warships were to comprise two main groups of ships, Forces Z and X. Force Z, under Vice-Admiral Syfret with his flag in *Nelson*, was to provide heavy cover and air support. To Syfret's battleships and carriers were assigned a large number of destroyers, some of which were to be available for detached duties. Force X was the through-escort of cruisers and destroyers, under Burrough in *Nigeria*. The subsidiary groups consisted of Force R, the refuelling detachment operating in the western Mediterranean;[15] Force Y, consisting of the two destroyers *Matchless* and *Badsworth*, which were to carry out Operation ASCENDANT, the reciprocal escort of *Troilus* and *Orari* from Malta to Gibraltar; and the 'local escort' from Malta, which would consist of the minesweepers and motor launches sent to the island during Operation HARPOON. Finally, submarine patrols were to be mounted to the north of Sicily by *Safari* and *Unbroken*, with *Utmost*, *United*, *Uproar*, *Ultimatum*, *Unruffled* and *P222* stationed between Malta and Tunisia.

Initially, as the convoy cleared the North Channel and headed out into the Atlantic at 12 knots, the ships destined to form these differing groups were variously deployed. Burrough was joined by a second cruiser, *Kenya*, and then from Scapa Flow by Syfret in *Nelson*, with *Rodney* in company. Numerous destroyers[16] arrived to form a screen, while the convoy, now proceeding south at 14 knots through rough seas, was subjected to extensive manoeuvres and exercises.

On the 4th the convoy was manoeuvred from four to two columns, to practise executing the change of deployment neces-sary prior to the night dash through the Sicilian Narrows. As the ships resumed their four-column formation, Burrough signalled: 'Exercises today were not so well carried out as I expected ... we must practice over and over again.' At 11.00 next morning a destroyer on the port wing hoisted the black flag indicating she was in contact with a U-boat, whereupon *Nelson* 'gave a pro-longed howl on her siren and the great convoy did a 45° turn to starboard'. It was PEDESTAL's first contact with the enemy and came to nothing, although a long-range Focke-Wulf Kondor was spotted in the distance the same evening.[17] Syfret continued to drill the ships throughout Friday. They executed emergency turns and zigzags and practised altering speed, wheeling, and changing the cruising disposition by both visual signal and short-range wireless telegraphy. The merchant ships carried out gun-drill, practising laying their weapons on bearings, angles of sight, and range judging. The naval liaison officers lectured the anti-aircraft guns' crews on what to expect from the enemy air forces, impressing upon them the enemy's proficiency at co-ordi-nated attacks, and that they should not allow themselves to become distracted, but must concentrate upon their own arcs of defensive fire. Alarm bells were tested for action stations, as were signals to check firing in order to avoid hitting friendly aircraft. Everything from fire-extinguishers to fenders and mooring wires was made ready as these laden vessels, no longer mundane mer-chantmen, were patiently metamorphosed into His Majesty's Military Transports.

Meanwhile the short-ranged destroyers fuelled, in choppy weather, from the cruisers and battleships. All the men-of-war practised high-angle shoots, which included the 16-inch main armament of *Nelson* and *Rodney* whose shells made a 'colossal bang when they went off at 10,000 feet'. This impressive display provoked debates on how the battleships' massive turrets could traverse quickly enough to react to multiple air attacks.

AT 07.00 on Saturday, 7 August, WS21s was overhauled by the first of the carriers, the flat-topped *Furious* and her air-guard, the cruiser *Manchester* with two destroyers, including the Polish *Blyskawica*. The carrier was loaded with Spitfires destined for

Malta. These, a later mark than had been shipped before, with a larger propeller diameter, had posed a potential problem in flying them off *Furious*'s odd flight deck, which thanks to the old ship's original two-stage conversion from a battle-cruiser was not flush. However, a successful trial of the Mark VB Spitfires had been run early on 5 August, and as fog came down that night *Furious* and *Manchester* set off after the convoy at speed.

The remaining aircraft-carriers which were to join Force Z were under the command of Rear-Admiral Lyster, flying his flag in *Victorious*, which bore new Sea Hurricanes of No. 885 Squadron, Fleet Air Arm. The carriers had been drawn from a number of sources. Lyster's flagship had left Scapa on 31 July and joined forces with *Argus* from the Clyde, screened by the cruiser *Sirius* and six destroyers;[18] *Indomitable*, covered by *Phoebe* and three destroyers,[19] had come north from Freetown, diverted from the Indian Ocean. A further three destroyers[20] and the carrier *Eagle* joined at the rendezvous from Gibraltar; *Eagle* had sixteen of her Sea Hurricane B1s fully operational and four in reserve, there being insufficient room to deploy all of them.

On 5 August, well out in the Atlantic to the west of Gibraltar, Lyster mustered his three main carriers, *Victorious*, *Indomitable* and *Eagle*. Anti-aircraft fire was provided to each carrier by an attached cruiser – *Sirius* stood air-guard to *Victorious*, *Phoebe* to *Indomitable*, and *Charybdis* to *Eagle* – and each had an anti-submarine destroyer detachment. *Argus* was present as fighter-director, and in support was a refuelling force from Freetown consisting of the oiler *Abbeydale* and corvettes *Burdock* and *Armeria*. Lyster now subjected the three fleet carriers to an intensive programme of tactical exercises designed to stretch both the ships and the seventy-two fighter aircraft aboard them.[21] They also taxed the air- and anti-submarine guards which had to follow the carriers as they headed into the wind, constantly changing course and speed as they worked their squadrons. Known as Operation BERSERK, the carrier exercise established the ships' intended tactical roles, with *Victorious*, having the higher proportion of Fulmars, providing low-altitude air cover while *Indomitable* and *Eagle*, with Martlets and Sea Hurricanes, would give the convoy high cover. Many of the embarked aircrews lacked combat experience and the exercises proved invaluable, though they ended with the regrettable loss of one of *Victorious*'s aircraft and her pilot. Unfortunately, Operation

BERSERK generated so great a number of radio transmissions that it was feared it gave warning of something major under way to the German radio intelligence service in Berlin.

Meanwhile the destroyers oiled amid the usual shambles of slow pumping, leaking connections, and inclement weather which parted the wires and compelled Lyster to send *Wishart* and *Derwent* to bunker in Gibraltar. On completion of Operation BERSERK the carriers proceeded to join up with Syfret's main force of convoy and escort on the 8th. Having carried out her fighter training duties *Argus*, with an escort of destroyers, was sent ahead into Gibraltar, and took no further part in the main operation.

As the main body of ships approached Gibraltar from the west, Coastal Command provided reassuring anti-submarine air-patrols. There now began the necessary shuffle of ships into the harbour to refuel, which occupied the night hours of 8/9 and 9/10 August. *Indomitable* and her screen refuelled first, followed by *Sirius*, *Manchester* and *Phoebe*. *Nigeria* and *Kenya* were replenished from *San Claudio* and *Brown Ranger*, although problems arose from incompatible equipment aboard the former, a chartered commercial tanker. The trail of thirsty destroyers entering Gibraltar seemed endless, for the offshore arrangements had been poor, especially the facility of *Abbeydale*. Vice-Admiral Sir Frederick Edward-Collins, now Flag-Officer, North Atlantic, at Gibraltar therefore had to cope with an unplanned modification to an already complicated bunkering schedule, reaping the harvest of neglect of replenishment-at-sea techniques during the pre-war years. Such was the disorder that *Indomitable* and *Manchester* had to be sent in twice to fill their tanks to capacity. Here *Wrestler* too dropped out of the operation, with a defective condenser.

Having run slightly ahead of its timing, the convoy was slowed and turned to the westward, which somewhat aided those sorting out this muddle. Aboard the warships the final briefings took place, given a poignant twist in those Home Fleet destroyers who had lately come from the humiliating débâcle of PQ17. Lieutenant-Commander Hill of *Ledbury* cleared the lower deck and addressed his ship's company. Confident of their ability to throw up an anti-aircraft barrage, Hill concluded: 'You know what happened on PQ17; as long as there is a merchant ship afloat, we shall stay with it.' There was gruff approval and grins all round. 'I felt a warm response,' Hill wrote later; 'we were spoiling for a fight together. As I climbed back to the bridge I thought that the ship would never be in better spirit or training for action. There was a strong touch of desperation and bloody-mindedness following PQ17 which applied, of course, much more strongly to myself.'[22]

While the men-of-war scrambled in and out of Gibraltar, those warships left with the convoy, as well as the merchantmen, continued to exercise. About noon on 8 August Lyster's carriers arrived; after dark these too joined the Gibraltar shuttle, but during the afternoon their aircraft subjected the convoy to mock air attacks, concluding with a fly-past intended to familiarise the multitude of gunners on the mass of shipping with the silhouettes of friendly aeroplanes.

As evening approached the convoy, now heading east again, moved in and out of fog patches through which the land came intermittently into sight. Spanish fishing boats were out in force, able to see the long lines of slow-moving ships.

Still the warships ran to and fro, in and out of Gibraltar under cover of night, as Forces Z and X completed fuelling. Aboard *Santa Elisa* the crew heard an enemy broadcast in which the merchant ships in WS21s were mentioned by name: it was clear the enemy were well aware of what was happening, and in some detail, possibly informed by the Spanish tunny fishermen. Anxious as he was about their failure to maintain security, Syfret found one consolation in the fact that the assorted ships had 'attained an efficiency in manoeuvring comparable to that of a fleet unit'.

In two columns, WS21s continued to steam through clusters of fishing boats. After dark these were all brightly lit and stretched across the strait 'like a necklace'. By 23.00 Cape Spartel lighthouse was abeam, and visibility then shut in again. Fog buoys were streamed, and as the ships of Operation PEDESTAL approached the entrance to the Mediterranean the convoy encountered two neutral merchant ships, one of which, a Vichy French passenger ship on a reciprocal course, passed down the centre of the convoy. As the ships took evasive action fog settled again, and this caused a degree of disruption. In this state they passed Gibraltar in the early hours of 10 August 1942.[23]

*

Unsurprisingly, Italian agents at Algeciras had alerted Rome to the movement of numerous ships. Two cruiser squadrons, at Cagliari and Messina, were ordered to prepare for sea, while torpedo-boats, aircraft and submarines were alerted, some of the latter being diverted to intercept what was thought at first by certain members of the Italian staff to be either a major landing force or a large delivery of aircraft to Malta. The magnitude of the fleet, however, inclined Comando Supremo to assume at first that the British intended the neutralisation of Axis airfields on Sardinia, for it was judged too great to be simply a convoy to Malta. Yet since the presence of merchant ships argued that an attempt might be made to reach the island, air reconnaissance was ordered for dawn on 11 August, and the submarine dispositions were finalised with eight boats north of Algiers, six off Bizerta, five off Cape Bon and one, *Asteria*, to the west of Malta.[24] The Axis response would depend upon whether the British, if they were intending to attempt to push supplies through to Malta, reversed the course of their heavy ships off the Skerki Bank, as was customary, or whether the extra muscle was used to reduce the odds in getting the transports through to the beleaguered island. In the course of the deliberations in Rome doubt was expressed as to whether there was sufficient oil fuel for Iachino's battleships – either a genuine indication of Supermarina's plight, or merely a deployment of the usual argument against using Italy's capital ships. Whatever the case, Da Zara was to command a combined cruiser strike force if the British battleships and carriers turned back.

On the assumption that Supermarina *would* mobilise the battleships of the Regia Marina as it had against MW11, and to 'prevent the enemy directing the full weight of surface and air forces against the convoy being run from Gibraltar',[25] Admiral Harwood had been instructed to mount a diversionary operation in the Eastern Mediterranean, code-named MG3.

With Rommel at the borders of Egypt and Axis submarines harrying British coastal shipping and laying mines off the coast, Harwood had withdrawn from Alexandria, and his flag now flew from a sloop at Ismailia in the Suez Canal. The dismantling of dockyard facilities at Alexandria was witnessed by Admiral Godfroy's French squadron, still languishing there. The *Queen Elizabeth* had been undocked on 27 June and sent through the canal *en route* to America for permanent repairs, and the depot and repair ships were moved south of the canal by way of Port Said. One of these, *Medway*, was sunk off Port Said by *U372* with the consequent further loss of valuable facilities, torpedoes, ammunition and stores. Meanwhile the Mediterranean Fleet, or what was left of it, had withdrawn to Port Said, Haifa and Beirut. Yet there were a few glimmers of light illuminating these dark days. At Malta, Leatham was of the opinion that the 10th Submarine Flotilla could return to Marsamxett, since Doram's minesweepers had cleared the approaches. They would need diesel fuel, but this was optimistically expected in *Ohio*. In the eastern basin of the Mediterranean the destruction of Axis submarines by British aircraft and warships continued relentlessly, and an enemy supply convoy had been attacked by Fleet Air Arm Albacores after the British biplanes had been boldly refuelled in the desert, behind enemy lines.

Operation MG3 was to make a westwards feint from Port Said and Haifa, using the remnants of MW11, redesignated convoy MW12. At 20.00 on 10 August, therefore, the three Ellerman liners, *City of Pretoria*, *City of Lincoln* and *City of Edinburgh*, left Port Said under the escort of the cruisers *Arethusa* (Captain Chapman, Senior Officer), *Euryalus* and *Coventry*, with ten destroyers.[26] Under Captain Deighton, the master of the *City of Pretoria*, who was to act as commodore, these three sister-ships constituted convoy MW12a. Its counterpart, MW12b, left Haifa at 05.00 the following morning, and consisted of *Ajax*, under the escort of Vian in *Cleopatra*, with *Dido* and five destroyers.[27] The two forces joined up just before daylight, turning and steaming west throughout the daylight hours of 11 August until roughly due north of Alexandria. After dark Vian led most of the warships away to bombard Rhodes, while the Ellerman and Blue Funnel liners turned back.[28] *City of Pretoria*, escorted by *Eridge* and *Hursley*, returned to Port Said; *City of Edinburgh* and *Ajax*, with *Beaufort*, *Belvoir*, *Croome* and *Tetcott*, proceeded to Haifa; while *City of Lincoln*, with *Dulverton* and *Hurworth*, made for Beirut as though on 'normal traffic routes'. The illusion of the continuing westwards progress of convoy MW12 was kept up by false radio transmissions and some flares dropped by aircraft. Operation MG3 not only passed off 'without incident' – it failed to elicit any action from the Italians. It is an irony that Harwood might well have been able to run MW12 through to Malta.

Indeed, as his report concluded, 'the only point of interest was that considerable disappointment was expressed by the merchant ships taking part, when they found they were not going through to Malta.'

While Operation MG3 was in progress and the PEDESTAL ships were debouching into the Mediterranean, the ships of Operation ASCENDANT left Malta after dark and headed west. Having languished in Grand Harbour for seven weeks, *Orari* and *Troilus* were to be extricated. Life aboard *Orari* had been uncomfortable because of the list necessary to repair the mine damage, but the dockyard, 'working with scratch materials under very difficult conditions', managed to patch the hole, and the ship was returned to an even keel. Socially, the ship's company had enjoyed playing 'several naval and military teams at football, cricket and water polo.' *Troilus* had been caught in the last of the air raids and covered in debris, but both ships emerged 'to load about 2,000 tons of scrap metal and empty ammunition cases, together with a large number of worn-out gun barrels ... A large and gratifying percentage of the scrap consisted of the wreckage of Axis planes ... '[29] Before sailing, the ships embarked captured Axis aircrews and some sick and wounded naval personnel. The departure of the two cargo-liners, under the escort of the patched-up destroyers *Matchless* and *Badsworth*, was supposed to be secret, 'but thousands of troops and Maltese lined the walls and bastions and gave [them] a really rousing send-off'. After dark, Italian recognition stripes of red and white were painted across the ships' decks as they steamed south-west to the Tripolitanian coast. Offshore they turned north and slowed, behaving like an Italian convoy until darkness should allow them to slip round Cape Bon; during this tense day they were overflown by indifferent Italian transport aircraft. At dark they fell into line ahead and increased speed, *Matchless* leading *Orari* and *Badsworth* bringing up the rear astern of *Troilus*. Heading close into the coast at 21.30, *Matchless* suddenly turned away to starboard as she opened fire on a dimly perceived shape no more than half a mile away on her port bow. This was the Italian destroyer *Lanzerotto Malocello*, engaged in minelaying, and the ships following *Matchless* consequently gave the *Malocello* a wide berth. According to British sources, fire was feebly returned, though the Italians claimed that they used false recognition lights to deceive the British, who disappeared in the darkness.[30]

By daylight all the British ships except *Matchless* had scrubbed off their Italian markings and this 'seemed to puzzle the few German and Italian aircraft which discovered us before the day was far advanced. They snooped round very inquisitively, but took no action ... until one Ju88 came so close that *Badsworth* [and *Orari* simultaneously] ... opened fire ... Both ships scored hits and he sheered away to the coast, pouring out smoke and losing height as he disappeared.'

There were no further encounters with the enemy, who were now concentrating on the PEDESTAL ships, the arcs of whose tracer shells could be seen on the northern horizon from the bridges of the westbound ships. Air escort arrived next day, the 13th, and at 11.00 on 14 August the four vessels arrived at Gibraltar to congratulatory signals from Edward-Collins and Leatham; the latter was 'very pleased that our little subterfuge had worked'.[31] There was also an exchange with the *Durham*, then still lying damaged at Gibraltar, whose officers were well known to those of *Orari*. The *Orari* and the *Troilus* left Gibraltar the following evening, and in due course finally parted company off Holyhead. The Blue Funnel liner headed for her home port of Liverpool while *Orari* went on to Glasgow, discharged her PoWs and received a visit from the Lord Provost, representatives of the Admiralty, the MoWT, and her owners.

The provision of fuel to the short-ranged destroyers in Operation PEDESTAL dominated the early progress of the principal operation. The refuelling group, Force R, had sailed from Gibraltar at 21.30 on the 9th to work ahead of the approaching ships.

In the small hours of 10 August the main force passed The Rock, the ships awaiting a clearance of the fog in order to restore order to the disrupted formation. Visibility improved at 05.00 and at daylight 'not a breath of wind ruffled the surface of the azure sea'. Meanwhile the transports, having slowed in the fog, increased speed to 13.5 knots and resumed a four-column cruising disposition, two on either side of a central column consisting of the two battleships and the carriers. Beyond this, the destroyers formed an anti-submarine screen. All day the remaining warships were arriving from Gibraltar to join the fleet, and by 16.00 the last carrier group, that of *Eagle*, had completed the muster.

The day should have passed peacefully, but the failure of RAF Hudsons flying anti-submarine patrols on behalf of the force to use their identification beacons resulted in the scrambling of combat air patrols from *Victorious*, the leading carrier. To Syfret's annoyance this broke the radio silence carefully maintained, despite the fog, since entering the Strait the previous evening.

Then, at 17.00, a Vichy French civilian airliner flying from France to Algeria was seen above the convoy, and its broadcast report was monitored. Two British battleships, it was announced to the world, with aircraft-carriers, cruisers and destroyers, were escorting twelve merchant ships east at a steady speed – information which was soon in the hands of the enemy in Rome.

19

'You men cannot be replaced'

(Operations BELLOWS *and* PEDESTAL, *with Convoy WS21s)*

THE REFUELLING CONTINUED, and at 21.30 on the evening of 10 August Captain Onslow led off in *Ashanti* with seven other destroyers to make a rendezvous with Force R and initiate the next phase of bunkering.[1] It was now that the first attack on the PEDESTAL ships was made, by Tenente di Vascello Targia. At 03.40 the hydrophones of his submarine, *Uarsciek*, submerged on her war patrol station, picked up the distant engine noises of Force R. Targia surfaced and ran west, sighting what he erroneously reported as an aircraft-carrier and battleship. Circling, he fired a salvo of three torpedoes, which missed their target and appear to have exploded impotently at the termination of their runs, though two torpedoes were seen to break surface by lookouts aboard the escorting corvette *Coltsfoot*.[2]

Meanwhile, at daylight Onslow's destroyers began to screen Force R as the tankers started refuelling the cruisers *Phoebe* and *Sirius*. They were then themselves topped up, after which individual ships either remained with Force R as other destroyers and *Cairo* arrived, or were sent back to join the main body. During the early forenoon the tug *Jaunty* left Force R, transferring to the convoy. About 18.30 that evening Onslow was to be relieved by Hutton's *Laforey*, and at 20.30, with *Brown Ranger* down to 100 tons, refuelling was broken off for the night. The two tankers had by now refuelled three cruisers and twenty-four destroyers. The following morning *Dingledale* transferred 1,000 tons into the Royal Fleet Auxiliary – but long before this the enemy had struck at the convoy, with fatal results.

Enemy aerial reconnaissance had located the fleet early on the morning of 11 August. Although co-operation between the Axis powers was poor, even when united in a major joint operation, the Luftwaffe's ability to transfer resources swiftly was startling. During 10/11 August several units of Fliegerkorps II were switched from Cyrenaica to Trapani in Sicily; they included a Stukagruppe, and they were joined by ten Heinkel HeIII H2s.[3] Further reinforcements in the form of Ju88s from Fliegerkorps X based in Crete were flown to Sicily on 11 and 12 August, and more aircraft from several units were scrambled to operate against the British in the next few days as they became available. Some of them flew from Sardinia to complete their sorties in Sicily; others, including bombers from Kampfgeschwader 54, flew sorties from Pantelleria.

The Axis commanders met on the morning of 11 August, when Kesselring informed the Italians that his aircraft would be unable to supply air cover to the Regia Marina. It seems that, despairing of the Italians achieving much, he preferred to take matters into his own hands: the Luftwaffe units, he told Comando Supremo, were fully committed, with fighter escorts being furnished to the bomber groups assigned to act against the British convoy. He suggested to Comando Supremo that the Italians should lay minefields. The Chief of the Italian Naval Staff, Ammiraglio Riccardi, considered the existing minefields to be adequate, and turned to the head of the Regia Aeronautica, Generalissimo Fougier, for air support for the Regia Marina's surface units. Fougier considered the movement of the British Mediterranean Fleet, Operation MG3, to be the more important, a view which was vehemently opposed by Ammiraglio Sansonetti, who feared both the western force and its carrier-borne capacity to strike at the battered airfields of Sardinia. Sansonetti cogently pointed out that a raiding party, landed on 9th August from the British submarine *Una*, had been picked up near Cagliari. Could it have been the precursor of something more sinister?

The meeting revealed the split between the air and naval arms, and the Italians' reliance upon the Luftwaffe to provide fighter air cover for their warships. Fougier spoke of 'cleaning the sky', but he had only fourteen Macchi Mc202 fighters immediately available, and preferred a rapid reinforcment of his western units in Sardinia and Sicily. He also placed great faith in radio-controlled aircraft which, each armed with 1,000-pound bombs, were to be directed at the British aircraft-carriers.

The meetings seem to have come to no real conclusions, beyond that of returning the repaired cruiser *Muzio Attendolo* from Naples to Da Zara's squadron, then at Cagliari, instead of sending the ship to Navarino. That afternoon a second conference was held. The Chief of the Army Staff, Count Cavallero, considered the capability of Malta-based British aircraft to be a threat, and Riccardi added this to his lack of oil to rule out action by Iachino's battleships. It was an indecisive muddle, based on false assumptions and old anxieties, fatal to the Italian cause. Although the initiative lay within grasp of the Italian high command, it contented itself with advancing stale excuses and adopting worn-out and half-hearted measures. There was talk of matters improving when they had access to the Caucasian oil-fields; in the meantime the British convoy from Gibraltar would be harried by the submarine patrols lying between Formentera and Algiers, and off Cape Bon. After this, an attack by *MAS*-boats from Pantelleria would further damage it, while Da Zara, combining his own 7th with Parona's 3rd Division, would fall upon the enemy with his cruisers.

The Regia Aeronautica were to supply the bulk of the torpedo bombers, SM79s which, along with some other torpedo-armed aircraft and their covering fighters, were deployed during 10 and 11 August; Fougier's air forces, which would finally number in all more than three hundred aeroplanes, would not be ready to attack until the 12th. So in the meantime matters would be left to Kesselring, who was preparing a probing attack for that evening. In the event, despite the failure of Comando Supremo to seize the opportunity by mobilising all its available resources, the air-assault was to prove formidable enough.

At 08.15 on 11 August the British aerial surveillance radars in the fleet detected the presence of shadowing aircraft; from then onwards, enemy snooping was continuous. At daylight the carriers, each with her guarding cruiser astern, had spread out across the rear of the convoy in line abreast, and air patrols took off. The long-range Ju88s were flying at 20,000 feet, and proved elusive; nevertheless, five interceptions were made, in which one Ju88 was shot down by Sea Hurricanes from *Indomitable*. One of these fighters was forced to ditch during the afternoon, but a circling Fulmar 23 miles away to the north led *Westcott* to the floating pilot. During this day a defective Fulmar was also lost, but its pilot was rescued.

By late morning Vice-Admiral Edward-Collins at Gibraltar had informed Syfret of a monitored enemy transmission from Rome. Broadcast to 'all units and stations', it had alerted enemy forces to the position and progress of the PEDESTAL fleet. Only a few minutes later, at 11.28, lookouts aboard both *Nelson* and *Charybdis* shouted out that torpedoes had been seen breaking surface on the starboard quarter of the convoy. This was ominous; the notorious changes of salinity and density in the extreme west of the Mediterranean Sea, where the warmer waters flowed west over a cold influx of the Atlantic, provided a perfect cloak for submarines to work close to the convoy without detection by sonar.

By noon the ships were some 580 miles west of Malta, zigzagging at 13 knots on a mean line of advance of due east. The day remained fine and sunny. Destroyer crews who had come from the Arctic revelled in the warmth, and eyes tended to be drawn upwards, in expectation of the inevitable air attack. Overhead flew eight fighters, four of them Sea Hurricanes from *Eagle*. At 12.18 the carrier *Furious*, slightly astern of the main body and screened by *Lightning* and *Lookout*, edged out to the north. Aboard *Furious* the flight deck crews prepared to launch forty Spitfires to fly on to Malta in the subsidiary Club Run known as Operation BELLOWS. Ten minutes later the first Spitfire successfully roared down the humped flight deck and lifted into the sky, followed by fifteen more, until the operation was abruptly broken off at 13.15, as all the ships were shaken by a rapid series of four underwater explosions. Staring round for the victim, the astonished cry was quickly raised on a score of bridges: 'It's the *Eagle*!'

The dispersal of the destroyers throughout the fleet had necessarily diluted the anti-submarine screen, although their comings and goings had frustrated watching and waiting enemy submariners whose hydrophones had alerted them to the approaching convoy and who had already made several unsuccessful attacks.

Now, the immutable laws of physics favoured Kapitänleutnant Rosenbaum. Having sighted the convoy approaching from the west, he ducked below the impenetrable density interface and worked *U73* through the destroyer screen, undetected by British sonar. Rosenbaum's orders from Admiral Kreisch at La Spezia were to target the aircraft-carriers rather than the merchantmen, and a mixture of fortune and skill now made of him the *Eagle*'s nemesis. Just in the rear of *Wairangi*, the aftermost transport in the starboard column, the British carrier loomed in the Zeiss optics of Rosenbaum's attack periscope. He fired a salvo of four torpedoes, all of which hit the *Eagle* along her port side. Rosenbaum sent his crew forward and dived deep. *U73* was not in the best condition, and her commander was anxious to minimise the effects of the inevitable counter-attack.

The carrier, steaming at 13 knots, rapidly listed to port and slewed to starboard, shedding the parked Sea Hurricanes on her flight deck into the sea in a succession of splashes. As the ship rolled over, a handful of men walked round her bilge; others jumped overboard as the screams of those trapped below rose through the vent pipes. In eight minutes *Eagle* drove under the surface, her four bronze propellers still revolving as she did so. The shock waves rippled through the convoy. 'Immediately [*Nelson*] gave the warning [on her siren] and we did a 45° turn to port, then another,' wrote Dickens aboard *Dorset*, 'and after a few minutes a 90° one to starboard ... Speed was increased to 15.9 knots - the extreme.'

About twelve minutes after he had fired his salvo, Rosenbaum's submarine was shaken by the awesome explosions of the plunging *Eagle*'s boilers. The concussion experienced by the carrier's survivors, bobbing in their hundreds in the water, was agonising.

Quickly on the scene, the tug *Jaunty* picked up 198 men. She was joined by *Lookout*, hurriedly detached by Syfret from screening *Furious*, and *Laforey* was also soon assisting, though to the men in the water the destroyers seemed 'to be busy doing something else and some were dropping depth charges far too near for comfort.'[4] The counter-attack was mounted by Commander Broome in *Keppel*, leading a group of five destroyers which were coming up from Gibraltar after bunkering in order to escort *Furious* west, on completion of Operation BELLOWS. One, *Malcolm*, was detached to help Hutton but the rest sought

Rosenbaum, in vain.[5] 'For about an hour and a half after the sinking of *Eagle*', Syfret recorded, 'numerous sightings of submarines and torpedoes and asdic contacts were reported but there is no conclusive proof of a second U-boat being in the vicinity.' Rosenbaum had escaped, coming to periscope depth later to report his success, for which he was awarded the Ritterkreuz.

Meanwhile, at 13.50, Operation BELLOWS had resumed. During the launching of the forty Spitfires, radar had detected an enemy aircraft flying at great height, and the huge 16-inch guns of *Nelson* and *Rodney* threw up a radar-controlled barrage for a few minutes. Their target was a single Ju88 on a photo-reconnaissance mission. Despite this, an hour later thirty-eight Mark VB Spitfires were flying towards Malta. One had to land almost immediately on *Indomitable* with defects, while another failed to reach its destination. The *Furious*'s escorts were still astern of the fleet, engaged in the hunt for *Eagle*'s attacker. The tug and Hutton's two destroyers had by now picked up 927 survivors from the carrier's crew of 1160, including Captain L. Mackintosh. *Jaunty* was 'an astounding sight ... literally hidden by a mass of bodies'.[6] His task accomplished, Hutton now rejoined the main force, soon afterwards followed by Broome, whereupon Syfret ordered one of Broome's destroyers, *Amazon*, to take the much slower *Jaunty* under her wing and join Force R. The detachment of the tug as a rescue vessel was later seen, at a time when her presence would have proved invaluable, to have been a mistake.

Having gathered all the destroyers, Syfret ordered the survivors aboard *Laforey* to transfer to *Keppel* and those in *Lookout* to be put aboard *Venomous*. The flat calm enabled this to be done by running each pair of destroyers alongside, and when it had finished at about 18.30 Hutton left to relieve Onslow's *Ashanti* with Force R, and to bunker *Laforey* and *Lookout*. At this time Broome's *Keppel*, with *Venomous*, *Malcolm*, *Wrestler* and *Wolverine*, joined Captain Bulteel in *Furious*, and the old carrier and her screen turned back for Gibraltar.

Bulteel and Broome steamed west into the sunset. After midnight the officer of the watch aboard *Wolverine* called his captain, Lieutenant-Commander Gretton, informing him that he had a radar contact. Gretton, rightly assuming the echo to be a surfaced submarine, altered course towards it. Steaming at 26 knots, Gretton impetuously ran down the bearing and 'hit her fair and

square at the after end of the conning tower ... The shock was terrific. The ship seemed to come up all standing, the impact throwing off their feet all those not holding on ... we seemed to lift out
of the water, then silence followed by a heavy explosion.' Gretton
had destroyed the Italian submarine *Dagabur* (Tenente di
Vascello Pecori), which had been running on the surface.
Wolverine was severely damaged forward and a main steam pipe
had fractured, filling her engine room with superheated steam
and causing its evacuation. However, the boilers were undamaged, and in about forty minutes the starboard turbine was again
working. Broome sent *Malcolm* back to stand by and in due
course Gretton's elderly destroyer limped west at some 6 knots,
her company rigging hand gear and recovering one anchor cable
which hung down from the wrecked bow. The following
morning *Malcolm* was diverted to assist Sunderland *TK7R* from
Gibraltar which was attacking the Italian submarine *Giada*.
Although damaged, *Giada* escaped destruction, and the
destroyer broke away. In due course *Malcolm* was to be sent east
again at high speed, but the attack on the leaking *Giada* was not
over. Her commander, Tenente di Vascello Cavallina, was later
forced to surface, to be spotted and bombed by a second
Sunderland, *TK7C*, which she was compelled to engage. After
the aircraft had further shaken the *Giada*, Cavallina's gunners
succeeded in hitting the Sunderland, which blew up in the air
while making her second attack. *Giada* thereupon ran for the
neutral though sympathetic Spanish port of Valencia, from
where, on 14 August, she limped back to La Maddelena.

Gretton's battered *Wolverine* was met at dawn on the 13th by
the corvettes *Burdock* and *Armeria*, and berthed at Gibraltar at
noon.[7] *Furious*, protected by Broome and her own anti-submarine Albacores, had long since arrived at Gibraltar and gone
directly into dock, a circumstance that led the Italians to think
she had been torpedoed; in fact the docking helped the loading
of a second consignment of Spitfires, ready for Operation BARI-
TONE.

The main body of Operation PEDESTAL had passed the first
patrol line of Axis submarines by the late afternoon of 11 August,
a number of evasive turns having been made, especially by the
carriers, as alert and nervous lookouts reported what they took
to be torpedo tracks.[8] A light breeze had sprung up and this

caused 'sufficient white horses ... to conceal a submarine's peri-scope feather'. Well before dark the deep-draughted battleships, cruisers and merchantmen streamed their paravanes, and while this task was in hand Syfret received further intelligence from Gibraltar that a dusk air-attack was probable. With Captain Hutton, the senior destroyer officer, still oiling from Force R, which the convoy had now overtaken, Onslow was ordered to extend the distance between the destroyer screen and the convoy. This opened up the formation in preparation for incoming bombers, and at the same time the Hunts were positioned so that they could give flank covering fire in the column intervals. Shortly after this, three shadowers made their presence felt and the British fighter patrols were kept 'extremely busy'.

Hutton had retained one of *Eagle*'s survivors 'to act as a most useful aircraft warning liaison and fighter direction officer'.[9] *Laforey*'s tanks were now topped up and Hutton, leaving Force R well astern, increased speed to take station at the head of the convoy in the advanced screen. He was just in time. Radar picked up a formation of enemy aircraft at 20.30, and Syfret was relieved to find his destroyer force at full strength at a crucial moment. 'At 20.35', recorded Dickens, 'Q flag was hoisted sig-nifying for all ships to be ready for air attack in 7 minutes. Then B was hoisted, "Prepare for instant air attack".' The carriers' Sea Hurricanes were vectored out to intercept, but the Ju88s evaded them with little trouble, arriving over the convoy ahead of their pursuers.

The enemy made their first bombing attack from 8,000 feet and at 20.56, a quarter of an hour after sunset, the destroyers opened fire, to be quickly followed by the rest of the ships. The barrage was tremendous, the noise deafening, and the rising shells exploded in puffs of smoke. *Laforey*'s first two salvoes burst behind an arrow-head formation of five Junkers Ju88 bombers, then the third 'corrected salvo pockmarked the sky, bursting right among [the aircraft] ... One fell away, trailing smoke and flames, and plummeted into the sea a couple of miles to port. A second plane showed a trail of smoke behind one engine but flew on, maintaining formation. Almost at once, the whole sky round the aircraft blackened with myriad shell bursts ... The bombs dropped by the remaining planes exploded harmlessly within the lines of merchant ships. Later, in the dusk, a half-hearted attack on the convoy with torpedoes dropped at long range by

over thirty Heinkel and Junkers [*sic*] bombers proved unsuccessful, while four of them were shot down by fleet gun fire.'

Aboard *Empire Hope* dusk had brought the gunners a stand-
down from their quarters, but within two minutes 'we were back
at action stations ... Tracers everywhere ... The noise [was] deafening. Bursting shells and great white plumes of water shot into
the air by near miss bombs. On top of all this din we had ... sirens
whooping, ordering emergency turns ...'[10]

In the middle of this assault the sonar operator aboard the
destroyer *Quentin* obtained a response and, while throwing up
his contribution to the barrage, Lieutenant-Commander Noble
conned *Quentin* into a series of three sub-surface attacks before
breaking off an inconclusive action on a submarine. The
destroyer rejoined her place in the forward screen at 21.40, just as
the air attack was driven off. As it ended the Sea Hurricanes
returned, their fuel running low. Arriving back over the convoy,
their pilots were met by a sight which took their breath away:
'The light was slowly dying, and the ships were no more than
patterns of the grey steel plate of the sea; but where we had left
them sailing peaceably through the sunset, now they were
enclosed in a sparkling net of tracer and bursting shells ... Every
gun in the fleet and convoy was firing, and the darkening air was
laced with threads and beads of flame.'[11]

But returning to their carriers was not to prove easy: 'We
moved round the fleet, and the bursts of fire followed us; and the
truth could no longer be disregarded. They were firing at anything that flew.' The airwaves were filled with the plaintive pleas
of pilots increasingly desperate to set their empty fighters down.
The Hurricanes were compelled to make their approaches
through the barrage and several, their tanks empty, crash-landed
on *Victorious* as she turned under full helm, the flashes of exploding empty fuel tanks lighting up the deepening dusk. Seeing the
plight of his Hurricanes, Captain Troubridge broke out of the
destroyer screen, illuminated his deck lights and steamed a
straight course at 26 knots to enable the dejected Fleet Air Arm
pilots to land on *Indomitable*.

Suddenly there was silence. 'Fagged out', men lay down to
sleep at their action stations. Syfret claimed only three of of the
thirty-six attacking Ju88s and HeIIIs as having definitely fallen to
the fleet's 'spectacular' barrage, one almost certainly to *Cairo*.
Several ships reported seeing mines being dropped. The German

aircraft also attacked and bombed Force R and *Jaunty*, though no hits were scored. In the air, the failing light prevented the fleet's fighters from achieving anything; they had to be landed perilously after dark, 'and in doing so some were fired on by our own ships.'

Having probed the British defences, the Luftwaffe withdrew. It was clear to observers that 'no attempt was made to bomb merchant ships', but several reported the carrier *Victorious* to have been the target. Captain Bovell had had to take drastic action, manoeuvring his ship under full helm as sticks of bombs fell uncomfortably close. From *Rochester Castle* it seemed that 'the attacks were not pressed home, the enemy showing [a] marked inclination to avoid the barrage'.[12] 'Soon after dark, action stations fell out and everyone settled down to snatch as much sleep as watch-keeping duties would allow.' One cadet in *Empire Hope* recalled ruefully: 'Galley shut down so no hot food for anyone.' Lack of food was to prove not the least of the problems confronting these predominantly young men during the next three days, though things were better aboard the warships: 'We relaxed into three watches, overhauled the guns, got up ammunition, had a hot stew and tried to think of everything needed for the next day.'[13]

In July Air Vice-Marshal Sir Keith Park had taken over from Lloyd as Air Officer Commanding at Malta. The very night he did so he mounted a series of small but disruptive air raids on enemy air fields in Sardinia, Sicily and Pantelleria with fifteen Beauforts, all that were available from combining the resources of Nos 39, 86 and 217 Squadrons of the Royal Air Force. The Beauforts, led by Wing-Commander R. Gibbs, were escorted by fifteen Beaufighters from Nos 235 and 252 Squadrons, led by Wing-Commander Shore. Other raids were made at dusk, on Elmas and Decimomannu airfields, by nine Beaufighters of No. 248 Squadron led by Wing-Commander Pike, and these were followed up later in the night by bombing raids by four American Liberators borrowed from the Middle East. Pike overflew Italian submarines, but the alerted defences at Elmas frustrated his attack, though one enemy plane was hit. At Decimomannu he had better luck, destroying four SM79s and a Cant Ca164 and inflicting damage on eleven others. On his return flight Pike spotted Da Zara's 7th Cruiser Division and its destroyer screen as they left Cagliari steering east. Receiving this information, Park sent off the radar-equipped Wellington *O-Orange*, which made an unsuccessful bombing attack on Da Zara at 01.30 on 12 August before returning to Malta.

Da Zara, with the cruisers *Eugenio di Savoia* and *Raimondo Montecuccoli*, screened by the destroyers *Gioberti* and *Oriani*, steamed east to meet the third cruiser of his own division, the *Muzio Attendolo*, along with Parona's heavy cruisers *Gorizia* and *Bolzano* from Naples. Also due on the rendezvous at 19.00 that evening from La Spezia was the heavy cruiser *Trieste*.

At the earliest glimmer of light on the 12th, radar located the day's first enemy shadowers. Long-range Ju88s and Cant Z.1007bis aircraft reported the convoy's progress. It was 05.30, and as the ships' crews went to action stations two Sea Hurricanes and two Fulmars were launched from *Victorious* and *Indomitable*. Forty minutes later another twelve fighters took off from the British carriers, lifting into the clear dawn air while the convoy drew the cruisers and Hunts close about it. However, Syfret had been warned to expect the second line of Axis submarines in the vicinity of Galita Island, and Hutton was therefore instructed that the intervals between his fleet destroyers should not be excessive.The presence of the suspected submarines was confirmed at 07.41, when *Kenya*'s helm went over to comb the track of three torpedoes. Her station in the rear of the convoy, between the two battleships, suggested the enemy were after either *Nelson* or *Rodney*.

By now the sun had risen high in the blue, cloudless sky; it was a perfect Mediterranean morning. Shortly before 09.00 the first wave of nineteen Ju88s approached from the east to make a high-level bombing pass over the convoy. The fleet barrage was again formidable and the fighter defence proved more effective than the previous evening, though it failed to interdict the powerful Ju88s, merely hampering their approach and forcing a few to jettison their bombs; moreover, the leader of *Victorious*'s No. 885 Sea Hurricane Squadron, Lieutenant Carver, was shot down. British claims of damage to the enemy were excessive, but six German aeroplanes were lost,[14] without damage to any ship. Hardly had the Junkers bombers droned away than Hutton's destroyer gained and attacked a sonar contact. Its source eluded *Laforey*, but a few minutes later, at 09.35, a contact was picked up by *Fury*, stationed on the starboard wing of the screen, and she was soon joined by *Foresight*. In accordance with standing orders, when fleet destroyers broke away from the screen the supporting Hunts were to move into the gaps to prevent penetration; *Bicester* and *Ledbury*, on the flanks of the leading outer transports, *Deucalion* to port and *Glenorchy* to starboard, therefore closed up.

As the convoy approached the new enemy submarine patrol line, several of those already passed remained in pursuit: *Uarsciek* was still in sight of the rear of the convoy, *U73* was not far off, and *Giada* was trying to catch up when she was attacked by the patrolling Sunderland and *Malcolm* in the closing phases of BELLOWS, mentioned earlier. *Fury* and *Foresight*, however, were in sonar contact with *Brin*, and Tenente di Vascello Andreotti slipped away to elude Lieutenant-Commanders Campbell and Fell by a deep dive. As two further destroyers peeled off to join in, Hutton recalled all four: the progress of the convoy was ultimately more important than actually killing an enemy boat, while a weakening of the screen exposed the transports, capital ships and carriers to attack from undetected submarines ahead of the fleet.

In the respite from air attack the shadowers edged in to probe the defence, but intermittent bursts of gunfire from the outer ring of destroyers drove them off. During the lull, two Fulmars from *Victorious*'s No. 884 Squadron were painstakingly vectored up-sun to shoot down a Savoia Marchetti shadower. A second long-range SM79 was similarly trapped, but the Italian aircraft was so well defended in the chase that its gunners damaged the pursuing Fulmars, which had to return to their carrier.

A little less than two hours later *Pathfinder*, on the port wing, steamed off to run down a sonar bearing and drop depth charges on a contact. She was supported by *Zetland*, but after fifteen minutes they had lost their quarry. In the face of the two destroyers Korvettenkapitän Reschke had abandoned his approach, and *U205* escaped destruction. Disappointed, Gibbs in *Pathfinder* led his colleague back to the screen.

It was now noon, and a large formation of aircraft was located ahead of the fleet, flying towards it. Whatever the deficiencies of the Regia Aeronautica at a strategic level, the tactical effect of this wave from Sardinia proved impressive, based as it was on a carefully co-ordinated mass attack. The Fleet Air Arm fighters were soon embroiled in aerial combat as the first group of enemy aircraft approached. The Sea Hurricanes were engaged with the escorting fighters, the fourteen Macchi Mc202s from Decimomannu with which Fougier was intending to sweep the sky clean. The approaching mass of aircraft was first seen from the fleet by lookouts in *Ashanti*, who spotted the smoke trail of a damaged SM84 at 12.10. A moment later the barrage opened up as ten SM84 bombers dropped motorised mines, *motobombas*, infernal devices which drove themselves round in a circle of several kilometres' diameter by means of compressed air, and which were persistently referred to in British reports as ordinary mines.[15] Seeing the descending parachutes, Syfret immediately ordered an eight-point turn and the fleet swung away to the north, reverting to the mean line of advance some minutes later. The evasion avoided contact, but by then a squadron of obsolete Fiat CR42 Falco biplanes had mounted diversionary attacks to draw the destroyers' fire. Despite being mauled by *Indomitable*'s Martlets, a few flew gallantly on to drop small bombs, near-missing *Lightning*.

Superaereo, the Regia Aeronautica's high command, had intended a mass attack, but the distances to be flown had slightly retarded the units and they failed to overwhelm the British defence by *force majeure*; instead they arrived in three distinct waves, and it was now that the third, consisting of the main for-mation, arrived. There were thirty-three SM79s and ten SM84s, all armed as torpedo-bombers and covered by twenty-six Caproni-Reggiane Re2001s. The carriers' fighters had somewhat disrupted this assault, breaking up the SM84s of 130 Gruppo, but the SM79s roared in from either side of the fleet. Many dropped their torpedoes early, deterred by the furious flak thrown up from the destroyers and a splash barrage laid down by salvoes from *Nelson* and *Rodney*, but a few bravely pressed home their approach, heading determinedly for *Nelson*, though two Savoias and a Reggiane were shot down. As the aircraft withdrew, the Luftwaffe's supporting contribution of thirty-seven Ju88s from Sicily arrived in small groups at heights of 10,000 to 15,000 feet. This was too high for the Sea Hurricanes, which were forced to wait until the Ju88s had made their attacks, and eight Fulmars were therefore scrambled from the two carriers. One tailed an incoming Ju88 so hard that, having forced it to jettison its bomb-load, the Fulmar was driven off its target by the fleet's barrage.

Flying doggedly in through the destroyers' curtain of fire, about a dozen Ju88s dived on *Cairo* and the transports.

Leading the port column as convoy guide, *Deucalion* was soon in trouble. At 13.00 a stick of bombs fell about her. One hit the starboard after well deck, abreast the mainmast, pierced the ship and did not explode; the second struck the port gunwhale of No. 1 Lifeboat slung outboard on the bridge deck, scraped the side and exploded as it hit the water; and the third burst against the ship's starboard bow at the after end of No. 1 Hatch. Despite *Deucalion*'s massive scantlings, 'it seemed as if the ship almost went on her beam ends with the explosion and she seemed to start to settle rapidly and was evidently badly damaged'. The electric power failed, and with the operation of the ship hampered Captain Ramsay Brown stopped the faltering engines, then ordered the chief officer and carpenter to sound the wells and had the lifeboats lowered to the embarkation deck. The following ships in the port outer column, *Clan Ferguson* and *Rochester Castle*, ploughed steadily past *Deucalion*.

The British fighters sped after the withdrawing Junkers, one pursuing south over Galita Island only to be counter-attacked by enemy fighters and riddled with shot-holes. The commanding officer of No. 806 Squadron's Martlets, Lieutenant R. Johnston, severely wounded, landed on *Indomitable* but was lost when his arrester hook snapped and his Martlet plummeted over the side and sank. The remaining Martlets were unable to hit any retreating Junkers, but shot down a Cant Z.1000 bis.

The British carriers were seen by the enemy as the greatest threat to any success their own operations against PEDESTAL might enjoy, and with this in mind the Regia Aeronautica now employed their most secret aerial weapon. Italian ingenuity had already enjoyed considerable success against the Royal Navy, and great expectations were now entertained of these remotely-directed bombers. The Italians had automated an adapted SM79 to make its final run into the targeted aircraft-carrier under radio control. Flown to within sight of its objective, the SM79 was abandoned by its pilot and, loaded with a 630-pound armour-piercing bomb, was guided towards the target from a second plane, in this case a Cant.

The two aeroplanes launched against *Indomitable* were escorted by five Fiat G50 fighters. On coming under nominal control of the Cant as its pilot baled out, the wilful Savoia flew straight on, to crash into the mountainous Algerian coast with a violent explosion. With this failure the combined attack was almost over, and the Sea Hurricanes began to land on their parent carriers. However, at 13.45 two Reggiane Re2001s succeeded in joining the British fighters stacked above *Victorious* as they waited to land on, deceiving those watching, who mistook them for Hurricanes. The RE2001s suddenly made approaches at high speed, diving on the carrier and dropping small bombs. Although six men were killed and two wounded, the bombs bounced along the flight deck, one causing splinter damage and the other exploding as it went over *Victorious*'s bow. Meanwhile the two daring Italian pilots were chased with a sudden, tardy and inadequate stream of tracer as they made good their escape.

The bomb explosions along the starboard side of *Deucalion* had destroyed No. 1 Lifeboat, but the crew mustering at their boat stations began to lower the other boats as ordered. Unfortunately, at this juncture 'some greasers and assistant stewards took it upon themselves to lower Nos 3 and 6 Lifeboats and pulled away from the ship', a circumstance which infuriated the preoccupied Brown. They were men who had been drawn from the Merchant Navy pool and put aboard *Deucalion* as replacements for her normal Chinese crew of 'Holt's men'. Reporting afterwards, Brown was scathing about these 'weak reeds', fulminating that he 'could never have imagined that any Britishers could have shown up in such poor colours'.[16]

The damage had by now been located. The ship's shell had been sprung, but although Nos 1 and 5 Holds were full of water, reducing the *Deucalion*'s freeboard to three feet aft, Brown thought she could make way. Although badly shaken, the ship was not therefore in immediate danger.[17] Syfret, meanwhile, had ordered *Bramham* to stand by *Deucalion* as she fell astern of the convoy. Seeing the lifeboats pulling towards his ship, Lieutenant Baines ordered them back to *Deucalion* and an hour was lost in rehoisting them. By this time Mr Campbell, *Deucalion*'s chief engineer, had restored power to the ship's services, particularly the steering motor, and Brown told Baines he could make way at 10 knots. Baines replied that they would attempt to close the coast and edge east in the hope of getting through to Malta. With *Deucalion* under way and heavily down by the head, the two ships turned to the south-east and the transport worked up to 12 knots. The convoy was now well to the eastwards of them.

Leaving *Deucalion* and *Bramham* astern the fleet passed on, and in the succeeding two hours the destroyers were occupied with several probing attempts by Italian submarines to slip through their guard. Commander Tyrwhitt, in *Tartar*, broke away from the starboard quarter of the screen to attack the *Granito*, which had been spotted on the surface. Tenente di Vascello Sposito submerged and Tyrwhitt dropped depth charges to discourage pursuit. Then at 14.17 *Zetland* 'was seen to alter course and steam to the southward at high speed', but Lieutenant Wilkinson was recalled since the enemy submarine 'was no danger'. Syfret's primary concern, the integrity of the screen, is clear from the restraint he imposed on the impetuous young men in command of the destroyers. Instead the location of the submarine was passed to Baines in *Bramham*, since it was felt she posed a greater threat to the wounded *Deucalion*, and to deter the enemy submarines Burrough suggested that the flanking destroyers should periodically lob depth charges overboard, to which Syfret agreed. From 14.00 until 19.00 the sea was pocked every ten minutes by their explosions.

On the starboard quarter *Tartar*'s men raised the alarm again with a torpedo-sighting at 16.40. Tyrwhitt immediately counter-attacked as lookouts, appropriately enough in *Lookout*, saw a periscope, and Commander Brown swung his destroyer out of station to join Tyrwhitt. Tenente di Vascello Franco in *Eno* had been stalking the convoy for half an hour and was about to fire on *Victorious* when he was frustrated by the fleet zigzagging. Instead, Franco loosed a salvo at a cruiser. None of his torpedoes hit anything, exploding at the ends of their runs or detonating as they crossed the wake of one of the destroyers. Franco was swiftly discomfited when Tyrwhitt's and Brown's depth charges exploded round *Eno*, and withdrew – as did his colleague Priggione in *Avorio*, not far away. It was *Avorio*'s periscope which *Lookout* had seen and mistaken for *Eno*'s, and thus Priggione's own approach was frustrated. On the opposite side of the convoy, Tenente di Vascello Amicarelli was meeting his own fate.

On the port wing at 16.16 *Pathfinder* had gained a sonar contact, and with *Zetland* in support Commander Gibbs made depth-charge attacks until the danger was passed, whereupon the destroyers rejoined the screen. Gibbs and Wilkinson had severely damaged *Cobalto*, driving her deep. In her crew's fight to regain control the submarine broke surface on the port quarter of the convoy, and was spotted by lookouts aboard *Ithuriel*. On receipt of the sighting, Lieutenant D. Maitland-Makgill-Crichton immediately swung *Ithuriel* towards *Cobalto*, as she suddenly plunged out of sight.[18] Picking up a sonar contact, 'Champagne Charlie' ran *Ithuriel* down the bearing and smothered *Cobalto* with a pattern of charges. Tenente di Vascello Amicarelli was forced to surface again astern of his tormentor. Crichton swung *Ithuriel* round to make a final approach at speed, intending to ram, his forward 4.7-inch guns firing at the enemy's conning tower. *Ithuriel* struck *Cobalto* just abaft the conning tower. Crichton's precipitate action mortally wounded the Italian submarine, but before a boarding party could retrieve any confidential books *Cobalto* foundered, and *Ithuriel* picked up Amicarelli and forty of his crew.

Two further attacks were made by Italian submarines, the *Avorio* and *Dandolo*, but both were broken up by the close approach of the escorts and abandoned.

By this time Syfret was making preparations to detach the ships of Force Z. In place of the absent *Bramham* he ordered Lieutenant Northey in *Wilton* to join Burrough's flag as part of Force X. At this time, several radar reports of circling enemy air formations were confirmed by the news of the standing air patrols going into combat. Thirty miles out, small groups of Ju87s of I Stukageschwader 3 were milling about, escorted by Fiat CR42s, and then at 17.49 four Stukas fell upon *Ithuriel*, some way astern after picking up *Cobalto*'s survivors and shoring up her own wrecked bow, the result of Crichton's impetuosity. The destroyer was now capable of 20 knots, and Crichton drove off his attackers and hurried back towards the convoy as it swung round onto a mean course of east-south-east, heading for the Skerki Channel. It was at this juncture that Syfret passed word that Force Z would turn to the west at 19.15.

At 18.30 the incoming bombers appeared visually, Syfret reporting '100 to 120 enemy aircraft in the vicinity, many of them fighters'. The strike force actually consisted of nine Italian manned Stukas from 102 Gruppo, twenty-nine Luftwaffe Stukas under Major Mossdorf and fourteen SM79 torpedo-bombers of

132 Gruppo under Capitano Rivoli. The major element of the fighter cover was to have been the replenished Reggianes of the morning's attack, transferred to Sicily from their base at Monserrato in Sardinia, but these were in no condition for action and their participation was cancelled; the Italian Stukas had therefore been flown to Pantelleria to meet Rivoli's Savoias from Trapani. A few fighters, Macchi Mc202s, Reggiane 2001s and Fiat CR42s, were provided by the Regia Aeronautica, with Me109s and Me110s covering Mossdorf.[19]

The initial air interception was by Sea Hurricanes from *Victorious*. Aboard both carriers the support crews were working like demons to refuel and rearm the aircraft, while coping with battle-damage and the normal run of oil leaks and minor defects. Soon all twenty-two of the airborne Fleet Air Arm fighters were intercepting the approaching enemy in a series of running dog-fights. These gallant actions were however insufficient to prevent the bombers drawing closer to the convoy from the south. The torpedo-bombers attacked in two groups, the first from the star-board flank; the ships altered course and evaded all the torpedoes dropped, most from a range of about two miles. Under cover of their escort of Macchi Mc202s the Italian Stukas dropped out of the sky, to swoop on the large British warships. Two were shot down, but *Rodney* was near-missed as Captain Rivett-Carnac threw the battleship's helm hard a-starboard. Astern of *Rodney*, on the port quarter of the fleet, Mossdorf's Stukas also attacked *Indomitable*, 'appearing suddenly from up sun out of the smoky blue sky' astern of the carrier and hammering down to 1,000 feet before releasing their bombs. One swooped lower, flattened out as she hurtled the length of *Indomitable*'s flight deck, and released her bombs. At least three of the Stukas' bombs exploded on *Indomitable*'s after flight deck, wrecking it and rendering it useless. Standing air-guard on the carrier, the gunners of *Phoebe* had been preoccupied by a flight of SM79s which appeared to be working round the convoy prior to making their run in.

In the mêlée the SM79s had left the carrier to the Stukas and made a further attack on the screen, torpedoing *Foresight*. The destroyer was hit aft: the torpedo 'just blew the stern away and we could see men spread-eagled, flying through the air', the hor-rified American Armed Guard gunners aboard *Almeria Lykes* re-collected. *Foresight*'s steering compartment was destroyed, her shafts were wrecked and her back was broken. She slewed round and came to a shuddering halt under a 'black cloud' as *Tartar* approached to stand by her.

The *Indomitable* was now a useless liability. While her aircraft were diverted to *Victorious*, her ship's company attacked the fire burning in her hangar forward, where it was igniting ready-use ammunition for the adjacent 4.5-inch guns which had themselves been destroyed, with most of their Royal Marine crews. The forward lift was damaged, as was the after, where a second bomb had blown a hole in the flight deck, under which a second fire was burning. Near-misses had heavily distorted a section of the carrier's shell plating level with the upper hangar, set-in plating on the port quarter below the waterline, and penetrated a port oil tank, so that sufficient water entered the ship to induce a list. All these explosions had caused extensive collateral damage and heavy casualties, destroying the aircrew of No. 827 Squadron whose Albacore pilots and observers had been off-duty. In all, fifty men were killed and fifty-nine wounded.

Syfret detached *Charybdis*, *Lightning*, *Somali* and *Lookout* to assist. It was 18.55, just twenty minutes from Syfret's proposed turnabout time. His concerns now multiplied, for Rivett-Carnac reported that *Rodney* had a boiler defect and her speed was likely to be reduced. With the enemy bombers withdrawing, Syfret gave the order for Force Z to reverse course immediately. As the two groups began the manoeuvre of parting company, concern about extricating *Indomitable* prompted Syfret to order *Lookout* to go alongside to help with fire-fighting parties. Mercifully, however, Troubridge soon reported both fires under control and *Indomitable* capable of 17 knots. This quickly rose to 20, then 28.5, but was offset by *Rodney*'s inability to exceed 18.

Aboard *Victorious*, meanwhile, the flight deck was becoming congested as she took aboard her own and *Indomitable*'s aircraft; she was already playing host to those aircraft from *Eagle* which had been airborne when their own carrier sank. In the scrimmage one Martlet ran out of fuel and had to ditch, though fortunately her pilot was picked up by the zealous *Zetland*. In due course a patrol of four Fulmars took off and engaged the retiring enemy fighters, with the loss of one of their company against one enemy aircraft shot down. A little after 20.00 the last air patrol of Sea Hurricanes took off, but with the onset of nightfall they had landed again within the hour.

*

Convoy WS21s had just lost its first merchant ship. Away to the south-west, *Bramham* and *Deucalion* had worked inshore towards the neutral waters of Tunisia, to pass close south of Galita. Campbell gradually increased *Deucalion*'s speed to 16 knots, and with this the hopes of Brown and his crew rose correspondingly as they headed east again, the dun cliffs of the coast on the starboard beam seamed with purple shadows as the sun began to wester. But the heavy head trim and increased speed produced an immense strain on the bulkhead between Nos 1 and 2 Holds and Brown was compelled to reduce to 12.5 knots again, although he remained pugnaciously optimistic that they could still 'get the vessel to Malta'. During the afternoon *Bramham* acquired, attacked and lost a sonar contact before a shadowing aircraft was sighted at 17.00. It was driven off by the combined gunfire of *Bramham* and *Deucalion*, but they now expected the worst, and it was not long in coming. At 19.46, two Junkers Ju88s made 'a sharp attack.' The *Deucalion* bucked and shook as the near-misses lifted her bodily in the water, and wallowed heavily as she settled on her way again with a slight port list.

Having passed Galita, course was altered at 19.40 to pass north of Cani Rocks, some fifteen miles further east. At 21.20, 'after sunset when the light was very bad', with the coast to the south now in shadow, two torpedo-bombers came in low with their engines shut off, one on the port quarter, the other on the starboard bow. Engaged by *Deucalion*'s guns, 'The first plane flew along the port side without attacking, then flew off, whilst the second bomber sail-planed to within half a mile of the starboard bow, opened up engines and flew about 50 feet high parallel with the ship not more than 200 feet away. All guns that could bear opened fire and ... [scored] several hits. Nevertheless, as the plane drew level with the bridge ... an object [left] it, evidently fired by an explosive charge, and travel[led] horizontally towards the ship.' This struck *Deucalion* aft and 'a tremendous fire broke out at once' as the aviation spirit and kerosene in No. 6 'Tween-deck exploded. A sheet of flame shot skywards, 'twice the height of the mast', and the whole after end of the ship became 'a raging inferno'. 'The chances of extinguishing it were hopeless from the outset,' a crew member afterwards remarked. Brown ordered the ship abandoned as Baines approached in *Bramham*. The boats were hurriedly lowered, and a fall of No. 3 slipped on the staghorn; one end of the boat dropped, spilling those in her into the warm sea, to struggle across the water towards the looming destroyer.

Down aft, the men round the poop guns were isolated from the rest by the intense heat and searing flame of the burning cargo. One of the guns' DEMS crew, Henderson, was already dead from machine-gun fire; another, Gunner Mead, was badly hurt with a broken arm, smashed femur and lacerations to arms and face. He lay pinned under a heavy Carley float, 'very close indeed to the flaming hatch'. From their stations aft by the guns Midshipmen Gregson and Bracewell saw Mead's plight, and after a struggle managed to extricate him from beneath the heavy float. Getting him to the ship's rail, they dropped him overboard and dived in after him. Gregson then swam with Mead towards *Bramham*, a quarter of a mile away, an action described by Brown as 'a really gallant and plucky action by a boy of only 18'.

Captain Brown and Chief Officer Ogilvie were 'the last to leave at about 21.25, the after deck by this time being awash, [the] ship burning fiercely, and the ammunition in the square of No. 6 hatch exploding at intervals. We pulled round picking up the men from the water and off the rafts, then rowed over to the destroyer.'

By 22.00 all the survivors were aboard *Bramham*, where Baines, seeing what he took to be the lights of Vichy French vessels approaching, was anxious to get away. He swung *Bramham* in towards the blazing ship and threw a depth charge, but 'it landed on deck and did not explode'. The noise of detonations came from *Deucalion*'s hull, however, and she now began to settle by the stern as the fire worked inexorably forward. Informed by Brown that she had TNT aboard, Baines was convinced *Deucalion* was doomed. At 22.40 he made off, heading south of Cani Rocks at 22 knots to regain contact with the fleet as soon as possible. In the distance he could see the flashes of explosions and knew the convoy was under attack. Then, at 22.40, there was a brighter flash astern as *Deucalion* herself blew up.[20]

As Syfret's ships turned away towards the setting sun, there was a short flurry of farewell signals. Burrough's warships and the convoy drew swiftly away to the east. From *Nigeria* came the signal ordering Force X and the convoy to assume the two-column formation for the passage of the Skerki Channel. For the men aboard the transports who watched the heavy ships turn back as the necessary helm orders were passed, the sight was

chilling. *Indomitable* was out of the order of battle: 'The last we
saw of her she was on a westerly course and we could still see
the columns of smoke until the darkness hid them.' But it was
more than that; with the major British naval force withdrawn, the
forthcoming onset of darkness over the wide sea, always a lonely
and emotional moment, seemed preternaturally bleak and forbidding.[21]

But darkness had not quite fallen when, moments later as it
approached the Skerki Channel, the convoy received its body-
blow. Here, in comparatively shallow water, lay more Italian submarines. Already at 19.38, having worked *Dessiè* undetected into
a position one mile from the approaching convoy, Tenente di
Vascello Scandolo had fired a salvo of four torpedoes, all of
which missed. Quite unaware of the close proximity of enemy
submarines, Syfret and Burrough had parted company, and now
the process of forming two columns was under way. The formation should have consisted of Burrough's *Nigeria* leading the port
column of seven transports, supported midway by *Cairo*, with
Kenya (Captain A. Russell) in the van of the starboard column of
six transports, with *Manchester* (Captain H. Drew) half-way
down it. This narrowing of the convoy was intended to tuck it
neatly astern of the minesweeping destroyers. These had already
lost *Foresight*, but *Intrepid*, *Icarus* and *Fury* drew ahead and
streamed their sweeps, while *Pathfinder*, *Ledbury* and *Bicester*
began to screen the starboard and *Ashanti*, *Penn* and *Derwent* the
port flanks. *Wilton* meanwhile dropped back to bring up the rear,
and the cruisers began to work themselves into their new stations, *Nigeria* and *Kenya* speeding up, and *Cairo* slowing down.

From her base at Cagliari Tenente di Vascello Ferrini's submarine *Axum* had arrived that morning on her patrol station 30 miles
north-west of Cape Bon. At 18.21, on a calm sea and with excellent visibility, Ferrini observed two columns of smoke rising on
the western horizon; these were from *Indomitable*. Submerging,
he began his approach, not rising to periscope depth for an hour,
when he swung parallel to the east-bound British convoy and
studied his objective, maintaining his station, helped by the
convoy's zigzagging. At 19.37, just as his colleague Scandolo
made his abortive attack, Ferrini closed the range and continued
patiently to stalk and observe. Suddenly, a quarter of an hour
later, seeing three ships begin to overlap as they changed stations, he swung to attack, loosing four torpedoes at 19.55.

The spread of Ferrini's torpedoes was fortuitously successful as it struck the British fleet, caught in the very act of redeploying. Steaming at 14 knots, *Nigeria* was hit on her port side, below her bridge. Her armour did not save her and she began to flood immediately, heeling to port as the forward boiler-rooms quickly filled. Power failed and her faltering steering motor jammed her rudder, so that she turned to port as she slowed. Counter-flooding reduced her list, but it was clear the cruiser's duty as Burrough's flagship was over, and the rear-admiral was now confronted by serial disaster.

The anti-aircraft cruiser *Cairo* had dropped her speed to fall back into her new station when two of Ferrini's torpedoes blew her stern off and water cascaded into her. Close to *Nigeria*, the tanker *Ohio* was hit in the pump-room, the explosion tearing the deck plating back to her centreline, ripping her shell open amidships, severing her telemotor pipes and rendering her main steering inoperable. A gout of flame shot up, the heat so fierce as to be felt aboard the stricken *Nigeria*, and as fires broke out in the exposed kerosene tanks adjacent to the pump-room, *Ohio*'s engine room was abandoned on Captain Mason's orders. Extraordinarily, the sea washing into the pump-room and across the deck assisted the crew, who were quickly pouring foam from extinguishers onto the fire, subduing it in a very few moments. The bomb blast had also extinguished *Ohio*'s boilers, but after the fire had been doused, the engine room was remanned and steam raised again.

At the same time, about 20.15, Captain Onslow, having chased the circling flagship on her outboard quarter, succeeded in running *Ashanti*'s bow alongside *Nigeria* and embarked Burrough and some of his staff, to the cheering of a party on *Nigeria*'s upper deck. *Bicester* and *Wilton* had also come up to the assistance of the torpedoed ships and, as *Cairo* could not be towed, Burrough ordered them to take off her crew, instructing Gibbs to sink her from *Pathfinder*. *Cairo* 'lay quietly', with her stern deep in the water[,] her bows riding high ...' Gibbs then had the humiliating experience of discovering that, though fired at close range, his torpedoes had malfunctioned and failed to do their job. A fourth torpedo detonated, but did not sink the old cruiser; Gibbs then dropped depth-charges, again without success. Anxious to return to his position on the screen, Gibbs instructed Commander Wright of *Derwent* to administer the *coup de grâce* by gunfire.

While all this was in progress *Nigeria* had fallen far astern of the disordered convoy, as *Ashanti* hurried after it. *Bicester* and *Wilton* with *Cairo*'s survivors now mounted guard on *Nigeria* as her company sought to regain control of their ship, and they were joined by *Derwent* after she had finally dispatched *Cairo*.

The convoy, in the process of executing Burrough's order to form two columns at the time of *Axum*'s attack, had achieved a degree of conformity and was in two loose lines at the fatal moment. The incomplete manoeuvre of changing stations quickly degenerated into disarray, however, combined as it was with the disaster affecting the convoy's port column, an emergency turn to starboard, and collision avoidance. Captain MacFarlane's *Melbourne Star* was not far astern of *Ohio*, which was immediately astern of *Port Chalmers*, when the tanker was hit. MacFarlane was compelled to throw his helm over and reverse his engines to avoid colliding with the vessels ahead of him. The transports following MacFarlane also drew out of their half-formed line ahead and sheered away from the obvious direction of the attack as they executed the emergency starboard turn. This forced those trying to form up in the starboard column further over to the south-east, and thus within a few minutes had the cumulative effect of destroying the hitherto tight formation. The professional instincts that made Onslow and his colleagues Northey and Bennetts in *Bicester* and *Wilton* close up on the flagship similarly motivated the merchant masters to preserve their own ships, mindful that the convoy must go on, and that mopping-up was a naval chore. In four minutes at 15 knots a ships travels a mile, while an alteration of course of twenty degrees produces a lateral offset of three-tenths of a mile. Effectively, therefore, Ferrini's attack had not merely hit three ships, it had dispersed the convoy.[22]

Deprived of *Foresight*, his fourth minesweeping destroyer, and hampered by streamed paravanes and sweep-wires, Commander Kitcat in *Intrepid*, with *Icarus* and *Fury*, maintained station leading the remnant van. Astern, the cruisers *Kenya* and *Manchester* stood on in their wake. Some aircraft high overhead were fired at, no one in the cruisers realising they were a patrol of Beaufighters from Malta trying to make contact with the fleet. At the extremity of their own operational range, the Beaufighters swung away frustrated, for *Nigeria* and *Cairo*, the only fighter direction ships capable of communicating with them, were gone.

At 20.35, with Force X and the convoy spread against the last gleam of daylight in the west, thirty Ju88s from Kampfgeschwaders 54 and 77 and seven HeIII torpedo-bombers of VI Kampfgeschwader 26 flew in from the north-east. They were escorted by six Messerschmitt Me110s of VI Zerstörergeschwader 26 and had been circling in the offing, awaiting the opportune moment. Now, ordered to attack after a shadower had reported the detachment of Syfret's heavy ships, they roared in, twenty minutes after sunset, to strike the disorganised 'scrummed-up' mass of shipping in a half-hour-long attack that caused mayhem.

Aboard *Ohio*, the tanker's engine had by now been restarted and hand steering had been engaged. Captain Mason was able to make way at 7 knots as *Ashanti* caught up from attending *Nigeria*. A near-miss on *Ashanti* caused a boiler to blow back and start a fire, whereupon the imperturbable Onslow, bringing *Ashanti* alongside *Ohio* at full speed, coolly ordered it 'put out, please'. As the destroyer ran parallel to the tanker, Burrough acknowledged Mason's refusal of a tow, noted that he had lost his compasses and promised him an escort, and instructed him to proceed by the inshore route. As *Ashanti* sped on, a handful of *Ohio*'s crew were still waiting in their designated lifeboat. A near-miss threw the boat into the air and tipped the two army gunners, a steward and the galley boy into the sea as their ship drew away. Galley boy Guidotte kept one of the gunners afloat until, by the greatest good fortune, they were later rescued by *Bicester*, still searching for survivors from *Nigeria*.

Everywhere enemy aeroplanes were attacking in a concerted and determined manner as the light finally failed. *Icarus* swung aside and avoided a torpedo, but it was now the transports against which the enemy planes struck. Spread out, their targets lacked the cumulative protection of a massed barrage, though every gun was firing. *Kenya* and *Manchester* put about to provide what anti-aircraft fire they could, while the flanking Hunts blazed away at every opportunity. As the Ju88s dived their machine-guns raked the exposed guns on the transports which, because of their *ad hoc* nature, gave less protection than if they had been part of the ships' structure.

One HeIII made a run at *Brisbane Star* and her torpedo struck the ship's forefoot, blowing a hole through both sides of the vessel. The ship began to take on water and slowed, but she did not stop. Captain Riley was informed that although No. 1 Hold was flooding, No. 2 was dry. Unable to keep up with the convoy, Riley boldly elected to proceed independently, passing word to Gibbs as *Pathfinder* slid up alongside. Moving away, *Brisbane Star* headed to round Cape Bon and keep inshore until morning, when Riley would decide whether 'to creep along the coast, or adventure on'.[23]

Almost simultaneously, and having eased his speed to avoid being rammed by *Brisbane Star* as Riley swung across his bow to evade his attackers, Captain Williams in turn yawed *Empire Hope* to dodge the falling bombs. The ship suffered eighteen near-misses before a bomb-burst stove in her side, stopping the engines. Coming to a standstill, *Empire Hope* attracted several bombers. Blast showered the deck with splinters, blowing men out of the gun-pits and filling with scattered coal those lifeboats that had escaped total destruction. At 20.50 *Empire Hope* took two direct hits in No. 4 Hold. In seconds ammunition and aviation spirit were exploding and the stern of the vessel was ablaze. Cadet P. Andrews was flung overboard and was soon joined by others. With the ship's helm jammed and burning gasolene spilling over the surrounding sea, Williams ordered his ship abandoned. In the water men were already screaming as their seared flesh came in contact with salt water. One boat prematurely lowered by army gunners was saved by the presence of mind of Cadet McCallum, who shipped the plug just in time to prevent it sinking. Having drawn away from the ship, the boats discovered that Captain Williams and Chief Engineer Leffler were still on board. One turned back, to find that in the interim Leffler had slipped out of his boiler-suit; he left the ship in full uniform, determined not to fall into enemy hands as an ordinary civilian. In due course most of *Empire Hope*'s crew got away, to be picked up by *Penn* shortly afterwards. Lieutenant-Commander Swain fired a torpedo into *Empire Hope* and left her still burning, but unsunk. To Andrews, still in the water, the jarring of Swain's exploding torpedo was terribly painful. Extraordinarily, he was picked up by *Manchester*.[24]

An aerial torpedo from another Heinkel struck *Clan Ferguson* at 21.02, almost coincidental with the two previous attacks, as she steamed at 15 knots towards Zembra Island. At the lookout's cry of alarm Captain Cossar threw his helm over to starboard; but it was too late, and with a tremendous explosion and flash 2,000

tons of aviation spirit ignited and counter-mined 1,500 tons of
ammunition. Incandescing gasolene was flung outboard in a
great shower as the flimsy cases burst asunder, propelled by the
multiple detonations of the ammunition below. *Clan Ferguson*
settled by the stern, surrounded by a ring of fire, the radiated
heat searing the stunned observers in *Glenorchy* and *Wairangi*,
steaming past her. It seemed impossible that anyone could
emerge from the inferno. *Clan Ferguson*'s second officer, Mr A.
Black, 'could see flames coming up from the engine room sky-
light and ship's side. The hatch covers were blown off No. 4 Hold
and two landing craft stowed on top were blown off ... There was
a violent explosion in No. 5 Hold and the ship appeared to sink
about seven minutes after being hit. The oil blazed on the water
for forty-eight hours and petrol cans kept floating to the surface
and catching fire, as did the oil [fuel], causing thick black smoke.
In all sixty-four men got away and were eventually equally
divided on the four rafts, which drifted apart.' On one of these,
Cadet Allison rescued several men.

Immediately astern of *Clan Ferguson* steamed *Rochester Castle*.
She had sustained structural damage from near-misses, fumes
from which had been drawn into the engine room by the ventilation fans. Her anti-aircraft fire dissuaded any further assaults
and she veered aside and passed the blazing Clan liner.

Dawn the next morning found about forty of *Clan Ferguson*'s
people in a single lifeboat. 'The sea was covered in oil, and
debris, the sky grey from the fires. No ships could be seen ...' In
due course the boat landed on Zembra Island and the men were
picked up by a Vichy minesweeper, to be interned in Bon Fichu
camp near the coast. Some of the rafts were located next morning
by the Italian submarine *Bronzo*. Tenente di Vascello Buldrini
questioned the survivors, and that afternoon a German Dornier
flying-boat landed and picked up the worst of the wounded. In
the evening an Italian seaplane, marked with red crosses,
rescued as many men as it could carry. Captain Cossar's raft had
worked its way close inshore, and here it was intercepted by a
MAS-boat which picked up Cossar and took him, a prisoner-of-
war, to Sicily.[25]

At the moment of Ferrini's attack during the change of deployment, the convoy commodore's ship, *Port Chalmers*, had been
coming up astern of *Cairo* to overtake her. As the cruiser was

torpedoed, Captain Pinkney of *Port Chalmers* only avoided collision by going astern. In the succeeding minutes, seeing the disintegration of his charges from the bridge of *Port Chalmers*,
Commander Venables, the convoy commodore, became increasingly concerned. As darkness fell the 'burning ships made visibility like daylight and after seeing a submarine to port I
decided to ... leave the convoy by the rear'. *Port Chalmers* turned
round and proceeded at full speed to the westward, signalling
'turn back' to MacFarlane in *Melbourne Star* and Tuckett in *Dorset*.
These two ships had fallen in astern of *Port Chalmers* and, seeing
them turn, Captain Henderson of *Almeria Lykes*, dutifully watching the commodore's motions, followed suit. After a few
moments' conformity, consultations on the bridges of the two
British ships persuaded their masters to change their minds:
Tuckett and MacFarlane both decided that they 'did not wish to
return' to Gibraltar, and hauled back round to the east-south-
east.

Seeing the plight of the merchant ships in those few eventful
minutes of the air assault, Lieutenant-Commander Hill had
turned *Ledbury* in towards the centre of the transports, between
what was left of the two lines. Noticing the four ships turning
away, Hill ran up alongside *Almeria Lykes* and hailed Henderson,
telling him that 'all the English ships are heading for Malta'. This
was clearly not the case, although as he drew away from the
American freighter both *Melbourne Star* and *Dorset* were disobey-
ing Venables and turning round to the east again. To MacFarlane
and Tuckett, Hill flashed the course of 120 degrees, passing the
news that Burrough was in *Ashanti* to the south, close to the coast
'and waiting for them'. A few minutes later MacFarlane signalled *Almeria Lykes* 'I am going to Malta, will you follow?', to
which Henderson replied 'Yes', and the American ship also
turned back to the east-south-east.

As this last air attack of the day petered out in the darkness, with
Ashanti, Penn, Pathfinder and *Ledbury* doing their best to round up
the merchant transports in the rear, the undamaged cruisers
Kenya and *Manchester* led on at a slightly lowered speed to reduce
their distance astern of Kitcat's minesweeping destroyers.
Glenorchy and *Wairangi* were the only merchant ships keeping
well up with this vanguard in the gloom, Captain Gordon having
survived an attack from a Heinkel by taking *Wairangi* between

the two approaching torpedo tracks. Catching them up were *Waimarama*, the fast American C2 transport *Santa Elisa* and, in somewhat extended order, *Melbourne Star*, *Dorset* and *Almeria Lykes*, all of which had fought off the assault of the bombers.

It was now about 21.12 and the minesweeping destroyers had just cleared the Skerki Channel, while those astern were still running the gauntlet. Tenente di Vascello Puccini had been observing the air attack on the convoy for some time. His submarine, *Alagi*, had been undergoing running repairs to two of her forward torpedo tubes, but they were serviceable by the time he was in a position to act. Seeing a cruiser in his attack-periscope, Puccini fired a salvo, but a vigilant lookout aboard *Kenya* raised the alarm. Captain Russell threw his helm over and two torpedoes passed clear astern, while a third ran deep. Unfortunately the fourth struck the cruiser's bow, inflicting serious damage. Many of her forward compartments were flooded, four men were killed and one injured; but the ship was capable of keeping up the convoy speed, and Russell was soon catching up with *Manchester*. To resolve the obvious muddle astern of him and unaware of Burrough's whereabouts, Russell transmitted a signal to all ships that he was in command of Force X. This did not help an already highly confused situation, but by now *Pathfinder* was coming up from astern, with *Penn* still in the rear.

Far to the west, Force Z headed into the twilight. Aboard *Indomitable*, men had paraded on the flight deck, the fifteen-year-old bugler had played the Last Post and she had buried her dead, the ensign snapping above her island at half-mast. As the naval obsequies concluded, the carrier's marine band struck up the hauntingly beautiful Evening Hymn.

Syfret received the news of the disaster to Burrough just after sunset. From *Nelson*'s towering forebridge he could see, stabbing the night sky astern, the flashes of the action which was destroying the convoy so lately under the protection of his capital ships. He immediately ordered *Charybdis*, *Somali* and *Eskimo* to reinforce Force X, and at 21.15 these ships tore past the wallowing *Nigeria* and her three escorting Hunts on their own halting passage back to Gibraltar. Syfret also ordered *Malcolm*, far to the west assisting Sunderland *TK7R* operating against *Giada*, to steam east and join the destroyers assisting *Nigeria*. Wise though these moves were, far too many of the useful Hunts remained clustered about the stricken cruiser, destroyers which would have been better disposed about the convoy, to whose escort they had been assigned.

Of the Hunts remaining in close escort, Hill's *Ledbury* stuck tenaciously to her task. After speaking with *Almeria Lykes*, Hill caught sight of and then closed the *Ohio*, resolving one of Mason's problems by providing him with a blue light on *Ledbury*'s stern to steer by, as both ships headed for Cape Bon. Although she was only able to keep station on *Ledbury* by means of a line of men passing directions to the bridge, from where a telephone line communicated with the clumsy hand-steering right aft, *Ohio* was cautiously worked up to 15 knots. It was now necessary to pass through the area of the air raid and, silhouetted against the blazing oil from *Clan Ferguson* and the still-burning hulk of *Empire Hope*, the two ships worked steadily east in the 'warm, clear night', heading for Cape Bon. At 23.48, not long after the tanker and destroyer had passed *Empire Hope*, the Italian submarine *Bronzo* sent a torpedo in to her still blazing hulk.

It was just before midnight when Kitcat's *Intrepid* led the three minesweeping destroyers in the van of Force X round Cape Bon, altering course to steer south towards Kelibia Point and the Gulf of Hammamet. Most of the ships of the disrupted convoy trailed astern of them as the lighthouses on Cape Bon and Kelibia Point in neutral Tunisia flashed indifferently. The revolving beams passing across the faces of the anxious men on the ships' bridges and at the guns made them feel horribly conspicuous. To the south-west, *Brisbane Star* proceeded independently; astern, *Penn* remained in the area of the air attack, still searching for survivors, while *Port Chalmers* headed west.

Coming up from the vicinity of Cani Rocks with *Deucalion*'s survivors, *Bramham* encountered *Port Chalmers* at 00.45 next morning. Venables placed himself under Baines's escort and turned east again. A few minutes later the two ships encountered *Penn*, and Lieutenant-Commander Swain took *Bramham* and *Port Chalmers* under his wing. The three vessels proceeded in line ahead, across the minefield off Cape Bon. To the south-east they could see that the convoy was embattled again: the night was not to offer any respite.

*

During 12 August the cruisers of the Regia Marina had steamed to their rendezvous in the Tyrrenhian Sea, north of Ustica, which they made at about 19.00. Da Zara now had under his command *Muzio Attendolo*, *Raimondo Montecuccoli*, *Eugenio di Savoia*, *Gorizia* and *Trieste*, with twelve escorts. The Italian admiral began to move south-west, intending to round the western extremity of Sicily and fall upon the convoy off Pantelleria. Since Comando Supremo estimated the British air forces on Malta as formidable, Da Zara expected heavy air cover himself.[26]

Comando Supremo still considered the British operation might constitute a landing force bound for Libya, and made submarine and destroyer dispositions in the eastern Mediterranean accordingly. They also scraped together an air-escort of forty-five Italian fighters for Da Zara for the following day, 13 August. In Rome, Mussolini was sanguine that the dawn would bring a decisive naval engagement, and he could well have been right.

But Air Vice-Marshal Park, who was soon aware of the plight of the PEDESTAL ships, kept his aircraft in touch with the Italian cruisers. Radar-equipped Wellingtons from Malta took over surveillance, making their presence obvious by playing searchlights on the Italian ships and transmitting plain-language sighting reports. One made an ineffective bombing run and several deceptive signals were made *en clair* by Park, indicating the approach of Liberator bombers and emphasising to the shadowing Wellingtons the importance of maintaining contact with Da Zara's force. Park also prepared what was effectively his only striking force, fifteen torpedo-equipped Beauforts and fifteen Beaufighters, to move against the Italian squadron at daylight. In his turn Da Zara watched the circling British aircraft, thanks to a German radar set fitted to the Soldati-class destroyer *Legionario*.

This contact with the British aircraft combined with Park's signals to alarm Supermarina, the members of which, like those of Comando Supremo, judged Malta's air strike capability to be considerable. There was further concern when *Alagi* and *Bronzo* reported British surface reinforcements – in the form of *Charybdis*, *Somali* and *Eskimo* – coming up from the west, to which both submarine commanders had signalled by lamp, thinking them Italian ships.

Vizeadmiral Weichold, head of the German Naval Command, Italy, supported Supermarina's plea for cover by Kesselring's fighters, which the latter again refused, despite Weichold's belief that this would 'mean missing a big chance of annihilating the largest [British] convoy undertaken so far in the Mediterranean after the heavy forces, superior in numbers and arms, have withdrawn'.[27] At Supermarina, the nerve of Riccardi and his staff now failed them entirely. Fearful of another fatal night-action, they appealed to Mussolini. The Duce cancelled the operation after telephoning Hitler, who insisted that the British convoy be left to his own aircraft.[28] Having wasted tons of scarce fuel, Da Zara and Parona, now thirty miles north of Marittimo, were recalled shortly after midnight.

The distinction between the Axis and British naval commands is nowhere displayed in starker contrast than on this occasion. As the ships of the Royal Navy supporting the merchant transports in their joint endeavour were sacrificed to the greater objective of the convoy's integrity, the Italians failed to capitalise on the damage they and their ally had already wrought upon this diminishing British asset, referring to Hitler at the critical moment. The Regia Marina had yet to inflict its final wound, but the cancellation of Da Zara's sortie must be regarded as a major blunder.

It was also to end in humiliation. The Wellingtons reported Da Zara's retreat into the Tyrrhenian Sea, and Leatham signalled the submarines *Safari*, patrolling north of Palermo, and *Unbroken*, off the Aeolian Islands: 'Enemy cruisers coming your way.'

Since the enemy knew of his presence and frequently carried out vigorous anti-submarine operations in the area, Lieutenant A. Mars had abandoned his official patrol zone south of Vulcano Island and withdrawn *Unbroken* north; at 03.15 on the morning of 13 August, when he received Leatham's signal, he was lying off Panarea. Courageously backing a hunch that the enemy would not retire on Messina by way of an area known to be the cruising ground of British submarines, Mars remained where he was. Then, through his periscope at 07.25, he observed four cruisers in line ahead steering towards him, intending to round Salina and head for the Strait of Messina. Guessing that some of the escorting destroyers would pass very near, Mars held his nerve and waited; three passed him so close that on the after deck of one of them he could see a seaman smoking.

Mars had selected a heavy cruiser as his primary target, and since a consort was slightly overlapping he was hopeful of success. Firing a salvo of four torpedoes, he dived and increased to *Unbroken*'s full underwater speed of 9 knots.

The first explosion came from impact with the heavy cruiser *Bolzano*, where an oil tank was ignited, and the adjacent magazines had to be flooded. Although only one man was killed, the flooding endangered the ship and Capitano di Vascello Mezzadra beached her on Panarea, where she lay for two days before being refloated and taken to Naples for repair. Mars's second hit blew the bows off the *Muzio Attendolo*, and though Capitano di Vascello Schiavuta reached Messina at 19.00 that evening under his own power, his light cruiser did not see further service and, like *Bolzano*, was broken up after the war.

Despite a heavy counter-attack, *Unbroken* escaped retribution and, empty of torpedoes, returned to Malta on 18 August.[29] The Italian cruisers had returned to port by midday, Da Zara's *Eugenio di Savoia* and *Raimondo Montecuccoli* arriving at Naples, Parona's *Gorizia* and *Trieste* entering Messina. Weichold afterwards summed the sortie up: 'A more useless waste of fighting power cannot be imagined.'

As the order to recall Da Zara took effect, the Regia Marina and Kriegsmarine were engaged in what amounted to the most successful of the several attacks upon the ships of Operation PEDESTAL. Lying in ambush beyond Cape Bon, in the narrow waters between Pantelleria and the Tunisian coast, was a mixed force of Italian and German *MAS*-boats and *Schnellboote*.[30] Against aircraft, even the merchant ships were well armed; but against fast attack craft, both they and the warships were curiously vulnerable. The speed with which the enemy boats fell upon the strung-out ships generated an element of surprise against which even radar faltered, for the returns from small, largely wooden craft, moving fast and kicking up masses of sea-clutter, presented interpretational difficulties to the radar operators and consequent delay in transferring the information to the gunnery directors. The difficulties were only made worse by a choppy sea. Though local control of the guns might seem to have presented the best means of dealing with this problem, the darkness of the night, combined with poor visibility and the impossibility of using star-shell for fear of exposing the vastly more vulnerable British ships to the enemy, precluded its use. Moreover, the guard rails fitted to many of the lighter weapons in the merchantmen prevented the depression of the Oerlikon and Bofors guns, so that the ships were only able to respond with lighter Hotchkiss and Breda machine-guns.

The convoy track doubled Cape Bon and followed the southerly trend of the Tunisian coast until beyond Kelibia Point, where it broke away to the east-south-east. When it was about seventy miles south of Pantelleria, it turned to run directly towards Malta. The first torpedo-boat attack occurred at 00.40 and was made from the eastwards on the leading minesweeping destroyers, *Intrepid*, *Icarus* and *Fury*, who were then steaming south with Kelibia light almost on their starboard beam, not far from the beached wreck of the British destroyer *Havock*.

The Italian 18th Squadron of four boats raced in towards the destroyers but were met with a sharp fire, and although torpedoes were fired and one hit was claimed, they drew off in search of easier prey astern. There now followed four hours of confusion in which the night was seamed by the palely bio-luminescent wakes of the active torpedo-boats and the tracks of their torpedoes. The British vessels, men-of-war and merchantmen alike, heeled and turned as their captains and commanders strove to avoid the deadly stings of their tormentors. The defending gunners were easily confused, and although several Italian transmissions monitored aboard *Ashanti* seemed to indicate that at least one and possibly two of the torpedo-boats had been knocked out, none was in fact destroyed. Several were damaged, however, *S58* particularly badly, though she was able to limp back into Port Empedocle.

An element of confusion also existed on the enemy side. Axis expenditure of torpedoes was heavy and there were many misses, evidence of ill-governed impetuosity. Oberleutnant-sur-Zee Muller, operating just north of Cape Bon, claimed a strike on a tanker for *S59* which might have been a miss on *Ohio*, while Capitano di Corvetta Manuti, commanding the 2nd Squadron, having lain in ambush in the radar shadow of *Havock*, had the mortification of watching his own torpedo run wide as he made an attack from the landward side. His target was a cruiser following in the wake of Kitcat's leading destroyers and astern of which came *Almeria Lykes* and *Glenorchy*. Manuti redoubled his efforts a few minutes later. Together with Tenente di Vascello Mezzadra in *MS22*, Manuti in *MS16* sped towards the passing cruiser, undetected until he was less than half a cable from

Manchester. As the alarm was raised Captain Drew put *Manchester's* helm down, and his forward 6-inch turrets depressed and fired.

Manuti and Mezzadra loosed their torpedoes and withdrew into the darkness. Seconds later *Manchester* was hit in the starboard side, in way of her after engine room. Thirteen men were killed instantly as the cruiser heeled and lost speed, her after boiler room, 4-inch ammunition magazine and fuel tanks all flooding fast. Two generators dropped off the distribution board and all power failed. Drew's avoiding action slewed *Manchester* to port across the bows of the fast *Almeria Lykes*, which had caught up with and overtaken *Glenorchy*. The American freighter turned in *Manchester's* wake and then stood on to seaward, across the stern of the listing cruiser. Captain Leslie gave a double ring for full astern and prevented *Glenorchy* from ramming *Almeria Lykes*, aboard which Henderson and his liaison officer, Lieutenant-Commander Mitchell, had agreed to break out of the ambush. Leslie stood on along the planned track, hopeful of keeping contact with *Kenya*. Next astern came *Waimarama*, and she too had to go hard a-port to scrape past *Manchester* as the cruiser ran the last of her way off.

Hearing of Drew's situation Burrough, still astern in *Ashanti*, ordered *Pathfinder* to stand by *Manchester*. Gibbs had been keeping company with *Melbourne Star* and *Dorset* and now ran alongside *Manchester*, leaving the merchantmen to proceed alone. It was now 01.40. Hailed by Drew, who thought he could save *Manchester*, Gibbs pleaded the greater necessity of escorting the merchant transports, to which Drew readily agreed, taking the opportunity of transferring 158 men of *Manchester's* complement over to *Pathfinder*. Gibbs then started off after *Melbourne Star* and *Dorset*, but soon received orders to rejoin Burrough.

On the merchant transports' bridges, a sense of being thrown back on their own initiative was evident, particularly for those masters and liaison officers who had witnessed the torpedoing of yet another cruiser. Aboard *Almeria Lykes*, Henderson and Mitchell considered heading independently for Malta but were deterred by the minefields, and swung back to the south-south-east, cutting the corner of the inshore dog-leg south of Kelibia Point, which in due course brought them back to Kitkat's destroyers. MacFarlane's *Melbourne Star* had lost contact not only with *Pathfinder* but also with *Dorset*. Ahead of him MacFarlane could see 'great activity ... gun flashes, coloured tracers, red, gold and pale green. My ship was herself giving a wonderful firework display from her exhaust which could not be stopped.'[31]

Meanwhile *Dorset* had had a lucky escape. A *MAS*-boat, having fired a torpedo which missed the ship's bow by a few feet, instead of turning away ran right under *Dorset*'s forefoot, so close that the guns could not be sufficiently depressed to fire at her and 'the shouts of the crew could be plainly heard [as] it missed the ship by a bare six feet'. After this, Captain Tuckett and his liaison officer decided to leave the area and to head north of Pantelleria; *Dorset*'s course was altered accordingly. Aboard *Rochester Castle*, Captain Wren put the same idea to his liaison officer, Lieutenant Binfield, who argued the presence of a minefield to the north of the Italian island. Wren remarked that there was one to the south anyway, and the paravane gear would keep them out of trouble, so *Rochester Castle* also headed to pass north of Pantelleria.

It was now almost 02.00, and the extempore flagship *Ashanti* was fast approaching Kelibia Point, round which Kitcat had passed some time before. Ahead of Burrough *Glenorchy*, having dodged round *Manchester* and succeeded in hitting an enemy boat after a brief exchange of fire, was doing 18 knots in the wake of Kitcat's destroyers. Now, however, Leslie found *Glenorchy* suddenly illuminated by a searchlight, in the glare of which two torpedoes fired by Tenente di Vascello Calvani from *MS31* briefly gleamed. In an attempt to avert disaster Leslie swung *Glenorchy* towards the searchlight, which was promptly extinguished. Calvani, briefly fired upon by an after gun on *Fury*, escaped as his torpedoes blew in the port side of *Glenorchy*'s engine room, the explosion blasting upwards and wrecking the ship's port lifeboats.

Chief Engineer Threlfall and five of his staff were killed instantly; Second Engineer Brunskill found himself trapped by his lifejacket under a grating, water pouring into the ship above him. After a struggle he broke free, able to breathe but blinded by oil. Familiarity with the layout of the engine room enabled him to heave the fourth engineer out and reach the deck. Partially regaining his sight, Brunskill watched a lifeboat being lowered, but he was exhausted and felt unable to clamber over the rail. A shipmate grabbed him and hove him unceremoniously overboard and into the boat, where he struck his head and passed out.

On the bridge Leslie had given the order to abandon *Glenorchy*. Aware of the aviation spirit stowed all over the deck, a few gunners on the poop threw a Carley float over the side and jumped overboard. In a more orderly fashion, Second Officer Skilling mustered the crew and began lowering the starboard boats and rafts. Once they were in the water Leslie hailed Skilling in No. 3 Boat, thanked the men for their fine behaviour, and told them the coast was only four miles away to the west. Leslie also asked if the chief engineer was present, and learnt that he was not. Third Officer Simon, having made his rounds of the ship, reported to Leslie that apart from the losses in the engine room all 124 souls on board, including the twenty-five passengers, were accounted for. Leslie ordered Simon to dump the confidential books, then follow the others into the boats; Simon asked if he were not following, whereupon Leslie replied 'You are a young man, Mr Simon, and life is just beginning for you', which Simon thought 'rather ridiculous'. When Skilling's boat came back alongside, Simon climbed down the boarding ladder and looked back to see Leslie descend three or four rungs, and then disappear back on deck. Skilling next pulled his boat across to No. 1 and transferred *Glenorchy*'s doctor to attend wounded men in No. 3 Boat. Leslie hailed them again, but still refused to leave the ship. Skilling now encountered the chief officer, Mr R. Hanney, who approached on a Carley float with five men. Learning that Leslie had remained on board, Hanney protested, 'We're not going to leave him!' and put back to persuade the master to abandon *Glenorchy*; on the way he rescued a further three men who had dived overboard from the poop when *Glenorchy* was hit. Unfortunately, his next encounter was with the Italian torpedo-boat which had sunk his ship and now loomed out of the black night. Her commander, Calvani, assumed Hanney to be *Glenorchy*'s master and took him and the eight men on the raft prisoner.

After this Skilling was unable to persuade his men to return to the ship. Oil was spreading out across the water and the air was filled with its pungent and flammable stench. With the two boats Skilling pulled away, hoping for rescue by a British destroyer, but nothing came in sight and the flashes of the battle offshore were drawing farther away. At daylight a low-flying bomber passed overhead and Skilling reluctantly headed west, landing his men just south of Kelibia at about 08.00. He immediately called for volunteers to return to the ship, still lying in sight of them. Simon, two engineers, two of *Glenorchy*'s own midshipmen, an able seaman, three greasers and a naval rating agreed to join him, but as they were relaunching the boat there was a violent blast and the oil about the derelict caught fire. They pulled out three miles nevertheless, in the vain hope of rescuing Leslie, but it was clear the master had died with his sinking ship, about which aircraft and a torpedo-boat were now seen circling. This last was Calvani returning in *MS31*, having picked up Hanney and his Carley float. Skilling put back ashore, to find his shipmates now surrounded by a crowd of curious children who brought them water-melons. In due course the survivors gave themselves up to the Vichy French coastguard, to be interned with other survivors near Sfax.[32]

Aboard *Manchester*, Captain Drew had finally given up his attempt to get his cruiser back to Gibraltar. He had brought her into port damaged before, but now she was found to be too badly wounded to make way, and was slowly sinking. At 02.45 he therefore sadly ordered the remainder of his ship's company over the side. 'You men cannot be replaced,' he said, wishing them Godspeed.

They took to the boats and the Carley floats, and the scuttling charges were fired, but *Manchester* did not give up the ghost for three hours. Her weary crew pulled six miles to the shore, landing after daylight to become prisoners of the Vichy French. In due course they were interned in Bon Fichu, with the survivors from *Glenorchy* and *Clan Ferguson*.

As these individual trials were enacted, the seething mêlée about the advancing ships of the convoy continued relentlessly. *Pathfinder* fought a sharp action in pursuit of *MS26*, Sottotenente di Vascello Bencini, whose boat had made several unsuccessful torpedo attacks during the previous half-hour. Gibbs sought to ram the enemy craft, pinning her in the beam of his big search-light and firing with every gun which would bear. Bencini laid smoke and made off, and Gibbs broke off the chase when he saw another boat, *M31*, approaching a merchantman.

Poor Burrough had only the haziest idea of the situation about him. Shortly before 03.00 he had the satisfaction of finding *Charybdis*, *Eskimo* and *Somali* coming up astern to join him, but the damaged *Kenya* was still some miles distant, still in contact with the *Santa Elisa* and *Wairangi* on the port wing of the dog-gedly proceeding minesweeping destroyers. By this time these were losing what effectiveness they possessed, though they occa-sionally fired at the torpedo-boats or threw starshell ahead, to illuminate any boats lying in wait.

Following in their wake, *Ashanti* had spotted several drifting horned mines, presumably cut adrift by Kitcat's ships, but Campbell of *Fury* was later disparaging about the effectiveness of his ship and its comparative inactivity in the face of the torpedo-boats, which he considered the greater danger. This opinion was doubtless prompted by the fact that *Fury* and *Icarus* had lost both their sweeps, while *Intrepid* was reduced to one.

A brief lull followed the loss of *Glenorchy* and *Manchester*, but just after 03.00 a second wave of *MAS*-boats and *Schnellboote* inter-cepted the British ships as they began to break away from the Tunisian coast. Shaw Savill's *Wairangi* was the next ship to be sunk, during an attack by *MAS552* and *MAS554*, the former of which was engaged by *Kenya*. Sottotenenti di Vascello Perasso and Calcagno launched their torpedoes within seconds of each other. From *Wairangi*'s bridge, the torpedo tracks were seen at the same instant as the boats. The *Wairangi* was hit forward, in her port side, striking a deep tank in No. 3 Hold. The explosion was not loud and 'there was no flash, but a large column of water'. The adjacent hold spaces and the engine room quickly flooded. *Wairangi* began to list to port, fighting off circling *MAS*-boats with gunfire.

Mr Chalmers, the chief engineer, tried to combat the flooding, but his pumps were inadequate and the engines would not restart. Captain Gordon was aware that *Wairangi* had become a hulk; he did not wish his dead ship to fall into enemy hands, and with no means of towing to hand, he decided she must be scut-tled. The boats were lowered and the charges set, but they failed to sink the ship. Anxious to expedite matters, Chalmers led a party of volunteers back aboard. The main cooling water pipe was smashed and the forward and after water-tight doors were opened to increase the influx of water. The ship now settled but still did not founder, and daylight found Gordon's boats huddled disconsolately around the waterlogged *Wairangi*. By 06.00 German HeIIIs were circling, but two pairs of torpedoes still failed to dispatch the ship, since both inexplicably missed.

Two hours later a destroyer appeared on the scene and Gordon flashed an Aldis light at her. She proved to be *Eskimo*, searching for *Manchester*'s survivors, and now lifted seventy-nine of *Wairangi*'s company from their boats and rafts.

At about 03.30 the German *Schnellboote S30* and *S36*, commanded respectively by Oberleutnants-sur-Zee Weber and Brauns, made a concerted run at the *Almeria Lykes*. The American ship was hit forward, in No. 1 Hold, where a stow of bags of flour absorbed much of the explosion and prevented counter-mining among the dangerous commodities elsewhere in the ship. The American crew, on their own evidence, knew little of the importance of Malta. 'Had we known,' one afterwards reminisced, 'we would have fought our ship better.'[33] As it was, with the engines stopped and No. 1 Hold full of water, Henderson ordered *Almeria Lykes* abandoned, and this was carried out in an orderly fashion, 105 people getting clear in three boats. Daylight exposed them to aerial reconnaissance, and in the distance they could see *Wairangi* being circled by enemy planes; the crew were therefore reluctant to answer Henderson's call for volunteers to reboard the still floating *Almeria Lykes*. In the event Henderson, his British liaison officer Mitchell, an engineer, a deck cadet and the purser returned to the ship and prepared scuttling charges. These were ineffective, but Cadet Harris returned to the boats with the ship's cat. *Almeria Lykes* was still afloat when *Somali* arrived, in company with *Eskimo*, and rescued the dejected Americans – though not before they had jettisoned their valuables, thinking her an Italian. Henderson suggested to Commander Currey of *Somali* that he should sink *Almeria Lykes*, but Currey and Le Geyt in *Eskimo* considered it better to leave *Wairangi* and *Almeria Lykes* afloat in the hope that they might yet be towed in to Malta. In his report Henderson spoke highly of his Armed Guard and their commander, Ensign Hirschbegg: 'The gun crews behaved nobly. All were young lads with little experience but as long as there was anything to shoot at, they kept up the fire.' In his turn, Mitchell commended Henderson, but gave grounds for Syfret's conclusion in his final summary that 'the *Almeria Lykes* ... could well have continued steaming to Malta. The tale ... of the abandonment of his ship is one of shame.' The indifferent performance of the remainder of the crew of the *Almeria Lykes* has to be set against the inexperience of the American merchant marine at this stage of the war, and the psychological effects of the previous days' bombardment on men manning ships loaded with highly inflammable cargoes. There is little doubt that an element of indifference to the military objectives of the war existed, as it did in the British merchant service; but self-preservation is a powerful motive, and many of this necessarily polyglot and somewhat anti-British crew retained peacetime prejudices merely sharpened by the rigours of war, and regarded themselves as cannon-fodder sacrificed by greedy owners.[34]

Keeping inshore, MacFarlane's *Melbourne Star* steamed south alone. *Pathfinder* had drawn away, and when a second destroyer came up and signalled MacFarlane 'to turn round and rejoin the main body of the convoy which [is] astern of us', he demurred, considering his ship better placed as she was to reach Malta alone. The destroyer was *Ashanti,* and her signal lamp flashed curtly 'I am the admiral'. MacFarlane, relieved that order was being re-established, 'had nothing more to say ... [but] turned and rejoined the convoy ...'

Away to the north, *Rochester Castle* was following a dimly perceived shape thought quite erroneously to be *Brisbane Star;* she was probably *Dorset.* Captain Wren had intended to pass north of Pantelleria, but at 01.21, on receipt of a signal from *Ashanti,* he altered course to rejoin Burrough. He dodged to the eastwards of the first torpedo-boat attack, but this brought *Rochester Castle* through the second wave of enemy torpedo-boats. She appears to have been unsuccessfully attacked by *MAS564* and *S30,* though she was unaware of it; but at 03.29 a *MAS*-boat (probably *MAS564* re-engaging) was 'observed stopped close on to starboard bow'. The helm was put over to head for the enemy, and fire was opened from the starboard bridge Oerlikon and forecastle Bofors. The ship's tracers were seen to strike the torpedo-boat and she was thought to have been able only to limp away, but at '03.30 torpedoes [were] observed' and these struck the starboard side by No. 3 Hold. The confidential books were dumped, even though the ship 'appeared to be steaming well and not in immediate danger of sinking'. Wren zigzagged and steamed by the stars until his dislodged compasses settled down again. Down below, dunnage toms were being hammered into place to shore up the forward bulkhead, which separated the engine room from the flooded hold. The pumps were kept going and *Rochester Castle* pressed along, 'merrily doing 13 knots'. At about 04.15 *Kenya*, *Charybdis* and *Melbourne Star* were seen ahead, and at dawn Wren's lookouts saw more merchant ships and escorting destroyers. *Rochester Castle* had rejoined the convoy.

Not far from *Wairangi* and *Almeria Lykes*, the second American ship, *Santa Elisa*, had also met her end. During the confusion of the previous evening's final air attack she had been told to steer 120 degrees and that 'Spitfires from Malta' would be with her 'in the morning'. But Captain Thomson, seeing ahead the torpedo-boat attack off Kelibia Point, had brought *Santa Elisa* to a stop, and remained hove-to for some time, a tense period which induced long moments of prayer from several of her crew kneeling in their messroom. Then, deciding to make a run for it, Thompson rang on full ahead. *Santa Elisa*'s engines 'revved up and went like the clappers'.

A little later, she was attacked from astern by *MAS557*. She replied with heavy fire from her Oerlikons and Bofors, though some could not depress enough as the torpedo-boat came so close. Having loosed a torpedo which missed, the enemy boat raced past, strafing *Santa Elisa* with machine-gun fire and killing four of her British army gunners. A second boat, *MAS564* commanded by Tenente di Vascello Iafrate, closed in from the starboard side and fired a torpedo at point-blank range into *Santa Elisa*'s starboard bow. The ship had no flour in No. 1 Hold to soften the blow, and the detonation took place amid a stow of aviation spirit. 'There was a terrific flash and explosion forward. Instantly a large amount of water came up over the ship and into the wheelhouse.' A gunner forward felt 'a terrible shudder as the torpedo hit. A searing blast cramped the lungs up.' He was blown over the side, and found the water warm. Burning petrol spilled overboard onto the sea and its ignition flashed skywards. 'When the flame subsided, Nos 1 and 2 [Holds] were seen to be heavily on fire, and there was also a small fire aft, which it is thought was caused by burning petrol from the forward hold. In view of the highly explosive nature of the cargo and the extremely small chance of controlling the fire, the Master decided to abandon ship.' The way was taken off and the crew were sent to the boats. 'All hands who could reach the boats abandoned ship in three lifeboats. The guns' crews on the forward gun platform were unable to get past the burning hatches and either jumped or were blown into the sea by the explosion.'[35]

The *Santa Elisa*'s people were picked up by *Penn* which, with *Bramham* and *Port Chalmers*, had now come up from the west. Warned by the flashes off Kelibia Point, Swain of *Penn* had avoided contact with the torpedo-boats by cutting the corner off and passing through the minefield. It was daylight, about 06.00, when *Penn* stopped to embark the survivors from the American ship. Swain went on to return *Port Chalmers* and her commodore to the convoy, leaving Baines in *Bramham* to dispatch *Santa Elisa*, but at 07.15 a Ju88 arrived and 'carried out a deliberate attack on *Santa Eliza* [*sic*], hitting her with a stick of bombs and sinking her within five minutes.' Baines turned away to the east-south-east, increasing speed to 22 knots. At about 09.00 *Bramham* rejoined the reassembling convoy, taking station on *Dorset*'s port quarter.

Captain Tuckett's *Dorset* had successfully passed north of Pantelleria during during the night after her close shave with the lone torpedo-boat. At daylight enemy aircraft flew overhead, and although they did not attack *Dorset* but headed further south to bomb the inert *Glenorchy*, *Almeria Lykes*, *Wairangi* and *Santa Elisa*, Tuckett did not need much encouragement from Binfield to rejoin the convoy and had just done so when *Bramham* arrived.

The concentration of Kesselring's pilots on the derelicts was a foolish error, as it gave the British sufficient time to regroup. Force X now consisted of *Ashanti*, still flying Burrough's flag, with *Kenya* and *Charybdis*, *Intrepid*, *Icarus*, *Fury*, *Pathfinder*, *Penn* and *Bramham* back in company. The merchantmen now in the slow process of reassembling under Burrough's flag and Venables' broad pendant flying in *Port Chalmers* were the *Rochester Castle*, *Waimarama*, *Melbourne Star*, and *Dorset*.

Also rejoining from the west were *Ledbury* and the damaged *Ohio*. Hill reported the positions of the damaged ships they had passed as they ploughed through the debris astern of the convoy. Earlier, at 07.12, Burrough had sent *Somali* and *Eskimo* back to search for *Manchester*'s survivors and, as previously noted, on their way west Le Geyt and Currey picked up men from *Wairangi* and *Almeria Lykes*. Finally, at 10.40, they rescued 150 of *Manchester*'s men from Carley floats close inshore. Not half a mile away on shore they saw 'several hundred of, apparently,

Manchester's ship's company being marched away. Having recovered all survivors, HM Ships *Eskimo* and *Somali* proceeded to Gibraltar.'

The ships of Operation PEDESTAL, leaving Pantelleria and the Tunisian cost astern, set off on their final leg to the east-south-east, heading for the entrance to the swept channel into Grand Harbour about a hundred miles away. Along their route lay the patrol line of six British submarines. But on the horizon, having sunk *Wairangi*, *Santa Elisa* and the *Almeria Lykes*, Kesselring's Heinkels and Junkers dive-bombers were again circling.[36]

20

'The enemy will ... proclaim this a great victory'

(Operation PEDESTAL)

IN DISTANT MOSCOW, Churchill was conferring with Stalin. He had met Roosevelt in late June, and this was his first personal encounter with the Soviet premier. Already enjoying the confidence of the American president, Churchill now needed to establish as similar a relationship with Stalin as might be possible. Unfortunately the meeting was overshadowed by the terrible aftermath of PQ17, and the need to tell Stalin that no more convoys would be run to North Russia until the dark nights of the Polar autumn set in. Of even more import to Stalin, who was clamouring for his western Allies to relieve the enormous pressure on the retreating Red Army, was the news that there would be no Second Front opened in Europe until 1943. Churchill was to tell Stalin that this would strike Italy, the underbelly of the Axis, and was predicated upon the preservation of Malta as a base.

Immediately before meeting Churchill, Stalin had given his momentous order that the Soviet army should make a stand at Stalingrad, and he was in no mood to compromise. Referring to PQ17 and the situation in the Western Desert, Stalin made his remarks that the Royal Navy had run away, and that if the British were to try fighting, they might find they liked it. Churchill's rebuttal to these insults was so impassioned that the translators failed to keep up with him, though as he was without a single victory to adduce as proof of British valour, it is doubtful whether the most careful translation of each word and nuance of Churchill at his most eloquent would have impressed the wily Soviet leader, who knew only too well how politicians could obscure the truth with a mask of words.[1]

More than the simple objective of replenishing Malta therefore rested upon the outcome of Operation PEDESTAL: beyond the practical imperative lay the matter of Churchill's own credibility, and that of the nation he led. If the operation failed, so too would that nascent, delicate process of diplomacy which would bind himself and Roosevelt to Stalin, and thereby expand the Grand Alliance. Without Malta, the planned invasion of Italy would be still-born, the relief of the Red Army would not take place, and the danger of another accommodation between Fascism and Communism would become a possibility. Operation PEDESTAL was elevated beyond a task of mere maritime logistics; it became, in that Churchillian phrase, a component, perhaps *the* component, of 'the hinge of fate'.

Thus an anxious Churchill in Moscow was in close contact with London, where the First Sea Lord kept him appraised of the progress of the operation. He was informed of the loss of *Eagle* during a banquet on his first evening in Russia; greatly depressed, Churchill left early, declining Stalin's offer of a film show, and in private instructed Pound to upgrade his next situation report. It was almost midnight. In the Mediterranean the convoy was soon to encounter the torpedo-boats, and further devastation; but it was in the forenoon of that day, 13 August 1942, that Operation PEDESTAL approached its climax.

At daylight in the Mediterranean, Burrough was expecting air cover in the form of Beaufighters, and great efforts were made to rig up a temporary air communications network on *Ashanti*'s bridge. But although Beaufighters were seen, the lack of fighter-direction was keenly felt, their presence was largely ineffective, and the failure of air support at this crucial time resulted in further losses. It was shortly after 08.00 when the Junkers Ju88s made their first attack on what remained of the convoy, spread out as it was. *Dorset*, coming in to rejoin from the north-west under one engine, was being circled by a Savoia bomber; *Ohio* and *Ledbury* were 'thundering up at 16 knots' from some few miles astern; and *Port Chalmers* was still catching up. The two surviving cruisers, *Kenya* and *Charybdis*, screened by the rest of the destroyers, *Intrepid, Icarus, Fury, Pathfinder, Penn* and *Bramham*, afforded protection to the remaining transports. Tucking themselves astern of the cruisers, *Rochester Castle* was followed by *Waimarama* and *Melbourne Star* in the wake of the *Charybdis*. MacFarlane's ship had run ahead of the main body and had been turned back at daylight by Burrough as he sought to round up the scattered vessels,[2] and *Melbourne Star* took station astern of *Waimarama*, a position which confronted MacFarlane with an appalling decision when two Ju88s made a concerted attack against the large Shaw Savill liner.[3]

On the bridge of *Waimarama*, Captain Pearce was eating his breakfast off a tray. In the chart room, Radio Officer Jackson was talking to the ship's naval liaison officer, Lieutenant Withers. Apprentice Treves had left the saloon amidships, having found the chief steward there, the worse for drink, and was on his way forward again to his action station under the forecastle. Withers and Jackson heard the sudden crescendo of the diving aircraft and made to step out onto the bridge-wing, Withers leading; as Jackson followed, a sheet of flame separated them.

Four bombs hit *Waimarama*, and all seem to have detonated amid the after deck cargoes of high octane spirit and ammunition. A vast sheet of flame roared high up into the sky, completely engulfing the second aircraft as it came in to attack. The 'flames were hundreds of feet high and a great expanse of sea was covered in rolling smoke and flames'.[4] Treves was flung through the open door into the forecastle onto a stow of bags of lime, with Able Seaman Bowdory falling heavily on top of him. Driven backwards by the searing heat, Jackson turned and made his way down to the boat deck though the accommodation. Hearing shouts from the water Jackson, a non-swimmer, jumped over the side. The bow of *Waimarama* reared up as she fell over to starboard. A gunner on the starboard bridge-wing looked aft and saw the figure of a young man in flames. Beyond him there was nothing. 'In two minutes the lot was gone.'

Two cables astern of the disintegrating *Waimarama*, Captain MacFarlane's *Melbourne Star* was showered by debris as a third Junkers dropped a stick of bombs ahead of and alongside her. MacFarlane, conning his ship from the monkey island, had little time to react, putting *Melbourne Star*'s helm hard a-port to avoid running into the blazing wreck of *Waimarama*. With great presence of mind Second Officer Richards in the wheelhouse below rang on full ahead, and the *Melbourne Star* pressed right through the burning sea. On her forecastle, the guns' crews ran aft as, surrounded by flames which threatened to ignite *Melbourne Star*'s own highly inflammable deck cargo, the ship stood on and successfully broke out of the ring of fire. On the poop, however, expecting their own ship to explode as the flames swept aft along the *Melbourne Star*'s sides, thirty-three men of the 6-inch and Bofors guns' crews jumped for their lives over the stern.[5]

Following, Captain Mason also veered round the burning grave of *Waimarama*, equally anxious lest *Ohio* should ignite from the fire, while close ahead *Rochester Castle*'s stern received a shaking from the explosion; she too was under violent helm movements as she dodged torpedoes fired at her at the same moment. Exposed on her bridge, passing instructions by telephone from the bridge to the after guns, Cadet Lockhead was severely injured by a shower of splinters from the exploding *Waimarama*.

Shortly after the attack, as *Port Chalmers* and *Ohio* finally reached their stations, Burrough ordered a two-column formation. The port column was led by *Kenya*, followed by *Rochester Castle*; the starboard, led by *Charybdis*, consisted of *Melbourne Star*, *Ohio* and *Port Chalmers*. By mid morning, *Dorset* had also fallen in astern of *Rochester Castle*.

Waimarama's Third Radio Officer Jackson, floundering desperately and fearing for his life, was helped to a piece of floating wreckage by Treves, who then turned back to see sixty-one-year-old Able Seaman Bowdory, who had been delegated to look after him, standing on a raft, silhouetted against the encroaching flames. Treves never forgot the sight of his friend, arms outspread, drifting away. Unable to reach Bowdory before the flames engulfed him, the seventeen-year-old swam away towards a gap in the fire. In the ensuing moments, as he got clear of the flames, he began to muster those who had survived, blowing on his standard issue whistle.[6] Then, incredibly, through the smoke loomed the sight of *Ledbury*'s sharp bow.

Burrough had signalled to *Ledbury* 'Survivors, but don't go into the flames.' It did not seem to Hill than anyone could have survived the pyre of *Waimarama*, but men were seen in the water and, having lowered his whaler in the charge of his gunner, Hill then edged *Ledbury* forward, defying Burrough's order. 'I cannot speak too highly of the sheer guts of these men. They were singing and encouraging each other,' Hill wrote in his report.[7] Speaking over *Ledbury*'s public address system, Hill reassured the men in the water as he manoeuvred his ship, while boarding nets were thrown over the destroyer's side. The collective remorse felt aboard *Ledbury* over the abandonment of convoy PQ17 prompted several of Hill's crew to leap over the side to assist *Waimarama*'s survivors, many of whom were 'burned black'. The enemy aircraft were still attacking, and at one point Hill went astern with the announcement that he was 'just going to deal with these buggers', but would be back. With his high-angle guns blazing, Hill withdrew. Described by Baines as 'a rumbustious, not to say erratic fellow, full of zip, zap and go', Hill was quite clear about his motives for doing what he did. Some might consider his action foolhardy; certainly those he rescued thought him inordinately brave; but for Hill it was a simpler, more seamanlike matter: he had 'the greatest admiration for the merchant seamen' and felt 'I was redeeming myself for leaving those ships in PQ17'.

Ropes were flung, and by a slow process of individual rescue, numerous men were recovered. As the flames roared higher than *Ledbury*'s mast, Hill was making a final withdrawal when his coxswain shouted from the wheelhouse that through its small port he could see a man remaining on a raft beneath the canopy of smoke which was choking Hill and the men on *Ledbury*'s bridge. Hill went ahead again, shouting to his first lieutenant to be quick, but *Ledbury*'s cook, coming on deck at that moment, kicked off his shoes and went overboard, swam to the survivor and, getting him off the raft, splashed back to the ship's side and a dangling scrambling net. With flames roaring towards him, Hill bawled out for the cook, named Walker, to hang on, and went astern.

'I thought that's the end of Cookie, but when I eased to stop, there he was with the man he'd rescued, still clinging on.' Having whipped the two men inboard, Hill then recovered his gunner, Mr Musham, commanding the whaler, in which were further survivors. In all, some eighteen men from *Waimarama*'s crew were pulled from the water, along with all those who had jumped from *Melbourne Star*. Eighty-seven were lost with the ship, and one of the survivors died as *Ledbury* steamed to catch up with the convoy. He was buried 'with full military honours', and shortly afterwards *Ledbury* was once again dodging bombs from Ju88s.[8]

At 09.25, escorted by Maachi fighters, Italian torpedo-bombers dropping their *motobombas* about the convoy were accompanied by Stukas in a second attack. They were targeting *Ohio*, close to which Onslow's *Ashanti*, flying Burrough's flag, was providing special anti-aircraft cover. *Ohio* was near-missed by a 500-pound bomb exploding on her port bow, inflicting more damage. One Ju87 was shot down by *Ashanti*, whose gunnery officer, Sub-Lieutenant Lewin, had already been at his post in her director for twenty-four hours. The Junkers crashed on *Ohio*'s poop, wrecking the after, low-angle gun, but mercifully did not explode. Although the four Beaufighters of No. 248 Squadron assigned to provide air escort failed throughout the day to find the ships, short- and long-range Spitfires were sent out to break up the enemy formations approaching from Sicily. In view of the enemy successes against the convoy, these must be regarded as having been of only partial effectiveness. Nevertheless, Spitfires did attack the enemy bombers, and claimed to have shot one down; certainly the gunners aboard *Dorset* accidentally shot down a Spitfire, with the loss of her pilot.

Twenty minutes later, however, the situation began to alter again. The renewed attack at 09.41 near-missed *Kenya*; then, at about 10.00, with Italian aeroplanes deploying the circling *motobombas* ahead of the convoy, about twenty German Ju88s, attacked from ahead as Stukas screamed down out of the blue sky in defiance of the British fighters now vigorously contesting the air-space above the ships. One Ju88 was hit by the barrage and skidded down across the sea, driving into the side of *Ohio* in a welter of flames. As she had dropped her bomb, no explosion took place, but this and near-misses from other aircraft blew out the boilers in *Ohio* and stopped the remaining engine in *Dorset*. Burrough ordered *Penn*, *Bramham* and *Ledbury*, the last still coming up from astern, to stand by the tanker.

During this attack two more Spitfires were shot down by the barrage as the ships sought to ward off their assailants. The Ju88s fell upon *Rochester Castle*, near-missing her with violent bombbursts under her bows which lifted the vessel bodily. The engines were put out of action and red-hot splinters lanced through the ship, starting small fires. These were quickly extinguished by fire parties under Chief Officer Culpin, though the after small-arms magazine had to be flooded, which affected the ship's steering gear. After about ten minutes the engines were restarted and in due course telemotor steering was resumed, but the ship was now even more sluggish and, with an estimated 4,000 tons of water in her, her freeboard was down to six feet. Like *Port Chalmers* and *Melbourne Star*, however, *Rochester Castle* pressed on.

At 11.20, twelve SM79 torpedo-bombers, escorted by fourteen Mc202s which were engaged by Spitfires, made another attack. Tired and fed up with his passive role, his exhausted gunners stimulated after a dose of Benzedrine, Gibbs took *Pathfinder* out of the screen at 30 knots, heading for the centre of the line of torpedo-bombers approaching at masthead height. Engaging on both sides, *Pathfinder* opened fire with every gun which would bear. 'The noise was tremendous ...,' wrote Gibbs afterwards; '... the whole formation was surrounded by shell bursts and streams of tracer bullets through which they dived, twisted and climbed, dropping their torpedoes in almost all directions except the convoy. One SM79 caught fire ... as they scattered and steered back to Sicily. The attack broken up, we turned under full rudder to rejoin the convoy ...' Gibbs was wrong in one particular: one torpedo *had* got through to the convoy. *Port Chalmers* had thus far avoided all bombs and 'experienced extraordinary good fortune'. This did not now desert her, for the torpedo only fouled her starboard paravane, its fins 'having caught in the guard of the paravane tail'. The ship was stopped and went astern, drawing the paravane clear. The gear was then slipped. 'The torpedo exploded on [the] bottom in 400 fathoms, but the uplift was tremendous though [the] ship was clear.'[9]

Burrough, who was still unaware that *Manchester* had sunk and that most of her crew were ashore on Vichy territory, now sent Hill back to look for more survivors from the cruiser. Hill was equally unaware of *Manchester*'s fate and, anxious to take on fuel, thought he would get some from the cruiser when he found her. *Ledbury* headed for the Gulf of Hammamet at full speed.

Burrough left *Penn* and *Bramham* to stand by *Dorset* and *Ohio* and led the three remaining transports towards the entrance to the swept channel. The pitiful remains of convoy WS21s now gradually acquired the belated but increasingly effective air umbrella of the Royal Air Force. At 12.30 short-range Spitfires were above the three transports and the escort, and two hours later Burrough met the fleet minesweepers of the local Malta Escort Force. Commanded by Acting Commander Jerome in *Speedy* (Lieutenant-Commander Doram), *Hebe*, *Hythe* and *Rye* now joined forces and at 16.00, at the entrance to the swept channel, Jerome's vessels streamed their gear and led the three cargo liners north, to round Delimara Point and make the final approach to Grand Harbour.

Having seen his charges thus far, Burrough left *Penn* and *Bramham* with *Ohio*, and *Dorset* and *Ledbury* in the Gulf of Hammamet, and headed west for Gibraltar. As he passed the labouring *Ohio*, he signalled his valediction: 'I am proud to have known you.'

After leaving Burrough off the Skerki Bank before sunset on 12 August, Vice-Admiral Syfret had cruised off the Algerian coast, providing distant cover in case the Regia Marina's capital ships should emerge. In the event, just before noon next day, the 13th, he sent *Indomitable*, the defective *Rodney* and the damaged *Ithuriel* on to Gibraltar, escorted by *Amazon*, *Antelope*, *Westcott*, *Wishart* and *Zetland*.

That same evening saw the end of *Foresight*, which since the air attack the previous afternoon had been under the watchful eye of Commander Tyrwhitt in *Tartar*. Tyrwhitt had run alongside and secured to *Foresight* and the two destroyers had limped past Galita Island when, at about 20.00, aircraft were seen in the distance. In slipping from *Foresight*, *Tartar* fouled a wire in her screws. Fortunately the aircraft, which may well have been the Beaufighters seen briefly above the convoy, withdrew. A little later *Nigeria* and her screen of Hunts hove in sight, with *Bicester* approaching to signal Tyrwhitt before returning to the task of seeing *Nigeria* into Gibraltar.

As the seamen aboard *Tartar* strove to clear their fouled screws, two Ju88s made an attack but were driven off without too much trouble. Work resumed, only to be broken off again when fast ships were seen to the north. Thought briefly to be Italians, these were then identified as friendly, but *Charybdis*, *Eskimo* and *Somali*, speeding east to reinforce Burrough, ignored Tyrwhitt's flashed signal for assistance. Finally unscrambling the tangle of wires under his transom, Tyrwhitt took *Foresight* in tow and worked up to 7 knots. *Foresight* was badly flooded aft, and during the night slowly settled by the stern. Such was the drag caused by the waterlogged hulk that the tow parted at 05.15, and although it had been reconnected by dawn, *Foresight*'s iron deck was now awash. By 08.30 shadowing aircraft had located the two destroyers, and a periscope was seen. This was the assiduous Rosenbaum in *U73*, seeking to regain contact with the enemy after sinking *Eagle* and making an unsuccessful attack on *Nigeria* and her Hunts. *Tartar* slipped her tow and attacked, but not before Rosenbaum had let fly a salvo, none of which hit the disabled *Foresight*. Having saturated the area with depth-charges, Tyrwhitt concluded that without assistance, *Tartar* was inadequate to her task: *Foresight* must be scuttled. Removing her crew, at 09.55 Tyrwhitt sank her with a torpedo and headed *Tartar* at high speed for Gibraltar. On passage he overhauled *Nigeria*, *Bicester*, *Wilton* and *Derwent*, arriving at Gibraltar in their company early in the morning of the 13th. Also arriving back under the shadow of The Rock were Force R, the tankers and corvettes of the replenishment force.

Burrough's ships, *Ashanti*, *Kenya*, *Charybdis*, *Intrepid*, *Icarus*, *Pathfinder* and *Fury*, headed west, their speed limited by the damaged *Kenya*. The cruiser, throwing up a huge wave from her damaged bow, nevertheless managed 20 knots, and Force X was off Cape Bon at 01.30 on 14 August before it encountered the enemy. Here the British were attacked by at least one torpedo-boat, *MAS556*, but she was driven off without trouble by gunfire from *Kenya*. At 04.50, however, when they were off the Fratelli Rocks, having negotiated the minefield in line astern of *Intrepid*'s one remaining sweep, the Italian submarine *Granito* fired a salvo of torpedoes which narrowly missed *Ashanti*. *Kenya* gamely swung to ram, but her turning circle was too wide. The speed of Force X enabled the ships to outrun the danger, but at daylight enemy reconnaissance aircraft appeared, and a determined onslaught on the retiring warships began. In a succession of attacks which lasted from 10.00 to 13.00, twenty-six Ju88s, thirteen Ju87s, fifteen SM84s and a score of SM79s dropped high- and low-level bombs, torpedoes and *motobombas*. Apart from another near-miss which shook *Kenya* and started a small fire in her forward boiler-room, necessitating a brief reduction in speed, Force X continued west undamaged. Not only that, but the concentration of Fliegerkorps II on Burrough's ships had served to divert them from the destruction of *Ohio*. At 18.00 that evening, off Algiers, an Albacore from *Victorious* sighted Force X; shortly after this Burrough rejoined Syfret's Force F, and the combined squadrons headed for Gibraltar, arriving there at 18.00 on 15 August, their part in PEDESTAL complete.

For the ships' companies of Force X there was the luxury of cleaning up and sleeping. Burrough was still covered in the oil he had accumulated in transferring from *Nigeria*, and *Ashanti* was desperately short of water, but the admiral decided that clean he would be. He therefore 'descended, wrapped in a towel, to the upper deck and took a salt-water shower in full view of an interested ship's company'. Last to arrive, at 05.30 on 15 August after a strafing by a single Ju88 on the 13th, were *Somali* and *Eskimo*, with the remnant few from *Manchester*.

Because of the severity of the injury to Cadet Lockhead, *Rochester Castle*, a gaping hole in her side, was the first of the three transports to enter Grand Harbour, followed by *Port Chalmers* and *Melbourne Star*. It was half past six in the evening of 15 August 1942, and the ramparts were black with people. Unused to any fanfare at times of arrival and departure, the exhausted, grimy and hungry merchant seamen found the occasion deeply affecting. 'We really thought we must have done something significant' was the prevailing emotion, as the cheers finally released each of them from the fearful tension of his individual solitude. They had been at continuous action stations for thirty-six hours.[10]

Offshore to the south and east of Malta, the ordeal was not yet over for the wreckage of the convoy. Far to the west that afternoon, Hill's *Ledbury* had steamed towards the Gulf of Hammamet, the crew at cruising stations, Hill dozing on his bunk. Suddenly he was summoned to the bridge as two aircraft flew in low. Thinking they were Beaufighters, Hill secured his 4-inch guns; realising his mistake, he alerted the pom-pom and Oerlikon crews, ordering them to hold fire until he gave the order, and to first target the aircraft to port. With a withering burst, *Ledbury*'s fire shot first one and then the other Savoia Marchetti down. The second loosed her torpedo; putting the helm hard a-port, Hill avoided it by inches. As the destroyer left astern a column of brown smoke rising from the wrecked air-craft, Hill ordered the mainbrace spliced and a tot of extra rum issued. 'This success', he wrote in his report, 'came at a very apt time, as the ship's company were showing signs of very great fatigue and the survivors were, most understandably, jumpy.' Closing the coast at 16.30 near Ras Mahmur, *Ledbury* turned south without wearing her ensign and steamed parallel with the coast. Answering a request from the signal station at Hammamet to hoist her identifying 'numbers', Hill added 'I' to the three-flag hoist for splicing the mainbrace and thus masqueraded as an Italian warship, though he had no Italian ensign to hoist aft. By 19.00 they had found no trace of *Manchester*, and it became clear that she and her company had disappeared. Hill headed back east, through an uneasy night of partial rest and anxiety, intend-ing to rejoin the effort being made to bring in the last merchant ships.

There were three of these: *Brisbane Star*, still proceeding independ-ently through neutral waters, and the two left behind by the convoy. On the afternoon of 13 August, as Burrough withdrew to the west, Hill headed for Ras Mahmur and Wren's *Rochester Castle* led her consorts into Grand Harbour, *Dorset* and *Ohio* both lay immobile and almost derelict on the calm Mediterranean Sea. *Dorset* had been severely damaged by near-misses which 'had blown the starboard side of her engine room in and knocked out the auxiliary generators as well as the main engines',[11] so there were no means of fighting the fire in No. 4 Hold. The adjacent hold, No. 5, contained cased petrol, and although both spaces were partially flooded, 'once the fire had got a grip' Captain Tuckett had decided he must abandon the ship; at about 11.00 *Dorset*'s crew had therefore lowered their boats. Shortly after-wards *Bramham* arrived to assist. According to Baines, *Dorset*'s crew 'had no desire to go back to her', and an attempt to pass a tow was abandoned when two Ju88s appeared and Baines hauled off to give effective anti-aircraft fire. When he returned to the task, *Dorset* had settled further.

At 13.05, faced with the reality of the problem, Baines had decided to 'act on a carte blanche' from Burrough and sink *Dorset*, but 'was instructed not to do so at 13.18' by Leatham, who urged the men-of-war offshore to make every effort to bring in *Dorset* as well as *Ohio*. Leatham was fast regretting the loss of the

tug *Jaunty*, so blithely sent back to Gibraltar on the second day of
the operation. Baines, meanwhile, in accordance with Leatham's
order, was preparing to go back alongside when Swain in *Penn*
ordered him to assist in covering *Ohio*, which was bearing the
brunt of continued bombing. Baines was relieved by the arrival
of the Malta-based minesweeper *Rye*, whereupon he returned to
Dorset, only to be attacked by five Ju88s. *Bramham* and *Dorset*
shuddered from near-misses, but Tuckett, his naval liaison
officer Lieutenant Bernard, chief officer and chief engineer, now
reboarded *Dorset* using one of the ship's lifeboats, manned by
Able Seamen Brown and Harvey, hoping to renew an attempt to
tow from alongside. The heat was intense, and again the imprac-
ticability of the task became obvious. Then, 'at 19.00, four more
Ju88s attacked, near-missing *Dorset* aft, and firing [*sic*] her badly
forward. She sank in 20 minutes.' Tuckett's party reboarded
Bramham, Baines requesting that they bring all the lifeboat stores
with them, so short of food was he for the numerous survivors
aboard his overcrowded destroyer. Apprentice Dickens, watching from the destroyer, shortly afterwards wrote: 'Gradually that
majestic looking ship went lower and lower and by 19.55 *Dorset*
was no more.' With her invaluable cargo, she was only seventy-
two miles short of her destination.

It had been apparent from noon that neither *Penn* nor *Bramham*
could manage their respective charges single-handed.[12] As she
ran back towards *Ohio* at 23 knots, *Bramham* was 'extremely
heavily attacked by a mixed force of ten Ju88s and Stukas'.
Joining *Penn* at 20.30, *Bramham* began the task of providing anti-
submarine defence to *Ohio*.

While these events were taking place, Captain Riley had been
living on his nerves and his wits in roughly equal parts as he
nursed the *Brisbane Star* towards her destination. It will be
recalled that *Brisbane Star* had been torpedoed in the bow during
the attack at sunset on 12 August. With No. 1 Hold and the forepeak spaces flooded or open to the sea, Riley decided to 'push
along on the bulkheads. Mr Nichol, Chief Engineer, was then
informed of the position and I let him know that I would travel
along to Cape Bon, some 35 miles ahead, and then decide
whether to creep along the coast the next day or adventure on in
the hopes of connecting up with the other ships at daylight.'
Making 5, then 10 knots, *Brisbane Star* picked her solitary way

along the coast, passing a darkened and stationary warship, and at daylight on 13 August rounded Ras Mahmur within sight of the burning hulk of *Glenorchy*. Off the headland they were investigated by a Savoia Marchetti torpedo bomber, but as they were in neutral waters and wore no ensign, Riley held his fire. The aeroplane returned about 10.00, but although it passed closely overhead, the aircrew did nothing. Several signal stations along the coast called up *Brisbane Star*, making the usual request for the ship to show her distinguishing 'numbers'. Riley asked to be excused the formality, and was not pressed. Meanwhile his naval liaison officer, Lieutenant Symes, had transmitted a signal to Leatham, outlining *Brisbane Star*'s position and Riley's intentions.[13] The Vichy authorities at Hammamet asked Riley to come inshore and anchor. He demurred, replying that his anchors were foul, 'which they were'. Asked if he required salvage, Riley ignored the question and resumed his course at 5 knots. Soon afterwards the crew reported a periscope trailing them, though neither the master nor Symes definitely observed this.

The request to stop was repeated at 17.00 by the signal station at Sousse, which then declined to excuse Riley the flying of his numbers, and ordered him to stop. Not complying, Riley soon found himself pursued by a French naval gun-boat, so headed *Brisbane Star* seawards, increasing speed to 10 knots, until a shot 'fell ten yards off our bow'. Incapable of outrunning the gun-boat, Riley slowed to a standstill and rounded-to. Two French officials boarded, the harbourmaster from Sousse and an armed naval officer. Taking his visitors down to his cabin and producing a bottle of whisky, Riley apologised to the harbourmaster for not wearing colours. He was told that *Brisbane Star* was to be carried in to the neutral port and impounded. As Riley reported afterwards, 'I replied that I would not let him do it.' The harbourmaster 'replied that he was sorry, but that those were his orders. I then asked him if he was a seaman, he replied yes. I then informed him I was in a difficult position and asked him if he would be a brother seaman, be kind to me, forget me and let me go. He looked at the naval officer for a few minutes, then caught hold of my hand and said "Goodbye, Captain, a safe voyage and good luck." As he was going away I took the opportunity to ask if he would take away a couple of wounded men ... He readily agreed and we put Corfield on the boat. The other seaman, Armitage, preferred to remain with us.'

Brisbane Star then stood east, zigzagging, at 10 knots. The escape from Sousse was 'of a happy nature in a day made most unpleasant for me by members of the ship's personnel whose sense of duty and ... honour I am sorry to say sank that day to a spring low water mark' – Riley had suffered the indignity of several delegations from the ship's departments to his bridge. He had dismissed them, even as the after guns' crews were reporting the trailing periscope again. 'It was at this period that Lieutenant Symes approached me and stated that my chances of getting to Malta were nil for as soon as I left the coast the submarine reported as following us would put ... torpedoes into us and we would be blown sky high ... the time had come for me to scuttle.' Symes had had his telegraphist monitoring the Italian frequencies, and was aware of enemy reports of the position of *Brisbane Star*. The sea transport officer, Lieutenant Eva, concurred with his colleague, and while Riley's chief officer, Mr White, was sympathetic to the master's dilemma, he pointed out the sense of their advice. 'The atmosphere ... was against me,' Riley reported, 'and I don't think ... I am far wrong when I say that close to 100% were wanting the ship scuttled and to get ashore ... It was at this time that we received a signal from Malta informing us that Beaufighters would be meeting us in the morning.'It may or may not have been this news which swayed those on *Brisbane Star*'s bridge, but Riley reported that the contrary opinions of his officers 'were short lived'.[14]

In fact the day's 'unhappiness', which received some public empurplement and added to the tales of reluctance among merchant seafarers to pull their weight, had arisen from a discussion in the messrooms as to the fate of the civilian merchant seamen if *Brisbane Star* should be interned. The Vichy French had acquired a nasty reputation among them, and their civilian status, along with the cessation of pay on the day the ship's articles of agreement were ended with her capture or sinking, inclined the ship's crew to go on. However, news of this 'combination' reached the ship's bridge and resulted in the crew being ordered onto the foredeck, where the naval liaison officer threatened them: if they did not obey orders, the military and naval personnel under his orders would turn the guns on them. With that the debate ended 'with a scatter'. When asked afterwards by seventeen-year-old Quartermaster Sanders if they would have opened fire on their shipmates, the gunners replied that they would obey the last order. 'I then realised', Sanders recollected, 'why I was in the Merchant Navy and could have a mind of my own.' After this unpleasant incident there was 'no more trusting service people, and anything we talked about was in a guarded tongue'.[15] Thus the matter blew over.

Despite *Brisbane Star's* forward draught of 38 feet and a broad, foamy wake, the night passed quietly. At 06.00 on 14 August 'three or four RAF Beaufighters were sighted escorting us', but these did not prevent a Ju88 flying in low from the port side, strafing the ship as it came. *Brisbane Star's* guns fired on the attacker and hit the aeroplane's port engine. Dropping bombs into the water, it then jettisoned the rest and flew off low over the sea, trailing smoke. One man was wounded by shrapnel as the bombs exploded, but this was the only outcome.

Shortly after this, RAF Spitfires were in touch 'and they remained with us until our arrival'. At 09.00 an attacking Italian torpedo-bomber was pounced on by a Beaufighter and shot down. Approaching the entrance to the swept channel, *Brisbane Star* was met by an escort of motor launches and the minesweepers *Hythe* and *Hebe*, which swept her in. At 15.30 on 14 August *Brisbane Star* passed the boom and entered Grand Harbour to proceed to No. 7 Berth. She wore her red ensign as she passed the crowds lining the Upper and Lower Barrakka Gardens but, Sanders recalled, there was 'no band to greet us, like the early arrivals. We were late.'

During the forenoon of 13 August, *Ohio* and *Ledbury* had rejoined the convoy in some style, at 16 knots. *Ohio* was shaken severely during the destruction of the *Waimarama* and her engines were briefly stopped. Still steering erratically, Mason had asked Tuckett to take station ahead of *Ohio* when *Dorset* rejoined about 09.00. In the subsequent attacks, with *Ohio* the principal target, the tanker was constantly shaken by near-misses. One Ju87, having dropped its bomb, was shot down by gunfire from *Ohio* and

> crashed alongside, the wing hitting the after part of the bridge and other large pieces being flung all over the ship ... Shortly after this another heavy attack took place by Ju88s, *Ohio* got four or five near-misses and the ship stopped ... both electric fuel pumps were found to be defective. The ship was once more got under way using the steam fuel pump, but the condensers were also damaged

and could not maintain a vacuum. Speed was now down to 20 rpm, about 4 knots. This was maintained for a short time, then reduced to 2.5 knots and finally stopped altogether. At the time, steam was being kept [up] and the ship could have been towed satisfactorily since [the] emergency steering was still working.[16]

It was at this point that *Ledbury* was ordered to search the Gulf of Hammamet, and Lieutenant-Commander Swain approached *Ohio* in *Penn*, intending to tow the tanker. During the heaving across of a heavy 10-inch manila hemp rope from the tanker, *Ohio*'s water-tube boilers finally failed and the tanker 'was left with no power of any sort and no means of steering'.

Swain's attempt to tow ended in failure when the hawser parted at 14.30. With her port side shell plating torn outwards by the original torpedo strike and acting like a drogue, *Ohio* was constantly veering to port, and moved in a languid and frustrating circle. All attempts to steer by hand proved too slow to be effective, and this drogue-effect continued to bedevil the entire operation of trying to move her ahead. *Penn* stood off as aircraft attacked, *Bramham* doing likewise near *Dorset*, not far away.

An impasse had been reached. Lieutenant Barton, the naval liaison officer aboard *Ohio*, reported that 'by this time everyone was feeling the strain of the last 48 hours, and it seemed impossible under the present conditions that any progress could be made unless some other ships could assist in the tow. It seemed that the ship was nothing more than a sitting target.' Swain now received a signal from Leatham that *Rye* and two attendant motor launches, *ML121* and *ML168*, were on their way to help. It was therefore agreed between Mason and Swain that *Penn* should come alongside and withdraw *Ohio*'s crew until darkness when, with assistance, they would have a better chance of moving the tanker. This was accomplished by 13.30. Everywhere, exhausted men collapsed about *Penn*'s decks. Some simply slept, others became cataleptic and inert. A few of the traumatised survivors from the merchant ships lay trembling uncontrollably, while other men acted irrationally, singing or, in one case, appearing on deck wearing a lampshade. A few were hallucinating, and at one point action stations were rung when someone mistook an aerial insulator for an attacking aircraft.

The arrival of *Rye* and her launches in the late afternoon prompted another attempt to tow, which Swain was eager to get on with. When he had conferred with Lieutenant Pearson of *Rye* and with Captain Mason, *Ohio*'s crew were returned to their ship. Swain took *Penn* ahead of the tanker and her heavy wires were hauled across to *Ohio*. Meanwhile *Ohio*'s engineers disconnected the steering gear and her seamen, under the chief officer, Mr Gray, rigged relieving tackles on the quadrant in an attempt to apply counter-helm to offset the effect of the torn plating. *Rye* made fast ahead of *Penn*, so that when Swain moved forward, *Rye* assisted by breaking the sheer induced by the drag of *Ohio*'s dead-weight.

Progress was 'almost nil' as the two small warships found they were unable to overcome *Ohio*'s perverse tendency to go her own way. Then, at 19.00, eight Ju88s attacked. *Penn* slipped the tow to open fire as a near-miss blew the *Ohio*'s rudder off. Another bomb penetrated the boat deck, starting a fire, and exploded in the engine room, which flooded, settling *Ohio* further into the sea and bringing a ventilator crashing down across one of the Bofors guns. Mortally wounded, Gunner Brown was dragged clear and later taken aboard *Penn*. All the vessels were shaken, *ML168* so badly that she was sent back to Valletta.

It was now quite impossible to steer *Ohio*. Consulting his chief engineer, Mr Wyld, Mason considered *Ohio* to be sinking and ordered her abandoned. Most crew members joined *Penn* by way of the lifeboats, including Wyld and Gray. Mason, Barton and the second officer were taken off with a dozen seamen in *ML121*. As the evening wore on it became clear that although *Ohio* was foundering slowly, she was not in immediate danger of sinking. 'We did not return', Barton reported, 'as there was nothing more that could be done to assist the towing ships', which still persisted in their endeavour, though they were achieving little. Mason's comment was that 'it was no good remaining on board to risk life when stopped, and the attempt at towing was proving hopeless'.

In the period before darkness two more bombing attacks were made by Ju88s which, despite the barrage put up by *Penn* and *Rye*, succeeded in further damaging *Ohio*'s structure. This increased Swain's difficulties, but not far away, at approximately 19.55, *Dorset* had finally sunk, and Baines was approaching in *Bramham* to help.

The drama now entered its final phase. *Ohio* had ceased to be a viable ship; she had been abandoned, and was slowly sinking. With Mason and his crew at the ends of their tethers and dropping with fatigue, Swain and his colleagues effectively took over

Ohio. She became a joint venture, Swain orchestrating the combined effort of the resources now available. After dark, as most of *Ohio*'s withdrawn crew slept, *ML121* went alongside *Penn* 'to transfer a working party to *Ohio* to make fast the tow again'. Led by *Penn*'s executive officer, Lieutenant Marten, *Rye* was secured ahead, with *Penn* on a line astern, to try to keep *Ohio* on a straight course. This was accomplished about 23.50, and all personnel were withdrawn from the tanker. While he was aboard, Barton had noticed that 'further damage to the ship had been done and that the deck was now buckled right across ... She had obviously broken her back and was well down aft, having settled some six feet since ... [we left] her at about 17.30. It seemed unlikely that she could remain afloat much longer.'

With *Bramham* slowly circling to provide anti-submarine cover, Swain gallantly tried to drag the inert mass of *Ohio* to the east, but his progress was pitiful. Lieutenant Baines – watching, one senses, with a touch of youthful impatience – brought *Bramham* close to *Penn* at about 01.15 and 'suggested that we should secure one each side of *Ohio* and that we might make 6 or 7 knots'. Theoretically this method would impart both power and a degree of directional control to the derelict; how much of the latter, would have to be determined empirically. At 02.30 *Rye*'s wire parted, and Swain agreed to Baines's suggestion. *Bramham* went directly alongside, to be followed by *Penn* half an hour later. Swain found, however, that the projecting plating prevented him getting *Penn* properly secured, and he had perforce to break away; Baines, disappointed, unable to achieve anything alone, followed suit.

By now everyone was exhausted, from the officers on the warships' bridges to the sweating and swearing seamen heaving heavy wires hither and thither as the situation changed as rapidly as the ideas of their commanders. It was decided to take a short break and await the dawn.

At daylight on the 14th Captain Mason woke to find that the destroyers' attempts to tow *Ohio* during the night had been unsuccessful. *Ohio* he observed to be 'settling considerably by [the] stern and [the] maindeck at [the] pumproom buckling'. It was now that German aircraft began a series of attacks that were to last all day. The irrepressible Hill arrived too, guided by the gun flashes of *Penn* and *Bramham*. *Ledbury* was also full of survivors, and many of these merchant seamen had had gunnery training. They were put aboard *Ohio* to man her guns; others assisted with clearing the ship of wreckage, and efforts were redoubled in a curious display of bloody-minded tenacity.[17] Hill sent Musham, his adaptable gunner, aboard *Ohio*, both to assist with connecting the tow and to supervise the volunteers in getting the tanker's damaged Oerlikons back in service. Also vital at this time was the bosun of *Waimarama*, whose knowledge of *Ohio*'s windlass proved invaluable.

An attempt was made to tow with *Rye* ahead and *Ledbury* astern, but this too failed. Next *Rye* secured ahead of *Ledbury* in a tandem tow, with *Penn* adding her power alongside *Ohio*'s starboard side. By now the minesweeper *Speedy* had arrived from Valletta, and Lieutenant-Commander Jerome took over as senior officer. A little progress was made, but at about 11.00 an attack by nine Italian Stukas developed, to be met by ferocious anti-aircraft gunfire. The Stukas dropped oil bombs in an attempt to ignite *Ohio* and Musham, manning one of *Ohio*'s Oerlikons, shot one down as Spitfires intervened, chasing the Stukas off but only destroying one more.

The disruption of this attack left the operation in complete disorder, all direction lost, *Ohio* lying inert, the small warships about her festooned in bights of ropes and wires. It was a morning of deep frustration under the hot sun. The enemy buzzed about and the appearance of Malta-based Spitfires, with no means of talking to them, seemed perversely brief and disjointed. At this point a second Stuka attack developed, and *Bramham* drew off to put up a deterrent fire. *Rye*'s tow wire again parted, and Hill slipped *Ledbury*'s as the veering tanker threatened to drag the little destroyer out of his grasp. Heaving away, Hill signalled *Ohio* that he would be back as soon as the enemy had been driven off. Near-misses shook all the warships as they threw up their barrage; one Stuka penetrated it, to put another bomb under *Ohio*'s stern, blowing a hole into the after-peak.

As the Stukas withdrew, Swain, still alongside *Ohio*'s starboard side, ordered *Bramham* to secure to port, and by 11.30 Baines had eagerly complied. Ahead, *Rye* took up the tow again and speed was worked up to a gratifying 6 knots, with a steady enough course. Morale rose accordingly. To cheer everyone up, Swain had 'Chattanooga Choo-Choo' played loudly, over and over again, on *Penn*'s PA system.[18]

*

From Malta Leatham was updating the Admiralty in London, who were passing on the news to Moscow. Even while *Ohio*'s fate remained uncertain, Churchill sent Stalin a note which tacitly admitted the losses of the convoy, but acknowledged that just sufficient shipping had arrived to justify the cost. Referring to the proposed invasion of Italy, he concluded: 'The enemy will no doubt proclaim this a great victory at sea, and so it would be but for the strategic significance of Malta in view of future plans.'

Meanwhile *Penn*'s engineer officer, Lieutenant-Commander (E) Smeall, had put an air compressor aboard *Ohio* and 'showed enterprise in taking steps to improve the [tanker's] buoyancy'.[19] Mason, more optimistic after his rest, sent a message to *Penn* that Gray and Wyld would assist as much as possible. Wyld and his men followed Smeall's lead in pumping air into the oil tanks and in passing a salvage line into *Ohio*'s engine room. Mason was transferred to *Penn* and reboarded *Ohio* where, in concert with Swain, Smeall, Wyld and Gray, a final effort was made to save the tanker. Mason recorded the water level in the engine room rising by six inches every hour, but he was decidedly inspirited by his short sleep. 'I think with luck we'll last twelve hours,' he reported to Jerome, 'and that should be enough for you to get us to Malta.'

It was a bold claim; by the afternoon *Ohio*'s freeboard was 'only 2 feet 6 inches and [the] stern half of [the] vessel [was] expected to part at any time as vessel appeared to be buckling more'.[20] That afternoon Mason buried Gunner Brown from the stern of *Penn*.

Rye's head tow now parted yet again, but progress was unimpaired and, with *Ledbury*, *Speedy* and *Rye* providing escort, *Ohio* was forced bodily towards the swept channel, girded by *Penn* and *Bramham* – 'the real heroes', as Hill called them – thrusting the tanker forward. The tenacity and obduracy of the young destroyer commanders were beginning to pay off. By the afternoon, as *Ohio* was patiently nudged along, a standing patrol of short-range Spitfires was overhead.

By the evening of 14 August, Malta was in sight. All concerned were exhausted with battle fatigue and the heat, Baines, Swain and Hill in particular, for they bore a heavy burden. It was scarcely surprising that an element of farce should have dominated the last miles of the passage. Arrangements had been made to hand the *Ohio* over to tugs at 20.00, and the tug *Robust* was seen coming out from Malta, loaded with spectators and intending to add her power ahead of *Ohio*. Aboard *Penn* the wardroom was full of survivors enjoying a festive meal when suddenly the destroyer's side was stove-in by *Robust* as the tug, having made fast the tow, was girded and rammed the destroyer.[21] Swain, furious, ordered her to return to Malta forthwith.

At 02.00 the entrance to the swept channel was reached. The directional stability of *Ohio* now became critical: there were two large and difficult turns ahead, to be negotiated by tired men, not helped by a fresh cross-wind and the mines flanking the swept channel. To complicate matters further, more harbour craft came out to meet them and sightings of submarine periscopes and torpedo-boats were received. The shore batteries, alerted to this danger, played their huge searchlight beams to seaward, illuminating *Ohio* and firing several salvoes of heavy artillery, to the fury of Swain, Hill and Baines. Scarcely able to credit the stupidity of the army gunners, they signalled 'For Christ's sake, stop firing!'[22]

With *Penn* and *Bramham* edging *Ohio* along the shore, *Ledbury* lent her power to shove the tanker's bow through the arc necessary to make the turns off Delimara and Zonqor Points, Hill remaining as escort between these bouts of activity. Men slumped at their guns, many, especially the young cadets aboard *Ohio*, suffering the pangs of hunger. Others had raided the tanker's stores, initiating stories of 'looting' that angered Mason and caused recriminations later, in the aftermath of reaction.[23]

At about 06.45 the King's Harbour Master and senior pilot arrived with more tugs and the minesweepers *Hythe* and *Hebe*. The tugs secured fore and aft and a third afterwards relieved *Penn* on the starboard side, while *Bramham* clung on to her port flank. In this way *Ohio* made her final approach astern of the sweepers. There was to be one final alarm, however: 'When the *Ohio* was about to enter Valletta harbour, two planes flew low out of the sun. The first escaped, the second was not so lucky. It was hit by three Bofors shells [from *Ohio*]. As it dived into the sea, it was seen to be a Spitfire [which] had been chasing a Jerry ... the first plane had dropped a bomb under the stern of the *Ohio* which [had] failed to explode.'[24]

At 08.00 on 15 August 1942, the feast of Santa Marija, the broken-backed and almost derelict hulk of *Ohio* made the tight turn inside the mole, rounded Ricasoli Point, and headed up

Grand Harbour. It was a sublime moment. The stupefied men were greeted by crowds, 'cheering like mad', lining the ramparts and bastions while bands played 'God Save the King', 'The Star-Spangled Banner' and 'Rule, Britannia!' in an emotional, competing din of noise. It was, as Hill recalled fifty years later, 'the most wonderful moment of my life' – even though, along the shore, Maltese children shouted, 'We want food, not oil!' Tears stung red-rimmed eyes as the *Ohio* proceeded ponderously towards the wreck of the Royal Fleet Auxiliary *Plumleaf*, alongside which she was secured at 09.30. Baines finally relinquished *Bramham*'s place to the auxiliary *Boxhall*, bringing out the connectors and pipes ready to discharge *Ohio*'s precious cargo.

As Operation PEDESTAL concluded, Operation CERES also reached its final phase. The cargoes of *Port Chalmers*, *Rochester Castle* and *Melbourne Star* had been unloaded, and the discharge of *Ohio* and *Brisbane Star* was rapidly completed. As for the tired warships, they moored in French Creek. 'All the chaps we'd picked up in *Ledbury* went to hospital', Hill recalled, 'and I went to sleep.'

Operation PEDESTAL has come to be regarded, quite erroneously, as the quintessential British convoy of the Second World War. It was in fact not a convoy at all, in the ordinary sense of the word. It was a major naval operation which had at its core a handful of British and American merchantmen transformed for the occasion into military transports. It had a fixed objective, and much of the quality of a forlorn hope, for when Syfret withdrew and the fighter-directing cruisers were lost, the material advantage effectively fell to the enemy.

PEDESTAL's chief asset was the synthesis that bound its constituent collection of warships and merchantmen. Despite the occasional faltering of unnerved men and the premature abandonment of at least one ship, in the end, sheer tenacity wrested the advantage from the enemy. Despite all its vicissitudes and the Pyrrhic cost, it succeeded by the skin of its bared teeth. The young men who finally brought the *Ohio* into Grand Harbour were a determined and desperate hotch-potch drawn from several ships, the survivors of lost merchantmen working cheek-by-jowl with the officers and ships' companies of a handful of minor warships.[25]

Nothing more, and most certainly nothing less.

21

'The unloading proceeded undisturbed'

(Operations BARITONE, TRAIN, CRUPPER, STONEAGE, PORTCULLIS,
QUADRANGLE *A, B, C, and D,* SURVEY *and MH2, with Convoys
MW13, 14, 15, 16, 17, 18 and 19, and ME11, 12, 14, 15, 16
and 17)*

───────────────

THE PLAUDITS FOR the great achievement poured in. Churchill spoke of the 'magnificent crash through of supplies to Malta' and congratulated the destroyers who had dragged *Ohio* into Grand Harbour. The price had been worth paying, Churchill asserted; writing to Cunningham, Pound concurred; and in view of the outcome, they were correct. In the following month Rommel was denied 300,000 tons of stores as forces from Malta reverted to the offensive, *Ohio*'s cargo providing fuel for Simpson's submarines and Park's aircraft. Between 31 August and 2 September Rommel was checked at Alam Halfa, then defeated on 23/24 October by Montgomery's Eighth Army at El Alamein. A few days later Montgomery went over to the offensive. At the other end of the Mediterranean, on 8 November Operation TORCH saw Allied forces under General Eisenhower landed in Vichy French North Africa. In this the Royal Navy and British merchant ships played their full part as the strategy to which Churchill had alluded in his communication to Stalin moved forwards.

Nor had Churchill been wrong about the enemy, who crowed in exaggerated terms their achievement in 'destroying' PEDESTAL. But the Italian moment of triumph was short-lived, for although the siege was not yet lifted, Italian fortunes had long passed their apogee.

For the merchant seamen, officers and ratings, landed in Malta, the turn of the tide was less obvious. Marched ashore, issued with basic clothing and accommodated on short rations in the hotels of Sliema, they were at least made welcome. Ill-clad survivors were invited to dances and embarrassed young men, wondering at the courage of a population that had endured the destruction evident all around them, were moved by the expressions of gratitude many of them received. For the authorities, the 568 PEDESTAL survivors remained a liability, and they were moved out of Malta as quickly as possible. Two hundred and seven of them left on 18 August in *Penn*, *Ledbury* and *Bramham* for Gibraltar. Transferred there, these men finally reached Britain in a variety of ships, including the damaged *Ithuriel* and *Indomitable*.[1] The rest were evacuated from Malta by submarine or aircraft, as the opportunity arose. The *Dorset*'s cadets, for instance, were taken aboard the submarine *Clyde*, and quartered in the vacated battery space used as a cargo hold on the outward passage. *Clyde* left Valletta on 3 September, *Proteus* followed on the 29th, and the Magic Carpet runs continued from both ends of the Mediterranean.

Less happy were the men supervising the discharge of the *Brisbane Star*. The provisions of Operation CERES were more than adequate to deal with the three transports which had arrived on 13 August, and *Rochester Castle*, *Port Chalmers* and *Melbourne Star* were emptied in double-quick time, the Axis making no attempt to interfere; *Ohio* was drained of her kerosene and diesel; but aboard *Brisbane Star*, Lieutenants Eva and Fearfield found 'pilfering was rife and appeals to the police were unavailing'. 'After a day or so' the two officers 'stopped it with strong measures'. Arming themselves, they 'threatened to shoot anybody caught pilfering or smoking near petrol being discharged. After a few shots had been fired at men in *dghaisas* in the vicinity of octane, and a few looters had been threatened with a revolver, there was little trouble.'[2] By 23 August the general cargoes had been landed, totalling 12,000 tons of coal and about 32,000 tons of mixed commodities. These would enable Malta to eke out an independent existence until mid November.

By this time more Spitfires had been flown in, during Operation BARITONE. Leaving Gibraltar on 16 August, *Charybdis* and twelve destroyers[3] escorted *Furious* to the flying-off position south of Formentera; the following morning thirty-two Spitfires took off. One crashed immediately and two turned back, but the rest landed at Malta at 13.00.[4]

Throughout October submarines continued their Magic Carpet passages. On the 2nd *Rorqual* arrived with stores from Beirut, the next day *Parthian* was swept in from Gibraltar, *Clyde* followed on the 6th 'with petrol and stores'. She left for Beirut two days later, laden with more survivors, returning on 9 November. Meanwhile a further Club Run, Operation TRAIN, was mounted between 28 and 30 October. Captain Agnew in *Aurora*, with *Charybdis* and eight destroyers,[5] again escorted *Furious* to the flying-off position, and twenty-nine Spitfires were sent east; two, suffering from engine defects, returned to the carrier. Ten Italian submarines[6] were on patrol, but although several contacts were attacked, no kills were made. *Furious*'s air-craft[7] kept enemy planes at a distance until 15.15 on the 29th, when a single Ju88 attacked and dropped a bomb five cables astern of the carrier.[8] The continuing deliveries of Spitfires were necessary since the enemy, instead of using the slower bombers, were now attacking Malta with fast fighter-bombers making hit-and-run raids.

Conditions on the island remained at subsistence level and, in addition to the submarines, unescorted merchantmen were again sent to run the gauntlet, in particular to maintain stocks of aviation spirit. On 1 November a former Italian prize and convoy veteran, the *Rodi*, now renamed *Empire Patrol* and commissioned as a naval transport, left Alexandria loaded with 1,200 tons of cased petrol and 300 tons of cased benzine; a refrigerated ship, she also carried food. She was to make a passage east of Cyprus under Turkish colours, then head for the Ionian Sea under the Italian ensign. On sailing she suffered from a failure in her steering motor, and her departure was delayed for some minutes. However, by 09.00 she was heading north, escorted by the Greek destroyers *Spetsai* and *Condouriotis*. Later that day a failure in the fuel-oil transfer pumps caused another short breakdown.

The following morning *Empire Patrol* parted company with her Greek escorts. By noon she had broken down again, and during the rectification of a faulty fuel valve she was circled repeatedly by a Dornier bomber. She was commanded by a Lieutenant RNR[9] with wide discretionary orders, whom the further sighting of a submarine periscope persuaded that *Empire Patrol*'s passage was compromised. She accordingly made her way to Famagusta, where she arrived early on the morning of 3 November.

A similar ruse, Operation CRUPPER, was mounted from the other end of the Mediterranean as the large convoys ran south to Gibraltar with stores for the North African landings. Sent out from Britain with convoy KMS1, the Yeoward Brothers' *Ardeola* (2,609 grt) and the British and Continental Steamship Company's *Tadorna* (1,947 grt) were conspicuous in peacetime paint schemes, both loaded chiefly with concentrated foodstuffs and dried milk for the civilian population. Detaching from the convoy, they passed independently through the Strait of Gibraltar. In the planning of TORCH it was assumed that French resistance would be minimal, but in fact the Vichy forces opposed the Allies with some vigour. When the *Ardeola* and *Tadorna* were shelled and ordered to stop by batteries at Cape Bon their masters tried, like Riley, to bluff their way out of trouble. They were boarded by French naval officers from torpedo-boats; neither master could scuttle his ship, and both vessels were taken into Bizerta, where their cargoes were unloaded and seized.[10]

Partially to compensate for these losses, *Manxman* sailed from Alexandria on 10 November, escorted part of the way by a screen of six destroyers and arriving alone in Grand Harbour on the 12th with 'much needed powdered milk, dried cereals and pre-served meat'. She left for Gibraltar the same day to load a con-signment of mines brought out from Britain in the minelaying cruiser *Adventure*; thereafter she laid a minefield off Cape Bon. Meanwhile, running east from Gibraltar as far as Algiers with shipping operating in support of the TORCH landing, *Welshman* arrived with a second consignment of supplies on the 18th.[11] She returned to Gibraltar but was then sent the length of the Mediterranean to Haifa, where she loaded torpedoes, delivering them for use by the 10th Submarine Flotilla at Marsamxett on 1 December and leaving again for Gibraltar on the 4th.[12]

Malta's long ordeal was now approaching its end, for despite the continuing loss of naval ships to Axis forces, bitter fighting in North Africa and the laying of further minefields off Cape Bon by the Regia Marina, the activities of British submarines and air-craft had robbed the Axis of its command of the Mediterranean. German arms were on the verge of defeat not only in the desert but also in the Soviet Union, where on 19 November the Red

Army counter-attacked across the Don to the north and south of Stalingrad; four days later the Wehrmacht's Sixth Army was encircled.

It was in this period that the relief of Malta was finally achieved. For some time Harwood's chief duty had been to supply and support the Eighth Army, but on the evening of 16 November convoy MW13 left Port Said under the escort of the 15th Cruiser Squadron, now commanded by Vian's relief, Rear-Admiral A. Power. *Cleopatra*, *Arethusa*, *Dido*, *Euryalus* and *Orion*, with the 14th Destroyer Flotilla,[13] took under their escort the Glen and Shire Line's *Denbighshire* (8,983 grt), the Dutch *Bantam* (9,312 grt), owned by Rotterdamsche Lloyd, and two American vessels, Seas Shipping's 7,000-ton *Robin Locksley* and Moore-McCormack Line's *Mormacmoon* (7,939 grt), in what was designated Operation STONEAGE. These four cargo-ships had made a rendezvous in Suez Bay, the *Bantam* and *Denbighshire* having loaded at Port Sudan on the Red Sea. Here they were protected by additional sandbagging around the bridge and gun-positions (lessons learnt from PEDESTAL), and *Denbighshire* embarked the convoy commodore on her arrival at Suez. The four ships passed into the canal on Sunday, 15 November, to anchor in the Great Bitter Lake until early the next morning, when they began the remainder of the transit of the Suez Canal, arriving at Port Said at 16.00 and 'stopping only long enough to load extra ammo'.[14] Passing north of Alexandria the following day, the 17th, the escort was temporarily relieved by ten Hunt class destroyers of the 12th Flotilla.[15] Having refuelled in Alexandria, Power's cruisers and destroyers caught up with the convoy and escort at dawn on 18 November, as the weather began to deteriorate. By noon enemy aircraft had located and attacked the convoy, but without any result, although 'the noise of both our guns and the guns of the other ships ... was frightening down in the engine room [of *Denbighshire*] especially as you are constantly watching the main engines for any sign of a fault'.

But at about 18.00, when they were off Derna, the *Arethusa* was hit forward by an aerial torpedo. She listed to port, as though turning under full helm. On deck there was 'a lot of smoke swirling around, small huddles of men standing around [and] quite a number lay badly burned ... there seemed to be an awful silence everywhere. There was a sick smell of burnt flesh.'[16] Several serious fires had been started and 155 men were killed, including most of the marine detachment. With many others, Captain Chapman had been badly burnt, but 'as night fell, the flames were contained and apart from a lot of smoke, the situation was more or less under control'. Command of *Arethusa* fell upon Commander Colleville, 'a quiet, calm man', and initially the cruiser was taken in tow by *Petard*.[17] Escorted by *Jervis* and *Javelin* and fighting a heavy head sea, Lieutenant-Commander M. Thornton began to drag *Arethusa* back to Alexandria, signalling that he could manage alone, and the two fleet destroyers returned to the convoy. But the tow parted, and in the end Colleville had the hands heave *Arethusa*'s anchor cables aft to lighten her bow and submerge her starboard screw, so that the cruiser could steam astern. For three days, under intermittent attack, *Arethusa* battled east, assisted by *Petard*, finally arriving at Alexandria on the evening of 21 November. She was the last warship operating in support of Malta to be damaged by the enemy.

The convoy and its depleted escort continued until they were some eighty miles east of the island, when they came under the fighter cover of Malta's Spitfires. Here Power detached, leaving *Euryalus* and the Hunts to see the four laden cargo-vessels into Grand Harbour in the early hours of 20 November. Met by the minesweeper *Speedy* and her consorts, the merchantmen were inside the boom by 01.30. 'In the moonlight, the harbour seemed full of sunken ships'; despite the hour, people watched the ships come in, 'and the cheers that went up were quite terrific'.

The discharge of the ships began at 03.00, and by the 26th 'the state of siege existing in Malta was considerably eased ... the greater part of the cargoes of the four ships ... were dispersed or under rock'.[18] Some light air attacks had been delivered by the enemy, but the greater danger had come from a fire aboard *Denbighshire*, when petrol fumes in an empty hold ignited. The flash-fire was soon extinguished 'without serious damage'.

The stiff resistance put up by the Wehrmacht in North Africa after the TORCH landings delayed the taking of the Cape Bon area by Allied forces and caused the cancellation of a fast convoy designed to run from Gibraltar concurrently with Operation STONEAGE. However, a consignment of 175 tons of seed potatoes was sent through with other essential stores aboard *Welshman* on her last supply run to Malta, to avoid them spoiling and to catch the planting period on the island.

But the quantity of supplies landed from MW13 eased the situation considerably and meant that the Magic Carpet runs could cease. More importantly, it meant that the submarines based on the island could step up their offensive, and that Rear-Admiral Power could resuscitate Force K, with *Dido*, *Euryalus* and the fleet destroyers of the 14th Flotilla. No. 821 Squadron of Fleet Air Arm Albacores was transferred to Malta, along with a motor-torpedo-boat flotilla and the British answer to the *maili*, the human chariots. In due course, working in co-operation with their colleagues from Bône, now in Allied hands, Force K and the British air forces achieved notable successes against the attempts of the Axis to reinforce their armies in North Africa. British submarines continued to damage enemy communications, but not without considerable losses to themselves. British warships were also sunk or damaged,[19] but these events had no direct bearing upon Malta, which was, in the words of Leatham, 'building up supplies of stores, ammunition and fuel … which it is hoped, will place [her] in a position to take a foremost part in the attack on the enemy's southern flank when the time comes'.[20]

This reinforcement followed the arrival of Operation STONE-AGE, which of itself deferred the infamous 'target date' to January 1943. A last major convoy to Malta, MW14, the mercantile component of Operation PORTCULLIS, left Port Said on 1 December and consisted of the American cargo vessels *Agwimonte* (6,679 grt, owned by the New York and Cuba Mail Steamship Company) and *Alcoa Prospector* (6,797 grt, owned by the Alcoa Steamship Company), the British Federal liner *Suffolk* (13,890 grt) and the Glen Liner *Glenartney* (9,795 grt). The latter bore a naval crew, the circumstances of whose embarkation were somewhat unusual. *Glenartney* had loaded the usual diverse 'military cargo' at Port Tewfik at the southern end of the Suez Canal and then sailed south into the Red Sea to confuse enemy agents, her master, Captain D. Evans, holding secret orders. She was then ordered in to Port Sudan, where her entire cargo was discharged and reloaded, her 2,000 tons of petrol in more robust containers than the twin cases used previously. By now uncertainty over *Glenartney*'s destination had been fomented into industrial action by members of the ship's Chinese crew, who were drawing all due pay and threatening to strike. Evans arranged for a dozen soldiers to be embarked under his orders and the poop Marlin machine-guns above the crew accommodation were disabled as *Glenartney* made for the rendezvous at Suez. On her arrival a tough, gaitered RNR lieutenant-commander boarded at the head of an armed party of forty men, and 'amid howls of dismay and some tears' the majority of the Chinese crew were removed ashore and interned for the duration of Operation PORTCULLIS, rejoining when the ship returned to Suez 'very much ashamed of themselves and with much loss of "face" '.[21] The naval crew 'performed splendidly throughout under the Merchant Navy officers, and', reported *Glenartney*'s second officer, Mr J. Atkinson, 'seemed thoroughly to enjoy their novel experience' during the operation. *Glenartney* took aboard her last cargo at Ismailia in the canal. With *Suffolk* she passed through Port Said and, joining *Agwimonte* and *Alcoa Prospector*, entered the Mediterranean. The crews were still uncertain of their destination.

Convoy MW14 was joined from Benghazi by the 7,000-ton American-owned but Panamanian-flagged tanker *Yorba Linda*, escorted by two Hunts, which brought the escort strength up to seven destroyers: *Aldenham*, *Belvoir*, *Croome*, *Exmoor*, *Hursley* and *Tetcott*, and the Greek *Pindos*. The following day the cruiser *Orion* and three more destroyers, *Pakenham*, *Petard* and the Greek *Vasilissa Olga*, joined from Alexandria. On 4 December, to the south-west of Crete, Power with *Cleopatra* and Force K, consisting of *Dido*, *Euryalus*, *Jervis*, *Javelin*, *Kelvin* and *Nubian*, also arrived from Malta. The convoy speed was 16 knots and the passage progressed in relative quiet, torpedo-bombers making only half-hearted attacks. Indeed, despite the restowing of her cargo, *Glenartney*'s crew were most affected by the leaking petrol containers, some of which 'had resembled watering cans ... The [hold] wells must have been overflowing with loose spirit. As the tops of the ventilators were level with the bridge ... difficulty [was experienced] in keeping ... awake whilst on watch ...'[22]

Convoy MW14 entered Grand Harbour on the morning of 5 December and received 'a memorable reception ... early on a fine crisp morning. There were thousands of people lining the battlements cheering each ship as it passed through the narrow entrance. Soldiers at various points stood to attention as each ship passed. Never have we seen such gratitude, as was displayed by these hardy people.' What had become a traditional welcome was given unstintingly to these ships, the last merchant transports to arrive in a convoy specifically tasked to Malta. With their safe arrival Malta's long ordeal of two and a half years under siege was fully over, and the island was relieved.

Grand Harbour presented a scene 'of devastation ... Ruin is everywhere', recorded *Glenartney*'s second engineer, R. Scott, as soldiers swarmed aboard to begin the discharge, working twelve-hour shifts and delighted with the sandwiches supplied by *Glenartney*'s crew. Sugar was such a rarity that aboard *Euryalus*, where a seemingly endless lunch was put on for visitors, her gunnery officer counted one wardroom guest put ten spoonfuls into a mug of tea.

By now Grand Harbour was congested with empty shipping. As the unloading of the general cargo ships of PORTCULLIS 'continued uninterrupted by air raids', convoy ME11 got under way on the morning of 7 December when *Rye* swept out to sea nine ballasted merchantmen.[23] These were the ships which had arrived with Operations PEDESTAL and STONEAGE, plus the quickly-discharged tanker *Yorba Linda* from PORTCULLIS. Convoy ME11 (Operation MH2) was escorted by *Orion* and eleven destroyers,[24] and although it was attacked several times by enemy aircraft on the evening of the 7th, several times on the 8th and again on the following day, no ships were damaged. Sadly, during action on the second day Sub-Lieutenant Roxburgh and two ratings aboard *Dulverton* were killed by friendly fire, a fact 'deeply regretted aboard the commodore's ship', *Melbourne Star*. These later convoys were no longer run at speed, and this one was further hampered by Captain Polidori's *Yorba Linda*, which was so slow that she was detached to Alexandria. Commenting upon the performance of the merchantmen, the naval liaison officer aboard *Melbourne Star* remarked upon the difference in the levels of experience of the various ships' companies. *Melbourne Star* had 'been twice to Malta since the siege began ... [she] was organised throughout like a warship. Her guns' crews plainly knew their jobs, and their guns were efficient.'

Off Derna on 9 December *Orion* and the five Hunts, *Aldenham*, *Croome*, *Dulverton*, *Exmoor* and *Hursley*, detached to meet the next Malta-bound ships of convoy MW15, leaving ME11 to make for Port Said, where it arrived on the 11th. The station-keeping and manoeuvring of the convoy had been 'of the highest standard and great credit is due to the Master. The only smoke observed was that of *Yorba Linda* who could be excused as she was always flat out.'[25] Victory was inducing a new air of tolerance.

Operation QUADRANGLE A covered the eastward passage of convoy MW15 and consisted of a spur run off the new regular convoy route from Port Said to Benghazi. This practice of running towards Benghazi until off Barce (Al Marj), where the Malta-bound merchantmen would be met and convoyed thither by escorts for Grand Harbour, continued until the summer of 1943. At the rendezvous, the laden transports would exchange with empty ships from Malta. Convoy MW15 consisted of two ships, the *American Packer* of 6,750 grt, of the United States Maritime Commission, and British India's 6,895-ton *Ozarda*, both of which arrived at 21.00 on the 10th, escorted by *Orion, Paladin, Hurworth, Dulverton, Hursley, Croome, Aldenham* and *Exmoor*. They were followed by MW16, Operation QUADRANGLE B, the *Clan Macindoe* and the 6,200-ton Dutch tanker *Erinna*, which arrived escorted by *Exmoor, Croome, Hurworth, Hursley, Aldenham* and *Belvoir*, and was swept into Grand Harbour by *Speedy*.[26]

The MW13 ships from PORTCULLIS had discharged their 28,577 tons of cargo by 9 December and formed the eastbound convoy ME12. *Alcoa Prospector, Agwimonte, Suffolk* and *Glenartney* left Grand Harbour on the 17th, escorted by *Orion, Croome, Hursley, Aldenham, Belvoir, Hurworth, Exmoor, Petard* and *Vasilissa Olga*. The convoy was 'ineffectively attacked by a few Ju88s' on 18 December. Some of the escort exchanged with ships from Alexandria and, having handed ME12 over off Barce, *Orion, Pakenham, Dulverton, Beaufort, Tetcott* and *Pindos* picked up QUADRANGLE C, or convoy MW17, the *Fort Tadoussac* (6,000 grt), managed by Ellerman and Bucknall on behalf of the MoWT, and the Hogarth-managed *Ocean Voyager* (7,174 grt), for the return passage to Malta.

At this time, on the 18th, the enemy made their only heavy air raid on Malta during December 1942, hitting Luqa and destroying nine Wellington bombers and four Spitfires with the loss of only one Ju88. Despite the concentration of the enemy on Luqa rather than on Grand Harbour, the new Vice-Admiral, Stuart Bonham-Carter, who had just relieved Leatham, noted that 'full precautions for the safety of the valuable cargoes being landed were still taken, ... and it was endeavoured to combine swift unloading with safe dispersal ...'

The Malta-based minesweepers had by now settled down to the routine of sweeping the channels daily, but they still attended important shipping movements such as the arrival or departure of a convoy and escort. Occasionally they forayed further afield. On 20 December *Hebe* was dispatched to recover Sub-Lieutenant

Kempson, whose Fleet Air Arm Swordfish had crashed in the sea. Kempson, suffering from shock and exposure, had been adrift in his dinghy for nine days.

There was no convoy ME13, but ME14, consisting of *American Packer*, *Clan Macindoe*, *Erinna* and *Ozarda*, left Malta on 28 December, escorted by *Euryalus*, *Dulverton*, *Tetcott*, *Beaufort* and *Pindos*. That same day QUADRANGLE D, convoy MW18, the tanker *Yorba Linda* and the new American Liberty ship *Daniel H. Lownsdale*, left for Malta escorted by *Paladin*, *Nubian*, *Exmoor*, *Hurworth*, *Aldenham* and *Hursley*. They arrived on 2 January 1943.

By the end of December the position of Malta had been transformed. Some 58,500 tons of general and military stores and supplies and 18,200 tons of fuel oils had been brought in. Bonham-Carter reported that

> the supply position, from being most precarious, became in this one month, established on a firm footing. The amount of aviation and motor transport spirit brought in relieved anxiety on this score and it was possible to increase the civilian rations, thus improving morale, and saving a falling off in the general health of the population, which was imminent ... The change from the defensive to the offensive both at sea and in the air, the good news from North Africa and Russia, and last but not least, the improvement in the rations, and the inclusion of a few long absent luxuries, brought everyone onto their toes. The civil labour worked with a great will unloading the merchant ships and combined with the Naval and Military to put these operations through in excellent time. Considerable progress was made in the Dockyard, clearing debris and repairing workshops ...

Convoy MW19, Operation SURVEY, sailed from Alexandria on 7 January 1943 and consisted of the British *Greystoke Castle*, whose master Captain W. Harper was convoy commodore, the American Liberty ships *Pierre S. Dupont* and *O. Henry*, and two Dutch vessels, the freighter *Tosari* and the tanker *Erinna*. Escorted by the Hunts *Dulverton*, *Beaufort*, *Hurworth*, *Tetcott*, *Hursley*, *Aldenham*, *Belvoir* and *Exmoor*, and *Vasilissa Olga*, the convoy was attacked by torpedo-bombers at twilight on the 8th, but with no damage. In a second raid after dark bombs fell near *Pierre S. Dupont* and *Beaufort* on the starboard rear of the formation, and a torpedo attack was made on *Aldenham*.

The following day the convoy ran into a gale, *Erinna* in particular labouring in the heavy seas, and the consequent reduction in speed to a mere 6 knots caused a delay in the interception of Captain Bush's Force K from Malta. MW19 was eventually met by *Euryalus*, *Jervis* and *Kelvin*, and as the weather improved, so did the convoy's speed. Fighter cover was provided by Beaufighters for most of the passage, and these were vectored onto an approaching HeIII, which was forced to jettison its torpedoes before making off, damaged. During the afternoon of 11 January a lone Ju88 was driven off, and that evening *Speedy* and accompanying motor-launches brought the convoy, whose conduct had been 'particularly good', into Grand Harbour.[27]

Convoy ME15 departed from Grand Harbour on 13 January 1943, consisting of the *Fort Tadoussac* and *Daniel H. Lownsdale*, escorted by *Orion*, *Pakenham*, *Nubian*, *Javelin*, *Aldenham*, *Hursley*, *Paladin* and *Belvoir*. It was dispersed in heavy weather that evening and located next morning by four Focke-Wulf FW200 Kondor aircraft, which were driven off by Malta-based Beaufighters. Later that day fire was opened by three of the destroyers on a submarine conning tower, but the enemy boat appears to have escaped, although a sinking was claimed. At 20.30 *Orion*, *Pakenham*, *Nubian* and *Javelin* turned back to Malta, leaving the convoy and remaining escorts to proceed to Port Said.[28]

Convoy ME16 followed, and on 13 February ME17 departed, escorted by *Jervis*, Captain Pugsley, with *Tetcott*, *Belvoir* and *Pindos*. The convoy of three ballasted merchantmen made their way east undetected by German aircraft, though a Beaufighter covering the convoy was seen to crash and her pilot was picked up dead. Making a rendezvous with a convoy from Benghazi and metamorphosing into TX1, *Jervis* was joined by *Paladin*, *Condouriotis* and *Kelvin*, releasing the Hunts. A submarine attack was foiled and counter-attacked. Later, course was adjusted to keep clear of the westbound convoy MW21, and ME17 arrived at Alexandria on the evening of 18 February.[29]

And so it went on. There were thirty-five MW convoys, MW35 arriving in June 1943.[30] Two further ships were sunk, both on 1 May 1943 off Barce by the Luftwaffe. These, part of MW27, were the British India cargo-liner *Erinpura*, of 5,143 tons, then carrying more than a thousand troops, and the British Tanker Company's *British Trust* of 8,466 tons. By this time, with North Africa in Allied hands, supplies for Malta were arriving mainly from the west as part of through-convoys, with empty vessels returning to Gibraltar. The first of these had arrived at Grand Harbour on 24 May, having detached from convoy KMS14. Malta's war was not over, nor was the Royal Navy's Mediterranean campaign, and warships continued to be sunk, but Malta was no longer beleaguered; instead she had become an important staging post in the world-wide ebb and flow of Allied shipping.

It was not possible to abandon the convoy system until the summer of 1944, since the Luftwaffe continued to operate from bases in south-eastern France and German U-boats were still to be encountered in the western Mediterranean. The Regia Aeronautica made its last raid on 26 February 1943, the Germans their last heavy raid from Italian bases in the early hours of 20 July. Merchantmen no longer brought in to Malta only those commodities essential to her survival, but constantly increased the build-up of *matériel* for Operation HUSKY, the invasion of Sicily.

This transformation was marked on 20 June, when a solitary white uniformed figure saluted the cheering crowds thronging the bastions and revetments of Valletta and the Three Cities from a specially constructed platform above the bridge of the cruiser *Aurora* as she bore King George VI into Grand Harbour.

Aftermath

THERE WERE TO be other illustrious visitors to Malta. Cunningham came back with the Allied Supreme Commander, General Eisenhower, for Operation HUSKY and the invasion of Sicily. Admiral Harwood and Generals Alexander and Montgomery arrived from Egypt. Cardinal Spellman visited from New York. And on 19 November, Winston Churchill drove through the wrecked streets of Valletta. By this time Mussolini had resigned and fled, leaving Marshal Badoglio to form a new government which dissolved the Fascist Party the next day, 26 July 1943. On 3 September the Italians surrendered, though the Germans continued to contest the possession of the Italian peninsula, installing Mussolini as puppet head of a state in the north.

On 11 September, as the bastions of Valletta once more filled up with spectators, Admiral Cunningham was able to inform London 'that the Italian Battle Fleet now lies at anchor under the guns of the fortress of Malta'. The hyperbole was excusable, but the Italians perhaps found the more appropriate metaphor: 'Malta', the Regia Marina's Intelligence Assessment concluded, 'was the rock upon which all our hopes in the Mediterranean foundered.'

When peace came to Malta, there was much wreckage to clear out of Grand Harbour. Among the sunken ships lay the destroyers *Jersey*, *Maori*, *Legion*, *Lance* and *Kingston*, the submarines *P36*, *P39*, *Pandora* and the Greek *Glaukos*. The minesweeper *Abingdon*, the oiler *Plumleaf*, many of the harbour craft and *No. 8 Floating*

Dock all required dispersal. As for the merchantmen, the broken-backed *Ohio* was gingerly eased out to sea from Rinella Bay in 1946 and sunk by naval gunfire. *Pampas* followed her, but *Talabot* proved less tractable, and there was a delay before she could be towed out and sent to the seabed – revenge, perhaps, for the treatment of her 'uncleanly' crew.

The veteran *Breconshire* was refloated bottom uppermost in August 1950, after the removal of much of her submerged super-structure had been accomplished by, ironically enough, Italian divers. She was sold to Leopoldo Rodriguez of Messina, towed by the naval tug *Brigand* to Messina on 1 September, and beached. Two years later she was resold, to Navigazione Libera Triestina, who had plans to rebuild her. Taken to Taranto, she was parbuckled upright, but in 1954 she was moved to Trieste and finally broken up.

The damaged *Essex*, which had remained in Malta since her arrival in January 1941, was surveyed in the spring of 1943, when it was decided that, in view of the shortage of shipping, she should be repaired. Captain R. Dunning was sent out to take command, and found himself responsible for parading the 150 officers and men of the Merchant Navy then in Malta for the visit of King George VI. Dunning was next ordered to clear *Essex* from the harbour in preparation for the Sicilian invasion fleet, and on 1 July, manned largely by naval ratings and assisted by tugs, *Essex* was shifted to an anchorage off Gozo where Dunning set about recruiting a crew, helped by the Maltese and augmented by the delivery crew of a boom defence vessel which had recently arrived in Grand Harbour. Loading two lifeboats from the sunken Dutch merchantman *Tanimbar*, *Essex* sailed west on 21 August under the tow of the tug *Jaunty* and escorted by the cor-vette *Jonquil*. On the 25th they were joined by the tug *Charon*, and on the 27th *Essex* arrived at Algiers, where the owners provided a crew under Chief Officer I. Norrie. The four vessels departed on the 29th, arriving at Gibraltar on the evening of 1 September. Here *Essex* languished for three months while repairs were put in hand and on 24 November, in the charge of the powerful Dutch salvage tug *Zwarte Zee*, she joined a convoy of low-powered ships, two more of which, the British *Pinzon* and American *Cape Mochigan*, were also under tow. Escort was pro-vided by the corvette *Camellia* and eight anti-submarine naval trawlers. Despite the slow convoy speed of 4 knots the tug *Roode*

Zee and her tow, the *Cape Mochigan*, failed to keep up, and the three tows were left astern with three trawlers.

The tugs and their charges crawled up the Iberian coast, passing Cape Finisterre on 1 December. In the early hours of 3 December, in the Bay of Biscay, the ships and tugs were dispersed and all three tows parted at the height of a north-westerly gale. *Essex* lay wallowing in the trough of the heavy seas – her rudder stock had carried away and the rudder hung by a single pintle – until Captain Vet of *Zwarte Zee* successfully reconnected his hawser during a moderation in the weather on the 4th. Finally, on 11 December 1943, *Essex* was brought in to Falmouth, where she was drydocked and fully reconditioned. She sailed from Liverpool with a military cargo for Australia in November 1944, then brought home the first consignment of Tasmanian apples since the beginning of the war.

In 1947 she was transferred to P. & O. under the name *Paringa* and later reverted to Federal colours as *Norfolk*, though she was owned and managed by the New Zealand Shipping Company until her sale and scrapping in 1956. Her history, one of durability through the vicissitudes of peace and war service, is typical of that of her versatile type, the cargo-liner, now superseded by the container ship. Her passing was unremarkable and unremarked; the life left her as her last crew went ashore, the acetylene torch reducing her again to an inanimate thing, as she had once been on the building ways.

Of all battlefields, the sea is unmarked by the events which momentarily disfigure its bleak beauty. The ships whose transient passages disturb its surface pass from the scene of everyday affairs, yet one hundred and ten such passages were made by merchant ships to sustain Malta between June 1940 and December 1943. There were seventy-nine arrivals, of which three ships were soon sunk in Grand Harbour. Only one was sunk on the return passage. Of the seven independent supply runs, all but one failed; three ships were sunk, two were taken into internment by the Vichy French, and one abandoned her attempt.

Naval losses were huge: one battleship, two aircraft-carriers, four cruisers, one fast minelayer, a score of destroyers and minesweepers and forty submarines, all sunk, along with immense damage to many other ships and losses to other minor vessels. About 1,600 civilians and 700 soldiers were killed in the siege.

The Royal Air Force lost 547 aircraft in combat, a further 160 on the ground, and about 900 of its personnel killed. Of Britain's sea services, the supply of Malta cost the Royal Navy about 1,700 submariners and 2,200 personnel in surface ships, while approximately 200 merchant seafarers died. But the survival of Malta beyond the last Target Date for surrender, 7 September 1942, ensured that the Middle East did not fall to the Axis, and that the Western Allies were able to go over to the offensive in the summer of 1943. The island, initially dismissed by military opinion as indefensible, had proved instead to be indestructible, thanks to the extraordinary efforts of mostly ordinary people.

Half a century later Malta, the British merchant service and the Royal Navy have all changed radically in their status and in their role in the world order. But in the early 1940s the three combined to provide a pivotal point in the defence of democracy. It is impossible to predict how the war would have progressed had they failed, though the outcome would surely have been fundamentally different.

But they succeeded.

Notes

PREFACE

1. Like his predecessor in the First World War, Woodrow Wilson, Roosevelt had reassured the American public that he would never sanction 'our boys' to fight on foreign soil.
2. During her brief war with the United States (1812–14), Britain had inflicted a crippling blockade upon the American coast. Roosevelt was sensible of the parallels: if Britain were to be defeated by Nazi Germany, the United States might be subjected to another such threat. In 1940 Japan was already a first-class naval power in the Pacific and if the German Kriegsmarine were to be augmented by ships from the Royal Navy, surrender of which Britain might be compelled to acquiesce in as part of the price of submission, the United States would find both the eastern seaboard and the Pacific littoral dominated by hostile and powerful navies.
3. Warlimont, *Inside Hitler's Headquarters, 1939–45*, p. 131. Warlimont also tells of a 'curious incident' which followed this decision, when Hitler's senior aide, Colonel Schmundt, 'demanded' that the staff officers make no mention of the difference of opinion in their records, perhaps because Goering favoured the Cretan project. Hitler's War Directive No. 32 of 11 June 1941 also clearly outlines the long-term intentions of the Axis 'after the destruction of the Soviet Armed Forces', calling for commanders to begin the planning of operations to assault 'the British positions in the Mediterranean and Western Asia ... by converging attacks launched from Libya through Egypt, from Bulgaria through Turkey, and ... from Transcaucasia through Iran'. Gibraltar was to be seized and Arab revolt fomented, and German staff officers had already considered an attack on India through Afghanistan.
4. See Martienssen, *Hitler and his Admirals*, pp. 123 *et seq.*, and Trevor-Roper, *Fuehrer Conferences on Naval Affairs*, page 263. Raeder reported that 'the most significant fact ... is that not a single heavy British ship in the Mediterranean is fully seaworthy. The Axis rules both the sea and the air in the Central Mediterranean ... the ... situation is definitely favourable at the moment.' This was the critical period when the plight of Malta, and thus of British fortunes, hung in the balance.
5. See J.M.A. Gwyer, *Grand Strategy*, vol. 3, p. 172, HMSO.
6. See B. Liddell Hart, *The Other Side of the Hill: Germany's Generals, their Rise and*

Fall, with their own Account of Military Events, 1939–45, Pan, 1978, pp. 230 *et seq.*, which contains both Thoma's assessment and Student's revelation.

CHAPTER 1: 'THE ADVENTURE BEGINS'

1. This lighthouse was managed by International agreement.
2. J. Christopher Herrold, *Bonaparte in Egypt*, Hamish Hamilton, 1963, p. 45. Herrold goes on to say: 'The mamelukes, whom the Knights had fought five centuries earlier, and whom Bonaparte was to fight five weeks later, showed no such signs of modernity.'
3. Among these was the poet Laurie Lee whose picaresque trek through Spain, recorded in *As I Walked Out One Midsummer Morning*, ends with this impressively improbable but true evacuation.
4. Hinsley (ed.), *British Intelligence in the Second World War*, vol. 1, pp. 62–3, 199–200. The principal value of these decrypts was to verify intelligence from other sources.
5. Ciano's *Diary*, 12 May 1939, p. 101.
6. *Lebensraum*, 'living space' for the German people, was what Hitler claimed from his invasion of Russia and in particular the Ukraine. Ciano's pious imitation is a pathetic exculpation for an act of unwarrantable aggression, an attempt to gloss it with an 'acceptable' justification.
7. ADM223/82, Admiralty Operational Intelligence daily Italian situation report for 30 April 1940.
8. *Glorious* was not flying combat air patrols and was proceeding independently from the main body of the fleet largely because her captain was anxious to return to Scapa Flow to court-martial two officers. Her accompanying destroyers sacrificed themselves with the customary gallantry; there were 2 survivors from *Ardent*, 1 from *Acasta* and 43 from *Glorious*. About 1,500 men died. The survivors were picked up by Norwegian trawlers and became PoWs: conversations with Tim Slessor, but see John Winton, *Carrier Glorious, the Life and Death of an Aircraft Carrier*, Arrow, 1986.
9. Envy of Great Britain and her empire in diplomatic circles extended from the drawing-rooms of Washington to the closets of the Emperor of Japan. The Japanese ambassador to Rome, seeking an audience with Mussolini from Ciano, said he considered the Axis Alliance 'an aggressive instrument by which to obtain from Great Britain "the many things she owes to us all"'.
10. The often profound influence of disease upon history is too often ignored. While recognition is afforded when a pandemic overwhelms a population and produces socio-economic change, the effects of pathogens such as *treponema pallidum* on individuals seems too indelicate a matter to engage the interest of many historians. Suggestions that Adolf Hitler also suffered from the same infection add at least a cogency to the Axis dictators' repudiation of even lip-service to the so-called civilised values that were fondly thought to guide the enlightened principles of European political life. Mussolini's case is mentioned as a matter of established and well-known fact in the diary of his son-in-law, Count Ciano. (Ciano was the son of an admiral and himself a pilot. He was entirely the Duce's creature, though apprehensive of war and ultimately estranged from his father-in-law, who acquiesced in his imprisonment. He was executed in January 1944.) In an entry for 27 December 1939, Ciano mentions Arturo Bocchini, Mussolini's Chief of Police, recommending 'the Duce should take an intensive anti-syphilitic cure … because Mussolini's psychic condition is due to a recurrence of his old illness'. The dictator's 'restlessness' had been

'noticed by all his colleagues'. Nevertheless, the attribution of mental distur-
bance is specific enough, and on 21 October 1941 Giuseppe Bottai, then Minister
of Education, member of the Grand Council and Civil Commissioner in Greece,
'called Mussolini "a product of syphilis"'. Bottai is recorded as saying: '"The
Duce has decayed intellectually and physically. He doesn't attract me any more.
He is not a man of action; he is presumptuous and ambitious and expects only
to be admired, flattered and betrayed."' (These were prophetic words; Bottai
collaborated in Mussolini's overthrow and was thought to have escaped into
the post-war French Foreign Legion.) Ciano makes no attempt to defend his
father-in-law, and when accusations are made that Mussolini contracted syphilis from his mistress, Clara Petacci, Ciano considers the argument silly: infection had clearly occurred much earlier. As a young teacher, Mussolini's sexual
excesses cost him his job and he became a promiscuous and indiscriminate
seducer, regarding women as 'objects to plunder'. He seems to have caught
syphilis while teaching at Tolmezzo in the Alps, perhaps from his landlady, with
whom he had an affair. This would account for his unstable megalomania, a
possible symptom of the tertiary stage of the disease, by the late 1930s.

11. Count Ciano's *Diary* for March 1939 contains two denials of German interest in
the Mediterranean (17 and 20 March).

CHAPTER 2: 'THE MORAL IS TO THE MATERIAL AS THREE IS TO ONE'

1. So great was this emphasis on speed that their builders received a bonus for
every knot by which each hull exceeded the specification. Unsurprisingly, the
matter formed the core of many jokes in the British fleet.

2. It was Italian divers operating from the *Artiglio* who had set up new records
between the wars when salvaging gold from the *Laurentic*, and it was Italian
inventiveness which devised the manned torpedoes employed later with such
effect against British capital ships in Alexandria harbour.

3. Benito Mussolini, *Mussolini's Memoirs 1942–1943*, Weidenfeld and Nicolson,
1949, p. 8.

4. Nor was contemporary British naval opinion in much doubt about this. Almost
exactly a year before Italy entered the war, on 8 June 1939, Ciano had handed
Mussolini an intercepted report from the C-in-C, British naval forces at Hong
Kong. Admiral Sir Percy Noble, later the first C-in-C, Western Approaches and
the founder of victory in the Atlantic, had submitted an appreciation of naval
operations against the Axis. It was 'couched in pessimistic terms, especially as
regards the Mediterranean, dominated in his opinion by the aerial, naval and
under-sea-forces of Fascist Italy'.

5. Alessandro Malaspina, after whom a submarine was named, made a significant circumnavigation in the late eighteenth century, but like Columbus and
Cabot was in the service of a foreign nation, in his case Spain.

6. Compare this with the presence of a small number of heavy German ships in
Norwegian waters which tied the Home Fleet down at Scapa. See Richard
Woodman, *Arctic Convoys 1941–1945*, John Murray, 1995. The Germans, inci-
dentally, also suffered from a lack of fuel for their large warships.

7. Tunstall, *World War at Sea*, 'The Italian Navy', p. 150.

8. See particularly Andrew Gordon, *The Rules of the Game*, John Murray, 1996.

9. See Barnett, *Engage the Enemy More Closely*, chapters 1 and 2.

10. The belief that sonar had overcome the submarine threat was a tenet of pre-war
naval orthodoxy. Churchill himself appears to have been deluded chiefly by a
demonstration off Portland in which attacking destroyers had no trouble in

echo-locating an obliging submarine by means of Asdic (the British acronym then used for sonar). He was manifestly satisfied with this exercise, witnessed by Captain Maurice Usherwood, RN, who related an account of it to the author in 1994. For the 'Cinderella' status of anti-submarine warfare, see Captain R. Whinney, DSC, RN, *The U-Boat Peril*, Arrow, 1989.

11. A reduction in pay had caused sailors in the Atlantic fleet to strike at Invergordon shortly before the outbreak of the Second World War. Perceived as a mutiny by the naval authorities, the incident was symptomatic of the Royal Navy's pre-war muddle-headedness and the refusal of Their Lordships to acknowledge the social changes which had occurred in post-1918 Britain.

12. Reinforcement and improvements in Singapore's defences, though planned, were continually postponed.

13. Rapid expansion of the Royal Canadian Navy in particular occurred after the outbreak of war and the force made a major contribution to victory in the Atlantic, while units of the Royal Australian Navy operated in the Mediterranean.

14. Part of the cause lay in the moratorium on battleship building, which had had a bad effect upon the decay of plant, in particular that necessary for the production of naval guns.

15. See E.H.H. Archibald, *The Fighting Ship in the Royal Navy 897–1984*, Blandford Press, Poole, 1984, p. 240. The efficacy of the 4-inch weapons against aircraft was confirmed in 1993 in conversation with the author by Rear-Admiral J. Lee-Barber who formerly commanded the destroyer *Opportune*.

16. In fact the battlecruiser *Tiger* was fitted with an experimental Argo clock and performed noticeably better than her sisters at Jutland.

17. This squadron, which should have consisted of an aircraft carrier as well as the new battleship *Prince of Wales* and the refitted battlecruiser *Repulse*, was destroyed off Malaya by Japanese aircraft in December 1941. In 1937 the Admiralty had commissioned the new carrier *Ark Royal*, and at the outbreak of war increased the carrier-building programme. *Illustrious*, completed in 1940, was to play a significant part in the Mediterranean. It was the absence of her sister *Indomitable* on 10 December 1941 that sealed the fate of Force Z, which was commanded by Vice-Admiral Sir Tom Phillips, an officer whose previous appointment had been Deputy Chief of the Naval Staff in London and who was well-known for his entrenched views about naval aviation. In conversation with the late Lieutenant-Commander Peter Kemp, whose work in the Admiralty brought him into close proximity with the DCNS, the author was left in no doubt that Kemp held very considerable misgivings about Phillips. See also Barnett, p. 138.

18. Even the exemplary Spitfire entered service twelve months late. By contrast, the Hawker Hurricane, the equally outstanding fighter which bore the brunt of the Battle of Britain and which, with the Supermarine Spitfire, was to play so important a part in the air defence of Malta, was built to a diminutive government order. However, one of Hawker's staff, a young man named Frank Murdoch, happened to be shown the Heinkel production line on a private, pre-war visit to Germany; reporting back to his management, he convinced them of the inevitability of war with Germany to such effect that Hawker's consequently went into full production of Hurricanes *as a speculation*! Thus sufficient machines existed during the spring of 1940 to combat the Luftwaffe.

19. Coastal Command was for too long the 'poor relation' arm of the RAF and did not come into its own until the Short Sunderland flying boats had been augmented by American long-range Liberators and Catalinas. Fortunately the

maritime background of the head of Coastal Command meant that the best was made of a bad job, and co-operation between the Royal Navy and Coastal Command became seamless. There is, however, very little doubt today that the Royal Air Force's obsession with the bombing offensive was wasteful of resources, less than effective, and delayed the ascendancy of the Allied forces waging the Battle of the Atlantic.

20. In the training of RNVR officers, due emphasis was placed on such recondite skills as sword-drill! Many suitable ratings from the conscripted ranks of the lower deck proved excellent officers, and officers from both the professional reserve (the ex-merchant naval RNR officers) and the 'amateurs' of the RNVR produced some outstanding commanders and exponents of naval warfare. See also Smithies and Bruce, *War at Sea, 1939–45*, pp. 137 *et seq*.

21. The poor performance of the Home Fleet against the *Bismarck* in May 1940, less than a fortnight before Italy entered the war, was an example of this problem, but it was echoed in other instances of a less prominent nature.

22. Many of these losses occurred in the Mediterranean, but before the sinking of the *Ark Royal* on 13 November 1941 when she was operating in support of Malta, the Royal Navy had already lost the battleship *Royal Oak*, torpedoed by *U48* while anchored in Scapa Flow; the battlecruiser *Hood*, to plunging shot from *Bismarck*; the fleet carriers *Courageous* and *Glorious* (see above); the cruisers *Bonaventure, Calcutta, Calypso, Curlew, Effingham, Fiji, Gloucester, Latona, Southampton* and *York*; ten armed merchant cruisers including *Rawalpindi* and *Jervis Bay*; fifty-six destroyers and thirty submarines; and this tally ignores minor warships such as anti-submarine trawlers (of which over 150 were lost), together with auxiliaries and many other craft.

23. See Richard Woodman, *The History of the Ship*, Conway Maritime, 1997, Chapter 16, and Ronald Hope, *A New History of British Shipping*, Chapter 20, for more detailed analyses of this first phase in the decline of Britain's merchant fleet.

24. *Ocean* consisted of the Ocean Steamship Company and the China Mutual Steam Navigation Company, whose ships were outwardly indistinguishable and collectively and colloquially known as The Blue Funnel Line. The company also owned the Glen and Shire Lines. Blue Funnel ships were named after Homeric characters, the Glens after Scottish valleys and the Shires after Welsh counties. The whole fleet was privately owned and managed by Alfred Holt and Company of Liverpool. Units of the Ocean fleet were destined to play a significant part in the Malta campaign, several of the superb *Glenearn* class commissioning under the white ensign and others serving with distinction in relieving operations. Alfred Holt and Co. were unusual in shipping circles in that the company's eponymous founder was a professional and highly innovative engineer, and they were much concerned with the betterment of mankind. The company inspired a fierce, almost regimental loyalty in its officers.

25. See Lane, *The Merchant Seaman's War*, a particularly fine and objective study of the men of the merchant marine.

26. Brodie, *A Layman's Guide to Naval Strategy*. A would-be latter-day Mahan, Brodie's wartime essay eloquently evaluates the factors dominating the sea war undertaken by the two great maritime allies in the Second World War. His views have the freshness of contemporary opinion. The italics are his and have a particular relevance to the Mediterranean theatre, as much as to the Atlantic. As an American, Brodie is more charitable to Britain's predicament than many post-war assessments based upon Fleet Admiral King's views. For a modern American view, however, see also W. Haskell's *Shadows on the Horizon*, Chatham Publishing, 1998.

CHAPTER 3: 'SUSTAINED BY THE VOLUME OF PRAYER'

1. See Cunningham, *A Sailor's Odyssey*, p. 236.
2. Philip Macdougal, 'Gibraltar Dockyard: Problems of Recruitment, 1939–45', *Mariners' Mirror*, vol. 82, No. 4, November 1996.
3. Ciano's *Diary*, 1 May 1940, p. 242.
4. Built in the First World War, *Warspite* had undergone extensive modernisation. Armed with a main armament of 15-inch guns, she was one of the *Queen Elizabeth* class which also included *Malaya*, *Valiant*, and *Barham*. All had had some form of modification, though this was least extensive in *Barham*. All were to serve in the Mediterranean.
5. The 3rd Cruiser Division consisted of the 8-inch cruisers *Pola*, *Trento* and *Bolzano*; the 1st and 8th of the 8-inch cruisers *Zara*, *Fiume* and *Gorizia*, and the 6-inch *Duca degli Abruzzi* and *Giuseppe Garibaldi*.
6. Godfroy's cruisers were *Duquesne*, *Tourville*, *Suffren* and *Duguay Trouin*.
7. Hinsley, *British Intelligence in the Second World War*, vol. 1, p. 206.
8. Somerville's Report of Proceedings, 27 June–4 July 1940, from HMS *Hood*, Gibraltar, 26 July 1940, in *Somerville Papers*.
9. *Ibid.*, Somerville to his wife, 4 and 5 July 1940.
10. Roskill, *The War at Sea*, vol. 1, p. 245.
11. *Ibid.*, p. 297.
12. Churchill, *The Second World War*, vol. II, p. 563.

CHAPTER 4: 'A MORAL EFFECT QUITE OUT OF PROPORTION TO THE DAMAGE'

1. I. Hay, *The Unconquered Isle*, The Right Book Club, 1944, p. 86.
2. *Ibid.*, p. 102.
3. Operational denominations applied to warship orders and the convoys were given separate identities. Other eastern Mediterranean convoys were running in the Levant and to Greece at this time, hence the numbering of this as the third.
4. This amazing tale is best told in Cunningham's own words in Chapter XXI of *A Sailor's Odyssey*. He had the advantage of enjoying a personal relationship with Godfroy with no language difficulties. The proximity of the ships and the co-operation previously enjoyed between the two fleets made possible the drastic action of going over Godfroy's head. This undoubtedly saved the lives of many men, on both sides. Cunningham sadly records Godfroy's fate, stuck on his under-manned flagship, marginalised, but always writing sympathetically when Cunningham's fleet suffered a loss, or to congratulate a success. He even expressed annoyance that he could not fire his guns to defend Alexandria when it was under bombing attack. Godfroy's squadron finally re-entered the war alongside the Royal Navy. His ships were *Lorraine* (battleship), *Duquesne*, *Suffren*, *Tourville*, *Duguay Trouin* (cruisers), the destroyers *Basque*, *Le Fortuné* and *Forbin*, and the submarine *Protée*.
5. Connell, *Mediterranean Maelstrom*, p. 55.
6. This refers to the reinforcing destroyers *en route* from Gibraltar, of which *Jervis* was one.
7. There were 25 Italian submarines at sea at this time.
8. See Somerville's Report of Proceedings, 6–11 July 1940, his letter to his wife of 10 July written at sea, and his letter to Pound of 13 July, in *Somerville Papers*; and also Macintyre, *Fighting Admiral*, pp. 73 and 74.
9. Built in 1915, this old battleship was incapable of more than 21 knots and had

trouble making 20. She was passed to the Soviet Navy at the end of the war and re-commissioned as *Archangelsk*.

10. O'Conor's ship was the first to send such a signal in the Mediterranean since the days of Nelson: see Cunningham, *A Sailor's Odyssey*, p. 260.

11. The Italians claimed to have avoided these by manoeuvring, but the possibility of malfunction, which dogged the weapon, cannot be ruled out entirely.

12. For Cunningham's official account of the action, see the *London Gazette*, 27 April 1948 and also *A Sailor's Odyssey*, pp. 260 *et seq*.

13. These were the 7th (*Freccia, Saetta*), the 9th (*Alfieri, Oriani, Carducci, Gioberti*), the 11th (*Artigliere, Camicia Nera, Aviere, Geniere*), the 12th (*Lanciere, Carabiniere, Ascari, Corazziere*) and the 14th (*Pancaldo, Vivaldi*).

14. Cunningham thought that a Swordfish from *Eagle* had hit the *Bolzano*.

15. Commanding Officer, HMS *Diamond*, Report of Proceedings 18 July 1940, in ADM199/92.

16. Commanding Officer, HMS *Stuart*, Report of Proceedings, 16 July 1940, in ADM199/92. Waller makes no mention of the submarine contacts, being more concerned with *Knight of Malta*'s poor performance, the signalling difficulties with all the merchant ships due to lack of signalling lamps, and deficiencies in the codes held aboard the hurriedly arranged convoy.

17. Ciano, *Diary*, 13 July 1940, p. 276.

CHAPTER 5: 'THE DOOR-KEEPERS'

1. Roskill, *The War at Sea*, vol. 1, p. 307. This amounted to 690,000 tons of shipping by fast convoy between June and December 1940. Losses amounted to less than 2 per cent. The Italians were able to achieve this when they knew the Mediterranean fleet were elsewhere. See Hinsley, *British Intelligence in the Second World War*, vol. 1, p. 212.

2. Cunningham, *A Sailor's Odyssey*, p. 267.

3. No. 813 Squadron, also embarked in *Eagle*, had sunk the Italian destroyer *Zeffiro* and a freighter at Tobruk on 5 July. By August the Fleet Air Arm were also using Dekheila, an airfield west of Alexandria, when *Eagle* was in port, and operating nearer the front from RAF airstrips to harry Italian shipping to the westward.

4. The Savoia Marchetti 79 was a capable torpedo-bomber powered by three Alfa-Romeo engines. It had a speed of 267mph at 13,120 feet and possessed a range of 1,180 miles.

5. Some authorities say 545 survived from *Colleoni*. Novaro died of his wounds on 23 July. *Bande Nere* was commanded by Capitano di Vascello Maugeri.

6. On 2 August 1940 Somerville wrote to his wife: 'My responsibility is very heavy and I'm not prepared to be a "yes man" so as to provide Winston [Churchill] with some squib to let off in the House [of Commons].'

7. See Churchill, *The Second World War*, vol. II, Chapter XXII.

8. *Malaya* suffered from frequent and serious problems with her condensers, into which salt water, the cooling agent, penetrated through leaking joints.

9. It was Daladier's government which had fallen on 20 May 1940. He had retained a cabinet post until the final French surrender a few days later, when he attempted to organise resistance in North Africa but was captured. It was his return to Vichy France that *Enterprise* was intended to intercept. Daladier was imprisoned in Buchenwald and Dachau, freed in 1945, and died in 1970.

10. This position was 37° 40' N 007° 20' E, some 350 miles from Malta and about 120 south-west of Cagliari.

11. For Operation HURRY, see *Somerville Papers*, Reports of Proceedings, 30 July–9 August 1940, and his letters to his wife, 2 and 5 August 1940.
12. Such was the Royal Navy's shortage of them that many of the destroyers which appeared in the Mediterranean shuttled back and forth between the Middle and the Barents Sea, alternately taking part in complex operations in the Med and escorting Russia-bound convoys. The regime was punishing on both the men and their ships. The constant and unremitting demands put great strain on the young, often very young, men who commanded them. *Argus* was to fly further reinforcements from Takoradi in West Africa overland across the desert to Egypt before appearing again in the Med.
13. These mine barrages were to account for damage to HMS *Gallant* on 10 January 1941 and the loss of *Hostile* a few days later on 23 August. *Hostile* had to be sunk by her sister-ship *Hero*.
14. The Italians were to carry supplies from Taranto to Leros in the Dodecanese in their submarines *Atropo* and *Foca*.
15. HMAS *Stuart* (Senior Officer), HMSs *Diamond, Juno* and *Ilex*.
16. *Bedouin, Mashona, Tartar* and *Punjabi*.
17. The elderly, slow and vulnerable battleship *Resolution*, though part of Force H, was left at Gibraltar.
18. Boiler oil stocks at Malta had to be maintained at a high level because many of Cunningham's ships operating from Alexandria to the central Mediterranean required refuelling at Malta. This meant that the other ships had to wait south of the island for their colleagues to rejoin, exposing them to air attack.
19. The Cant Z506B Airone seaplane was an effective, triple-engined reconnaissance aircraft capable of carrying bombs or torpedoes, with a range of some 1,700 miles. A variant was used in an air–sea rescue role. The Cant Z501 was a single-engined flying-boat with a range in excess of 1,300 miles.
20. The actual position was 38° 06′ N 010° 51′ E.
21. Somerville's Report of Proceedings, 30 August–3 September 1940. Somerville commended to Their Lordships' notice Lt-Cdr M. Johnstone and Lt T.W.B. Shaw, the pilot and observer who had led both attacks on Cagliari.
22. Chamberlain was on his first voyage to sea. See Cameron, *Red Duster, White Ensign*, Chapter 2.
23. ADM199/75, Captain P.J. Mack, Secret Report 0898 and enclosed Narrative, Convoy M.F.2. 29 August–2 September 1940. Also Narrative of Medical Officer transferred from HMS *Juno*, 31 August 1940. SS *Cornwall*, Commander's Report, 4 September 1940. This, Pretty's own report, was forwarded by Vice-Admiral Ford to Cunningham and described as 'characteristically modest'. The *Cornwall* remained at Malta undergoing repair for several months. Captain Pretty was shipped home and transferred to command the Federal Steam Navigation Company's new *Nottingham*, 8,532 grt. On 7 November 1941 *Nottingham* was off Greenland proceeding independently from Glasgow to New York when she was torpedoed and sunk by *U74* (Kentrat). All hands were lost.
24. See Cunningham, *A Sailor's Odyssey*, p. 272–3.
25. *Calcutta* did not have radar, though *Coventry* did.

CHAPTER 6: 'MARE NOSTRUM IS AN ESTABLISHED FACT'

1. Events surrounding operations against Vichy France were to result in an infamous Churchillian search for a scapegoat in which Somerville narrowly avoided the obloquy which fell instead upon the hapless flag officer at Gibraltar, Sir Dudley North.

2. Attacking a military convoy approaching Durazzo during the latter part of September, *Osiris* sank the torpedo-boat *Palestro*.
3. Cunningham, *A Sailor's Odyssey*, p. 276 *et seq*.
4. Quoted in Winton, *Cunningham*, p. 107.
5. Photographs of *Royal Sovereign* belching funnel smoke and emerging from a carpet of near-miss bombs were cited as clear evidence of 'A British battleship on fire'.
6. The Blue Funnel Line's *Memnon* was actually owned by Alfred Holt's China Mutual Steam Navigation Company. She was subsequently torpedoed in the Atlantic in March 1941.
7. The destroyers involved were *Dainty, Decoy, Defender, Hyperion, Havock, Hero, Hasty, Hereward, Ilex, Imperial, Jervis, Janus, Juno, Nubian, Stuart, Vampire, Vendetta, Voyager, Waterhen* and *Wryneck*.
8. This consisted of the destroyers *Mirabello* and *Riboty*, the torpedo-boats *Antares, Altair, Andromeda, Aretusa, Calatafimi, Castelfidardo, Curtatone, Confienza, Cantore, Fabrizi, Medici, Monsambano, Prestinari, Solferiono* and *Stocco*, the patrol/escort vessels *Capit, Cecchi, Lago Tana, Lago Zuai* and *Ramb III*, and four *MAS*-boats.
9. Although given the designation A-22 by the United States Army Corps, the Maryland, a fighter-bomber, was never adopted for US service use. Two hundred and twenty-five were used by the RAF. They had a range of 1,210 miles, a ceiling of 26,000 feet and a speed of 278 mph.
10. See Spooner, *Supreme Gallantry*, pp. 22 *et seq*.
11. *Dainty, Decoy, Defender, Diamond, Hyperion, Havock, Hero, Hasty, Hereward, Ilex, Jervis, Juno, Janus, Mohawk* and *Nubian*.
12. All the destroyers carried 50 men each, *Barham* had embarked 700, *Berwick* 750 and *Glasgow* 400.
13. Although the Cagliari raid was led by the experienced Mervyn Johnstone, *Ark Royal* had received new drafts of fighter pilots during her recent return to Britain. See Somerville's Report of Proceedings, 7–11 November 1940 and letter to his wife, 10 November 1940, in *Somerville Papers*.
14. 14th Destroyer Squadron of the Regia Marina: *Vivaldi, Da Noli, Pancaldo* and *Malocello*.
15. The other submarines were *Mamelli, Corallo, Bandiera* and *Topazio*.
16. Quoted in Barnett, *Engage the Enemy More Closely*, p. 248.
17. All four merchant ships were lost. They were *Antonio Locatelli* (5,700 grt), *Catalani* (2,430 grt), *Capo Vado* (4,400 grt) and *Premuda* (4,430 grt).
18. Ciano mentions these in his diary entry of 12 November 1940.
19. Admiral Isoroku, C-in-C of the Japanese fleet, sent officers to Taranto to study the results of the British attack.
20. Two attacks on the nights of 24 and 25 September sank the armed trawler *Stella Sirius*.

CHAPTER 7: 'THE USUAL CROWDED PROGRAMME'

1. The precise disposition of British destroyers during this operation has proved difficult to unravel, but these appear to have been *Defender, Greyhound, Griffin* and *Hereward*.
2. Report of Convoy ME4, Commanding Officer, HMAS *Vendetta*, in ADM 199/92.
3. Lancelot Holland transferred to *Hood* in May 1941 as C-in-C Battlecruiser Force and was lost with that ship on 24th of the same month.
4. See *The Somerville Papers*, Report of Proceedings 19–29 November 1940.

5. Four submarines, *Alagi, Aradam, Axum* and *Diaspro*, were south of Sardinia, with *Tembien and Dessiè* off Malta.
6. The 7th (*Freccia, Saetta* and *Dardo*) and the 13th (*Granatiere, Fuciliere, Bersagliere* and *Alpino*).
7. The 9th Flotilla (*Alfieri, Carducci, Gioberti* and *Oriani*).
8. Sansonetti's cruisers were *Trieste, Trento* and *Bolzano*, his destroyers *Lanciere, Ascari*, and *Carabinieri*.
9. This would have been *Ramillies, Newcastle* and *Berwick*, together with *Coventry*, and the destroyers *Defender, Greyhound, Gallant, Griffin* and *Hereward*.
10. Quoted in Macintyre, *Fighting Admiral*, p. 93.
11. The disabled 'cruiser' was probably the destroyer *Lanciere* which had received a hit in the brief action and was afterwards towed away.
12. *The Somerville Papers*, p. 209, Cork and Orrery to Somerville, 7 December 1940.
13. Somerville to his wife, 28 November 1941, on his way back to Gibraltar.
14. Quoted Macintyre, *Fighting Admiral*, p. 99. The criticism of Somerville, though personally hurtful to him, undoubtedly enhanced his standing with his staff, his captains and his fleet generally. A few days later, embarked in *Ark Royal*, he flew as an observer with one of his young Fleet Air Arm Pilots. He had, he impishly reported, 'by climbing to high altitudes … rid my system of poison which recent events might have engendered.'
15. This consisted of a battle squadron comprising the *Vittorio Veneto, Andrea Doria* and *Giulio Cesare* with a destroyer flotilla under Iachino and Brivonesi; the heavy cruisers *Zara, Pola, Gorizia* and *Fiume* and two destroyer flotillas under Cattaneo; the heavy cruisers *Trieste, Trento* and *Bolzano* with one destroyer flotilla under Sansonetti; the light cruisers *Duca d'Aosta, Eugenio di Savoia, Raimondo Montecuccioli* and two destroyer flotillas under Legnani; the light cruisers *Muzio Attendolo, Duca degli Abruzzi* and *Giuseppe Garibaldi* and one destroyer flotilla under Marenco; and, under the direct command of Supermarina, the light cruisers *Giovanni delle Banda Nere* and *Armando Diaz* with two destroyer flotillas. *Pola* was damaged in a British air attack on Naples on 14 December 1940.
16. Consisting of *Eagle, Barham* and *Malaya*, the monitor *Terror* and the gunboats *Aphis, Gnat* and *Ladybird*, together with the Australian destroyers *Voyager, Vampire, Vendetta* and *Waterhen*.
17. Cunningham, *A Sailor's Odyssey*, pp. 296 *et seq.*
18. The destroyers Cunningham mentions in his autobiography appear to include the three named and attached to CS7, plus *Dainty, Defender, Diamond, Greyhound, Gallant, Griffin, Mohawk* and *Nubian. Vampire, Vendetta, Voyager* and *Wryneck*, the corvettes *Gloxinia, Hyacinth, Peony and Salvia*, together with the cruiser *Calcutta* and the *Chakla*, formed the close escort to both convoys, while *Hyperion, Havock, Hero, Hasty, Hereward* and *Ilex* screened *Malaya*.
19. These five were under *Duncan* (Captain (D) 13th Destroyer Flotilla), whose boilers had been repaired after their failure, *Encounter, Isis, Jaguar* and *Wishart*, which had returned from her impromptu escort duty to Malta.

CHAPTER 8: 'THINGS STARTED TO GO WRONG'

1. *Empire Trooper*, 14,000 grt, had been the German liner *Cap Norte*, captured in October 1939 off the Faeroes by HMS *Belfast*. She was under the management of the MoWT. Later that day *Admiral Hipper* sank the independently sailing *Jumna*, 6,078 grt, owned by James Nourse Ltd. On the 28th *Bonaventure* sank the German supply ship *Baden*. In WS5A were the carriers *Argus* and *Furious* with aircraft for Egypt. These were flown off to cross the desert from Takoradi in

West Africa to Egypt. 'WS' signified a special, military convoy, one of 'Winston's Specials'.

2. Owned by the Prince Line, *Northern Prince*, built in 1929, grossed 10,917 tons and was capable of 16.5 knots. She was afterwards refloated and proceeded to Suez via the Cape of Good Hope. It is a measure of the importance attached to these cargo-liners that they are more formally referred to as 'merchant transports' in naval reports.

3. Cunningham's acting rank of Admiral had been made substantive on 3 January 1941.

4. Cunningham, *A Sailor's Odyssey*, p. 301.

5. *Pandora*'s patrol was off the east coast, but *Upholder* and *Triumph* covered an enemy approach from the north while the EXCESS ships were passing between Galita Island and the Skerki Bank.

6. The fourth of Pridham-Wippell's original cruisers of Force D, *Ajax*, had been detached to join Rear-Admiral Rawlings in *Barham* who, with *Eagle* and *Ajax*, had intended to raid the Dodecanese, a plan foiled by bad weather.

7. See Cunningham, *A Sailor's Odyssey*, pp. 302 *et seq. Gallant* reached Malta but was not repaired.

8. See Winton, *Ultra at Sea*, p. 11.

9. In his autobiography, Cunningham is defensively, and understandably, mute about the degree of surprise achieved by the Luftwaffe. In fact little advantage could have been derived from Enigma decrypts, such was the speed of Geisler's concentration; Cunningham and Somerville had left their respective bases almost before Geisler had arrived at his.

10. Cunningham, *A Sailor's Odyssey*, pp. 302 *et seq.*

11. Quoted in Cameron, *Red Duster, White Ensign*, p. 38.

12. Attard, *The Battle of Malta*, pp. 65 and 68.

13. By the end of January long-range bombers, dive-bombers and fighters were based in southern Italy and Sicily in strength. These comprised Ju87s, Ju88s, He111s and Me110s at Catania, Comiso, Trapani and Palermo. These were to operate against Malta in the coming months supported by large numbers of Italian aircraft. A few Italian squadrons were equipped with Stukas.

14. See Dobbie, *Grace under Malta*, pp. 43 *et seq.* Miss Dobbie states that 'Most of the civilian population had been evacuated earlier, and those that remained had access to excellent rock shelters, so that the loss of life was not severe. But the loss of property was appalling and irreplaceable historic buildings were destroyed.'

15. See Waters, *Ordeal by Sea*, pp. 71–8. *Essex* was managed but not owned by the Federal Steam Navigation Company. Her beneficial owners were actually P. & O. See Chapter 22.

16. *Clan Cumming* was torpedoed but not sunk by the Italian submarine *Neghelli* on 19 January. *Neghelli* was attacked and sunk by the escorting destroyer *Greyhound*.

17. Captain Rowley is quoted in the Admiralty Battle Summary No. 18 (CB 3081 (11), now unclassified), p. 9.

18. Quoted in Connell, *Mediterranean Maelstrom*, p. 79.

19. Rawlings flew his flag in *Barham*, and had with him *Eagle* and *Ajax* with a destroyer screen.

CHAPTER 9: 'EVEN A GUNNERY OFFICER CANNOT MISS'

1. In early March the last four Italian submarines, *Perla, Archimede, Guglielmotti* and *Ferraris*, withdrew from the Red Sea and proceeded to Bordeaux via the

Cape, being supplied on passage by the German raider *Atlantis* and the supply ship *Nordmark*.

2. Mine-watching, under the supervision of Vice-Admiral, Suez Canal, Sir James Pipon, occupied three and a half battalions of British troops until they were relieved by Egyptians. The magnetic mines were a real menace, often allowing more than twenty ships to pass over them before detonating, and were very difficult to sweep, hence the necessity to have them spotted as they fell into the water, after which divers deactivated them.

3. To run supplies to Tobruk Cunningham used the *Chakla* and *Fiona*, small passenger vessels owned by the British India Steam Navigation Company 'splendidly commanded by officers of the Royal Naval Reserve with part Indian crews', and Christian Salvesen's British but South African-based whalers *Southern Floe, Southern Isle, Southern Maid* and *Southern Sea*. The first-named was mined off Tobruk on 11 February 1941.

4. See Cunningham, *A Sailor's Odyssey*, pp. 312 *et seq.*

5. See Wingate, *The Fighting Tenth*, pp. 12 *et seq.*

6. *Aldebaran* was sunk by Fleet Air Arm Swordfish of No. 815 Squadron off Valona on 18 March 1941.

7. On 4 March Cunningham was made a Knight Grand Cross of the Bath, news he later stated he had welcomed with the remark 'I would sooner have had three squadrons of Hurricanes.' The air defences in the Western Desert were very poor; all the AA guns moved up to Benghazi had been withdrawn for the Greek campaign, and the losses of the small ships essential to get into Benghazi, which was within range of the Luftwaffe in Sicily and Calabria, were mounting.

8. See Cunningham, *A Sailor's Odyssey*, pp. 219 *et seq.*

9. Like Alfred Holt's Blue Funnel Line whose ships were actually owned by subsidiary companies, the main Ellerman fleet was divided up between the Ellerman Bucknall Line, the Hall Line and the City Line. All were indistinguishable in outward appearance, and all named after cities. Ellerman's short sea traders, the Ellerman Wilson Line and Ellerman and Pappayani Lines, named their ships differently, all their names ending in 'o'. The Wilson ships also wore a different livery. A merchant ship's owners and her managers were usually essentially the same interests, subdivided either for historical reasons or, more pragmatically, for purposes of trade, insurance or taxation. During the Second World War, enemy prizes and the ships of occupied nations were either run directly under the management of the Ministry of War Transport (often, but not always, renamed with an '*Empire*' prefix), or handed over to a British company with the expertise and capacity to manage them. See also Chapter 8, Note 15.

10. See Winton, *Cunningham*, p. 133.

11. Eden was Foreign Secretary and very close to Churchill in thought and methodology. Highly principled and a brilliant negotiator, he acted as Churchill's close aide. General Sir John Dill was Chief of the Imperial General Staff until replaced by Alan Brook in late 1941. Clever and cautious, he was afterwards very successful as Head of the British Joint Staff Mission in Washington.

12. Matapan was the first Mediterranean operation to be based upon Signal Intelligence: see Hinsley, *British Intelligence in the Second World War*, vol. 1, pp. 404–405.

13. German Naval Liaison Officer to Italian Naval Staff, 19 March 1941.

14. 2nd, Captain Nicholson, *Ilex, Hasty, Hereward, Havock* and *Hotspur*; 10th, Captain Waller, RAN, *Stuart, Greyhound* and *Griffin*; 14th, Captain Mack, *Jervis, Janus, Mohawk* and *Nubian*. The elderly HMAS *Vendetta* later dropped out of the action due to engine trouble.

15. The 13th consisted of *Alpino, Bersagliere, Fucilere* and *Granatiere*; the 9th of *Alfieri, Carducci, Gioberti* and *Oriani*; the 16th of *Nicoloso da Recco* and *Emmanuele Pessagno*; the 12th of *Corazziere, Carabiniere* and *Ascari*.

16. Angelo Iachino was Italian Naval Attaché in London 1931–34 and had some insight into British naval methods. He wrote an account of the action, *Gavdo and Matapan*, in which he describes the impact of Taranto and the increasing demoralisation of the Regia Marina despite their superb ships. For a fully detailed account of the battle, see Pack, *The Battle of Matapan*, bearing in mind Hinsley's later revelations about the contribution of Enigma decrypt analysis, to which Note 12 above refers.

17. Fisher is quoted by Pack, *The Battle of Matapan*, p. 49; he was Pridham-Wippell's Staff Officer Operations, and therefore aboard *Orion*.

18. Lieutenant F.H.E. Hopkins, Saunt's observer, quoted by Pack, p. 62.

19. Fisher, quoted by Pack, *ibid.*, pp. 62 *et seq.*

20. Barnard, quoted by Pack, *ibid.*, p. 63.

21. Hopkins, quoted by Pack, *ibid.*, p. 66.

22. Cunningham, *A Sailor's Odyssey*, p. 329.

23. Pack, *The Battle of Matapan*, p. 71.

24. Barnard, quoted by Pack, *ibid.*, p. 75. Afterwards, the two admirals' staffs had great difficulty reconciling their respective track plots, the difference between them amounting to ten miles. In the end the C-in-C's had to be matched.

25. Fisher, quoted by Pack, *ibid.*, p. 78.

26. Iachino, quoted by Pack, *ibid.*, p. 92.

27. Barnard, quoted by Pack, *ibid.*, p. 98. In his autobiography, Cunningham informs us that he 'paid respectful attention' to the opinions of his staff.

28. Williams failed to make Suda Bay, but ditched near *Juno* and was rescued by boat.

29. Cunningham quoted by Pack, *The Battle of Matapan*, p. 35.

30. Cunningham, *A Sailor's Odyssey*, p. 332.

31. Lee-Barber, quoted by Pack, *The Battle of Matapan*, p. 127. As a result of bomb damage received while in Grand Harbour, Valletta, all *Griffin's* forward fuel tanks were open to the sea and Lee-Barber had only his after tanks to call upon.

32. Many of *Pola's* crew had jumped overboard and there was evidence of drinking from the numerous empty Chianti bottles Mack's boarding party found. There were also signs of looting in the officers' cabins.

33. The late 'Johnnie' Lee-Barber, DSO, commander of *Griffin*, later commanded the destroyer *Opportune* in the Arctic and took part in the torpedoing of *Scharnhorst* in the Battle of North Cape. He retired as rear-admiral. See Woodman, *Arctic Convoys*, John Murray, 1995.

34. Once again Cunningham was niggardly in his rewards, for the squadron commander, Dalyell-Stead, received only a posthumous Distinguished Service Order, rather than a Victoria Cross.

CHAPTER 10: 'A MEMORABLE ACHIEVEMENT'

1. Somerville's Report of Proceedings, 1–4 April 1941. The 'island' was the carrier's superstructure amidships. The Italian submarines in question were *Corallo, Santarosa* and *Turchese. Aradam* and *Onice* were off Cyrenaica.

2. Cruisers, *Orion* (flag), *Ajax, Phoebe, Calcutta, Carlisle* and *Coventry*; destroyers, *Stuart, Voyager, Vendetta, Vampire, Waterhen, Wryneck, Diamond, Defender, Decoy, Griffin, Hasty, Havock, Hero, Hotspur, Hereward, Isis, Nubian, Kandahar, Kingston* and *Kimberley*; sloops, *Auckland, Flamingo* and *Grimsby*.

3. Among these were Ellerman Wilson's *Cavallo*, the Holland America Line's *Pennland* of 16,322 grt (on charter to the British MoWT), Reardon Smith's tramp *Santa Clara Valley* and the armed yacht *Calanthe*. The *Clan Fraser*, having transited the Cape with a cargo of ammunition since she left Malta and arrived at Gibraltar, was bombed in the Piraeus. Her explosion did immense damage to harbour installations, thirteen other merchant ships and numerous lighters and coasters. See Roskill, *The War at Sea*, vol. 1, p. 436.
4. Dobbie, *Grace under Malta*, pp. 122 *et seq.*
5. On 24 April and 4 May 1941 the Italian torpedo-boats *Simone Schiaffino* and *Giuseppe la Farina* were lost to these extensive minefields off Cape Bon, which constituted an ever present and indiscriminate danger to surface warships of the combatant powers.
6. The light cruiser *Dido* was one of a class laid down between 1937 and 1939 armed with 5.25-inch dual-purpose twin mountings, capable of high- and low-angle fire, which had been developed as secondary armament for the *King George V*-class battleships. The *Didos* were to prove very successful, especially against aircraft, and figured prominently in the Mediterranean war. Among the class operating in the Mediterranean were *Bonaventure, Cleopatra, Euryalus, Hermione, Naiad, Charybdis* and *Phoebe*.
7. Force H consisted of *Renown* (flag), *Ark Royal, Sheffield, Faulknor, Fearless, Foresight* and *Fortune*. See Somerville's Report of Proceedings, 24–28 April 1941.
8. See Lennox Kerr, *Touching the Adventures of Merchantmen*, pp. 140 *et seq*, the account of Stanley Sutherland, a member of *Parracombe*'s crew. Mr Bilmeir, who gave his crews bonuses of ten pounds, was the architect of similar single-ship runs through the Barents Sea to North Russia which were no more successful. See Woodman, *Arctic Convoys*, Chapter 16. Hook and several members of his crew were decorated by King George VI after repatriation in 1943. Sutherland makes no bones about the toughness of the Glaswegian crew.
9. The southbound convoy was escorted by *Euro, Fulmine, Castore, Orione* and *Procione*; the northbound by *Folgore, Saetta, Strale* and *Turbine*, with distant cover being provided by the cruisers *Trieste, Eugenio di Savoia* and *Bolzano*, screened by the destroyers *Ascari, Carabiniere* and *Gioberti*.
10. Air raids at this time wrecked the already damaged fleet minesweeper *Fermoy* in No. 5 Drydock and the destroyer *Encounter* in No. 2 was badly damaged.
11. One of these was the 'convoy service ship' *Chakla*, formerly a 3,081-ton British India steamship, built in 1914 and employed on the trade known as 'the goat and coolie run'. Having been requisitioned and converted to an armed boarding vessel at Bombay, she was re-equipped at Alexandria with an AA armament which heartened other ships in company. After serving as a convoy escort and operating with the inshore squadron harrying the Axis advance in Cyrenaica and carrying out the salvage of a large tanker, the *Desmoulea, Chakla* was sunk in Tobruk on 29 April 1941 when resupplying the garrison, though her AA guns were subsequently salvaged. Her CO was Lieutenant-Commander A.J. Hattie (see R. Osborne, *Conversion for War*, World Ship Society monograph No. 6).
12. Stitt, *Under Cunningham's Command*, pp. 127 *et seq.*
13. The Cape-routed balance of the original WS7 consisted of the Dutch freighter *Abbekerk*, the British liners *Aronda, Dominion Monarch, Empress of Asia, Empress of Russia, Highland Chieftain, Reina del Pacifico* and *Strathaird* and the Polish ship *Sobieski*.
14. *Empire Song* was a 9,228-ton standard refrigerated ship built in Greenock in 1940, managed by Cayzer Irvine and Co. on behalf of the MoWT: see Stitt, *Under Cunningham's Command*, p. 135. The master's drunkenness and other

details are mentioned in the Imperial War Museum's *Book of the War at Sea*, edited by Julian Thompson, p. 115, which quotes Salter.

15. On the German invasion of Norway in the spring of 1940, the decision by the Norwegian government to order its merchant ships at sea to place themselves under British command meant that a number of fine modern tankers were available from Norwegian companies. To Britain's shame, her own tanker fleet was neither numerous nor modern, a fact which complicated the supply of Malta.

16. Sources for the disposition of escort vessels in TIGER are conflicting, and complicated by the frequency with which they were changed, usually in response to critical fuel levels. It appears that the following took part, either in the close escort of MW7 A and B, or in screening Cunningham's fleet: destroyers *Jervis, Juno, Jaguar, Kandahar, Kimberley, Kingston, Napier, Nizam, Imperial, Griffin, Hotspur, Havock, Decoy, Defender, Greyhound, Ilex, Isis, Hero* and *Hereward; Hasty, Janus* and *Nubian* are also believed to have been present. One of the corvettes was *Gloxinia* and another is listed as *Swona*, a minesweeping whaler of 313 tons hired in April 1940 and later purchased as a dan-buoy layer.

17. The Italian cruisers were *Duca degli Abruzzi, Giuseppe Garibaldi, Giovanni delle Banda Nere* and *Conte di Cadorna*, with five destroyers.

18. See Cunningham, *A Sailor's Odyssey*, pp. 363 *et seq*.

19. *Alpino, Bersagliere, Fuciliere, Maestrale, Scirocco, Da Recco, Usodimare, Pessagno* and *Pancaldo*.

20. Force H for SPLICE consisted of *Renown, Sheffield* and *London*, with the destroyers *Hesperus, Havelock, Harvester, Faulknor, Foxhound, Fury* and *Forester*.

21. Force H for ROCKET: *Renown, Sheffield, Faulknor, Foxhound, Foresight, Forester, Fearless* and *Fury*. Force H for TRACER: *Renown, Faulknor, Fearless, Foresight, Forester, Foxhound, Hesperus* and *Wishart*.

22. Force H for RAILWAY, Phases One and Two: *Renown, Hermione, Faulknor, Fury, Forester, Fearless, Foxhound, Lance* and *Legion*. See Somerville's Report of Proceedings, 22 June–1 July 1941, which is at variance with accounts claiming eight Hurricanes were prevented from taking off due to the fire.

CHAPTER 11: 'ON THE VERGE OF DISASTER'

1. Cunningham, *A Sailor's Odyssey*, p. 364.
2. Petty Officer Alfred Sephton of HMS *Coventry* was awarded a posthumous Victoria Cross for continuing to carry out gunnery direction duties though shot through the spine and mortally wounded in the attack.
3. Cunningham, *A Sailor's Odyssey*, p. 391.
4. *Georgic* was afterwards salvaged, and towed to Karachi, an operation in which *Sydney Star* and *Clan Campbell* assisted. Here she was rebuilt, re-entering service as a troopship.
5. Cunningham, *A Sailor's Odyssey*, p. 396.
6. On 26–27 May, by the torpedo boats *Circe, Calliope, Clio* and *Perseo*.
7. During June and July several sorties were made by the 7th Division under Casardi (*Eugenio di Savoia, Duca d'Aosta* and *Muzio Attendolo*), and the 4th under Giovanola (*Banda Nere, Di Giussano, Pigafetta, Da Mosto, Da Verazzano, Da Recco, Usodimare, Gioberti* and *Scirocco*). The minefield off Tripoli was later to have a devastating effect on Force K. See Chapter 14.
8. Wingate, *The Fighting Tenth*, p. 83.
9. *Ibid.*, pp. 83 and 84. Newton and his men were PoWs until liberated in 1943. The Italians enjoyed another minor success at the beginning of August when

the submarine *Delfino*, operating off Mersa Matruh, shot down and captured the crew of an attacking Sunderland flying-boat.

10. Cunningham, *A Sailor's Odyssey*, pp. 404–5.
11. See Cameron, *Red Duster, White Ensign*, pp. 51 *et seq*. See also Lennox Kerr, *Touching the Adventures of Merchantmen*, pp. 203 *et seq*. Launched in Amsterdam, the *Jacob van Heemskerck* was completed in a British yard in February 1940.
12. See Somerville's Report on Operation 'Substance', 4th August 1941, in ADM199/830.
13. In his annual summary for Force H's first twelve months, Somerville pointed out that *Faulknor* had spent 266 days at sea and run 84,000 miles, a few more than the second most active ship, *Ark Royal*, with 83,780 miles in 230 days. *Renown* had 74,164 miles to her credit in 232 days, *Sheffield* 'over 75,000' in 240 days. See Document 169 in *The Somerville Papers*.
14. A total of eight submarines were detailed to support Operation SUBSTANCE. These were: Naples, *Olympus* (Dymott) and the Dutch *O21* (van Dulm); Palermo, *Urge* (Tomkinson); Marittimo, *Upholder* (Wanklyn); Cagliari, *P32* (Abdy); North Messina, *Utmost* (Cayley); South Messina, *Unique* (Collett) and *Upright* (Wraith).
15. Correspondence with Mr L.E. Bone of *Sydney Star*.
16. For instance, Swordfish patrols reported *Leinster* in company, and her grounding position was initially thought to have been Tarifa.
17. Somerville's Report on Operation SUBSTANCE, 4th August 1941, *loc. cit.*
18. Rosenthal's Report of Proceedings, 28th July 1941, in ADM199/830. *Diaspro* was one of the two Italian submarines on patrol north of Bougaroni at this time, on the lookout for incursion by Force H; the other was *Alagi*.
19. Somerville's Report on Operation SUBSTANCE, 4th August 1941, *loc. cit.*, also Pugsley's Report of the loss of HMS *Fearless*, 24th July 1941, from HMS *Forester*, in ADM199/830.
20. Cameron, *Red Duster, White Ensign*, p. 52. The difficulties of adjusting the constant-running diesel engines of a merchant vessel, designed for individual performance and not for acting in company or station-keeping, were rarely appreciated by naval officers bred to precision in such matters. Such admonishments were a constant irritant to experienced masters and to their officers and engineers attempting to regulate machinery not intended for such niceties of operation.
21. Lennox Kerr, *Touching the Adventures of Merchantmen*, Account by Captain Higgs, p. 209.
22. Pugsley's Report of Proceedings, *loc. cit.*
23. Somerville's Report of Proceedings, *loc. cit.*
24. *Ibid*. Syfret reported to Somerville that a torpedo track had been seen to pass close to *Edinburgh* during this attack and was thought to have been fired by a submarine. In fact no Italian submarine which was at sea in the area through which GM1 and Force X passed fired her torpedoes.
25. *Ibid*.
26. *Ibid*.
27. Cameron, *Red Duster, White Ensign*, p. 56.
28. Rosenthal's and Somerville's Reports. The very much lower manpower available in merchantmen compared with warships frequently occasioned delay and provoked such implied criticisms of the former by the latter, whose commanding officers' reports survive while the points of view of the merchant ships' officers are lost. At this time all the *Sydney Star*'s officers would have been fully occupied and damage would have to be specially investigated, probably by the chief officer and the carpenter, then reported back. The time

necessary for this has to be set against the reaction time of *Nestor*, which in her turn seems to have failed to notice the condition of *Sydney Star*, beyond reporting her course as 'opposite ... to that of the convoy'. Experienced master mariners felt that the shortcomings implied in reports arising from such incidents showed them in a poor light and resulted from a basic ignorance of their own difficulties. Out of such vague misunderstandings an enduring resentment grew.

29. See Cameron, *Red Duster, White Ensign*, p. 58. The reports were written from opposite perspectives. Horn undoubtedly thought his ship was seriously damaged at the time, and Rosenthal doubtless urged him to do all in his power to save her. Somerville's Report has the unfortunate effect of giving all the credit to Rosenthal and casting aspersions upon Horn.
30. Rosenthal's and Somerville's Reports of Proceedings. This derives from Rosenthal carrying a Lieutenant Stoner back to Gibraltar. On the outward passage Stoner had been liaison officer aboard *City of Pretoria*, and told Rosenthal 'that it was believed in that ship that *Sydney Star* was holed by a projectile fired by one of the escort'.
31. Taprell-Dorling, *Blue Star Line at War*, p. 82. The author, a retired naval officer, is better known as the novelist 'Taffrail'. Commissioned by Blue Star to write the company's war history, he makes no mention of Somerville's rather pejorative spin on events.
32. Cameron, *Red Duster, White Ensign*, p. 60.
33. See Rosenthal's Report, *loc. cit*. The other side is expressed in correspondence with Mr L.E. Bone, a member of *Sydney Star*'s crew who was ordered into the boats under the Third Officer.
34. Somerville's Report of Proceedings.
35. From position 37° 42' N 007° 17' E.
36. Somerville's Report of Proceedings.
37. Somerville's Report of Proceedings. Those lost were Sub-Lieutenant K.G. Grant, RNVR and Acting Leading Airman H. McLeod.
38. *Ibid*.
39. Somerville reports in paragraph 122: 'The other aircraft whose crews [*sic*] consisted of Lieutenant A.T.J. Kindersley and P.O. Airman F.A. Barnes was seen by *Sikh* to crash vertically into the sea at high velocity. There were no survivors.'
40. Somerville's Report of Proceedings. In his report of the loss of *Fearless*, Commander A.F. Pugsley commends highly the conduct of Surgeon-Lieutenants E. Yates of *Fearless* and C.J. Vaughan of *Forester* for their care of the wounded. Nine more ratings died of their wounds, largely burns, during their passage aboard *Forester*.
41. Somerville's Report of Proceedings.
42. Roskill, *A Merchant Fleet at War*, pp. 135 and 147.
43. Admiralty to Air Chief Marshal Sir Wilfrid R. Freeman, KCB, DSO, MC, 15 September 1941, in ADM199/830.
44. Dickson, Report of Proceedings, 28th July 1941, in ADM199/830.

CHAPTER 12: 'A MOST HECTIC AFTERNOON'

1. Hay, *The Unconquered Isle*, pp. 143 *et seq*.
2. Successes achieved by these craft led Churchill to enquire what the British equivalent was. On being told there was none, he immediately ordered the matter rectified.
3. Correspondence with author by leading stoker in *Arethusa*.

4. Somerville to North, 26 August 1941, *Somerville Papers*.

5. Pilcher's report was quoted in *Sea Breezes*, April 1946, pp. 249 *et seq*. Pilcher, MacDougall and Newlyn were all decorated.

6. Holman, *In the Wake of Endeavour*, p. 165. Before the penny dropped, Pilcher had sought a meaning from the International Code: KIA meaning 'you should send for orders' and ORA signifying 'I wish some people taken off'.

7. Roskill, *A Merchant Fleet at War*, pp. 147–8.

8. The troop convoy was escorted by *Aviere, Da Noli, Camicia Nera, Gioberti, Usodimare* and *Pessagno*; the northbound by *Euro, Oriani, Pegaso, Calliope* and *Orsa*.

9. This convoy was escorted by *Dardo, Da Recco, Folgore, Strale, Ascari* and *Lanciere*.

10. *Centaure* and *Polluce*.

11. The destroyers *Oriani* and *Fulmine* and the torpedo-boats *Procione, Pegaso, Orsa, Circe* and *Perseo* formed the escort.

12. Raeder's Report to the Fuehrer at Wolfsschanze in the afternoon of September 17, 1941. See Trevor-Roper, ed., *Fuehrer Conferences*, pp. 231 *et seq*.

13. Ciano's *Diary*, 25 September, 1941.

14. Somerville to Cunningham, 7 September 1941 (*Somerville Papers*). Somerville also wrote to North next day, telling him that he, Somerville, had given Churchill his views on 'Oran & Dakar and what really happened ... He [Churchill] gave several disturbed grunts but wouldn't argue or discuss the matter at all ...'

15. Somerville's Report of Proceedings for 12 September, dated 14th.

16. See Woodman, *Arctic Convoys*, pp. 297 *et seq*.

17. Macintyre, *Fighting Admiral*, quoted pp. 148–9.

18. HM Destroyer *Gurkha* had actually been built as HMS *Larne*, but was given the Tribal name after the original Tribal-class *Gurkha* sank off Norway in April 1940.

19. *Denbydale* was afterwards raised and used as a storage hulk. *Durham*, holed in No. 6 Hold, lay beached until a year later, 4 September 1942, when she was towed back for dry-docking and repair in Falmouth. After the war, *Durham* resumed trading as a cadet ship.

20. Macintyre, *op. cit.*, quoted p. 152.

21. The *Göben* group, named after an Imperial German cruiser that had successfully transited the Mediterranean in the First World War to the embarrassment of the British, consisted of *U75, U79, U97, U371* and *U559*.

22. Somerville's Report of Proceedings, 14–24 September 1941.

23. Details from Somerville's Report on Operation HALBERD, 24–30 September 1941, ADM199/831.

24. Clarke appears to have been a stickler for station-keeping. Senior Officer of the close ocean escort of WS11x, 22–24 September, he had the converted ack-ack auxilaries HMSs *Ulster Monarch* and *Royal Scotsman* stationed between *Sheffield* and the convoy's starboard wing, near *Breconshire*, then leading the centre column: '*Ulster Monarch* was continually out of station, and on many occasions grossly so ...' *Royal Scotsman* was as bad: 'A marked improvement in their handling is required. Incidentally, they could not have added anything to the credit of the Royal Navy in the eyes of the Merchant Service present.' (In ADM199/831.)

25. Correspondence with the late Mr R. Thomas, crew member of *Rowallan Castle*.

26. McBeath's Report of Proceedings in ADM199/831. Phillips received no special honour for this exploit, though he was commended and later received a CBE 'for long and meritorious service in the Merchant Navy'.

27. Oliver's Report of Proceedings, in ADM199/831.

28. Ford's complaint is in ADM199/831. Despite this and Somerville's initial mis-

givings, Burrough went on to play an important part in Operation PEDESTAL and to command escorts to Arctic convoys with distinction.

29. Somerville's Report on Operation HALBERD, 24–30 September 1941, para. 144.
30. Correspondence with Captain J.C.W. Reid, whose father served in *Nelson*.
31. During her stay in Grand Harbour, Captain Higgs of the *Port Chalmers* had dined with General Dobbie (an unusual occurrence, arising from the fact that both men were members of the same dissenting Protestant sect). Higgs had taken with him his young Fourth Officer, Derek Thompson, to whom I am indebted for details of his ship.
32. The master of *City of Pretoria*, as commodore, had sent 'Help Major' at 17.30, followed by 'Major now alright' at 18.15. For 'making her numbers', please see Chapter 20, Note 13.
33. Somerville's Report on Operation HALBERD . . . para 170.

CHAPTER 13: 'THE BLACKEST OF DAYS'

1. In early October the British submarine *Perseus* had sunk a ship of 2,100 tons and British bombers had sunk the 6,000-ton *Rialto*, both bound for Libya, while the Dutch submarine *O21* sank a ship of 1,400 tons in the western Mediterranean. In the middle of the month the large new Italian submarines *Saint Bon* and *Cagni*, together with the older *Atropo*, carried 354 tons of oil fuel to Bardia in spite of being attacked by air.
2. The actions of the Mediterranean Fleet in support of Tobruk are beyond the scope of the present narrative, but the efforts of the Royal Navy at this time were prodigious, tinged as they were with the inevitability of ultimate defeat in the surrender of the fortress.
3. The Australian destroyers led by *Stuart* and commanded by Captain Waller had finally gone. All were old vessels, and *Stuart* had been reduced to one engine before her departure. They had distinguished themselves in the supply of Tobruk.
4. See Cameron, *Red Duster, White Ensign*, pp. 79 *et seq*. *Empire Guillemot* was managed by W.A. Souter Ltd., trampship owners of South Shields, on behalf of the MoWT. *Empire Guillemot* signed on her crew at her loading port of South Shields, directly from the 'pool', and their quality was sometimes in contrast to those in the cargo-liners.
5. *Balilla* (2,469 grt) and *Marigola* (5,996 grt).
6. Hinsley, *British Intelligence*, vol. 2, pp. 283–4.
7. These were Captain A. Nicholl (*Penelope*), Lieutenant-Commander R. Northcott (*Lance*) and Lieutenant-Commander W. Hussey (*Lively*).
8. Ciano's *Diary*, 9 November 1941. Ciano believed Force K to consist of 'two battleships'.
9. Roskill, *The War at Sea*, vol. 1, p. 533.
10. Ciano's *Diary*, 9 and 10 November 1941.
11. Taken over on the stocks, *Athene* had been laid down as *Clan Brodie* and was one of a pair (the other was *Engadine*, ex *Clan Buchanan*). She had been completed in September and was naval-manned. Capable of carrying crated or built aircraft, these ships were usually independently routed.
12. Somerville's Report of Proceedings, 10–13 November 1941, in *Somerville Papers*.
13. Somerville to his wife, 14 November 1941, *loc. cit.*
14. Somerville to Cunningham, 25 November 1941, *loc. cit.*
15. Macintyre, *Fighting Admiral*, p. 167.
16. Somerville to his wife, 21 November 1941, *loc cit.*

17. Slader, *The Fourth Service*, pp. 209 *et seq.*
18. The crews were interned with the crews of *Havock, Manchester, Parracombe* and *Empire Guillemot* at El Kef. There had been a visit by the American consul at Tunis in January 1941. He discovered 'an open expression of communistic sentiments' among the ratings, as a result of differing conditions of diet between the ships' officers and themselves. See Lane, *The Merchant Seaman's War*, pp. 201 *et seq.*

CHAPTER 14: 'THE CRISIS IN OUR FORTUNES'

1. See Cunningham, *A Sailor's Odyssey*, p. 423. Correspondence with Mr L.E. Bone of *Sydney Star*, whose ship had had her No. 3 Hold repaired by September, confirms his ship's participation, which is also mentioned in Joseph Caruana's monograph *The Malta Convoys*, prepared for the World Ship Society.
2. Roskill, *The War at Sea*, vol. 1, p. 536, which most other British accounts follow, states this was the *Duca degli Abruzzi*. German sources are emphatic that it was *Trieste*, and that it was the second attack that hit the *Abruzzi*.
3. These were the destroyers *Vivaldi, Da Noli, Granatiere, Fuciliere, Corazziere, Carabiniere, Alpino* and *Turbine* and the torpedo-boat *Perseo*.
4. The other patrolling submarines were *Delfino, Squalo, Tricheco* and *Corallo*.
5. Gordon, *HMS* Pepperpot! *The* Penelope *in World War Two*, p. 73. These were J. Mountfield in *Lance* and J. Griffin in *Lively*.
6. The movements of these U-boats were not known to Bletchley Park, who were having little luck with the naval Enigma code at this time (Hinsley, *British Intelligence*, vol. 2, p. 328). It was January 1942 before a separate Submarine Tracking Room was set up in Alexandria.
7. Cunningham, *A Sailor's Odyssey*, p. 424. Archive film exists of this awesome event, and disagrees with Cunningham's account in one detail. Other witnesses, who state that *Barham* was still moving ahead, some say at 20 knots, confirm what is clearly visible on film.
8. Connell, *Mediterranean Maelstrom*, J. Edmunds and J. Ellis, quoted p. 137.
9. Cunningham, *op. cit.*, p. 425.
10. The others were *Bragadino, Otaria, Dandolo, Emo, Millo, Menotti, Cagni, Settimo, Saint Bon, Mocenigo* and *Veniero*.
11. *Porpoise*, Lieutenant-Commander E. Pizey, had recently arrived at Malta with a cargo of fuel for the RAF Hurricanes there. She was the first submarine to be fitted with proper cargo tanks for the carriage of aviation spirit.
12. At about this time Vian's cruisers become referred to as Force B. While Rawlings' force subsumed Force K, the designation is retained for Agnew's ships, which often continued to act separately.
13. The others were *Unbeaten* and *Utmost*. See Ciano's *Diary*, 13 December 1941: 'The usual naval woes ... The fact is our naval losses become more serious every day and I wonder whether the war won't outlast our navy.'
14. *U81, U205, U431, U557* and *U565* now joined *U79, U331* and *U559*.
15. Vian's Report of Proceedings, 15–19 December 1941, in ADM199/897.
16. Cunningham, *op. cit.*, p. 431.
17. Captain Agnew's Report of Proceedings, HMS *Aurora*, 22nd December 1941, in ADM199/897.
18. Capitano di Fregata Bragadin, *The Italian Navy in World War II*, quoted by Pack, *The Battle of Sirte*, p. 21. Ciano's contemporary record in his diary states that 'the convoy has gone through without battle and without trouble'!
19. O'Conor's attack was considered intemperate. The ships were very close

inshore, still at 24 knots, in waters which it could only be in the enemy's interest to mine. Both Agnew and Nicholl were more experienced in the kind of
operation Force K had been engaged in, but O'Conor was six months senior to
Agnew and therefore superseded him.
20. Cunningham, *op. cit.*, pp. 433 *et seq.*
21. I am indebted to the late Graham Sibly, former third officer of HM Transport
Ajax, for permission to quote from his account of *Ajax*'s exploits in the
Mediterranean. This was written in collaboration with Glyn Powell, the ship's
second electrician.
22. Hitler's War Directive No. 38, quoted in Trevor-Roper, *Hitler's War Directives*,
pp. 163 *et seq.*

CHAPTER 15: 'AT VERY GREAT HAZARD'

1. Ciano's *Diary*, 4 January 1942.
2. *Carabiniere, Alpino, Pigafetta, Da Noli, Ascari, Aviere, Geniere*, and *Camicia Nera*.
3. *Pisani, Onice, Dandolo, Alagi, Aradam, Axum*, and *Tricheco*.
4. *Beilul, Dessiè, Galatea* and *Zaffiro*.
5. There was in fact only one aircraft available for air reconnaissance:
Cunningham, *A Sailor's Odyssey*, p. 438.
6. Interviewed by Simpson, this German survivor revealed that passage through
the Strait of Gibraltar had been made at 260 metres (850 feet), a depth far
exceeding that at which British submarines could operate, and 350 feet deeper
than British depth charges were capable of being set. Simpson communicated
this vital intelligence to the Admiralty, but it was over a year before British
depth-charge pistols were modified to work at depths exceeding 500 feet. See
Wingate, *The Fighting Tenth*, pp. 137 *et seq.*
7. Vice-Admiral (Malta), War Diary, February 1942, in ADM199/424. This
emphasises the importance of small quantities of essentials brought in by submarines.
8. Ford was afterwards posted to Rosyth.
9. Correspondence with the late Roy Thomas, a member of *Rowallan Castle*'s crew.
10. *Lively* and *Zulu* had sunk two Italian coasting vessels west of Sicily on 8
February 1942. The destroyer *Fortune* had arrived at Malta with the cruiser
Cleopatra on 11 February; as she entered Grand Harbour an air attack was in
progress and the cruiser was hit on her forecastle by a bomb.
11. Vice-Admiral (Malta), War Diary, *loc. cit.*
12. Martin was later landed with pneumonia, and his first lieutenant said he had
not seen the signal before making the attack. Other submarine commanders
claimed that *Lucania*'s special distinguishing marks were not clear (she had
been granted immunity from attack on previous occasions). Martin was flown
home and had to explain his actions personally to the Foreign Secretary,
Anthony Eden. He later commanded *Tuna* and sank *U644*, winning the DSO.
See Wingate, *The Fighting Tenth*, pp. 143 *et seq.* Ciano records on 12 February
1942 that the British 'really broke their word and there is no justification for it'.
13. Attard, *The Battle of Malta*, p. 134.
14. I am grateful to Captain Hedley Kett, one of a handful of reserve officers to
command submarines and who served as first lieutenant in *Clyde*, for this
information. One submarine had provided a lighter moment in the gloom.
Returning from a patrol on 17 February, *Unique* ran aground on the Maltese
coast: one of her crew landed, and reached the dockyard to report the boat's
predicament without once being challenged. This embarrassing event was
headlined in *The Malta Times* as MALTA INVADED!

15. Churchill, *The Second World War*, vol. II, p. 261.
16. *Thunderbolt* arrived from Alexandria with personnel, kerosene and stores on 7 March; *Porpoise* arrived with passengers and petrol on the 9th, sailing with passengers on the 12th. On the 20th *Olympus* arrived from Gibraltar with passengers and petrol, leaving two days later with stores. Vice-Admiral (Malta), War Diary, *loc. cit.*, February 1942.
17. See Cunningham, *op. cit.*, p. 442.
18. *Ibid.*, p. 443.
19. The first by *Vivaldi, Malocello, Premuda, Zeno, Strale* and the torpedo-boat *Pallade*; the second by *Pigafetta, Pessagno, Usodimare, Maestrale, Scirocco* and the torpedo-boat *Circe*.
20. The battleship by *Ascari, Camicia Nera, Aviere* and *Geniere*; the cruisers by *Alpino, Da Noli* and *Oriani*.
21. Palmas's report is quoted by Wingate, *The Fighting Tenth*, p. 150.
22. *Pigafetta, Da Noli, Bersagliere, Vivaldi, Fuciliere, Scirocco, Astore, Cigno, Procione, Pallade* and *Castore*. The submarines covering Operation V5 and Operation SIRIO were *Corallo, Millo, Veniero, Uarsciek* and *Onice*.
23. Some accounts state that the cruiser sank 'against the last of the daylight', others that it was 'after dark'. It seems that the sinking was during the period of nautical twilight when an observer low down in a destroyer looking astern might have seen a lighter sky than an observer in a cruiser astern of *Naiad* and looking east.
24. Shortly after this, Philip Mack returned to Britain to become flag captain to Admiral Tovey, C-in-C Home Fleet in *King George V*. Later still he was promoted to rear-admiral, and was lost in an air crash when on his way back out to the Middle East. He was an exceptional officer with a very high reputation. Another change in Cunningham's command in the early months of 1942 was the return home of Rear-Admiral Rawlings.
25. Bush, quoted by Pack, *The Battle of Sirte*, p. 27. Grantham rose to full admiral and was a later Governor of Malta.
26. These consisted of *Southwold, Beaufort, Dulverton, Hurworth, Avon Vale, Eridge* and *Heythrop*.
27. Captain C. Hutchinson, Report of Proceedings, 20–23 March 1942, HMS *Breconshire*, in ADM199/681. Details of delay to *Clan Campbell* and about *Talabot* from Lieutenant G. MacFarlane, Rough Narrative and Remarks of Naval Liaison Officer to SS *Talabot*, 18–25 March 1942, in ADM199/681.
28. *Cossack*'s commanding officer Robert Sherbrooke, who later fought a brilliant destroyer action in the Barents Sea, was replaced in *Cossack* for this operation by Vian (conversation with Mrs Rosemary Sherbrooke).
29. See Stephen, *The Fighting Admirals*, pp. 150 *et seq*. Further insight into Vian's character provided in conversation and correspondence with Captain C.K.S. Aylwin, former gunnery officer, HMS *Euryalus*.
30. Bush, quoted by Pack, *Battle of Sirte*, p. 29.
31. Nicholl of *Penelope* reported that his radar did not work during the battle, but that his 'experts' had 'reported triumphantly' that it was functioning after his return to Malta. 'Half an hour later it was blown to smithereens by a near-miss'! Recorded by Pack, *op. cit.*, p. 134.
32. Nicholl, quoted by Pack, *op. cit.*, p. 44.
33. Fisher of *Hero*, quoted by Pack, *op. cit.*, p. 46.
34. St Clair-Ford, quoted by Pack, *op. cit.*, p. 69.
35. Poland, quoted by Pack, *op. cit.*, p. 68.
36. Capitano di Fregata Bragadin, quoted by Pack, *op. cit.*, p. 73.
37. Lieutenant-Commander J. Wright, Report of Naval Liaison Officer to SS

Pampas dated 12 April 1942 and written aboard HMS *Queen Elizabeth* at
Alexandria, in ADM199/681.

38. Edkins, quoted by Pack, *op. cit.*, pp. 75–7.

39. MacFarlane, Rough Narrative and Remarks, *loc. cit.* This officer provides a full
analysis of the air attack techniques. He remarks that the initial air defence of
the Hunts was wasteful, but later most effective. 'Despite the destroyers' fire,'
MacFarlane reported, '… most attacks were very determined, and in the
opinion of an RAF Wing-Commander aboard [*Talabot*] were skilfully made
considering the high wind blowing.'

40. This quotation comes from Pack, *op. cit.*, p. 75 and is rather in the nature of an
explanation made by Captain Hutchinson with hindsight, in view of what happened.

41. See Hutchinson's Report of Proceedings, *loc cit.*, in which he orders Operation
'B' (the dispersal plan) executed at 19.00. The course was 280°, and the dispersal position reckoned as 33° 30′ N, 017° 10′ E, but the ships were ordered to
'only spread 5 degrees'. This seems not to have been carried out. Logically
Breconshire, since she was the fastest ship in the convoy and could cover the
greatest distance, should have been on the most southerly course. A spread of
8° to 10° to port of *Clan Campbell*'s 280° would approximate to *Breconshire*'s
course of 255°. But Wright, aboard *Pampas*, claims to have steered the 'most
southerly course', without saying what this was, and this would seem roughly
corroborated by that ship's course of 327° after 21.00 (when she shaped a
course for Malta), whereas *Breconshire* steered 318° from this time.

42. Wright, Report of Naval Liaison Officer to SS *Pampas*, ADM199/681.

43. British Admiralty Battle Summary No. 32, Malta Convoys 1942, page 12.

44. John Slader in his *The Red Duster at War*, p. 194, records that 'The chief mate
who survived was very bitter about the way the Royal Navy had mishandled
the whole business.'

45. Jellicoe's Report of Proceedings, quoted in Cameron, *Red Duster, White Ensign*.

46. Both Wright and MacFarlane reported very favourably on the behaviour of the
service personnel, DEMS gunners and merchant crews of both nationalities,
with the exception of one Norwegian deck officer 'who took to the bottle in his
cabin as soon as the surface action commenced'.

47. Attard, *Battle of Malta*, pp. 160 *et seq.*

48. Vice-Admiral (Malta), War Diary, March 1942, in ADM199/424.

49. *Ibid.*

50. *Ibid.*

51. *Ibid.*

52. Report by C-in-C Mediterranean on Operation MG1 (p. 6), signed by Admiral
Harwood (see next chapter), in ADM199/681.

53. Beauforts of No. 39 Squadron from Egypt, Albacores of No. 828 Squadron, Fleet
Air Arm from Malta.

54. Woods, quoted by Pack, *Battle of Sirte*, p. 86.

CHAPTER 16: 'A QUESTION OF SURVIVAL'

1. Force H comprised *Malaya, Hermione, Laforey, Lightning, Anthony, Wishart,
Duncan, Active, Blankney* and *Whitehall*.

2. In February about 1,000 tons were dropped, in March about 2,000, and in April
6,700 tons.

3. Several former merchant seamen alluded to being mildly abused by the local

population on this score, particularly those whose ships had been sunk and
who had therefore not succoured the island. The Victualling Superintendent's
complaint was actually made in July 1941, when *Talabot's* Norwegian crew had
been on short commons in Malta for *four months*. It is in Malta General,
ADM199/2406.

4. The decision had been made by the Flag Officer Submarines, Sir Max Horton.
5. So much so that when Mussolini pressed for the invasion of Malta to go ahead
a few days later, Hitler, preparing to renew the offensive against Russia,
decided against it, although Kesselring himself wanted the island occupied
and the matter settled beyond doubt. The strivings of a joint 'Malta staff' at
OKW were thus dismissed and 'the key section of the OKW order on future
strategy in the Mediterreanean resulting from the 4 May [1942] agreement
[between Mussolini and Hitler] ... falls to the ground.' See Warlimont, *Inside
Hitler's Headquarters, 1939–45*, p. 237. Ciano's *Diary* for 22 April 1942 mentions
that Kesselring, on his return from Germany, 'brought Hitler's approval for the
landing operation on Malta'. Ciano follows this with his usual misgivings
about the danger of the undertaking.
6. Operation LUPO had passed three two-ship convoys to Tripoli between 2 and
4 April, which were attacked by Beauforts from Egypt at the extremity of their
operational range. Five out of the eight aircraft were lost. Extensive minefields
were also laid in the Narrows by Italian and German craft.
7. Churchill, *The Second World War*, vol. IV, p. 269.
8. Flight-Lieutenant Barnham, quoted by Ian Cameron in *Red Duster, White
Ensign*, and Ernle Bradford in *Siege: Malta 1940–43*, from his own book *One
Man's Window* (William Kimber, 1956). One Spitfire failed to arrive, its
American sergeant-pilot, according to Jack Greene and Alessandro Massignani
in their *The Naval War in the Mediterranean*, footnote p. 333, flying to Vichy
North Africa and claiming to be a 'lost civilian pilot in need of repatriation'.
This man, presumably an American volunteer in the RAF, may well have been
appalled at the British bungling.
9. In his official history *The War at Sea* Captain Stephen Roskill does a comprehensive whitewashing job of the disaster, while Churchill fudges it completely.
10. The naval writer 'Bartimeus' (Lieutenant-Commander Ricci), quoted by
Winton, *Cunningham*, p. 265.
11. Cunningham, *A Sailor's Odyssey*, p. 454.
12. Winton, *op. cit.*, p. 265.
13. Such an impression provided justifiable fuel for American doubts as to British
standards of efficiency, doubts which were echoed later in the Pacific War.
14. *Wasp* returned to Scapa Flow on 3 May.
15. Vice-Admiral (Malta), War Diary, May 1942, in ADM199/424.
16. See Connell, *Mediterranean Maelstrom*, pp. 162 *et seq.*
17. See Roskill, *The War at Sea*, vol. 2, p. 63.
18. I am indebted to the late Peter Kemp, who observed Cunningham's style when
First Sea Lord. For another assessment of Cunningham, see Stephen, *The
Fighting Admirals*, pp. 156–7.
19. *Westcott, Antelope, Wrestler, Wishart, Partridge* and *Ithuriel.*
20. *Westcott, Antelope, Wrestler, Wishart* and *Ithuriel.*
21. *Westcott, Antelope, Wrestler, Wishart, Patridge* and *Ithuriel.*
22. The Italians also lost the destroyer *Antoniotto Usodimare* off Cape Bon on 9 June
when she was mistakenly sunk by the Italian submarine *Alagi.*
23. *Bedouin, Escapade, Icarus, Onslow, Marne, Matchless, Badsworth, Blankney,
Middleton* and *Kujawiak* (Polish).
24. Built 1938 in Odense as the *Hulda Maersk*, she had been requisitioned by the

Americans and ran under the United States Maritime Commission. I am indebted to Captain Peter King for extracting this information from *With Constant Care ... A.P. Moller: Shipowner 1876–1965*, by Ove Hornby.

25. These were Nos *121, 134, 135, 168, 459* and *462*.
26. See Admiralty Battle Summary No. 32, Malta Convoys 1942, p. 16.
27. *Malachite, Velella, Bronzo, Emo, Uarsciek, Giada, Acciato, Otaria* and *Alagi* off Algeria; *Corallo, Dessiè, Onice, Ascianghi* and *Aradam* off Lampedusa; *Axum, Platino, Micca, Zoea* and *Atropo* east of Malta; *Galatea, Sirena, U77, U81, U208, U431, U453* and *U559* off Crete.
28. Battle Summary. No. 32, Malta Convoys 1942, pp. 18 *et seq*.
29. Doram claimed he had sunk the submarine *Alagi*, but this was not correct.
30. Scurfield's account was written from prison camp to his wife and is in the War Veterans' Newsletter *Malta Remembered, No. 4*. Scurfield had distinguished himself on several previous occasions: commanding the *Hunter* in 1937 when she was damaged in an illegal attack during the Spanish Civil War, and in command of *Broke* in April 1941, when he removed 180 men from the burning Armed Merchant Cruiser *Comorin* in heavy weather and mid Atlantic in a feat of outstanding seamanship. Taken prisoner by the Italians after the action off Pantelleria, he was tragically killed by an RAF Hurricane while being marched through Germany after the Italian surrender.
31. Battle Summary No. 32, p. 24, ascribes the retreat of the Italian forces to the error of a 'friendly' air attack.
32. Commodore Pilditch's Report of Proceedings for Operation HARPOON, dated 7 July 1942, in ADM199/835. In peacetime Holt's ships carried their own insurance, and Blue Funnel and Glen Line officers were made aware of this circumstance from their induction into the company.
33. I am indebted to Mr J.W.N. Rice, son of Captain Rice, for copies of *Orari*'s log and his father's Report of Proceedings and letter to his owners, from which there are several quotations in this chapter. After returning home, Rice was interviewed for the BBC by Freddie Grisewood, who immediately annoyed Rice by referring to him as a '*Merchant Navy Skipper*'. Rice had served his apprenticeship, as had so many of his generation, in sail. He had earned the OBE for gallantry on convoy work, and the HARPOON operation gained him the CBE.
34. I am indebted to Joseph Caruana for his kind permission to quote from his paper on the mining of convoy GM4, from which the details of this incident are largely drawn. Mr Caruana also provided additional details of the action off Pantelleria, culled from several sources.
35. Hutchinson's Report is in ADM199/835.
36. See Report of Proceedings – Escort *Brown Ranger*, 24 June 1942, in ADM199/1110. This mentions that the oiler was further east than was intended, and was within 100 miles of Sardinia at daylight on 14 June. *Liverpool* and her attendants and *Partridge* were both seen heading west.
37. See Appendix to Malta No. 344/682/1 of 27 July 1942, in ADM199/1110. The experience, born out of the errors of MW10, resulted in Operation CERES being prepared for the PEDESTAL convoy.
38. See Vice-Admiral (Malta), Report on Operation BRASSO, 27 July 1942, in ADM199/1110.
39. Vice-Admiral (Malta), War Diary, June/July 1942, in ADM199/424.

CHAPTER 17: 'AN IMPERIAL BALLS-UP'

1. Dobbie's signal of 1 April 1942 to the War Office had summarised Malta's situation. Staples of wheat and flour would last until early June, as would already

inadequate rations of fodder. Meat stocks were 'entirely exhausted' but other 'minor foodstuffs' would last until the end of June. Of the white oils, benzine would last until mid June, kerosene until early July and aviation spirit until mid August. There were 920 tons of diesel oil, which amounted to five weeks' supply, and 2,000 tons of boiler oil. This was entirely earmarked for the ships currently undergoing repair in the dockyard: 'Black oil position is thus becoming precarious and very urgent action appears necessary to restore it.' There was enough coal to last until mid June, but only sufficient Welsh steam coal to provide power until the end of May. Anti-aircraft ammunition was sufficient for about 45 days.

2. The submarines were *Uproar, Ultimatum, Umbra, Taku, Thorn, Thrasher, Proteus, Porpoise* and *Una.*
3. MTBs Nos *259, 261, 262* and *264.*
4. The Hunts were *Airedale, Aldenham, Beaufort, Croome, Dulverton, Eridge, Exmoor* and *Hurworth.*
5. Sibly, G., third officer of *Ajax,* private narrative. See also Report of Naval Liaison Officer, Lieutenant P. Aylwin, aboard *Ajax* and dated 22 June 1942, in ADM199/1244. Aylwin states that: 'The behaviour under air attack of all the Merchant Navy Officers was excellent throughout. I cannot speak too highly of the Master, Captain [J.R.] Scott, a man of 40 years' sea service, and approaching 60 years of age. He remained calm throughout and accepted without hesitation any advice I had to give for taking avoiding action during air attacks.'
6. Destroyers *Kelvin* and *Zulu,* which had escorted *Centurion* from Port Said and were attached to her, and *Pakenham, Fortune* and *Paladin;* corvettes *Delphinium, Erica, Primula* and *Snapdragon.*
7. Four Greek submarines, *Papanicolis, Triton, Katsonis* and *Nereus,* operated from the Greek depot ship *Corinthia* based, until her evacuation on 29 June 1942, at Alexandria.
8. See Courtney, G., *SBS in World War Two* (Robert Hale, 1983), p. 28 and Mediterranean War Diary for Saturday, 13 June 1942 (in ADM199/414). The earlier raiding parties, landed near Cape Trikala on the night of 6/7 June, intending to attack Kastelli and Timbaki as well as Maleme, found Timbaki abandoned. They did wreck seven planes and some fuel at Kastelli. Jellicoe's raid may not have wrecked all the planes claimed.
9. In the order of their Captain (D)'s seniority: 7th (Australian) Flotilla, *Napier* (Arliss, RN), *Nestor, Norman* and *Nizam;* 14th, *Jervis* (Poland), *Kelvin* and *Javelin;* 12th, *Pakenham* (Stevens), *Paladin* and *Inconstant;* 22nd, *Sikh* (Micklethwait), *Zulu, Hasty* and *Hero;* 2nd, *Fortune* (Lt-Cdr Pankhurst), *Griffin* and *Hotspur.* SO of the 5th was Lt-Cdr Petch in *Dulverton.* The 7th, 12th and 2nd Flotillas were from the Eastern Fleet.
10. Admiralty Battle Summary No. 32, Malta Convoys 1942, p. 28.
11. Lieutenant Freeman's Report of Proceedings, HMS *Malines,* 21 June 1942 and the appended Report of Surgeon-Lieutenants H. Darlow and J. Innes, RNVR, in ADM199/1244. The services of such obscure ships are largely unrecorded.
12. Wuppermann's 3rd Flotilla consisted of *S54, S55, S56, S58, S59* and *S60.* The Admiralty Battle Summary, drawing on the Mediterranean War Diary, states incorrectly that *Hasty* was sunk by a submarine.
13. 7th Flotilla, *Legionario, Folgore, Freccia* and *Saetta;* 11th Flotilla, *Aviere, Geniere, Camicia Nera* and *Corazziere;* and 13th Flotilla, *Alpino, Bersagliere, Mitragliere* and *Pigafetta.*
14. British Admiralty Battle Summary No. 32, Malta Convoys 1942, p. 31.
15. *Ibid.,* p. 32.
16. Spooner, *Supreme Gallantry,* p. 158.

17. Signals quoted in British Admiralty Battle Summary, No. 32, pp. 32 *et seq*. The effect on morale in British merchant ships had this unequivocal order been carried out can only be measured against the outcome of the scattering of the Russia-bound convoy PQ17 some three weeks later. Such a betrayal of the delicate but vital trust that existed between the Royal Navy and Merchant Navy might have provoked an unprecedented revolt among the latter. As it was, midsummer 1942 marks the absolute nadir of the British merchant seamen's war. See Woodman, *Arctic Convoys*, Chapters 12 and 13.
18. In addition to *U205*, these were *U77, U81, U431, U453, U559, Atropo, Axum, Galatea, Micca, Sirena* and *Zoea*.
19. *Ajax* went on to Haifa where she discharged her cargo and was released from transport duties after taking part in Operation MG3 and convoy MW12 (see next chapter). She then returned to Port Said and loaded a full cargo of battle-damaged tanks for New York. On opening the hatches, the holds were found to be teeming with rats which had infested the tanks, living on the grease.
20. This is contained in the War Diary signals log and answers a prompt from London timed at 17.42 on the 15th. Harwood's reply begins 'I fully appreciate dire necessity of getting a convoy to Malta ...' and was transmitted to London at 00.42 local time (GMT plus 3) on the 16th, repeated to Leatham in Valletta.
21. Harwood's Report on Operation VIGOROUS, dated 22 June 1942, in ADM199/1244. This piece also contains the short reports submitted by the various naval liaison and sea transport officers embarked in the merchant ships, upon which I have drawn for minor details. Of *Potaro*, Lieutenant Murdoch says: 'I wish to state, that the co-operation onboard between all four Services was excellent, and that the conduct of the Master, his officers and crew throughout the voyage was of the very highest standard of that noble Service to which they belong.' Like all the VIGOROUS ships, *Potaro* had, in addition to her own crew and the naval detachment, RAF and army personnel on board, all of whom had defence stations allocated to them.

CHAPTER 18: 'THE LARGEST POSSIBLE CONVOY'

1. For the full circumstances and argument over PQ17, see Woodman, *Arctic Convoys*.
2. These submarines were *Atropo, Bragadino, Corridoni, Micca, Narvalo, Santarosa, Sciesa, Toti* and *Zoea*.
3. See Cabinet Papers, 3 July 1942, in CAB 65.27.12251.
4. See Strategic Report MEP 02/1663.
5. Viscount Cranbourne, Secretary of State for the Colonies, reported Dobbie's concern about Maltese morale to Churchill as early as 27 February 1942, while Cunningham's War Diary for January 1942 remarks that: 'Labour troubles now constitute the main difficulty in Malta dockyard. There are signs of this improving, but there is still a high proportion of absentees, and little work gets done if there seems likelihood of a raid.' Dobbie's signal sent on the failure of MW10 has been quoted in Chapter 16 (it is in PREMIER 3/266/2).
6. Prime Minister to Lord Gort, Personal Telegram No. T.683/2, 4 May 1942, in PREMIER 3/266/1 and Ditto, Personal Telegram No. T.1023/2, 18 July 1942, in PREMIER 3/266/2.
7. Gort to Churchill, 27 July 1942, in PREMIER 3/266/5.
8. Chiefs of Staff meeting, 22.30 on 15 June 1942, Minute 3, MALTA, in PREMIER 3/266/2.
9. *Ohio* had done well at her trials, with a speed of 17.2 knots, and had been imme-

diately earmarked by the US Navy Department as a 'National Defence Tanker'. The hull contained nine centre tanks, with a pump-room amidships. The wings were divided into six spaces on each side, two of which were each further sub-divided into three small tanks for parcel cargoes. *Ohio*'s main fuel tank ran right across the ship abaft the main cargo tanks, just forward of the engine room.

10. Correspondence with Philip Andrews of *Empire Hope*.

11. Correspondence with the late Ron Peck of *Empire Hope*.

12. See Commander Venables' report on Operation PEDESTAL, dated 15 August 1942, in ADM199/1243. Conversation with Patrick Murphy of *Deucalion*.

13. Conversation with Frederick Treves of *Waimarama*, 1996. Treves was afterwards interviewed in London by Lord Justice Tucker. The Middle East drafting offices were open sources of knowledge of transfer of service personnel for Malta and this had been reported after VIGOROUS.

14. I am indebted to Captain D.A.G. Dickens for permission to draw details from his account of PEDESTAL written in November 1942 after his experiences as a cadet aboard *Dorset*. Like Treves and other midshipmen, apprentices and cadet officers, Dickens was in his teens, as were numerous junior radio officers, deck and galley boys in the ships of WS21s.

15. There were in fact eleven 'Force' designations, some with temporary existences within the overall operation. PEDESTAL itself was, like JULIUS, a superior code containing several subsidiary operations. Force R comprised the corvettes *Jonquil* (Lieutenant-Commander R. Partington, RNR), *Spiraea*, *Geranium* and *Coltsfoot*, the fleet oiler *Brown Ranger* and the auxiliary oiler *Dingledale*. The tug *Salvonia* was added at the last moment with the loss of *Ark Royal* in mind.

16. *Amazon, Bicester, Bramham, Derwent, Zetland, Ledbury, Malcolm, Venomous, Wilton, Wolverine, Wishart, Ashanti, Tartar, Eskimo, Somali, Pathfinder* and *Quentin. Penn* was delayed with boiler problems and later caught up. Some of these did not join until later as, like *Ledbury*, they were escorting another WS convoy, bound for the Middle East round the Cape, which had left the North Channel on 30 July and in the wake of which WS21s was to proceed, looking like a second convoy bound on the same track.

17. See Report of Naval Liaison Officer aboard *Empire Hope*, dated 16 August 1942, in ADM199/1243.

18. *Sardonyx, Buxton* (which did not pass Gibraltar), *Foresight, Fury, Intrepid* and *Icarus*. The last four were fitted for minesweeping.

19. *Laforey, Lightning* and *Lookout*.

20. *Vansittart, Westcott* and *Wrestler*.

21. These consisted of 46 Sea Hurricanes, 10 Grumman Martlets (Wildcats) and 16 Fulmars, aboard *Victorious, Indomitable* and *Eagle. Victorious* and *Indomitable* also carried 28 Albacores. Fleet Air Arm Squadrons involved were: *Victorious*, Nos 809 and 884 (Fulmars), No. 885 (Sea Hurricanes) and Nos 817 and 832 (Albacores); *Indomitable*, Nos 800 and 880 (Sea Hurricanes), No. 806 (Martlets), Nos 827 and 831 (Albacores); *Eagle*, Nos 801 and 813 (Sea Hurricanes).

22. See Hill, *Destroyer Captain*, p. 62; also correspondence between the author and Roger Hill.

23. It is interesting that the C-in-C's Mediterranean War Diary for 10 August 1942 notes: 'Lieutenant-General B.L. Montgomery assumed command of the Eighth Army *vice* General Auchinleck' (in ADM199/414).

24. Between Algiers and Formentara, *Brin, Dagabur, Giada, Uarsciek, Volframio, U73, U205* and *U331*; off Bizerta, *Avorio, Cobalto, Dandolo, Emo, Granito* and *Otaria*; off Cape Bon, *Alagi, Ascianghi, Axum, Bronzo* and *Dessiè*.

25. C-in-C's Mediterranean War Diary, 10 August 1942, *loc. cit.*
26. *Pakenham, Paladin, Jervis, Kelvin, Dulverton, Hurworth, Eridge, Hursley, Beaufort* and *Belvoir.*
27. *Sikh, Zulu, Javelin, Tetcott* and *Croome.*
28. *Dido,* suffering from defects, was sent separately to Port Said with *Pakenham, Paladin* and *Jervis.*
29. Details from Captain Rice's report to the owners of *Orari.*
30. See Greene and Massignani, *The Naval War in the Mediterranean,* p. 243.
31. Details from Captain Rice's report to the owners of *Orari.*

CHAPTER 19: 'YOU MEN CANNOT BE REPLACED'

Accounts of this phase of PEDESTAL are understandably contradictory, even accounts by those reporting on events only a few hours past. Evidence of fatigue and confusion permeates the primary sources. My reconstruction has been based largely upon those official reports available, interpreted in light of the known movements of the ships and the written contemporary and retrospective evidence of eyewitnesses, and spiced with some material from verbal accounts given fifty years later by veterans. These, recorded on video, have been relied upon chiefly for personal details, but occasionally they have reconciled discrepancies thrown up by both original reports and subsequent historical works. Nowhere else have I felt more strongly Voltaire's definition of history, that it is a fable we agree upon, though I have tried to avoid the victor's point of view, being somewhat sceptical, on this occasion, as to from whose perspective this truly derives.

1. The others were *Ledbury, Zetland, Wilton, Bramham, Bicester, Foresight* and *Derwent.*
2. There seems not to be any corroborating evidence of this attack being made on any aircraft-carrier or of counter-attacks being mounted by British destroyers, as some accounts state, though Onslow's destroyers were probably in company at this time. The longitude given by *Coltsfoot* seems too far to the east to give any credibility to Targia attacking anything other than Force R. *Coltsfoot*'s report is mentioned in Syfret's Diary of Events, Appendix B, Passage of the Straits, Operation PEDESTAL, in ADM199/1242.
3. It is interesting to note that the Germans, having transferred several groups of torpedo-bombers to Norway to operate against PQ17 in early July, had failed to return them to the Mediterranean a month later to operate against PEDESTAL. On the other hand, dire necessity had driven the British to send south Home Fleet units which had been in the Barents Sea during that unhappy operation.
4. See Crosley, *They Gave Me a Seafire,* for an account of *Eagle*'s sinking. *Eagle*'s airborne fighters were directed to the other carriers.
5. Broome, who had commanded the close escort to PQ17, now had with him *Amazon, Venomous, Wolverine* and *Wrestler.*
6. See Gretton, *Convoy Escort Commander,* p. 90.
7. *Wolverine* had a temporary bow fitted at Gibraltar and then went home for permanent repairs.
8. See Report of Naval Liaison Officer, MV *Empire Hope,* 16 August 1942, in ADM199/1243.
9. I am indebted to P. Durham of *Laforey* for this and subsequent details from his private account.
10. I am indebted to P. Andrews of *Empire Hope* for this and subsequent details from his private account.

11. Quoted by Peter Smith, *PEDESTAL, The Malta Convoy of August 1942*, p. 73.
12. See Report of Naval Liaison Officer, MV *Rochester Castle*, 15 August 1942, in ADM199/1243.
13. See Hill, *Destroyer Captain*, p. 65.
14. Syfret's report claims the barrage shot two down (by *Pathfinder* and *Deucalion*) and one was observed flying off, losing height and making smoke due to the barrage; he also claims '8 certain, 3 probable and 2 damaged'.
15. Two of the SM84s of 132 Stormo (Colonel Leone) were shot down by the defending fighters and it was the smoke of one which had been spotted from *Ashanti*. Every one of the remainder was damaged so the unit was rendered non-operational.
16. See Roskill, *A Merchant Fleet at War*, p. 196. Needless to say, much was made of such incidents, particularly by naval officers who rarely appreciated the small number of supervising officers who ran merchant ships. Undoubtedly the pool system produced many bad hats, men who after the harsh and heartless years of the Depression felt they owed little allegiance to anyone. It is important to set these in context, for the majority of merchant personnel behaved well. Moreover, these transports were all floating bombs: the quantities of inflammable materials on board were enough to speed departure, if departure were decided upon or in the balance. These men, however, unsupervised, had abandoned ship without orders.
17. See Report of Naval Liaison Officer, M.V. *Deucalion*, 15 August 1942, in ADM199/1243, and subsidiary personal evidence from crew, in ADM199/1242.
18. The late D.H. Maitland-Makgill-Crichton, a dashing, aristocratic officer nicknamed 'Champagne Charlie' from his style, is chiefly remembered for his prodigious ability to master languages: he was fluent in more than forty. In the Cold War he became an expert in Russian, and was a crucial expert witness in the conviction of the post-war Portland spy ring. Syfret considered that 'the expensive method chosen … to sink [*Cobalto*] … was unnecessary. Moreover I was disturbed at the resulting absence of the *Ithuriel* from the screen when an air attack was impending.' These events thus removed two front line destroyers, *Ithuriel* and *Wolverine*, from operational duties for some time.
19. The accounts of this attack vary widely, both in terms of the numbers of aircraft engaged and in the enemy losses. The damage that they achieved is, however, incontrovertible.
20. Interviews with Dr Patrick Murphy, Mr John Gregson and the Reports of the Naval Liaison Officer and Commanding Officer, HMS *Bramham*. Also Captain Ramsay Brown's Report to Shipping Casualties Section, Admiralty Trade Division. Gregson was awarded the Albert Medal which, on its official withdrawal, was replaced by a George Cross. Brown and Campbell each received the DSC; Bosun McCaughey and Carpenter Owen, the DSM; the Chief Officer, Mr Ogilvie, Fourth Officer Price, Extra Second Engineer Ward, Midshipman Bracewell, DEMS Gunner Ward and Yeoman of Signals Collins were all mentioned in despatches. Of his engineers, Brown wrote that he 'had nothing but praise for the ship's Engineers, who carried out their trying duties in the best tradition of their calling'. See also account in Roskill, *A Merchant Fleet in War*. Many decorations were also made to the officers and men of the Royal Navy involved in PEDESTAL.
21. The effect of the withdrawal of these ships was profound, as several members of the remaining crews pressing on afterwards testified. Fifty years later it still rankled, causing some embarrassment at a reunion of PEDESTAL veterans.
22. I am entirely at odds with the accounts of other commentators, which imply

that the confusion arose from the inexpertise of the merchant masters. The lack
of collisions is evidence of expertise of a high order, and the distractions posed
by the naval ships at this time are entirely understandable. In fact, Commander
Kitcat of *Intrepid* was ordered to 'leave' the convoy at this time, a silly error in
transposition for 'lead', but one which is unsurprising, given the speed and
magnitude of events. That Scandolo and Ferrini were entirely undetected, for
whatever reason, seems the prime cause of the disaster, for it was little else.

23. See Captain Riley's Report to his owners, dated 16 August 1942, held by the
    National War Museum Association, Valletta; and Report of the Naval Liaison
    Officer, MV *Brisbane Star*, 16 August 1942, in ADM199/1243.
24. See Reports of Proceedings of Commanding Officer, HMS *Penn*, 17 August
    1942, in ADM199/1242, and of the Naval Liaison Officer in *Empire Hope*,
    ADM199/1243; also personal account of Philip Andrews.
25. The loss of *Clan Ferguson* is from an account by a DEMS naval gunner, L.C.
    Hedge, in the George Cross Island Association's South East Area Branch
    Newsletter No. 37, July 1998. Black is quoted in Peter Smith's *PEDESTAL, The
    Malta Convoy*, p. 121. Some 'histories' claim all hands were lost, but this is not
    the case, though the rescue of so many men is remarkable.
26. Da Zara's escorts were *Ardito, Ascari, Aviere, Camicia Nera, Corsaro, Fuciliere,
    Geniere, Gioberti, Grecale, Legionario, Maestrale* and *Oriani*. Italian estimates of
    Malta's aircraft strength were correct in terms of numbers, but grossly over-
    estimated the numbers of strike-aircraft. The preponderance of fighters there-
    fore achieved a moral if not a material ascendancy, and this was to impact on
    the final decisions.
27. German Naval Staff War Diary, 12 August 1942, quoted Smith, *PEDESTAL, The
    Malta Convoy*, p. 149.
28. After the war Admiral Burrough met Weichold and was informed that at one
    stage in the operation Mussolini had personally telephoned Hitler, putting
    forward the suggestion that the Regia Marina should intervene in force with a
    view to annihilating the convoy. Hitler's reply was apparently short, to the
    effect that Mussolini should do no such thing, and that the Luftwaffe would
    see to the matter. The anecdote was told by Burrough to Captain D.A.G.
    Dickens, by then an Elder Brother of Trinity House, to whom I am indebted for
    the information.
29. Alastair Mars was decorated for this exploit and wrote his memoirs in
    Unbroken – The Story of a Submarine (Frederick Muller, 1952). His post-war con-
    frontation with the Admiralty and the Establishment is told in his book *Court
    Martial* (Frederick Muller, 1954).
30. The torpedo-boats assigned to the task appear to have been: Italian, *MAS533,
    MAS543, MAS548, MAS552, MAS553, MAS554, MAS556, MAS557, MAS560,
    MAS562, MAS563, MAS564, MS16, MS22, MS23, MS25, MS26* and *MS31*;
    German, *S30, S36, S58* and *S59*. Sources: Joseph Caruana, and Rohwer and
    Hummelchen.
31. Quoted by Smith, *PEDESTAL*, p. 130.
32. See Roskill, *A Merchant Fleet at War*, pp. 199 *et seq.* Hanney and his men were
    interned in Sicily, then Italy, until the surrender, after which they were marched
    to Germany. Brunskill wrote a personal account of the crew's imprisonment.
    Several of the other men held with Skilling in Le Kef died of dysentery before
    they were moved to Sfax under a more compassionate regime. After the Allied
    invasion of North Africa, the survivors were offered the option of taking to the
    hills or awaiting events. Led by the camp commandant, a Lieutenant Morrell
    of the Spahis, they reached the Allied front line and were repatriated to the
    Clyde in *Orontes*, arriving on 3 December 1942.

33. Video evidence by Bob Waxman, engineer cadet, and Harold Bennett, deck cadet.
34. The United States did not confer veteran status on their merchant seamen until many years after the war. As late as 1995 John Follansbee, a former American purser in PEDESTAL, wrote: 'I might mention that you folks seemed to appreciate your Merchant Marine much more than the merchant seamen and officers were in the U.S.' His letter to the author then set out a body of evidence to prove it.
35. See Report of Liaison Officer in SS *Santa Eliza* [sic], 16 August 1942, in ADM199/1243. The author has also seen an account by an American officer, who wished to remain anonymous.
36. Additional details derived from documents relating to Operation PEDESTAL in ADM199/1242.

CHAPTER 20: 'THE ENEMY WILL ... PROCLAIM THIS A GREAT VICTORY'

1. The British army had lost in France and Norway, been beaten in Malaya, and surrendered Singapore; Burma was all but taken by the Japanese; Greece and Crete had gone; the Germans were in Tobruk, preparing to invade Egypt. The Royal Navy was thinly deployed in four theatres and while it had sunk the *Bismarck*, its ability to protect convoys, as evidenced by its conduct in regard to PQ17, suggested it was impotent. As for Malta, the stepping-stone by means of which the Western Allies were proposing to invade Italy, she teetered on the brink of surrender. Churchill's promises must have seemed to Stalin the very epitome of decadent bombast.
2. Several naval reports refer to these ships as 'stragglers', a somewhat pejorative noun, given the disintegration of the convoy and the fragmentation of its dispersed escort. The convoy commodore, Commander Venables, who ordered *Port Chalmers* onto a *westerly* course at the height of the bombing attack on the evening of the 12th, and whose 'return' order was defied by other masters, states in his report that: 'The evening of 12th August was a severe trial to all, *as escort afloat had also vanished* [my emphasis: R.W.] at a critical moment, after the disaster at [the] entrance to [the] Skerki Channel.'
3. It is noteworthy that the 'definitive' summarised account of PEDESTAL, compiled by Syfret's staff, signed by the vice-admiral and held in the Public Record Office, states that this attack blew up *Clan Ferguson*, which had long since been sunk.
4. Hill, *Destroyer Captain*, p. 73.
5. See Report of Naval Liaison Officer, SS *Melbourne Star*, 16 August 1942, in ADM199/1243; also video evidence of J. Jackson and interview with F. Treves.
6. Frederick Treves, later in life a well-known actor, was awarded the British Empire Medal and Lloyd's War Medal for his courage, particularly the rescue of John Jackson. In the Operation PEDESTAL documentary made for Channel 4's *True Stories* series he expressed his deep remorse at not being able to do the same for AB Bowdory. I am indebted to him for his candour during our subsequent meeting, and for his permission to quote his harrowing experience for its value as history.
7. See Report of Proceedings from Commanding Officer, HMS *Ledbury*, 18 August 1942, in ADM199/1243.
8. See Hill, *Destroyer Captain*, pp. 72–4; also correspondence with the author. Further video evidence is available in the Imperial War Museum from material for the documentary mentioned in Note 6. Hill's own account is characteristically modest. A man of great humanity, he was much affected by the abandonment of PQ17. Walker was promoted and awarded a DSM for 'outstanding bravery'.

9. See Report of Commodore, Operation PEDESTAL, 15 August 1942, in ADM199/1243.
10. One apprentice from *Dorset*, who wishes to remain anonymous, when interviewed on 7 March 1995 recalled of his ordeal: 'A few events stuck in the mind, but the rest was hoping someone would stop by with something to drink or eat, and a longing for sleep. To be honest, I was scared to death and the noise [of the barrage] was unbelievable.' For an analysis of recollections of Operation PEDESTAL, see *The Mariner's Mirror*, November 1993, vol. 79, No. 4, p. 437.
11. Interview with anonymous apprentice from *Dorset*.
12. Details from Report of Proceedings from Commanding Officer, HMS *Bramham*, 17 August 1942, and Report of Naval Liaison Officer in MV *Dorset*, 17 August 1942, both in ADM199/1243.
13. Every ship has an individually allocated four-letter signal known colloquially as her 'number', from which derives the phrase to 'make one's number'. The uppermost flag distinguishes her nationality, and in territorial waters it was then obligatory to exhibit this if requested, as well as to wear one's national ensign. It was by the use of 'I' that Hill's *ruse de guerre* implied Italian nationality. Riley's refusal was an admission that he did not wish to be identified, and thereby roused Vichy suspicions.
14. Details from Riley's report to his owners, dated 16 August 1942 and reprinted in the Maltese *National War Museum Association Newsletter No. 101*, July/September 1997; the Association now holds the report at Fort St Elmo, Valletta. See also Report of Naval Liaison Officer, HM Transport *Brisbane Star*, 16 August 1942, in ADM199/1243.
15. Private account and conversation with R.A. Sanders, Quartermaster, MV *Brisbane Star*.
16. Report of Naval Liaison Officer, SS *Ohio*, Operation PEDESTAL, 15 August 1942, in ADM199/1243.
17. In addition to some naval personnel and the army and naval gunners embarked in the transports sunk, these included cadets and seamen from *Waimarama*, *Dorset* and *Empire Hope*, and Third Officer Larsen and Cadet Dales from *Santa Elisa*.
18. Correspondence with Jack Follansbee, purser of *Santa Elisa*, then aboard HMS *Penn*.
19. See Report of Proceedings from Commanding Officer, HMS *Penn*, 17 August 1942, in ADM199/1242, from which the chronology for the *Ohio* incident is drawn. Swain's report is more detailed for this than that of either Baines or Hill, who at this stage came under his orders.
20. See Captain Mason's report to his owners, reprinted in Fall 1994 edition of *Steamboat Bill*, the Journal of the Steamship Historical Society of America. The report of Mr J. Wyld, Chief Engineer of *Ohio*, is also published in this journal.
21. Anecdotal accounts call this tug *Robert*. Swain's report refers to *Robust*, which Roger Hill confirms.
22. The Italian submarine *Asteria* was tasked with a final attack, but failed to reach her target and was not off Delimara Point at this time.
23. Captain Mason reported: 'Vessel had been looted throughout night as two Destroyers had approximately 400 survivors aboard besides own crew[s] of nearly 400.' At least one apprentice, a survivor from another ship, was later reprimanded by Mason for taking foodstuffs without permission.
24. I am indebted to the late Ron Peck, a survivor from *Empire Hope*, for this information. He concludes: 'If [the bomb] had exploded, the outcome of the war might have been vastly different. I have never seen this incident recorded anywhere.'

25. Numerous awards were given to men of both sea services, including George Crosses to Mason and Petty Officer Cook Walker, of *Ledbury*; Distinguished Service Orders went to Captains MacFarlane, Pinkney, Riley and Wren, and to Chief Engineer Wyld; Distinguished Service Crosses to Gray and other officers of *Ohio*; and seven Distinguished Service Medals were distributed among her crew.

CHAPTER 21: 'THE UNLOADING PROCEEDED UNDISTURBED'

1. *Ohio*'s Chief Officer, Mr Gray, volunteered to command an elderly steamer, the *Omega*, for the homeward passage from Gibraltar. She only made 4 knots and Gray had to proceed alone, shooting down a German bomber and winning an OBE in the process. In Gibraltar one steward from *Waimarama* became insane as a result of his ordeal; other men suffered from nervous breakdowns.
2. See Report of Naval Liaison Officer, SS *Deucalion*, *loc. cit.*
3. *Laforey, Lookout, Lightning, Antelope, Wishart, Derwent, Keppel, Malcolm, Bicester, Eskimo, Somali* and *Venomous.*
4. See War Diary, Vice-Admiral Malta, *loc. cit.*
5. *Westcott, Bramham, Wishart, Cowdray, Verity, Achates, Vanoc* and *Blyskawicka.*
6. *Emo, Brin, Corallo, Turchese, Topazio, Axum, Nichelio, Porfido, Argo* and *Asteria.*
7. In addition to her consignment of Spitfires, *Furious* carried eight Seafires of No. 801 Squadron FAA, and four Albacores of No. 822 Squadron. Captain Bulteel emphasised the inferiority of the Seafire when in combat with a Ju88. See Report of Proceedings, Operation TRAIN, HMS *Furious*, 31 October 1942, in ADM199/897.
8. See Report of Proceedings of Operation TRAIN, HMS *Aurora*, 2 November 1942, in ADM199/897.
9. Regrettably I am unable to decipher this officer's name from his Report of Proceedings, and it was not naval practice for an officer to type his name under his signature. *Empire Patrol* was commissioned as one of HM Ships, classed as a 'closed petrol ship'.
10. *Ardeola* and *Tadorna* were passed to the Italians and renamed *Aderno* and *Balzac*. Both were sunk by British submarines, the first on 27 July 1943, the second on 7 March 1943.
11. See War Diary, Vice-Admiral Malta, *loc. cit.*
12. *Welshman* made a further delivery of stores to Malta at the end of the year, with an operational visit in late January 1943. Returning to Alexandria, she was torpedoed by *U617* (Korvettenkapitän Brandi) on 1 February. She took three hours to founder, with the loss of 152 men.
13. These were *Jervis, Javelin, Kelvin, Nubian, Pakenham, Paladin* and *Petard.*
14. Private account of Gordon Knox, Third Engineer, TSMV *Denbighshire.*
15. *Aldenham, Beaufort, Belvoir, Croome, Dulverton, Exmoor, Hursley, Hurworth, Tetcott* and the Greek Navy's *Pindos* (ex *Bolebroke*).
16. Private account by a crew member of *Arethusa*, in the author's possession.
17. *Petard* had played a noteworthy role during the fighting in the Eastern Mediterranean when in company with *Pakenham, Hero, Dulverton* and *Hurworth*, and supported by an RAF Wellington, at the end of October 1942: *U559* had been forced to surface, and a boarding party from *Petard* had captured the U-boat's code-books and *Wetterkurzschlüssel*, or short-weather cypher. Two of her men were lost trying to remove the M4 cypher machine as *U559* sank, but the trophies enabled Bletchley Park to break the Triton code, on 13 December.

18. See War Diary, Vice-Admiral, Malta, *loc. cit.*
19. It is outside the scope of this work to detail the actions associated with the attacks on Axis shipping. However, it is worth making the point that although the tide had turned irrevocably against the enemy, British ships continued to be lost or severely damaged in action. At the beginning of December the destroyer *Quentin* was sunk by bombing, *Manxman* was torpedoed and damaged by *U375* on the 1st, the destroyer *Porcupine* was sunk by *U602* and the corvette *Marigold* by an aerial torpedo on the 9th, *Blean* by *U443* on the 11th, *Partridge* by *U565* on the 18th. This U-boat also sank the trooping liner *Cameronia* on the 22nd. The corvette *Snapdragon* was sunk on the 19th, the trooping liner *Strathallan* was sunk by *U562* on the 21st, and the Italian submarine *Mocenigo* damaged the cruiser *Argonaut*. Against these successes, Axis losses were correspondingly high. Three out of four convoys were recalled, while the fourth was destroyed, all four merchant ships being sunk, one of the escorts damaged and another, *Folgore*, sunk. Other convoys were attacked and many freighters were sunk. *Jervis, Javelin, Janus* and *Kelvin* massacred the Italian torpedo-boat *Lupo* on 2 December. The Italian cruiser *Muzio Attendolo* was wrecked by an American bombing raid on Naples on 4 December, and the submarines *Porfido* and *Corallo* were lost to *Tigris* and *Enchantress; Uarsciek* was detroyed by *Petard* and the Greek destroyer *Vasilissa Olga* on the 15th. And so it continued.
20. See War Diary, Vice-Admiral Malta, *loc. cit.*
21. See Roskill, *A Merchant Fleet at War*, p. 248. Not all the Chinese were removed, and Roskill seems to be in error when citing the chief cook as ringleader, for he remained with the ship. Two excellent fitters also remained aboard, as did the officers' stewards, including Evans's 'tiger', as his personal steward was called. All members of *Glenartney*'s crew were being paid a war bonus.
22. Personal account by Reg Scott, Third Engineer, TSMV *Glenartney*. Among the ship's midshipmen was a member of the owner's family, Mr Julian Holt. The naval liaison officer, who boarded in the Canal with three signals ratings, was Lieutenant Woods, one of the few to have escaped from the submarine *Thetis* when she sank on trials off the Mersey in 1939.
23. *Bantam, Brisbane Star, Denbighshire, Melbourne Star, Mormacmoon, Port Chalmers, Robin Locksley, Rochester Castle* and the tanker *Yorba Linda*. The ex PEDESTAL ships received civic welcomes when they returned to Britain. *Brisbane Star* had had her bow filled with cement in Malta, and received more substantial repairs at Cape Town. Here one of her crew was mugged, and drowned when he was thrown into the docks.
24. *Pakenham, Petard, Aldenham, Belvoir, Croome, Dulverton, Exmoor, Hursley, Tetcott,* and the Greeks *Vasilissa Olga* and *Pindos*.
25. See Report of Proceedings, Commanding Officer, HMS *Pakenham*, 11 December 1942, in ADM199/1316.
26. Details from War Diary, Vice-Admiral Malta, *loc. cit.*
27. See Reports of Proceedings, Commanding Officers, HMS *Euryalus, Dulverton* and *Exmoor*, dated 14, 18 and 11 January 1943, respectively, in ADM199/1030.
28. See Report of Proceedings, Commanding Officer, HMS *Orion*, 17 January 1943, in ADM199/1030.
29. See Report of Proceedings, Commanding Officer, HMS *Jervis*, 18 February 1943, in ADM199/1030.
30. There were three further convoys, numbered MW36, 37 and 38, but they were so-named for security reasons and were actually part of Operation HUSKY.

Bibliography

(Place of publication London unless otherwise stated)

General Background

Churchill, W.S., *The Second World War*, Penguin, 1985
Ciano, G., *Diary, 1939–43*, Heinemann, 1947
Gilbert, M., *Second World War*, Fontana, 1989
Hinsley, F.H. (ed.), *British Intelligence in the Second World War* (3 vols), HMSO, 1979–1984
Hitler, A., *Hitler's War Directives, 1939–45*, Pan, 1966
Hough, R., *Former Naval Person*, Weidenfeld and Nicolson, 1985
Howard, M., *The Mediterranean Strategy in the Second World War*, Greenhill Books, 1993
Lash, J., *Roosevelt and Churchill, 1939–1941*, Andre Deutsch, 1977
Lewin, R., *Ultra Goes to War*, Hutchinson, 1978
Martienssen, A., *Hitler and his Admirals*, Secker and Warburg, 1948
Reader's Digest, *The World at Arms*, 1989
Trevor-Roper, H., *Hitler's War Directives*, Pan, 1966
——Ed., *Fuehrer Conferences on Naval Affairs 1939–45*, Greenhill Books, 1990 (Reprint)
Tunstall, B., *World War at Sea*, Secker and Warburg, 1942
Warlimont, W., *Inside Hitler's Headquarters, 1939–45*, Presidio, Novato, 1964
Winton, J., *Ultra at Sea*, Leo Cooper, 1989

Maltese Background

Attard, J., *The Battle of Malta*, William Kimber, 1980
Bradford, E., *Seige: Malta, 1940–1943*, Hamish Hamilton, 1985
Dobbie, S., *Grace Under Malta*, Drummond, 1944
Elliott, P., *The Cross and the Ensign: A Naval History of Malta, 1798–1979*, Granada, 1982
Gerard, F., *Malta Magnificent*, Cassell, 1943
Hay, I., *The Unconquered Isle*, Right Book Club, 1944
Hogan, G., *Malta: The Triumphant Years, 1940–43*, Hale, 1978
Lucas, L., *Malta: The Thorn in Rommel's Side*, Penguin, 1993
Micallef, J., *When Malta Stood Alone, 1940–43*, Private Publication, Malta, 1981

Owen, C., *The Maltese Islands*, David and Charles, Newton Abbot, 1969
Ritchie, L., *The Epic of Malta*, Odhams, 1945
Spooner, T., *Supremè Gallantry*, John Murray, 1996
Vella, P., *Malta: Blitzed But Not Beaten*, Progress, Valletta, 1985.

General Naval Background

Barnett, C., *Engage the Enemy More Closely*, Hodder and Stoughton, 1991
Brodie, B., *A Layman's Guide to Naval Strategy*, Oxford University Press, 1943
Hardy, A., *Everyman's History of the War at Sea* (3 vols), Nicholson and Watson, 1948
HMSO Reprint, *British Vessels Lost at Sea 1939–45*, Patrick Stephens, Wellingborough, 1988
Jones, G., *Submarines Versus U-Boats*, William Kimber, 1986
—— *Autumn of the U-Boats*, William Kimber, 1984
Kemp, P., *Victory at Sea*, Muller, 1957
Lipscomb, F.W., *The British Submarine*, A. & C. Black, 1954
Padfield, P., *War Beneath the Sea*, John Murray, 1995
Rohwer, J. and Hummelchen, G., *Chronology of the War at Sea* (revised edn), Greenhill, 1992
Roskill, S., *The War at Sea* (3 vols), HMSO, 1954–61
Terraine, J., *Business in Great Waters*, Leo Cooper, 1989
Thompson, J. (Ed.), *Imperial War Museum Book of the War at Sea*, 1996.

Merchant Naval Background and Company Histories

Behrens, C., *Merchant Shipping and the Demands of War*, HMSO, 1955
Bowen, F., *The Flag of the Southern Cross, 1939–45*, Shaw Savill, c. 1949
Bushell, T., *Eight Bells: Royal Mail Lines War Story 1939–45*, Trade and Travel, 1950
Doughty, M., *Merchant Shipping and War*, Royal Historical Society, 1982
Grove, E. (Ed.), *The Defeat of the Enemy Attack on Shipping, 1939–45*, Ashgate/Navy Records Society, Aldershot and London, 1997
HMSO, *Merchantmen at War*, 1944
Holman, G., *In the Wake of Endeavour*, Charles Knight, 1973
Hope, R., *A New History of British Shipping*, John Murray, 1990
Hope, S., *Tanker Fleet, The War Story of Shell Tankers*, Anglo-Saxon Petroleum Company, 1948
Lane, T., *The Merchant Seaman's War*, Manchester University Press, Manchester, 1990
Lennox Kerr, J. (Ed.), *Touching the Adventures of Merchantmen*, Harrap, 1953
Lucas, W., *Eagle Fleet, The Story of a Tanker Fleet*, Weidenfeld and Nicolson, 1955
McBrearty, R., *Seafaring 1939–45, As I saw it*, Pentland Press, 1995
Mitchell, W. and Sawyer, L., *Empire Ships of World War Two*, Sea Breezes, Liverpool, 1965
Moore, A., *A Careless Word, a Needless Sinking* (revised edn), American Merchant Marine Museum, 1988
Murray, M., *Union-Castle Chronicle 1853–1953*, Longmans Green, 1953
Osborne, R. (Ed.), *Conversion for War*, World Ships Society Monograph No. 6, Kendal, 1983
Pearce, F., *Heroes of the Fourth Service*, Robert Hale, 1996
Roskill, S., *A Merchant Fleet at War: Alfred Holt and Co., 1939–1945*, Collins, 1962
Russell, A.G., *Port Line*, privately published, 1985
Slader, J., *The Fourth Service, Merchantmen at War 1939–45*, Hale, 1994
—— *The Red Duster at War*, William Kimber, 1988

'Taffrail' (Captain Taprell-Dorling, RN), *Blue Star Line at War, 1939–1945*, Foulsham, 1973
Waters, S., *Ordeal by Sea*, New Zealand Shipping Company, 1949
Young, J., *Britain's Sea War*, Patrick Stephens, Wellingborough, 1989

Numerous Articles in *Sea Breezes, Warships Supplements* and World Ship Society publications.

Operations in the Mediterranean

Cameron, I., *Red Duster, White Ensign*, Muller, 1959
Connell, G., *Mediterranean Maelstrom, HMS* Jervis *and the 14th Flotilla*, William Kimber, 1987
Divine, A., *Destroyer's War*, John Murray, 1942
Gordon, E., *HMS* Pepperpot!: *The* Penelope *in World War Two*, Hale, 1985
Greene, J. and Massignani, A., *The Naval War in the Mediterranean, 1940–1943*, Chatham, 1998
Ireland, B., *The War in the Mediterranean, 1940–43*, Arms and Armour, 1993
HMSO, *East of Malta, West of Suez*, 1943
—— *The Mediterranean Fleet*, 1944
Langmaid, R., *'The Med'*, Batchworth Press, 1948
Macintyre, D., *The Battle for the Mediterranean*, Batsford, 1964
Pack, S., *The Battle of Sirte*, Ian Allan, 1975
—— *The Battle of Matapan*, Batsford, 1961
Poolman, K., *The British Sailor*, Arms and Armour, 1989
Russell, H. and Pursey, H., *Ark Royal*, The Bodley Head, 1942
Hankland, P. and Hunter, A., *Malta Convoy*, Fontana, 1963
Smith, P., *PEDESTAL: The Malta Convoy of August 1942*, William Kimber, 1970
Stitt, G., *Under Cunningham's Command*, Allen and Unwin, 1944
Wingate, J., *The Fighting Tenth*, Leo Cooper, 1991

Biography and Personal

Crosley, M., *They Gave Me a Seafire*, Airlife, 1986
Cunningham of Hyndhope, Viscount [A.B.], *A Sailor's Odyssey*, Hutchinson, 1951
Edwards, K., *Seven Sailors*, Collins, 1945
Gretton, Sir P., *Convoy Escort Commander*, Cassell, 1964
Hill, R., *Destroyer Captain*, William Kimber, 1975
Macintyre, D., *Fighting Admiral*, Evans Brothers, 1961
Simpson, M. (Ed.), *The Somerville Papers*, Scolar/Navy Records Society, 1995
Smithes, E. and Bruce, C., *The War at Sea, 1939–45*, Constable, 1992
Stephen, M., *The Fighting Admirals*, Leo Cooper, 1991
Vian, P., *Action this Day*, Muller, 1960
Winton, J., *Cunningham*, John Murray, 1998
—— (Ed.), *Freedom's Battle*: Vol. 1, *The War at Sea 1939–45*, Hutchinson, 1967

Unpublished Material

Aylwin, K., *Maritime Forces Supporting Malta During the Seige of 1940–43*. A detailed list, with supporting documentation, of all vessels engaged in the relief of Malta
—— Typescript account of experiences in HMS *Euryalus*

Brunshill, T., Typescript of talk detailing the personal experiences of the Second Engineer of *Glenorchy* during Operation PEDESTAL

Bunker, K., Typescript account of an airman's experiences in HMS *Euryalus*

Dickens, D., *Malta Convoy (PEDESTAL), August 1942*. Contemporary typescript written by Apprentice Dickens of *Dorset* for his family, November 1942

Durham, P., HALBERD *and* PEDESTAL, private account by Gunnery Control Officer of HM Destroyer *Laforey*

Fowler, J., *Santa Marija Corvette*, private account of PEDESTAL by a member of the crew of HM Corvette *Spiraea*

Knox, G., STONEAGE, typescript account by the Third Engineer of *Denbighshire*

Malins, C., *As I Remember*, the privately published memoirs of Captain C.W. Malins, DSO, DSC, RN, then First Lieutenant of *Pathfinder*

Rogers, K., *Malta, 1942, The Blitz and the Siege*. A fighter pilot's account.

Sibly, G., *The Forgotten Convoys* (1994), a typescript account prepared for publication in *Sea Breezes* magazine by the then Third Mate of HM Transport *Ajax*

Further information has been culled from various editions of *The Naval Review, The Mariner's Mirror* and *Sea Breezes*.

The author has conducted a number of interviews and also consulted other private accounts whose originators did not wish to make them known to a wider public. These include material from Americans serving in Malta-bound convoys.

Acknowledgements

My thanks are extended to a number of people who have contributed in one way or another to the production of this book. I was prompted to write it by the late Admiral of the Fleet, The Lord Lewin, to whom I owe a great debt, not only for his encouragement but also for his practical help. When we first discussed the idea, I said that I was not proposing to write a purely naval history and that I would wish to emphasise the part played by the merchant service. Lord Lewin's appreciation of merchant seafarers was unusual among senior naval officers, who generally regard merchant ships as an anonymous collection of undistinguished vessels, and he replied with some emphasis that such an approach was only right and proper. Sadly he is unable to see the book published or to provide the proposed foreword, though he knew of the work's completion before his death.

The book could not have been completed without the constant support of my wife Chris, the tolerance of my publisher, John R. Murray, and the assistance of my agent, Barbara Levy. Tremendous help was provided by Captain Ken Aylwin, who read every word and put me straight on not a few. I am also hugely indebted to Ian McCafferty for his enthusiastic assistance in research, his advice and suggestions, his faith in the project and his unfailing sense of humour during the long process of gestation. I tested the bonds of friendship to the limit, for he too toiled through my drafted chapters, conscious of the burden of information, yet determined that we should capture as much as possible.

Unexpected and serendipitous assistance came from two sources. Noreen Molloy, Executive Producer of a documentary on Operation PEDESTAL made for Channel 4's *True Stories* series, kindly made available to me much of her own research, including video footage of the interviews of veterans. Her encouragement was sustaining. A second heart-warming contribution came from Joseph Caruana, of Senglea, who not only gave freely of his own published work on Malta Convoys, but updated me in the light of his own research in the Maltese archives subsequent to our meeting.

My thanks must also go to the following for permission to use private accounts and journals, for supplying information, advice or photographs, or for allowing me to invade their privacy and interview them: Philip Andrews, Jim Bayley, L.E. Bone, J. Bore, Captain Graeme Boxall, Tom Brunskill, B.H. Clinkard, Sid Crowe, Ian Cubitt, Mike Curtis, John Dalgleish, Commander James Davidson, Stan Deighton, Captain Desmond Dickens, John Follansbee, Jim Fowler, John Gregson, GC, Rodney Hazlitt, Commander Roger Hill, Lewis Jukes, Captain Hedley Kett,

Captain Peter King, Gordon Knox, Captain Jerry Lawton, Sandy Mackenzie, Donald J. MacLeod, the late Captain C.W. Malins, Ian A. Millar, J.R. Moxley, Dr Patrick Murphy, Commander Felix Neville-Towle, Ken Nicholls, Charles Owen, Ron Peck, Leonard A. Perrigo, Glynn Powell, Captain John Reid, John Rice, Robert M. Ritchie, Peter Rothwell, R.A. Sanders, Commander M. Scott, Reg Scott, the late Graham Sibly, Bill Skilling, the late Tony Spooner, the late Roy Thomas, Derek Thompson, Frederick Treves, Commodore John Wacher, Charles Walker, the late Captain John Wells, Captain Cornelis Wenninck, and C.H. Wilson.

For allowing me to quote from her late husband's work, I would like to thank Mrs D. Pack, and for permission to quote material from other previously published books I wish to acknowledge the following: Messrs Cassell plc of London for the use of quotations from Winston S. Churchill's *The Second World War*, and The Presidio Press of California for permission to quote from General Warlimont's *Inside Hitler's Headquarters, 1939–45*.

Great help in securing illustrations was rendered by Alfred Coldman, introduced to me by John Agius in Valletta, and I should like to record my thanks to the members of the National War Museum Association of Valletta for permission to reproduce material from their splendid collection of photographs. My gratitude is also owed to the Trustees of the Imperial War Museum in London, the staff at the Public Records Office at Kew, my local library, and John Willis of Orwell Photography.

The finished product owes much to Gail Pirkis of John Murray Ltd; to Liz Robinson, who worked assiduously on the typescript and dealt tactfully with my infelicities; and to Douglas Matthews, for his meticulous compilation of the Index. Notwithstanding this, unless clearly attributed all opinions are my own, as are the mistakes and errors I fear still lurk in these pages.

Richard Woodman
Harwich, 1999

Additional corrections to this paperback edition have been suggested by Joseph Caruana, James Gibson, Dr Eric Grove, Bryan Knights, Vice Admiral Sir Ian McGeoch, Jack Harvey, Captain Tony Sainsbury, Commander Brian Wainwright and Oliver Woodman. I am most grateful to them for their interest and assistance. James Gibson wished credit to be given to one unknown figure behind the story of Malta convoys. In bonded warehouses at Alexandria in Egypt and under extensive tarpaulins in fields near Didcot in England every mixed cargo destined for Malta was assembled. These huge consignments were then despatched to the loading ports of the fast cargo-liners. The officer responsible for this was Paymaster-Commander Robert Jackson (afterwards Sir Robert Jackson KCVO CMG OBE), Secretary to the Staff Officers' Committee in Malta, then an officer on Ford's staff on secondment from the RAN. Jackson flew frequently to Didcot and Alexandria to supervise this careful preparatory work.

Richard Woodman
Harwich, 2003

Index

528 *Index*